Law and Society

Second Canadian Edition

Steven Vago
Professor Emeritus
Saint Louis University

Adie Nelson
University of Waterloo

PEARSON
Prentice
Hall

Toronto

D1511190

Library and Archives Canada Cataloguing in Publication

Vago, Steven
    Law and society / Steven Vago, Adie Nelson. — 2nd Canadian ed.

Includes index.
ISBN-13: 978-0-13-201689-6
ISBN-10: 0-13-201689-3

    1. Sociological jurisprudence—Textbooks. I. Nelson, Adie, 1958-
II. Title.

K370.V33 2008   340'.115   C2006-905870-9

ISBN-13: 978-0-13-201689-6
ISBN-10: 0-13-201689-3

Editor-in-Chief, Vice-President of Sales: Kelly Shaw
Acquisitions Editor: Ky Pruesse
Executive Marketing Manager: Judith Allen
Developmental Editor: Patti Altridge
Production Editor: Kevin Leung
Copy Editor: Anne Borden
Proofreader: Robert Giannetto
Production Coordinator: Avinash Chandra
Composition: Laserwords
Art Director and Cover Design: Julia Hall
Cover Image: Firstlight

    4 5   12 11 10 09

Printed and bound in the United States of America.

Contents

Preface

The objective of this book is to serve as an undergraduate text in courses on law and society. Although the book was written primarily for university and college students, anyone with an interest in law and society will find it useful, informative, and provocative. The classroom-tested and -refined material has been organized and presented in a logical fashion, and each chapter builds on the previous one. Should one prefer a different organization of the contents, it would not detract from the value of the book. For example, if one desires, Chapter 9, Researching Law in Society, can be read after Chapter 2, Theoretical Perspectives, rather than at the end of the book.

Our purpose has been to prepare a book that is pedagogically sound, full of ideas and insights, informative and provocative to read, and distinctive in its coverage of the subject. We have attempted to produce a book that is clear and readable, and includes new trends, concerns, and controversies. Wherever possible, we have emphasized clarity of language at the expense of professional jargon.

Knowledge about law and society has accumulated haphazardly. Intellectual developments in the field are influenced by a number of theoretical perspectives, resulting in a variety of strains of thought and research. In writing this book, we recognize that it may well be the case that more questions will be raised than answered. However, it is the abundance of unanswered questions and unexpected developments that keeps the study of law and society challenging and appealing.

Writing a book always requires the cooperation, support, and encouragement of many people. At Pearson Education Canada, we wish to thank Ky Pruesse, Patti Altridge, Kevin Leung, and Anne Borden. We would also like to thank the reviewers who commented on and constructively criticized this book prior to its publication: Chloe Atkins, University of Calgary; Marilyn Belle-McQuillan, University of Western Ontario; Robert Carley, University of Guelph; Jane Dickson-Gilmore and Dawn Moore, Carleton University; David Howes, Concordia University; Randy Lippert, University of Windsor; and Jane McMillan, York University. Although we have not been able to incorporate all of their valuable suggestions, we gratefully acknowledge their insights and thoughtful comments.

New to this edition

More Canadian content and examples which includes the following:

- Chapter 3—Federal Accountability Act and the impact on lobbyists
- Chapter 4—Heather Crowe case and International Tobacco Control policy
- Chapter 5—New data on drug addiction and the opening of federally-run drug treatment courts; new federal legislation designed to combat human trafficking
- Chapter 7—Walkerton and the limitations of law on social change as regards corporations and environment issues
- Expanded focus on aboriginal people throughout entire text
- New Tort law section covered in Chapter 3
- End-of-chapter critical thinking questions

Instructor Supplement

Instructors will be able to make use of the online Test Item File for Law and Society, Second Canadian Edition. This supplement can be downloaded by instructors from a password-protected location on Pearson Education Canada's online catalogue (at vig.pearsoned.ca). Simply search for the text, then click on "Instructor" under "Resources" in the left-hand menu. Contact your local sales representative for further information.

Student Supplement

A new text enrichment website is available for students at **www.pearsoned.ca/text/vago**. By visiting the text website, students may download their own glossary of the key terms. These key terms, which are bolded in the text, are listed by chapter for easy reference. The site also gives students additional reading suggestions on a chapter-by-chapter basis.

chapter one

Introduction

With the advent of the 21st century, law increasingly permeates all forms of social behaviour. Its significance and pervasiveness resonate on all walks of life. In subtle and at times not-so-subtle ways, a complex and voluminous set of laws governs our entire existence and our every action. It determines registration at birth and the distribution of possessions at death. Laws regulate prenuptial agreements, marriage, divorce, and the conduct of professors in the classroom. Laws set the speed limit and the length of school attendance. Laws control what we eat and where, what we buy, when and how we use our computers, and what we can see in movie theatres. Laws protect ownership and define the boundaries of private and public property. Laws regulate business, raise revenue, provide for redress when agreements are broken, and uphold social institutions, such as the family. Laws protect the prevailing legal and political systems by defining power relationships, thus establishing who is superordinate and who is subordinate in any given situation. Laws maintain the status quo and provide the impetus for change. Finally, laws, in particular criminal laws, not only protect private and public interests but also preserve order. There is no end to the ways in which the law has a momentous effect upon our lives.

The foremost mission of this book is to serve as a text in undergraduate courses on law and society. Because the book has been written originally for the undergraduate student, we opted for an eclectic approach to the often controversial subject matter without embracing or advocating a particular position, ideology, or theoretical stance. To have done so would have been too limiting for a text, since important contributions would have been excluded or considered out of context. Thus, the book does not propound a single thesis or position; instead, it exposes the reader to the dominant theoretical perspectives and sociological methods used to explain the interplay between law and society in the social science literature. Should any reader care to follow up on a theoretical perspective or practical concern, the chapter topics and references will, hopefully, provide the necessary first step toward the further exploration of many law and society-related issues.

OVERVIEW

In every human society throughout history there have been mechanisms for the declaration, alteration, administration, and enforcement of the rules by which people live. Not all societies, however, utilize a formal legal system (courts, judges, lawyers, and law enforcement agencies) to the same degree. For example, throughout the developing world, the formal systems of property rights taken for granted in advanced nations simply do not exist. As the renowned economist Hernando de Soto (2001) points out in his influential book *The Mystery of Capital,* 80 percent of the poor people in the developing world cannot identify who owns what, addresses cannot be verified, and the rules that govern property vary from neighbourhood to neighbourhood or even from street to street. The notion of holding title to property is limited primarily to a handful of elites whose assets are "paperized" in the formal documents and legal structures common in the West (see also Blomley, 2003).

Further, traditional societies rely almost exclusively on custom as the source of legal rules and resolve disputes through conciliation or mediation by village elders, or by some other moral or divine authority (Pottage and Mundy, 2004). As for law, such societies need little of it. Traditional societies are more homogeneous than modern industrial ones. Social relations are more direct and intimate, interests are shared by virtually everyone, and there are fewer things to quarrel about. Since relations are more direct and intimate, nonlegal and often informal mechanisms of social control are generally more effective.

As societies become larger, more complex, and modern, homogeneity gives way to heterogeneity. Common interests decrease in relation to special interests. Face-to-face relations become progressively less important, as do kinship ties. Access to material goods becomes more indirect, with a greater likelihood of unequal allocation, and the struggle for available goods becomes intensified. As a result, the prospects for conflict and dispute within the society increase. The need for explicit regulatory and enforcement mechanisms becomes increasingly apparent. The development of trade and industry requires a system of formal and universal legal rules dealing with business organizations and commercial transactions, subjects that are not normally part of customary or religious law. Such commercial activity also requires guarantees, predictability, continuity, and a more effective method for settling disputes than that of trial by ordeal, trial by combat, or decision by a council of elders. As one commentator has noted, "The paradox . . . is that the more civilized man [sic] becomes, the greater is man's [sic] need for law, and the more law he [sic] creates. Law is but a response to social needs" (Hoebel, 1954:292).

In the eloquent words of Oliver Wendell Holmes, Jr. (1881:5), "The law embodies the story of a nation's development through many centuries," and every legal system stands in close relationship to the ideas, aims, and purposes of society. Law reflects the intellectual, social, economic, and political climate of its time. Law is inseparable from the interests, goals, and understandings that deeply shape or compromise social and economic life (Morales, 2003; Posner, 2001; Sarat and Kearns, 2000). It also reflects the particular ideas, ideals, and ideologies that are part of a distinct "legal culture"—those attributes of behaviour and attitudes that make the law of one society different from that of another—that make, for example, the law of the Inuit different from the law of the French (Friedman, 2002).

In sociology, the study of law embraces a number of well-established areas of inquiry (Cotterrell, 1994; Friedrichs, 2001). The discipline is concerned with values, interaction patterns, and ideologies that underlie the basic structural arrangements in a society, many of which are embodied in law as substantive rules. Both sociology and law are concerned with norms—rules that prescribe the appropriate behaviour for people in a given situation (Etzioni, 2000). The study of conflict and conflict resolution are central in both disciplines. Both sociology and law are concerned with the nature of legitimate authority, the mechanisms of social control, issues of human rights, power arrangements, the relationship between public and private spheres, and formal contractual commitments (Baumgartner, 1999; Hagan and Levi, 2005). Both sociologists and lawyers are aware that the behaviour of judges, jurors, criminals, litigants, and other consumers of legal products is charged with emotion, distorted by cognitive glitches and failures of will, and constrained by altruism, etiquette, or a sense of duty.

Historically, the rapprochement of sociology (along with economics, psychology, and other social sciences) (Kapardis, 2003; Roesch, et al., 1999; Posner, 2001) and law is not novel. North American sociologists in the 20th century emphasized the various facets of the relationship between law and society. E. Adamson Ross (1922:106) considered law as "the most specialized and highly furnished engine of control employed by society." Lester F. Ward (1906:339), who believed in governmental control and social planning, predicted a day when legislation would endeavour to solve "questions of social improvement, the amelioration of the conditions of all the people, the removal of whatever privations may still remain, and the adoption of means to the positive increase of the social welfare, in short, the organization of human happiness."

The writings of these early sociologists have greatly influenced the development of the school of legal philosophy that became a principal force in sociological jurisprudence. *Sociological jurisprudence* is the study of law and legal philosophy, and the use of its ideas in law to regulate conduct (Lauderdale, 1997:132). It is based on a comparative study of legal systems, legal doctrines, and legal institutions as social phenomena and considers law as it actually is—the "law in action" as distinguished from the law as it appears in books. Roscoe Pound, the principal figure in sociological jurisprudence, relied heavily on the findings of early sociologists in asserting that law should be studied as a social institution. For Pound (1941:18), law was a specialized form of social control that exerts pressure on a person "in order to constrain him [sic] to do his [sic] part in upholding civilized society and to deter him [sic] from anti-social conduct, that is, conduct at variance with the postulates of social order."

Interest in law among sociologists grew rapidly after the Second World War, which ended in 1945. In North America, some sociologists became interested in law almost by accident. As they investigated certain problems, such as race relations, they found law to be relevant. Others became radicalized in the mid- and late 1960s, a period of social unrest, and their work began to emphasize social conflict and the functions of stratification in society. It became imperative for sociologists of the left to dwell on the gap between promise and performance in the legal system. By the same token, those sociologists defending the establishment were anxious to show that the law dealt with social conflict in a legitimate fashion. These developments provided the necessary impetus for the field of law and society which got its start in the mid-1960s with the formation of the Law and Society Association and the inauguration of its official journal, the *Law & Society Review* (Abel, 1995:9; *Law & Society Review,* 1995:5; Tomlins, 2000). Feminist legal scholarship emerged in Canada during the decade that followed with the release of the 1970 report of the Royal Commission on the Status of Women and gained momentum when the Canadian Charter of Rights and Freedoms came into effect on April 17, 1982 (Brockman and Chunn, 1993:5). The National Association of Women and the Law, a national, non-profit women's organization that promotes the equality rights of women through legal education, research, and law reform advocacy, was established in 1974. In 1985, the Women's Legal Education and Action Fund, "a research and litigation organization with a mandate to initiate, and to intervene in, cases affecting women" (Mossman, 1998:193), was created and the *Canadian Journal of Women and the Law* began publication (Dawson, Quaile, and Holly, 2002:105). The *Canadian Journal of Law & Society*, an interdisciplinary journal, was also founded in 1985. Initially based at the University of Calgary's Research Unit for Socio-Legal Studies, the journal seeks to promote and publish research on law and legal systems as social phenomena.

But interest in law and society is not confined to North America. Adam Podgorecki, a Polish sociologist, has analyzed a number of distinct national styles in social science work related to law. Scandinavian scholars have emphasized the social meaning of justice. In particular, they have investigated knowledge of the law and attitudes toward it. Italian social scientists have been concerned with empirical investigations of judges and the process of judging. With the end of the Soviet Union, the legitimacy of its law also died. Russian social scientists, encouraged and supported by the March 2004 re-election of President Vladimir Putin, are looking into the processes involved in the transformation of socialist legal systems into more Western, market-oriented ones with studies on privatization, joint-ventures, leadership successions, and the reintroduction of juries in criminal cases. German sociologists are studying the socio-legal implications of reunification, changing demographic composition of the population due to immigration, the assimilation of large numbers of guest workers, and the ways of coping with economic contrast and rising nationalism. Additionally, there is a flourishing interest in law and society in Japan, initiated by the many problems Japan experienced with the reception of European law and more recently by the growing anti-Japan sentiments brought about by perceptions of "unfair" trade practices and internal pressures to modernize the quasi-feudal criminal justice system (*Economist*, 2004). Both nationally and internationally, a number of organizations have been formed and centres established to study the multi-faceted interaction between law and society (Rehbinder, 1975:13). The International Institute for the Sociology of Law was founded in 1988 by the International Sociological Association (Research Committee on Sociology of Law) and the Basque government. The Institute is located in the Old University of Onati (Spain), and by the mid-1990s it had a full-fledged master's program and an International Doctorate in Sociology of Law program. By early 2004, the success and reputation of the Institute had created a long list of applicants anxious to gain admission. The Institute also has a sought-after program for a cadre of international visiting scholars.

Few sociologists concerned with the study of law and society would question Eugen Ehrlich's oft-quoted dictum that the "centre of gravity of legal development lies not in legislation, nor in juristic science, nor in judicial decision, but in society itself" (Ehrlich, 1975:Foreword; see also Kagan, 1995). We share I.D. Willock's (1974:7) position that "in so far as jurisprudence seeks to give law a location in the whole span of human affairs it is from sociology that it stands to gain most." Sociological knowledge, perspectives, theories, and methods are not only useful but also axiomatic for the understanding and possible improvement of law and the legal system in society.

But the study of law by sociologists is somewhat hampered by difficulties of interaction between sociologists and lawyers. Language-based approaches to issues are different in the two professions (Conley and O'Barr, 1998; Noreau, 2000), and as Edwin M. Schur correctly notes, "In a sense . . . lawyers and sociologists don't 'talk the same language,' and this lack of communication undoubtedly breeds uncertainty in both professions concerning any involvement in the other's domain, much less any cooperative interdisciplinary endeavours." He goes on to say, "Sociologists and lawyers are engaged in quite different sorts of enterprises," and notes that "the lawyer's characteristic need to make decisions, here and now, may render him [sic] impatient with the sociologist's apparently unlimited willingness to suspend final judgment on the issue . . ." (Schur, 1968:8). The complexity of legal terminology further impedes interaction. There is a special rhetoric of law (Garner, 2001; Sarat and Kearns, 1994) and it has its own vocabulary; terms like *subrogation* and *replivin* and *respondeat superior* and *chattel lien* abound. Lawyers use a special arcane writing style, at times replete with multiple redundancies such as *made and entered into, cease and desist, null and void, in full force and effect,* and *give, devise, and bequeath.* Not surprisingly, "Between specialized vocabulary and arcane style, the very language of the law defies lay understanding" (Chambliss and Seidman, 1982:119). There is a move underway to combat such legalese, and lawyers and law schools are beginning to learn that good English makes sense (Gest, 1995). The "linguistically challenged profession" (Glaberson, 2001) is further beset by difficulties involving the complexities of legal writing and the need to translate it into plain English (Garner, 2001), and the forms of irritating documentation called sentence citations that tend to position references (e.g., *Ominayak v. Norcen Energy Resources Ltd.,* 29 Alta. L.R. (2d) 151, [1984] 4 C.N.J.R. 27, additional reasons at [1984] 4 C.N.L.R. 34, 52 A.R. 395 (*sub nom. Lubicon Lake Indian Band v. Norcen Energy Resources Ltd.*), affirmed 36 Alta. L.R. (2d) 137, [1985] 3 W.W.R. 193, [1985] 3 C.N.L.R. [1], 58 A.R. 161, leave to appeal to S.C.C. refused 58 N.R. 122n, application to rehear leave to appeal quashed 36 Alta. L.R. (2d) Ixin, [1985] 3 C.N.K.R. 111 at 112 (S.C.C.)) in mid-sentence. Not surprisingly, there is now a move underway to clean up legal documents by putting citations at the bottom of the page. Legal citations can include references to the date, volume, and page number of legal publications where precedents can be found.

Problems of interaction are also brought about and reinforced by the differences in professional cultures (Strathern, 2005). Lawyers are advocates; they are concerned with the identification and resolution of the problems of their clients. Sociologists consider all evidence on a proposition and approach a problem with an open mind. Lawyers, to a great extent, are guided by precedents, and past decisions control current cases. In contrast, sociologists emphasize creativity, theoretical imagination, and research ingenuity. Law represents specific individuals and organizations within the legal system (Walker and Wrightsman, 1991:179). The pronouncements of law are predominantly prescriptive: they tell people how they should behave and what will happen to them if they do not. In sociology, the emphasis is on description, on understanding the reasons why certain groups of people act certain ways in specific situations. The law *reacts* to problems most of the time; the issues and conflicts are brought to its attention by clients outside the legal system. In sociology, issues, concerns, and problems are generated within the discipline on the basis of what is considered intellectually challenging, timely, or of interest to funding agencies.

These differences in professional cultures are, to a great extent, due to the different methods and concepts that lawyers and sociologists and other social scientists (Mattei, 1997) use in searching for "truth." Legal thinking, as Vilhelm Aubert (1973:50) explains, is different from scientific thinking for the following reasons:

1. Law seems to be more inclined toward the particular than toward the general (e.g., what happened in a specific case).

2. Law, unlike the physical and social sciences, does not endeavour to establish dramatic connections between means and ends (e.g., the impact the verdict has on the defendant's future conduct).

3. Truth for the law is normative and nonprobabilistic; either something has happened or it has not. A law is either valid or invalid (e.g., did a person break a law or not).

4. Law is primarily past- and present-oriented and is rarely concerned with future events (e.g., what happens to the criminal in prison).

5. Legal consequences may be valid even if they do not occur; that is, their formal validity does not inevitably depend on compliance (e.g., the duty to fulfill a contract; if it is not fulfilled, it does not falsify the law in question).

6. A legal decision is an either-or, all-or-nothing process with little room for a compromise solution (e.g., litigant either wins or loses a case).

Of course, these generalizations have their limitations. They simply highlight the fact that law is an authoritative and reactive problem-solving system that is geared to specific social needs. Since the emphasis in law is on certainty (or predictability or finality), its instrumentation often requires the adoption of simplified assumptions about the world. The lawyer generally sees the law as an instrument to be wielded, and he or she is more often preoccupied with the practice and pontification of the law than with its consideration as an object of scholarly inquiry.

Perhaps the question most frequently asked of any sociologist interested in law is, "What are you doing studying law?" Unlike the lawyer, the sociologist needs to "justify" any research in the legal arena and often envies colleagues in law schools who can carry out such work without having to reiterate its relevance or their own competence. Yet, this need for justification is not an unmixed evil, since it serves to remind the sociologist that he or she is not a lawyer but a professional with special interests. Like the lawyer, the sociologist may be concerned with the understanding, the prediction, and perhaps even the development of law. Obviously, the sociologist and the lawyer lack a shared experience, a common quest. At the same time, increasingly, sociologists and lawyers work together on problems of mutual interest (such as research on jury selection, conflict resolution, crime, demographic concerns, and consumer problems) and are beginning to see the reciprocal benefits of such endeavours. Sociologists also recognize that their research has to be adapted to the practical and pecuniary concerns of lawyers if it is to capture their interest. In view of the vocational orientation of law schools and the preoccupation of lawyers with legal doctrine, it is unlikely that research aimed at theory building will attract or retain the attention of most law students and professors (Posner, 1996:327).

CONCEPTUALIZATIONS OF LAW

In ordinary parlance, the term "law" conjures up a variety of images. For some, law may mean getting a parking ticket, not being able to get a beer legally if under age, or complaining about the local "pooper-scooper" ordinance. For others, law is paying income tax, signing a prenuptial agreement, being evicted, or going to prison for growing marijuana. For still others, law is concerned with what legislators enact or judges declare. Law means all the above and more. Even among scholars, there is no agreement on the term. The purpose here is to introduce some of the classic and contemporary conceptualizations of law to illustrate the diverse ways of defining it.

The question "What is law?" haunts legal thought, and probably more scholarship has gone into defining and explaining the concept of law than into any other concept still in use in sociology and jurisprudence. Comprehensive reviews of the literature by Ronald L. Akers and Richard Hawkins (1975:5), Lisa J. McIntyre (1994:10), and Robert M. Rich (1977) indicate that there are almost as many definitions of law as there are theorists. E. Adamson Hoebel (1954:18) comments that "to seek a definition of the legal is like the quest for the Holy Grail." He cites Max Radin's warning: "Those of us who have learned humility have given over the attempt to define law." In spite of these warnings, law *can* be defined. In any definition of law, however, we must keep Julius Stone's (1964:177) admonition in mind that "'law' is necessarily an abstract term, and the definer is free to choose a level of abstraction; but by the same token, in these as in other choices, the choice must be such as to make sense and be significant in terms of the experience and present interest of those who are addressed."

In our illustrative review of the diverse conceptualizations of law, let us first turn to two great jurists, Benjamin Nathan Cardozo and Oliver Wendell Holmes, Jr. Cardozo (1924:52) defines law as "a principle or rule of conduct so established as to justify a prediction with reasonable certainty that it will be enforced by the courts if its authority is challenged." Holmes (1897:461) declares that "the prophecies of what the courts will do in fact, and nothing more pretentious, are what I mean by the law." For Holmes, judges make the law on the basis of past experience. In both of these definitions, the courts play an important role. These are pragmatic approaches to law as revealed by court-rendered decisions. Although implicit in these definitions is the notion of courts being backed by the authoritative force of a political state, these definitions of law seem to have a temporal character: what is the law at this time?

From a sociological perspective, one of the most influential conceptualizations of law is that of Max Weber. Starting with the idea of an *order* characterized by legitimacy, he suggests: "An order will be called *law* if it is externally guaranteed by the probability that coercion (physical or psychological), to bring about conformity or avenge violation, will be applied by a *staff* of people holding themselves specially ready for that purpose" (Weber, 1954:5). Weber argues that law has three basic features that, taken together, distinguish it from other normative orders, such as custom or convention. First, pressures to comply with the law must come externally in the form of actions or threats of action by others regardless of whether a person wants to obey the law or does so out of habit. Second, these external actions or threats always involve coercion or force. Third, those who instrument the coercive threats are individuals whose official role is to enforce the law. Weber refers to "state" law when the persons who are charged to enforce the law are part of an agency of political authority.

Weber contends that customs and conventions can be distinguished from law because they do not entail one or more of these features. **Customs** are rules of conduct in defined situations that are of relatively long duration and are generally observed without deliberation and "without thinking." Customary rules of conduct are called *usages*, and there is no sense of duty or obligation to follow them. **Conventions**, by contrast, are rules for conduct and they involve a sense of duty and obligation. Pressures, which usually include expressions of disapproval, are exerted on individuals who do not conform to conventions. Weber

(1954:27) points out that unlike law, a conventional order "lacks specialized personnel for the instrumentation of coercive power."

Although a number of scholars accept the essentials of Weber's definition of law, they question two important points. First, some contend that Weber places too much emphasis on coercion and ignores other considerations that may induce individuals to obey the law. For example, Philip Selznick (1969:4) argues that the authoritative nature of legal rules brings about a special kind of obligation that is not dependent on the use or threat of coercion or force. Many laws are obeyed because people feel it is their duty to obey. The second point concerns Weber's use of a special staff. Some scholars claim that Weber's definition limits the use of the term "law" in cross-cultural and historical contexts. They argue that the word "staff" implies an organized administrative apparatus that may not exist in certain illiterate societies. E. Adamson Hoebel (1954:28), for instance, proposes a less restrictive term by referring to individuals possessing "a socially recognized privilege," and Ronald L. Akers (1965:306) suggests a "socially authorized third party." Of course, in modern societies, law provides for a specific administrative apparatus. Still, these suggestions should be kept in mind while studying the historical developments of law (see, for example, Mundy, 2002; Pottage and Mundy, 2004).

From a different perspective, Donald Black (2002:118), a leading figure in law and society studies, contends that law is essentially governmental social control. In this sense, law is "the normative life of a state and its citizens, such as legislation, litigation, and adjudication." He maintains that several styles of law may be observed in a society, each corresponding to a style of social control. Four styles of social control are represented in law: penal, compensatory, therapeutic, and conciliatory. In the **penal style of social control**, the deviant is viewed as a violator of a prohibition and an offender to be subjected to condemnation and punishment (for example, a drug pusher). In the **compensatory style**, a person is considered to have a contractual obligation and, therefore, owes the victim restitution (for example, a debtor failing to pay the creditor). Both of these styles are accusatory where there is a complainant and a defendant, a winner and a loser. According to the **therapeutic style**, the deviant's conduct is defined as abnormal; the person needs help, such as treatment by a psychiatrist. In the **conciliatory style**, deviant behaviour represents one side of a social conflict in need of resolution without consideration as to who is right or who is wrong (for example, marital disputes). These last two styles are remedial, designed to help people in trouble and ameliorate a bad social situation. Elements of two or more of these styles may appear in a particular instance, for example, when a drug addict is convicted of possession and is granted probation contingent upon his or her participation in some kind of therapy program.

The foregoing definitions illustrate some of the alternative ways of looking at law. It is the law's specificity in substance, its universality of applicability, and the formality of its enactment and enforcement that set it apart from other devices for social control. Implicit in these definitions of law is the notion that law can be analytically separated from other normative systems in societies with developed political institutions and specialized law-making and law-enforcement agencies. The paramount function of law is to regulate and constrain the behaviour of individuals in their relationships with one another. Ideally, law is to be employed only when other formal and informal methods of social control fail to operate or are inadequate for the job. Finally, law can be distinguished from other forms of social control primarily in that it is a formal system embodying explicit rules of conduct, the planned use of sanctions to ensure compliance with the rules, and a group of authorized officials designated to interpret the rules and apply sanctions to violators. From a socio-logical perspective, the rules of law are simply a guide for action. Without interpretation and enforcement, law would remain meaningless. As Henry M. Hart (1958:403) points out, law can be analyzed sociologically as a "method" of doing something. In this context, law can be studied as a social process, instrumented by individuals during social interaction. Sociologically, law consists of the behaviours, situations, and conditions for making, inter-preting, and applying legal rules that are backed by the state's legitimate coercive apparatus for enforcement.

TYPES OF LAW

The content of law may be categorized as substantive or procedural. **Substantive laws** con-sist of rights, duties, and prohibitions administered by courts—which behaviours are to be allowed and which are prohibited (such as prohibitions against murder or the sale of nar-cotics). **Procedural laws** are rules concerning just how substantive laws are to be admin-istered, enforced, changed, and used by players in the legal system (such as filing charges, selecting a jury, presenting evidence in court, or drawing up a will).

At times a distinction is made between public law and private law (Johnson, 1977:59). **Public law** is concerned with the structure of government, the duties and powers of offi-cials, and the relationship between the individual and the state (Tomkins, 2003). "It includes such subjects as constitutional law, administrative law, regulation of public utilities, crimi-nal law and procedure, and law relating to the proprietary powers of the state and its polit-ical subdivisions" (Davis, 1962:51). **Private law** is concerned with both substantive and procedural rules governing relationships between individuals (the law of torts or private injuries, contracts, property, wills, inheritance, marriage, divorce, adoption, and the like).

A more familiar distinction is between civil law and criminal law. As noted, **civil law**, like private law, consists of a body of rules and procedures intended to govern the conduct of individuals in their relationships with others. Violations of civil statutes, called *torts*, are private wrongs for which the injured individual may seek redress in the courts for the harm he or she experienced. In most cases, some form of payment is required from the offender to compensate for the injury he or she has caused. Similarly, one company may be required to pay another a sum of money for failing to fulfill the terms of a business contract. The complainant firm is thus "compensated" for the loss it may have suffered as a result of the other company's neglect or incompetence. **Criminal law** is concerned with the definition of crime and the prosecution and penal treatment of offenders. Although a criminal act may cause harm to an individual, crimes are regarded as offenses against the state or "the peo-ple." A crime is a "public," as opposed to an "individual" or "private," wrong. It is the state, not the harmed individual, that takes action against the offender. Furthermore, the action taken by the state differs from that taken by the plaintiff in a civil case. For example, if the case involves a tort, or civil injury, compensation equivalent to the harm caused is levied. In the case of crime, some form of punishment is administered. Henry M. Hart suggests that a crime "is not simply antisocial conduct which public officers are given a responsibility to suppress. It is not simply any conduct to which a legislature chooses to attach a 'criminal' penalty. It is a conduct which, if duly shown to have taken place, will incur a formal and solemn pronouncement of the moral condemnation of the community" (1958:404). In Hart's view, both the condemnation and the consequences that follow may be regarded as constituting the punishment. Occasionally, a criminal action may be followed up by a civil suit, such as in a sexual assault case where the victim may seek financial compensation in addition to criminal sanctions.

A distinction can also be made between civil law and common law. In this context, civil law refers to legal systems whose development was greatly influenced by Roman law, a collection of codes compiled in the Corpus Juris Civilis (Code Civil). Civil-law systems are codified systems, and the basic law is found in codes. These are statutes that are enacted by national parliaments. France is an example of a civil-law system. The civil code of France, which first appeared in 1804, is called the Code Napoléon and embodies the civil law of the country. By contrast, common law resisted codification. Law is not based on acts of parliament but on case law, which relies on precedents set by judges to decide a case (Friedman, 1998, 2002). Thus, it is "judge-made" law as distinguished from legislation or "enacted" law. While most countries subscribe to either civil law or common law or a blend of the two, "Canada is unique from a legal perspective . . . in that part of the country utilizes the substantive and procedural law of two legal families as a basis for its legal system" (Terrill, 2003:152). The historical importance of both England and France in the founding and colonizing of this country has resulted in not only two distinct cultures, but also a dual legal culture that is most evident within the field of private law. While the private law of Quebec has its basis in the Romano-Germanic, or civil law, tradition, the private law elsewhere in Canada derives from the common law of England.

Law in Canada may be further divided into the following branches: constitutional law, case law, statutory law, administrative law, and royal prerogative. *Constitutional law* is a branch of public law. It determines the political organization of the state and its powers while also setting certain substantive and procedural limitations on the exercise of governing power. Constitutional law consists of the application of fundamental principles of law based on that document, as interpreted by the Supreme Court. The Constitution is "the supreme law of Canada" and establishes the basic organizational framework of government and the limits on government (Statistics Canada, 1998:511). Although Canada's constitution consists of more than 30 statutes, the two most important sources of constitutional law are the *Constitution Act, 1987* (formerly the *British North America Act, 1867*), which establishes the division of powers between the federal and provincial governments, and the *Constitution Act, 1982* (which includes the *Canadian Charter of Rights and Freedoms*), which imposes limits on the ability of governments to infringe upon specified rights and freedoms of Canadians. **Case law** is enacted by judges in cases that are decided in the appellate courts. **Statutory law** is legislated law—legislation passed by elected officials in legislative assemblies. Finally, **administrative law** is a body of law created by administrative agencies in the form of regulations, orders, and decisions. **Royal prerogative or prerogative powers**, the residue of discretionary authority that is legally left in the hands of the Crown, are another source of law. These powers, which originate in common law, are vested constitutionally in the Crown, as represented by the governor-general and the provincial lieutenants-governor. These various categories of law will be discussed and illustrated later in the text.

MAJOR LEGAL SYSTEMS

In addition to the types of law, there is a large variety of legal systems (see, for example, Johansen, 1998; Kritzer, 2002). The dominant legal systems that exist in various forms throughout the world are the Romano-Germanic (civil law), common law, socialist law, and

Islamic law. The Romano-Germanic systems predominate in Europe, in most of the former colonies of France, Germany, Italy, Spain, Portugal, and Belgium, and in countries that westernized their legal systems in the 19th and 20th centuries. Common-law systems are predominant in English-speaking countries. Islamic systems are found in the Middle East and some other parts of the world to which Islamic religion has spread. Socialist legal systems prevail in the People's Republic of China, Vietnam, Cuba, and North Korea. Remnants of socialist systems are still found in the former Soviet Union and Eastern European countries.

Romano-Germanic System

The Romano-Germanic, or civil, law refers to legal science that has developed on the basis of Roman *ius civile* or civil law (Abel and Lewis, 1988, Vol. 2; Mousourakis, 2003). The foundation of this system is the compilation of rules made in the sixth century A.D. under the Roman emperor Justinian. They are contained in the Code of Justinian and have evolved essentially as private law, as means of regulating private relationships between individuals (see, for example, Mears, 2004). After the fall of the Roman Empire, the Code of Justinian competed with the customary law of the Germanic tribes that had invaded Europe. The code was reintroduced in law school curricula between A.D. 1100 and 1200 in northern Europe, then spread to other parts of the continent. Roman law thus coexisted with the local systems throughout Europe up to the 17th century. In the 19th century, the Napoleonic codes, and subsequently the code of the new German Empire of 1900 and the Swiss code of 1907, are examples of the institutionalization of this legal system.

Codified systems are basic laws that are set out in codes. A **code** is simply a body of laws (see, for example, Kevelson, 1994; Mears, 2004). These statutes are enacted by national parliaments that arrange entire fields of law in an orderly, comprehensive, cumulative, and logical way. Today, most European countries have national codes based on a blend of customary and Roman law that makes the resulting systems members of the Romano-Germanic legal tradition. While Quebec's legal system today is best described as mixed, this system is also reflected in Quebec's Civil Code and Code of Civil Procedure, which regulates the relationships between and transactions among persons (e.g., the status of individual persons, the law of marriage and relations between married persons, the law of property and the law of contracts, and responsibility for civil wrongs) subject to Quebec law.

Common-Law System

Common law is characteristic of the English system, which developed after the Norman Conquest in 1066. The law of England, as well as those laws modelled on English law (such as the laws of Canada, the United States, Ireland, and India), resisted codification. Law is not based on acts of parliament but on case law, which relies on precedents set by judges in deciding a case (Friedman, 2002). Thus, it is "judge-made" law as distinguished from legislation or "enacted" (statutory) law. The doctrine of "precedent" is strictly a common-law practice. The divisions of the common law, its concepts, substance, structure, legal culture, vocabulary, and the methods of the common-law lawyers and judges are very different, as will be demonstrated throughout the book, from those of the Romano-Germanic, or civil, law systems.

Socialist Legal System

Although there are multiple versions of it, the origins of the socialist legal system can be traced back to the 1917 Bolshevik Revolution, which gave birth to the Union of Soviet Socialist Republics. The objectives of classical socialist law are threefold. First, law must provide for national security. Ideally, the power of the state must be consolidated and increased to prevent attacks on the socialist state and to assure peaceful coexistence among nations. Second, law has the economic task of developing production and distribution of goods on the basis of socialist principles so that everyone will be provided for "according to his or her needs." The third goal is that of education: To overcome selfish and antisocial tendencies that were brought about by a heritage of centuries of poor economic organization.

The source of socialist law is legislation, which is an expression of popular will as perceived by the Communist Party. The role of the court is simply to apply the law, not to create or interpret it. Even today, for example, judges in China are not required to have any legal training, and few do. Most hold their positions because they have close connections with local governments, which are eager for quick convictions (Diamant, Lubman, and O'Brien, 2005; Oleinik, 2003; Smith, 2001).

Socialist law rejects the idea of separation of powers. The central notion of socialist law is the notion of ownership. Private ownership of goods has been renamed "personal ownership," which cannot be used as a means of producing income. It must be used only for the satisfaction of personal needs. Socialist law is unique with respect to "socialist" ownership, of which there are two versions: collective and state. A typical example of collective ownership is the *kolkhozi*, or collective farm, which is based on nationalized land. State ownership prevails in the industrial sector in the form of installations, equipment, buildings, raw materials, and products. In a socialist legal system, the real question of property is not who owns it, but by whom and how such property is exploited (David and Brierley, 1985). Versions of this type of legal system still exist in China, Cuba, North Korea, and Vietnam (see, for example, Calvi and Coleman, 2004; Zatz, 1994).

The collapse of communism in the Soviet Union and the former Eastern-bloc countries, the dissolution of the political and economic institutions that guaranteed the conservation of communist structures, the reintroduction of a multiparty system, and the general democratization of political life had immediate implications for the socialist legal system (Priban, Roberts, and Young, 2003; Tismaneanu, 1992). These developments brought about by transitions require a reconceptualization of the basic notions of property, authority, legitimacy, and power, and even of the very idea of law (see, for example, Elster, 1995).

As part of the unexpected and unforeseen dramatic transformations that are still taking place in Eastern Europe and the former Soviet Union (Collins, 1995), the newly established independent states are experimenting with workable alternatives to the socialist rule of law in their attempts to create a climate for a system of laws receptive to and facilitative of democratic forms of market economies and civil liberties (Alexander and Skapska, 1994; Bryant and Mokrzycki, 1994; Milor, 1994; Priban, Roberts, and Young, 2003). Although the problems involved in the transition vary from country to country according to unique historical and political circumstances, all the states face common concerns, such as establishment of a new political ideology, creation of new legal rights, the imposition of sanctions on former elites, and new forms of legitimization. Among the practical problems are the creation of new property rights; the attainment of consensus in lawmaking; the formulation and instrumentation of new laws on such matters as privatization; joint ventures;

restitution for and rehabilitation of victims of the overturned regime; revision of criminal law; the rise of nationalistic, anti-foreign, and anti-Semitic sentiments; and multi-party electoral behaviour (Oleinik, 2003). There is also a whole slate of legal issues previously denied public attention by socialist law, such as prostitution, drug abuse, unemployment, and economic shortages. There are also significant structural changes taking place that are composed of newly democratic parliamentary lawmaking, conversion of the judicial system, and the awakening of alternative political parties. There are, finally, concerns with the development of new law school curricula, selection of personnel, and replacement or resocialization of former members of the Communist Party still occupying positions of power.

So far, the transition has been slow, uneven, and limited in scope. There has been no effort to remove judges who grew up under the old regime. The constitutions have yet to be revised, although there is much talk about them (Klingsberg, 1992). There is a shortage of defence lawyers (Erlanger, 1992). Since November 1993, Russian law has allowed accused criminals to request a trial by jury (Stead, 1994). But the powers of prosecutors have remained largely unreformed since Stalin's day. They remain hugely influential, heavy-handed, unaccountable, and corrupt, and prosecutors can get almost anyone arrested under Russia's vague and contradictory laws, and usually convicted too (Oleinik, 2003). Shelley (2002) argues that crime and corruption in Russia are "embedded" in Russia's state structure and identifies the following contributing factors: the low salaries of state personnel; corrupt law enforcement officers; a lack of protective devices for those who confront organized crime; selective prosecution; the failure of the Putin administration to remove corrupt leaders with links to organized crime; a historical legacy of passivity that makes the Russian people unwilling or afraid to challenge state authority; and the failure of Russia's educational system to instill in its students a meaningful sense of respect for the law (see also Hendley, 2004).

A significant task facing the new lawmakers is the creation of a legal climate aimed at stimulating foreign investments. Westerners need to be assured about the safety of their investments, which requires the creation of a legal infrastructure based on democratic principles. New laws are needed on repatriation of profits, property rights, privatization, and the movement of goods. However, perhaps the greatest challenge confronting the post-Communist regimes is crime management (see, for example, Friedman, 2000; Oleinik, 2003). In Russia and in its former satellites, the Soviet criminal code has not been significantly altered, and this has resulted in some unexpected developments. It is better suited to catch political dissidents than to inspire respect for law and order. The laws are aimed at defending the totalitarian state, not the individual. Presidential decrees and legislative acts have expanded the boundaries of life—from the right to buy and sell property to the freedom to set up banks and private corporations—but the notoriously inefficient courts have no legal basis for interpreting these decrees, much less enforcing them. Consequently, the police cannot formally tackle organized criminal activity since under present law only individuals can be held criminally culpable. Not surprisingly, the number of organized criminal groups in Russia more than quadrupled during the last decade of the 20th century (Friedman, 2000; Priban, Roberts, and Young, 2003).

Criminal groups now operate in every region and the *Mafiya* is ubiquitous internationally and nationally (Friedman, 2000). For example, prostitution networks in Western Europe, involving several hundreds of thousands of women each year from former Soviet-bloc countries, are run mostly by Russians and Ukrainians and generate huge profits. They collect several thousand dollars per woman at each stage of her odyssey (passport, journey, placement, etc.) and "middlemen" average about $20 000 per person (Paringaux, 1998:18).

In cities all across the nation, gangs operate with near impunity, practising fraud and extortion, conducting illegal trade, bribing and corrupting officials, and viciously murdering anyone who gets in their way. One base of support for the Russian Army's invasion of Chechnya in late 1994 was competing crime syndicates elsewhere in Russia (Meier, 1995; Oleinik, 2003). In 1993, Russia saw 335 000 crimes officially designated as racketeering and nearly 30 000 premeditated murders. In Moscow, the slaughter included over 1400 gangland assassinations, with probably thousands more that went unrecorded. By the end of the first quarter of 1994, the toll was running at 84 murders a day, giving Russia the dubious distinction of surpassing the United States' homicide rate—in fact, more than doubling it. The bulk were contract killings due to conflicts in commercial and financial activities (Viviano, 1995). In 2003, the murder rate in Moscow was about 18 per 100 000 residents (Wines, 2004), compared with around 5 per 100 000 in New York City and 2.86 in Winnipeg (the Canadian census metropolitan area with the highest homicide rate in that year) (Statistics Canada, 2005).

Almost every small business across Russia pays protection money to some gang. Some authors even raise questions such as: "Is Sicily the future of Russia?" (Varese, 2001). Vast fortunes in raw materials—from gold to petroleum—are smuggled out through the porous borders in the Baltic region by organized groups who have bribed their way past government officials, and ministries and municipal governments peddle property and favours. Official corruption is rampant and, along with tax instability, licensing confusion, and disregard for intellectual property rights, serves, as a disincentive to the kind of private Western investment Russia needs to create jobs and a functioning market economy (Erlanger, 1995).

Despite attempts to establish a "dictatorship of law" in the new Russia (Priban, Roberts, and Young, 2003; Wines, 2001), the conditions remain chaotic, and the authors of an influential paper in the *Brookings Review* contend that many Russians still believe that organized crime is beneficial for the economy (Gaddy et al., 1995). Businesspeople perceive organized crime as a necessary evil. Although it is hard to acknowledge, the Mafia confers certain benefits. The protection rackets offer security against other types of "disorganized" crime that might affect their clients. Dispute resolution is another Mafia service. But perhaps the biggest contribution of the Mafia to orderly market transactions is contract enforcement. In today's Russia, contracts have little force. Failure to adhere to a contract—to pay for goods or services ordered or delivered—exacts virtually no official sanctions. Close to half of the aggregate volume of accounts receivable in all Russian industry are delinquent. Since the Russian state is unwilling or unable to provide public enforcement of private contracts, the interim alternative is to privatize enforcement. It is one of the private solutions business people use when they need protection for their transactions. It also makes a nice argument in support of functionalist theorizing in sociology.

Islamic Legal System

Islamic law, unlike the previously discussed systems, is not an independent branch of knowledge. Law is integral to Islamic religion, which defines the character of the social order of the faithful who create laws in the name of God (Ahmed, 2001; Cooper, et al., 2000; Hallaq, 2004). "Islam" means "submission" or "surrender" and implies that individuals should submit to the will of God. Islamic religion states what Muslims must believe and includes the *Shari'a* ("the way to follow"), which specifies the rules for believers based on divine command and revelation. Unlike other systems of law based on judicial decisions, precedents, and legislation, Islamic law is derived from four principal sources. They include the *Koran*, the word of God as given to the Prophet. This is the principal source of Islamic law. The second source is the *Sunna*, which are the sayings, acts, and allowances of the Prophet as recorded by reliable sources in the Tradition (*Hadith*). The third is *judicial consensus*; like precedent in common law, it is based on historical consensus of qualified legal scholars, and it limits the discretion of the individual judge. *Analogical reasoning* is the fourth primary source of Islamic law. It is used in circumstances not provided for in the Koran or other sources. For example, some judges inflict the penalty of stoning for the crime of sodomy, contending that sodomy is similar to the crime of adultery and thus should be punished by the same penalty the Koran indicates for adultery. In the same vein, a female would get half the compensation a male would receive for being the victim of the same crime, since a male is entitled to an inheritance twice that of a female. In addition to these principal sources, various supplementary sources, such as custom, judge's preference, and the requirements of public interest, are generally followed.

Shari'a legal precepts can be categorized into five areas: acts commanded, recommended, reprobated, forbidden, and left legally indifferent. Islamic law mandates rules of behaviour in the areas of social conduct, family relations, inheritance, and religious ritual, and defines punishments for heinous crimes including adultery, false accusation of adultery, intoxication, theft, and robbery. For example, in the case of adultery, the proof of the offence requires four witnesses or confession. If a married person is found guilty, he or she is stoned to death. Stones are first thrown by witnesses, then by the judge, followed by the rest of the community. For a woman, a grave is dug to receive the body. The punishment for an unmarried person is 100 lashes (Lippman et al., 1988:42). For theft, the penalty of hand amputation is often used. From time to time, the classic retribution forwarded in the spirit of *lex talionis* (punishment of the same type) makes the phrase "eye for an eye" accurate in a literal sense. For example, in December 2003, a judge in Bahawalpur, a city in the eastern Pakistani province of Punjab, ruled that a man convicted of attacking and blinding his fiancee with acid be blinded with acid himself. "This is an Islamic way of doing justice," the judge wrote in his verdict and ordered that a doctor perform the punishment publicly at a sports stadium (*Seattle Times*, 2003:A8). This severe punishment may be an attempt at deterrence since violence against women, including acid attacks, is reportedly common in Pakistan, particularly in rural and deeply conservative tribal regions.

Although such practices are susceptible to interpretations that can and do create conflicts between religious doctrine and human rights (see, for example, Ghanea, 2004; Mayer, 1999; Saeed, 2004), they must be examined within the philosophy of Islam and in the spirit of true theoretical inquiry for justification—or even understanding—for Islamic justice is based on religious and philosophical principles that are quite alien to most Western readers (Souryal and Potts, 1994; Roach, 2005). Punishments and rules not defined by historical sources of *Shari'a* are left to decision by contemporary government regulations and Islamic judges. This practice permitted an evolution of *Shari'a* law to reflect changing social, political, and economic conditions.

It is important to remember that the sanctions attached to the violation of Islamic law are religious rather than civil. Commercial dealings, for example, between Muslims and Westerners are covered by governmental rules comparable to administrative law in Canada. The fundamental principle of Islam is that of an essentially theocratic society, and Islamic law can be understood only in the context of some minimal knowledge of Islamic religion and civilization (see, for example, Sechzer, 2004). Thus, care should be exercised in discussing or analyzing components of Islamic law out of context and in isolation.

FUNCTIONS OF LAW

Why do we need law, and what does it do for society? More specifically, what functions does law perform? As with the definition of law, there is no agreement among scholars of law and society on the precise functions, nor is there consensus on their relative weight and importance. A variety of functions are highlighted in the literature (see, for example, Rawls, 2001), depending on the conditions under which law operates at a particular time and place. The recurrent major themes include social control, dispute settlement, and social change. We shall now consider them briefly. These functions of the law will be examined in detail in the chapters dealing with social control, conflict resolution, and social change.

Social Control

In a small, traditional, and homogeneous society, behavioural conformity is ensured by the fact that socializing experiences are very much the same for all members. Social norms tend to be consistent with each other, there is consensus about them, and they are strongly supported by tradition. Social control in such a society is primarily dependent upon self-sanctioning. Even on those occasions when external sanctions are required, they seldom involve formal punishment. Deviants are mostly subjected to informal mechanisms of social control, such as gossip, ridicule, or humiliation. Although they exist, banishment or forms of corporal punishment are rare.

Even in a complex, heterogeneous society such as Canada, social control rests largely on the internalization of shared norms. Most individuals behave in socially acceptable ways, and, as in simpler societies, fear of disapproval from family, friends, and neighbours is usually adequate to keep potential deviants in check. Nevertheless, the great diversity of the population; the lack of direct communication between various segments; the absence of similar values, attitudes, and standards of conduct; economic inequities; rising expectations; and the competitive struggles between groups with different interests have all led to an increasing need for formal mechanisms of social control. Formal social control is characterized by "(1) explicit rules of conduct, (2) planned use of sanctions to support the rules, and (3) designated officials to interpret and enforce the rules, and often to make them" (Davis, 1962:43).

In modern societies, there are many methods of social control, both formal and informal. Law is considered one of the forms of formal social control. In the inimitable words of Roscoe Pound (1941:249): "I think of law as in one sense a highly specialized form of social control in developed politically organized society—a social control through the systematic and orderly application of the force of such a society."

Lawrence M. Friedman calls attention to two ways in which law plays an important role in social control:

In the first place, legal institutions are responsible for the making, care and preservation of those rules and norms which define deviant behaviour; they announce (in a penal code, for example) which acts may be officially punished and how and which ones may not be punished at all. In the second place, the legal system carries out many rules of social control. Police arrest burglars, prosecutors prosecute them, juries convict them, judges sentence them, prison guards watch them, and parole boards release them. (1977:11)

Of course, as we shall see, law does not have a monopoly on formal mechanisms of social control. Other types of formal mechanisms (such as firing, promotion, demotion, relocation, compensation, manipulation, and so forth) are found in industry, academe, government, business, and various private groups (Selznick, 1969).

Dispute Settlement

As Karl N. Llewellyn so aptly put it:

What, then, is this law business about? It is about the fact that our society is honeycombed with disputes. Disputes actual and potential, disputes to be settled and disputes to be prevented; both appealing to law, both making up the business of law . . . . This doing of something about disputes, this doing of it reasonably, is the business of law. (1960:2)

By settling disputes through an authoritative allocation of legal rights and obligations, the law provides an alternative to other methods of dispute resolution. Increasingly, people in all walks of life let the courts settle matters that were once resolved by informal and nonlegal mechanisms such as negotiation, mediation, or forcible self-help measures. It should be noted, however, that law deals only with disagreements that have been translated into legal disputes. A legal resolution of conflict does not necessarily result in a reduction of tension or antagonism between the aggrieved parties. For example, in a case of employment discrimination on the basis of race, the court may focus on one incident in what is a complex and often not very clear-cut series of problems. It results in a resolution of a specific legal dispute, but not in the amelioration of the broader issues that have produced that conflict.

Social Change

Many scholars contend that a principal function of law in modern society is social engineering: purposive, planned, and directed social change initiated, guided, and supported by the law. Roscoe Pound captures the essence of this function of law in stating:

For the purpose of understanding the law of today, I am content to think of law as a social institution to satisfy social wants—the claims and demands involved in the existence of civilized society—by giving effect to as much as we need with the least sacrifice, so far as such wants may be satisfied or such claims given effect by an ordering of human conduct through politically organized society. For present purposes I am content to see in legal history the record of a continually wider recognizing and satisfying of human wants or claims or desires through social control; a more embracing and more effective securing of social interests; a continually more complete and effective elimination of waste and precluding of friction in human enjoyment of the goods of existence—in short, a continually more efficacious social engineering. (1959:98)

In many instances law is considered a "desirable and necessary, if not a highly efficient means of inducing change, and that, wherever possible, its institutions and procedures are preferable to others of which we are aware" (Grossman and Grossman, 1971:2). Although some sociologists disagree with this contention (for example, Quinney, 2002), law is often used as a method of social change, a way of bringing about planned social change by the government. Social change is a prominent feature of modern welfare states. For example, part of the taxes a government collects goes to the poor in the form of cash, medical and legal benefits, and housing (Friedman, 2002). We shall return to this social change function of the law in the discussion of law and social change in Chapter 7.

DYSFUNCTIONS OF LAW

Although law is an indispensable and ubiquitous institution of social life, it possesses—like most institutions—certain dysfunctions that may evolve into serious operational difficulties if they are not seriously considered. These dysfunctions stem in part from the law's conservative tendencies, the rigidity inherent in its formal structure, the restrictive aspects connected with its control functions, and the fact that certain kinds of discriminations are inherent in the law itself.

The eminent social scientist Hans Morgenthau (1993:418) suggests that "a given status quo is stabilized and perpetuated in a legal system" and that the courts, being the chief instruments of a legal system, "must act as agents of the status quo." Although this observation does not consider fully the complex interplay between stability and change in the context of law, it still contains an important ingredient of truth. By establishing a social policy of a particular time and place in constitutional and statutory precepts, or by making the precedents of the past binding, the law exhibits a tendency toward conservatism. Once a scheme of rights and duties has been created by a legal system, continuous revisions and disruptions of the system are generally avoided in the interests of predictability and continuity. Social changes often precede changes in the law. In times of crisis, the law can break down, providing an opportunity for discontinuous and sometimes cataclysmic adjustments. Illustrations of this include the various first-aid legal measures used during an energy crisis, such as the rationing of gasoline purchases.

Related to these conservative tendencies of the law is a type of rigidity inherent in its normative framework. Since legal rules are couched in general, abstract, and universal terms, they sometimes operate as straitjackets in particular situations. An illustration of this is the failure of law to consider certain extenuating circumstances for a particular illegal act; for example, stealing because one is hungry or stealing for profit.

A third dysfunction of the law stems from the restrictive aspects of normative control. *Norms* are shared convictions about the patterns of behaviour that are appropriate or inappropriate for the members of a group. Norms serve to combat and forestall *anomie* (a state of normlessness) and social disorganization. Law can overstep its bounds, and regulation can turn into overregulation, in which situation control may become transformed into repression. For example, public administration is sometimes hampered by an overly restrictive use of the law, which tends to paralyze needed discretionary exercises in governmental power (Pound, 1941:12).

Donald Black's (1989) contention that certain kinds of discrimination are inherent in law itself can also be construed as a fourth dysfunction. Rules, in principle, may apply to everyone, but legal authority falls unevenly across social place. A quote from Anatole France's (1894) *The Red Lily* aptly illustrates this point: "The law in its majestic equality . . . forbids the rich as well as the poor from sleeping under bridges, begging in the streets, and stealing bread" (quoted in Black, 1989:72). Black argues that social status (regardless of race), the degree of intimacy (for example, family members versus friends versus strangers), speech, organization, and a number of other factors all greatly influence the use and application of law. For example, when a black person is convicted of killing a white person in America, the risk of capital punishment far exceeds every other racial combination.

In Ohio, the risk of capital punishment is approximately 15 times higher than when a black is convicted of killing another black; in Georgia, over 30 times higher; in Florida, nearly 40; and in Texas, nearly 90 times higher.

Undoubtedly, the list of dysfunctions of law is incomplete. One may also include a variety of procedural inefficiencies, administrative delays, and archaic legal terminologies. At times, justice is denied and innocent people are convicted (Yant, 1991). There is the cost of justice to the middle class and its unavailability to the poor, to the consumer, and to minority-group members. Questions can also be raised regarding the narrowness of legal education and the failure of ethical indoctrination, and the polarization of faculty and students along economic, racial, and gender lines that has abated, but endures, during the early years of the first decade of the 21st century. One can also talk about laws being out of date, inequitable criminal sentencing, the lack of clarity of some laws resulting in loopholes and diverse interpretations, and the dominating use of law by one class against another (Ruddell, 2005). Finally, critics of the law point to the rage for procedure and to "government by judges" as being particularly dysfunctional in a world as complex as ours (Crozier, 1984:116).

PARADIGMS OF SOCIETY

Sociological discussions of law in society often take place in the context of one of two ideal conceptions of society: the **consensus** and the **conflict** perspectives. The former describes society as a functionally integrated, relatively stable system held together by a basic consensus of values. Social order is considered as more or less permanent, and individuals can best achieve their interests through co-operation. Social conflict is viewed as the needless struggle among individuals and groups who have not yet attained sufficient understanding of their common interests and basic interdependence. This perspective stresses the cohesion, solidarity, integration, co-operation, and stability of society, which is seen as united by a shared culture and by agreement on its fundamental norms and values.

The conflict perspective, in direct opposition, considers society as consisting of individuals and groups characterized by conflict and dissension and held together by coercion. Order is temporary and unstable because every individual and group strives to maximize its own interests in a world of limited resources and goods. Social conflict is considered intrinsic to the interaction between individuals and groups. In this perspective, the maintenance of power requires inducement and coercion, and law is an instrument of repression, perpetuating the interests of the powerful at the cost of alternative interests, norms, and values.

But, as Ralf Dahrendorf aptly points out, it is impossible to choose empirically between these two sets of assumptions: "Stability and change, integration and conflict, 'function and dysfunction,' consensus and constraint are, it would seem, two equally valid aspects of every imaginable society" (1958:174). When law in society is viewed in one of these two perspectives, not surprisingly, quite disparate conceptions of its basic role emerge (see, for example, Dahrendorf, 1990). Let us examine in some detail the role of law in these two perspectives.

The Consensus Perspective

The consensus perspective considers law as a neutral framework for maintaining societal integration. One of the best-known and most influential legal scholars, Roscoe Pound

(1943, 1959), views society as composed of diverse groups whose interests often conflict with one another but are in basic harmony. He considers certain interests as essential for the well-being of society and maintains that the reconciliation between the conflicting interests of the diverse groups in society is essential to secure and maintain social order. In his words, law:

> is an attempt to satisfy, to reconcile, to harmonize, to adjust these overlapping and often conflicting claims and demands, either through securing them directly and immediately, or through securing certain individual interests, or through delimitations or compromises of individual interests, so as to give effect to the greatest total of interests or to the interests that weigh most in our civilization, with the least sacrifice of the scheme of the interests as a whole. (Pound, 1943:39)

In Pound's view, law in a heterogeneous and pluralistic society such as Canada is best understood as an effort at social compromise with an emphasis on social order and harmony. Pound argues that the historical development of law demonstrates a growing recognition and satisfaction of human wants, claims, and desires through law. Over time, law has concerned itself with an ever wider spectrum of human interests. Law has more and more come to provide for the common good and the satisfaction of social wants (Pound, 1959:47). He considers law a form of "social change" directed toward achieving social harmony. Pound argues that the purpose of law is to maintain and to ensure those values and needs essential to social order, not by imposing one group's will on others, but by controlling, reconciling, and mediating the diverse and conflicting interests of individuals and groups within society. In brief, the purpose of law is to control interests and to maintain harmony and social integration.

Talcott Parsons (1962:58) concurs with this view by suggesting that "the primary function of a legal system is integrity. It serves to mitigate potential elements of conflict and to oil the machinery of social intercourse." Other sociologists, such as Harry C. Bredemeier (1962), accept this perspective and believe that it is necessary for society to supplement informal mechanisms with formal mechanisms for generating and sustaining interpersonal co-operation. Proponents of the consensus perspective further maintain that law exists to maintain order and stability. Law is a body of rules enacted by representatives of the people in the interests of the people. Law is essentially a neutral agent, dispensing rewards and punishments without bias. A fundamental assumption of this perspective is that the political system is pluralistic, that society is composed of a number of interest groups of more or less equal power. The laws reflect compromise and consensus among these various interest groups and the values that are fundamental to the social order (Chambliss, 1976:4). This perspective will be alluded to in various sections of this book.

The Conflict Perspective

In marked contrast to the consensus perspective, the conflict view considers law as a "weapon in social conflict" (Turk, 1978) and an instrument of oppression "employed by the ruling classes for their own benefit" (Chambliss and Seidman, 1982:36). From this perspective, the transformation of society from a small, relatively homogeneous social group to a network of specialized groups is brought about by the evolution of both distinct sets of interests and differences in real power between groups. When diverse groups come into conflict, they compete to have their interests protected and perpetuated through the formalization of their interests into law. On the basis of this idea, Richard Quinney argues that rather than being a device to control interests, law is an expression of interests, an outgrowth of the inherent conflict of interests characteristic of society. According to Quinney:

> Society is characterized by diversity, conflict, coercion, and change, rather than by consensus and stability. Second, law is a *result* of the operation of interests, rather than an instrument that functions outside of particular interests. Though law may control interests, it is in the first place *created by* interests of specific persons and groups; it is seldom the product of the whole society. Law is made by men [sic], representing special interests, who have the power to translate their interests into public policy. Unlike the pluralistic conception of politics, law does not represent a compromise of the diverse interests in society, but supports some interests at the expense of others. (1970:35)

Proponents of the conflict perspective believe that law is a tool by which the ruling class exercises its control. Law both protects the property of those in power and serves to repress political threats to the position of the elite. Quinney (1975:285) writes that whereas the state, contrary to conventional wisdom, is the instrument of the ruling class, "law is the state's coercive weapon, which maintains the social and economic order" and supports some interests at the expense of others, even when those interests are that of the majority.

But advocates of this position overstate their case. Not all laws are created and operated for the benefit of the powerful ruling groups in society. Laws prohibiting murder, robbery, arson, incest, and assault benefit all members of society, regardless of their economic position. It is too broad an assumption that powerful groups dictate the content of law and its enforcement for the protection of their own interests. As we shall see in Chapter 4, all kinds of groups are involved in lawmaking, although the powerful groups do have a substantial voice in the lawmaking process.

These two perspectives of society—consensus and conflict—are *ideal types* (that is, abstract concepts used to describe essential features of a phenomenon). Considering the operation of legal systems in society, there may be an element of truth in both. Sociologists who are influenced by Karl Marx, Georg Simmel, Lewis Coser, and Ralf Dahrendorf generally tend to embrace the conflict perspective of law in society (Goldstein, 2004). One of their justifications for taking this theoretical stance is that this approach emphasizes the role of special-interest groups in society. For example, the power of economic and commercial interests to influence legislation is illustrated by William J. Chambliss in his study of vagrancy statutes. He notes that the development of vagrancy laws paralleled the need of landowners for cheap labour during the period in England when the system of serfdom was collapsing. The first of these statutes, which came into existence in 1349, threatened criminal punishment for those who were able-bodied and yet unemployed—a condition that existed when peasants were in the process of moving from the land into the cities. The vagrancy law served "to force labourers (whether personally free or unfree) to accept employment at a low wage in order to insure the landowner an adequate supply of labour at a price he could afford to pay" (Chambliss, 1964:69). Subsequently, vagrancy statutes were modified to protect the commercial and industrial interests and to ensure safe commercial transportation. In the late 19th and early 20th centuries, vagrancy laws were used again to serve the interests of the wealthy (Chambliss and Seidman, 1982:182). This is just one illustration to show how law came to reflect the particular interests of those who have power and influence in society (see also Banner, 2000). We shall return to the role of interest groups dealing with decision-making processes in the context of lawmaking in Chapter 4.

OPTIONS FOR SOCIOLOGISTS

As with the approaches to the study of law and society, divergences of opinion also characterize the question of what role sociologists should play in such endeavours. This question, to a substantial degree, polarized the discipline. Some sociologists consider their role primarily to synthesize material and to provide instructional packages for students and interested laymen (see, for example, Friedrichs, 2001; Sutton, 2001). Others consider their role as describing and explaining social phenomena objectively. They are concerned with the understanding of social life and social processes, and they go about their research in an alleged value-neutral and empirical fashion. They accept as scientific only those theoretical statements whose truth can be proven empirically. They are guided by Max Weber's notion of sociology as "a science which seeks to understand social action interpretively, and thereby to explain it causally in its course and its effects" (Weber, 1968:3). They believe that the discovery of causal laws is the ultimate goal of sociology, but the understanding of people's motives is central.

Others, however, go beyond the notion of *verstehen* (to understand). Sociologists who claim to be **dialectical** and critical in their orientation do not seek merely to describe and explain social events. They, as scientists, assert their right to criticize. The standards of evaluation upon which their criticism is based, and which these sociologists deduce from the nature of human beings and from considerations about social development, cannot always be empirically tested. To them, empirical research is necessary insofar as it provides and explains the data, but it is, so to speak, only a first step toward the essential criticism. They believe that the task of sociology is to account for human suffering. They aim at demystifying the world; to show people what constrains them and what their routes are to freedom. Their criticisms are prompted by their belief that the human condition and the social order have become unbearable. These critics believe that they have a responsibility not only to identify the factors that have precipitated a deleterious condition but also to provide, through theoretical and empirical efforts, ways of rectifying or redressing the condition.

Finally, for some sociologists, criticism is interconnected with practice. They endorse the role of being simultaneously a student and an agent of social action. They are guided by **praxis**, or the wedding of theory and action. Because of their knowledge of social conditions, they are obligated to take action (see, for example, McLaren and Farahmandpur, 2004; Schram, 2002). This position is associated with a Marxist tradition. It is based on the notion that knowledge generated from an analysis of a specific historical situation may be used as an argument for intervention, and politically engaged scholarship can contribute to the struggle for social justice. Sociologists in such situations try to demystify, clarify, and show individuals the source of their misery and the means of overcoming it. In a Marxian context, praxis means what people do, as contrasted with what they think. "Praxis is a revolutionary form of social practice (i.e., it contributes to the humanization of people by transforming reality from alienation to a hopefully better future). The concept is both a means of consciously shaping historical conditions and a standard for evaluating what occurs in any historical order. Marx maintains that a dialectical relationship exists between theory and praxis" (Reasons and Rich, 1978:431). Thus, sociologists of this perspective actively advocate changes in law and legal institutions wherever needed and work for the reformation of both the criminal system and the criminal law when warranted (Munger, 2001; Nelson, 2001).

These controversies beset the "proper" role of sociologists in the discipline. Based on one's values, ideologies, and conception of sociology, and a plethora of other considerations, one may prefer to be a detached observer of social life, a critic of the social order, or an active agent of change. These roles, fortunately, are not mutually exclusive. Depending on the nature of the issue under consideration, the degree of commitment to and involvement in that issue, one may freely select among these alternatives (Lempert, 2001). As an intellectual enterprise, sociology is flexible enough to accommodate diverse positions. In a sense, sociologists contribute to a greater understanding of the complicated interplay between law and society.

SUMMARY

- In sociology, the study of law touches on a variety of well-established areas of inquiry. It incorporates values, ideologies, social institutions, norms, power relations, and social processes.
- Since World War II, there has been a growing interest in law among sociologists both in this country and elsewhere. Some of the examples of the study of law and society include the effectiveness of law, the impact of law on society, methods of dispute resolution, and research on judicial, legislative, and administrative processes.
- The content of law may be considered as substantive or procedural. A distinction is made also between public law and private law, as well as between civil law and criminal law. Common law generally refers to "judge-made" law or "case" law, as differentiated from statutory or enacted law.
- The principal legal systems in the world today include the Romano-Germanic (civil law), common law, socialist law with its current ramifications and problems of transition, and Islamic law.
- Sociological analyses of law and society are generally based on two ideal views of society—consensus and conflict perspectives. The former considers society as a functionally integrated, relatively stable system held together by basic consensus of values. The latter conceives of society as consisting of groups characterized by conflict and dissension on values and held together by some members who coerce others.
- There is dispute over the "proper" role sociologists should play in the study of law and society. Some sociologists maintain that their role is to try to understand, describe, and empirically analyze social phenomena in a more or less value-free context. Others argue that it is the responsibility of social scientists to criticize malfunctioning components of and processes in a social system. Still others are guided by the notion of praxis; they seek to combine theory with practice, and their objective is to try to redress deleterious social conditions by means of legal action.

CRITICAL THINKING QUESTIONS

1. Robert Kagan (1995) has identified four factors as playing a powerful role in the rapid growth of legislation over the last few decades: the intensification of international economic competition; rapid technological change; a growing concern with the environment; and increased geographic mobility. In this context, he observes, three agendas have become dominant in sociolegal research: the first "focuses on determining the

social, political and economic forces that explain law and institutional forms, the second focuses on the performance of legal institutions, and the third tries to assess the effects of legal processes on social life." While Kagan suggests that greater attention should be directed to the third, which of these research "agendas" do *you* find most compelling? Why?

2. Richard Vatz (1980:160) observes that "'The law' to most citizens comprises a massively complex, but well ordered and ultimately equitable and fair system of adjudications of disputes and alleged law breaking by which all citizens benefit. One need not belabour the metaphors of balanced scales of justice to comprehend this widespread mythology." However, it is his contention that faith in the law is "analogous to and no less than religious faith'" and he proclaims that the image of the law as orderly, rational in its composition, and sure in its execution is simply a "myth." According to Vatz, public confidence in "the law" arises as the result of "experiencing communications *about* the law which convinces them that 'the law' is functioning in a way worthy of the public's considerable reverence."

In what ways are positive impressions of the law urged upon us by opinion leaders in the socialization process (e.g., the family, the school, the peer group, and the mass media)? What are the advantages/disadvantages of this inculcated "mythos"?

Theoretical Perspectives

This chapter examines the evolution of legal systems and reviews some of the principal classical and contemporary theories of law and society. At the outset, it should be acknowledged that there is no single, widely accepted, comprehensive theory of law and society (or of anything else in the social sciences). The field is enormously complex and polemical, and individual explanations have thus far failed to capture fully this complexity and diversity. This is, of course, not due to lack of effort. On the contrary, sociological theories of law abound (Arrigo, 1999; Banakar, 2003; Banakar and Travers, 2002). Of the vast amount of literature, this chapter deals briefly with only a few of the important classical and contemporary theories of law and society. This approach serves certain purposes. It provides the reader with some conception of the development and content of these different theories and how they relate to one another. Although the discussion of these theories clearly shows the complex and multi-faceted nature of the relationship between law and society, it also serves as a means of differentiating, organizing, and understanding a great mass of material. Thus, although the concern is to suggest the magnitude and diversity of the field, an attempt is also made to lend order to that magnitude and diversity.

A cautionary note is in order with regard to the procedures followed in this chapter for grouping various theories. It will become clear that many theories of law and society tend to overlap. For example, the reader may find that a theory that has been placed under the heading of "The European Pioneers" will contain similar elements to those embodied in "Classical Sociological Theorists." Any such effort at classification of theories should be viewed as essentially a heuristic device to facilitate discussion rather than to reflect the final status of the theories considered. Just as with general sociological theories (see, for example, Adams and Sydie, 2002; Shoemaker, Tankard, and Lasorsa, 2004), there are many ways of categorizing the more specific law and society theories. They may be considered from the disciplinary perspectives of jurisprudence, philosophy of law, sociology of law, and anthropology of law. They can also be listed under the headings of sociology of civil law, sociology of criminal law, sociological jurisprudence, and anthropology of law; grouped by various theoretical trends, such as natural law, historical and analytical jurisprudence, utilitarianism, positivism, and legal realism; or categorized under various perspectives such as Marxian, Weberian, and Durkheimian (see, for example, Pottage and Mundy; Trevino, 1996). Any attempt to categorize theories under particular labels is open to question. The present effort should not be an exception. The categories used are in some ways arbitrary, since they can be increased or decreased depending on one's objectives. These categorizations simply provide some semblance of order for the principal theoretical approaches to law and society. In the schema employed, the diverse theories are presented in a chronological order, with an emphasis on influential classical and contemporary theories.

EVOLUTION OF LEGAL SYSTEMS

Formal codified law emerges when the social structure of a given society becomes so complex that regulatory mechanisms and methods of dispute settlement no longer can be dependent on informal customs and social, religious, or moral sanctions (see, for example, Zifcak, 2005). Formal and institutionalized regulatory mechanisms come into being when other control devices are no longer effective. Changes in the organization of a society from kinship and tribe to a territorially based political organization inevitably result in changes in the legal system. The basic content of the law and legal system concomitantly will become more complex, specialized, and statutory as the economy grows more complex and diversified, industrialization increases, and social institutions become more stratified and specialized.

Historically, legal development and industrialization, urbanization, and modernization are closely intertwined. In a small, homogeneous society with little division of labour and a high degree of solidarity, informal sanctions are sufficient to keep most behaviour in line with the norms. An ideal example is the community on Tristan da Cunha, an isolated island in the middle of the South Atlantic Ocean. A few hundred people live there, growing potatoes and catching fish. When social scientists visited the island in the 1930s, they were amazed to see how "law-abiding" these people were, even though they had nothing resembling law as we know it. There was no serious crime on the island that anyone could recall, no police, courts, jails, or judges. There was no need for them. People in the community relied on informal mechanisms of social control such as shaming and open disapproval, which can be effective and severe in their own way. Such forms of control work in small, homogeneous, face-to-face communities (Friedman, 2002; Ellickson, 1991).

But in a modern, heterogeneous, and complex society, formal norms and sanctions are necessary to control behaviour so that society can continue to function in an orderly and predictable fashion. The presence of law and a legal system is essential to the maintenance of social order (see, for example, Kritzer, 2002).

The reciprocal relationships between society and the legal system during their parallel development are perplexing issues that have been conceptualized vaguely in the sociological literature. Jonathan H. Turner points out:

> [L]inkages between law and society are often left implicit; change in the relative importance of these linkages is frequently not discussed; and there is a tendency to place too heavy an emphasis on single variables and thereby ignore the multiplicity of institutional influences on legal development. (1974:3)

Turner (1972:242) views legal development as a form of institutional adjustment to the ubiquitous problems of control and coordination facing modernizing society. He reasons that modernization inevitably generates conflict, tension, strains, and disjunctures that can force the modernization of law in society. It should be noted, however, that although there is some overall pattern of legal development, the specifics vary from society to society as a result of unique conditions such as geographical location, historical events, conquest, and prevailing political and social forces. As a result, it is impossible to trace legal development from a primitive to a modern profile for one society because changes in geographical boundaries, wars, and other events would obscure unilinear development. For instance, a highly developed system of Roman law was imposed upon traditional legal systems during the expansion of the Empire, "with the result that a developmental jump occurred in these primitive legal systems" (Turner, 1972:242).

Developmental models, although controversial, have been used in almost every field of social science. Their use is justified by the attempt to make sense of history, which requires an appreciation of directionality, growth, and decay (Nonet and Selznick, 2001:19). The early sociologists all believed in the progressive development of social patterns over long periods of time (Vago, 2004:51). Similar beliefs are also present in psychology. Consider, for example, the stages of growth to psychological maturity in Freudian theory, or the development of personality in the theories of Piaget (1932/1965). Similarly, in economics, Walt W. Rostow (1961) talks about the stages of economic growth from preconditions for takeoff to the age of high mass consumption. In the same vein, students of modern organization talk rather freely of three stages: prebureaucratic, bureaucratic, and postbureaucratic (Bennis, 1966:3). Developmental models can deal with transformations at various levels in society, such as individual, group, community, organization, and social institutions, or they may deal with the transformation of entire societies. The underlying theme in developmental models is the identification of forces that, having been set in motion at one stage, produce a characteristic outcome in another stage.

Thus, it is not surprising that Pound (1959:366), among others, finds it "convenient to think of . . . stages of legal development in systems which have come to maturity." The law and society literature suggests that the more complex the society, the more differentiated the legal system (Schwartz and Miller, 1975). Underlying this proposition is the notion that legal development is conditioned by a series of integrative demands stemming from society's economic, political, educational, and religious institutions. Based on the complexity and magnitude of the interplay among these institutions and between these institutions and the law, several types of legal systems may be identified in the course of societal development. There is practically no limit to the variability of legal systems, and many scholars have developed typologies to capture this diversity (such as Mundy, 2002; Pottage and Mundy, 2002).These typologies seldom correspond fully to the real world, but they are essential in an analytical discussion dealing with the types of legal systems. From a developmental perspective, some general types can be isolated, and following Turner's illustrative and timeless categories (1972:216), the "primitive," transitional, and modern legal systems will be examined. However, given that the terms "primitive" and "traditional" law and legal systems are often used interchangeably in the literature (see, for example, Rouland, 1994), we have elected to use the latter term, recognizing that the former conveys a pejorative connotation.

Traditional Legal Systems

Traditional legal systems are typically found in hunting and gathering and simple agrarian societies. The laws are not written or codified; they are permeated by customs, tradition, religious dogma, and values. Traditional laws often coexist with ancient norms and are also comparatively undifferentiated. There is, however, some distinction between substantive and procedural laws. **Substantive laws** consist of rights, duties, and prohibitions concerning what is right, wrong, permissible, and impermissible. **Procedural laws** are rules regarding just how substantive law is to be administered, enforced, changed, and used in the mediation of disputes. Subsequent differentiation of types at later stages of legal evolution can be encompassed under these two general types of law.

The functions of law in traditional societies are essentially the same as those in more advanced societies (Rouland, 1994:153). Laws preserve important cultural elements; they coordinate interaction, settle disputes, check deviance, and regularize exchanges. Laws also legitimize existing inequalities. In addition: "By codifying, preserving, and enforcing certain key kinship rules (usually descent and authority), religious rituals and dogmas, and the chief's right to enact laws, differences in power and privilege are preserved and made to seem appropriate" (Turner, 1972:220).

In traditional societies, there are no well-developed political subsystems, and the polity is composed of kin leaders, councils of elders or chiefs, and various religious leaders. Legislators are political bodies and, as such, do not formally exist in traditional societies. In such societies, judges and political leaders (elders and the like) are one and the same. The emphasis is on court-enacted law (common law) rather than legislative law enacted by political bodies (statutory law). Although the distinction between the two in traditional societies does not exist (because courts are political and their decisions constitute legislation), chiefs or elders can enact both substantive and procedural laws. Because there are no written laws, the chief-legislator can strike, rescind, or change old laws more easily than the modern legislator; and if such action appears reasonable, little resistance is offered. Obviously, getting old laws off the books in modern societies is rarely that easy.

Courts, like the police force, are temporarily assembled and then dispersed as disputes arise and are settled. Although they are provisional, the courts comprise at least two clearly differentiated roles: that of the judges, who hear evidence and make decisions in accordance with laws, and that of litigants, who have to abide by the judges' decisions. Occasionally, a third role can be identified in such courts, that of a representative "lawyer" who pleads the case for a litigant. As the legal system develops, these roles become more clearly differentiated. In traditional societies, however, these three procedures are sufficient to maintain a high degree of societal integration and coordination.

Transitional Legal Systems

Transitional legal systems are characteristic of advanced agrarian and early industrial societies where the economic, educational, and political subsystems are increasingly differentiated from kinship relationships. As a result of increases in integrative problems, the legal subsystem becomes more complex and extensive, as evidenced by a clear-cut differentiation in basic legal elements—laws, courts, enforcement agencies, and legislative structures. In the transitional stage, most of the features of the modern legal system are present, but not to the same degree. Law becomes more differentiated from tradition, customs, and religious dogma. There is a distinction between **public law** and **private law**. The former is concerned with the structure of government, the duties and powers of officials, and the relationships between the individual and the state (the latter regulates relations among non-political units). Criminal law also becomes distinguishable from torts. **Criminal law** denotes wrongs against the state, the community, and the public. **Torts** are laws pertaining to private wrongs of parties against each other rather than against the state or the public. There is, similarly, a clearer differentiation between procedural and substantive laws, and as the types of laws increase, laws become systems of rules (Friedman, 1975:291).

The increased differentiation of laws is reflected in the increased complexity of the courts. Accompanying this differentiation is the emergence of at least five distinct types of statuses: judge; representative or lawyer; litigant; court officials and administrators; and jurors. The roles of judges and lawyers become institutionalized, requiring specialized training. In transitional legal systems, written records of court proceedings become more common, contributing to the emergence of a variety of administrative roles, which, in turn, leads to the initial bureaucratization of the court.

With the development of clearly differentiated, stable, and autonomous courts, legal development accelerates for the following reasons:

> (1) Laws enacted by the growing legislative body of the polity can be applied systematically to specific circumstances by professionals and experts. This means that laws enacted by the centralizing polity have institutional channels of application. (2) Where political legislation of laws is absent, an established court can enact laws by handing down Common-Law precedents. Such common laws tend to fit nicely the structural conditions in a society, since they emerge out of attempts to reconcile actual and concrete conflicts. (Turner, 1972:222)

Initially, courts are localized and characterized by common-law decisions. In time, their conflicting and overlapping rules provide an impetus for the unification of a legal system, eventually leading to a more codified system of laws.

There is also the emergence of explicit, relatively stable, and somewhat autonomous police roles in transitional legal systems. Concomitant with the development of police roles is the emergence of legislative structures. This results in a clear differentiation of legislative statuses from judicial (courts) and enforcement (police) statuses. Legislating new laws or abolishing old ones is no longer a matter of a simple decree. In transitional legal systems, a small cluster of statuses, whether organized in a forum, a senate, or a royal council, can enact laws. Initially, these laws are dominated by a political elite and are responsive to its demands. Later on, legislative changes become more comprehensive, involving a group of laws pertaining to general problem areas. With the enactment of more comprehensive statutes and codes, a system of civil law begins to emerge to supplement common law. The development of civil codes is stimulated by an established court system and police force, a pool of educated lawyers and judges, a background of common law, and a degree of political and national unity. The functions of law in transitional legal institutions are essentially similar to those in traditional systems—perhaps a bit more complex, and at the same time, less successful in resolving integrative problems. Structural differentiation becomes more complex. Political development increases, bringing with it inequities in power and wealth. In such situations, civil law tends to legitimize these inequalities.

Modern Legal Systems

In modern legal systems, we find all the structural features of transitional systems present, but in greater and more elaborate arrangements. Turner notes: "Laws in modern legal systems are extensive networks of local and national statutes, private and public codes, crimes and torts, common and civil laws, and procedural and substantive rules" (1972:225). A distinctive feature of modern legal systems is the proliferation of public and procedural laws, referred to as **administrative law**. Another aspect is the increasing proportion of statutory law over common law. Legislation, as a result of political development, becomes a more acceptable method of adjusting law to social conditions. There are also clear hierarchies of laws, ranging from constitutional codes to regional and local codes.

Courts, in modern legal systems, have an important role in mediating and mitigating conflict, disputes, deviance, and other sources of malintegration. The roles of lawyers and judges become highly professionalized, with licensing requirements and formal sanctions. The various administrative statuses—clerks, bailiffs, and prosecutors—specialize, proliferate, and become heavily bureaucratized. The jurisdictions of courts are specified with clearly delineated appeal procedures. Cases unresolved in lower courts can be argued in higher courts that have the power to reverse lower court decisions.

In modern legal systems, laws are enforced and court decisions are carried out by clearly differentiated and organized police forces. Each force possesses its own internal organization, which becomes increasingly bureaucratized at the higher levels. In addition to police forces, regulatory agencies regularly enforce and oversee compliance with laws. Administrative agencies, as will be discussed in Chapters 4 and 5, also make and interpret laws in the context of their own mandates.

> Legislative bodies at various levels proliferate. There is a greater emphasis on integrative problems and on enacting comprehensive laws. Accompanying the emergence of a stable legislature, well-planned and comprehensive law enactment can become an effective mechanism of social change. (Zifack, 2005)

Inherent in modern legal systems is the notion of "modern" law. Marc Galanter (1977), in a classic and influential article, "The Modernization of Law," sets forth a comprehensive conceptualization of contemporary law that remains among the most widely cited even today. His model, not a description, includes 11 salient features that characterize the legal systems of the industrial societies of the last century, and many of them can be found in modern societies as well. He argues that "modern law consists of rules that are uniform and unvarying in their application" (1977:1047). The same rules and regulations are applicable to everyone. Modern law is also "transactional." Rights and duties stem from "transactions." They are not "aggregated in unchanging clusters" prescribed to an individual by ascribed status. Galanter insists that modern legal norms are "universalistic"; that is, their application is predictable, uniform, and impersonal. Further, the system, to be uniform and predictable, operates on the basis of written rules and has a regular chain of command. The system is "rational" in the Weberian sense, and "rules are valued for their instrumental utility in producing consciously chosen ends, rather than for their formal qualities" (1977:1048). Such a system is run by full-time professionals whose "qualifications come from mastery of the techniques of the legal system itself, not from possession of special gifts or talents or from eminence in some other area of life" (1977:1048). Professionals run the law; lawyers replace "mere general agents" as the legal system grows more complex.

The system is "amenable." It can be changed and it does not have "sacred fixity." Says Galanter: "Legislation replaces the slow reworking of customary law" (1977:1048). It is also "political"—that is, tied to the state, which has a monopoly on law. Finally, legislative, judicial, and executive functions are "separate and distinct" in modern law.

Thus far, we have identified some of the preconditions necessary for the development of modern legal systems. Let us now consider some of the theories accounting for those developments.

THEORIES OF LAW AND SOCIETY

The preceding section dealt with some general types of legal systems as they correspond to various stages of modernization and social development. The present section addresses two questions emerging from the previous discussion: Why did changes in the legal system take place? And what factors contributed to legal development from a historical perspective? In answering these questions, we can distinguish two general issues. The first is the issue of legal development in any society. The second concerns forces that produce or prevent change in the legal system.

Theorists of law and society have long been preoccupied with efforts to describe the broad historical course of legal development and to analyze the factors that influence legal systems. The literature is extensive, going back several centuries. The investigation of legal development has traditionally been the concern of scholars in a variety of fields. In view of the limits set for this study, no attempt is made here to provide a comprehensive and systematic review of principal theories and schools. Certain prominent theorists will, however, be considered.

Among the theorists to be presented, there is more or less general agreement that societal and legal complexities are interrelated. Beyond that, there is little consensus. The particular theorists differ as to detail and interpretation of the general relationship between legal change and social change. It is hoped that the following sample of theorists from various disciplines, historical periods, and countries will provide a better understanding of the diverse issues involved in the investigation of the multi-faceted relations between law and other major institutions of society.

The European Pioneers

For centuries in Europe, law has been considered as an absolute and autonomous entity, unrelated to the structure and function of the society in which it has existed (see, for example, Feinberg and Coleman, 2003). The idea of **natural law** constitutes the basis for this exposition of law (see, for example, George, 2003). The origins of natural law can be traced back to ancient Greece. Aristotle maintains that natural law has a universal validity and is based on reason that is free from all passion (see, for example, Brooks and Murphy, 2003). St. Thomas Aquinas argues that natural law is part of human nature, and through natural law, human beings participate as rational beings in the eternal laws of God.

The idea of natural law is based on the assumption that through reason the nature of human beings can be known, and that this knowledge can provide the basis for the social and legal ordering of human existence (see, for example, Belliotti, 1992:17). Natural law is considered superior to enacted law. It is "the chief tenet of natural law that arbitrary will is not legally final" (Selznick, 1961:100). An appeal to higher principles of justice is always permissible from the decrees of a lawmaker. When enacted law does not coincide with the principles of natural law, it is considered unjust. For example, pro-life proponents argue that laws providing for abortion on demand are contrary to the tenets of natural law.

Under the influence of natural law, many European scholars believed that law in any given society was a reflection of a universally valid set of legal principles based on the idea that through reason, the nature of human beings can be ascertained. This knowledge could then become the basis for the social and legal order of human existence. From the middle of the 19th century, however, the idea of natural law was largely displaced by historical and evolutionary interpretations of law, and by **legal positivism**, which considered the legal and the moral to constitute two quite separate realms. These two views of the law sought to explain the law causally in terms of ethnological factors, or by reference to certain evolutionary forces that pushed the law forward along a predetermined path. Many theorists sought to discourage philosophical speculation about the nature and purposes of law and concentrated on the development and analysis of positive law as laid down and enforced by the state. The most notable among these scholars include Baron de Montesquieu in France, and Herbert Spencer and Sir Henry Sumner Maine in England. We shall now consider their theories in some detail.

Baron de Montesquieu (1689–1755). Montesquieu challenges the underlying assumptions of natural law by presenting a radically different conceptualization of law and society. He considers law integral to a particular people's culture. The central thesis of his *Spirit of Laws* (1886) is that laws are the result of a number of factors in society such as customs, physical environment, and antecedents, and that laws can be understood only in the context of particular societies. He further posits that laws are relative and that there are no "good" or "bad" laws in the abstract. This proposition ran contrary to the opinions of the day. Each law, Montesquieu maintains, must be considered in relation to its background, its antecedents, and its surroundings. If a law fits well into this framework, it is a good law; if it does not, it is bad.

But Montesquieu's fame rests above all on his political theory of the separation of powers. According to this theory, a constitution is composed of three different types of legal powers: legislative, executive, and judicial, each vested in a different body or person. The role of the legislature is to enact new laws; of the executive, to enforce and administer the laws as well as to determine policy within the framework of those laws; and of the judiciary, simply to interpret the laws established by the legislative power. This neat classification had considerable influence on the form of constitution subsequently adopted by the newly created United States of America after the Declaration of Independence (Bodenheimer, 1974:49) and would greatly affect constitutional thinkers in other countries as well throughout the late 18th and 19th centuries.

Leopold Pospisil (1971:138), in his analysis of Montesquieu's contributions, aptly remarks: "With his ideas of the relativity of law in space as well as in time, and with his emphasis on specificity and empiricism, he can be regarded as the founder of the modern sociology of law in general and of the field of legal dynamics in particular."

Herbert Spencer (1820–1903). Contrary to the doctrines of natural law, in 19th-century England, Herbert Spencer provides the philosophical underpinnings for the theory of unregulated competition in the economic sphere. Strongly influenced by Charles Darwin, Spencer draws a picture of the evolution of civilization and law in which natural selection and the survival of the fittest are the primary determining factors.

Evolution for Spencer consists of growing differentiation, individuation, and increasing division of labour. Civilization is the progress of social life from primitive homogeneity to ultimate heterogeneity. He identifies two main stages in the development of civilizations: a primitive or military form of society, with war, compulsion, and status as regulatory mechanisms, and a higher or industrial form of society, with peace, freedom, and a contract as the controlling devices.

Spencer is convinced that in his second stage, human progress is marked by a continual increase in individual liberty and a corresponding decrease in governmental activities. Government, he believes, must gradually confine its field of action to the enforcement of contracts and the protection of personal safety. He strongly opposes public education, public hospitals, public communications, and any governmental programs designed to alleviate the plight of the economically weaker groups in society. He is convinced that social legislation of this type is an unwarranted interference with the laws of natural selection (Spencer, 1899).

Spencer's ideas on law influenced a number of early North American sociologists (McCann, 2004). For example, William Graham Sumner advocates a position essentially similar to that of Spencer. He, too, sees the function of the state limited to that of an overseer who guards the safety of private property and sees to it that the peace is not breached. He favours a regime of contract in which social relations are regulated primarily by mutual agreements, not by government-imposed legal norms. He argues that society does not need any supervision. Maximum freedom of individual action should be promoted by law. He considers attempts to achieve greater social and economic equality as ill-advised and unnatural.

> Let it be understood that we cannot go outside of this alternative: liberty, inequality, survival of the fittest; not liberty, equality, survival of the unfittest. The former carries society forward and favours all its best members; the latter carries society downward and favours all its worst members. (Sumner, 1940:25)

Reflections of the economic and social philosophies of Spencer and Sumner are still discernible in current conservative attitudes that place the rights of wealthier groups above those of the disfavoured members of society. One may also consider, in this context, resistance to legislative policies designed to equalize the bargaining power of management and labour, to protect the health and subsistence of marginal groups, or to interfere with that freedom of contract which was considered the true birthmark of an advancing civilization.

Sir Henry Sumner Maine (1822–1888). The founder and principal proponent of the English historical school of law, Maine was among the first theorists to argue that law and legal institutions must be studied historically if they are to be understood. He contends that legal history shows patterns of evolution that recur in different societies and in similar historical circumstances. He argues that there do not exist infinite possibilities for building and managing human societies; certain political, social, and legal forms reappear in seemingly different garb, and if they reappear, they manifest themselves in certain typical ways. For example, Roman feudalism produced legal rules and legal institutions strikingly similar to English feudalism, although differences can also be demonstrated. One of his general laws of legal evolution is set forth in his classical treatise, *Ancient Law*:

> The movement of the progressive societies has been uniform in one respect. Through all its course it has been distinguished by the gradual dissolution of family dependency and the growth

of individual obligation in its place. The Individual is steadily substituted for the Family, as the unit of which civil laws take account. The advance has been accomplished at varying rates of celerity, and there are societies not absolutely stationary in which the collapse of the ancient organization can only be perceived by careful study of the phenomena they present. But, whatever its pace, the change has not been subject to reaction or recoil, and apparent retardations will be found to have been occasioned through the absorption of archaic ideas and customs from some entirely foreign source. Nor is it difficult to see what is the tie between man [sic] and man [sic] which replaces by degrees those forms of reciprocity in rights and duties which have their origin in the Family. It is Contract. Starting, as from one terminus of history, from a condition of society in which all the relations of Persons are summed up in the relations of Family, we seem to have steadily moved towards a phase of social order in which all these relations arise from the free agreement of Individuals. (1861:170)

Thus, Maine arrives at his often-quoted dictum that "the movement of the progressive societies has hitherto been a movement from Status to Contract" (1861:170). Status is a fixed condition in which an individual is without will and without opportunity. Ascribed status prevails; legal relations depend on birth or caste. It is indicative of a social order in which the group, not the individual, is the primary unit of social life. Every individual is enmeshed in a network of family and group ties. With the progress of civilization, this condition gradually gives way to a social system based on contract. Maine argues that a progressive civilization is manifested by the emergence of the independent, free, and self-determining individual, based on achieved status, as the primary unit of social life. He suggests that the emphasis on individual achievement and voluntary contractual relations set the conditions for a more mature legal system that uses legislation to bring society and law into harmony. In essence, his argument is that in modern societies legal relations are not conditioned by one's birth but dependent on voluntary agreements.

Classical Sociological Theorists

Early sociologists have recognized the essential interrelation between legal institutions and the social order. In this section, the influential theoretical explanations of law and society of Karl Marx, Max Weber, and Emile Durkheim are explored.

Karl Marx (1818–1883). Of all the social theorists, few are as important, brilliant, or original as Karl Marx. Part philosopher, part economist, part sociologist, and part historian, Marx combines political partisanship with deep scholarship. Marx, and the subsequent ideology of Marxism, may have caused more social change than any other force in the modern world, in both developed and developing societies (see King and Szelenyi, 2004).

Marx postulates that every society, whatever its stage of historical development, rests on an economic foundation. He calls this the "mode of production" of commodities, which has two elements. The first is the physical or technological arrangement of economic activity. The second is "the social relations of production," or the indispensable human attachments that people must form with one another when engaged in economic activity. In his words:

> The sum total of these relations of production constitutes the economic structure of society—the real foundation, on which rise legal and political superstructures and to which correspond definite forms of social consciousness. (Marx, 1959:43)

For Marx the determinant variable is the mode of production. Changes in this produce changes in the way in which groups are attached to production technology. This economic determinism is reflected in Marx's theory of law.

Marx's theory of law, which has greatly influenced social and jurisprudential thinking throughout the world, may be summarized in three principal assumptions: (1) law is a product of evolving economic forces; (2) law is a tool used by a ruling class to maintain its power over the lower classes; and (3) in the communist society of the future, law as an instrument of social control will "wither away" and finally disappear.

The idea that law is a reflection of economic conditions is integral to the doctrine of "*dialectical materialism*." According to this doctrine, the political, social, religious, and cultural order of any given epoch is determined by the existing system of production and forms a "superstructure" on top of this economic basis. Law, for Marx, is part of this super-structure whose forms, content, and conceptual apparatus constitute responses to economic developments. This view maintains that law is nothing more than a function of the economy but without any independent existence.

In societies with pronounced class distinctions, the means of production are owned and controlled by the ruling class. Marx's theory of law is the characterization of law as a form of class rule and dominance (Collins, 1996). While addressing the bour-geoisie of his day in his *Communist Manifesto*, Marx (Marx and Engels, 1955:47) writes: "Your jurisprudence is but the will of your class made into a law for all, a will whose essential character and direction are determined by the economic conditions of existence of your class." Marx further argues that law, as a form of class rule, is sanc-tioned by public authority, which has the power of enforcement through the use of armed bodies.

Finally, Marx suggests that after the revolution, when class conflict is resolved and the institution of private property is replaced by a communist regime, law and the state, hith-erto the main engines of despotism and oppression, will "wither away." There will be no need for coercion, since everyone's needs will be fulfilled and universal harmony will prevail. According to this view, there will be no need for law in the future—a future that will be the final stage of humanity's evolution because stateless and lawless communism shall exist forever.

Max Weber (1864–1920). Max Weber holds a central position among the law and soci-ety theorists and remains among the most influential social thinkers of our time (see, for example, Camic, Gorski, and Turbek, 2005; Ringer, 2004). Weber's typology of legal sys-tems is based on two fundamental distinctions (1954:63). First, legal procedures are ration-al or irrational. *Rational* procedures involve the use of logic and scientific methods to attain specific objectives (see also Berg and Meadwell, 2004). *Irrational* procedures rely on ethi-cal or mystical considerations such as magic or faith in the supernatural. Second, legal pro-cedures can proceed, rationally or irrationally, with respect to formal or substantive law. *Formal* law refers to making decisions on the basis of established rules, regardless of the notion of fairness. *Substantive* law takes the circumstances of individual cases into consid-eration along with the prevailing notion of justice. These two distinctions create four ideal types, which are seldom, if ever, attained in their pure form in specific societies.

1. *Substantive irrationality.* This exists when a case is decided on some unique religious, ethical, emotional, or political basis instead of by general rules. An example of this

would be when a religious judge makes a decision without any recourse to explicit rules or legal principles.

2. *Formal irrationality*. This involves rules based on supernatural forces. It is irrational because no one tries to understand or clarify why it works and formal because strict adherence is required to the procedures. The Ten Commandments, for example, were enacted in a formally irrational way: Moses, claiming direct revelation, presented the tablets and announced, "This is the Law." Other examples would include the use of ordeals and oaths.

3. *Substantive rationality*. This is based on the application of rules from nonlegal sources such as religion, ideology, and science. It is rational because rules are derived from specific and accepted sources and substantive because there is a concern for justness of outcomes in individual cases. The efforts of Ayatollah Khomeini in Iran to make decisions on the basis of the Koran would be an example of substantive rationality.

4. *Formal rationality*. This involves the use of consistent, logical rules independent of moral, religious, or other normative criteria that are applied equally to all cases. An example of this is modern Canadian or Western law.

While referring to both formal and substantive rationality, Weber identifies three types of administration of justice: (1) *Kahdi* justice, (2) empirical justice, and (3) rational justice. **Kahdi** justice is dispensed by the judge of the Islamic *Shari'a* court. (See Chapter 1 for a detailed discussion of Islamic law and Huff and Schlucter, 1999.) It is based on religious precepts and is so lacking in procedural rules as to seem almost completely arbitrary. The *Koran* contains the revealed word of God, and this bible forms the heart of the Islamic legal system in such countries as Iran and Pakistan. **Empirical justice**, the deciding of cases by referring to analogies and by relying on and interpreting precedents, is more rational than *Kahdi* justice, but notably short of complete rationality. Weber argues that modern law is rational, whereas traditional and primitive laws were irrational, or at least, less rational. Rational justice is based on bureaucratic principles. The rational legal system is basically universalistic; the irrational is particularistic. The rational legal system looks toward contract, not toward status (Parsons, 1964:339). Rationality can be further based on adherence to "eternal characteristics" (observable, concrete features) of the facts of the case. However, Weber perceives that Western law, with its specialized professional roles of judges and lawyers, is unique in that it is also reliant on the "logical analysis of meaning" of abstract legal concepts and rules.

Modern society differs from its past in many ways, which Max Weber sums up in a single concept: the **rational**. Modern society is in pursuit of the rational. Weber contends that the modern law of the West has become increasingly institutionalized through the bureaucratization of the state. He points out that the acceptance of the law as a rational science is based on certain fundamental and semi-logical postulates, such as, that the law is a "gapless" system of legal principles, and that every concrete judicial decision involves the application of an abstract legal proposition to a concrete situation. There is little doubt that Weber captures, in his idea of rationality, a crucial feature of modern legal systems (Wilson, 2002). It is rather ironic that soon after Max Weber's death in 1920, rational law in Germany was in part replaced by a faith in the intuition of a charismatic leader—Adolph Hitler.

Emile Durkheim (1858–1917). Durkheim outlines his thesis on law in society in his influential work *The Division of Labour in Society* (1964). While tracing the development of social order through social and economic institutions, Durkheim sets forth a theory of legal development by elucidating the idea that law is a measure of the type of solidarity in a society. Durkheim maintains that there are two types of solidarity: mechanical and organic. **Mechanical solidarity** prevails in relatively simple and homogeneous societies where unity is ensured by close interpersonal ties and similarity of habits, ideas, and attitudes. **Organic solidarity** is characteristic of modern societies that are heterogeneous and differentiated by a complex division of labour. The grounds for solidarity are the interdependence of widely different persons and groups performing a variety of functions.

Corresponding to these two forms of solidarity are two types of law: repressive and restitutive. Mechanical solidarity is associated with **repressive** and **penal law**. In a homogeneous, undifferentiated society, a criminal act offends the **collective conscience** (i.e., the "totality of social likenesses" [Durkheim, 1965:80]) and punishment is meant to protect and preserve social solidarity. Punishment is a mechanical reaction. The wrongdoer is punished as an example to the community that deviance will not be tolerated. There is no concern with the rehabilitation of the offender.

In modern heterogeneous societies, repressive law tends to give way to **restitutive law** with an emphasis on compensation (see, for example, Strickland, 2004). Punishment deals with restitution and reparations for harm done to the victim. Crimes are considered acts that offend others and not the collective conscience of the community. Punishment is evaluated in terms of what is beneficial for the offender and is used for rehabilitation.

Stated concisely, Durkheim's position is that penal law reflects mechanical solidarity. Modern society is bound together by organic solidarity—interdependence and division of labour flowing out of voluntary acts. Society is complex—its parts are highly specialized. Through contracts, which are the main concern of modern law, people arrange their innumerable, complex relationships. Contracts and contract laws are central to modern society and influence the course of societal development through the regulation of relationships.

Although Durkheim's concern is not with the elaboration of a general framework or methodology for the sociological analysis of law, his interest in law "resulted in the school that formed around him developing a considerable interest in the study of law as a social process" (Hunt, 1978:65). His ideas on law have also provided an important background to subsequent discussions concerning the nature of primitive law and the nature of crime. Although it may be questionable that "he made a serious contribution to the development of systematic legal sociology" (Gurvitch, 1942:106), he certainly made an important contribution to our understanding of the relationship between law and social solidarity and legal evolution (McIntyre, 1994:77).

Sociolegal Theorists

The theorists that will be considered in this section argue that law cannot be understood without regard for the realities of social life. Since the beginning of the 20th century, scholars of jurisprudence and of related disciplines on both sides of the Atlantic have reflected the influence of the social sciences in their analysis of legal development. The more prominent scholars included in our analysis are Albert Venn Dicey, Justice Oliver Wendell Holmes, Jr., and E. Adamson Hoebel.

Albert Venn Dicey (1835–1922). Dicey offers what has become a classic theory on the influence of public opinion on social change. He traces the growth of statutory lawmaking and the legal system in the context of the increasing articulateness and power of public opinion. He notes that the process begins with a new idea that "presents itself to some one man

[sic] of originality or genius." He has in mind such individuals as Adam Smith and Charles Darwin. Next, the idea is adopted by supporters who "preach" it to others. As time passes, "the preachers of truth make an impression, either directly upon the general public or upon some person of eminence, say a leading statesman [sic], who stands in a position to impress ordinary people and thus to win the support of the nation" (Dicey, 1905:23). As Dicey points out, however, something must happen so that people will listen to a truly new idea and change their values. He talks of "accidental conditions" that enable popular leaders to seize the opportunity. As an example he gives the Irish famine, which enabled Cobden and Bright to gain acceptance of Adam Smith's doctrine of free trade.

Public opinion, for Dicey, is "the majority of those citizens who have at a given moment taken an effective part in public life" (1905:10). Dicey talks of the "gradual, or slow, and continuous" (1905:27) developments of tides of public opinion in England. Generally, he maintains, there are few abrupt changes. Ideally, legislators should reflect and act upon public opinion, but judges (even more than legislators) lag behind public opinion. Dicey concedes that although judges are "guided to a considerable extent by the dominant current of public opinion" (1905:363), "they are also guided by professional opinions and ways of thinking which are, to a certain extent, independent of and possibly opposed to the general tone of public opinion" (1905:364). He then concludes, "they are men [sic] advanced in life. They are for the most part persons of a conservative disposition" (1905:364).

Dicey is also known for his famous doctrine of "the rule of law." The doctrine has three aspects. First, no one is punishable except for a distinct breach of law and, therefore, the rule of law is not consistent with arbitrary or even wide discretionary authority on the part of the government. Second, the rule of law means total subjection of all classes to the law of the land, as administered by the law courts. Third, individual rights derive from court precedents rather than from constitutional codes.

From a sociological perspective, Dicey's most crucial contribution to law and society is the recognition of the importance of public opinion in legal development. As Lord Tangley (1965:48) observes: "We are indebted to Professor Dicey for many things—he established for all time the relationship between public opinion and law reform and traced its course through the nineteenth century."

Oliver Wendell Holmes, Jr. (1841–1935). A distinguished judge and legal philosopher, Holmes is considered one of the founders of the "legal realism" school (White, 2000). The basic contention of legal realists is that "judges make law rather than find it" (Schur, 1968:43). Judges must always exercise choice when making a decision. They decide which principle will prevail and which party will win. According to the legal realists' position, judges make decisions on the basis of their conceptions of justness before resorting to formal legal precedents. Such precedents can be found or developed to support almost any outcome. The real decisions are based on the judge's notion of justness, conditioned, in part, by values, personal background, predilections, and so forth. They are then rationalized in the written opinion (Holmes, 2004).

Holmes stresses the limits that are set to the use of deductive logic in the solution of legal problems. He postulates that the life of law has been experience and not logic, and maintains that only a judge or a lawyer who is acquainted with the historical, social, and economic aspects of the law will be in a position to fulfill his or her functions properly.

Holmes assigns a large role to historical and social forces in the life of law, while deemphasizing the ethical and ideal elements. He considers law largely as a body of edicts representing the will of dominant interests in society, backed by force. Although he admits that moral principles are influential in the initial formulation of the rules of law, he is inclined to identify morality with the taste and value preferences of shifting power groups in society. Schwartz notes: "Holmes was part of the generation that had sat at the feet of Darwin and Spencer and he could never shed his Darwinist outlook" (1974:151). His basic philosophy is that life is essentially a Darwinian struggle for existence and that the goal of social effort was to "build a race" rather than to strive for the attainment of humanitarian ethical objectives.

In his often-quoted essay "The Path of the Law," Holmes (1897:458) outlines some of his basic propositions and states that "a legal duty so called is nothing but a prediction that if a man [sic] does or omits certain things he [sic] will be made to suffer in this or that way by judgment of a court." A pragmatic approach to law, he declares, must view the law from the point of view of the "bad man" [sic]. Such a person does not care about the general moral pronouncements and abstract legal doctrines. What is important is simply what the courts are in fact likely to do. Holmes argues that any sense of absolute certainty about the law was bound to be illusory.

> Behind the logical forms lies a judgment as to the relative worth and importance of competing legislative grounds, often an inarticulate and unconscious judgment, it is true, and yet the very root and nerve of the whole proceeding. You can give any conclusion a logical form. (Holmes, Jr., 1897:465)

Lawyers and judges should be aware of this and should "consider the ends which the several rules seek to accomplish, the reasons why those ends are desired, what is given up to gain them, and whether they are worth the price" (Holmes, Jr., 1897:476).

E. Adamson Hoebel (1906–1993). A highly respected and influential scholar in the field of anthropology of law, Hoebel was much influenced by Karl N. Llewellyn, a brilliant lawyer with social science skills and interests. The two men collaborated on an analysis of the "law ways" in traditional Cheyenne society. The emphasis on the "law-jobs" having both a "pure survival" or "bare bones" aspect for the society and a "questing" or "betterment" value (Llewellyn and Hoebel, 1941) contributed significantly to the development of a modern functional approach to the legal system. We shall return to this point in the discussion on the functionalist approach later in this chapter.

Hoebel's (1954) views on the development of legal systems are presented in the concluding chapter, entitled "The Trend of the Law," in his book *The Law of Primitive Man*. Hoebel (1954:288) notes that "there has been no straight line of development in the growth of law." His description of trends in legal development is based on the assumption that cultures of contemporary traditional societies exhibit characteristics that are similar "to those that presumably prevailed in the early cultures of the infancy" of humankind (1954:290). He considers law and the legal system as a property of a specific community or subgroup of a society, and states: "Without the sense of community there can be no law. Without law there cannot be for long a community" (1954:332). Consequently, law exists to some extent even in the simplest societies.

Hoebel begins his description of the trend of law with a discussion of the "lower primitive societies"—the hunters and gatherers, such as the Andaman Islanders. Almost all relations in such a society are face-to-face and intimate. The demands imposed by culture are relatively few. Ridicule is a potent mechanism of social control. Taboo and the fear of supernatural sanctions control a large area of behaviour. Special interests are few, for there is little accumulated wealth. Conflict arises mostly in interpersonal relations. Repetitive abuse of the customs and codes of social relations constitutes a crime, and the offender may be beaten or even killed by the members of the community. Hoebel writes: "Here we have law in the full connotation of the word—the application, in threat or in fact, of physical coercion by a party having the socially recognized privilege-right of so acting. First the threat—and then, if need be, the act" (1954:300).

Among the more organized hunters, the pastoralists, and the rooter-gardening peoples, such as the Cheyenne, Comanche, Kiowa, and Indians of the northwest coast of North America, the size of the group and the increased complexity of the culture make possible a greater divergence of interests between the members of society. Conflicts of interest grow, and the need arises for legal mechanisms for settlement and control of the internal clash of interests. Private law emerges and spreads, although many of the internal social control problems are handled on a non-legal basis.

In the tribes, a more formalized chieftainship develops, with a tendency toward hereditary succession (Hoebel, 1954:309). Although homicide and adultery still represent major difficulties, the development of criminal law remains weak.

"The real elaboration of law begins with the expansion of the gardening-based tribes," such as the Samoans and the Ashanti (Hoebel, 1954:316). The gardening activity provides an economic foundation for the support of larger populations that can no longer maintain face-to-face relationships. With the formation of more communities: "The pressures to maintain peaceful equilibrium between the numerous closely interacting communities become intensified. The further growth of law and a more effective law is demanded" (1954:316). The attempt to establish the interest of the society as superior to the interests of kinship groups is the prime mover of law in this type of society. Allocation of rights, duties, privileges, powers, and immunities with regard to land becomes important, and "the law of things begins to rival the law of persons" (1954:316). "Clear-cut crimes" (1954:319) are established in the legal systems of these societies, and action for damages becomes even more frequent than on the preceding level.

For Hoebel, the "trend of law" is one of increasing growth and complexity in which the tendency is to shift the privilege-right of prosecution and imposition of legal sanctions from the individual and the kinship group to clearly defined public officials representing the society as such. Hoebel notes: "Damages have generally replaced death as penalties in civil suits" (1954:329). Hoebel maintains that this is how law developed in human societies through the ages, but the laws of particular societies have not followed a single line of development through fixed, predetermined, and universal stages. The development of legal systems in particular societies is characterized by a trend that only in general exhibits the features described here.

Contemporary Law and Society Theorists

A brief explanation is necessary for the inclusion of the particular contemporary theorists. Comprehensive macrolevel theoretical works on law and society are few. Our intention in this section is to describe influential (and possibly controversial) theoretical developments that have taken place since the 1970s. The rationale for this preference is to illustrate some of the relatively recent advances in sociolegal theorizing on law and society. There are, of course, a number of other theorists (who will be alluded to in specific contexts) who could have been discussed. They include Raymond A. Belliotti (1992), *Justifying Law*; William

Chambliss and Robert Seidman (1982), *Law, Order, and Power*; William M. Evan (1990), *Social Structure and Law: Theoretical and Empirical Perspectives*; Hyman Gross (1979), *A Theory of Criminal Justice*; Alan Hunt (1993), *Explorations in Law and Society: Toward a Constitutive Theory of Law*; Philippe Nonet and Philip Selznick (2001), *Law and Society in Transition: Toward Responsive Law*; Harold E. Pepinsky (1976), *Crime and Conflict: A Study of Law and Society*; Charles E. Reasons (1974), *The Criminologist: Crime and the Criminal*; and Charles Sampford (1989), *The Disorder of Law: A Critique of Legal Theory*. As illustrations of contemporary theorists, these and similar works tend to be limited in scope. By contrast, the ones chosen for examination attempt to account for law and society in their treatises from different but complementary perspectives. Their alternative viewpoints are also broad enough to include both the older theoretical perspectives and the more contemporary, specialized advancements.

Donald Black. In *The Behaviour of Law*; *Sociological Justice*; and *The Social Structure of Right and Wrong*, Donald Black (1976, 1989, 1998, 2002) sets forth a theory of law that he contends explains variations in law from a cross-national perspective, as well as among individuals within societies. As noted in Chapter 1, he considers law as governmental social control, which makes use of legislation, litigation, and adjudication. He distinguishes between behaviour that is controlled by these means from behaviour that is subject to other forms of social control, such as etiquette, custom, and bureaucracy.

Black contends that law is a quantitative variable that can be measured by the frequency by which, in a given social setting, statutes are enacted, regulations are issued, complaints are made, offences are prosecuted, damages are awarded, and punishment is meted out. Consequently, the quantity of law varies from society to society and from one historical period to another in a given society. Different organizations in a society may have more or less law both for themselves and in regards to other groups and organizations.

The direction of law (that is, the differential frequency and success of its application by persons in different social settings) also varies. So does the style of law that, as we mentioned earlier, may be accusatory (with penal or compensatory consequences) or remedial (with therapeutic or conciliatory consequences).

Next, Black develops a number of propositions that explain the quantity, direction, and style of law in regard to five measurable variables of social life: stratification; morphology; culture; organization; and social control. **Stratification** (inequality of wealth) can be measured in such ways as differences in wealth and rates of social mobility. **Morphology** refers to those aspects of social life that can be measured by social differentiation or the degree of interdependence (for example, the extent of division of labour). **Culture** can be measured by the volume, complexity, and diversity of ideas, and by the degree of conformity to the mainstream of culture. **Organization** can be measured by the degree to which the administration of collective action in political and economic spheres is centralized. Finally, the amount of nonlegal **social control** to which people are subjected is a measure of their respectability, and differences between people indicate normative distance from each other.

On the basis of sociological, historical, and ethnographic data, Black arrives at a number of conclusions. He points out that the quantity of law varies directly with stratification rank, integration, culture, organization, and respectability, and inversely with other forms of social control. Thus, stratified societies have more law than simple ones, wealthy people have more law among themselves than poor people, and the amount of law increases with the growth of governmental centralization.

The relationships between the quantity of law and the variables of differentiation, relational distance, and cultural distance are curvilinear. Law is minimal at either extreme of these variables and accumulates in their middle ranges. For example, law relating to contractual economic transaction is limited in simple societies where everyone engages in the same productive activity and in the business world where manufacturers operate in a symbiotic exchange network.

The style of law varies with its direction. In relation to stratification, law has a penal style in its downward direction, a compensatory or a therapeutic style in its upward direction, and a conciliatory style among people of equal rank. In regard to morphology, law tends to be accusatory among strangers and therapeutic or conciliatory among intimates. Less organized people are more vulnerable to penal law and more organized people can count on compensatory law.

These patterns of stylistic variation explain, for example, why an offence is more likely to be punished if the rank of the victim is higher than that of the offender, but is more likely to be dealt with by compensation if their ranks are reversed, why accusatory law replaces remedial law in societies undergoing modernization, why members of subcultures are more vulnerable to law enforcement than conventional citizens, and why organizations usually escape punishment for illegal practices against individuals.

Over the years, Black's theory of law has generated considerable critical debate and analysis (see, for example, Cooney, 2003; Cooney and Phillips, 2002; Wong, 1998). It has been referred to as a "crashing classic" (Nader, cited by Gottfredson and Hindelang, 1979:3) and as "the most important contribution ever made to the sociology of law. It is that and more" (Sherman, 1978:11). However, it has also been derided as "circular" (Michaels, 1978:11) and lambasted for a purported "absence of logical connections between the propositions" (Friedrichs, 2006:134). As well, empirical testing has provided only limited support, at best, for some of the propositions that are derived from Black's theory (see, for example, Borg and Parker, 2001; Geiger-Oneto, 2003). Nevertheless, Black's theory of law continues to provide the impetus for much empirical work (see, for example, Cooney, 1997; Phillips and Cooney, 2005). His propositions are likely to be subjected to further testing, criticism, revision, reformulation, and possible rejection, especially his recently compiled ideas on the "geometry of law" (Black, 2002). But, as Sherman presciently noted shortly after the publication of *The Behaviour of Law*, "whatever the substance or method, social research on law cannot ignore Black" (1978:15).

Roberto Mangabeira Unger. In *Law in Modern Society* (1976), Unger revives the sweeping scope of Max Weber's theorizing on law and places the development of rational legal systems within a broad historical and comparative framework. Unger locates the study of law within the major questions of social theory in general: the conflicts between individual and social interests, between legitimacy and coercion, and between the state and society. His main thesis is that the development of the rule of law, law that is committed to general and autonomous legal norms, could take place only when competing groups struggle for control of the legal system and when there are universal standards that can justify the law of the state.

Unger's analysis emphasizes the historical perspective. His goal is an understanding of modern law and society. He examines the nature of society, and compares rival systems (for example, the Chinese) with the Western tradition with the range of special types of law—customary or interactional law, regulatory law, and autonomous legal order. Customary or interactional law is "simply any recurring mode of interaction among individuals and groups, together with the more or less explicit acknowledgment by these groups and individuals that such patterns of interaction produce reciprocal expectations of conduct that ought to be satisfied" (1976:49). Bureaucratic or regulatory law for Unger "consists of explicit rules established and enforced by an identifiable government" (1976:50). This type of law is not a universal characteristic of social life: "It is limited to situations in which the division between state and society has been established and some standards of conduct have assumed the form of explicit prescriptions, prohibitions, or permissions, addressed to more or less general categories of persons and acts" (1976:51). Unger calls the third type of law the legal order or legal system, which is both general and autonomous, as well as public and positive (1976:52). From an evolutionary perspective, these different types of law turn out to be stages, for they build upon one another, regulatory law upon customary law, the autonomous legal order upon regulatory law.

For Unger, law is indicative of the normative structure of social life. He contends that there are two competing forms of normative integration: consensual and instrumental. "Consensual law expresses the shared values of a group or community and manifests the stable structure in recurring interactions. Regulatory law is instrumental social control by political institutions through positive and public rules" (Eder, 1977:142). Unger considers autonomous law as both instrumental and consensual.

Unger accounts for these different types of law in an evolutionary context. The change of customary law into bureaucratic law is characterized by an extension of instrumental rules that have normative quality (state law, governmental sanctions). This extension of the instrumental rule is dependent upon the recognition of the consensual basis of law. Unger argues that sacred and natural law can provide the cultural context within which instrumental norms can be legitimized. The development of an autonomous legal order brings about a further extension of instrumental rules to everybody. Everyone can pursue his or her personal objectives as long as they do not infringe upon those of others. Laws set these limits. He notes, however, that this situation requires a further legitimization of the principles of law, and consensus must be generated by social contract and by agreement upon the criteria of substantive justice.

Unger is a prolific writer and provides a fresh and unified, albeit somewhat controversial, solution to a number of problems in social theory—the problem of social scientific method, the problem of social order, and the problem of modernity (Sampford, 1989:145). His theory of law is useful for the analysis of changes in law, and he has generated a number of testable propositions that enable sociologists to study law at the synchronic and diachronic levels (Eder, 1977:143). His works are becoming increasingly recognized and appreciated in sociological circles.

CURRENT INTELLECTUAL MOVEMENTS IN LAW

As we have shown in Chapter 1, sociological discussions of the role of law in society generally take place in the context of two ideal conceptions of society: the consensus and conflict perspectives. The consensus perspective is grounded in the functionalist approach, and the conflict perspective in the conflict and Marxist approaches to the study of law in society. These are the two prevailing approaches in the sociological literature. Most sociologists opt for either a version of the functionalist approach or the conflict and Marxist approach to law and the legal system.

Functional analysis examines social phenomena with respect to their consequences for the broader society. Proponents of this approach ask specific questions such as: What does a kinship system do for society? What does law do for society? What are the "functions" of government, of social classes, or of any social phenomenon? (Turner, 2003:11). In the context of the analysis of law, functionalists are concerned with the identification of the characteristics of legal phenomena, as well as indicating how legal institutions fit into the workings of the overall structure. Theorists embracing conflict and Marxist approaches emphasize the structuring of economic relations that provide, for them, the foundation for various specific studies of legal trends. We shall now consider these two approaches in some detail.

The Functionalist Approach

"Functionalism," writes Robert A. Nisbet (1969:228), "is without any doubt the single most significant body of theory in the social sciences in the present century. It is often thought to be essentially a theory of order, of stability, of how society is possible." Historically, functionalism was brought into sociology by borrowing directly, and developing analogies for, concepts in the biological sciences. Biology, since the middle of the 19th century, frequently referred to the "structure" of an organism, meaning a relatively stable arrangement of relationships between the different cells, and to the "function" of the organism that considered the consequences of the activity of the various organs in the life process. The principal consideration of this organic analogy was how each part of the organism contributed to the survival and maintenance of the whole.

Sociologists distinguish between the manifest and the latent functions (Merton, 1957:19). **Manifest functions** are those that are built into a social system by design. They are well understood by group members. **Latent functions** are, by contrast, unintentional and often unrecognized. They are unanticipated consequences of a system that has been set up to achieve other ends. For example, one of the oldest interventionist policies of governments in Canada—minimum wage legislation—arose from a desire to protect the most vulnerable of workers, women and children, from overt exploitation. In 1918, British Columbia and Manitoba introduced minimum wage legislation which focused solely on women workers, and by 1920, four other provinces (Nova Scotia, Quebec, Ontario, and Saskatchewan) had followed this gender-specific approach. When, in 1925, British Columbia enacted its *Men's Minimum Wage Act*, it became the first Canadian province to legislate a minimum wage for men as well as for women. Ironically, however, while minimum wage laws were enacted as a palliative against the worst of the market's inequities, the inequitable treatment of women workers became further entrenched with the passage of the 1925 Act. On the assumption that men, and not women, were or ought to be their families' principal providers, the minimum wage set for men was higher than the minimum wage set for women. Moreover, some maintain that, even today, minimum wage laws exacerbate the vulnerability of those groups that they purportedly protect. Specifically, it is argued that minimum wage laws contribute to reduced job prospects of low-wage earners and increase their risk of unemployment as companies hire fewer, and more highly skilled workers. This "disemployment" is noted to disproportionately affect the young and women (Schenk 2001:3).

The basic tenets of functionalism are summarized in the following key assumptions (Van den Berghe, 1967:294):

1. Societies must be analyzed "holistically as systems of interrelated parts."

2. Cause and effect relations are "multiple and reciprocal."

3. Social systems are in a state of "dynamic equilibrium," such that adjustment to forces affecting the system is made with minimal change within the system.

4. Perfect integration is never attained, so that every social system has strains and deviations, but the latter tend to be neutralized through institutionalization.

5. Change is a fundamentally slow adaptive process, rather than a revolutionary shift.

6. Change is the consequence of the adjustment of changes outside the system, growth by differentiation, and internal innovations.

7. The system is integrated through shared values.

In sociology, functional analysis is as old as the discipline. Comte, Spencer, Durkheim, Malinowski, Radcliffe-Browne, Merton, and Parsons, to name a few, have engaged in the functional analysis of the social world (Turner and Maryanski, 1979:xi). The early theorists viewed the world in systematic terms (Turner and Maryanski, 1995:49). For them, such systems were considered to have needs and prerequisites that had to be met to ensure survival. They viewed such systems as having normal and pathological states, thus suggesting a system of equilibrium and homeostasis. The social world was seen as composed of mutually interrelated parts, and the analysis of these connected and interdependent parts focused on how they fulfilled the requisites of the systems as a whole and how, thus, system equilibrium was maintained.

Ever since the classical sociological theorist Emile Durkheim postulated the notion that deviance could serve certain social functions in a society, sociologists have looked for evidence to support this contention. Durkheim had in mind the idea that a society needed deviance to continually reaffirm its boundaries of propriety. Functional arguments for the importance of deviance are intriguing. They provide a novel way of showing how certain institutions in a society, if not the society itself, continue to operate. Durkheim points out, for example, that without the existence of sinners, a church could not exist. Their very existence provides the opportunity for believers to reaffirm the faith that has been offended by the sinner. Thus, the worst thing that could happen to a church is to completely eliminate sin from the world and completely propagate the faith to society.

Functionalism is also present in legal anthropology. For example, in *The Cheyenne Way,* Karl N. Llewellyn and E. Adamson Hoebel (1941) outline their law-job theory about society as a whole. For societies to survive, there are certain basic needs that must be met. It is within this context that the wants and desires of individuals, their "divisive urges," assert themselves. The conflicts produced are unavoidable, but at the same time, essential to group survival. "The law-jobs entail such arrangement and adjustment of people's behaviour that the society (or the group) remains a society (or a group) and gets enough energy unleashed and coordinated to keep on functioning as a society (or as a group)" (1941:291). They consider the law-jobs as universal, applicable, and necessary to all groups and to all societies.

Functionalism is also evident in other writers. For example, in Jerome Frank's (1930) *Law and the Modern Mind,* the entire discussion of the "basic legal myth" and the associated "legal magic" is grounded in an examination of their functional consequences for the legal system. Similarly, Thurman Arnold's (1935) concern with the role of symbolism within legal institutions is consciously functionalist. Felix Cohen (1959) resorts to functional analysis in his elaboration of "functional jurisprudence." The writing of Lon Fuller (1969) on law morality, Julius Stone's *Law and the Social Sciences in the Second Half Century* (1966), Philippe Nonet's (1976) ideas on jurisprudential sociology, and Andra Sajos' (2003) study of the nature and politically determined functions of governmental corruption in post-Communist transition and how political structure itself creates corrupt practices that become a structural feature of transition societies are illustrative of the functionalist approach to the study of law and society.

Almost from the beginning, however, the functionalist approach was attacked both for alleged theoretical shortcomings and on ideological grounds. Criticisms have included complaints that the whole notion of function is oversimplified. Questions such as "Functional for whom?" were raised, and not without grounds, for the interests and needs of different groups in a society are often in conflict. What may be functional for one group may be dysfunctional for another. Others argue that functional analysis is a static, antihistorical mode of analysis with a bias toward conservatism. Some sociologists even suggest that there is an implicit teleology in functional analysis, in that this mode of analysis inappropriately attributes purposes to social institutions as if they were conscious beings. As expected, a sizable amount of literature in the field has been devoted to both formulating and refuting these charges (see, for example, Turner and Maryanski, 1995). In spite of these criticisms, some maintain that "most sociology of law theorists are adherents to structural-functionalist theory" (Reasons and Rich, 1978:153).

Conflict and Marxist Approaches

Conflict and Marxist approaches are based on the assumption that social behaviour can best be understood in terms of tension and conflict between groups and individuals (see, for example, Goldstein, 2004). Proponents of these approaches suggest that society is an arena in which struggles over scarce commodities take place. Closely intertwined with the idea of conflict in society is the Marxian notion of **economic determinism**. Economic organization, especially the ownership of property, determines the organization of the rest of society. The class structure and institutional arrangements, as well as cultural values, beliefs, and religious dogmas, are, ultimately, a reflection of the economic organization of a society.

According to Marx, law and the legal system are designed to regulate and preserve capitalist relations. For the Marxists, law is a method of domination and social control used by the ruling classes. Law protects the interests of those in power and serves to maintain distinctions between the dominated and domineering classes. Consequently, law is seen as a set of rules that arise as a result of the struggle between the ruling class and those who are ruled. The state, which is the organized reflection of the interests of the ruling class, passes laws that serve the interests of this domineering class.

This breakdown of society into two classes—a ruling class that owns the means of production and a subservient class that works for wages—*inevitably* leads to conflict. Once conflict becomes manifest in the form of riots or rebellions, the state, acting in the interest of the ruling class, will develop laws aimed at controlling acts that threaten the interests of the status quo. As capitalism develops and conflict between social classes becomes more frequent, more acts will be defined as criminal.

It is not surprising, therefore, that many sociologists interested in law and, in particular, criminal law, have espoused this perspective. The conflict view of criminal law is most noticeable in the now controversial writings of Marxist criminologists. Quinney (1974), for example, argues that law in capitalist society gives political recognition to powerful social and economic interests. The legal system provides the mechanism for the forceful control of the majority in society. The state and the legal system reflect and serve the needs of the ruling class. In *The Critique of Legal Order,* Quinney (2002:16) argues that as capitalist society is further threatened, criminal law is increasingly used in the attempt to maintain domestic order. The underclass will continue to be the object of criminal law as the dominant class seeks to perpetuate itself. To remove the oppression, to eliminate the need for further reward, would necessarily mean the end of that class and its capitalist economy.

Similarly, William Chambliss and Robert Seidman take a conflict approach in their analysis of law. While emphasizing conflicting interests in society, they argue that "the state becomes a weapon of a particular class. Law emanates from the state. Law in a society of classes must therefore represent and advance the interests of one class or the other" (1982:72). For them, law is an instrument sought after and employed by powerful interest groups in society. Chambliss (1978:149) further reinforces the notion of law as an instrument of the powerful in society by specifically pointing out that "acts are defined as criminal because it is in the interests of the ruling class to so define them." Austin Turk (1978) also sees law as "a weapon in social conflict," an instrument of social order that serves those who are in power. The control of legal order represents the ability to use the state's coercive authority to protect one's interests. The control of the legal process further means the control of the organization of governmental decisions and the workings of the law, which diverts attention from more deeply rooted problems of power distribution and interest maintenance. Reasons (1974:103) considers crime as a phenomenon created by special interests who, with their definition of rectitude, create the laws of society.

Conflict theorists point out that most of our criminal law comes directly from English common law. C. Ray Jeffery (1957) contends that acts such as murder, theft, trespassing, and robbery, problems that were once resolved in the kinship group, became crimes against the state when Henry II, King of England, centralized political power and declared them wrongs against the crown. Jerome Hall (1952) traces the growth of property and theft laws to the emergence of commerce and industrialization. With the advent of commerce and trade, a new economic class of traders and industrialists emerged, and the need to protect their business interests grew. As a result, new laws were established to protect the interests and economic well-being of the emergent class. These laws included the creation of embezzlement laws and laws governing stolen property and obtaining goods under false pretense. According to conflict theorists, notions of crime have their origins less in general ideas about right or wrong than in perceived threats to groups with the power to protect their interests through law.

Critics have not been kind to this type of argumentation, holding that it involves enormous simplification, reification, and absence of sensitivity to the complexity of social interaction (Manning, 1975:12). There are many who concede the validity of conflict and interest-group arguments but who, at the same time, contend that bold assertions about the "ruling class" conceal more than they reveal. Surely, lawmaking phenomena are more complex than implied in these statements that hint at a monolithic ruling class that determines legislative behaviour and the creation of rules. In spite of these and other criticisms, Marxism exists in contemporary sociological theorizing and "must exist—because alienation exists. *Alienation* refers to the way in which human beings under capitalism do not control their work, but instead are dominated by their work and by the requirements of the profit-system" (Agger, 1979:1). Elements of the Marxist approach enter into a number of sociological studies on law and society and are influential on epistemological, methodological, and theoretical approaches (see, for example, Caudill and Gold, 1997). Although the collapse of the Soviet planned economy ended the most extensive attempt to implement Marxism ever, Marxism can be expected to retain its allure as an approach to the study of law in society.

The Critical Legal Studies Movement

Critical legal studies (CLS, but also referred to as CRITS) is a vibrant, refreshing, controversial, and enduring addition to the ongoing jurisprudential debate on law, legal education, and the role of lawyers in society (see, for example, Kennedy, 2004; Kramer, 1995; Neacsu, 2000). It is widely considered, by critics and followers alike, to comprise some of the most exciting sociolegal scholarship around, and one sociologist of law described it as being "where the action is" (Trubek, 1984). The movement began with a group of junior faculty members and law students at Yale in the late 1960s who have since moved to other places. In 1977, the group organized itself into the Conference of Critical Legal Studies, which has over 400 members and holds an annual conference that draws more than 1000 participants.

The movement has been greatly influenced by Marxist-inspired European theorists, and its roots can be traced back to American legal realism (Tomasic, 1985:18). Legal realists in the 1920s and 1930s argued against the 19th-century belief that the rule of law was supreme. They contended that because a good lawyer could argue convincingly either side of a given case, there was actually nothing about the law that made any judicial decision inevitable. Rather, they pointed out, the outcome of a case depended largely, if not entirely, on the predilections of the judge who happened to be deciding it. Thus, far from being a science, the realists argued, law was virtually inseparable from politics, economics, and culture. They rejected the idea that law is above politics and economics.

Proponents of the movement reject the idea that there is anything distinctly legal about legal reasoning. As with any other kind of analysis, legal reasoning, they maintain, cannot operate independently of the personal biases of lawyers or judges, or of the social context in which they are acting. Furthermore, law is so contradictory that it allows the context of a case to determine the outcome. That attribute of law—its inability to cover all situations—is called **indeterminacy** (Trubek, 1984:578). Because law consists of a variety of contradictions and inconsistencies, judicial decisions cannot be the self-contained models of reasoning that some scholars claim them to be. Decisions rest on grounds outside of formal legal doctrine which are inevitably political.

Critical legal scholars also reject law as being value-free and above political, economic, and social considerations. Laws only *seem* neutral and independent, even those that reflect the dominant values in society. Moreover, laws legitimize those values that predominate in society. Therefore, laws legitimate the status quo. They maintain that law is actually part of the system of power in society rather than a protection against it.

Although proponents of the movement insist that their ideas are still tentative and evolving, their attacks on law and legal training have created a good deal of criticism. The movement has been called Marxist, utopian, hostile to rules, and incoherent. Critical legal scholars have been accused of favouring violence over bargaining, of advocating the inculcation of leftist values in legal education, and of being preoccupied with "illegiti-mate hierarchies" such as the bar (Schwartz, 1984); their approach to law is termed "nihilistic," and they are accused of teaching cynicism to their students, which may result in "the learning of the skills of corruption." Purportedly, these "nihilistic" law teachers (with a proclivity for revolution) are likely to train criminals, and they have, therefore, "an ethical duty to depart from law school" (Carrington, 1984:227). It is unlikely that the con-troversy between proponents and opponents of the movement will be settled in the fore-seeable future (Trubek and Esser, 1989). Further, although the movement has been fairly successful in questioning the validity of the Western legal system, it has failed, as the fol-lowing sections will demonstrate, in its major objective of developing and gaining broad-er support for new legal doctrines that are more representative of class, gender, and race differences. So far, the most useful function of the movement is indicating the extent to which politics influences the legal system (Goodrich, 1993).

Feminist Legal Theory

Feminist legal theory is another intellectual movement of substantial influence, impor-tance, and impact. It is concerned with issues that are central to a broader intellectual and political feminist movement: equality in the workplace, reproductive rights, domestic vio-lence, sexual harassment, and sexual assault, just to mention a few (see, for example, Kolmar and Bartkowski, 2005; Rhode and Sanger, 2005). It draws from the experiences of women and from critical perspectives developed in other disciplines in analyzing the relationship between law and gender (Greenberg, Minow, and Roberts, 1998; Poutanen, 2002; Sangster, 2002; Sullivan, 2004; Williams, 2004). Unlike critical legal studies, which started in elite law schools and were inspired predominantly by notions of contem-porary Marxism, feminist legal theories emerged against the backdrop of mass political movements organized around such issues as equality rights, abortion, sexual subordination and exploitation in the profession of law, and the general prevalence of sexism in most walks of life (see, for example, Chesney-Lind and Pasko, 2004a, 2004b; Leiper, 2006).

A dominant tendency in feminist legal theories is to regard patriarchy as the source of women's problems (Naffine, 1990:20; Wing, 2003). There is a strong conviction that male-dominated jurisprudence perpetuates women as objects (Dawson, 2003; Eskridge and Hunter, 1997). Society is viewed as basically patriarchal, organized and dominated by men, and, as a result, not very hospitable to women. Not surprisingly, proponents of the theory consider it one of the most crucial challenges to contemporary law and legal insti-tutions (Bartlett and Kennedy, 1991:1).

There are at least three predominant, although by no means mutually exclusive, themes in feminist legal literature (see, for example, Delamont, 2003). The first deals with women's struggle for equality in a male-dominated legal profession and in the broader society. Feminists challenge legal claims of fairness and the impartiality of law in dealing with women. The argument is that men directly or indirectly have endeavoured to maintain their own power and to keep women "in their place." There are many structural constraints that perpetuate inequality. One is law's respect for precedent. But for feminists, the empha-sis on precedents raises two concerns. First, existing precedents tend to support and rein-force a status quo that may be more favourable to male than to female interests. Second, reasoning not based on precedent or accepted doctrine is often viewed as extreme and is less likely to be successful than arguments based on precedents. An example of these two concerns is suggested by the Supreme Court of Canada's 1993 decision that the cost of childcare did not qualify as a legitimate "business deduction" (i.e., expenditures incurred for the purpose of gaining or producing income from business) as defined under section 18 of the *Income Tax Act of Canada*. However, and in marked contrast, "the courts have . . . permitted men to deduct club fees because men like to conduct business with each other over golf" and to deduct the costs of driving a Rolls Royce, "[b]ecause some men believe expensive cars enhance their professional image." According to Macklin (1992), "[A]s long as business has been the exclusive domain of men, the commercial needs of business have been dictated by what men [think they] need to spend in order to produce income . . . . [O]ne might reasonably demand a reconceptualization of 'business expense' that reflects the changing composition of the business class" (see also Johnson, 2000).

In the second broad theme of feminist legal scholarship, it is argued that the law is androcentric and that this androcentricity is pervasive. The law, according to this theme, is a reflection of a typical male culture, a masculine way of doing things. Law, therefore, is corrupted for women by its inherent masculinity. The task that feminists face is to come up with a completely new law for women. Such law should be devoid of norms and characteristics that reinforce male prerogatives and female powerlessness about gender roles and private intentions. For example, it is argued that the male legal culture dismisses or trivializes many problems that women face, such as sexual harassment and date rape (Brockman, 2000; Stein, 1999). Feminist legal scholars address issues such as the different subjective experiences of shared social realities: for the man, an office pass may be defined as sex (and pleasurable); for the woman, it may be defined as harassment (and painful). Many gender-specific injuries are still dismissed as trivial (sexual harassment on the street); consensual (sexual harassment on the job); humorous (nonviolent marital rape); deserved or private (domestic violence, date rape); or non-existent (pornography).

The third dominant theme challenges the very concepts law invokes to support its contention that it is a just and fair institution. Contrary to professed notions, law is not value-neutral, objective, rational, dispassionate, and consistent. This is because law defines those concepts in a typically masculine way, ignoring or devaluing the qualities associated with the experiences of women. Essentially, the problem is that law is claimed to be neutral in relation to the sexes (and other social categories); yet, the very way this neutrality is argued is gender-biased (Boyd, 2000; Dossa, 2000). The particular style of maleness can best be illustrated by the concept of "rational person," a mythical legal subject who is coherent, rational, acts on *his* free will, and in ordinary circumstances can be held fully accountable for *his* actions (Bender, 2003; Lahey, 2003; Shaffer, 2003).

Many feminists are pragmatists (Chafetz, 1997; Radin, 1991) and rely on feminist legal methods (Bartlett, 1991; Jarviluoma, Moisala, and Vilkko, 2003; Ramazanoglu and Holland, 2002) to advance their cause. Feminists contend that without understanding feminist methods, law will not be perceived as legitimate or "correct." These methods, although not unique to feminists, seek to reveal features of a legal concern that more traditional approaches tend to ignore or suppress. There are three such basic methods (Bartlett, 1991:370).

One method asks the **woman question**, which is designed to probe into the gender implications of a social practice or rule (see, for example, Lamarche, 2000; Scott, 2003). Asking the woman question compensates for law's failure to take into account experiences and values that are more typical of women than of men. Feminists ask the woman question in many areas of the law. In the case of sexual assault, they have challenged the 1983 legislation that enshrined the defence of "honest but mistaken belief" and asked why this defence dealt with the perspective of the defendant and what he "reasonably" thought the woman wanted, rather than the point of view of the woman and what she "reasonably" thought she conveyed to the defendant (Bonnycastle, 2000). Pursuing the woman question entails continuing to ask why conflict between family and work responsibilities is still often considered a private matter for women to resolve rather than a public concern involving the restructuring of the workplace (Condon, 2000; Johnson, 2000). Essentially, the woman question shows how the predicament of women reflects the organization of society rather than the inherent characteristics of women.

Another method, **feminist practical reasoning,** deals with features not usually reflected in legal doctrine. The underlying assumption is that women approach the reasoning process differently from men, that women are more sensitive to situation and context, and that they tend to resist universal generalizations and principles. Feminist practical reasoning challenges the legitimacy of the norms of those who claim to speak on behalf of the community, and they seek to identify perspectives not represented in the dominant monolithic male culture.

A third method, **consciousness-raising,** provides an opportunity to test the validity of legal principles through personal experiences of those who have been affected by those principles. The idea is to explore common experiences and patterns that come about from shared recollection of life events. It enables feminists to draw insights from their own experiences and those of other women and to use these newly formed insights to challenge dominant versions of social reality. In consciousness-raising sessions, women share their experiences publicly as victims of marital rape, pornography, sexual harassment on the job, or other forms of oppression or exclusion based on sex (Robson, 1994; Williams, 2004), in an attempt to alter public perception of the meaning to women of practices that the dominant male culture considers acceptable or innocuous. There is also a call for the development of a lesbian legal theory, "a theory about law that is relentlessly and intelligently lesbian," as a component of contemporary legal scholarship (Robson, 1992:37, 1998; see also Gavigan, 2000).

Of course, feminist legal theory and its methods are not without their detractors. In part as a reaction to feminist legal scholarship, there is a nascent intellectual movement of critical studies of masculinity (see, for example, Collier, 1995; Hearns, 1992). The contention is that men are oppressed within patriarchy in a fashion comparable to women's oppression. It is not yet an institutionalized attempt at "men's liberation," albeit there are already efforts to legitimize the endeavours of politically powerful individuals and organizations to "improve" the legal rights of men (Collier, 1995:26).

Critics charge that the assumption of a dominant androcentric homogeneous legal culture is an exaggeration. They argue that the accusation itself is more of a rhetorical than a factual contention. Specifically, they maintain that while the classical Marxist polarization of the sexes into a dominant and a subordinate class, with the concomitant proletarianization of gender, represents a forceful argument, it is one of limited intellectual substance and appeal. For example, critics emphasize that, in depicting the benefits that accrue to men in what is considered an essentially sexist institution, many feminists have neglected to consider that not all men benefit equally from legal sexism. That is, allusions are made only to successful white middle-class males, with their unique form of white middle-class masculinity, while minority and gay males are excluded (Keen and Goldberg, 1998). A close examination of the principles and methods of law also reveals that there are many people who are omitted or maltreated on the basis of class, race, age, and ethnic background, in addition to gender. Thus, to assume that we are dealing with a clear-cut issue of "us versus them," gender-based exploitation would seem an oversimplification.

There are also some perplexing dilemmas confronting feminists. For example, there is no consensus in the literature about various options. That is, while some feminists maintain that equality is best realized by treating men and women the same (with accommodation made only for such sex-irreducible differences as pregnancy, lactation, and childbirth), others insist that equality necessitates that the sexes be treated differently. "To overstate and oversimplify, the division, as old as feminism itself, pits those who focus on the similarities between men and women and hold up an ideal of common humanity against those who focus on what is unique, special, different and worthy in women's culture and experience as contrasted to men's culture and experience and hold up an ideal in which women are empowered to speak in their own voice and project their values into the public realm" (Williams, 1987:120). This difference-versus-similarity argument carries over into a variety of other areas and leads to protests that feminists cannot have it both ways (Williams, 1991). Feminist legal theory has also been accused of failing to address issues of democracy and citizenship (Higgins, 1997), and of neglecting to formulate a positive theory of female sexuality (Franke, 2001). Still, in spite of such criticisms, feminist legal theory and its methods represent an important intellectual movement that challenges traditional legal doctrine both in Canada and elsewhere (see, for example, Bartlett, Harris, and Rhode, 2002; Greer, 2000; Williams, 2006).

Critical Race Theory

Critical race theory (CRT) is an eclectic, dynamic, and growing movement in law with over 700 leading law review articles and a dozen books devoted to it (see, for example, Ayres, 2003; Delgado, 2004; Delgado and Stefancic, 2000; Valdes et al., 2002).

Like feminist legal theory, critical race theory is concerned with questions of discrimination, oppression, difference, equality, and the lack of diversity in the legal profession (Johnson, 1997). Although its intellectual origins go back much farther, the inception and formal organization of the movement can be traced back to a 1989 workshop on critical race theory in Madison, Wisconsin (Delgado, 1994, 2004; Delgado and Stefancic, 2000). Many of the proponents have been previously involved with critical legal studies or feminist jurisprudence, and the 1989 conference effectively ratified critical race theory as an important component of legal theory. The critical race theory movement attempts to rectify the wrongs of racism while acknowledging that racism is an inherent part of modern society (see, for example, Bender, 2004; Valdes, 1997, 2002). Racism is embedded in the system, and proponents recognize that its elimination is impossible; but at the same time they insist that an ongoing struggle to countervail racism must be carried out.

In a way, the word "critical" reflects a continuity between critical legal studies and critical race studies. Both seek to explore the ways in which law and legal education and the practices of legal institutions work to support and maintain a system of oppressive and nonegalitarian relations. But CLS do not generally look outside of the law to identify the forces that actually determine the content of legal rules, while critical race theory prompts a recognition of the urgency of racial problems and an uncompromising search for real solutions rather than temporary and comforting stop-gap measures (Chang, 1993; Culp, 1994; Farber, 1994). The basic premise is that indigenous peoples and racialized minorities are oppressed and that oppression creates fundamental disadvantages for those who are so treated. Critical race theory focuses on the experiences and situations of oppressed people and provides an outlet for the concrete experiences of subordinates (Scheppele, 1994). Because of oppression, racialized minorities perceive the world differently from those who have not had such experience. Critical race theory scholars can thus bring to legal analyses perspectives that were previously excluded. Through narratives and "storytelling," some scholars share their experiences or the experiences of other racialized minorities to make their presence felt in legal scholarship. For example, Crenshaw (1989) has argued that the experiences of visible minority women cannot be presumed to be interchangeable with the experiences of visible minority males or nonvisible minority females. The term "**intersectionalism**" is forwarded to "capture some of the unique dimensions and circumstances of being both a woman and a person of colour" (Friedrichs, 2006:108).

Critical race theorists extend traditional civil rights scholarship to locate problems beyond the surface of doctrine to the deep structure of law and culture. Racism is viewed not only as a matter of individual prejudice and everyday practice, but also as a phenomenon that is deeply embedded in language and perception. Racism is a ubiquitous and inescapable feature of modern society, and despite official rhetoric to the contrary, race is always present even in the most neutral and innocent terms. Concepts such as "justice," "truth," and "reason" are open to questions that reveal their complicity with power. This extraordinary pervasiveness of unconscious racism is often ignored by the legal system.

Proponents of critical race theory have a commitment to a vision of liberation from racism through reason and efforts to separate legal reasoning and institutions from their alleged racist roots. It is believed that justice is attainable and that with the correct theory of race and racism, enlightenment, empowerment, and eventually emancipation will follow.

As with all other intellectual developments, critical race theory has its detractors (see, for example, Ayres, 2003). One concern is that CRT articulates its conception of race as a social construction at the macro level, focusing primarily on legal and sociopolitical processes. It has not paid attention to the interpersonal ways in which race is produced. That is, CRT often ignores the racial productivity of the "choices" people of colour make about how to present themselves as racialized persons. As a general matter, CRT's race-as-a-social-construction thesis does not include an analysis of the race-producing practices reflected in the daily negotiations people of colour perform in an attempt to shape how (especially white) people interpret their nonwhite identities.

There also seems to be a contradiction between CRT's commitment to radical criticism and its emphasis on racial emancipation. If the very language used to describe justice is infected by racism and gradations of power, some query, what is the objective of critique? Another criticism is that it lacks a standard methodology and a set of common tenets. Further, it is also seen as a reformist project, not really new and distinguishable from traditional civil rights scholarship, which set out to eliminate discrimination but failed to fully achieve its stated objective. In the final analysis, critical race theory is a young intellectual movement which has the potential to have a profound effect on legal scholarship in the coming years.

Law and Literature/Rhetoric

In recent decades, "law and literature" has emerged as "a significant movement in American jurisprudence . . . a growing part of the law school curriculum and . . . [received] significant attention from the legal academy and practicing bar" (Scallen, 1995:705). By the early 1990s, 84 of North America's 199 law schools offered some variation of a law and literature course (Luyster, 1997). The law and literature/rhetoric movement has continued to flourish in the new millennium, inspiring communities of scholars not only in Canada and the United States, but also in Italy, France, the UK, Scandinavia, Germany, the Netherlands, Australia, and China (Weisberg, 2005). However, the "law and literature" label is, in itself, at least somewhat misleading for it seems to invite the assumption that scholars within this field are engaged upon a singular quest. Instead, perhaps the most notable features of this movement are its rich intellectual diversity and its avowedly inter-disciplinary nature, attracting not only scholars in the field of law but also in literary criti-cism and poetics, in linguistics and communication studies, in sociolinguistic and cultural history, in critical theory and in cultural, race, and gender studies (see, for example, Freeman and Lewis, 1999; Ost, 2006; Peters, 2005).

It is common that law and literature is divided into two sub-areas, using a dichotomy that is typically (but not always; see, for example, Yoshino, 2005) credited to American civil rights lawyer Ephraim London (1960). The first, "law-in-literature," directs attention to the depiction of law and jurisprudential questions within fiction. The second, "law-as-literature," adopts a more radical vantage point, which approaches legal opinions and arguments as works of literature or as a type of creative writing. Others, however, have found it useful to forward more elaborate categorizations of the law and literature move-ment that employ different names and boundary markers. For example, Scallen (1995:705) identifies three "schools" within law and literature studies: (1) the "law in lit-erature school," which emphasizes legal themes and characters within works of fiction and employs these fictionalized accounts as prisms to scrutinize legal proceedings; (2) the "legal literary/rhetorical criticism school," which employs the methods and/or theories of literary and rhetorical criticism to study various types of actual legal discourse (e.g., con-stitutional provisions, judicial opinions); and (3) the "legal storytelling school," a hybrid that "blurs whatever distinction exists between the first two schools by making extensive use of personal use of personal narratives as evidence in legal scholarship."

The "law in literature school" is the oldest of these three "schools," with legal schol-ars exploring the implications of law as it is depicted in literary classics. This endeavour, which is often traced back to Dean John Wigmore's (1913) compilation of lists of fiction-al works featuring lawyers or law-related themes, was "rather singlehandedly reinvigorat-ed and given new life by the work of a single scholar, James Boyd White" (Elkins, 2002) in the 1970s with the publication of his pioneering work, *The Legal Imagination* (1973). The use of great works of literature as a source of insight into the nature of crime and judg-ing, the paradoxes of equity, the relationship between customs, norms, law, power, and the political order, has continued to attract such scholars as Robin West (1988a, 1988b), Richard Posner (1988, 1990), and Richard H. Weisberg (1996, 1998). It has been argued that many benefits accrue to lawyers who engage in the critical analysis of literary works. Some maintain that doing so improves their abilities to write and to examine complex texts with care and critical thought, encourages the development of empathy, allows them to "liberate themselves from the narrow-mindedness that comes from specializing in law . . . sensitize themselves to the timeless moral and ethical issues that stories of law and jus-tice raise . . . [and] gain a critical perspective on what it means to be a lawyer or a non-lawyer engaged with the law" (Scallen, 1995:706; see also Heilbrun and Resnick, 1990; Possner, 2005).

The more recently developed "legal literary/rhetorical criticism school" derives, in part, from the same claims and concerns that spawned the critical legal studies movement (which, as earlier noted, argue that legal doctrine and arguments often attempt to shore up existent and unjust power structures). Scallen (1995:707) observes that if the CLS critique "seems to say that law has no inherent logic, that its meanings are limited only by the skill or audacity of its interpreters," some scholars have found it appealing to turn toward literary and rhetorical theory and to the interpretive strategies of critical social theory (e.g., post-structuralism, deconstructionism, intentionalism, neopragmatism, and cultural studies) "in an attempt to find some limits to the process of interpretation and some justification for the study of it." This agenda has broadened the field of inquiry as legal scholars have "begun to accept the idea that law could be viewed as the cultural and literary discourse of a group of people who have adopted a particular form of communication for doing what they do when they do 'law'" (Minda, 1997:246; see also Milovanovic, 2003; Mundy, 2002).

The most recent of the three schools, legal storytelling, employs narratives as an essential part of a scholarly argument; these personal stories are not viewed as digressions or as illustrations of a point but, instead, as evidence for the argument that is being advanced. For example, Peter Brooks insists that "if the law paid more attention to the narrative analysis of what it's up to, it might learn something from that. It would learn that—first of all—storytelling is not innocent. The way you talk about it makes a lot of difference to the result you come up with" (in Couch, 2002). Similarly, Elkin (2001) observes that, while "[l]awyers are storytellers, and always have been," the legal profession and legal educators "are becoming more conscious of the ways lawyers tell stories and the effect of their stories." He notes, for example, that "[c]ourtroom trials have never been forums reserved for truth-telling; lawyers have always been rhetoricians (of the classic and not so classic sort); and jurors are not today, nor have they ever been, paragons of rationality and objectivity who can step out of their prejudices and reach beyond their culturally shaped understanding of the world." Scallen (1997:714) observes that, for writers within this school, "rhetoric, in the form of their stories, is truth and their method of communicating it to the majority who, under the banner of truth, have only told stories that protect their interest."

Like each of the movements discussed earlier, the law and literature movement has its critics. A fundamental criticism is that this movement lacks a clear definition of its subject matter, its constituency, and its goals. Rather than a unified body of knowledge and an agreed upon set of procedures for resolving analytic difficulties, the law and literature enterprise seems to have only a tenuous unity. Moreover, while Scallen's (1995) identification of three distinct schools within law and literature may function as a helpful pedagogical tool, it should be stressed that their boundaries are actually more porous than concrete. Thus, while Scallen positions James Boyd White within the "law in literature school," his writings might be better described as "law and literature with jurisprudential aspirations" (Elkins, 2002). It is notable that White's now-classic study of *The Legal Imagination* (1973) did not only concern itself with law and literature, but it also directed attention to judges and lawyers as storytellers and how law is accomplished through the telling of stories (e.g., client to lawyer, lawyer to client, lawyer to judge, trial judges listening to stories and so on). His writings also thoroughly explore the narrative and storytelling perspective (see, for example, Boyd, 1990; 1994). In *When Words Lose Their*

Meaning (1984), Boyd argued that the law is best viewed as "a set of social and intellectual practices that have their own reality, force and significance. It provides a place that is at once part of the larger culture and apart from it, a place in which we can think about a problematic story by retelling it in various ways and can ask in a new and self-conscious way what it is to mean."

Scallen (1997:713) notes that a further criticism of the law and literature movement is that "its proponents are unclear as to the scope of their project—to what degree are they attempting to be theoretical, to state 'overarching inductive generalities [Morawetz, 1993:501]?" She observes that some authors, in their attempt to state unified theories of law and literature, forward grand claims that are "expressed at a level of abstraction that makes them inaccessible and even incomprehensible to those who need it most—legislators, judges, lawyers and the public." Echoing this sentiment, Domnarski (2003:109) charges that "[C]ritical theorists seem invariably to have taken up ideologically-based (pluralist, feminist, radical) approaches that use literature to set the real world straight by reforming, deconstructing, or excoriating the texts which they associate with hegemony. . . . Much of this ideological critique may turn out to be of little relevance to students as they take up the practice of law."

Proponents of the law and literature movement within law schools have also been charged with ignoring the works of minority writers. As Judith Resnick (1990:221) early observed, "The question is that of the canon: what (and who) is given voice; who privileged, repeated, and invoked; who silenced, ignored, submerged, and marginalized. Law and literature have shared traditions—of silencing, of pushing certain stories to the margin and of privileging others. An obvious example in literature is the exclusion of certain books from the canon of the 'great books.'" More than a decade later, Desai, Smith, and Nair (2003) asserted that while "[l]iterature was urged upon the law school with creative pluck" the agenda stalled after the inclusion of Homer and Melville: "For the most part, studies in Law and Literature still do not venture outside a narrow range of standard, Harvard-and-its-sisters approved literature."

In the 1980s and 1990s, feminist investigators, such as Carolyn Heilbrun and Judith Resnick (1990), reported that the law and literature movement showed a decidedly masculinist bias with prominence given to male authors. More recently, Desai, Smith, and Nair (2003) have charged that the "law and literature canon" has failed to incorporate the works of ethnic minority authors. They observe that the two major journals in the field of law and literature share a disappointing track record in this regard: "In the twelve years plus that *Cardozo Studies in Law and Literature* [first published in 1989] has been in business, it has published one article explicitly on a minority writer . . . and one that is centrally concerned with issues of race. . . . In the twelve years plus that the other major journal in the field, the *Yale Journal of Law and the Humanities* [first published in 1988] has been existence, it has published one article explicitly concerned with the intersections of race in the field of law and literature." In addition, they claim that a broader search of law reviews and full-length texts also reveals a "telling silence," with works that analyze literary texts by ethnic minorities "few and far between." In an attempt to redress this situation, more than 300 academics interested in analysis of multi-ethnic literature gathered in New Orleans in 2000 for a conference on "Multi-Ethnic Literatures and the Idea of Social Justice." The explicit intent of the conference was "to engage in the active de-canonization of the field and literature, and to show through example how the inclusion of literature emerging from a wide variety of ethnic experience . . . would challenge the settled assumptions of the field" (in Desai, Smith, and Nair, 2003).

Finally, it should be emphasized that the use of narratives and storytelling as evidence is not confined to scholars within one specific "class" within one delimited "school" within the law and literature movement (see, for example, Elkins, 2002; Longride, 2006; Tushet, 1992). As noted, both critical race theory and feminist legal theory champion analyses which raise the "voices" of previously ignored (or "silenced") groups of women and men. In addition, ethnographers within the social sciences have long directed attention to the importance of language as "the essential mechanism through which the power of law is realized, exercised, reproduced, and occasionally challenged and subverted" (O'Barr and Conley, 1998:129; see also Conley and O'Barr, 1990, 2003; Popp et al., 2003; White, 1991).

SUMMARY

- In a historical context, legal development, industrialization, urbanization, and modernization are closely intertwined. Legal development is conditioned by a series of integrative demands, stemming from society's economic, political, educational, and religious institutions.

- What distinguishes the traditional, transitional, and modern legal systems from each other is the comparative degree of differentiation between basic legal elements. Accompanying the emergence of laws, court systems, police forces, and legislation is a trend toward increasing size, complexity, differentiation, and bureaucratization.

- Efforts at explaining the interplay between law and society should be seen in the context of the intellectual, political, and social climates of the particular theorists. In each historical epoch, every interpretation of social reality posits certain questions and provides certain answers.

- Sociologists embracing the functionalist approach attempt to account for law in society within the overall framework of the theory that society consists of interrelated parts that work together for the purpose of maintaining internal balance. Sociologists advocating conflict and Marxist approaches to the study of law in society consider conflict inevitable and ubiquitous in societies, as a result of inescapable competition for scarce resources.

- Proponents of the critical legal studies movement maintain that law is riddled with contradiction and prejudice and that it is heavily in favour of the wealthy and powerful. Feminist legal theorists challenge the impartiality of law in dealing with women and argue that law is androcentric and reflective of male culture. Critical race theorists argue that the root causes of racial inequality still persist in our society, embedded in law, language, perception, and structural conditions. The law and literature movement positions the language of law and its narratives as focal concerns.

CRITICAL THINKING QUESTIONS

1. The legal definition of "homicide" varies across time and space. Examine the forms of culpable homicide contained in the Canadian Criminal Code. What is included? What is excluded? In what ways does the Code's definition of criminal homicide reflect a general consensus of the Canadian population? In what ways may it suggest elitist control over the relatively powerless?

2. Reflect upon a literary work that you have read with a law-related theme (e.g., George Orwell's *1984* or *Animal Farm*; Fyodor Dostoyevsky's *The Brothers Karamazov*; Margaret Atwood's *The Handmaid's Tale*; or Toni Morrison's *The Bluest Eye*, *Beloved*, or *Tar Baby*). How did it present the relationship between law, norms, and power? Did reading this work encourage you to challenge customs, norms, and/or laws that you had previously accepted in an uncritical way?

chapter three

The Organization of Law

The Civil Proceedings section of this chapter was written by Gregory P. Brown, Chair of the Department of Sociology, Criminal Justice and Social Welfare of Nipissing University.

Nowadays, in one way or another, law touches all of us. The contact may be pleasant or unpleasant, tangible or intangible, direct or indirect, but it is nonetheless a constant force in our lives. For a sociological understanding of law in society, we need to know about the social organization of law, the types of social arrangements and relations involved in the legal process, and the social characteristics of people who interpret and administer the law (see for example, Sarat, 2004). This chapter examines the social organization of legal systems in the context of the judicial, legislative, administrative, and enforcement agencies that carry out the official (and at times unofficial) business of law.

COURTS

One of the most important functions of courts is to process disputes (see, for example, Mays and Gregware, 2001). By definition, a **dispute** is a conflict of claims or rights—an assertion of right, claim, or demand on one side, met by contrary claims on the other. When courts hear disputes, they attempt to decide (adjudicate) between or among those who have some disagreement, misunderstanding, or competing claims. Such disputes may arise between individuals, between organizations (private or governmental), or between an individual and an organization. When a judge renders the official judgment of the trial court in a civil or a criminal case as to the defendant's guilt or innocence, the process is called **adjudication**.

Unlike legislative and administrative bodies, courts do not place issues on their own agendas (see, for example, Abraham, 1998). Judges generally do not decide to make rulings about same-sex marriages, a parent's right to spank his or her children, or the extent of freedom of expression in cases involving pornography, hate, and advertising and then announce their "decisions." Rather, courts are passive; they must wait until matters are brought to them for resolution. The passivity of courts places the burden on citizens or organizations to recognize and define their own needs and problems and to determine which require legal judgments. As Donald Black (1973:138) notes, this method of acquiring cases "assumes that each individual will voluntarily and rationally pursue his [sic] own interests." The courts are indifferent to those issues or disputes that individuals or organizations fail to notice or wish to ignore. This reactive nature of courts ensures that they consider disputes only after the injuries have taken place or the problems have developed.

In theory, courts differ from other kinds of dispute-regulation methods in that they are available to all members of society. In principle, everyone who has a dispute for which there is legal redress ought to be able to use the courts. Unlike dispute-settlement methods that are available only to specific groups in society (for example, university grievance committees or religious tribunals), courts are truly public. Judicial resolution of disputes entails both the application of legal knowledge and the interpretation of events. The role of courts is to interpret and to apply law. Such judicial interpretation of law is expected to be impartial. Judges are expected to be governed by legal principles, not by personal preferences or by political pragmatism. (In other countries, such as China, courts also have a propaganda function in adjudication and sentencing that carries images and messages about the state, order, legitimacy, and the consequences of punishment and is part of a wider program of social control and socialization [see, for example, Trevaskes, 2004]).

Dispute Categories

The dispute-processing function of Canadian courts, which will be discussed in detail in Chapter 6, is on the increase (see, for example, Bogart, 2002; Sauvageau, Schneiderman, and Taras, 2006). To understand what courts do, it is necessary to examine the kinds of disputes they process. Sheldon Goldman and Austin Sarat (1989:4) suggest that there are three important categories of dispute that provide the bulk of work of courts. The first is called the **private** dispute. This kind of dispute is characterized by the absence of any initial participation by public authorities. For example, when a husband and wife quarrel, when two businesspeople debate the terms of a contract, or when two automobiles collide, these events are likely to give rise to private disputes. Although they may occur in public places and may involve competing interpretations of law, they remain private as long as the government is not a party. Since these disputes arise more or less spontaneously in the course of normal social life, they are usually processed and managed without the intervention of government. Many of these private disputes can be dealt with in the general context of ongoing relationships or through some kind of bargaining and negotiation. For example, the husband and wife may seek marriage counselling, the businesspeople may arrive at a compromise through negotiation, and a settlement may be reached for the car accident through an insurance company. At times, however, nonlegal intervention is insufficient for the disputing parties. The courts may be asked to settle disputes in a large variety of civil cases where a party seeks legal redress in a private interest, such as for a breach of contract or the use of a copyrighted story without permission.

The second category of disputes is called the **public-initiated** dispute. It occurs when the government seeks to enforce norms of conduct or to punish individuals who breach such norms. These kinds of public disputes emerge when society attempts to control and channel social behaviour through the promulgation of binding legal norms. An illustration of the public-initiated dispute is the ordinary criminal case in which the state, or some official acting on its behalf, seeks to use the courts to determine whether a particular breach of law has occurred and whether sanctions should be applied. It is unique because it always involves and is governed by the law of the entire community. In the case of criminal law violation, dispute processing must occur in a public forum, for no society could allow the development of private mechanisms for the enforcement of breaches of public norms, since that could easily lead to anarchy. It should be noted, however, that not all public-initiated disputes are resolved or processed by means of judicial action. A variety of informal mechanisms, ranging from the warnings that a police officer may give to a traffic violator, to the prosecutor's choice not to go ahead with a criminal case, to the practice of plea bargaining, may be used to deal with breaches of public norms (Fisher, 2003). Furthermore, disputes involving the breach of public norms are, at times, not called to the attention of public authorities. For instance, the husband who beats his wife has committed a violation of public norms, but until a complaint is lodged with law enforcement agencies, their dispute remains private.

The third kind of dispute is the **public defendant** dispute. In this type, the government participates as a defendant. Such disputes involve challenges to the authority of some government agency or questions about the propriety of some government action that may be initiated by an individual or by an organization. In such cases, the courts are called upon to review the action of other branches of government. These disputes involve claims that the government has not abided by its own rules or followed procedures that it has prescribed. For instance, the case of *B. (R.) v. Children's Aid Society of Metropolitan Toronto* concerned the right of parents to refuse a blood transfusion for their child on the basis of their religious belief, and whether the forced blood transfusion constituted a violation of the parents' rights and freedoms as enshrined in the *Canadian Charter of Rights and Freedoms*. This case involved parents who belonged to the Jehovah's Witnesses faith and who had refused a blood transfusion for a one-month-old infant daughter that the child's doctors believed necessary to save her life. Protection proceedings were instituted by the Children's Aid Society (CAS) to gain wardship of the child and, while the child was in their care, she was given a blood transfusion. The child was later returned to her parents. The parents appealed the wardship orders, but the appeal was dismissed, as was their appeal to the Court of Appeal. The parents next appealed to the Supreme Court of Canada, arguing that the Charter right of "liberty" gave them unconstrained freedom and the right to make decisions of fundamental personal importance, such as the general right to nurture their child and make decisions about their child's welfare and medical care. (While the Supreme Court of Canada did not disagree, it ruled in 1995 that intervention was reasonable and justified when the conduct of parents fails to meet a socially accepted standard and places the lives and well-being of children at risk.) In general, such disputes come to court only after the aggrieved party has failed to remedy his or her grievance either through the political process or through procedures provided by the offending government agency.

These three types of dispute—private, public-initiated, and public defendant — represent, for the most part, the workload of Canadian courts. It should be noted that, contrary to widespread beliefs, courts, in general, process rather than solve disputes. A court decision is seldom the last word in a dispute. For example, after a divorce decree, the aggrieving parties may continue to argue, not about settlements, but about visitation rights or proper supervision of children (see, for example, Sarat and Felstiner, 1995). Thus, it should be remembered that whether the disputes involve only two individuals who bring the case to court or whether cases have broader ramifications, court decisions are seldom the final word in a dispute. Let us now consider the structure of courts where decisions are rendered.

The Organization of Courts

Since Canada is a federal state, legislative powers are divided between two levels of government: federal and provincial. Under the *Constitution Act, 1867*, the provinces were granted the power to create and maintain provincial courts that would deal with matters that fell within their jurisdiction. In addition, the Act gave federal Parliament the authority to establish "a general court of appeal for Canada" as well as "any additional courts for the better administration of the laws of Canada." As a result, Canada's court system is complex; it is composed of a range of courts that have varying jurisdictions and "questions of jurisdiction can be difficult to sort out, especially since courts that share the same functions may go by different names" (Department of Justice, 2005).

As Figure 3.1 indicates, Canada's courts can be distinguished into four basic levels. In ascending order, these levels are: (1) provincial/territorial courts; (2) provincial/territorial superior courts and the Federal Court; (3) provincial/territorial courts of appeal and the Federal Court of Appeal; and (4) the Supreme Court of Canada, which is the highest court in Canada and the final court of appeal from all other Canadian courts. During the 2002–03 fiscal year, governments spent $1.2 billion (slightly more than $37 for every person in Canada) operating the court system. In that year, a total of 12 069 people were employed in provincial, territorial, and federal courts. Of this number, 10 001 (83 percent) were court staff and 2068 (17 percent) were judges (Statistics Canada, 2004).

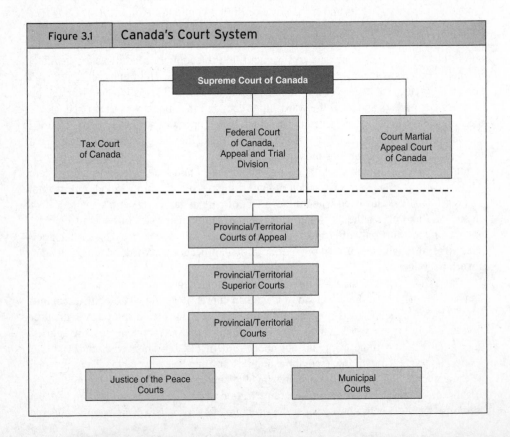

Figure 3.1	Canada's Court System

Provincial/Territorial Courts. Every Canadian province and territory, with the notable exception of Nunavut, has a provincial/territorial court; in Nunavut, cases that would ordinarily be heard in a provincial/territorial court are heard by the Nunavut Court of Justice, a court that "combines the power of the superior trial court and the territorial court so that the same judge can hear all cases that arise in the territory" (Department of Justice, 2005).

The role of provincial/territorial courts is the same across the country even though the names and divisions of these courts may vary. "Provincial/territorial courts deal with most criminal offences, family law matters (except divorce), young persons in conflict with the law (from 12 to 17 years old), traffic violations, provincial/territorial regulatory offences, and claims involving money, up to a certain amount (set by the jurisdiction in question). Private disputes involving limited sums of money may also be dealt with at this level in Small Courts. In addition, all preliminary enquiries—hearings to determine whether there is enough evidence to justify a full trial in serious criminal cases—take place before the provincial/territorial courts" (Department of Justice, 2005).

There are a number of courts at the provincial/territorial level that are devoted entirely to particular types of offences or offenders. For example, the **Drug Treatment Court** (DTC) program was first introduced into this country in 1998 in Toronto and, since then, has spread to Vancouver, Edmonton, Regina, Winnipeg, and Ottawa. DTCs attempt to address the needs of non-violent individuals who are charged with criminal offences that are motivated by their addictions (see Chapter 5). In some provinces and territories (e.g., Manitoba, Alberta, Ontario, the Yukon), **Domestic Violence Courts** have been established in an attempt to "improve the response of the justice system to incidents of spousal abuse by decreasing court processing time; increasing conviction rates; providing a focal point for programs and services for victims and offenders; and, in some cases, allowing for the specialization of police, Crown prosecutors, and the judiciary in domestic violence matters" (Department of Justice, 2005; see also Comack and Balfour, 2004; Shaffer and Bala, 2004). **Youth Courts** address cases in which a young person, aged 12 to 17, is charged with an offence under federal youth justice laws.

Provincial/Territorial Superior Courts. Every Canadian province and territory has superior courts. The superior court of original jurisdiction is the highest court at the provincial level and variously called, in different provinces, the Court of Queen's Bench, the High Court of Justice, the Superior Court of Justice, the Supreme Court Trial Division, or the Division Court. The superior courts have jurisdiction to hear all civil and criminal cases (unless a statute specifically says otherwise). In most provinces and territories, the superior court has special divisions (e.g., the family division). While superior courts are administered by the provinces and territories, superior court judges are appointed and paid by the federal government.

Appellate courts are provincial institutions which hear appeals of a decision of the provincial superior court and are variously referred to as the Court of Appeal, the Supreme Court Appeal Division, or Appellate Division. "The justices in a provincial court of appeal . . . do not in most instances rehear witnesses, testimonies or accept evidence" (Yates et al., 2000:99). Rather, they examine the written transcripts of a trial and listen to legal arguments that are presented by lawyers representing the parties involved in the dispute. In addition, courts of appeal also hear constitutional questions "that may be raised in appeals involving individuals, governments, or governmental agencies" (Department of Justice, 2005a).

The Federal Courts. The Federal Court of Canada, which replaced the Exchequer Court in 1971, consists of a trial division and a court of appeal. "The Federal Court and Federal Court of Appeal are essentially superior courts with civil jurisdiction. However, since the Courts were created by an Act of Parliament, they can only deal with matters specified in federal statutes (laws)" (Department of Justice, 2005a). The jurisdiction of these Courts includes interprovincial and federal-provincial disputes, intellectual property proceedings (e.g., patents, trademarks, copyright), *Competition Act* cases, citizenship appeals, and cases involving Crown corporations or departments of the Government of Canada. "As well, only these Courts have jurisdiction to review decisions, orders and other administrative actions of federal boards, commissions and tribunals; these bodies may refer any question of law, jurisdiction or practice to one of the Courts at any stage of a proceeding" (Department of Justice, 2005a).

Specialized Federal Courts. In an attempt to deal more effectively with certain areas of law, the federal government has created specialized courts. These include the Tax Court of Canada and courts that serve the Military Justice System. In 1983, the Tax Court of Canada was created to address disputes that arose from the assessment of federal taxes. This court, which is independent of the Canada Revenue Agency and all other government departments, hears disputes between taxpayers and the federal government after a taxpayer has exhausted all of the other options for appeal under the *Income Tax Act*. Canada's *National Defence Act* provides for the establishment of military courts to hear cases involving the Code of Service Discipline—"a system of disciplinary offences designed to further the good order and proper functioning of the Canadian Forces"—and "applies to all members of the Canadian Forces as well as civilians who accompany the Canadian Forces on active service" (Department of Justice, 2005). The role of the Court Martial Appeal Court is to hear appeals from military courts. The function of this court is similar to that of a provincial/territorial appeal court and its powers are the same as those of a superior court.

The Supreme Court of Canada, created by federal statute in 1875, is Canada's highest court of law. Originally, decisions of the Supreme Court could be appealed to the Judicial Committee of the Privy Council in the British House of Lords. However, these types of appeals were abolished in 1933 for criminal cases and in 1949, for civil cases. As a result, the Supreme Court of Canada now acts as the court of last resort. "It is the final authority on the interpretation of the entire body of Canadian law, whatever its source" (Hogg, 1997:217). It has jurisdiction over disputes in all areas of the law (e.g., constitutional law, administrative law, criminal law, civil law) and is the final court of appeal from all other Canadian courts. However, "[b]efore a case can reach the Supreme Court of Canada, it must have used up all available appeals at other levels of court. Even then, the Court must grant permission or 'leave' to appeal before it will hear the case" (Department of Justice, 2005). "Leave to appeal" is not routinely granted; rather, it occurs only when a case "involves a question of public importance; if it raises an important issue of law or mixed law and fact; or if the matter is, for any other reason, significant enough to be considered by the country's Supreme Court" (Department of Justice, 2005). McCormick (2006) reports that "[m]ost applications for leave are rejected—in recent years, the success rate varies between 11 percent and 15 percent." In some cases, however, the right to appeal to the Supreme Court is automatic. For example, a person who has been acquitted at trial but found guilty by a court of appeal automatically has the right to appeal to the Supreme Court. Moreover, "no leave is required in criminal cases where a judge on the panel of a court of appeal has dissented on how the law should be interpreted" (Department of Justice, 2005).

The Supreme Court of Canada is additionally empowered to rule on the legality of bills submitted by the government and to declare the law on questions referred to it by the federal cabinet. "The government may ask the Court to consider questions on any important matter of law or fact, especially concerning interpretation of the Constitution. It may also be asked questions on the interpretation of federal or provincial/territorial legislation or the powers of Parliament or the legislatures" (Department of Justice, 2005). Between 1892 and

2005, there were 76 federal references. For example, in the *Constitutional Patriation Reference* (1981), the Supreme Court ruled that the federal government could patriate the constitution without the consent of the provinces even though it would violate a political tradition if it did so without securing "a substantial degree" of provincial consent. In the *Quebec Secession Reference* (1998), the Supreme Court unanimously ruled that while a unilateral declaration of independence by a province (i.e., Quebec) would be illegal according to the Canadian Constitution and international law, Quebec had the right in principle to negotiate a separation agreement and that a constitutional amendment would make secession possible. The court also said that if a clear majority of Quebeckers voted for secession in a referendum, the rest of Canada would be obliged to negotiate the terms of independence and that these negotiations would have to respect democracy, federalism, the rule of law, and the protection of minorities. Other noteworthy reference cases in recent decades include the *Anti-Inflation Act Reference* (1976); the *Senate Reference* (1980); the *Newfoundland Continental Shelf Reference* (1984); the *Manitoba Language Rights Reference* (1984); the *Ng Extradition Reference* (1991); the *David Milgaard Conviction Reference* (1991); the *Quebec Sales Tax Reference* (1994); the *Firearms Act Reference* (2000); and, most recently, the *Reference re: Same-Sex Marriage* (2004; see Chapter 7).

The role of the Supreme Court in particular and the role of Canadian courts in general have been expanded by the *Constitution Act, 1982*, and its *Canadian Charter of Rights and Freedoms*. Although Canadian courts have long possessed the power to declare laws or actions of government to be invalid, this power was fairly narrow prior to 1982. The only basis for striking down legislation was if the government who introduced it had exceeded its legislative authority under the *Constitution Act, 1867* (the *BNA Act*). That is, the federal government was not allowed to legislate on matters that fell under provincial jurisdiction (e.g., property and civil rights, administration of justice, education, health and welfare, municipal institutions, and matters of a local or private nature) and the provincial governments were not permitted to legislate on matters that fell under federal jurisdiction (e.g., criminal law, employment insurance, postal service, regulation of trade, external relations, money and banking, transportation, citizenship, Indian affairs, and defence). However, provided that the legislation was not *ultra vires* (Latin for beyond, or in excess of, the power that passed it) and did not encroach on the legislative authority of the other, it was valid.

The powers of the courts expanded when the *Constitution Act* became law in 1982. The requirement that federal Parliament and the provincial legislatures must now comply with constitutional provisions, including the *Canadian Charter of Rights and Freedoms*, has made the Supreme Court, and the judges who compose it, the supreme guardians of our constitutionally defined rights. As Sauvageau, Schneiderman, and Taras (2006:8) pointedly remark, "The adoption of the Charter of Rights and Freedoms in 1982 transformed Canadian political life. It placed the Supreme Court at the nexus of societal power and change. Judges had to give life to the Charter, and in doing so it can be argued that they redefined and reordered much of the Canadian social contract." Legislation or government actions that infringe or deny any of the fundamental rights and freedoms recognized by the *Canadian Charter of Rights and Freedoms* may be struck down by the courts, and the Supreme Court has the final say on this matter.

The Supreme Court, which is composed of eight puisne justices and one Chief Justice, hears cases in either panels of three, five, or seven members or as an entire body. It is a "lawyers court: lawyers typically appear before it to argue points of law, but the parties to a dispute do not appear" (Boyd, 1998:141). Although a decision of the Supreme Court of Canada "is binding on all courts within Canada at every level . . . [when it] hears a case requiring its interpretation of a provincial statute, its decision will only be applicable to those provinces having similar statutory provisions in place" (Yates et al., 2000:28). In addition, a ruling of the Supreme Court that concerns the application of the civil law in Quebec will not apply outside of that province.

Sauvageau, Schneiderman, and Taras (2006:16) observe that the Supreme Court "has dominated the Canadian political landscape" in terms of both credibility and prestige. They point to the results of a 2001 Gallup poll that found that Canadians had "greater respect and confidence in the Supreme Court than they did in almost all other Canadian institutions, including churches, newspapers, banks, large corporations, the federal government, the House of Commons and provincial government" (2006:16). Nevertheless, they note that surveys have found that approval for the court's performance has fallen since the onset of the new millennium; while about 90 percent of respondents voiced approval of the court's performance in 2001, this declined to just 65 percent in 2003 and, in that year, less than 20 percent of survey respondents expressed strong confidence in the court. Moreover, they acknowledge that the Supreme Court has been the target of significant criticism. For example, they observe that "[g]overnments and nationalists within Quebec have traditionally viewed the court as a leaning Tower of Pisa that always leans in the same direction, a centralist one"; for western populists, the Supreme Court has long been thought to symbolize "the entrenched power of the East" (24).

Participants in Court Processes

Courts, as dispute-processing institutions, are composed of four distinct groups of participants—litigants, lawyers, judges, and juries. These participants, in turn, bring to the judicial process diverse interests, values, and perspectives that influence the ways in which disputes are processed. We shall discuss them separately.

Litigants. Since the principal function of courts is to process disputes, the most obvious participants must be the disputants. This group includes individuals, organizations, and government officials who are trying to settle disagreements and to regulate their own behaviour and the behaviour of others. Clearly, not all individuals, groups, or organizations can or are willing to resort to courts in their attempts to settle disputes. Questions of cost, efficiency, availability, the fulfillment of the legal requirements of a suit, and the nature of the dispute affect differently the potential users of courts. Consequently, two distinct types of litigants emerge.

In a classic study, Marc Galanter (1974) designates the two types of litigants as "one-shotters" and "repeat players" who have not changed over the years. They are distinguished by the relative frequency with which they resort to court services. As will be shown in Chapter 6, those who use the courts only occasionally are called **one-shotters**. Illustrations of one-shotters include an author suing her/his publisher for breach of contract, and a professor filing charges against a university for sexual or racial discrimination in promotion. **Repeat players** are those who engage in many similar litigations over a period of time. Whereas one-shotters are usually individuals, repeat players are organizations, such as finance companies, moving companies, or insurance companies. Their investment and interest in a particular case is moderately small. Because of their high frequency of participation in litigation, repeat players are more concerned with the ways a decision may affect the disposition of similar cases in the future than with the outcome of a single case (Ross, 1980). Repeat players can also invest greater resources in litigation than one-shotters, and their frequent appearances in court enable them to develop expertise. Such expertise is reflected in the way in which they select cases for litigation and in the manner in which they carry on disputes that have been transformed into lawsuits.

By contrast, participants who have only a one-time interest in litigation are generally more concerned with the substantive result of their case than the way in which the outcome may affect other cases. For example, the author in the preceding illustration is more concerned with winning her/his case against the publisher than with setting a precedent for similar cases. Organizations, in general, participate in litigation as plaintiffs, and individuals participate as defendants. Both governmental and non-governmental organizations have greater access to resources, and they are the most frequent initiators of court cases to process disputes between themselves and private individuals with whom they are dealing.

Research suggests that repeat performers (generally organizations) using the courts for the routine processing of clients have the highest success rates and do better as both plaintiffs and defendants than one-shotters (generally individuals) (Galanter, 1975; Relis, 2002). Refining these categories and applying them to the courts of appeal, Peter McCormick's "party capability" theory suggests that senior levels of government (federal/provincial) will fare better than their municipal counterparts, "and that the Crown will do better still because it acts against isolated individuals in a clearly defined legal background that maximizes returns to experience and organization" (McCormick, 1994:156). Moreover, he suggests that, compared to "small" businesses, "big business" (e.g., banks, insurance companies, and major corporations such as C.P.R., Hydro Quebec, or the Irving business empire in the Maritimes) will enjoy greater success and that individuals will be least successful.

In his research, which considered the performance of various categories of litigants on the basis of a sample of provincial appeal court decisions (including all reported decisions for the second and seventh year of every decade since 1920), McCormick found confirmation of his hypothesis:

> The government category was the most successful as both appellant and respondent; appeals by governments succeeded well over 50 percent of the time. The rank ordering within the government category (Crown, federal/provincial, municipal) was also as expected. Business as a whole was slightly less successful, with a combined success rate of just over 50 percent. However, the spread between 'big business' and 'other business' is surprisingly large, so much so that big business litigants rank above the federal/provincial government category and second only to the Crown. Unions and individuals bring up the rear, with combined success rates well below 50 percent. (McCormick, 1994:158)

With regard to the surprisingly poor performance of trade unions, McCormick suggests that while these large organizations are "repeat players" that have "considerable resources and access to first-rate legal advice," they are most effective when they appear as respondents (successfully defending the trial court decisions more than half of the time) rather than as appellants. Adopting the argument of Wheeler et al. (1988) that the "normative tilt of the law" favours one type of interest over another, McCormick suggests that the courts are more likely to take the side of capital in its clashes with labour (159).

In addition, McCormick analyzed the 3993 decisions of the Supreme Court of Canada that were reported in either the *Supreme Court Reports* or the *Dominion Law Reports*. Although there are certain methodological problems with this research which he acknowledges (e.g., the role and procedures of the Court changed greatly over the time period investigated), he again reports confirmation of the party capability thesis. Here too, the general category of government was most successful as both appellant and respondent, and the rank ordering of their likelihood of success was as expected (e.g., Crown, federal, provincial, municipal). While business as a whole evidenced a combined success rate of just under 50 percent, "the spread between 'big business' and 'other business' . . . [was] so large that big business litigants . . . [ranked] above provincial governments" (p. 163). Once again, unions and individuals had success rates well below 50 percent. He concludes: "The general message remains the same, during as before the age of the Charter: governments, especially the Crown, are more successful than business litigants, who in turn are more successful than unions or individuals. The gap between government and business may have narrowed slightly, but the gap between business and other litigants has grown" (p. 165) (see also Flemming and Krutz, 2002; Flemming, 2004; McCormick, 2006).

Lawyers. Law is a technical game and the players are highly trained in its complex rules and elusive categories (see Hutchinson, 2005). Without the assistance of lawyers, most individuals would be unable to activate the courts on their own behalf. The operation of courts is based on special standards and rules established by law. The process of identifying and applying rules requires special training and expertise, which is provided by members of the legal profession. Lawyers occupy an intermediary position between disputants and courts and transform litigants' complaints into legal disputes. Disputants generally need to retain the services of lawyers to receive advice about legal rules and how they apply to specific issues in dispute. By being familiar with both court operations and legal rules, lawyers are instrumental in determining whether a particular dispute warrants judicial intervention. Lawyers, in effect, play the role of gatekeepers for the judiciary (Hughes, 1995:109).

Lawyers are repeat players in the adjudication process. Only a small proportion of lawyers are involved in actual litigation. Most are concerned with specific non-trial activities, such as writing wills or carrying out routine transactions. As will be discussed in Chapter 8, some lawyers specialize in particular areas of the law (such as divorce or criminal law), and others represent only particular kinds of clients (such as corporations or universities) or limit themselves to particular clients within specified areas of law (such as taxes). Jonathan Casper (1972) distinguishes among types of trial lawyers by the manner in which they perceive their clientele. He argues that a small number of lawyers view themselves principally as representatives of public interests. These lawyers are concerned, for example, with consumer interests or with the protection of the environment. For them, individual cases are simply vehicles for achieving broad public objectives that generally necessitate major changes in the law. They prefer to take only cases they believe involve significant issues. The second type of lawyer represents particular interests or organizations. For example, some companies have in-house lawyers whose principal role is to represent members of the organization.

The third type of lawyer, typically criminal defence lawyers, is most often involved in actual court work and, therefore, will be considered in greater detail. These lawyers are legal specialists who most closely approximate the public's preconception of lawyers. They handle a broad range of criminal cases and only rarely deal with traffic or personal injury cases (Wice, 1978:29). Although the role of defence lawyers is most often couched in the general term of "defending a client," they perform a number of specific roles. These include the roles of advocate, intermediary, and counsellor (Cohn, 1976:261). In the primary role of *advocate,* defence lawyers take all possible steps within legal and ethical bounds to achieve a victory for the client, while protecting the rights of the client at each step of the criminal justice process. Often, this can best be accomplished by acting as an *intermediary* between the client and the law, working through negotiation and compromise to secure the best possible benefits from the system. The third role is that of *counsellor.* It is the responsibility of defence to give advice to the client as to what to expect and what appears to be in the client's best interest. Although most people would agree that defence attorneys should perform the foregoing functions, it is often suggested that they fail to do so. For example, Abraham S. Blumberg echoes some of the still prevailing criticisms of defence lawyers. He argues:

> The real key to understanding the role of defence counsel in a criminal case is the fixing and collection of his [sic] fee. It is a problem which influences to a significant degree the criminal court process itself, not just the relationship of the lawyer and his [sic] client. In essence, a lawyer-client "confidence game" is played. (Blumberg, 1979:242)

Blumberg charges that defence lawyers make sure that their clients know that there is an important connection between fee payment and the zealous exercise of professional expertise, secret knowledge, and organizational "connections" in their behalf. He contends that defence lawyers manipulate their clients and stage-manage cases to offer at least the appearance of services. He calls the criminal lawyer a "double agent" because the main concern is to maintain good relations with members of the court organization. The defence lawyer may give the impression of being an impartial professional who will do everything possible for the client; however, he or she is, in reality, dependent on the goodwill of the prosecutor and the court.

The fourth type of trial lawyer perceives a lawyer's role primarily as serving individuals who retain him or her. These lawyers are often referred to as "hired guns" (Blumberg, 1979:238). They are interested only in the case in which they are involved, and they will do everything within legal and ethical limits to ensure favourable outcomes for their clients. In their view, they serve a case, not a cause. These different types of lawyers behave differently in advising clients whether to litigate and in preparing strategies of litigation.

Judges. Although a variety of officials work around courtrooms, none has the prestige of the judge, who is responsible for the administration of the court and its reputation for honesty and impartiality. The courtroom is designed so that attention is focused on the judge, who sits on a pedestal above the other participants. Any visitor to a courtroom will notice that the visitors' gallery never rises above the judge and that those who work in the courtroom are not allowed to sit or stand at the judge's level. When the judge enters the courtroom, everyone rises, and all attention is directed at him or her. The judge is addressed as "Your Honour," regardless of individual predilections (Jacob, 1984:10). The judge alone interprets the rules that govern the proceeding, although this power may be shared with a jury of laypersons, and the judges see themselves as autonomous decision-makers whom nobody bosses around (Jacob, 1997:3). Moreover, while one may speak disparagingly of our prime minister or criticize our elected representatives with relative impunity, showing disrespect toward a judge (or engaging in any act "which is calculated to embarrass, hinder or obstruct a court in the administration of justice, or which is calculated to lessen its authority or its dignity") may result in an individual being charged with "contempt of court." (These offences, which are punishable summarily, are also referred to as "criminal contempts.")

In 2002–03, about half of all judges in Canada, or 1030, were appointed by the federal government. Four in 10 (40 percent) worked in superior courts, 6 percent worked in appeal courts, and 4 percent in federal courts (Statistics Canada, 2004). While the judiciary accounted for only 17 percent of those employed in Canada's provincial, territorial, and federal courts in 2002–03, they received almost half (44 percent) of the total amount spent on salaries and benefits.

While Canadian judges enjoy high occupational prestige, salaries (see Chapter 8), and job security, their freedom is limited by virtue of their role. Specifically:

> A judge must avoid anything that creates a conflict of interest. He or she must give up director-ships or other management positions in corporations and business ventures. A judge must also be very careful when speaking on public matters that he or she may later be required to adjudi-cate. If charged with traffic or other minor offences, a judge is expected not to contest the charge, in order to avoid embarrassing colleagues by having to appear before them. (Yates et al., 2000:113)

Nevertheless, while in theory judges may be removed from office if they breach the requirements of good behaviour, in practice, they would appear to be relatively immune from sanctioning. Under the *Judges Act*, the process to assess alleged breaches of conduct by federally appointed judges falls to the Canadian Judicial Council (CJC), established in 1971 by an Act of Parliament. One of the four responsibilities of the CJC is to investigate complaints about the conduct of federally appointed judges (the others being: making rec-ommendations, generally in conjunction with the Canadian Superior Courts Judges Association, on judicial salaries and benefits; continuing education of judges; and devel-oping consensus among Council members on issues involving the administration of jus-tice). On receipt of a complaint that a judge has breached the requirements of good behav-iour, the CJC must decide whether or not the judge has become "incapacitated or disabled from the due execution of the office of judge" by reason of "age or infirmity; having been guilty of misconduct; having failed in the due execution of office; or having been placed, by conduct or otherwise, in a position incompatible with the due execution of that office" (Canadian Judicial Council, 2002:11). The CJC receives between 150 and 200 complaints annually and received 1632 between 1991 and 2001. However, its 2000–01 Annual Report acknowledges that "[i]n only five cases during the Council's nearly 30-year history have complaints led to formal Inquiry Committees. In addition, in five instances there have been formal inquiries directed by a Minister. *Only once since 1971 has the Council recom-mended to the Minister of Justice that a judge be removed from the bench*" (Canadian Judicial Council, 2002:11; italics added). Between 2001 and 2005, an additional 637 com-plaints were received, with 125 new complaints received on average per year. Of the 149 new complaints received in 2004–05, "two-thirds of complaints were found to be without merit and were closed without referral to the judge in question—a proportion consistent with results in past years" (Canadian Judicial Council, 2005:12). The largest single source of complaints (typically accounting for about half of all complaints) occurred in relation to family disputes (i.e., divorce and child custody cases) (Canadian Judicial Council 2005:9). While the CJC will generally issue a news release if a complainant has made his or her complaint public, "[o]ut of respect for the privacy of both the complainant and the judge, the Council will not make the fact of a complaint or its disposition public on its own initiative" (Canadian Judicial Council, 2002:10).

Judges come from the middle or upper classes and have a history of party identification, if not activism (Carp and Stidham, 2001:210; McCormick and Greene, 1990:66). As we note in Chapter 8, while virtually all judges are lawyers in Canada, only a small fraction of lawyers are, or ever become, judges (Friedman, 2002). Other than their experience as barristers and solicitors, Canadian judges "are not required to have any formal training on how to be a judge before they are appointed" (Department of Justice, 2005). Nevertheless, once appointed, Canadian judges do "have access to a range of programs at both the provincial/territorial and federal levels on all aspects of judging, as well as areas of the law. The National Judicial Institute, in particular, coordinates and delivers educational programs for all federal, provincial, and territorial judges" (Department of Justice, 2005).

In civil-law countries, such as France and Italy, judges are civil servants and have different training and experience from practising lawyers. Those who aspire to become judges take a competitive examination after law school. The ones who pass will become judges with a career of their own. Previous practice of law is not required. It is also unlikely that they will ever practice law. Their roles and functions are also different from their Canadian counterparts of the adversarial system. Unlike in common-law countries, judges rely on the inquisitorial method, which has its roots in ecclesiastical courts. The French criminal trial is a good example of this method. The main figures at the trial are the investigating magistrate and the presiding judge. The magistrate is responsible for the investigation. He or she sends the material to the trial, where the judge dominates the proceedings and interrogates the defendant and the witnesses, who are the same for both the defence and the prosecution. Obviously, there is no "coaching" of witnesses. The interrogation of the judge resembles more a conversation than a cross-examination (Loh, 1984:497). The judges are much more active than in Canada. They play a greater role in building and deciding a case, they put the evidence together, and they go far beyond the "refereeing" role characteristic of common-law judges.

Juries. An ancient Welsh king, Morgan of Glamorgan, established trial by jury in A.D. 725, and the origins of the Canadian jury system can be traced back to civil and criminal inquiries conducted under old Anglo-Saxon law in England (Abramson, 2000; Vidmar, 2000). The original concept of the jury was most likely imported to England after the Norman Conquest. The Normans started the practice of placing a group of local people under oath (hence the term "juror") to tell the truth. Early jurors acted as sources of information on local affairs, and they gradually came to be used as adjudicators.

Before the 12th century, criminal and civil disputes were resolved by ordeal. It took many forms. There was ordeal by water. The accused person was bound by rope and dropped into a body of water. If the person floated, it was a sign of guilt; if he or she sank, it was a sign of innocence. There was also ordeal by fire—carrying heated stones or iron, and if the subsequent burn did not get infected in three days, the accused was declared innocent—and ordeal of the morsel that did or did not choke the accused. Civil disputes were often resolved by oaths on the assumption that a false oath would expose someone to the judgment of God.

The jury system came to Canadian shores with the British settlers in the mid-1700s. Although jury trials are most common in the United States, with an estimated 80 percent of all jury trials worldwide taking place in that country (Boyd, 1998:164; Hans and Vidmar, 1986:31; Cristol, 2002), juries are also used in criminal trials and, albeit less frequently, civil trials in Canada.

According to the *Canadian Charter of Rights and Freedoms*, a person accused of criminal activity "has the right, except in the case of an offence under military law tried before a military tribunal, to the benefit of trial by jury where the maximum punishment for the offence is imprisonment for five years or a more severe punishment." In consequence, criminal cases involving summary and minor indictable offences are tried without a jury. Although cases involving such serious offences as murder, treason, hijacking, intimidating Parliament or a legislature, or bribery by the holder of a judicial office require trial by jury in a superior court, this statutory requirement may be waived with the consent of the accused and the attorney general. An accused may also opt for a jury trial in cases involving many less serious indictable offences. In relation to civil proceedings that are governed by provincial statutes, cases such as libel, slander, malicious arrest or prosecution, and false imprisonment require a jury unless both sides agree to dispense with the services of a jury. In other cases, especially those that are highly complicated and very technical, the use of juries is very rare. "The right to civil jury trial is a common law right that is not specifically enshrined in the Charter, and its use has slowly eroded over the last two centuries" (Vidmar and Schuller, 2001:129). While there are still more than 1000 civil jury trials in Ontario each year, they occur far less frequently in some of the other English-speaking provinces (Vidmar and Schuller, 2001:129). In Quebec, the right to a jury trial has been abolished in civil matters, with the reasoning that a jury may fail to properly review and weigh the evidence before making a determination.

The selection and constitution of juries falls under provincial jurisdiction in Canada and, in consequence, qualifications vary somewhat. Until the 1950s, most provinces did not permit women to be jurors. Since 1972, however, the Criminal Code has stated that "no person may be disqualified, exempted or excused from serving as a . . . juror in criminal proceedings on the grounds of his or her sex." In addition, all provinces now allow women to serve as jurors for civil trials. In general, all Canadian citizens who are between 18 and 65 (or 69) years of age, who have not been convicted of an indictable offence (or have received a pardon for an indictable offence) and who are free from any mental or physical disability (e.g., blindness) that might impede their performance as a juror, are considered qualified to serve on a jury. Certain occupational groups (and sometimes their spouses) are exempted from serving as jurors. These groups include members of the Privy Council, provincial cabinets, the Senate, the House of Commons, and provincial legislatures, as well as lawyers, law students, judges, law enforcement officers, clergy, doctors, coroners, dentists, veterinarians, and some essential service providers (e.g., firefighters, nurses, persons required in the running of transportation or communication services). Lists of jurors are prepared each year from various sources such as voter registration lists and provincial lists of Medicare beneficiaries. The selection of names, often done by computer, must be random.

In criminal cases the jury is composed of 12 persons. In the past, criminal juries in the Yukon and the Northwest Territories could be composed of six persons; however, this provision was declared to be unconstitutional. The verdict of the jury in criminal cases in Canada must be unanimous. If the jury seems unable to reach agreement after a reasonable amount of time, the judge may set the case for retrial or call for a new jury to replace a "deadlocked" or "hung jury." In civil cases, fewer jurors are required and unanimity is not required. In general, agreement by five of the typically six jurors who compose the jury in a civil case will suffice.

Although they invented the jury system, the British have been steadily dismantling it for decades (Gunnell, 2000). There are no juries in British civil cases, except those involving libel or police misconduct. Around 93 percent of criminal cases are heard before panels of three lay magistrates. There is no **voir dire** (a trial within a trial to decide upon the admissibility of evidence), and cross-examination of juries and criminal cases do not require unanimous verdicts. Juries are used predominantly in common-law countries (Friedman, 1998, 2002). However, since November 1993, Russian law has allowed accused criminals to request a trial by jury. The old tribunal method, which only involved a judge and two assistants, was unfairly biased against the defendants, who now are entitled to a fair trial (Stead, 1994).

In the United States, generally "only criminal trials make extensive use of juries" (Jacob, 1984:165). In some jurisdictions, the prosecutor has the right to have a case tried by a jury. In such jurisdictions, the jury may be used even if the defendant prefers to have the case tried by a judge, although how the proceedings are carried out is determined by the trial judge. A prosecutor may seek a jury trial because of the belief that a jury is more likely to convict than a particular judge, that a jury is more likely to impose the desired sentence, or that a jury trial will attract more public attention to a defendant's heinous crime (US Department of Justice, March, 1992:7). Though the right to a jury trial is often waived, juries are essential to the operation of American courts. The jury is used in all death penalty cases, and a fundamental law in the United States is that no person may be convicted of a capital crime except by the unanimous verdict of a 12-member jury. That is the law in all of the 38 states that have the death penalty, as well as in federal cases. There is, however, one exception. A jury of five is all that is required to sentence a member of the armed services to death in a courtmartial (Bonner, 2001).

Dispute processing in trial courts involves two basic types of issues: issues of law and issues of fact. Issues of law emerge as participants in the dispute seek to identify and interpret norms that will legitimize their behaviour. In a sense, a trial is a contest of interpretation and legal reasoning. The judge has the authority to determine which interpretations of law are proper and acceptable, but a trial is more than a question of legal reasoning. It also provides the opportunity for a reconstruction, description, and interpretation of events (that is, issues of fact). The purpose of a trial is to answer the question of who did what to whom and whether such conduct is legal. Juries are called "triers of fact" and the function of the jury is to listen to and decide among competing and conflicting interpretations of events. The jury acts as a referee in an adversary contest dealing with the presentation of differing versions of the same event. By a crude division of labour, the jury is the authority on facts; the judge is the authority on law. But judges also control the jury, and the common law provides several mechanisms by which judges can and often do intervene to prevent juries from going overboard, including the discretion to exclude prejudicial evidence, the prerogative to instruct the jury in the law, the right to discharge a juror who cannot continue due to illness or any other reason, the use of special verdicts to ensure that factual determinations are rational, and so on (see, for example, Bogus, 2001). In addition, criminal juries in Canada do not participate in the sentencing of those who have been judged guilty; sentencing is strictly the duty of the judge.

In the United States, jury selection has become one of the most important functions of a trial lawyer (Donner and Gabriel, 2000). Indeed, some American lawyers now contend that by the time the jury has been chosen, the case has been decided. During the process of voir dire, prospective jurors in the United States are questioned first by the judge, then by the lawyers representing defence and prosecution. The purpose of the voir dire is three-fold. First, it is used to obtain information to assist in the selection of jurors and to ferret out any juror bias (Jonakait, 2003). Second, it enables the lawyers to develop rapport with potential jury members. Finally, there is an attempt by both sides to try to change the attitudes, values, and perspectives of jurors (Klein, 1984:154). If a juror admits to a racial, religious, political, or some other bias that would influence his or her decision, the lawyers whose client would be harmed can ask the judge to excuse the juror for cause.

Lawyers may employ various strategies that they perceive will maximize their side's chances for success (Dimitrius and Mazzarella, 1998; Hoffman, 2004). Reportedly, a significant number of lawyers embrace a **one-juror verdict theory** (Keeton, 1973) and look for a "key juror" who will be sympathetic to their case and able to influence the decision of the entire group of jurors. Adopting the premise that, "In general, an individual's status and power within the jury group will mirror his [sic] status and power in the external world" (Christie, 1976:270), lawyers attempt to select an influential individual who will favour their position and encourage others to do so as well. Other lawyers assume that likes will favour likes (e.g., Catholics will favour a Catholic litigant), a belief that is known as the **similarity-leniency hypothesis** (see, for example, Kunz and Kunz, 2001). While some evidence supports this position (most notably with respect to religious similarity), other research suggests a **black-sheep effect**. That is, while "in-group members" are generally favoured, those who are an embarrassment to the in-group or cast the group in a negative light may be treated especially harshly (Wrightsman et al., 1998:373). However, to maximize their side's chances of success, American lawyers have made increasing use of social scientists in jury selection (Hans, 1992:61).

Scientific jury selection, as it is termed, consists of three steps. First, a random sample is drawn from the population, and the demographic profile of this sample is compared with that of the prospective jurors (Pope, 1989). If the jurors were randomly selected, the profile should match. If there is substantial over- or under-representation of particular characteristics (ethnic groups, age, occupation, and so forth), the jury pool can be challenged. Second, after it is established that the prospective jurors represent the population at large, a random sample is drawn from the jury pool to determine the demographic, personal, and attitudinal characteristics considered to be favourable to one's own side. Third, after establishing the psychological and demographic profile of a "favourable" juror, the social scientist can make recommendations for selection of individual jurors (Loh, 1984:400). This basic procedure is often supplemented with additional information. For example, in one trial, investigators for the defence questioned prospective jurors' neighbours and friends to learn about their attitudes. In another case, a research firm representing a corporate defendant called all potential jurors and questioned them, pretending to be conducting a random telephone survey.

An expansion of the technique is the use of a **shadow jury**. Some social scientists feel that since the opposing lawyers present conflicting views of the facts, jurors tend to make decisions based more on empathy than evidence. Thus, techniques of effective communication and persuasion need to be called to the attention of lawyers. To this end, simulated or "shadow" juries are used to gain feedback for lawyers on how to try their cases. Such mock trials are the most useful early in a case. They can help a lawyer pinpoint the main issue of a case and assemble pertinent evidence around it, as well as show jurors' probable reactions to arguments which might contradict their basic beliefs. Most mock trials are conducted by jury consulting or market research firms and contain abbreviated versions of all parts of a regular trial (Clifford, 1995; Fuente, Fuente, and Garcia, 2004).

There are serious reservations about the appropriateness of the use of scientific jury selection. Lawyers, when they are being candid, admit that their goal is not fairness but the selection of biases that benefit them. In the words of one lawyer, "I don't want an impartial jury. I want one that's going to find in my client's favour" (Hunt, 1982:85). But critics of the method contend that it tends to undermine the purpose of having an adversarial system of justice. Consider here that the techniques for surveying the community and assessing juror values during the voir dire are clearly designed to achieve juror partiality. It also leads to an imbalance in the composition of the jury. Thus, it is an advantage only to rich defendants in criminal cases and the richer side in civil suits. One with greater resources will have more lawyers, better lawyers, a larger staff. Jury research is one more such advantage. The ability of the adversary system to guarantee a fair and impartial jury and trial is obviously tested when the adversaries possess unequal resources.

There is also the danger that prosecutors may start relying on scientific jury selection if they lose too many cases because of the defendants' use of experts. As Amitai Etzioni points out, "Could any but the most affluent . . . compete with the state, once it began to apply these procedures to the prosecution?" (quoted in Andrews, 1982:73). Finally, there is the question of the public perception of the trial. There is a possibility that the legitimacy of the trial and subsequent verdict is undermined by the use of scientific methods in jury selection.

In stark contrast to the selection process in the United States, intensive questioning that places the juror on trial is contrary to both Canadian law and tradition. Only limited questioning of prospective jurors is allowed for in Canada, and in the vast majority of cases, jurors are selected without any questioning whatsoever (Vandor, 2001:16). Consider the contrast: while prospective jurors in the trial of O.J. Simpson were asked approximately 290 questions each (Vandor, 2001:16), potential jurors for the 1995 trial of Paul Bernardo were asked up to a maximum of eight questions (Vidmar and Schuller, 2001:127).

Although the only information readily available to Canadian lawyers about a potential juror is the juror's name, address, occupation, and whatever their physical appearance and general demeanour are thought to convey, three types of challenges can be used to eliminate prospective jurors. First, the jury list can be challenged if it can be shown that the list was fraudulent or partial or showed willful misconduct in selecting prospective jurors. For example, in *R. v. Nepoose* (1991) the jury was successfully challenged because it had too few women. In *R. v. Born with a Tooth* (1993), the Crown successfully challenged the jury panel selection procedure after a list of 200 persons who were selected at random from the city of Calgary was supplemented with the names of 52 Aboriginal persons living on three nearby reserves who were not randomly selected.

A **challenge for cause** can be made on the grounds that, for example, a prospective juror fails to meet the requirements of the provincial statute that governs juries (e.g., the person's occupation places him/her within an exempted category). On occasion, the challenge for cause procedure is used to screen potential jurors whose impartiality has been tainted by mass media coverage of a case or exposed to the rumours and gossip that may circulate in a small community about a crime. A challenge for cause may lead to a potential juror being asked, for example, if he or she has heard about the case or has any preconceived notions about the proper outcome of the case and so on. So long as a judge rules that a challenge for cause is valid, there are no limits placed on how many of these challenges can be made. The most controversial use of the challenge for cause procedure has been in relation to screening individuals for various types of prejudices, a topic we will return to shortly.

> In contrast to American practice, in which it is the judge who determines whether or not bias has been demonstrated, the jurors themselves are responsible for this decision . . . . This procedure is quite unique to Canada . . . . To begin the process, two individuals are randomly chosen from the jury panel and sworn to serve as "triers." . . . The two triers listen to the prospective juror's responses to the questions and, under instructions from the judge, render an unanimous decision on whether or not the individual is "impartial between the Queen and the accused." . . . If they find that the individual is "not impartial," another juror is called. This process continues until an unbiased juror is found. (Vidmar and Schuller, 2001:146)

The third type of challenge, a *peremptory challenge*, allows either the defence or the Crown prosecutor to eliminate a prospective juror without giving a specific reason. The number of such challenges is limited by the nature of the offence. For example, for charges of high treason or first degree murder, a maximum of 20 challenges are allotted to each side; in cases where the maximum sentence upon conviction would be less than five years, a maximum of four peremptory challenges are allowed. In using these challenges, lawyers rely on their private judgments about which jurors are likely to be unsympathetic to their side and eliminate those who worry them most. Decisions to exclude or include a juror may be based on a variety of considerations: gut reactions to the juror's looks and manner, advice passed down by other lawyers, and various maxims or rules of thumb (Wrightsman et al., 1998:371).

Various concerns have been expressed in relation to the involvement of jurors in dispute processing in courts (Duff and Findlay, 1997; Prentice and Koehler, 2003). The first is whether the presumption that juries are capable of assessing the facts presented to them in an impartial way is, indeed, valid. In *R. v. Sherratt* (1991), the Supreme Court of Canada observed that the "perceived importance of the jury and the Charter right to jury trial is meaningless without some guarantee that it will perform its duties impartially and represent, as far as possible and appropriate in the circumstances, the larger community." In *R. v. Williams* (1998), the Supreme Court explicitly acknowledged that four types of bias could potentially have an impact upon jurors. As identified by Vidmar and Schuller (2001), these are: **interest prejudice**, or biases that jurors may hold due to a direct interest in the case (e.g., a relationship to the accused or a witness); **specific prejudice**, attitudes or beliefs about the particular case that may affect one's ability to decide the case in a way that is fair; **generic prejudice**, beliefs about certain groups of people or certain types of crime (e.g., judging a person as guilty or innocent based on his/her race or sex or sexual orientation rather than on the facts of the case); and **normative prejudice**, "biases that occur when a juror perceives that there is such strong community interest in a particular outcome of a trial that he or she is influenced in reaching a verdict that is consistent with community sentiment rather than one based on an impartial evaluation of the trial evidence" (Vidmar and Schuller, 2001:134; see also Vidmar, 2002).

In *R. v. Williams* (1998), the Supreme Court of Canada ruled that a Native Canadian was entitled to a new trial because the original trial court had rejected his motion to ask jurors if they held any biases about Native Canadians. This decision, which explicitly acknowledged the potential impact of negative stereotypes of a particular group upon a jury, is expected to be far reaching. It also raises a number of controversial questions. As

Vidmar and Schuller (2001:151) point out, given that national surveys have revealed that "Arabs," "Moslems," "Indo-Pakistanis," and "Sikhs" are rated even more negatively than "Native Indians" (and "West Indian Blacks"), a number of questions must be asked. Does this mean that some jurors may be other than impartial "in judging accused who belong to one of these racial or religious groups? Does the issue of partiality relate to the victims and witnesses as well? What if the victim is of the same race as the accused person? And, finally, how might the race of the accused interact with the type of crime he or she is accused of committing?" (Vidmar and Schuller, 2001:151). They point out that researchers have already found evidence for the existence of crime-related racial stereotypes with "blue collar crimes" such as robbery and assault associated with blacks and "white collar" crimes such as fraud and embezzlement linked with whites (Gordon et al., 1996; Gordon, 1990, 1993). They additionally observe that research suggests that individuals judge a defendant more harshly if the defendant is accused of committing a race-stereotypic crime (e.g., a white charged with embezzlement or a black charged with robbery).

A second concern is whether or not juries are truly effective checks on judicial power. There is really no way of determining whether juries ensure that judges will be more restrained in using their power than they would otherwise. In a study by Harry Kalven and Hans Zeisel (1966), an attempt was made to determine the effectiveness of the jury in checking the judge's power by examining the percentage of cases in which the judges and juries involved in the same case agreed as to the appropriate verdict. The researchers found a high degree of agreement between judge and jury—approximately 75 percent. They also noted that in almost all criminal cases in which judge and jury disagreed, the jury tended to be more lenient. Whether the leniency of the jury can be construed as limiting the exercise of judicial power is open to question. It does, however, show that the participation of laypersons in the decision-making process does make a difference in the outcomes of court decisions.

Another issue deals with the question of representativeness of the jury. Ideally, a jury that is representative of the community it serves is one that provides judgment by peers. Studies show, however, that juries in various countries are not always representative, mainly because the sources from which potential jurors are drawn—typically voter registration lists—are not representative of the various ethnic, social, and economic groups in the community (Forman, 2004; Israel, 1998). Defence lawyers often complain that the urban poor, many of them minorities, are more mobile than the middle class and thus less easy to access as jurors. Therefore, fewer are located and called for jury service. Yet, having even a few members of a minority group on a jury panel can help enormously, because racist discussions are less likely to occur in a mixed-race setting (Kennedy, 1998). Obviously, the representativeness of juries is important, not only because of the need to ensure legitimacy of the jury, but also because different kinds of people bring different attitudes and values to the jury.

The representativeness of the jury is further jeopardized by the courts' generally lenient policy toward "no-shows," excuses, and deferments. Although anyone can theoretically get a temporary postponement for "undue hardship or extreme inconvenience," we have already noted that certain groups may be excused permanently. As a result, jury panels are more likely to be composed of people who have the time or can (or want to) take time off from their place of employment. In many occupations and professions, the prospect of being absent for a prolonged period is not welcomed. Thus, it is not surprising that juries draw disproportionately from the lower-middle and middle classes. At the same time, in a disproportionate number of cases, upper- and middle-class persons are chosen as jury forepersons over lower-class persons (Deosaran, 1993).

As we have previously noted, concerns have also been expressed about the ability of jurors to comprehend the judge's instructions so that they do not make up their mind about the sentence before the evidence is presented (Burnett and Badzinski, 2000; Sommer, Horowitz and Bourgeois, 2001) and about their bias against business and their competence in civil cases. Studies show that jurors tend not to be biased against business, they are generally skeptical of plaintiff tort claims against businesses, they question more the motivations and actions of plaintiffs than the responsibilities of business, and they tend to be conservative, in most cases, in awarding damages (Hans and Lofquist, 1992). Regarding competence, some observers argue that many disputes are so complex that an average person is incapable of understanding either the nature of the dispute or the complicated issues involved. For example, to decide whether IBM had monopolized various markets claimed in Memorex's $900 million antitrust suit, jurors needed a detailed understanding of things like "reverse engineering," "cross elasticity of supply," and "subordinated debentures." (And just try to imagine the complexity of cyber jargon in the widely-reported Microsoft antitrust case that lasted three years, from 2001 to 2004). The trial lasted 96 days. The jury heard 87 witnesses and examined some 3000 exhibits. Due to an inability to comprehend such complex issues, some jurors may become susceptible to appeals to their emotions, or increased levels of stress may influence their disposition toward the case (Fitzgerald, 2000; Whittemore and Ogloff, 1995). However, other research finds that juries generally do grasp the facts and that actual incompetence is a rare phenomenon (Greene and Johns, 2001; Horowitz and Bordens, 2002). Further, a study of nearly 9000 trials noted that judges award punitive damages as often as juries and generally in about the same proportion, suggesting that juries may be far less arbitrary, irresponsible, and incompetent than is widely believed. This study is expected to be controversial not only because it concludes that jurors may be more rational than they were believed to be, but also because it contradicts other research (*New York Times*, 2001).

While acknowledging juries' shortcomings, some observers maintain that juries can nevertheless play an essential and symbolically significant role within our system of law.

> The jury . . . serves as the conscience of the community because it is drawn precisely from the community in which the crime was committed. In addition, because the jurors can apply their own sense of fairness in reaching a verdict, never having to justify that decision, it can serve as a guardian against oppressive or rigid laws. (Vidmar and Schuller, 2001:130)

On occasion, the decision of a jury may transmit a powerful message from the community to the government. For example, after four separate jury trials in the 1970s and 1980s failed to convict Dr Henry Morgentaler for providing abortions in a non-accredited or approved hospital—even though his actions were in clear violation of the Criminal Code—the government was moved to amend the laws governing access to abortion (Schuller and Yarmey, 2001:159).

The Flow of Litigation

Several characteristics of the flow of litigation are significant. The processes by which cases are decided differ widely according to the type of dispute, the participants involved, and the stage of the judicial process at which the dispute is settled. In many instances, civil and criminal cases are quite different, and we shall review them separately.

Criminal Cases. A high degree of discretion is characteristic of every phase of criminal procedure (see, for example, Stolzenberg and D'Alessio, 2002). For example, to issue a search warrant to investigating officers, a justice of the peace must be satisfied that the officers have reasonable and probable grounds to search for evidence. A police officer also uses discretion in deciding whether or not to arrest a suspected lawbreaker. Once an arrest is made, a justice of the peace or judge must decide whether to release the accused prior to trial and whether conditions such as a surety (i.e., the deposit of money) should be imposed on the accused in addition to his/her promise to appear for trial. With hybrid offences, the Crown counsel decides whether to treat the offence as a summary conviction offence or to proceed by indictment. At a preliminary inquiry, a judge must decide whether there is sufficient evidence to proceed to trial or if the accused should be discharged. At trial, the judge or jury must decide that the Crown has proven its case "beyond a reasonable doubt." At sentencing, a judge may request that a probation officer prepare a pre-sentence report or receive a statement about the impact of the crime on the victim(s). The judge must also weigh the goals of sentencing, bearing in mind that the Criminal Code requires that "all available sanctions other than imprisonment that are reasonable in the circumstances should be considered for all offenders." At each stage in the criminal justice process, it is possible that the "wheels of justice" may turn in unexpected directions because of the use of discretion by agents of the criminal justice system.

Although determinations of guilt or innocence are ostensibly simple tasks for such fictional investigators as Sherlock Holmes and Hercule Poirot, in real life, these decisions can be difficult and extraordinarily complex. Consider the issue of eyewitness identification. While personal crimes such as assault and sexual assault usually involve parties who know each other (Linden, 2004), for other crimes, such as armed robbery, law enforcement agents are often unable to establish accurately the identity of the perpetrators on the basis of eyewitness testimony (Levi, 1998; Worrall and Hemmens, 2005). Moreover, while "eyewitnesses are among the most influential resources the prosecuting attorney uses to convict a defendant in a criminal trial" (Wrightsman et al., 1998:174) and jurors, in particular, attach great weight to eyewitness identification, there are actually significant limitations in the accuracy or reliability of such eyewitness testimony (Inbau et al., 1997:639; Worrall and Hemmens, 2005).

The unreliability of eyewitness identification and the fallibility of testimony on the witness stand are brought about by three general problems of human memory (Woocher, 1977). To start, the perception of an event is not merely a passive recording. People can perceive only a limited number of events at the same time, and the number remembered is even smaller. Even trained observers find it difficult to describe accurately such basic physical characteristics as height, weight, and age. Humans also find it difficult to judge time, and because of the amount and variety of activities that occur during an action-packed event such as a crime, there is a tendency to overestimate the length of time. Often, crimes take place under poor observation conditions, making subsequent recall difficult. The presence of stress and anxiety decreases perceptual abilities. As a result, witnesses often compensate for perceptual selectivity by reconstructing what has occurred from what they assume must have occurred. In essence, they state what they think should have taken place rather than what actually transpired. Finally, eyewitness accuracy is further reduced in situations of cross-racial identifications. People are poorer at identifying members of another race than of their own. For example, whites have greater difficulties recognizing Black or Asian faces than they do recognizing white faces.

The second problem is that memory decays over time. People forget quickly and easily. When it comes to recall at the police station or on the witness stand, people have a tendency to fill gaps in memory by adding extraneous details so "things make sense." For example, a witness may recall an individual accurately but be completely wrong in remembering the circumstances under which he or she encountered that person. A salesperson may identify the defendant as having been in the store with the murder victim when, in reality, the defendant had been in that store on a few earlier occasions but was out of town at the time of the crime.

Finally, the way in which information is recalled from memory invariably reduces the accuracy of eyewitness testimony. The recall of witnesses is influenced by the subtle suggestions they receive under questioning by a police officer or a lawyer (Wasby and Brody, 1997). Many people also feel compelled to answer questions completely in spite of incomplete knowledge in an attempt to please their interrogators. So they rely on their imagination to supplement factual information.

Despite the impression fostered by film and television representations of the criminal justice process, not all criminal defendants wind up exercising their right to a fair public hearing in court. **Plea bargaining** is a form of negotiation that can be traced back to the earliest days of common law (Nasheri, 1998). The term "plea bargain" has been defined by the Law Reform Commission of Canada as "an agreement by the accused to plead guilty in return for the prosecutor's agreeing to take or refrain from taking a particular course of action" (in Verdun-Jones and Tijerino, 2002:3). According to the Federal Prosecution Service Desk Book of the Department of Justice (which contains guidelines on plea bargaining that are binding on federal prosecutors), several things can be negotiated including "charges, procedure, sentences, and the facts of an offence for the purposes of a guilty plea." Verdun-Jones and Tijerino (2002:3) have identified three useful subcategories of plea bargaining: "(1) *Charge bargaining*, which involves promises concerning the nature of the charges to be laid; (2) *Sentence bargaining*, which involves promises relating to the ultimate sentence that may be meted out by the court; and (3) *Fact bargaining*, which involves promises concerning the facts that the Crown may bring to the attention of the trial judge."

Prior to trial, a defendant's lawyer may ask his or her client if the client wishes to plea bargain. In doing so, the lawyer may believe that the evidence against the client is very compelling and suggest that the client would be better off pleading guilty to a lesser charge with the expectation of receiving a lighter sentence. If the client agrees, the accused person, through his or her counsel, enters into negotiation with a crown prosecutor. In *R. v. Burlingham* (1994), the Supreme Court of Canada ruled that the Crown or police cannot enter into a plea bargain without the participation of a defence counsel, unless the accused specifically waives that right. This decision extended and reinforced the right, guaranteed in the *Canadian Charter of Rights and Freedoms*, of an accused to retain and instruct counsel without delay.

Plea bargaining generally takes place before the actual trial. However, it may also take place during the trial if unanticipated evidence is introduced that significantly increases the perception of the crown prosecutor that he or she will not secure a conviction or causes the defence counsel to feel that their client's chances of acquittal are slim. Simply put, plea bargaining functions to increase certainty. Both the Crown and the defence are aware that the Criminal Code provides judges, for most crimes, with wide discretion in sentencing a convicted offender. In addition, although both the Crown and the defence may privately believe that their side has the stronger case, the outcome of trials, whether before a judge alone or before a judge and a jury, are not 100 percent certain. In consequence, the Crown may perceive that a plea bargain simplifies the process of obtaining a conviction against the accused and guarantees that the person will be penalized in some way—albeit to a lesser degree than if the person was convicted at trial for a more serious charge. A negotiated guilty plea also saves the court time and costs, especially in lengthy and complicated proceedings, and eliminates the need to select a jury or call possibly traumatized victims to testify on the witness stand (see Auditor General of Canada, 2002:5). However, plea bargaining is subject to limitations. For example, while the Crown may recommend a specific sentence to the court, it is up to the court whether or not it will accept the Crown's recommendation. In addition, various appellate courts have ruled that the Crown is divisible. In other words, an agreement made by a prosecutor in a lower court does not bar the Crown from changing its position on appeal if it can demonstrate that it has a good reason for doing so.

In the not-so-distant past, plea bargaining was looked down upon as unseemly. For example, in its 1975 annual report, the Law Reform Commission of Canada haughtily referred to the practice as "something for which a decent criminal justice system has no place." Although plea bargaining has become a fairly routine part of the court process (Verdun-Jones and Tijerino, 2004), on occasion, its use has generated substantial controversy. For example, in 1993, Karla Homolka entered into a plea bargain that resulted in her receiving two 12-year sentences for manslaughter (to be served concurrently) for her role in the sexual assaults and murders of two teenage girls, Kristen French and Leslie Mahaffy. In exchange, Homolka agreed to serve as the Crown's key witness at the later trial of her husband, Paul Bernardo, who was charged with two counts of first-degree murder, kidnapping, unlawful confinement, and aggravated sexual assault, and one count of causing an indignity to a corpse. However, this case was highly unusual in a variety of ways and, contrary to popular belief, individuals who plead guilty do not, on the average, receive a lighter sentence than those who do not. Rather, it is most obviously the criminal justice system that benefits by saving time and the expense of conducting a trial. According to Ericson and Baranek (1982) this should not be surprising given that an uneven playing field exists in negotiations between the police and the Crown on one side, and the accused on the other.

Plea bargaining, as a form of negotiated justice, is a baffling and controversial topic in the sociological literature (see, for example, Lynch and Evans, 2004; Palermo et al., 1998). There are many objections to plea bargaining, the most common being that criminals are allowed to obtain "cheap" convictions (that is, ones in which they do not pay for the real crimes they committed), that it is moving criminal justice into an administrative process rather than an adversarial one, and that it is generating cynicism about criminal justice among the accused, the system's participants, and the public at large. As noted by the 2002 Report of the Auditor General of Canada (2002:5), the practice of plea bargaining has "the potential to undermine the integrity of the criminal justice system, in part because disclosure of the basis for agreements and accountability for the decisions have been inadequate. There are no reliable data on how often plea bargaining occurs and with what outcomes" (see Verdun-Jones and Tijerino, 2002, 2004 for a discussion of how victims' interests are jeopardized by plea negotiations).

In explaining the widespread use of plea bargaining, Arthur Rosett and Donald R. Cressey (1976:85) assert that court personnel, including prosecutors, "develop a group sense of justice" which differs from attitudes generally held in the community, and which is generally more humane and pragmatic than that of the public. They maintain that prosecutors use caseloads as their public excuse for bargaining (there is evidence that plea bargaining positively affects the courts' ability to move through serious cases quickly and efficiently [Holmes et al., 1992]) but rarely consider caseloads in deciding whether to deal with specific cases before them (such as whether to prosecute on the basis of initial charges or to negotiate). The real reasons for plea bargaining, they argue, are the weaknesses in cases that could result in acquittals; the desire to adjust the charges to more reasonable levels, depending on the facts and the character of the defendant; and the desire to comply with the courthouse consensus on concepts of fairness and justice. For a typical defendant, it is often his or her own defence lawyer who initiates negotiations and urges a settlement by plea bargaining. In one study, Abraham S. Blumberg (1979:223) found that over half of the 724 defendants entering guilty pleas indicated that their defence counsel first suggested the guilty plea, usually during the first or second meeting between lawyer and client. The situation is similar in Canada as well as in other countries. In England, barristers often justify the use of plea bargaining based on their desire to avoid going to trial, their belief that most defendants are guilty, and their desire to control crime (Mulcahy, 1994; Passas, 2003).

The final step in most criminal proceedings is sentencing the defendants who have been found guilty. Although sentencing decisions are made within a specific legal framework (see, for example, Savelsberg, 1992; Tonry, 1996), "[j]udges in Canada, like their counterparts in the United Kingdom and other common law countries, have a great deal of discretion with respect to the type and severity of sentences they can impose. A small number of offences carry minimum penalties, and an even smaller number carry a mandatory penalty" (Roberts, 2001:194). While those convicted of first-degree murder are sentenced to life imprisonment without the possibility of parole for 25 years, for the majority of other criminal offences, the Criminal Code only prescribes a maximum penalty.

In 1996, Parliament passed Bill C-41 and enacted a law codifying a set of sentencing principles that were to act as a guide for judges and reduce disparities in sentencing. According to the statement of purpose and principle contained in section 718 of the Code, "A sentence must be proportionate to the gravity of the offence and the degree of responsibility of the offender." This section identifies various objectives that are to be considered by a judge in sentencing:

(A) *Denunciation*: the attempt to censure an individual for culpable criminal conduct. The court imposes a sentence to denounce the crime of which the offender has been convicted.

(B) *Specific deterrence*: the attempt to prevent crime by arousing fear of punishment in the individual being sentenced. Individual offenders are inhibited from further offending by fear of what will happen to them if they are re-convicted.

(C) *General deterrence*: the attempt to prevent crime by creating fear of punishment among the general public. Potential offenders are said to be deterred by being made aware of the punishments imposed on criminal offenders.

(D) *Incapacitation*: the prevention of crime by the incapacitation of the individual offender for a specific period of time. This usually means incarceration.

(E) *Rehabilitation*: the attempt to change an individual by promoting law-abiding behaviour. This usually involves sentencing the offender to some alternative to custody, such as probation with conditions.

(F) *Reparation*: the court may order the offender to make reparations to individual victims or the community.

(G) Promote a sense of responsibility in offenders. (Roberts, 2001:190)

Among the options available to Canadian judges in sentencing are: imprisonment (which may be continuous, intermittent [served on weekends], or indeterminate [as is the case for those identified as Dangerous Offenders]); suspended sentence with probation; probation; the imposition of a fine; conditional and absolute discharge; restitutions; and various specific prohibitions (such as prohibiting the individual from being in possession of a handgun). In an attempt to reduce the use of incarceration as a sanction, the 1996 sentencing reforms created a variety of elements including a disposition called a "conditional sentence," which allows an offender to serve his or her sentence in the community provided that the individual complies with the conditions imposed. If the individual fails to abide by the conditions, he or she may be sent to prison. Not all individuals are eligible for this type of sentence. In applying this sentence the court must feel confident that "serving the sentence in the community would not endanger the safety of the community," and the sentence originally imposed must be for a period of incarceration that is less than two years.

In addition, sentencing reforms purposefully attempted to redress the overrepresentation of Aboriginal peoples within Canada's inmate population. Although Aboriginal peoples represent approximately 3 percent of Canada's population, they are overrepresented as a proportion of those incarcerated within both federal and provincial/territorial institutions (Correctional Service of Canada, 2005). According to Statistics Canada (2005) "the proportion of Aboriginal peoples among provincial/territorial sentenced custody admissions has remained stable at 21 percent since 2001–02. The proportion of Aboriginal peoples among sentenced admissions to federal facilities also remained stable at 18 percent." Among women sentenced to custody in Canada in 2003–04, approximately one-third were Aboriginal; Aboriginal men accounted for one-fifth of all men sentenced to custody during that time period. The overrepresentation of Aboriginal peoples is particularly marked in the Prairie provinces. A one-day snapshot survey of all inmates in Canada's adult correctional facilities found that while Aboriginals represent only 9 percent of Manitoba's population, they account for almost two-thirds (61 percent) of the adult inmate population. In Alberta, where Aboriginals make up 4 percent of the provincial population, one-third (34 percent) of adult inmates are Aboriginal (Robinson et al., 1999). In 1999–2000, Aboriginal people comprised the "majority of both federal and provincial/territorial sentenced admissions in Manitoba and Saskatchewan, as well as the majority of federally sentenced admissions in the Northwest Territories and Nunavut and the majority of territorial offenders in the Yukon" (Lonmo, 2001:8).

Section 718.2(e) of the Criminal Code specifies that "all available sanctions other than imprisonment that are reasonable in the circumstances should be considered for all offenders, *with particular attention to the circumstances of Aboriginal offenders*" (emphasis added). While being Aboriginal does not automatically result in a lesser sentence, the

Supreme Court of Canada has urged judges, when sentencing an Aboriginal offender, to recognize the "broad systemic and background factors affecting Aboriginal people" (Lonmo, 2001: 8).

Comack and Balfour (2004:107) note that, for some, section 718.2(e) is interpreted "as suggesting that there are two sets of principles of sentencing, one for Aboriginal peoples and one for other offenders" and/or as "advocating a more lenient treatment" of Aboriginal offenders. However, they point out that, in *R. v. Gladue* (1999), the Supreme Court addressed this charge of "reverse discrimination" and ruled that "The fact that a court is called upon to take into consideration the unique circumstances surrounding these different parties is not unfair to non-Aboriginal people. Rather, the fundamental purpose of s. 718(e) is to treat Aboriginal offenders fairly by taking into account their difference." Equal treatment, they commented, need not be synonymous with treating all offenders in the identical manner. Nevertheless, Comack and Balfour acknowledge that "[a] more fundamental difficulty" with section 718.2(e) is its presumption that the overincarceration of Aboriginal peoples is best understood as the "result of harsh sentencing decisions by judges—and not the more deep-rooted problem of social and economic oppression." They sombrely remark that "If the underlying problem is understood as being implemented in poverty, addressing it at the sentencing stage does not really attend to the reasons that the case came to court in the first place."

Sentencing circles (or "circle sentencing") represent a relatively recent attempt to implement more culturally appropriate forms of justice for Aboriginal peoples. "Sentencing circles operate within the Canadian criminal justice system, and therefore within parameters set out by the *Canadian Criminal Code* and case law/appeals, often taking the place of criminal court sentencing hearings, once guilt has been established" (Spiteri, 2002:2). Although circle sentencing has historic roots in the "healing circles" used by Aboriginal communities to address community wrong-doings (see, for example, Brown, 2002), the term and its practice was first introduced by judges in the early 1990s in the Yukon Territorial Courts. In *R. v. Morin* (1995), the judge noted that while punishment and retribution are focal concerns within the Canadian justice system, "healing circles"—as their name implies—emphasize rehabilitation, the healing of wounds, the restoration of balance and community harmony.

In circle sentencing, the court typically invites "interested members of the community to join the judge, prosecutor, defence counsel, police, social service providers, community elders, along with the offender, the victim and their families and supporters" (Spiteri, 2002:2) to meet and, within a circle, discuss the crime, factors that may have impacted upon its commission, sentencing options, and strategies through which the offender may be reintegrated into the community. Sentencing circles seldom hear cases which carry a minimum punishment of over two years' imprisonment. "Often only offenders who are eligible for a suspended or intermittent sentence, or a short jail term with probation, make it before a sentencing circle. Although some communities allow sexual assault cases to be heard by a circle, circles almost never hear offences such as murder" (Spiteri, 2002:2). It is common that the circle will forward a restorative community sentence that involves some type of restitution to the victim, community service and/or treatment/counselling services; only on rare occasions, it seems, do sentencing circles recommend a term of imprisonment. It should be noted, however, that judges are not bound to accept the recommendations of sentencing circles (Department of Justice, 2005).

The use of sentencing circles has not been without criticism. Critics have charged that the victim's inclusion within sentencing circles may be traumatic or the reluctant aftermath of family/community pressure (Razack, 1998). On occasion, sentences arrived at by sentencing circles have been decried as excessively lenient (CBC News, 2000). In addition, some have queried whether the use of sentencing circles within Aboriginal communities is truly empowering for those communities, observing that "[e]ven if communities have been able to retain and implement traditional justice practices, these practices are ruled over by the Canadian justice system in today's day and age" (Spiteri, 2002:2).

It is evident that judges do have some choice between sentencing options for most crimes, and they tend to exercise it. Factors that might influence a judge's decision include the race, sex, age, and socioeconomic and criminal background of the defendant, and the skill of the defence lawyer involved. The decision to plea bargain is also a factor. Although legal norms set the framework for the process, they do not control whether violators will be subjected to these legal norms. For example, in an examination of incarceration rates across nine Canadian jurisdictions for a limited number of offences, Roberts (2001:202) reports that "a considerable degree of the variation in sentencing patterns is accounted for by the judge rather than the legal characteristics of the case (the seriousness of the crime, the criminal history of the offender, etc.)."

Throughout the world in recent years there have been several developments in sentencing (see, for example, Tonry and Hatlestad, 1997). Most recently in Brazil, there are efforts underway to reform the judiciary, which according to the *Economist* (2004a) is "dysfunctional": agonizingly slow, best with frivolous cases designed to evade justice, and enmeshed in useless procedure. The 16 900 judges seem old-fashioned, out of touch, and unaccountable to the citizens they serve. A police operation called "Anaconda" in 2003 caught judges selling favourable sentences to criminals. Of the 49 000 murders committed annually in Brazil, just 7.8 percent every year are "prosecuted with success." Currently, the defendants have endless rights of appeal, not merely against a verdict but against minor decisions along the way. Since one court's rulings are not binding on another, a single legal question can be tried separately several times.

In the United States, the trends in sentencing include the use of mandatory minimums, various forms of determinate sentencing such as "three strikes and you are out," truth-in-sentencing, and guidelines-based sentencing. These measures are aimed at ensuring that some time will be served for violent offences, limiting judicial discretion in sentence variation for the same offences, and increasing the predictability of penalties (see, for example, Stolzenberg and D'Alessio, 1997).

As a response to the growing preoccupation with violent crime in the United States, a number of states have adopted mandatory sentencing laws to fight high crime rates. These laws require a minimum amount of incarceration upon conviction and were designed for specific offences such as rape, murder, drug trafficking, and dangerous weapons violations. Studies show that mandatory minimums have dramatically increased the number of offenders in prison, and the prison terms are longer. For example, a recent study by The Sentencing Project, "The Meaning of Life," found that no fewer than 127 000 persons— 1 of every 11 persons incarcerated in America's prisons—"is now serving a life sentence, at a potential cost of $1 million for each sentence"; over a quarter of these individuals (330 000) "have no option for parole and will spend the rest of their lives in prison" (The Sentencing Project, 2005). The study noted that the total number of lifers in that country

"represents a growth rate of 83 percent since 1992" and that "the growth of the lifer population was "due to changes in sentencing policy and not crime rates," with the lifer population including "substantial numbers of mentally ill persons, juveniles [and] abused
women." Moreover, it would seem that, other than keeping offenders off the streets for
longer periods of time, mandatory sentencing provisions do not act as a general deterrence
and have no measurable impact on crime rates (O'Connell, 1995; see also Chapter 5).

Other law-and-order initiatives such as the three-strikes and two-strikes (and you are
out) sentencing measures mandating life without parole for repeaters of certain violent or
drug-related crimes, first passed in Washington State in 1993 and in California in 1994,
did not fare much better (Garland, 2001; Rodriguez, 2003). They too fail to combat crime
and recidivism and ignore questions of rehabilitation and reform. A 2001 study by The
Sentencing Project, a nonprofit research group, showed that in California, these laws had
no significant effect on the state's decline in crime. In California, with three-strikes and
two-strikes laws, crimes dropped 41 percent from 1993 to 1999, while New York, with no
such laws, showed the same decline for the same period (Lewin, 2001). They also waste
precious jail space on minor offenders (the majority of convictions at least in California
are for property, drug, and other nonviolent offences), strain resources, contribute to the
aging of the prison population, denigrate the independence of the judiciary, and rob judges
of the discretion needed to tailor sentences to offenders and their life situations (Broderick,
1994; Franklin, 1994). In recognition of these concerns, some smaller states such as
Louisiana, Connecticut, Indiana, and North Dakota have quietly started to roll back some
of their most stringent anticrime measures, including those imposing mandatory minimum
sentences and forbidding early parole (Butterfield, 2001).

Truth-in-sentencing measures reflect continued attention to discretion and to the association between sentences and time served (Wood and Dunaway, 2003). Truth-in-sentencing is
intended to reduce the discrepancy between the sentence imposed upon those who are sent to
prison and the actual time they serve. Data indicate that violent offenders released from
American state prisons in 1992 served 48 percent of the sentence they had received—an average of 43 months on an average sentence of 89 months (US Department of Justice, 1995).

In US federal courts, the amount of discretion judges may exercise is limited by the
controversial *Sentencing Reform Act,* which took effect on November 1, 1987 (Margolick,
1992; see also Lax, 2004). One of the primary objectives of the act was to eliminate the
problem of unwarranted disparity—that is, that two similarly situated offenders could go
into two different courtrooms, even in the same courthouse at the same time, and come out
with two vastly different sentences. Under the guidelines, all crimes are ranked on a scale
from 1 to 43; the greater the heinousness and severity, the higher the number. For example, murder is assigned a score of 43; hijacking, 38; and blackmail, 9. The base score is
affected by a variety of aggravating and mitigating circumstances, such as acknowledgment of guilt and co-operation with the government. Since the implementation of the
guidelines, the range of sentences has been noticeably reduced. Critics complain, however, that it is difficult to master the complex guidelines (with amendments, the manual is three
inches thick), and at times it can be tricky. For instance, robbery has a base score of 20.
But if a post office or a bank is robbed, the score goes up to 22. If a weapon was fired, it
rises 7 more; if a gun was merely "used," it goes up by 6; and if the gun was "brandished,
displayed or possessed," by 5. In spite of these and other criticisms, the Act is working by
reducing and checking the power of judges and effectively eliminating what was sardonically referred to as a "system of roulette" in sentencing. It also filters out variations based

on the philosophies of particular judges and probation officers, docket pressures in some courts, and other criteria, such as race, sex, and socioeconomic background of the defendant, that have been considered decisive in the literature (see, for example, Albonetti, 1992). Not surprisingly, there is widespread dissatisfaction among federal judges with the sentencing guidelines, and they are loath to have much of their discretion in sentencing taken away (Reske, 1994).

CIVIL PROCEEDINGS

On August 17, 1985, Peter Galaske and his son Karl, age eight, were travelling in Erich Stauffer's truck, on their way to visit Mr Stauffer's vegetable garden. Karl sat in the front seat in the middle, between his father and Mr Stauffer. Although the truck was outfitted with seat belts for all of the occupants, none of them were wearing them. Through no fault of Mr Stauffer, the truck was struck by another vehicle. Both of the passengers were thrown from the vehicle. Peter Galaske died of his injuries. His son survived but was rendered paraplegic as a result of severe injuries. Mr Stauffer was not seriously injured.

On his behalf, Karl Galaske's guardian later filed an action in court against Mr Stauffer (the defendant), claiming that Mr Stauffer was negligent for failing to ensure that Karl was wearing a seat belt. The *British Columbia Motor Vehicle Act* requires that children under 16 years of age wear a seat belt at all times when travelling in a motor vehicle. Karl's lawyer argued that Mr Stauffer had a special duty to ensure that Karl, a young child, was wearing a seat belt.

The trial court and the British Columbia Court of Appeal dismissed the action, accepting Mr Stauffer's argument that it was the responsibility of Peter Galaske, the child's father, to ensure that Karl was wearing a seat belt.

Karl Galaske's lawyers appealed the lower court decision to the Supreme Court of Canada. In April 1994 the Supreme Court of Canada rendered its decision, finding that indeed, Mr Stauffer had, as the operator of the vehicle, a duty to ensure that young Karl was wearing a seat belt. The Supreme Court directed that the case should be sent back to the original trial judge to determine the degree to which Mr Stauffer should be held responsible for Karl's injuries and paraplegic state, and the financial costs attached to this.

Mr Stauffer's failure to ensure that Karl Galaske was wearing a seat belt was found by the Supreme Court of Canada to be a "tort." Fleming (1998:1) defines a *tort* as "a civil wrong, other than a breach of contract, which the law will address by an award of damages." In other words, unlike a crime which is an offence against the state, a tort is a private injury or harm that has occurred against an individual, corporation, or government.

The Supreme Court of Canada found that Mr Stauffer owed a duty of care to young Karl Galaske, to ensure that the young boy wore a seat belt while travelling in Mr Stauffer's vehicle. In failing to exercise this duty of care, Mr Stauffer both broke the law (the *B.C. Motor Vehicle Act*) and was found in civil court to be negligent. As a result, Mr Stauffer was required to pay damages or compensation to Karl Galaske.

Crimes versus Torts

A **crime** is a public wrong, an offence that has been committed against the public interest (Boyd, 2002). The definition of an act as a crime signals that the harm represented by the act is so serious as to require public condemnation and punishment. The goal of state-administered punishment is to deter the specific offender from committing further crimes (**specific deterrence**) and to deter members of the general public from committing offences by "making an example" (**general deterrence**). Owing to the fact that the commission of a crime is considered to be so serious an act, and the punishment so severe, the determination of who is responsible for (guilty) of the crime must be determined in court "beyond a reasonable doubt." Part of this determination requires that the person accused of the crime be shown to have been possessed of an evil intent (*mens rea*) when the evil act (*actus rea*) was committed.

A **tort** (as discussed in Chapter 1) is a wrong committed against the private interest of an individual, corporation, or government (Boyd, 2002). The wrong committed may be intentional or due to negligence. Torts are viewed as less serious than crimes, as the harm that has been done is limited to specific individuals or organizations. As a result, it is left up to the party that has been wronged (the plaintiff) to file an action in court to have the wrongdoer (the defendant) punished, usually in the form of a payment of damages. At the same time, because a tort is treated less seriously than a crime, a lower standard based on a balance of probabilities as to who is *probably* responsible is used to determine who is "at fault" (Fridman, 1978). In addition, unlike a crime, it is not a requirement in tort law that it be shown that the defendant intended to do harm; it is enough to show that the defendant's actions, intended or not, caused harm to someone else.

With increasing frequency, wrongdoing is being dealt with both in the criminal courts and as torts in civil court. The best-known example is the O.J. Simpson case. Simpson was accused of the 1994 murder of his wife Nicole Brown Simpson and her friend Ron Goldman. Though Simpson was found not guilty in the criminal trial, a civil court found that, on the balance of probabilities, Simpson was liable for their deaths, and was ordered to pay $33.5 million in damages to the Brown and Goldman families (*Gazette*, 27 January, 2001:B8). More recently, actor Robert Blake was ordered to pay $30 million in damages to the children of his former wife, Bonny Lee Blakley, whom the actor was accused of murdering in 2001 (*National Post*, 19 November, 2005:A3). In one of the first such types of legal action in Canada, an Ontario man who was found not guilty in a criminal court for the 1994 murder of his wife is being sued for $850 000 in civil court by his former mother-in-law who claims he is liable for her daughter's wrongful death (Levy, *Toronto Star*, 15 April, 2005:A3).

History of Tort Law

The term *tort* is derived from the Latin word *tortus,* which means "twisted" or "wrong" (*Oxford English Dictionary,* 1989). The term was introduced into English law following the conquest of England by William the Conqueror in 1066 (Fridman, 1978). Under William the Conqueror, a system of laws developed that recognized a distinction between actions or "offences" that threaten the "King's Peace" or the state (crimes), and harms that are solely a matter of a dispute between individuals (torts) (Fridman, 1978).

William's heirs introduced additional important changes into the English system of law. Under Henry II (1154–1189) a system of royal courts and "King's Justices" was established, promoting a consistent rule of law and judicial decision-making across England. To have a case heard before the court, the plaintiff applied to the King's Chancery office for a *writ*, a document that outlined the circumstances of the alleged wrong that had been committed against the plaintiff, and which granted permission to approach the court to have the matter heard (Fridman, 1978). Over time, the issuance of writs describing different types of wrongs (torts), and the decisions of the courts in relation to these matters, came to form the common law of torts, a growing body of legal precedents or "judge-made" laws that addressed the duties and responsibilities individuals living together in a society.

This tradition of the common law of torts continues into the present. Unlike criminal, family, or constitutional law, there are no books of statutes that direct how the law of torts is to be administered. Instead, as societies continue to develop and become more complex, new types of private disputes between individuals, corporations, or governments arise and are dealt with in the courts, adding to the storehouse of the common law of torts.

In Canada, there are two systems of tort law in operation. In Quebec, matters involving private wrongs are dealt with according to the law of delicts, or law of civil responsibility. In all of the other provinces and territories, a system of tort law derived directly from the English common law system is in effect. Over time, Canadian courts have combined the English tort system together with decisions from courts in Australia, New Zealand, Northern Ireland, and the United States (Osborne, 2003).

The Functions of Tort Law

Linden (2001) describes six functions that tort law serves in society:

1. compensation
2. deterrence
3. education
4. psychological function
5. market deterrence
6. ombudsman

First and foremost, tort law serves to compensate injured parties. Compensation is most often made in the form of an award of damages to the injured party, a sum of money designed to compensate them for their loss. Special damages are awarded when the losses to the injured party are specific and easily calculated, such as loss of wages, a damaged fence, or a broken car windshield. General damages are awarded when the cost of compensation cannot be precisely calculated, as in determining the cost of pain and suffering due to a chronic whiplash injury. On rare occasions, the court may order that exemplary or punitive damages also be awarded, to punish the wrongdoers (Ontario Law Reform Commission, 1991).

Tort law can be used for the purposes of deterrence, as a means to prevent both intentional and negligent acts in the future. For example, in a landmark 1998 Canadian ruling, a Toronto woman, "Jane Doe," sued the Toronto Board of Police Commissioners for failing to warn her of a known danger of sexual assault in her neighbourhood. The Toronto Police had decided not to alert women in the neighbourhood because they feared that the resulting hysteria might scare the perpetrator off, undermining their efforts to apprehend him. An Ontario court ruled that the police had failed to do their duty to warn Jane Doe of the danger to herself (and to other women), and awarded her $220 000 in general and specific damages. The monetary award was not, however, Jane Doe's goal. "It was a political action for me, and that was accomplished," she said following the trial. "I won the day the trial started" (OWJN, 2000). Jane Doe hoped that her successful suit against the Toronto Police would define a new standard for care that police across Canada must take into account when investigating sexual assault crimes (Honey, 1998; Linden, Klar, and Feldthusen, 2004).

The case of *Jane Doe v. Board of Commissioners of Police for the Municipality of Metropolitan Toronto* continues to spark controversy. While it is an important ruling, critics assert that few substantial changes in police practices related to sexual assault investigation have taken place as a result of the ruling (OWJN, 2001). As Childs and Ceyssens (2005:14) note, the *Jane Doe* case is but one in a long series of civil cases brought against police services. They observe that this growing number of civil cases calls for a "substantive response from police services and their governing bodies."

A third function of tort law is education. Williams (cited in Linden, 2001) suggests that making an individual or organization pay compensation may be "educationally superior to a fine" in that "it teaches a moral lesson." At the same time, tort law teaches about appropriate standards of conduct in society (Fridman, 1978). In *Waldick v. Malcolm,* Waldick fell on an icy parking area in front of the Malcolms' farmhouse residence near Simcoe, Ontario, sustaining an injury. Waldick brought suit against the Malcolms, claiming they had been negligent in not putting salt or sand down to make the area safe. The Malcolms responded in defence by claiming that it was not the practice to salt or sand driveways in their area, and so they should not be held liable for Waldick's injury. The Supreme Court of Canada ruled against the Malcolms, arguing that custom does not release anyone from taking reasonable precautions to ensure the safety of others; everyone has a duty toward others to take such care as is reasonable under the circumstances (Osborne, 2003).

Linden (2001) believes that tort law may also serve a psychological function in satisfying the thirst for revenge by those who have been wronged. In providing a legitimate means for revenge, in the form of damages and financial compensation, the tort law system thus serves to keep the peace in society, deterring wronged parties from seeking their own revenge in the form of feuds or vigilantism. In addition, tort proceedings in court "enrich our society with ritual and symbolism" (Linden, 2001:18), in much the same way that Durkheim argued in *The Elementary Forms of Religious Life* that ritual and symbols serve to bind society together in a common conscience and recognition of common norms and values.

Tort law can serve to reduce accidental injuries through **market deterrence**. By making activities that are accident prone more expensive, tort law serves to deter individuals from engaging in these activities, decreasing the likelihood of injuries (Linden, 2001). Bogus (2004) observes that, in the United States, the number of private and public swimming pools that are equipped with diving boards has declined due to personal injury lawsuits against diving board and pool manufacturers. Higher costs for equipment that meets diving and swimming pool standards along with higher costs to insure these pools have resulted in fewer diving boards being installed by private and public pool owners; the net effect may be to reduce the number of serious diving-related accidents and fatalities. Bogus observes:

> The removal of these [diving] boards will reduce the number of tragic SCI [spinal cord injuries] and perhaps some fatalities. Will some fun be eliminated as well? Of course it will. But it is difficult to argue that the trade-off—less fun for fewer SCI—is unreasonable. How many dives add up to the joy that is lost over a lifetime by a young person suffering a spinal cord injury? (2004:37)

Finally, tort law increasingly serves an ombudsman function in modern society. Tort law can put pressure upon those in power to address individual and collective wrongs. For example, in *Hollis v. Dow Corning Corp.* a Canadian woman, Hollis, brought suit against her doctor and the Dow Corning Corporation for failing to warn her of the risks involved in having breast implants, in particular the risk of rupture. In 1983, Ms Hollis had breast implant surgery performed to correct a congenital deformity. By 1985, the implant in her right breast had ruptured, beginning a series of health problems and surgeries. Evidence introduced at court showed that as early as 1979 Dow was aware that the implants could rupture and leak, causing serious health problems, but failed to fully inform physicians of the extent of the risk. The Supreme Court of Canada determined that Dow Corning Corporation was liable for damages related Ms Hollis's injuries. Dow removed the breast implants from the market, and later introduced a safer alternative.

Tort law actions have been used to address wrongdoing by government officials, including the police, health professionals, and politicians. Multinational corporations including automobile manufacturers, pharmaceutical companies, tobacco companies, and others have been taken to task in the form of class action lawsuits due to their marketing of defective or harmful products. Often, the threat of publicity arising from a tort action is enough to cause corporations and governments to address identified problems (Linden, 2001).

Intentional Torts versus Negligence

The law distinguishes between two main categories of torts. **Intentional torts** are actions taken by an individual or organization that are deliberately meant to cause harm. **Negligence** refers to actions that cause an unintentional harm because a person or organization has failed to take reasonable precautions to ensure that their actions do not endanger others (Yates and Bain, 2000:187).

Intentional torts are deliberate acts that cause harm to persons or property. Regardless of whether the actual extent of the damage caused was planned or foreseeable, it is sufficient to show that the wrongdoer intended some form of harm in order to be held liable. The harm caused can take the form of physical injury or mental anguish, destruction of property, economic loss, damage to reputation, nuisance, or loss of use or enjoyment of property (Fridman, 1978). Intentional torts include assault, battery, intentional infliction of mental suffering, false imprisonment, trespass, nuisance, defamation, and invasion of privacy.

In tort law, an assault is defined as "conduct that causes the victim fear or apprehension of imminent physical contact" (Yates and Bain, 2000:172). Battery, on the other hand, is a successful assault carried through that ends in some form of physical contact (Yates and Bain, 2000:172). In a landmark 1830s case in England, *Stephens v. Myers,* the defendant, Myers, during a heated argument at a local parish meeting, threatened to pull the plaintiff Stephens "out of his chair." Myers approached Stephens with his fist raised, but was prevented by the churchwarden from getting close enough to actually grab or strike. Though no physical contact was made, the court decided that the defendant clearly approached and intended to harm the plaintiff, and would have done so if not restrained. Consequently, an assault, but no battery, was deemed to have taken place.

Trespass occurs "when a person intentionally goes on to another person's land without justification or right" (Yates and Bain, 2000:178; Osborne, 2003). In *Dwyer v. Staunton,* the plaintiff, Dwyer, claimed that the defendant, Staunton, had trespassed on his farm and requested claimed damages in the amount of $520. In addition, Staunton petitioned the court to grant an injunction preventing the defendant from any further trespass. The major public highway running north and south near Dwyer's Lundbreck, Alberta farm was completely blocked by snow. Employees of an oil company working in the area, needing to reach the nearby town, bulldozed a road through, following the highway where possible, but at other points crossing farmer's fields, including that of the plaintiff, Mr Dwyer.

After the road was bulldozed through and the oil company employees had passed through to town, the defendant, Mr Staunton, a farmer and rancher in the area, used the makeshift road to get into town, travelling down it in his car accompanied by four or five trucks. As they crossed his farm property on the makeshift road, the plaintiff stopped the defendant. An argument ensued, but finally the plaintiff allowed the car and the trucks to pass; however, he warned that he would stop them if they tried to return across his property.

While in town, the defendant was informed that the municipal bulldozer had broken down and that the highway could not be plowed out that day. The defendant as well as others attempted to find an alternative route home, but all of the regular roads in the area were blocked by snow. Left with no alternative, the defendant, along with others, set out to return home along the makeshift road.

Once again, crossing the plaintiff's farm, the defendant was stopped. This time, the plaintiff was adamant in his refusal to allow the vehicles to pass. The defendant, seeing no alternative, pushed ahead in his vehicle, knocking down a wire gate. He was followed by the other vehicles. Having passed through the farm, the plaintiff offered to pay for any damages, or to go to court if necessary.

In court, the judge ruled that the trespass on the plaintiff's land occurred as a result of necessity, and so the defendant could not be held liable, citing previous tort law precedent that states: "Where a highway becomes impassable, travelers are entitled to deviate from the established road on to adjacent land, taking care to do no unnecessary damage."

The case of *Chaytor et al. v. London, New York and Paris Association of Fashion Ltd and Price* is an interesting example of the intentional tort of false imprisonment. Vera Chaytor and John Delgado Jr, two employees of Bowring Brothers Ltd, a St John's Newfoundland department store, decided to do some comparison shopping at the store of a competitor, the London, New York and Paris Association of Fashion Ltd. Their goal was to check out their competitor's merchandise and prices.

Shortly after entering their competitor's store, Chaytor and Delgado were stopped by Mr Price, the store manager, who accused them of being spies. Mr Price directed his store security to watch them while he called the police to have them arrested as "suspicious characters." When the police arrived, Chaytor and Delgado willingly accompanied the police to avoid embarrassment and because they felt they were required to do so. They were detained at the police station for approximately 15 minutes and then released without a charge being laid.

Ms Chaytor and Mr Delgado, plaintiffs, filed an action in court to claim damages against the defendants, the London, New York and Paris Association of Fashion Ltd, and Mr Price, the store manager, for false imprisonment. The court awarded the plaintiffs $100 each in damages against the London, New York and Paris Association of Fashion Ltd, and an additional $100 each against Mr Price.

As the common law body of torts has developed over time, each type of tort has come to have associated with it different remedies and defences. The defences typically used to counter claims for damages in intentional torts include consent, self-defence, defence of property, necessity, and legal authority (Boyd, 2002). In *Malette v. Shulman*, the defence of necessity was employed.

The plaintiff in the case, Mrs Malette, was a Jehovah's Witness. Mrs Malette was injured in an automobile accident near Kirkland Lake, Ontario. When she arrived in the emergency room of the hospital she was semi-conscious and in shock. Emergency room staff checked her purse for identification and discovered a card stating that the plaintiff was a Jehovah's Witness and, for religious reasons, no form of blood transfusion was to be administered under any circumstances.

The defendant Dr Shulman, the attending physician, was informed of this. Dr Shulman determined that a blood transfusion was, however, necessary to save the patient's life, and proceeded to administer one. The plaintiff recovered from her injuries and sued the defendant doctor for negligence, assault, and conspiracy.

In court, Dr Shulman's lawyer argued that the defendant had acted out of necessity to save a life, and that this justified his actions. Mrs Malette's lawyer argued that the defendant, knowing in advance that Mrs Malette was a Jehovah's Witness, had proceeded to ignore her wishes, violating her right to control her own body.

The court held the defendant Dr Shulman liable and awarded Mrs Malette $20 000 in damages. The defendant appealed the decision to the Ontario Court of Appeal, but was unsuccessful.

In *Barclay v. Fournier* the defence of self-defence was employed. A nine-year-old New Brunswick girl was being bullied and assaulted by a group of boys. The girl threw a rock at the boys in self-defence. The rock hit one of the boys, also nine years old, in the mouth, knocking out his front teeth. The court ruled that her action was "not excessive" under the circumstances, though its consequences were unfortunate and an unintended accident.

The defence of **consent** is based on the argument that the wronged or injured party consented to be part of an activity or practice that they knew could result in an injury. In March 2006, Colorado Avalanche hockey player Steve Moore filed suit against Vancouver Canucks player Todd Bertuzzi, seeking lost wages and damages for an attack that took place during a 2004 game (Pap, 2006). The attack left Moore with a concussion and three fractured vertebrae in his neck, putting his future hockey career into question. In the civil trial to come, Bertuzzi's lawyers will likely argue that, as a professional hockey player, Moore consented to be paid and play in a sport that is known for its rough play, brawls, and occasional serious injuries.

Defence of property is based on the idea that the owner of a property is allowed to take reasonable measures (fences, barbed wire) to deter others from entering the property without permission (Osborne, 2003). Similarly, the owner of a property may use a reasonable amount of physical force (not lethal force) to remove an intruder from the property. The defence of **legal authority** is most often based on a series of statutes found in the Canadian Criminal Code that pertain to the rights of police officers and other law enforcement officials to detain persons, make arrests, or use force against a person.

Negligence

Negligence is the most common category of tort claim (Boyd, 2002). **Negligence** is an act committed against persons or property that causes an unintentional harm. The harm caused can take the form of physical injury or mental distress, destruction of property, and economic loss (Fridman, 2002). Negligence is demonstrated by showing that the wrongdoer failed to take reasonable steps to ensure that their actions, however innocent, did not cause harm to others. "Reasonable steps" are determined by reference to the five core elements of a negligence action: the negligent act; causation; damage; duty of care; and remoteness of damage (Osborne, 2003). It is the responsibility of the wronged party, the plaintiff, to prove each of the elements.

In determining whether an act itself is negligent, tort law makes reference to the common law principle of the "reasonable person" as a normative standard. In effect, the court asks what steps a sensible person of normal intelligence would take to ensure that the act in question did not cause harm to others, and compares this standard to the factual conduct of the accused wrongdoer. If the court determines that the defendant did not act in a way that a normal and sensible person would, and if the court is also convinced that the defendant should have foreseen that their careless act could cause harm to others, then the act is found to be negligent, and the defendant is liable for damages stemming from negligence.

In *Amos v. New Brunswick (Electric Power Commission)* the court found that the Power Commission had failed to act as a reasonable person would in meeting its obligations. The plaintiff, a nine-year-old boy, was seriously injured when a tree branch he was climbing came into contact with a high-tension electric wire belonging to the New Brunswick Electric Power Commission. The plaintiff's lawyer claimed that the defendant, New Brunswick Electric Power Commission, was negligent in failing to cut down or cut back trees that had grown up through the wires, obscuring them from view. It was well known that children played in the general area. The Supreme Court of Canada agreed the risk posed by the combination of the overgrown trees and electric wires was something that a reasonable person would have foreseen to be a danger. The defendant was found liable for damages stemming from the negligent act.

In addition to the negligent act itself, the plaintiff must establish that the negligence is the cause of any injury or loss that has been suffered. Here, the "but for" test is traditionally applied; would the plaintiff's damage have occurred "but for" the defendant's negligent act? If the answer is no, the defendant's negligence is the "cause-in-fact" of the damage (Fridman, 2002). In the New Brunswick case *Snell v. Farrell,* a newer and broader standard of causation was employed, one that requires only that the negligent act be shown to have "materially contributed" to the damage (Fridman, 2002).

The plaintiff, Snell, was rendered blind in one eye following cataract surgery performed by Dr Farrell, the defendant. The defendant was found negligent at trial for continuing to operate after bleeding was observed in the plaintiff's eye. The decision to continue the operation even after the bleeding was noticed was found to be a possible cause of the blindness, though there might be other causes as well. The Court found that the defendant's act, though possibly not the sole cause of the blindness, materially contributed to the condition, and consequently the defendant was liable for an award of damages.

There can be liability for negligence only if the wronged party has suffered a form of damage that is recognizable, that is, an injury or loss that can be proven in court. The purpose of awarding damages is to restore the wronged party to the state they were in before the negligence caused the harm (Fridman, 2002).

The fourth element that must be proved by the plaintiff is that the defendant owed the plaintiff a "duty of care" (Osborne, 2003). In the 1932 English landmark case of *Donoghue v. Stevenson*, Lord Atkin of the British House of Lords established a general rule related to the duty of care that individuals in society have toward one another:

> The rule that you are to love your neighbour becomes in law, you must not injure your neighbour; and the lawyer's question, Who is my neighbour? receives a restricted reply. You must take

reasonable care to avoid acts or omissions which you can reasonably foresee would be likely to injure your neighbour. Who, then, in law is my neighbour? The answer seems to be—persons who are so closely and directly affected by my act that I ought reasonably to have them in contemplation as being so affected when I am directing my mind to the acts or omissions which are called into question.

In other words, we owe a duty to those who live around us, or with whom we may have formed a relationship, to exercise care in how we act so that we do not cause them harm.

Lord Atkin's ruling in *Donoghue v. Stevenson* continues to act as the standard against which a duty of care is measured in England, Canada, and many other countries. For example, in *Dobson v. Dobson* the plaintiff, Ryan Dobson, sued his mother, Cynthia Dobson, for failure in her duty of care to protect him from injuries sustained prior to his birth (Kerr, 2000).

Mrs Dobson, pregnant at the time with Ryan, was travelling in her car in winter on a slippery, windswept highway near Moncton, New Brunswick, following her husband who was in another car directly in front. Mr Dobson's vehicle hit a patch of slush and slid into the ditch. Mrs Dobson's vehicle hit another slippery patch on the road and veered directly into oncoming traffic, colliding with a pick-up truck. Mrs Dobson was rushed to the emergency room of a nearby hospital where, as a result of injuries sustained in the accident, an emergency caesarian section was performed. The child (Ryan) survived but now suffers from a severe form of cerebral palsy and will remain dependent on others for the rest of his life.

On behalf of Ryan, his grandfather (Mrs Dobson's father) filed suit against Mrs Dobson and her insurance company in order to receive insurance money to pay for Ryan's care. The plaintiff argued in court that his mother was negligent in her driving and failed to exercise her duty of care to protect her unborn child.

The case was eventually heard before the Supreme Court of Canada, where the majority of the justices ruled that, while a moral duty may be said to exist, a pregnant mother owed no legal duty of care to her unborn child.

Finally, "remoteness of damage" refers to the extent to which the negligent act can reasonably be linked to the damages claimed (Osborne, 2003). In a landmark British case, *Smith v. Leech Brain & Co,* the Court of Queen's Bench was asked to consider a case dealing directly with the remoteness element.

As a result of the defendant's negligence, the plaintiff's husband was injured at work when a piece of hot metal struck him in the lip, causing a burn. At the time, the burn was treated like any other normal burn. Later, however, it began to ulcerate and cancer was diagnosed. Several operations were performed and radiation treatments administered, all to no effect, and eventually the plaintiff's husband died as a result of the cancer.

The plaintiff filed an action for damages against the defendant, arguing that the employer's negligence was the cause of her husband's burn, his cancer, and his eventual death. The Court agreed with the argument and awarded damages to the plaintiff.

In effect, the British court accepted the principle, referred to as the "thin skull rule," that as long as it has been demonstrated that the injury to the plaintiff was due to a negligent act, the defendant is held liable for all of the consequences following an injury, irrespective of the physical or psychological characteristics of the injured party. Whether or not Mr Smith had a pre-existing physical condition predisposing him to the particular form of cancer caused by the burn is irrelevant; the negligent employer is still wholly at fault and liable for causing the burn that unleashed the unfortunate sequence of events leading to Mr Smith's death.

In other cases, it may be decided by the court that the cause of an injury is the consequence of a number of contributory negligent acts. For example, in *Harris v. TTC and
Miller* the Supreme Court of Canada held that the actions of a bus driver could only partially be held liable for an injury sustained by an infant child. The plaintiff, a young infant,
was a passenger on a bus owned by the Toronto Transit Commission and operated by the
driver, Miller. As the bus pulled away from a bus stop, it brushed against a steel pole that
was set in the sidewalk close to the road curb. Having extended his arm out the window of
the bus, the plaintiff's arm was crushed against the pole as the bus brushed against it, frac-
turing the arm. An action for damages was filed on behalf of the young infant.

At court, the trial judge found that the negligent act of the bus driver, in failing to exercise caution in pulling away from the bus stop, was a "proximate" or neighbouring cause
of the infant's broken arm, but not the only cause. In addition, the trial judge held that the
infant himself was negligent in putting his arm out of the window of the bus, given a clearly
posted warning below the window that said "Keep arm in." The trial judge divided the fault
for the injury, and apportionment of liability for damages, equally between the plaintiff and
the defendants, the Toronto Transit Commission and Miller. The decision of the trial judge
was upheld by the Supreme Court of Canada.

Defences to negligence claims include accident, voluntary assumption of risk, illegality, and contributory negligence (as in *Harris v. TTC and Miller* above). **Accident** is a legitimate defence when, for example, a driver swerves to avoid hitting a small dog that has
wandered out onto the road and subsequently drives over a freshly planted garden. The
driver cannot be held liable for negligent operation of the motor vehicle because the presence of the dog on the road was not foreseeable, and hence the destruction of the garden
was truly an accident (Fridman, 2002).

If an individual is injured or suffers a loss as a result of their involvement in an illegal
activity, they cannot normally recover damages by claiming negligence on the part of
another person. For example, in *Rondos v. Wawrin* a Manitoba court held that injuries sustained by Rondos as the result of the high speed, erratic driving of Wawrin that took place
following their theft of an automobile could not be considered a legitimate basis for a
claim of negligent damages (Fridman, 2002).

In *Dyck v. Manitoba Snowmobile Assn Inc,* the Supreme Court of Canada ruled that the
plaintiff, Dyck, could not recover damages from the snowmobile club after crashing his
machine at the end of the race, as Dyck had knowingly and voluntarily assumed the risks
of participating in the race, as outlined in the waiver that had been signed by Dyck prior
to the start of the race (Osborne, 2003).

The Future of Tort Law

As the volume of tort litigation has grown in modern countries, in particular the United
States, Canada, and Britain, calls to abolish the tort system have become louder and more
frequent (Rubin, 1995; Atiyah, 1970; 1997). US President George Bush has identified
"reducing the lawsuit burden of our economy" as an important initiative for the current
government (Executive Office of the President, 2003).

Tillinghast Towers Perrin (2004) estimate that in 2003, tort litigation costs in the US
exceeded $246 billion, or 2.23 percent of the entire US gross domestic product (GDP). In
Britain, tort litigation costs account for 0.6 percent of GDP (Tillinghast Towers Perrin,
2002; Broughton et al., 2004). In Canada, the annual costs of tort litigation are estimated

in 2003 to exceed $8 billion, or 0.8 percent of total GDP. Tort litigation thus costs each Canadian approximately $250 per year in higher costs for insurance, legal costs, medical care, automobiles, recreation equipment and facilities, wages and benefits, and a host of consumer products.

Some have suggested that expanded systems of no-fault and private liability insurance are solutions to the increasingly expensive tort law system (Sugarman, 1985; Feldthusen, 1993; Broughton et al., 2004). Under no-fault schemes like automobile insurance, public health insurance, and employee benefit plans, the insured person is automatically compensated for damages without having to resort to expensive legal action. Liability insurance automatically covers individuals and organizations for any losses they incur as the result of their actions (Linden, Klar, and Feldthusen, 2004). According to Osborne (2003) and Zywicki (2000), courts are perceived to have recently taken a much more liberal view of the scope of liability (for example, cancer deaths due to tobacco use), with the result that the balance of power in tort actions has tipped in favour of the plaintiff and increasingly expensive damage claims. Presumably, under an expanded system of no-fault and liability insurance, virtually everyone in society would be protected from injury and loss.

Chimerine and Eisenbrey (2005) argue that proposals to do away with the tort law system in favour of no-fault and liability insurance systems are likely to benefit insurance companies and corporate clients at the expense of individual victims. Critics like Bogus (2001; 2004) and Linden (2001) observe that such proposals make all in society directly responsible for the costs of the torts of a few and, more importantly, undermine the important deterrence function of tort law. The potential publicity resulting from wrongdoing serves as a strong deterrent to many corporations and government itself to exercise their duty to take care to protect the person and property of members of the public. At the same time, the tort law system provides the means, much as Alexis de Tocqueville identified in *Democracy in America* (1835), for even the simplest citizen of society to have recourse to the courts when a wrong has been done.

Linden (2001) and others (Fridman, 1978; Chimerine and Eisenbrey; Bogus, 2001; Osborne, 2003) attribute growth in the tort litigation both to its flexibility to adapt to arising issues, and to the expanded functions (outlined above) it serves in modern society. Wright (1967; in Linden, 2003:1) observes that:

> Arising out of the various and ever increasing clashes of the activities of persons living in a common society, carrying on business in competition with fellow members of that society, owning property which may in any of a thousand ways affect the person or property of others— in short doing all the things that constitute modern living—there must of necessity be losses, or injuries of many kinds sustained as the result of the activities of others. The purpose of the law of torts is to adjust these losses and to afford compensation for injuries sustained by one person as the result of the conduct of another.

Thus, as Maine (1861), Weber (1921), and Durkheim (1893) argued, development, differentiation, and growth in the complexity of societies brings forth a need for more law to govern the conduct and activities of individuals and organizations. At the same time, increasing emphasis and recognition of individual freedoms and rights, and consequent changes in the norms of a society can give rise to new tort litigation. For example, tort law has recently been proposed as a weapon in the battle against domestic violence, as a broader means of holding the abusing partner accountable for both past and present actions (Lehrman, 1996). Similarly, the rapid growth of computers and other forms of information technology has given rise to "cyber-torts" related to the responsibilities and duties of care of manufacturers and users of information technology, and those who use such technologies for harmful purposes (Osborne, 2003). In Canada, compensation for former students of Indian Residential Schools, for victims of 9-11, and for victims of the "tainted blood" scandal, and claims against tobacco companies for negligent marketing are new challenges that will be addressed by the tort law system, along with terrorism, illness, and deaths from dangerous products such as asbestos, Agent Orange, Vioxx, and a host of other products and practices in society. Increasingly in the future, Osborne (2003:404) predicts tort law will be used as a "political weapon to achieve social change."

Linden concludes that:

> For the present, at least, tort law is "far from dead or moribund". One day, we may fashion alternative institutions more responsive to all of our needs. Hopefully, it will not be too long before our social welfare programmes are integrated and rationalized, but this would not necessitate discarding tort law. We may choose to let it live in peaceful coexistence with social insurance. By opting for such a solution, tort law could continue to serve society, alongside whatever new techniques are devised. Individuals should not be prevented from suing cigarette-makers, movie and music producers, professionals, educators, alcohol and gun manufacturers and drug distributors when they have been damaged by them in the hope of obtaining compensation and of altering their careless conduct, if that can be proven. (2001:31)

Tort Law as Normative Process

According to Krawietz (2001:37) all law "gives effect to, mirrors, or is otherwise expressive of the prevailing social relations." Nowhere is this truer than in the case of tort law. In virtually all areas of social life, norms have been "re-institutionalized" (Bohannan, 1973) in the form of tort law principles governing individuals' rights and responsibilities toward one another.

Shapo (1997) argues that tort law is an important catalyst for social cohesion in modern society. The tort law system provides a means for individual justice according to social norms of responsibility and duty to others. At the same time, Shapo notes, the outcomes of tort cases depend for their acceptance on a general belief or consensus among members of the public that justice has been done. In this manner, the tort law system serves to connect individuals and the general public in a very direct and "consensus-building" way to social norms and laws surrounding individuals' conduct, rights, and responsibilities in society. Similar to Durkheim's (1912) reasoning, ceremonies like tort law court proceedings and decisions thus serve to bring together individuals to reaffirm "collective sentiments" of right and wrong, of justice, in society.

At the same time, recent evidence shows that the tort law system may be serving to redress some of the inequalities in power between individual plaintiffs and large corporate defendants, providing at least in part (*à la* Erin Brockovich) a mechanism for the powerless to be heard and even compensated for the wrongs that have been done to them.

LEGISLATURES

To begin the study of the organization of legislatures, we first need to look at what they do. A legislature is defined as a "group of people having the duty and power to make laws for a country, province or state. This group may be elected (as are members of Parliament and provincial legislature) or appointed (as are members of the Senate)" (Statistics Canada, 1998:474). The functions of the legislature, at both the federal and the provincial levels, are numerous. Of course, the hallmark of legislative bodies is their lawmaking function. Following the title, the initial words one reads in a Canadian statute or law are: "Her Majesty, by and with the advice and consent of the Senate and House of Commons of Canada, enacts as follows . . . . " Part of the next chapter will be concerned with how this function is carried out. Yet lawmaking takes up only a portion of the legislature's time. Legislative bodies are also engaged in conflict and integrative functions.

Conflict-Management Functions

Although conflict management is part of both the administrative and the judicial subsystems, the legislature may be distinguished by the extent to which compromise, as a mode of conflict management, is institutionalized in the system. The emphasis is on conflict management rather than on conflict resolution since, in a sense, few political decisions are final (Boulding, 1956:103).

The conflict-management functions of legislative bodies can be seen in the context of their deliberative, decisional, and adjudicative activities (Jewell and Patterson, 1986:5). Frequently, legislative bodies deliberate without arriving at a decision or taking action. However, the deliberation process itself and the rules under which it takes place contribute to the reconciliation of divergent interests. In addition to formal debates, deliberation is carried on in the hearing rooms, in the offices of legislators, or in lobbies and other meeting places. At times, these informal deliberations are more important, for they provide an opportunity to incorporate a variety of viewpoints and interests. Some adjudicative activities are routinely undertaken by legislative bodies, and the principles of dispute resolution currently being applied in the judicial system also benefit the legislators (Melling, 1994). For example, the work of some legislative committees has been adjudicative, as when hearings before investigating committees have been, in effect, trials during the course of which sanctions have been applied.

Integrative Functions

Legislative bodies contribute to the integration of the polity by providing support for the judicial and executive systems. They provide this support through authorization, legitimization, and representation (Jewell and Patterson, 1986:10). In Canada, for example, the prime minister's authority comes from the office, not from custom or the individual's personal attributes. As an elected Member of Parliament, as well as the national leader of the political party that holds the majority of seats in the House of Commons, the prime minister has a mandate to speak on behalf of Canada and to govern the country in a way that will, one hopes, benefit all Canadians.

In 1848, the provinces of Canada and Nova Scotia were granted "responsible government." This meant that cabinet members had to be drawn from sitting members of the legislature and that the Cabinet could only direct the administration of government so long as it enjoyed majority support in the legislature. Without this support it lost its mandate to govern. By the time of Confederation in 1867, responsible government—with the executive branch accountable to the legislature—had been achieved in all of the colonies. The executive could no longer tax and spend on its own authority or on the authority of the Crown. Rather, the legislature controlled the purse strings.

Continuing today, the Cabinet is responsible to the House of Commons, and if it fails to enjoy the support of the majority in the House of Commons it must, by convention, call an election or make way for a new government to be formed. In turn, the House of Commons is responsible to the people through the electoral process. In stark contrast, in the United States, a president may remain in office even if the bills he or she puts forward are consistently blocked by one or both houses of Congress. In addition, while both Canada and the United States are democracies and federal states, "the two systems of government grew out of opposite approaches to federalism: Canada's Fathers of Confederation envisioned a strong central government whereas the American version—as the name 'United States' implies—has always been highly decentralized" (Statistics Canada, 1998:479). Ironically, perhaps, Canada is becoming more decentralized due, in large measure, to the forces of globalization, while the United States is becoming less decentralized (Bricker and Greenspon, 2001:307).

Legislative bodies also authorize the courts to establish jurisdiction, to create their organizational machinery, and to qualify their members. Moreover, legislatures oversee bureaucratic activities and attempt to balance them against prevailing special interests in a community. The integrative functions are also promoted through legitimization of activities. Legislative actions are considered by most people as legitimate.

A characteristic of any constitution is the specific delegation of authority to different components of government. In Canada, the *Constitution Act, 1867*, remains the basis of our written constitution. It identifies which level of government has jurisdiction over which powers. The federal government's 29 areas of jurisdiction are set out in section 91, while the 16 areas of provincial jurisdiction are outlined in section 92. Although the *Constitution Act* established only two levels of government, the provinces have delegated some of their power to the third level of government—local municipalities (e.g., cities, towns, townships) that operate and pass bylaws to regulate their activities.

Debating political jurisdiction has sometimes been termed a "national pastime" of Canadians and, admittedly, the division of powers can sometimes appear to be inordinately complex. For example, "[a]s a result of legal interpretation, labour legislation (except that pertaining to certain industries) and social security (except employment insurance and shared power over pensions) come under provincial law" (Statistics Canada, 1998:480). In some areas (e.g., agriculture, immigration, and certain aspects of natural resources), responsibility is shared. However, when laws conflict, the national laws hold sway (the **doctrine of paramountcy**).

Aboriginal Peoples

One of the most contested powers given to the federal government under section 91 of the *Constitution Act, 1867* was the power to pass legislation with respect to Aboriginal peoples and the lands reserved for their use. This was accomplished without the involvement or consent of the Native peoples (who had previously made their treaty arrangements with England)—a fact that has become increasingly important as Natives continue their struggle to enforce the terms of original treaties (Yates et al., 2000:57; see also Chapter 7). A second point of controversy is that even though Aboriginal rights are constitutionally protected, these rights are not absolute in Canadian law.

Traditional First Nations forms of social organization have undergone significant changes as a consequence of contact with European cultures. Even prior to Confederation, assimilationist policies promoted the "civilization" and "Christianization" of Aboriginal peoples. The introduction of European law, which supported patrilineality and patrilocality, forcibly changed the descent rules and residence patterns of many First Nations cultures. Ever since the 1850 Act for the *Better Protection of the Lands and Property of Indians in Lower Canada* defined an "Indian," foreign criteria have been imposed on "Indian" status, the determination of band membership, and access to rights tied to status and membership. The *Gradual Civilization Act* of 1857 explicitly declared as its goal the assimilation of Aboriginal peoples. In 1868, following Confederation, the federal Parliament passed an *Act for the Gradual Civilization of Indian Peoples*, designed with the express intent of assimilating Aboriginal people through the use of three primary tools: "The first was the creation of reservations, which in most cases did not correspond to the traditional territories the tribes had occupied. Secondly, band councils with limited powers were appointed to replace tribal governments. The Act also defined who could be classified as Indian and to which band they belonged" (Yates et al., 2000:57).

The goal of assimilation would be furthered reinforced in the post-Confederation period by the *Enfranchisement Act* of 1869 and, most notably, by the *Indian Act* of 1876. This Act, although presented as a "temporary measure" for controlling "Indians" on reserves, clearly reflected the federal government's agenda: "to act as guardians over Aboriginal Peoples, giving them 'protection' but with the ultimate goal of assimilation and absorption into [the] general population" (Canadian Labour Congress, 2005:2.40). It defined who was an "Indian" under the law and what "Indians" could or could and not do. Some examples: "Status Indians" (persons who were registered as "Indians" for the purpose of special entitlements) were not eligible to vote; it was not until 1960 that First Nations members were extended the right to vote in federal elections (their right to vote in provincial/territorial elections was acquired in various years with Quebec the last province to grant this right in 1969). An early (1880) amendment also provided for the automatic "enfranchisement" (loss of status) of those who earned a university degree and of any Indian woman who married a non-Indian or a non-registered Indian. As a report by the Canadian Labour Congress (2005:2.11) observes, "The word 'enfranchisement' was used by the government to describe the process by which to deny one's right to register for Status under the *Indian Act*. However, the dictionary meaning of the term is 'certification.' In this case, therefore, it was actually a system which was used to 'de-enfranchise' (de-certification or loss of Status) the Aboriginal Peoples." In a 1920 House of Commons discussion of changes to the Indian Act, Deputy Superintendent General Duncan Campbell Scott clearly announced the intended purpose of the Act: "Our object is to continue until there is not a single Indian in Canada that has not been absorbed into the body politic and there's no Indian question, and no Indian department, that is the whole object of the Bill." It may be noted that the *Indian Act* is now widely regarded as having provided a framework for South Africa's apartheid system (abolished in 1994); it also currently holds the dubious distinction of being one of the few—if not the only—piece of legislation in the world that is aimed at a specific "racial group."

Although the Royal Proclamation of 1763 by King George III had recognized that Aboriginals lived as nations, acknowledged that they possessed traditional territories until they were "ceded to or purchased by" the Crown, established an Indian territory in which Whites could not settle or buy land, and "clearly stated that land cessations could only be made by Aboriginal Peoples through treaties with the Crown" (Canadian Labour Congress, 2005:2.3), following Confederation, the federal government allowed a persistent encroachment onto Aboriginal land. Moreover, in 1927 the federal government passed an amendment to the *Indian Act* which made it illegal to "receive, obtain, solicit or request from any Indian any payment for the purpose of raising a fund or providing money for the pursuing of any claim" without "the written consent of the Superintendent of Indian Affairs." In 1969, a federal government White Paper would candidly reject the notion of any "special status" for Aboriginal peoples and propose the repeal of the *Indian Act* and the abolition of all treaties (Canadian Labour Congress, 2005:2.13). In response, Aboriginal leaders presented their own Red Paper, tellingly entitled "Citizen Plus"; the term, in itself, directs attention to the status of Aboriginal peoples as the original occupation and founding members of Canadian status whose rights have never been extinguished by treaty or consequent and, explicitly, suggests that this status demands the extension of rights beyond those enjoyed by all Canadians.

In January 1973, the Supreme Court of Canada rendered its historic *Calder* decision—recognizing land rights based on Aboriginal title (i.e., based on an Aboriginal group's traditional use and occupancy of that land) and that "Aboriginal peoples who had never signed treaties, still hold some claim and title to the lands they traditionally used and occupied" (Canadian Labour Congress, 2005:2.28). Until this decision, the policy of the federal government in relation to Aboriginal title to land where a treaty had not been signed was simple: they denied its existence. The impact of the Supreme Court's ruling in Calder was momentous; "[b]ecause the majority of Native people north of the 60th parallel had never signed treaties, it meant that Inuit, Dene and Yukon Indians still potentially retained a legal right to lands covering one-third of Canada" (Canadian Labour Congress, 2005:2.28). In addition, it effectively forced the federal government to tend to Aboriginal land claims with a degree of seriousness and urgency that had been formerly lacking. In the aftermath of this decision, the federal government established an office to deal with Aboriginal land claims and recognized two broad classes of these claims: (1) *comprehensive* (based on ancestral rights to lands and natural resources that were not formerly dealt with by treaty and other legal means) and (2) *specific* (which address specific grievances that First Nations peoples may have in relation to the government's administration of Indian land and other assets and which allege non-fulfillment of treaties). Along with the resolution of land claims, there was also increased discussion of Aboriginal self-government. "A significant result of this was the recognition and affirmation in the *Constitution Act, 1982* of 'existing Aboriginal and treaty rights' for all Aboriginal peoples of Canada, Indian, Métis and Inuit" (Canadian Labour Congress, 2005:2.4).

Aboriginal rights, such as treaty rights, are recognized and affirmed by section 35 of the *Constitution Act, 1982*. The Supreme Court of Canada has also ruled that this section provides for the protection of a wide range of rights that may be asserted by Aboriginal people in respect of certain lands or activities (e.g., the legal recognition of customary practices in relation to marriage and adoption). These provisions are not subject to the "reasonable limits" of our rights and freedoms found in section 1 of the Charter. In addition, Section 25 provides that Charter rights cannot infringe on rights (including those rights and freedoms recognized by the Royal Proclamation of 1763 as well as those existing or acquired through land-claims agreements) pertaining to Aboriginal peoples. Stated somewhat differently, this section attempts to ensure that the Charter does not function as a way of abrogating or derogating the rights of Aboriginal peoples.

While Aboriginal rights have yet to be given a comprehensive definition in law, many Aboriginal peoples assert that these rights include the right to self-government. For example, it is pointedly noted that "[a] treaty in Canada is unique in that it is not an agreement between the conquerors and the unconquered. These were agreements between *autonomous nations*. By signing treaties, the Aboriginal Nations did not give up their Nationhood or their own ways of living, working and self-governing. Rather, it was a mechanism to achieve peace and harmony, to agree on rules of coexistence and solving disputes between Peoples, Nations and governments" (Canadian Labour Congress, 2005:2.16; emphasis added). In the early 1990s, the Charlottetown Accord proposed a constitutional amendment that would have explicitly recognized the Aboriginal peoples' "inherent right of self-government within Canada." However, a national referendum in 1992 rejected this initiative. The issue of Aboriginal self-government was additionally addressed by the Royal Commission on Aboriginal Peoples (RCAP) in its 1996 final report. The RCAP stressed "the need for a complete restructuring of the relationship between Aboriginal and non-Aboriginal peoples in Canada" and included, among its broader recommendations:

- governmental commitment to a new set of ethical principles that acknowledged and respected Aboriginal cultures and values, the historical origins of Aboriginal nationhood, and the inherent right to Aboriginal self-determination;
- that the further development of Aboriginal governments focus on Aboriginal nations rather than single communities, and that an Aboriginal parliament, composed of Aboriginal representatives, be established to advise Parliament on matters affecting Aboriginal peoples;
- the establishment of independent justice systems on reserves that would recognize an important role for elders in the community and reinforce values and traditions that are historically intrinsic to indigenous communities; and
- the creation of an independent lands and treaties tribunal that would oversee negotiations among federal, provincial, and Aboriginal governments on land issues.

However, in its response to the report, the federal government limited itself to pursuing four objectives: "renewing partnerships; strengthening Aboriginal governance; developing a new fiscal relationship; and supporting strong communities, people and economies" (Doerr, 1999:4).

In recent decades, various legal mileposts have been reached. For reasons of space, only a short chronology featuring merely some of these landmark cases can be noted here. In *R. v. Drybones* (1970), Drybones, an Aboriginal man, had been found intoxicated away from his reserve—an act that constituted an offence under the *Indian Act* of 1876. The Supreme Court ruled that Drybones had been punished for his race under a law whose penalty differed for other Canadians and, using a clause declaring equality before the law in the Bill of Rights, struck down this part of the *Indian Act*. After two Supreme Court challenges had failed to remove discrimination on the basis of sex from the *Indian Act*, "an extraordinary group of women from Tobique Reserve in New Brunswick who were in the forefront of Aboriginal women's struggle for equality" took the case of Sandra Love to the United Nations (Canadian Labour Congress, 2005:4.29). In *Lovelace v. Canada* (1983), the United Nations Human Rights Committee found that the *Indian Act* discriminated on the basis of sex and, as well, that this Act contained other provisions that were contrary to the Universal Declaration of Human Rights. In response, the federal government passed Bill C-31, *An Act to Amend the Indian Act*, which brought the *Indian Act* into line with Charter provisions.

In *R. v. Sparrow* (1990), the Supreme Court affirmed the rights of Aboriginal peoples in the *Constitution Act* and stated that these rights must be interpreted broadly. In this case, authorities had charged Sparrow, an Aboriginal man, with breaking a federal fishing law. However, Sparrow argued successfully that the right to fish was protected by treaty and the Constitution. The Court also established criteria for interpreting Aboriginal rights in the Constitution. In *R. v. Van der Peet* (1996) and *Delgamuukw v. British Columbia* (1997), the Supreme Court clarified aspects of the proof, identification, and content of Aboriginal rights and Aboriginal title. In the former, the Court stated that in order for an Aboriginal right to be established, it must meet all of the following criteria: the right must involve an activity that was a "practice, tradition, or custom [that] was a central and significant part of the [Aboriginal] society's distinctive culture; the activity must have existed prior to contact with European settlers; the activity, even if evolved into modern forms, must be one that continued to exist after 1982, when the *Constitution Act* was passed." In the latter, the "leading modern decision on the nature of Aboriginal title" (Elliott, 2005:310), the Supreme Court defined the content and extent of Aboriginal title to ancestral lands, requiring that Aboriginals who sought such title prove that they had occupied the territory before Canada's declaration of sovereignty. The Court also decided to consider admitting oral history as evidence. In its 1984 decision in *Guerin*, "the Supreme Court confirmed that the common law recognizes Aboriginal title based on occupancy and use of land" (Elliott, 2005:43).

The year 1998 brought the Nisga'a Final Agreement, the first modern land claims agreement to be signed in British Columbia. April 1, 1999, marked the creation of Nunavut, a new territorial government controlled, effectively, by the Inuit of northern Canada. Also in 1999, the Supreme Court ruled on the case of Donald Marshall Jr, a Mi'kmaq Aboriginal charged with various offences contrary to fishery regulation and who claimed, in response, that as a Mi'kmaq he had a right to fish based on the 1760–61 LaHave treaties. The Marshall case "was the first case in which the court analyzed treaty rights using section 35 of the *Constitution Act, 1982*" and also "the first time the court found that a treaty afforded a limited commercial right to fish" (Sauvageau, Schneiderman, and Taras, 2006:140).

The 2003 signing of the Tlicho Agreement marked "the first combined land claim and self-government agreement of its kind in the Northwest Territories," creating the "largest single block of First Nation owned land in Canada" and providing new systems of self-government for the Tlicho First Nations (formerly known as the Dogrib) (CRIC, 2006). A year later, Labrador Inuit voted to accept a historic land claim that would see the creation of a region of self-government in northern Labrador in which they will own 15 800 sq. km of northern Labrador and, in another 56 700 sq. km area, have limited resource and management rights. "Within these lands the Inuit will have resource rights, the ability to forge their own lands, and control of their own education system and social services" (CRIC, 2006).

Nevertheless, the slowness of progress in Canada's response to recognizing the rights of Aboriginal people in relation to self-determination and control over their lands and resources has drawn and continues to evoke criticism from the United Nations. As Fleras (2005:314) observes, if "within policy circles, most agree that Aboriginal peoples possess a right to self-government," there remain notable disagreements about "its scope and source." He identifies four prevailing self-government possibilities: (1) statehood, "with complete political independence, both internal and externally"; (2) nationhood, "with retention of authority and jurisdiction over all internal matters"; (3) municipality, "with control over delivery of services by way of parallel institutions"; and (4) institutional, "with meaningful decision-making through representation and involvement in mainstream institutions" (Fleras, 2005:316). He reports that, in general, "Aboriginal claims for self-government have been consistent with the model of 'domestic dependent nations' in the United States" and notes that, while "American First Nations do not possess external sovereignty (for example they cannot raise an army) . . . [t]hese 'domestic dependent nations' retain considerable control ('sovereignty') over those internal jurisdictions not preempted by federal and state authority." He observes, however, that while the Canadian government has "conceded the possibility of self-governing powers that go beyond a municipality status," the powers envisaged are "less than the powers of a nation or province."

Participants in the Legislative Process

The legislative process encompasses a variety of participants. In this section, we have chosen to give attention to participants who are particularly relevant to legislative activity: legislators and lobbyists.

Legislators. Who are the legislators who make laws? Do legislatures represent a cross-section of the population? What groups are "overrepresented" and "underrepresented" in the legislature? Social scientists have carried out a number of investigations on the social origins and occupational backgrounds of political decision-makers. A few of these studies have focused on legislators. In spite of substantial gaps in factual knowledge about legislative personnel, certain generalizations can be made.

Contrary to popular beliefs, legislators are not representative of the population at large, and obviously not all citizens have an equal chance to be elected to legislative office. As a group, legislators have a much higher educational attainment than the general population. In part, this high educational level can be accounted for by their relatively high social origins. Moreover, recruitment of legislators is also very selective by occupational status. By and large, those in the professional and business occupations dominate the legislative halls in Canada at both the federal and the provincial levels.

As Robert Brym (2001:479) has observed, "[o]nly people with high incomes, substantial wealth, and postsecondary education have the time, money, and social connections required for the most intense forms of political engagement." He points out that our senior federal and provincial politicians, along with senior federal bureaucrats and senior officials of large corporations, are disproportionately drawn from the wealthiest 10 percent of Canada's families who are "linked not just by class interests but by a host of social ties."

Protestant Anglo-Saxon males are also substantially overrepresented among legislators. The United Nations Development Program (1995:83) has observed that while "[n]o gender-specific training is required to be a parliamentarian . . . [and] [n]either public speaking, nor the ability to represent the opinions of the electorate, nor the art of winning public confidence requires exclusively masculine traits . . . politics remains an obstacle course for women." Nevertheless, Canada certainly has come a long way since 1921, the year of the first federal election in which women were allowed to vote and run for office. "Between 1921 and 2006, 3402 women candidates stood in the 39 general elections and won on 426 occasions" (Heard, 2006).

In the 1921 federal election, in which only four women ran for office, a Canadian first was achieved when Agnes Campbell McPhail was elected to the House of Commons. For the 2006 election, of the 1634 candidates confirmed by Elections Canada, 380 were women; in 241 of the 308 ridings, at least one woman candidate ran for office. A total of 244 men and 64 women (21 Liberals, 17 from the Bloc Québécois, 14 Conservatives, and 12 from the New Democratic Party) were elected to public office (Heard, 2006).

Some notable "firsts" have occurred in recent decades. In 1989, the election of Audrey MacLaughlin as leader of the New Democratic Party marked the first time that a woman had been elected leader of a national Canadian political party. On June 13, 1993, Kim Campbell was elected leader of the Progressive Conservative Party, and on June 25 was sworn in as Canada's first female prime minister. On September 8, 1999, when the Right Honourable Adrienne Clarkson was appointed Governor-General of Canada, she became the second woman and the first member of a visible minority to hold this (largely symbolic) role as the resident representative of the Crown. In 2001, the Liberal government appointed the first woman—Marlene Cattarall—to the post of chief government "whip" in the House of Commons. (Canadian MPs are expected to conform to their party's position, and each party selects one MP to act as the party whip—a person who is expected to figuratively whip the other MPs into line on policy issues and to corral MPs into attendance when their votes are needed.) Nevertheless, it remains true that women, Aboriginal peoples, visible minorities, and foreign-born Canadians are underrepresented in our legislatures. For example, Forcese and Freeman (2005:152) point out that, following the 2004 federal election, only 18 members of visible minorities (6 women and 12 men) were elected (accounting for 6 percent of the House of Commons versus 14 percent of the general population). They maintain that, for visible minority females (who comprised a mere two percent of the House of Commons) "the lack of representation in Parliament creates a 'double minority status.'"

In a 183-nation survey conducted by the Inter-Parliamentary Union which focused on the parliamentary representation of women (as of August 2004), Canada, with 21 percent representation in the House of Commons and 32 percent in the senate, was ranked 33rd; among 30 industrialized countries, Canada was ranked 16th (Inter-Parliamentary Union, 2004). Data collected by the United Nations for their 2005 Human Development Report indicates that, among 124 nations that provided information on the percentage of seats in their parliament that were held by women as of March 2005, Canada (at 21.1 percent) ranked 38th—well behind countries such as Sweden (45.3), Norway (38.2), Denmark (36.9), Finland (37.5), the Netherlands (36.7), Spain (36.0), and Belgium (34.7), but notably ahead of the United States (15.0), The United Kingdom (18.1), and Japan (7.1) (United Nations Development Program, 2005:316).

Some countries have responded to the lack of diversity in their legislatures by instituting quotas. In India, for example, an amendment passed in 1993 reserves one-third of all seats in local political contests for women. In Britain, a law passed in 1996 stipulates that a minimum of 20 percent of each party's candidates be women. Countries with similar policies include Finland, Germany, Mexico, South Africa, and Spain (Sheehan, 2000). In Sweden, each sex is guaranteed a minimum of 40 percent and a maximum of 60 percent of seats in Parliament. In New Zealand, four seats within that country's legislature are reserved for its indigenous Maori population. However, Forcese and Freeman (2005:152) report that, in this country, there appears to be "little appetite" for the introduction of quotas.

From the preceding discussion, it is evident that no legislature comes close to representing a cross-section of the population it serves. The political system inevitably has built-in biases, numerous devices for the containment of minority group aspirations for office and for the advancement of dominant segments of the population. Some groups win often; others lose often.

Lobbyists. Organizations and groups that attempt to influence political decisions that affect their members or their goals are called interest groups. At the most general level, the interest group system has a distinct bias favouring and promoting upper-class and predominantly business interests. Interest groups are usually regarded as self-serving—with some justification (Rozell and Wilcox, 1999). The very word "interest" suggests that the ends sought will primarily benefit only a segment of society. For example, Barlow and Campbell (1995:175) report that corporations have been able to exert political influence through the efforts of those who are paid to lobby on their behalf. "Lobbying," they observe, "has become a booming business in Ottawa—estimated at $100 million a year." Similarly, James Hackler (2000:27) suggests that the Canadian tobacco industry has long benefitted from its ability to hire influential people such as Bill Neville, "chief of staff when Joe Clark was prime minister . . . a member of Brian Mulroney's election campaign committee for 1988, . . . [and] president of the Canadian Manufacturer's Council since 1987" to intercede on their behalf. Still, not all the groups that attempt to influence legislative bodies profit directly. "Pressure groups or 'lobbies' are [also] formed by trade unions . . . ethnic groups, and other organizations to advise politicians of their members' desires" (Brym, 2001:478). In addition, there are quite a number of groups that claim to represent causes that are deemed progressive, such as consumer advocates, homeless advocates, children's advocates, gay rights advocates, animal rights advocates, and so on (Seligman, 1995). (Note that the word "advocate" sounds much better than "lobbyist.")

The lobbyist plays a variety of roles in the legislative process. As a contact person, the lobbyist's time and energies are devoted to walking the legislative halls, visiting legislators, establishing relationships with administrative assistants and others of the legislator's staff, cultivating key legislators on a friendship basis, and developing contacts on the staffs of critical legislative committees. As a campaign organizer, the lobbyist gathers popular support for his or her organization's legislative program. As an informant, the lobbyist conveys information to legislators without necessarily advocating a particular position. Finally, as a watchdog, the lobbyist scrutinizes the legislative calendars and watches legislative activity carefully. This way, the lobbyist can be alert to developments that might affect client groups (Jewell and Patterson, 1986).

Forcese and Freeman (2005:460) observe that although lobbying as a formal industry in Canada is relatively recent, originating with the 1968 formation of Executive Consultants Ltd (ECL) by two former executive assistants to Liberal Cabinet ministers, Bill Lee and Bill Neville, "the process of lobbying predates this, of course. In fact, law firms often billed themselves as 'Parliamentary Agents,' although this more often referred to the use of lawyers for certain statutory applications such as divorce or corporate charters than to the performance of lobbying roles per se." They note that, prior to the emergence of ECL, lobbyists were typically "party-connected lawyers and 'bagmen' who could fix a client's problems with a call to a minister." However, they argue, the lobbying industry changed dramatically in the 1980s when Prime Minister Mulroney, "[s]uspicious of a public service that had served successive Liberal governments for most of the previous two decades," opted to place a lesser degree of reliance than had his predecessors on the expertise of public servants and, instead, to position his ministers "at the centre of policy-making." This change, they suggest, prompted the lobbying industry to focus "increased attention on these ministers in their campaigns, and those with personal contacts with these ministers often sold their services for a premium" (Forcese and Freeman, 2005:461).

In an attempt to rein in the power of professional lobbyists and to curb the excesses of the lobbying industry, the *Lobbying Registration Act* was passed in 1988. The LRA focuses attention on those who are paid to lobby; it does not apply to those persons who engage in lobbying activities on a purely volunteer basis. The Act, which is administered by Industry

Canada, makes registration of the lobbyist in a public registry a key obligation; the registry identifies who lobbies for whom and on what subject and is open to public inspection. The LRA is intended to reveal who wields political influence and to make lobbying more transparent; the expectation is that "sunshine will be the best disinfectant, deterring suspect lobbying practices" (Forcese and Freeman, 2005:478). However, while the LRA is the primary instrument at the federal level for policing lobbying activity, it has provided for only modest legal regulation of lobbying activities for much of its history. For example, "the original Act took a largely hands-off approach to lobbying, imposing only minimal disclosure requirements when lobbyists registered under the Act" (Forcese and Freeman, 2005:465). Moreover, while amendments to the Act in 1995 obliged professional lobbyists to provide greater amounts of information about their contacts with government (e.g., disclosing the subject matter of their lobbying activities, identifying the corporations which controlled their clients as well as the members of a coalition who sponsored their lobbying efforts), the Act remained plagued by a sloppy definition of "lobbying." For example, its registration requirements did not apply to "any oral or written submissions made to a public office holder by an individual on behalf of any person or organization in direct response to a written request from a public officer holder, for advice or comment in respect" to a government decision that would ordinarily demand registration. As Forcese and Freeman (2005:470) point out, this exception provided a legal loophole that allowed lobbyists "to 'launder' their efforts to influence decisions by first seeking a *pro forma* invitation to submit those views from a public officer holder."

The LRA distinguished between two categories of professional lobbyists: "consultant lobbyists" and "in-house lobbyists." A "consultant lobbyist" was defined as "[e]very individual who, for payment, on behalf of any person or organization . . . undertakes to . . . communicate with a public office holder in *an attempt to influence*" a decision of the government decision (i.e., over grants, financial benefits, contracts, policies, programs, regulation, and so on). Included within this definition would be an undertaking to "arrange a meeting between a public office holder and any other person." For the purposes of this Act, a "public office holder" was broadly defined to include "any officer or employee of Her Majesty in right of Canada" (e.g., a senator, MP, and/or their staff). However, as noted by Industry Canada, "The focus on the expression 'attempts to influence' entails that in order to successfully obtain a prosecution one must demonstrate beyond a reasonable doubt that an individual had attempted to influence a public office holder. The criminal nature of the offence requires a very high standard of proof . . . thereby making it very difficult to secure a conviction under the LRA" (in Forcese and Freeman, 2005:462).

The second category of professional lobbyists, "in-house lobbyists," was divided into two subtypes: "in-house (corporate)" and "in-house (organizations)." The "in-house (corporate)" lobbyists provisions of the LRA apply "[w]here a person employs an individual a significant part of whose duties as an employee is to communicate with public office holders on behalf of the employer in an attempt to influence" government activities. With a few exceptions, these "government activities" are similar to those that were earlier described in relation to consultant lobbyists. An "in-house lobbyist (organization)" addresses "an organization [that] employs one or more individuals any part of whose duties is to communicate with public officer holders on behalf of the organization in an attempt to influence" government activities. Once again, the wording proved problematic. For example, in 1998, of the 15 companies awarded more than $1 million from Technology Partnerships Canada—a $250-million-a-year federal subsidy fund that is largely geared to aerospace research and development—only seven were registered as employing lobbyists to secure TPC investments. Among those that did not register were "the Canadian branches of some global aerospace heavyweights . . . [such as] US giant Raytheon's subsidiary . . . which got $3.3 million, and the Montreal operations of Europe's Sextant Avionique, awarded $9.9 million" (*Maclean's*, 1999). While negotiating for TPC was acknowledged to be a "very time-consuming" process, companies could take advantage of a loophole in the law that states that only those full-time employees whose lobbying efforts occupy a "significant part" of their job were required to register. Companies claiming that such efforts on the part of their employees do not absorb a "significant part" of their employees' time were allowed to remain in the shadows.

Although the LRA obliged lobbyists to file a form with the Lobbyists Registry within a specified period after beginning a lobbying activity (with the precise amount of time varying for different types of lobbyists) and could impose criminal penalties upon those who failed to comply with the Act's registration requirements, it remained "common knowledge in the industry that many lobbyists failed to register" (Forcese and Freeman, 2005:465). Not surprisingly perhaps, lobbyists grew in both number and in the amount of influence they wielded over the decades that followed. A 1997 issue of *Canadian Lawyer* magazine reported that, in this country, "lobbyists are becoming a new kind of power broker, a sort of surreptitious civil service that wields real clout"; "[b]etween 1995 and 2003, the number of 'hired-gun lobbyists'—what Canadian law calls 'consultant lobbyists' . . . grew from 290 to 980 (Forcese and Freeman, 2005:461).

Following a parliamentary review in 2001 by the House of Commons Standing Committee on Industry, Science and Technology, further amendments to the LRA were passed in 2003 as Bill C-15 (*An Act to Amend the Lobbyists Registration Act*). The amended Act, which came into force on June 20, 2005, acknowledges that lobbying "is a legitimate part of our democratic system" and that "[p]eople, organizations and businesses have the right to communicate, to decision makers, information and views on issues that are important to them" (Office of the Registrar of Lobbyists, 2005). It also continues to focus on the issue of transparency. However, it does impose some significant changes. Most notable among them: it changes the definition of lobbying. Unlike earlier versions of this Act, which defined lobbying as "attempting to influence a public office holder," the new definition is less subjective; it defines lobbying as "any oral or written communication made to a public office holder." Moreover, the exception for communications initiated by a public office holder has been removed. Among other changes, the revised Act requires all categories of lobbyists to file a disclosure every six months and requires former public office holders who become paid lobbyists to disclose the positions they previously held with the federal government. In addition, the Act's enforcement provisions have been strengthened. Notification of the appropriate police authorities is now required when the Registrar of Lobbyists, "in conducting an investigation into an alleged breach of the Lobbyists Code of Conduct, has reasonable grounds to believe that an offence has been committed" (Government of Canada, 2005).

In addition, in April, 2006, Prime Minister Harper introduced a proposed *Federal Accountability Act* and action plan that, in part, would purportedly "reduce the opportunity to exert influence with money by banning corporate, union, and large personal political donations . . . [and] give Canadians confidence that lobbying is done ethically with a five-year lobbying ban on former ministers, their aides, and senior public servants" (Treasury Board of Canada Secretariat, 2006). The stated intent of the *Federal Accountability Act* is to ensure that lobbying is done in an "ethical and transparent way" by: establishing a new Commissioner of Lobbying as an independent Agent of Parliament; providing the Commissioner with enhanced investigative powers and a mandate to enforce compliance with the proposed *Lobbying Act;* prohibiting ministers, ministerial staff, and senior public servants from registering and lobbying the Government of Canada for five years after leaving office; banning any payment or other benefit contingent on the outcome of a consultant lobbyist's activity, and requiring all government contracts and agreements to state that contingency fees will not be paid; requiring that contacts with senior public officer holders will be recorded; and doubling the criminal monetary penalties for lobbyists who fail to comply with the requirements of the *Lobbying Act* (Government of Canada, 2006).

All of these measures attempt to ensure that government decisions do not simply, or most primarily, reflect narrow special interests. However, some maintain that this goal requires more than lobbyist regulation. For example, Forcese and Freeman (2005:478) observe that while governments currently consult with citizens, these consultations often prove frustrating to both citizens and policymakers. "The source of frustration for both sides," they charge," is a poorly-organized citizenry that is not always given the tools to articulate its desires effectively, and in a language that is useful and understandable for policymakers." "Civil society" organizations, they argue, are also typically fettered in their ability to meaningfully engage government decision-makers in relation to policymaking and to counter monied lobby interests. For example, while organizations that wish to retain their charitable status are prohibited from devoting more than 10 percent of their resources to "advocacy" activities, the efforts of the "well-heeled lobbying industry" are not bound by such restrictions. In contrast, the efforts of industry lobbyists are facilitated by Canada's tax laws, which allow corporations to deduct from their taxable income the costs incurred for hiring lobbyists to influence policy to their advantage.

ADMINISTRATIVE AGENCIES

Like the study of legislation, the investigation of regulatory and administrative agencies has been neglected by legal sociologists, who tend to focus their attention primarily upon courts and litigations. As a result, there is a paucity of research and theorizing on administrative and regulatory bodies in the sociological literature (Tomasic, 1985:111). These agencies deal with an important sociological process, **social control**, which is a leading concern in the study of law and society. This section will briefly describe the context within which that control is exercised.

One of the most striking developments in Canadian law over the course of the last century was the growth in administrative law, the multiplication of administrative agencies, and the extension of their power and activities (Mullan, 2001). Federal and provincial legislatures have delegated legal authority to various administrative tribunals or boards to decide a range of issues. These include quasi-judicial determinations, such as whether an individual will receive social assistance benefits or a broadcasting licence, to broad policy rulings, such as whether to permit increases in prescription drug prices or local competition in the delivery of telephone or cable services. Examples of administrative tribunals include liquor control boards, the Canadian Radio-television and Telecommunications Commission

(CRTC), the Canada Council, and the Employment Insurance Commission. However, provincial law alone has established almost 1800 administrative boards. Two-thirds of these are lawmaking boards dealing with matters "related to human rights, labour and employment standards, land assessment and expropriation, public utilities, transportation, financial institutions and securities, immigration, employment insurance, police and parole, consumer protection, parks, entertainment and athletics" (Statistics Canada, 1998:519); the rest of administrative boards are simply advisory bodies.

Individuals are much more directly and much more frequently affected by the administrative process than by the judicial process (see, for example, Seib, 1995). A typical couple is awakened by the buzz of an electric clock or perhaps by a clock radio. This marks the beginning of a highly regulated existence. The clock or radio that wakes them up is run by electricity provided by a public utility agency. They listen to a radio station regulated by the Canadian Radio-television and Telecommunications Commission. When they go into the bathroom, they use products such as mouthwash and toothpaste, made by companies that are subject to the Canadian Food and Drug Regulations. The husband receives a disturbing phone call informing him that his plans to build a cottage have failed to meet the standards of the National Fire Code, the National Building Code, the Canadian Electrical Code, and the Canadian Welding Code. Meanwhile, his wife is trying to dress their child in clothes that have met with the approval of the Canadian General Standards Board (CGSB). After the child is dressed, her father pours a bowl of cereal for her from a box that carries a label showing the name, nature, volume, and weight of the product along with the name and address of the manufacturer—as required by the *Packaging and Labelling Act.*

The family leaves the house and gets into a car that contains a catalytic converter and other devices stipulated by the *Canadian Environmental Protection Act* (CEPA). On the way to work, they obey the *Highway Traffic Act* as well as a variety of municipal ordinances. The wife reminds her husband that they need to purchase a new set of tires (that must meet the specifications of the *Motor Vehicle Tire Safety Act*). It is evident that administrative decisions are ubiquitous and affect us all.

The Organization of Administrative Agencies

Administrative agencies are authorities of the government created for the purpose of administering particular legislation. They can be called commissions, bureaus, boards, authorities, offices, departments, administrations, or divisions. The powers and functions of an agency are generally contained in the legislation that created it (Breyer and Stewart, 1998:6) and that serves as the source of its authority. For example, in deciding whether or not to deny workers' compensation benefits, a decision-maker is not free to act capriciously or arbitrarily. The decision-maker's power derives from legislative authority and regulations passed under that authority.

As social life in general and economic activity in particular became more complex, legislative bodies were unable or unwilling to prescribe detailed guidelines for regulation. In consequence, agencies were established and given considerable discretion in determining the applicability of often vaguely written legislation to specific situations such as mass transport and communication. These agencies were expected to provide certain advantages over the courts in the instrumentation of public policy. These advantages included speed, informality, flexibility, expertise in technical areas, and continuous surveillance of an industry or an economic problem.

There is substantial variation in the responsibilities, functions, and operations of agencies. Some are concerned with only a few activities of a large number of firms (Harris and Milkis, 1989), and others oversee a great many matters involving a relatively small number of firms. Many agencies in the first category have the official mission of protecting the interests of the public in regard to health, safety, and activities in the marketplace. Most of the agencies in the second category are expected not only to perform public protection functions, but also to safeguard and promote the health of specific occupations, industries, or segments of the economy subject to their jurisdiction.

Yates et al. (2000:120) observe that "because there are as many different forms of tribunals as there are government bureaucracies, it is difficult to describe their structure and procedures." Nevertheless, they point out that, in general, certain basic rules of procedure that are sometimes referred to as "due process" or the "rules of natural justice" must be followed whenever government administrators assume a judicial or quasi-judicial function and make decisions that affect the rights of others (e.g., deciding whether or not a union should be certified or if an individual qualifies for parental benefits).

> Rules of natural justice are basically the rules of fair play, and primarily embodied in the idea of having a fair hearing. In fact, what constitutes a fair hearing may vary with the nature of the matter discussed. It may involve no more than allowing the interested party to write a letter describing his or her position. In other situations, it may require having the opportunity to appear before the decision-maker or to cross-examine a witness. (Yates et al., 2000:122)

While natural justice requires that a respondent be given the opportunity to make his or her case heard and to receive a decision that is made by an impartial decision-maker, the specific procedures adopted by the administrative tribunal can vary. Moreover, administrative tribunals are not bound by the stringent rules of procedure that govern the courts. For example, they need not follow strict rules of evidence (i.e., rules that govern the types of evidence that can be introduced and how that evidence must be obtained). "As long as the decision is made within the parameters of the rule of law and the rules of natural justice and the policies set out in the legislation, the decision-maker is free to make a decision and the agency to implement it" (Yates et al., 2000:124).

Nevertheless, there are certain curbs placed on administrative tribunals. As Judge Beverley McLachlin (1992:168) has noted, "We expect our administrative tribunals to be bound by the law, to render decisions in an equal and predictive manner and to act in accordance with law and social values." For example, administrative tribunals are bound to follow the terms of the *Charter of Rights and Freedoms* and cannot violate Charter rights by denying the liberty or security of the person, or violate the principles of fundamental justice that are set out in section 7 of the Charter. Tribunals are also required to act in a reasonable way, based on the available evidence that they possess (although it is possible for an administrative tribunal to argue that a seemingly unreasonable decision falls under section 1 of the Charter and is, in fact, a "reasonable limit prescribed by law"). If an individual who appears before an administrative tribunal believes that his or her Charter rights have been violated, that due process has not been followed, or that a decision made by a tribunal is unreasonable, that person may apply for a judicial review.

In general, the role of the court is to provide a counterbalance to the discretionary power wielded by government-appointed members of administrative tribunals. While members of tribunals are generally appointed because of their expertise and familiarity with a particular area of legislation, the court plays a supervisory role. The court may consider if the tribunal was operating within its territorial jurisdiction, if it was acting under appropriately passed legislation within that jurisdiction, respected the rights set out within the *Charter of Rights and Freedoms*, and followed the rules of natural justice. If the court finds that the tribunal failed to satisfy any of these conditions, it may review the decision and apply remedies. For example, an order of *certiorari* may be issued, quashing the decision or declaring it to be of no effect. An order of *prohibition* may be issued when administrators have made a decision that exceeds their jurisdiction. The court may make a *declaratory judgment* that announces the law that will apply in a situation. The complainant may also be granted compensation for an unfair decision. However, if "court[s] have always been protective of their supervisory right over other adjudicative bodies . . . legislators have been just as keen to stop courts from interfering" (Yates et al., 2000:125). Statutes empowering tribunals may contain *privative clauses* which state that a decision made by a board (e.g., the Workers' Compensation Board) is not reviewable by a court of law or that an order of *certiorari*, prohibition, etc. cannot be applied to any decision made by the board. However, these clauses are less iron-clad than they may appear, and the courts "have always treated such privative causes with a certain amount of resistance" (Yates et al., 2000:125).

The Administrative Process

Administrative agencies affect the rights of individuals and businesses by exercising powers of investigation, rulemaking, enforcement, and adjudication. The creator of an agency, which is generally the legislature, retains the power to destroy it or alter the rules governing it. The judiciary retains the power of final review of the determinations of administrative agencies, but this right is, as a practical matter, rather limited. The principal administrative processes include investigation, rulemaking, and adjudication. We shall consider these separately.

Investigation. The authority to investigate is given to practically all administrative agencies. Without information, administrative agencies could not regulate industry, protect the environment, collect taxes, or issue grants. Most administrative actions in both formal and informal proceedings are conditioned by the information obtained through the agency's prior investigation. As regulation has expanded and intensified, agencies' could not quests for facts have gained momentum. Some agencies are created primarily to perform the investigative function. This authority is one of the functions that distinguishes agencies from courts, and is usually exercised to properly perform another primary function, that of rulemaking.

Statutes usually grant an agency the authority to use several methods to carry out its information-gathering function, including requiring reports from regulated businesses and conducting inspections. Necessary information is often available from the staff, from the agencies' accumulated records, and from private sources. If these resources prove inadequate, the agency may seek further information by calling in witnesses or documents for examination, or by conducting searches. The authority of an agency to investigate is intertwined with the objectives of administrative investigation. The purposes of investigations vary, ranging over the entire spectrum of agency activity. For example, if an agency is responsible for enforcing a statute, its investigations may set the groundwork for detecting violations and punishing wrongdoers (e.g., inspecting employers' payroll records when checking for compliance with minimum wage laws).

Rulemaking. Rulemaking is the most important function performed by government agencies (Kerwin, 1999: xi). It defines the mission of the agency and essentially involves the formulation of a policy or an interpretation that the agency will apply to all persons engaged in the regulated activity. As quasi-legislative bodies, administrative agencies issue three types of rules: procedural, interpretive, and legislative. Procedural rules identify an agency's organization, describe its methods of operation, and list the requirements of its practice for rulemaking and adjudicative hearings. Interpretive rules are issued to guide both the agency's staff and regulated parties as to how the agency will interpret its statutory mandate. These rules range from informally developed policy statements announced through press releases to authoritative rulings binding upon the agency and issued usually after a notice and hearing. Legislative rules are, in effect, administrative statutes. In issuing a legislative rule, the agency exercises lawmaking power delegated to it by the legislature.

The rulemaking process, more often than not, is lengthy and complicated. Usually a lawyer's expertise is needed to master the procedural maze and technical requirements imposed by administrative agencies. Even so, an average person may initiate and participate in the process. Unlike legislatures and courts, access to administrative agencies is often direct. No intermediaries stand between agencies and their clients (Jacob, 1995).

Adjudication. Administrative agencies of all kinds and at all levels must settle disputes or mediate among conflicting claims. Adjudication is the administrative equivalent of a judicial trial. It applies policy to a set of past actions and results in an order against (or in favour of) the named party.

Much of this adjudication is handled informally through the voluntary settlement of cases at lower levels in an agency. At these levels, agencies dispose of disputes relatively quickly and inexpensively, and they take an immense burden off the courts. Moreover, they are handled by individuals who are experts in technical areas. But this practice is not without criticism. Many individuals—in particular, lawyers pleading cases before the agencies—have expressed concern over the extent of judicial power vested in agencies. They complain that administrators violate due process of law by holding private and informal sessions, by failing to give interested parties an adequate hearing, and by basing their decisions on insufficient evidence.

These complaints stem, in part, from the institutional differences between agency and court trials. Agency hearings tend to produce evidence of general conditions, as distinguished from the facts relating specifically to the respondent. This distinction is due to one of the original justifications for administrative agencies—the development of policy. Another difference is that in an administrative hearing, a case is tried by a trial examiner and never by a jury. As a result, the rules of evidence applied in jury trials, presided over by a judge, are frequently inapplicable in an administrative trial. The trial examiner decides both the facts and the law to be applied. Finally, the courts accept whatever cases the disputants present. As a result, their familiarity with the subject matter is accidental. By contrast, agencies usually select and prosecute their cases. Trial examiners and agency chiefs either are experts or at least have a substantial familiarity with the subject matter, since their jurisdictions tend to be restricted. As we have noted, however, the courts do have the power to overturn the agencies' judgments on points of law, as in cases where an agency has exceeded its authority, misinterpreted the law, or simply been unfair. Judicial review of agency activities also deals with procedural safeguards, such as more formalized hearings and proper notice of action (Edley, 1990). But the role of the courts is essentially limited to procedural matters—advising agencies, sometimes repeatedly, to go about their business in a fairer manner and to pay serious attention to all affected interests. In technical, complex disputes, courts cannot decide major issues. They will not set tariffs, allocate airline routes, or control the development of satellite communications (Breyer and Stewart, 1998).

LAW ENFORCEMENT AGENCIES

The word *police* comes from the Greek word *polis*, meaning "city." The word also includes the idea of the city's "government," and by more modern extension that of the state. The principal functions of the police are law enforcement, maintenance of order, and community service (see, for example, Langworthy and Travis, 2003; Thurman and Zhao, 2004). Like other components of the Canadian legal system, the origins of the Canadian police can be traced to early English history. In the ninth century, Alfred the Great started paying private citizens for arresting offenders. The population was broken down into units of 10 families or "tithings," and each person was responsible for watching over the others. Subsequently, the unit was expanded to the "hundred," and one person, designated as the constable, was in charge of maintaining order. In time, the hundred was increased to include the countrywide "shire" under the control of an appointed "shire-reeve," who later on became known as the "sheriff." The first citywide police force was created by Sir Robert Peel in London in 1829; in 2004, one in every 115 employed Londoners was a police officer (*Economist*, 2004b). Police officers were uniformed, organized along military lines, and called "Bobbies" after their founder. While Canadian municipal policing was initially modelled primarily on the example provided by the London Metropolitan Police, the more militaristic example provided by the Royal Irish Constabulary provided the model for the Northwest Mounted Police (the precursor of the Royal Canadian Mounted Police).

There are three levels of policing in Canada: federal, provincial, and municipal. The Royal Canadian Mounted Police (RCMP) is our national or federal police force. The Ontario Provincial Police (OPP) and the Sûreté du Québec (SQ) are the provincial police forces in Ontario and Quebec, respectively; in other provinces, the RCMP also serve as the provincial police force. At the third level are municipal police forces and services, such as the Edmonton Police Service and the Vancouver Police Department. In large metropolitan areas, municipal forces have been established under provincial laws. In small municipalities that do not have their own police forces, the RCMP, the OPP in Ontario, and the SQ in Quebec carry out this role under contract with the provinces.

Regardless of whether they are federal, provincial, or municipal police officers, all are responsible for protecting the safety, health, and morals of the public and enforcing the law. As of June 15, 2005, Canada had more than 61 000 police officers (Statistics Canada, 2005b). In that year, there were 189 police officers per 100 000 population—a figure that is lower than that of the United States, Australia, and the United Kingdom (where police strength ranges from 242 to 262 officers per 100 000 population). Within Canada, the highest number of police per capita is found in Saskatchewan (202 officers per 100 000 population), followed by Quebec (194), Manitoba (192), and Ontario (187). The fewest police per capita in 2005 were found in Newfoundland and Labrador (150) and Prince Edward Island (154). Women accounted for 17 percent of Canada's police officers in 2005, up from 10 percent a decade ago. The number of visible minority police officers has also grown, increasing by 61 percent between 1996 and 2001 (Statistics Canada, 2004b).

In addition, governments in Canada authorize other forms of police with powers that may be limited to specific areas or specific groups (military police, harbour police, etc.). Prior to July 1984, the RCMP Security Service was the principal authority in domestic intelligence work. However, since that time, the Canadian Security Intelligence Service (CSIS), an agency of the Department of the Solicitor General, has been charged with conducting security investigations within Canada that are related to suspected subversion, terrorism, and foreign espionage and sabotage. Although its members are not police officers, the agency can obtain judicial warrants to conduct searches and electronic surveillance.

Finally, no review of law enforcement agencies is complete without mention of the private police (Nemeth and Poulin, 2005; Williams, 2005). Indeed, within Canada, "an authority figure in a uniform is twice as likely to be a security guard as a police officer" (Gillespie, 2002). Although "[t]he number of security guards and private investigators in Canada increased 2 percent between 1996 and 2001, compared with a 6 percent increase in the number of police officers during that period," private security personnel "still outnumbered police officers in 2001, at 84 000 compared with 63 000" (Statistics Canada, 2004b). Compared with Canada's police officers, private security personnel in Canada are less likely to hold a university degree or college diploma (over one-half of police officers versus less than one-third of security personnel). They also earn appreciably less: Canadian police officers who worked full-time, full-year in 2002 earned an average salary of almost $60 000—an amount that was over one-and-a-half times the average income of private investigators and more than double that of security guards. "Private security personnel were also about seven times more likely than police officers to experience unemployment, and almost eight times more likely to work part-time" (Statistics Canada, 2004b).

Special needs of private sectors of the community require the services of private police patrols and investigation agencies. Businesses, industries, residential complexes, and others use private agencies, such as Securities Canada (the largest Canadian security firm), Brinks, and Wackenhut, to guard property, provide security at nuclear facilities and on university campuses, maintain order in some housing complexes, and detect fraud and embezzlement. Nationally, the private security industry in Canada generates over $2 billion a year in revenue. In Ontario alone, there were 600 licensed security firms employing 28 000 guards in 2002 (Gillespie, 2002). However, Burbidge (2005) sounds a cautionary note and suggests that the "growing presence of private police in our society, and especially the fact that they perform many policing functions traditionally regarded as the preserve of public police, raises fundamental questions of police government and accountability for a democratic society based on the rule of law and respect for human rights." He notes that, unlike public police agencies which "are governed by and accountable to democratically elected governmental authority and to the public, private police officers . . . are not subject to the same form of democratic governance and accountability." This situation, he argues, is unacceptable and in urgent need of redress.

The Organization of Law Enforcement Agencies

The rest of this section will be devoted to the structural features of nonprivate police departments. Police organizations have evolved in response to changes in technology, social organization, and political governance at all levels of society (Carter, 2002; Thurman and Jamieson, 2005). They are structured along the lines of complex bureaucratic organizations. A variety of organizational tables or patterns describe how the police divide up tasks. In every case, a formal and highly complex division of labour characterizes these systems. In addition to their bureaucratic characteristics, law enforcement agencies are structured like quasi-military institutions, which give these agencies their special character. Bittner notes: "Both institutions are instruments of force and for both institutions the occasions for using force are unpredictably distributed. Thus, the personnel in each must be kept in a highly disciplined state of alert preparedness. The formalism that characterizes military organization, the insistence on rules and regulations, on spit and polish, on obedience to superiors, and so on, constitute a permanent rehearsal for 'the real thing'" (1970:53).

This system of law enforcement is built on a subordinating chain of command (Loveday, 1998). Although all units of a particular department may be related to a central command, the overall chain of command is divided into units so that different divisions are immediately responsible to a localized authority. The functional divisions of police departments follow the kinds of activities they handle, such as traffic patrol, investigative work, sex crimes, homicide, undercover work (for example, in vice and narcotics), juveniles, and uniformed patrol, whose officers are popularly referred to as "cops"—which is the abbreviation of the British designation "constable on patrol."

Although recruitment policies vary with respect to education, most Canadian police forces require a high school diploma and at least some now prefer that recruits have post-secondary education. Although white males have been and remain the most likely applicants, equity requirements have increased the presence of women, visible minorities, and Aboriginals within Canadian police departments to some degree (Nelson, 1993). Although similar curricula exist in major regional recruit training centres, there is no "standard training" for Canadian police officers, and the duration of basic recruit training varies from 12 weeks in some municipal police forces to 22 weeks for RCMP officers at the Regina depot. Police training is pragmatic and brief and usually takes place in an individual police department. This training is generally followed by some type of mentoring or supervised in-service training for up to the first half-year on the job.

Most officers come from lower-middle-class or working-class backgrounds (Jacob, 1995). For many, becoming a police officer is an opportunity for upward social mobility. Compared with other occupational groups, there is a high degree of cohesion and solidarity among police officers (a fact that becomes readily apparent when an officer is killed in the line of duty and officers from around the country may attend the funeral). They are, by virtue of occupational expectations, suspicious and tend to be skeptical toward outsiders, and much of their outlook and conduct have an authoritarian character. Their subculture includes a code of silence, and fellow officers rarely incriminate each other. They socialize and make friends within the department, and some even conceal their police identity (Skolnick, 1994). Although the perception exists that policing is an extremely dangerous profession, "working life appears to be relatively safe for police officers; on average, there are 0.1575 deaths for every 1000 person-years of police work. Working as a law enforcement officer is only marginally more dangerous than working as a biologist, an occupation in which there are 0.1570 deaths for every 1000 person-years worked" (Statistics Canada, 1998:231). Suicide among police personnel is caused by a variety of factors such as job stress, frustration, easy access to firearms, alcohol abuse, and fear of separation from the police subculture (Violanti, 1995).

The activities of police both in Canada and in other parts of the world consist of routine patrol and maintaining order—such duties as attending to domestic disturbances, handling drunks, assisting motorists, controlling traffic, escorting dignitaries and funeral processions, and processing juveniles (Lyman, 2004; Thurman and Jamieson, 2005). Contrary to popular image, police officers, with the exception of detectives, spend about 20 percent of their time in criminal investigations.

The effectiveness of law enforcement agencies (as determined usually by arrest and clearance rates) depends on the size of the department and the way it is organized (Kerley, 2005). Small departments often lack the training or equipment for proper handling of serious crimes (Glaberson, 1992). Whether or not departments are organized along professional criteria also has a bearing on their effectiveness. In a classic study of a non-professionalized police department, James Q. Wilson (1968a) found that the members had no strong sense of urgency about police work and produced low rates of official actions on offenders. In a professionalized department, however, violations of the law were more likely to be detected, and offenders were more likely to be arrested, producing a higher crime rate.

In another well-known and influential study, Wilson (1968b) identified three styles of police work: the watchman style, the legalistic style, and the service style. Although elements of all three can be found in any law enforcement agency, different agencies tend to emphasize one style more than the others and, as a result, practise different law enforcement policies.

The **watchman** style emphasizes the responsibility for maintaining public order, as contrasted with traditional law enforcement (see, for example, Crank, 1994). The police officer in such an agency is viewed as a peace officer, ignoring or handling informally many violations of the law and paying much greater attention to local variations in the demand for law enforcement and maintenance of order. The role of peace officer is characterized by a great amount of discretion, since peacekeeping is poorly structured by law or by agency regulation. Underenforcement, corruption, and low arrest rates characterize watchman-style departments.

The **legalistic** style is just the opposite of the watchman style. Agencies characterized by this style tend to treat all situations, even commonplace problems of maintaining order, as if they were serious infractions of the law. Members of such agencies issue a high rate of traffic tickets, arrest a high proportion of young offenders, and crack down on illicit enterprises. The police typically act as if there were a single standard of conduct rather than different standards for different groups. As a result, some groups, especially youths, visible minorities, and Aboriginal peoples, are more likely to be affected by law enforcement than others considered "respectable" by the police. Although this style of law enforcement is characterized by technical efficiency and high arrest rates, it also results in inequality in law enforcement, with complaints of harassment and police brutality by groups who are disproportionately subjected to police scrutiny.

The **service** style combines law enforcement and maintenance of order. An emphasis is placed on community relations, the police on patrol work out of specialized units, and command is decentralized. The pace of work is more leisurely, and more promotional opportunities are available. This style differs from the watchman style in that the police respond to all groups and apply informal sanctions in the case of minor offences. It differs from the legalistic style in that fewer arrests are made for minor infractions, and the police are more responsive to public sentiments and desires. In this sense, the service style is less arbitrary than the watchman style and more attuned to the practical considerations of public service than the legalistic style. There is little corruption, and complaints against police in service-style departments tend to be low. Such departments are also characterized by community-oriented policing (COP). The emphasis is on problem-solving policing where attention is focused on the problems that lie behind incidents, rather than on the incidents only (Zhao and Thurman, 1997). It aims at reducing alienation and distrust between police and minorities and between police and the poor—potentially explosive situations that can escalate a simple traffic stop into a riot. Community policing tries to improve neighbourhood quality of life, involves citizens in crime fighting (in particular against drugs), and undertakes more concerted effort at crime prevention (Peak and Glensor, 2004; Thurman et al., 2001). Although it is more expensive and labour-intensive, community policing has become increasingly popular in Canada (Ontario Provincial Police Association, 1993). But the approach is not without criticism, and enthusiasm for it is being tempered by training needs, costs, and overall effectiveness (Joseph, 1994). Community policing, as a recent study contends, also colonizes community life and increases the capacity of police departments to shield themselves from criticism (Lyons, 1999).

Community policing is not limited to Canada. It is widely practised in the United States and many European countries (see, for example, *Economist*, 2004b), and it was more or less "invented" in Japan (Kristof, 1995). In Japan the police are highly respected and considered almost incorruptible. In every Japanese city, each neighbourhood has its own *koban*, or police box. It is a one- or two-room office, staffed around the clock by police officers called "Honourable Walkabouts," for they spend much of their time strolling or bicycling around the neighbourhood. They advise homeowners how to avoid burglaries, make teenagers rip up and throw away their cigarettes—"but in the trash can, not just on the ground"—issue a newsletter for the area, and visit homes at least once a year. The police have broad powers: they can stop people who look suspicious, they can ask them to come to the *koban* for a "discussion," to empty their pockets, or tell them to avoid the neighbourhood. The police also have the right to detain people for up to 23 days for questioning often without the presence of an attorney before being charged, to interview suspects without tape recording, to deprive suspects of sleep, and to make suspects feel guilty and confess. In fact, the police bring charges to court only when they have a cast-iron case, almost always based on confession (and the courts almost invariably convict [*Economist*, 2004c]). But despite appearances, Japanese police are much less powerful than their Canadian counterparts—they are usually not allowed to infiltrate subversive organizations, to pay informers, tap telephones, or plea-bargain with defendants. Even though the crime rate is much lower, Japan spends a greater proportion of its GNP on police than either Canada or the United States. Adopting the Japanese style of policing in Canada would increase costs substantially. Placing police in *kobans* tends to cost more than keeping them in station houses. But Japan does have the lowest crime rate in the industrialized world, and its highly efficient model of policing deserves further scrutiny.

Police Discretion

A significant feature of law enforcement—indeed of the entire judicial process and the criminal justice system—is the discretionary power officials can exercise in specific situations (Gilbert, 1997; Schulenberg, 2003). The exercise of discretion is integral to the daily routine of police officers in a large variety of activities ranging from routine traffic stops to responding to domestic violence calls (Campbell, 1999; Kane, 1999). Police discretion is highly institutionalized in our system of criminal justice, and questions about police discretion increasingly appear in lawsuits against the police (Worrall, 1998). Albert J. Reiss and David J. Bordua (1967) point out that police discretion and disparity stem in large part from the general organization of modern police work. As a largely reactive force, primarily dependent on citizen mobilization, the police officer functions in criminal law much as a private lawyer functions in civil law—determining when the victim's complaint warrants formal action and encouraging private settlement of disputes whenever possible. Among such private arrangements protected by the police are those of their own relationships with various categories of citizens, so that the degree to which formal legality is extended by police to different categories of individuals varies substantially. In view of the highly decentralized police operation, with minimal direct supervision, it is difficult to control such disparate treatment. Many of the decisions of police officers on the beat do not lend themselves to either command or review. As a result, police exercise a considerable amount of discretionary power, as reflected in disparities in the volume of arrests, parking tickets, and pedestrian stops. For example, Geiger-Oneto and Phillips (2003) recently surveyed American undergraduates (N=1192) in an attempt to investigate (1) whether a driver's race, sex, and social status influenced police behaviour (e.g., whether they were stopped, frisked, searched, ticketed, or arrested by police); and (2) which drivers were most likely to possess drugs in their cars. Their findings suggested that a driver's race, sex, and social status all shape police behaviour: "African American men and Hispanic men experience more social control than white men; all men experience more social control than women; and low status drivers experience more social control than high status drivers." They note, however, that while police direct attention to minority males, in their sample of respondents, it was white males who were the most likely to report carrying drugs in their cars.

Because of their discretionary power, "the police are among our most important policy-making administrative agencies. One may wonder whether any other agencies . . . make so much policy that so directly and vitally affects so many people" (Davis, 1975a:263; see also Cooney, 1994). The police need to make policy with regard to nearly all their activities, such as deciding what types of private disputes to mediate and how to do it, breaking up sidewalk gatherings, helping drunks, deciding what to do with runaways, breaking up fights and matrimonial disputes, entering and searching premises, controlling juveniles, and managing race relations. The police exercise discretion in both reactive and proactive policing.

Reactive police work is a response to citizen mobilization. But even before a citizen can reach a police officer, discretionary power is exercised by police dispatchers at the communication centre. A member of the dispatch crew answers the telephone call made to the police emergency number, interviews the caller to identify the nature and location of the reported problem, and decides whether to dispatch a patrol car. In a study of telephone calls to three departments, T. E. Bercal (1970) found that 20 to 40 percent of the calls are handled without dispatching a car. If the dispatcher decides to send a patrol car, the nature of the assignment (for example, an assault or a robbery) and which car to assign must be determined. When a car is dispatched, the officer may informally turn down the assignment, or may procrastinate on the way, or even lie about having investigated the call (Rubinstein, 1973:87). If the officer follows up on the call, he or she often has to decide whether a crime has been committed. Albert J. Reiss (1971:73) found that whereas citizens considered 58 percent of their complaints as criminal matters, officers responding to those dispatches officially processed only 17 percent as criminal matters. One study found in domestic violence cases that over half of the offenders were gone upon police arrival (Kane, 1999:68). Harold E. Pepinsky (1976:21) suggests that police officers' decisions are determined mainly by the dispatcher's characterization of the incident and officers' experience with similar cases in their jurisdiction.

A great deal of police work is undertaken on the initiative of the police themselves without citizen mobilization (Reiss, 1971:88). The activities of traffic and tactical divisions are primarily proactive policing, as are the various nondispatched activities of detectives and vice divisions. In proactive policing, discretionary power is exercised in the context of whether or not to stop a suspicious pedestrian or automobile for investigation (Cooney, 1997; Murdocca, 2004).

There is a thin line between discretion and discrimination in discretionary law enforcement (Skolnick, 1994). If the likelihood that an individual will be considered a criminal is dependent on the discretionary power of the police to respond to or to ignore a citizen's complaint, to arrest or to release a suspect, and the like, then the probability that any one person will be labelled a criminal increases or decreases depending on that person's correspondence to police conceptions of the criminal. Some individuals are more—or less—likely than others to have their behaviour treated as a crime by the police and, consequently, to be labelled as criminal (Nelson, 1994). Research suggests that young adults, poor citizens, minority members, and individuals who look disreputable by police standards are more likely to be stopped by the police, experience one or another form of police brutality, and to be arrested than are more "respectable" citizens (Skolnick, 1994; Wortley and Tanner, 2005). In general, the police are likely to sanction suspects who fail to defer to police authority, whether legal grounds exist or not (Black, 1980:77).

Police discretion not to enforce the law is attributed to a number of conditions. These include the police beliefs that (1) the legislative body does not desire enforcement; (2) the community wants non-enforcement or lax enforcement; (3) other immediate duties are more urgent; (4) the offenders promise not to commit the act again; (5) there is a shortage of police officers; (6) there is sympathy with the violator; (7) a particular criminal act is common within a subculture; (8) the victim is likely to get restitution without arrest; (9) non-enforcement can be traded for information; (10) the probable penalty is likely to be too severe; and (11) the arrest would unduly harm the offender's status (Davis, 1975a:264).

But as Kenneth Culp Davis (1975b:140) argues: "Police discretion is absolutely essential. It cannot be eliminated. Any effort to eliminate it would be ridiculous. Discretion is the essence of police work, both in law enforcement and in service activities. Police work without discretion would be something like a human torso without legs, arms, or head." Selective enforcement represents low-visibility interaction between individual officers and various citizens. The exercise of discretion is not guided by clear policy directives, nor is it subject to administrative scrutiny. For such reasons, selective enforcement can easily deteriorate into police abuse and discriminatory conduct. Although it cannot be eliminated, Joseph Goldstein (1960) proposes that an impartial civilian body should scrutinize the decisions as to which laws should be enforced. In that way, discretionary conduct would become more visible and might result in selective law enforcement that would then become a subject for open public dialogue. Discretionary law enforcement can also become an area in police-community relations (Thurman, et al., 2001).

SUMMARY

- This chapter has been concerned with the organization of law in society in the context of judicial, legislative, administrative, and enforcement agencies.
- Courts, as dispute-processing institutions, are composed of four distinct groups of participants—litigants, lawyers, judges, and juries.
- Although the flow of litigation is different in criminal and civil cases, a high degree of discretion at every level is characteristic of both.
- Although the principal function of legislative bodies is lawmaking, they also engage in conflict-management and integrative functions.
- Administrative agencies reach into virtually every corner of modern life and are created for the purpose of administering particular legislations. Administrative agencies have powers of investigation, rulemaking, and adjudication.
- An important characteristic of law enforcement is the strongly bureaucratic and militaristic organization of the police. The effectiveness of law enforcement agencies depends on the way in which departments are organized.

CRITICAL THINKING QUESTIONS

1. The recommendations of the Royal Commission on Aboriginal Peoples included recommendations for separate legal structures of self-government (e.g., an eventual separate Aboriginal parliament) as well as enhanced Aboriginal self-sufficiency and self-control in such areas as health, education, and housing. However, as David Elliott (2005:191) has rhetorically asked, "How much self-control can individual groups exercise within a large polity without threatening its viability or effective operation?" It is noteworthy that recent surveys suggest a lack of widespread support for Aboriginal aspirations for self-government. For example, Bricker and Greenspon (2001:277) report that while just over half (52 percent) of the Canadians surveyed agreed with the statement that "Aboriginals should have the rights and status they need to protect their culture and heritage, even if it means they may have certain rights that other Canadians do not have," 57 percent believed that "It isn't fair to displace people and businesses who currently depend on the land just to make up for wrongs committed against Aboriginal peoples many years ago." Almost two-thirds (61 percent) of Canadians felt that "Canada's Aboriginal people are too dependent on government," and more than eight in ten (84 percent) believed that "when treaties are signed, Aboriginal people should have the same rights as any other Canadians, no more and no less." A more recent survey, conducted in 2003 and based on a representative sample of 3204 Canadians found that, when asked whether they felt it "beneficial to all Canadians that the distinctive cultures of Aboriginal peoples remain strong," three-quarters agreed that it was beneficial. However, when asked to select which of two options would be better: (1) eliminating Aboriginal treaty rights and treating Aboriginal and non-Aboriginal peoples identically or (2) settling outstanding land claims with Aboriginal peoples and giving Aboriginal peoples the powers they needed to govern their own communities, just over half (53 percent) supported option #2. Similarly, when asked the question, "Do you think that Aboriginal peoples should have some type of preferential access to hunting and fishing grounds in areas where they have traditionally lived, or do you think that when governments regulate access to hunting and fishing grounds they should treat everyone the same?" 63 percent of Canadians felt that everyone should be treated the same. According to this survey, almost half (49 percent) thought that "few" or "none" of the land claims made by Aboriginal peoples were valid; this sentiment was also expressed by the majority of individuals surveyed in Atlantic Canada (54 percent) as well as in the provinces of Manitoba (51 percent), Saskatchewan (60 percent), Alberta (57 percent), and British Columbia (56 percent). In Quebec, however, the percentage of respondents who identified themselves as in favour of the territorial demands of Quebec's Aboriginal peoples grew from 36 percent in 1994 to 48 percent in 2003 (CRIC, 2004). Do you agree or disagree with the sentiments expressed by the majority of Canadians within these surveys? How would *you* answer Elliott's question? Explain your reasoning.

2. Discuss the strengths/weaknesses of the following assertion: Tort law very much defines in a formal way the obligations we have to treat each other with respect, to recognize and respect the property of others, to take care in the way we treat others—in short, tort law is, sociologically, the "ultimate" in normative prescriptions and proscriptions for everyday life.

chapter four

Lawmaking

Routinely and seemingly mechanically at the local, provincial, and federal levels, legislative, administrative, and judicial bodies grind out thousands of new laws each year. Each has its own distinct set of precipitating factors, special history, and *raison d'être*. Still, some generalizations are possible about how laws are formed, the sociological factors that play a role in lawmaking, and the social forces that provide an impetus for making or altering laws. This chapter focuses on the more important sociological theories of lawmaking; the ways in which legislatures, administrative agencies, and courts make laws; the roles of vested interests, public opinion, and social science in the decision-making process; and the sources of impetus for laws.

PERSPECTIVES ON LAWMAKING

The creation and instrumentation of laws are routine and ongoing processes (Ball, 2004; Cheney, 1998), and theoretical perspectives dealing with the many facets of lawmaking abound in the sociological literature (Chambliss and Zats, 1993; Monahan and Walker, 1998:125; Zander, 1999). Students of lawmaking have used a number of them in attempts to explain how laws are created or defeated. We will consider briefly four such theories to illustrate the diversity of perspectives—the rationalistic model, the functional view, conflict theory, and a "moral entrepreneur" thesis.

The **rationalistic** model proposes that laws (in particular, criminal laws) are created as rational means of protecting the members of society from social harm. In this perspective, crimes are considered socially injurious. This is the most widely accepted but also the most simplistic theory of lawmaking (Goode, 2005). One of the principal difficulties with this perspective is that it is the lawmakers and powerful interest groups who define what activities may be harmful to the public welfare. Value judgments, preferences, and other considerations obviously enter into the process of definition (for example, why are certain types of behaviours, like prostitution or gambling—which will be discussed in the following chapter—labelled as criminal?).

The **functionalist** view of lawmaking, as formulated by Paul Bohannan (1973), is concerned mainly with how laws emerge. Bohannan argues that laws are a special kind of "reinstitutionalized custom." Customs are norms or rules about the ways in which people must behave if social institutions are to perform their functions and society is to endure. Lawmaking is the restatement of some customs (for example, those dealing with economic transactions and contractual relations, property rights in marriage, or deviant behaviour) so that they can be enforced by legal institutions.

This view proposes that failure in other institutional norms encourages the reinstitution-alization of the norms by the legal institution. As noted earlier, this perspective implies a consensual model of lawmaking in a society. From the functionalist perspective, laws are passed because they represent the voice of the people. Laws are essentially a crystalliza-tion of custom, of the existing normative order. Although there are conflicts in society, they are relatively marginal, and they do not involve basic values. In this view, conflict and competition between groups in a society actually serve to contribute to its cohesion and solidarity.

The **conflict** perspective cites value diversity, unequal access to economic goods, and the resulting structural cleavages of a society as the basic determinants of laws. Specifically, the origin of law is traced to the emergence of an elite class. These elites, it is suggested, use social control mechanisms such as laws to perpetuate their own advantageous positions in society. In the event of conflict over the prescription of a norm, conflict theorists would argue that the interest group(s) more closely tied to the interests of the elite group would probably win the conflict. To define who the elites or the powerful groups of the society are, conflict theorists often employ structural indices of power. For example, William J. Chambliss (1964), as shown in Chapter 1, claims that the groups in England having the most power to create the vagrancy laws were those representing the dominant economic interests at the time. Perelman's (2003) more recent analysis of the development of intellectual prop-erty rights in the United States since the early 19th century also suggests the important role played by elite groups. He reports that while capitalist entrepreneurs were initially suspi-cious of the concept of intellectual property, "economic depressions during the mid-19th century and following WWII prompted corporate leaders to advocate stronger intellectual property rights in order to increase revenues." In addition, he argues that companies who were able to secure intellectual property rights effectively limited potential sources of com-petition and stresses that these results promoted the growth of monopolies within certain industries.

The **"moral entrepreneur"** theory attributes the precipitation of key events to the "presence of an enterprising individual or group. Their activities can properly be called *moral enterprise*, for what they are enterprising about is the creation of a new fragment of the moral constitution of society, its code of right and wrong" (Becker, 1963:146). The role of moral entrepreneurs in lawmaking is well-illustrated by Enakshi Dua's (1999) research on the historical discouragement of interracial marriage in Canada. She argues that laws prohibiting mixed-race marriages emerged in Canada, as well as other British, white set-tler colonies such as the United States, South Africa, Australia, and New Zealand, as part of "the project of creating a white settler colony with political power in the hands of white settlers" (p. 244). "As eugenicists linked miscegenation [interracial marriage] to the dete-rioration of the race and nation, sexual purity became a controlling metaphor for racial, economic and political power . . . " (Dua, 1999:253).

While the United States enacted a series of laws specifically prohibiting marriages between white settlers and those of African descent (Haney-Lopez, 1997; Sollors, 2000), "[i]n Canada the regulation of interracial sexuality took place through other legal mechanisms" such as the 1876 *Indian Act,* which was "employed to govern marriage and sexual relations between white settlers and First Nations people" (Dua, 1999:256). For example, until 1985, when the *Indian Act* was modified, an Indian woman who married a non-Indian man lost her Indian status, and both she and her descendants lost those benefits to which status Indians were entitled (Kallen, 2003:135). In addition, Tanis Das Gupta (2000:159) observes that in the early part of the 20th century, single male Chinese workers were seen as posing "a threat of miscegenation" and vilified in newspapers as sexual predators who lusted after white women. Such inflammatory, racist stereotypes were consequential and galvanized Protestant moral reformers, middle-class white women's groups, the owners of small businesses, and trade unionists to jointly campaign for legislation that prohibited Asian employers from hiring white women as employees.

> Fearful of the implications of the pronounced sexual imbalance within the Asian-Canadian community [an imbalance created by restrictive immigration policies], these groups decried racial intermarriage and fretted over the potential for coercive sexuality that suffused the employment relationship. White women were called into service as the "guardians of the race," a symbol of the most valuable property known to white society, to be protected at all costs from the encroachment of other races. (Backhouse, 1999:5)

Toward the end of "protecting" white womanhood and keeping the "races" pure, a Saskatchewan statute colloquially referred to as the "white women's labour law" was enacted in 1912. It specified that "No person shall employ in any capacity any white woman or girl or permit any white woman or girl to reside or lodge in or work in or, save as a bona fide customer in a public apartment thereof only, to frequent any restaurant, laundry or other place of business or amusement owned, kept or managed by any Japanese, Chinaman or other Oriental person." Similar statutes were also passed in 1913 in the province of Manitoba (where indications are that it was never actually proclaimed), in 1914 in Ontario, and in 1919 in British Columbia and remained in force for many years. Manitoba was the first province to repeal its act (in 1940); Ontario followed in 1947 and British Columbia in 1968. The Saskatchewan statute, "veiled in racially neutral language, was not repealed until 1969" (Backhouse, 1999:15).

It should be noted that the passing of a law may also symbolize the supremacy of the groups that support it. The creation of a law is a statement that the illegal behaviour is disreputable. Where groups differ significantly in prestige and status, or where two groups are competing for status, each sees the law as a stamp of legitimacy. They will seek to use it to affirm the respectability of their own way of life. According to Gusfield:

> The fact of affirmation through acts of law and government, expresses the public worth of one set of norms, or one subculture vis-à-vis those of others. It demonstrates which cultures have legitimacy and public domination, and which do not. Accordingly it enhances the social status of groups carrying the affirmed culture and degrades groups carrying that which is condemned as deviant. (1967:178)

The functionalist, conflict, and moral entrepreneur theories of lawmaking are currently prominent in the law and society literature. Yet, none of these theories can account for the creation of all laws. On the basis of research evidence, however, some models come closer to providing a general explanation than do others. But how much closer they come depends on one's theoretical perspective. Some would argue that "the paradigm that is most compatible with the facts is one that recognizes the critical role played by social conflict in the generation of . . . law" (Chambliss, 1976:67). Others, in a similar vein, would argue for the explanatory power of *their* respective theoretical stances. Because a large number of laws are made by the legislative, administrative, and judicial bodies each day, it is always possible to select a few examples that illustrate almost any conceivable theoretical position. At best, the theories we have discussed explain in part how laws are made. Probably all these theories are at least partially correct, but it is doubtful that any single theory fully explains the creation of law, although one or another may account for the formation of any particular law or kind of law. With these considerations in mind, let us now turn to an examination of the processes of legislative, administrative, and judicial lawmaking.

LEGISLATION

The foremost legal task of legislative bodies is to make law (Loewenberg, Squire, and Kiewiet, 2002). The term "legislation" describes the deliberate creation of legal precepts by a body of government that gives articulate expression to such legal precepts in a formalized legal document. In Canada, "[t]he ultimate source and maker of law . . . is the legislative body having jurisdiction in the area. Because Canada is a confederation with 11 legislative bodies, each must be considered supreme in its own right, and therefore they are the ultimate makers of law" (Yates et al., 2000:35). However, since the 1982 introduction of the *Charter of Rights and Freedoms* into the Constitution of Canada, Canada has adopted a limited judicial check on the supremacy of parliament in that any parliamentary enactment that violates the rights set out in the Charter can be struck down by the courts.

Legislation, as such, must be distinguished from normative pronouncements made by the courts. The verbal expression of a legal rule or principle by a judge does not have the same degree of finality as the authoritative formulation of a legal proposition by a legislative body. Consider here that while "[h]istorically, changes to the law, which were made by judges in the common law system, occurred slowly and minutely, almost imperceptibly . . . [a] new statute . . . can make drastic changes with the stroke of a pen"(Yates et al., 2000:38). Furthermore, although both adjudication and legislation involve the deliberate creation of laws by a body of government, it should be remembered that the judiciary is not a body set up primarily for the purpose of lawmaking. As pointed out earlier, its main function is to decide disputes under a pre-existing law, and the law-creating function of the judges should be considered incidental to their primary function of adjudication.

There are several other differences that should be kept in mind between legislative and judicial lawmaking. Judge-made law stems from the decision of actual controversies. It provides no rules in advance for the decision of cases but waits for disputes to be brought before the court for decision. Although legislators are chronically playing catch-up and most commonly act in response to the rise of a social problem, they may also formulate rules in anticipation of cases. A judicial decision is based on a justification for applying a particular rule, whereas a statute usually does not contain an argumentative or justificatory statement. It simply states: this is forbidden, this is required, this is authorized. An opinion supporting a court decision is normally signed by the judge who wrote it. By contrast, a statute carries no signature (Fuller, 1968:89). In general, legislators have much more free-dom to make significant changes and innovations in the law than do the courts. The accu-mulation of precedents and the growth of an ever more complex body of principles have inevitably narrowed the scope of most judicial innovations. Legislators are also more respon-sive to public and private pressures than judges. Whereas judges deal with particular cases, legislators consider general problem areas with whole classes of related situations. At times, the attention of legislative bodies is drawn to a problem by a particular incident, but the law it eventually passes is designed for general applicability. For example, when the Canadian government passed the *Anti-Terrorism Act* (Bill C-36) in 2001, the terrorist attacks on the United States of September 11 were fresh in their minds, but the law that was enacted was designed to deal with a whole class of such possible occurrences.

Legislative lawmaking, at times, represents a response to some kind of problem, one acute enough to intrude on the well-being of a large number of individuals and their organ-izations or on the well-being of the government itself, one conspicuous enough to attract the attention of at least some legislators. Consider here that within a year of the September 11 attacks, governments in no fewer than 50 nations worldwide enacted or proposed laws (e.g., the 2001 *USA Patriot Act*; Britain's *Anti-Terrorism Crime and Security Act 2001*) that shifted the balance between security and liberty away from a privacy-protective stance and toward a stance that emphasized the preservation of security. According to the human rights group Privacy International and the Electronic Privacy Information Centre (EPIC), four trends may be observed in the legislation created in the immediate aftermath of the September 11 attack: "the swift erosion of pro-privacy laws; greater data sharing among corporations, police and spy agencies; greater eavesdropping; and sharply increased inter-est in people-tracking technologies, such as face recognition systems and national ID cards" (McCullagh, 2002). In the United States, for example, the September 11 attacks led to the *USA Patriot Act*, signed into law by President Bush on October 26, 2001, which expanded all forms of electronic surveillance, allowing increased information sharing between the CIA and federal police, and encouraging Internet providers to work closely with police agencies. Although Posner (2001) argues that the erosion of civil liberties that has occurred in such national security initiatives should not trouble civil libertarians, main-taining that "[t]he safer the nation feels, the more weight judges will be willing to give to the liberty interest," he admits that "[h]uman security may be the precondition to liberty, but it should not be valued above liberty for, when so weighted, it is capable of destroying liberty. A society that exaggerates its security requirements can debase the values it cher-ishes." Cohen (2005:549) acknowledges that Canada's *Anti-Terrorism Act* has been "as beset by controversy and condemnation as other national initiatives" and notes that "state authorities now possess strong powers that they did not have in their arsenal before 9/11." He identifies, among areas of particular contention and concern, the Act's "listing proce-dure to identify terrorist entities and freeze and seize their assets; powers of preventive detention and compelled questioning; augmented search, seizure and wiretap capabilities; substantive offences of enlarged scope and breadth; [and] suspicious transaction/terrorist financing reporting requirements." While Cohen is cautiously optimistic that Canada's leg-islation contains elements of "cautious restraint" that distinguish it from other national security initiatives, he acknowledges that, "[t]he practice of democracy is more art than science. Obviously, calibrating the appropriate balance between the need to be secure and the requirements of liberty in a free society is a weighty responsibility" (2005: 569; see also Chapter 5).

Legislation can also be generated, among other ways, by social unrest, conflict, and environmental deterioration and technological innovation (Lazarus, 2004). For example, Susan Martha Kahn's (2000:2) *Reproducing Jews: A Cultural Account of Assisted Conception in Israel* notes that not only has Israel been a "global leader" in the research and development of the new reproductive technologies (e.g., artificial insemination, ovum donation, and in-vitro fertilization), but "Israeli lawyers have actively fought for legislation guaranteeing broad-based access to reproductive technology, whether by challenging existing regulations that limit access to these technologies or by drafting innovative legislation regarding their use." She reports that, in Israel, the issue of reproduction has "deep political and historical roots": "Some feel they must have children to counterbalance what they believe to be a demographic threat represented by Palestinian and Arab birthrates. Others believe they must produce soldiers to defend the fledgling state. Some feel pressure to have children in order to 'replace' the six million Jews killed in the Holocaust. Many Jews simply have traditional notions of family life that are very child centred. Finally, there are a range of cultural sensitivities to practices designed to limit Jewish births, given that such policies were often employed in various diaspora contexts as part of other anti-Semitic measures" (2000:3). In consequence, it is not, perhaps, surprising that Israel has shown unbridled enthusiasm for creating laws and implementing social policies which encourage and facilitate the use of these new technologies or that there are more fertility clinics per capita in that country than in any other country in the world: by the mid-1990s, Israel, with a population of 5.5 million, had 24 fertility clinics— four times the number per capita that existed in the United States. Similarly indicative of that country's embrace of these technologies, "every Israeli, regardless of religion or status, is eligible for unlimited rounds of in-vitro fertilization treatment free of charge, up to the birth of two live children"—a commitment which "theoretically obligates the state to subsidize hundreds of thousands of dollars of infertility treatment . . . as a standard part of the basic basket of health services." In 1996, when Israeli legislators passed the Embryo-Carrying Agreements Law, it became the first country in the world to legalize surrogate mother agreements.

Although the reality of a falling birth rate in Canada since the mid-1960s could have prompted legislators in this country to similar efforts, Canada has been far more cautious in its response to the new reproductive technologies (Caulfield, Knowles, and Meslin, 2004; Machado and Burns, 2000). In 1989, a Royal Commission on New Reproductive Technologies was established, issuing its final report (tellingly entitled *Proceed with Care*) in 1993. This report recommended that the government ban the sale of eggs, sperm, embryos, and fetal tissue, surrogate motherhood, and the sale of eggs in exchange for in-vitro services; close clinics that provide sex selection services; and control in-vitro fertilization. The introduction of Bill C-47, the *Reproductive and Genetic Technologies Act*, followed but died after first reading in the House of Commons when a federal election was called in the spring of 1997. After three more failed attempts to create a law to govern reproductive technologies, the *Assisted Human Reproduction Act* (Bill C-13) received Royal Assent on March 26, 2004. Canada's law currently bans "human cloning, commercial (but not volunteer) surrogacy contracts, the sale of human sperm and eggs, sex selection (if used for purposes other than the prevention, diagnosis and treatment of a sex-linked disorder or defect), genetic alteration, creation of artificial wombs and retrieval of eggs from fetuses and cadavers" (Dranoff, 2005:15).

The list of legislation proposed and/or passed in response to the emergence of new problems or to the successful dramatization of old ones could be extended infinitely. But neither legislators' recognition of a social problem nor their recognition of a group's particular claims for action is certain to lead to legislation. The probability of some form of legislative response increases when (1) powerful interest groups mobilize their members to seek legislative action; (2) the unorganized public becomes intensely concerned with an issue, or conversely, is indifferent to the particular measures advocated by an interest group; and (3) there is no pressure to maintain the status quo or opposition to the proposed legislation.

Typically, the introduction of a legislative plan is preceded by a series of pre-lawmaking "stages" of activity. The first stage is the *instigation and publicizing* of a particular problem (such as nuclear waste disposal). Typical instigators include the mass media (such as special TV programs or a series of articles or editorials in major newspapers or news magazines) or an author (as we shall see later in this chapter) who documents and dramatizes a social problem. The second stage is *information-gathering.* It entails collecting data on the nature, magnitude, and consequences of a problem; alternative schemes for solving the problem and their costs, benefits, and inherent difficulties; the likely political impact of each scheme; and the feasibility of various compromises. The third stage is *formulation,* or devising and advocating a specific legislative remedy for the problem. The fourth stage is *interests-aggregation,* or obtaining support for the proposed measure from other lawmakers through trade-offs and compromises (that is, if you support my proposal, I will support yours); the championing of one interest group over others; or mediating among conflicting groups. The fifth stage is *mobilization,* the exertion of pressures, persuasion, or control on behalf of a measure by one who is able, often by virtue of his or her institutional position, to take effective and relatively direct action to secure enactment. Whether an issue goes beyond the first three stages usually depends on the support it receives from individuals, groups, or governmental units that possess authority and legitimacy in the policy area, and on the support that the proponents of a proposal are able to muster from key figures in the legislature. The last stage is *modification*, the marginal alteration of a proposal, sometimes strengthening it, and sometimes granting certain concessions to its opponents to facilitate its introduction (Price, 1972:4).

These six stages, although they show a certain sequential character and complementarity, do not simply represent the components that the legislative process must "necessarily" include. They also illustrate the norms that govern the legislative process (for example, the airing of an issue and the attempt to accommodate diverse interests) and the thoroughly political character of the legislative lawmaking process.

ADMINISTRATIVE LAWMAKING

Administrative agencies engage in lawmaking through rulemaking and through the adjudication of cases and controversies arising under their jurisdiction. Administrative agencies pursue both civil remedies and criminal sanctions to promote compliance with regulatory and administrative laws (Beerman, 2003; Kerrigan et al., 1993). Administrative lawmaking plays an increasingly important role in modern society (Evan, 1990:89), and its consequences are felt in all walks of life.

The intent of this section is to examine the fundamental processes involved in that kind of lawmaking in the context of administrative rulemaking and adjudication.

Administrative Rulemaking

Administrative rulemaking refers to the establishment of prospective rules (Beerman, 2003). *A rule is a law made by an administrative agency.* Through rulemaking, a particular administrative agency legislates policy.

> For example, a workers' compensation board is created by provincial legislation called the *Workers' Compensation Act*, and the chairman [sic] of its board (or the minister responsible) is given the power under that act to make the regulations necessary to fulfill the goals of the legislation. The board's authority would include the power to specify under what circumstances a person will receive compensation, and how much. As long as the regulations are within the limits of the authority granted by the legislation, they have the force of law. (Yates et al., 2000:37)

The fact that the *Canada Gazette* (which contains notices about regulations of the federal government) grew from a 3120-page, 4-volume consolidation in 1955 to a 14 420-page, 18-volume set in 1978 and accumulated over 40 000 additional pages by 1987 (Bogart, 2002:29) is simply one indicator of the considerable increase in administrative rulemaking. Another is provided by the observation that the rules and regulations passed by federal and provincial bodies authorized to create such regulations "are more voluminous than the provincial and federal legislation authorizing them" (Yates et al., 2000:37).

The flexibility of agencies in rulemaking procedures is much greater than in administrative adjudication. Formal hearings are not held unless required by statute. Administrators are free to consult informally with interested parties and are not bound by the more rigid requirements of adjudicative hearings. The number of parties that may participate is also potentially far greater than in adjudicative proceedings, where only those directly affected by an administrative order have standing (that is, are directly involved in litigation).

Much of the immense code of federal regulations is composed of the substantive rules of administrative agencies. Consider that the rules and regulations of the *Income Tax Act* (a nearly 2000-page compendium) are amended so often that they are republished annually in book form (Statistics Canada, 1998). At this point, it should be noted that administrative agencies issue a variety of pronouncements less formal and binding than their "legislative" regulations, which are designed to clarify the laws they are administering (see, for example, Schwartz, 1995). Some of these are described as "interpretative regulations" (which, for example, set out under what circumstances a professor may deduct his or her office at home as a business expense). Moreover, in response to inquiries, agencies sometimes issue "advisory rulings," which interpret the law with reference to particular types of situations such as the disposal of certain types of potentially hazardous wastes. In addition, some agencies also publish instructions, guides, explanatory pamphlets, and so forth.

Regulatory agencies state many of their regulatory policies through rulemaking. Rate-setting proceedings (for example, the limits on fees brokerage houses may charge for a certain class of services) of regulatory bodies are also considered to be rulemaking. Outside of the regulatory realm, various government departments are constantly stating their general policies through the issuance of rules ranging from banking practices to dress codes in the military.

Administrative Adjudication

The second way in which agencies create rules is through their adjudicative powers. **Administrative adjudication** is the process by which an administrative agency issues an order. Adjudication is the administrative equivalent of a judicial trial. As we pointed out in

Chapter 3, adjudication differs from rulemaking in that it applies only to a specific, limited number of parties involved in an individual case before the agency. Administrative orders have retroactive effect, as contrasted with the prospective effect of rulemaking. In rulemaking, the agency is apprising in advance those under its jurisdiction of what the law is. When an agency opens proceedings with the intention of issuing an order, it must eventually interpret existing policy or define new policy to apply to the case at hand. The parties involved do not know how the policy is going to be applied until after the order is issued, giving the agency decision retroactive effect. Adjudicative lawmaking tends to produce inconsistencies because cases are decided on an individual basis. The rule of *stare decisis* (requiring precedent to be followed, which will be discussed in the context of judicial lawmaking) need not prevail (West, 1985:53), and the high turnover of top-level administrators often results in a lack of continuity.

Since many agencies have the power to both issue regulations and adjudicate cases, they can choose between the two methods of lawmaking. When an agency believes that the time has come to formulate a policy decision in an official text, it can draft and issue a regulation. But when an agency prefers to wait until the contours of a problem become clearer, it can continue to deal with the problem on a case-by-case basis, formulating a series of decisional rules couched in terms that ensure continuing flexibility (for example, individual workers' compensation claims). Furthermore, an agency, unlike a court, does not have to wait passively for cases to be brought before it. Its enforcement officials can go out looking for cases that will raise the issues its adjudicating officials want to rule on. And because the agency can decide for itself what enforcement proceedings to initiate, it can choose cases that present the issues in such a way that the court will be likely to uphold the agency's ruling if an appeal is taken.

JUDICIAL LAWMAKING

The role of the judiciary in the administrative state has been complex. In reviewing the historical record, Arthurs (1980:225) charges that "the courts utterly failed to deal with the most significant legal repercussions of the Industrial Revolution in the nineteenth century and with the revolution of rising expectations in the twentieth." William Bogart (1994:111) concurs that, historically, in areas such as workers' compensation, labour relations, and human rights, the courts almost invariably responded with a "distressing rigidity."

> In administrative issues our judges have mostly been the keepers of pure liberal ideology: the state assigned minimalist policing functions, and the market was the best distributor of goods and services. Whether it was in such matters as occupational health and safety, the development of human rights, or the advent of unions and collective bargaining, the courts' activities wove a pattern of indifference, even hostility towards state activities . . . . [U]nder the guise of principles that seemed to treat everyone equally, the health and safety of workers were ignored with abandon, poisons were dumped into the environment, and the most insidious acts of prejudice were taken as a hallmark of self-regarding behaviour. (Bogart, 1994:111)

Within these areas, Bogart (1994:116) observes, a common pattern emerged: (i) the courts' initial proposal of rules that extolled "strict liberal notions of individual responsibility, autonomy, and freedom centred on economic entitlement"; (ii) the adoption of a more communitarian perspective by legislatures that "inquired into the actual results, and recognized other values (such as the need for compensation, legitimacy of collective action, and claims to equal treatment)"; (iii) the creation of an administrative body; and, finally, (iv) the removal of these issues from the courts, "at least in terms of initial deci-sion-making and the creation of some administrative agency to decide such questions."

Although the record of the courts is not exemplary, in the postwar period, a number of countries have attempted to "harness litigation and the courts to effect social and political change" (Bogart, 2001:144). The most notable example is the United States, where, as early as the mid-19th century, Alexis de Tocqueville (1969:270) observed that there was "hardly a political question . . . which does not sooner or later turn into a judicial one." In the United States, there has been a steady increase in judicial lawmaking over the years (Canon and Johnson, 1999) and the "list of issues that have been placed before courts. . . in the last decades seems endless" (Bogart, 2001:160). There, in many instances, legisla-tors and administrators have shown considerable willingness to let judges take the heat for controversial actions, such as allowing or disallowing abortion, or ordering busing to desegregate schools. As a result, the judiciary in the United States has assumed an increas-ingly powerful role. As Henry J. Abraham has remarked, "It is simply a fact of life that in the United States all social and political issues sooner or later seem to become judicial" (1994:21). However, the question of whether or not courts *should* assume an enhanced role in society is of obvious interest to Canadians since the 1982 adoption of the *Canadian Charter of Rights and Freedoms.*

While the Charter, unlike the US Bill of Rights, explicitly provides that any rights are subject to "reasonable limits prescribed by law as can be demonstrably justified in a free and democratic society," it additionally empowers judges to strike down legislation and/or nullify actions of public officials that contravene the rights enumerated within the Charter. And, after displaying a certain initial timidity, Canadian courts have now tackled "ques-tions relating to abortion, mercy killing, assisted suicide, language rights, and a broad array of issues relating to the administration of criminal justice" (Bogart, 2001:151). Indeed, Sauvageau, Schneiderman, and Tara (2006:21) argue that there is a notable con-gruence between de Tocqueville's mid-19th century comments about the judiciary in America and a recent observation by Chief Justice Beverly McLachlin: "More and more, courts are being called upon to decide questions of central importance to great numbers of people in our society."

As Kelly (2004:124) observes, "Since the entrenchment of the Charter of Rights and Freedoms in the Constitution, there are some who take the view that [Canadian] judges have, to a certain extent, usurped or taken over the role of the legislature in the making of law." However, a number of questions remained unanswered. Among them: "Does equip-ping courts with the power to nullify the enactments of elected officials change the polit-ical process, making the forging of policy through popular politics more difficult? Do rights anchored in courts mean less agreement regarding the common good?" (2004:150). As well, given concern with maintaining a national identity in the shadow of the most pow-erful nation of the world, one might also ask, could the entrenchment of rights and the enhanced role of the judiciary lead to our country becoming progressively more indistin-guishable from the United States?

In the United States, courts have tended "to move from the byways onto the highways of policy making" (Horowitz, 1977:9). In fact, Nathan Glazer argues that Americans have developed an "Imperial Judiciary"—that is, the courts now have so much power, play such a great role in lawmaking, that they pose a threat to the vitality of the political system. Glazer contends that too much power has moved from the elected, representative branches of government to the judiciary, and that the courts "are now seen as forces of nature, difficult to predict and impossible to control" (1975:110). Judicial activity has now been extended, for example, to welfare, prison, and mental hospital administration, to education and employment policy, to road and bridge building, to automotive safety standards, and to management of natural resources. Some activist judges are described by Mary Ann Glendon (1994) as "romantic judges" who follow their passions of "do-gooding" and use due process and equal protection to justify making law rather than interpreting it. These judges are bold, creative, compassionate, and result-oriented, and they do not let tradition, precedent, or non-romantic readings of the Constitution get in the way.

However, leaving the formation of domestic policy—whether in relation to health care, education, support for families, welfare entitlement, or crime prevention—to "judicial activism" is highly controversial (Leo and Thomas, 1998). In the United States, questions have been raised about the policymaking role of judges in the American system of government. There, the role of judges is to apply the law, and the policymaking activities carried out by the Supreme Court in interpreting the Constitution in view of social changes is considered by some to be an impermissible expansion of the powers granted to the judicial branch. The increase in judicial activism, some have argued, has created a legislative body that is not accountable to the American people (Graglia, 1994).

In like spirit, William Bogart (2001:145) remarks that in Canada:

> Politicians, no matter how wrong-headed, can point to the power of the ballot as the source of legitimacy of their actions: the force they wield rests on the base of the democratic process. Life, for courts, is more complicated. Since the power they exercise can, by definition, be anti-majoritarian, proponents of an ambitious judicial role have to offer a rationale that does not depend on popular will or authority.

Prior to discussing when and how judges make law, it is important to review the salient features of the adjudicative process. Adjudication is focused. The typical question before the judge is simply: does one party have a right, or does another party have a duty? This should be contrasted with the question before legislators and administrators: what are the alternatives? Adjudication is also piecemeal, and the lawsuit is a good illustration of incremental decision-making. Furthermore, courts must act when litigants present their cases before them. In the end, a judgment cannot be escaped. Moreover, fact finding in adjudication is poorly adapted to the ascertainment of social facts. The unrepresentative character of the litigants makes it difficult to generalize from their situation to a wider context. Finally, adjudication makes no provision for policy review. Judges base their decisions on behaviour that antedates the litigation. Consequential facts—those that relate to the impact of a decision on behaviour—are equally important but much neglected. This results, as we have noted, in an emphasis on rights and duties rather than on alternatives.

Lawmaking by Precedents

Judicial formulation of rules is based frequently on the principle that judges should build on the precedents established by past decisions, known as the doctrine of *stare decisis* ("stand by what has been decided"), which is a deeply rooted common-law tradition (Carp and Stidham, 1996:295). By contrast, civil-law countries, such as France and Germany, have a codified legal system where the basic law is stated in *codes*. These are statutes enacted by the national parliament, which arranges whole fields of law (family law, housing law, and so forth) in an orderly, logical, and comprehensive way. The judges follow the basic principles of law found in acts of parliament. In common-law countries, judges base their decisions on *case law*, a body of opinion developed by judges over time in the course of deciding particular cases. The doctrine of precedent, the notion that the judge is bound by what has already been decided, is a strictly common-law doctrine (Friedman, 1998:2002).

In the common-law system, following precedents is often much easier and less time-consuming than reformulating solutions to problems that have already been faced. It enables the judge to take advantage of the accumulated wisdom of preceding generations. It minimizes arbitrariness and compensates for weakness and inexperience. It conforms to the belief that "like wrongs deserve like remedies" and to the desire for "equal justice under the law." More important, the practice of following precedents enables individuals (with the assistance of lawyers) to plan their conduct in the expectation that past decisions will be honoured in the future. Although certainty, predictability, and continuity are not the only objectives of law, they are certainly important ones. Many disputes are avoided, and others are settled without litigation simply because individuals are familiar with how the courts will respond to certain types of behaviour (see, for example, Geel, 2005).

But judicial formulations of rules are frequently revised and restated by the courts in cases presenting the same or similar problems. A judge may also be confronted with a case for which there are simply no precedents. To make a decision, judges must search through cases for any analogies that seem applicable. Through the selection of appropriate and desirable analogies (which is, indeed, a value judgment), judges make law in instances when they are not guided by precedents. In general, in view of the way courts deal with legal rules laid down in earlier decisions (by rephrasing, qualifying, broadening, narrowing, or changing such rules, or by analogies), a precedent must be considered a weaker and less authoritative source of law than a statute.

The Interpretation of Statutes

In interpreting statutes, judges determine the effects of legislative decisions. For many, a legislative decree is not a law until enforced and interpreted by the courts (Jacob, 1984:37). In the vast majority of cases involving the application of statutes, the courts have no trouble determining how to apply the statute. Most cases fall squarely inside or outside of the law's provisions.

In some cases, however, the intent of a legislature is ambiguous. Some statutes contain unintentional errors and ambiguities because of bad drafting of the law. Other statutes are unclear because those who pushed them through the legislature sought to avoid opposition by being vague or silent on potentially controversial matters. An important reason for the lack of clarity in many instances is that the proponents have not been able to foresee and provide for all possible future situations. This provides the courts with a potential opportunity to engage in lawmaking.

In order to forestall misinterpretation from occurring, a statute is generally crafted to begin with a section that defines terms used within it. There are also federal and provincial interpretations that outline certain rules of interpretation that apply to all statutes. Beyond these legislative interpretation rules, the courts have developed three main rules of statutory interpretation: the literal rule; the golden rule; and the mischief rule. The fore-most principle of interpretation, the **literal rule** (sometimes called the "plain meaning rule") sets out that the statute should be applied literally, regardless of whether or not the judge approves or disapproves of its result. As Olivo (2004:71) remarks of this rule, "If Parliament is supreme, then it may be unfair or absurd if it chooses to be, subject to limits on legislative action imposed by the *Charter of Rights and Freedoms*." The golden rule and mischief rule address ambiguous legislation. The **golden rule** specifies that in cases where the literal interpretation of a statute would lead to a "logical absurdity, an inconsistency or a repugnancy," the court can move from the literal interpretation—but "only so far as is necessary to remove the conflicting construction." The **mischief rule** states that when con-fronted by ambiguous statutes, "attention should be given to the problem the statute was created to solve" or "what mischief. . . the statute [was] designed to suppress, or what rem-edy is being advanced by it" (Yates et al., 2000:39).

In addition, judges may use a variety of external aids to assist their interpretation of statutes including scholarly and interpretive writings, interpretation statutes (which exist at both the federal and provincial levels), and the legislative history of statutes. Olivo (2004:73) notes that although "[i]n the search for legislative intent, it has long been tradi-tional in Canada and Britain to ignore Hansard (the official record of debates in a legisla-ture), committee reports, royal commission reports, ministers' speeches, press releases, and other such documents" with the assumption that "one need go no further than the words of the statute" to find its meaning, there is "some indication" that legislative history may have a legitimate interpretive role" in Charter of Rights cases. He reports a "growing use of the technique in constitutional cases as a way of gaining insight into the meaning of legislation under the constitutional challenge."

INFLUENCES ON THE LAWMAKING PROCESSES

Lawmaking is a complex and continuous process, and it exists as a response to a number of social influences that operate in society. The forces that influence lawmaking cannot always be precisely determined, measured, or evaluated. At times, a multitude of forces are in operation simultaneously. Although a variety of forces can exert influence on the law-making process, in this section we shall consider only the roles of vested interests, public opinion, and the social sciences—the ones most prominently discussed in the law and soci-ety literature.

Interest Groups

The interest group thesis contends that laws are created because of the special interests of certain groups in the population (Mahood, 2000). The image of society reflected by this view stresses cultural differences, value clashes, inequities, and social conflict (Hajnal and Clark, 1998). Examples of interest group influence in lawmaking abound (see, for exam-ple, Gioacchino, Ginebri, and Salbani, 2004; Rozell and Wilcox, 1999). Laws governing the use of alcohol, regulations concerning sexual conduct, abortion bills, pure food and drug legislation, and antitrust laws are all documented instances of interest group activity (Quinney, 1970:49). However, even when interest groups achieve their goal, their response may be inconsistent with their previously stated demands. For example, Nick Larsen

(1999:62) has observed that the manner in which police in Vancouver, Edmonton, Winnipeg, and Toronto implemented Bill C-49 (which effectively criminalized all public communication for the purposes of prostitution) was incongruous with the leading role that Canadian police played in the "concerted political campaign to force the federal government to enact much tougher laws for the control of street prostitution." Although crackdowns were initially instituted in all four cities following the proclamation of Bill C-49, they were short-lived and the police "frequently exhibited considerable ambivalence regarding the specific approaches that they applied to the implementation of the new law" (1999:71). In addition, he notes that none of the municipal governments in these cities ever attempted to formulate a long-term strategy by which to control street prostitution. He observes:

> Inasmuch as police and municipal politicians had extensively lobbied the federal government for tougher laws to control street prostitution, this omission is nothing short of incredible. It suggests that these groups either were not sincere in their calls for tougher legislation or else lacked the ability to implement the law in a coherent fashion. Unfortunately, neither conclusion speaks well for the integrity or competence of the police and local politicians. (1999:70)

Throughout the legislative process that resulted in the proclamation of Bill C-49, various groups (including, for example, the police, residents' groups, politicians, and prostitutes' rights groups such as POWER [Prostitutes and Other Women for Equal Rights]) were all involved in shaping the legislation to fit their interests or views. Some, obviously, were more successful than others. Often, interest groups act as a communication network for social movements, facilitating the dissemination of their ideas in a manner that helps to legitimize it, exerting public pressure for legal change, attracting some politicians to the movements' objectives and, in such ways, effecting policy change (Yarnold, 1992:115).

The nature of the interaction between interest groups and lawmakers varies to an extent based on the branch of the government. Judges, although they are not immune to interest group pressures, are generally not lobbied in the same way as legislators or administrators. To reach the courts, a lawyer must be hired, formal proceedings must be followed, and grievances must be expressed in legal terminology. To influence legislators, a group must be economically powerful or able to mobilize a large number of voters (Jacob, 1984:150). Minorities and the poor may find the courts more attractive because they are more readily available: if a group has enough money to hire a lawyer, it can seek court action to further its interests. Interest groups may also turn to courts because they assume that the judiciary may be more sympathetic to their objectives than legislators (Carp and Stidham, 2004:122; Cowan, 2005). However, the importance of wealth in accessing the courts or mobilizing an effective interest group should be apparent.

The techniques used by interest groups to influence courts are different from those used to influence legislative or administrative bodies. Notes Jacob: "The principal techniques are: to bring conflicts to a court's attention by initiating test cases, to bring added information to the courts through *amicus curiae* (friend of the court) briefs, and to communicate with judges indirectly by placing information favourable to the group's cause in legal and general periodicals" (1984:151). By instituting test cases, interest groups provide judges with opportunities to make policies by which they overcome the otherwise passive nature of the judicial process. Often, such briefs communicate relevant social science research findings to a particular case (Roesch et al., 1991). By providing information through *amicus curiae* briefs, interest groups expand the confines of the judicial process and build coalitions with other groups (McGuire, 1994). The final technique is to publish decisions in legal periodicals. Judges generally read these journals to keep abreast of legal scholarship and sometimes even cite them as authority for their ruling. Publication in these journals gets one's views before the courts and before their attentive public.

Interactions between interest groups and legislative and administrative lawmakers are more overtly political in nature. Many interest groups maintain offices staffed with people who keep track of developments in the legislative and administrative branches and attempt to influence their activities. Some groups pay for the services of law firms in dealing with legislators or administrators. These firms provide expertise in such areas as antitrust and tax regulations and use their personal contacts with important lawmakers on behalf of their clients.

A number of specific conditions can be identified that enhance the potential influence of interest groups on lawmakers (Ripley, 1980). In many instances, there may not be two competing groups on an issue. When only one point of view is presented, the group is likely to get much of what it wants. Similarly, if the groups on one side of a controversy are unified and coordinated on the principal issues they want to push (or if they can minimize their disagreements), they will enhance their chances of success. If certain key members of legislative bodies believe in the interest group's position, the probability of success is greatly enhanced. The visibility of an issue is another consideration in influencing lawmakers. When the issue is not too visible, or when interest groups seek single distinct amendments to bills (such as to alter soybean export quotas in addition to others proposed by farming interests), as contrasted with large legislative packages, the chances for success increase. Conversely, as the visibility of issues increases and public attention grows (such as wage-price controls), the influence of interest groups tends to diminish. Interest groups are likely to have greater influence on issues that coincide with the interests of the groups they purport to represent. For example, unions such as the United Steel Workers Canada or CAW Canada may be very influential in matters concerning working conditions, but they are likely to receive less attention from lawmakers when they advocate higher tariffs for imported goods or when they make attempts to guide foreign policy. Finally, interest groups are likely to have greater influence on amendments than on entire pieces of legislation. This is because amendments are generally technical and less understood by the public.

In general, the effectiveness of interest groups in influencing lawmakers is related to such considerations as their financial and information resources, their offensive or defensive positions, and the status of the group in the eyes of lawmakers. Financial resources determine the ability of an interest group to support court suits, lobbying, public relations, and other activities (Abramson, 1998). Interest groups that support the status quo have an advantage over groups trying to bring change, because whereas the latter must overcome several obstacles in the lawmaking process, the former may frustrate change at any of several points in the process. But the influence of an interest group depends mainly on its status as perceived by lawmakers. An interest group is particularly influential in situations where a lawmaker shares the same group affiliation (for example, when farm groups talk to legislators who are farmers), where the group is considered important to the legislator's constituency, and where the group is recognized as a legitimate and reliable source of information. In addition, a group's competence to influence lawmaking is enhanced by its ability to bring about social or economic disruptions. Threats of disorder, disruption, and violence have been, at times, effective bargaining weapons of relatively powerless groups. Similarly, the threat of a decline in the supply of such necessities as food, medical services, and energy have been used to influence lawmakers. There is little doubt that the ability of an interest group to create a crisis, whether a social disorder, an economic slowdown, or the reduction of supply of a needed product or service, gives it considerable clout in the lawmaking process.

Public Opinion

When the relationship between law and popular will was refined in the 19th century, theorists of law and society were concerned with the origins of law and the development of legal institutions (see Chapter 2 and Althaus, 2003). Legal development was viewed as a sequence of events. First, practices and sentiments occur in a group of people without their awareness that they are the "right" ones or the "only" ones. Eventually, particularly on occasions of deviance from prior practice, *a* way of acting or believing becomes *the* way of acting or believing. Custom becomes law.

It is easier to substantiate the association between popular sentiments and law in traditional societies (Llewellyn and Hoebel, 1941:10). As a society becomes more complex, there is a less direct correspondence between public opinion and the law. In a traditional society, one comes to know intimately the law of one's tribe. It is highly unlikely that today one can know, let alone tinker with, much of the law that could affect one's life. As a result of such limited awareness, there is a fair amount of selectivity involved in the expression of opinions toward the law. Some questions, therefore, arise in the discussion of the influence of public opinion on lawmaking. One concerns the timing of the relationship between public opinion and lawmaking. At what point does the accumulation of practice and belief make the reflection of those practices and beliefs in law an inevitability? For example, how many marijuana violations cause the law relating to marijuana to be changed?

A related question concerns the identification of those individuals whose opinion is expressed in lawmaking and the means of translating those opinions into legal outcomes. The *people* may mean a numerical majority, an influential elite, women, the poor, the middle class, the young, the aged, students, professors, and so forth. Popular views may be similar throughout all segments of the population, but on many important issues opinions will differ.

A more meaningful way of looking at the influence of public opinion on lawmaking would be to consider the diverse opinions of many "publics" (that is, segments of society) bearing on specific concerns such as sentencing offenders for particular crimes (Walker and Hough, 1988). These opinions are expressed through a multitude of channels, such as the media, political parties, and the various types of interest groups. Care should be exercised, however, not to overestimate the catalytic part played by public opinion in lawmaking. As Friedman states:

> The "public opinion" that affects the law is like the economic power which makes the market. This is so in two essential regards: Some people, but only some, take enough interest in any particular commodity to make their weight felt; second, there are some people who have more power and wealth than others. At one end of the spectrum stand such figures as the president of. . . General Motors; at the other. . . babies, and prisoners. (1975:163)

The differential influence of public opinion on lawmaking processes is a well-known phenomenon and is recognized by lawmakers. Lawmakers are aware that some people are more equal than others because of money, talent, or choice. Notes Friedman:

> They know that 100 wealthy, powerful constituents. . . outweigh thousands of poor, weak constituents. . . Most people do not shout, threaten, or write letters. They remain quiet and obscure,

unless a head count reveals they are there. This is the "silent majority"; paradoxically, this group matters only when it breaks its silence—when it mobilizes or is mobilized by others. (1975:164)

Lawmakers also know that most people have no clear opinions on most issues with which judicial, administrative, and legislative bodies must deal. This means that they have a wide latitude within which to operate. Thus, for example, when a legislator claims to be representing the opinion of his or her riding, he or she is, on most issues, representing the opinion of only a minority of the constituents, because most do not know or care about the issue at hand and do not communicate their views on it.

In spite of these considerations, public opinion does exert an influence on the law-making process (Carp and Stidham, 2004:296). Dennis S. Ippolito and his associates (1976) identify three types of influences that press lawmakers into formulating certain decisions. These three types are direct, group, and indirect influences.

Direct influence refers to constituent pressures that offer rewards or sanctions to law-makers. Rewards for compliance and sanctions for noncompliance may be votes in an election campaign, financial assistance, and other forms of pressure that could possibly range from the representative's standing in lawmaking bodies to prestige in his or her own particular community. But this kind of influence is not confined to legislators. Members of the judiciary are also pressured by partisan publications to make certain decisions consistent with opinions and interests that run throughout the jurisdiction of a particular court.

The second type of influence, **group influence**, is distinctly that of organized interest groups representing a special constituency. Political parties, interest groups, and citizen action groups are continually influencing the lawmaking process. In the area of administrative law, for example, special-interest groups press regulatory agencies for rules and regulations that are in keeping with their own immediate interests. Public opinion in these and other areas is represented by organization leaders. The motivation behind joining such groups is the perceived need for expressing a point of view in a manner that will influence lawmakers. In this context, public opinion becomes organized around a specific issue or an immediate objective (for example, the pros and cons of euthanasia or abortion). Through the process of organizing, interests are made specific, and public opinion backing is sought in the attempt to gain an advantage in pressing for change or redress through the legal machinery.

The third type of public opinion model, **indirect influence**, is that which influences the lawmaking process indirectly. Here a lawmaker acts in the capacity of an "instructed delegate." The decisions made are on behalf of the desires of a particular constituency, for example, those residents living around an airport who oppose expansion of facilities. Ippolito (1976:3) and his colleagues state that indirect influence occurs when legislators act in accordance with constituent preferences because they either share such preferences or believe such preferences should prevail over their own judgment. This type of influence is indicative of the importance attached to public opinion polls.

Public opinion polls seek to determine the aggregate view people hold in a community on current important issues. Polling is flourishing in Canada. Today, there are many well-established commercial firms that take public opinion polls. They often work jointly with major TV networks or newspapers and magazines. In addition, there are a variety of smaller, specialized public and private and university polling organizations. Scores of surveys have been commissioned by federal agencies and by various governmental bodies. A typical sample size for national polls is around 1500 respondents. Pollsters claim that with a sample of that size, there is a 95 percent probability that the results obtained are no more than three percentage points off the figure that would be obtained if every adult in the country were interviewed.

Opinion polls clearly influence what lawmakers do (Lipset, 1976). On a variety of domestic issues (for example, parental leave, abortion, no-fault divorce) public opinion has led or prompted lawmakers toward passage of a program that might have otherwise been delayed for months or years. However, in other instances (e.g., capital punishment, immigration policies, and treatment of refugee claimants) public opinion has either lagged behind government policy or tended to support measures that are repressive or dismissive of human rights.

Generally, the use of polls in lawmaking is encouraged. For example, Irving Crespi suggests that lawmakers could be more effective if they learned to draw upon the full fruits of survey research. Direct evidence—unfiltered by the interpretations of special interests or lobby groups—of the wants, needs, aspirations, and concerns of the general public needs to be accounted for in lawmaking activities. In lawmaking processes, Crespi argues, there should be, first, an attempt to determine the views of both the general public and that segment of the public that would be directly affected by a particular law. It could then make public opinion part of the formative stages of the lawmaking process, and not simply a force to be coped with after the fact. Says Crespi: "The difference between treating public attitudes and opinions as a relatively minor variable instead of an influence that should be authoritative is ultimately the difference between technocratic and democratic government" (1979:18). Yet, the issue may actually be more complex than Crespi's commentary would suggest. For example, one might rhetorically ask: if a democratic government enacts rights-enhancing legislation on a country whose population has been polled and revealed to oppose such legislation (or to be blatantly racist or misogynistic or homophobic), would that indicate bad government?

Lawmaking and Social Science

Lawmakers have long been aware of the contribution that social scientists can make to the lawmaking process (Zeisel, 1962:142). However, in an era increasingly dominated by scientific and technical specialists, it is not surprising that lawmakers increasingly reflect the quest for specialization and expertise. Experts abound in a variety of fields (Smith, 1992), and there is a growing reliance on social scientists and the research data they generate in diverse areas, ranging from consumer surveys in trademark suits to the impact of mandatory arrest policies for abusers in cases of domestic violence (Sherman, 1992; Berk and Newton, 1995). For example, in *R. v. Parks*, in which a black Jamaican was accused of killing a white person, the Ontario Court of Appeal noted "an ever growing body of studies and reports documenting the extent and intensity of racist beliefs in contemporary Canadian society"and ruled that the trial judge had erred in refusing a defence request to challenge potential jurors about whether or not they could be fair and impartial in evaluating this case. With the aid of social scientists, committees of legislative bodies have, at times, also produced important studies on such varied issues as insurance, investment banking, public utilities, prostitution and pornography, child abuse, and new reproductive technologies.

Efforts to bring social science to bear on lawmaking processes involve the use of both qualitative and quantitative social science data and the reliance on the social scientist as an expert witness in specific legal cases. Social science data may be collected and analyzed for academic purposes and later utilized by one or more sides of a dispute. Social science research may also be reactive in the sense that it is initially requested by parties in a dispute. In such instances, the materials may address facts in the case or initiate an intervention in a lawmaking process. Social science research may also be undertaken in a proactive fashion. In such a situation, a social scientist may undertake an investigation with the anticipation of subsequent use of the results by lawmakers. Recently, 40 researchers from Canada, the United States, the United Kingdom, Australia, Ireland, Thailand, Malaysia, South Korea, and China joined together in the International Tobacco Control Policy Evaluation Project; the aim of this project is to investigate and evaluate national-level tobacco control policies that will be introduced in the next few years in more than 100 countries. Their research, the first to evaluate the policies introduced by the first-ever international health treaty—The Framework Convention on Tobacco Control—is intended to establish the evidence base for FCTC policies by evaluating the effectiveness of such strategies as warning labels, advertising and promotion bans, higher taxes, and protections against secondhand smoke. According to the project's lead investigator, Canadian social scientist Geoffrey Fong, "Evidence from good science gives policymakers the courage to do what they know is right" (*University of Waterloo Bulletin*, 2006).

Social scientists can additionally participate in the lawmaking process as expert witnesses who testify typically for one of the litigants or appear before a legislative body. The demand for such service is evidenced by the various directories of expert witnesses and a growing body of literature on the intricacies of testifying in court or in front of legislative bodies (Brodsky, 2004). In *R. v. Edwards* (1996), the Ontario Court of Appeal relied on the testimony of Professor Anthony Doob, a Canadian criminologist and expert on sentencing research, to help resolve a sentencing appeal. In this case, the Crown appealed the sentence given to Edwards, who had been sentenced to nine years in prison (in addition to the one year he had already spent in prison at the time of sentencing) for the attempted murder of his former common-law wife. While the Crown sought to increase the sentence, arguing that cases involving domestic violence warranted harsher sentences as a deterrent to others, Doob "testified that research on general deterrence has shown that the magnitude of the penalty has little impact on potential offenders, since they assume that they will not be caught" and concluded his testimony by saying that "there is no evidence that suggests that more severe sentences would make offenders such [as this one] less likely to commit further offences" (in Roberts, 2001:193). In its ruling, the appellate court accepted Professor Doob's summary of research findings on this topic and dismissed the Crown's appeal.

At times, social scientists are asked to directly assist either the court or the legislator in the preparation of background documents pertinent to a particular issue or to serve on commissions intended for policy recommendations. However, there are controversies surrounding the role of social scientists in lawmaking. Daniel Patrick Moynihan (1979) proposes two general reasons why social scientists have been criticized for their involvement in lawmaking processes. First, he points out that social science is basically concerned with the prediction of future events, whereas the purpose of the law is to order them. Notes Moynihan: "But where social science seeks to establish a fixity of *relationships* such that the consequences of behaviour can be known in advance—or, rather, narrowed to a manageable range of possibilities—law seeks to dictate future performance on the basis of past *agreements*" (1979:16). For example, it is the function of the law to order alimony payments; it is the function of social science to attempt to estimate the likelihood of their being paid, of their effect on work behaviour and remarriage in male and female parties, or similar probabilities. The second reason he suggests is that "social science is rarely dispassionate, and social scientists are frequently caught up in the politics which their work necessarily involves" (1979:19).

Social scientists are, to a great extent, involved with problem solving, and the identification of a "problem" usually entails a political statement that implies a solution. Moynihan states: "Social scientists are never more revealing of themselves than when challenging the objectivity of one another's work. In some fields almost *any* study is assumed to have a more-or-less-discoverable political purpose" (1979:19). Furthermore, there is a distinct social and political bias among social scientists. As a result, the social sciences attract many people who are more interested in shaping the future than preserving the past. Moynihan feels that this orientation coupled with "liberal" tendencies and the limited explanatory power of social sciences results in a weakening of influence on lawmakers. He points out, for example, that after examining a number of recent studies concerning the effects of rehabilitation programs on criminals, no consistent effects could be shown one way or the other. Moynihan notes: "Seemingly, all that could be established for certain about the future behaviour of criminals is that when they are in jail they do not commit street crimes" (1979:20). Similarly, there are still controversies concerning the deterrent effects of the death penalty (see, for example, Chapter 5 and Wolfgang, 1998).

Obviously, when social science data yield uncertain results, the root causes of major problems remain elusive. When well-intentioned social scientists dispute about alternatives, it is not surprising that lawmakers are, at times, skeptical about social science and social scientists.

SOURCES OF IMPETUS FOR LAW

An *impetus* is a fundamental prerequisite for setting the mechanism of lawmaking in motion. Demands for new laws or changes in existing ones come from a variety of sources. In the following pages, several of the more widely analyzed and prominent sources of impetus for law creation are considered. These sources, which are not mutually exclusive, include detached scholarly diagnosis, a voice from the wilderness, protest activities, social movements, public interest groups, and the mass media.

Detached Scholarly Diagnosis

The impetus for law may come from a detached scholarly undertaking. From time to time, academicians may consider a given practice or condition as detrimental in the context of existing values and norms. They may communicate their diagnoses to their colleagues or to the general public through either scholarly or popular forums. In some cases, they may even carry the perceived injustice to the legislature in search of legal redress.

There have been a number of attempts by academics in a variety of disciplines to provide an impetus for lawmaking as an outgrowth of their investigations. Notable efforts include David Caplovitz's *The Poor Pay More* (1963) and *Consumers in Trouble: A Study of Debtors in Default* (1974), which argued for reform of consumer credit laws, and Amitai Etzioni's *Genetic Fix* (1973), which examined the implications of "human engineering." The source of impetus, however, is not limited to ivory towers. It can have other origins, as the following sections will demonstrate.

A Voice from the Wilderness

Through their writings, many people outside of academe succeed or even excel in calling public attention to a particular problem or social condition. For example, in the domain of environmental protection laws, it would be difficult not to consider the book *Silent Spring* by Rachel Carson (1962). It was the first time that the environmental threat posed by pesticides was announced to a wide audience. However, there is a long list of those whose literary efforts stimulated changes in the law. For our purposes, it will suffice to call attention to simply a few.

Around the beginning of the 20th century, there was a fair amount of concern in the United States about the quality of food products. In particular, numerous scandals had arisen over the quality of meat products. It was alleged that during the Spanish-American War, American soldiers were forced to eat cans of "embalmed beef." A number of horrible practices of manufacturers were revealed in the mass media, but a federal food and drug law had still not passed when, in 1906, Upton Sinclair published *The Jungle,* a novel about life in Chicago, which directed attention to the meat-packing industry. The first half of the book deals with a vivid description of conditions in the Chicago meat-packing plants. To illustrate:

> Tubercular pork was sold for human consumption. Old sausage, rejected in Europe and shipped back " mouldy and white," would be "dosed with borax and glycerin, and dumped into the hoppers, and made over again for home consumption." Meat was stored in rooms where "water from leaky roofs would drip over it, and thousands of rats would race about on it." The packers would put out poisoned bread to kill the rats; then the rats would die, and "rats, bread and meat would go into the hoppers together." Most horrifying of all was the description of the men in the "cooking rooms." They "worked in tankrooms full of steam," in some of which there were "open vats near the level of the floor." Sometimes they fell into the vats "and when they were fished out, there was never enough of them left to be worth exhibiting—sometimes they would be overlooked for days, till all but the bones of them had gone out to the world as Durham's Pure Leaf Lard." (Quoted by Friedman and Macaulay, 1977:611)

When it was published, the book created a furor. A copy was sent to President Roosevelt, who, in turn, appointed two investigators whose report confirmed Sinclair's findings. It is hard to say to what extent Sinclair's book provided an impetus for the passage of the US Pure Food and Meat Inspection Law in 1906, but it is indisputable that it played an important role in it.

Even a short list of influential authors would be incomplete without reference made to Ralph Nader and Isabel LeBourdais. Nader was an unknown young lawyer at the time he published *Unsafe at Any Speed* (1965), which alerted the public to the automobile industry's unconcern for safety in the design and construction of American cars. This book is a model of the kind of journalism that, at times, initiates the rise of public concern over a given issue. As a result of his book, and General Motors' reaction to it, Nader became front-page news, and his charges took on new weight. Perhaps more than anyone else, he has contributed to and provided the impetus for the passing of a substantial number of auto safety provisions (Buckhorn, 1972:226). LeBourdais was a Canadian journalist who, in 1966, published *The Trial of Steven Truscott*. At the age of 14, Truscott had been found guilty in the rape and murder of 12-year-old schoolgirl Lynn Harper and sentenced to hang. In her book, LeBourdais ravaged both the police investigation into Harper's killing and the conduct of Truscott's trial; simultaneously, she called into question a justice system that many people at the time believed to be infallible and beyond reproach. "Her argument that the court had erred and sentenced an innocent teen to death made front-page headlines and sparked public demonstration. The resulting uproar in Parliament led Lester Pearson's Liberal government to order a Supreme Court review" (CBC, 2004). Even though the Supreme Court ruled against Truscott being granted a new trial, Truscott became "the poster boy against capital punishment" (Halperin, 2004). His sentence was eventually commuted to life imprisonment and, after spending 10 years in prison, Truscott was paroled. Today, many experts believe that the controversy over the Truscott case, which had been prompted by LeBourdais's scathing analysis, led in 1976 to Canada's abolishment of the death penalty (CBC, 2004).

More recently, Canadian waitress Heather Crowe served as a both a poignant and potent "voice in the wilderness" in relation to the dangers of secondhand smoke in the workplace. In 2002, Crowe was informed that she had inoperable lung cancer, caused by her years of working in smoke-filled bars and restaurants. Crowe dedicated the remaining years of her life to travelling across Canada, promoting changes to municipal, provincial, and federal laws that would better protect workers from the dangers of secondhand smoke. In addition, she allowed her story to be told and retold in government advertisements and news stories. Crowe died in May of 2006; however, various organizations continue to honour her efforts and pursue her cause. The organization "Physicians for a Smoke-Free Canada," for example, maintains a "Heather Crowe Campaign" that seeks further legal protection of Canadian workers from the dangers of secondhand smoke.

There are other ways of transforming "private troubles into public issues" (Spector and Kitsuse, 1973:148). While some engage in a war of words to advance their concerns, others adopt more overtly confrontational tactics.

Protest Activity

Protest activity involves demonstrations, sit-ins, strikes, boycotts, and more recently various forms of electronic civil disobedience or "hacktivism" (Harmon, 1998; Jordan and Taylor, 2004) that dramatically emphasize, often with the help of the media, a group's grievances or objectives (Rooy, 2004). Consider, in this context, that when in June of 1990, Elijah Harper, "clasping an eagle feather in his hand, used procedural delays to block ratification of the Meech Lake Accord, which he felt did not adequately address the concerns of First Nations Canadians," he became a hero to at least some Canadians, with Indian leaders dubbing him "our Wayne Gretzky" (Morton and Weinfeld, 1998:320). In the same year, "members of the Kanesetake and Kahnawake reserves blockaded roads and a bridge to protest expansion of a golf course onto land at Oka that had been subject to Aboriginal claims since the 18th century" (Elliott, 2005:8). This protest activity, which was to escalate into violent confrontation between Aboriginals and members of the armed forces and police, "was followed by a series of Aboriginal occupations and blockages in support of claims and grievances throughout most of the rest of the 1990s" (Elliott, 2005:8).

Often, protest strategies have been considered tools of those who are unable or unwilling to engage in the more conventional lawmaking or who regard it as useless (Gamson, 1990). It should be noted at the outset that "the relationship among law, protest, and social change is neither unidirectional nor symmetrical—nor always predictable. One major function of protest may be to secure changes in the law as a means of inducing change in social conditions. Another may be to bring about change directly without the intervention of the law. Still a third may be to bring about legal change which ratifies or legitimizes social change accomplished by other means. These functions are not mutually exclusive" (Grossman and Grossman, 1971:357). But the impact of protest activities on law creation is clearly evident, for "the law in general, and the Court in particular, lacks a self-starter or capacity for initiating change on its own" (Grossman and Grossman, 1971:358).

Racial minorities, poverty organizations, antiwar groups, and opponents of nuclear power have been among those who have employed protest techniques in recent years in attempts to create laws in favour of their objectives. Much of this activity is designed to generate favourable media coverage and, through this, the support of organizations and persons important in the eyes of lawmakers. But the young, the poor, and minority groups have not been the only ones to use protest techniques such as strikes and boycotts. Strike action has long been a central tactic of organized labour, including the unions of public employers in pursuing political and economic goals. Boycotts have been used by consumers protesting high prices.

To what extent protest activities provide an impetus for lawmaking is difficult to say. But "few major social movements or great changes have occurred without the unrest and disorder which, if one approves is called protest or civil disobedience, and if one disapproves, it is called breaking the law, violence, or worse. Violence in particular is as much a part of enforcing the law as it is of seeking changes in the law" (Grossman and Grossman, 1971:358). Hooper's (1998) examination of the impact of 15 years of advocacy for the homeless poor notes that although advocacy groups engaged in a wide range of activities, including occupation of official buildings, fasts, lobbying, public demonstrations and marches, class-action litigation, and researching and writing newspaper articles, some advocates have expressed doubt about the efficacy of their actions. She notes, for example, that "[r]esort to emergency relief measures raises equity issues; gains won through litigation are insufficient or are undone in practice; strategic terrain thought to have been won must be fought for again; and local efforts to organize homeless persons have proved very difficult." In addition, she observes that for those who conduct applied research, "it has become increasingly difficult to participate in an enterprise that manages to 'explain' homelessness but seems powerless to eradicate it."

Social Movements

Over the years, there have been many examples of social movements that have culminated in proposals for or the actual creation of new laws and social policies (Almeida and Stearns, 1998; Snow, Soule, and Kriesi). By definition, a social movement is a type of collective behaviour whereby a group of individuals organize to promote certain changes or alterations in certain types of behaviour or procedures. Invariably, the movement has specified stated objectives, a hierarchical organizational structure, and a well-conceptualized and precise change-oriented ideology. The movement consciously and purposefully articulates the changes it desires through political, educational, or legal channels (see, for example, McAdam and Snow, 1997).

A good example is the movement to legalize abortion (Bennett, 2004). People had for some time regarded illegal abortion as dangerous, but efforts to prevent it (and thus end the death or serious injury of women) were unsuccessful. Then, the combined efforts of women's rights activists and trailblazing physician Dr Henry Morgentaler led to an organized campaign for the repeal of abortion laws that, in Morgentaler's words, "compelled the unwilling to bear the unwanted." Women's group leaders argued that a woman has an unassailable right over her own body and ought to be able to choose whether or not to terminate the pregnancy.

On occasion, tragic events have caused the claims advanced by a social movement to resonate forcefully. For example, on December 6, 1989, the largest mass shooting in Canada occurred when a 25-year-old man, armed with a Sturm Ruger Mini-14 semiautomatic rifle, knives, and bandoliers of ammunition, entered the Ecole Polytechnic in Montreal and killed 14 female students and wounded 13 other students (9 women and 4 men). His rampage, which had deliberately targeted women, ended with his suicide. The "Montreal massacre," as it has come to be known, prompted the Canadian government to proclaim December 6 the National Day of Remembrance and Action on Violence Against Women and to create a Panel on Violence against Women, which delivered its final report in 1993. In addition, it provided a catalytic environment for the inauguration of new legislation aimed at gun control and resulted in Bill C-68 receiving Royal Assent in December 1995. This legislation, which has as its centerpiece a licensing and registration system, is part of a wider framework of weapons control attempts to deter the use of firearms in criminal offences.

Of course, there are many other social movements, including ecology, civil rights, "crime without victims," and "law and order movements." However, it should be pointed out that not all social movements are successful in bringing about changes through laws. As a matter of fact, at any given moment, hundreds of groups with hundreds of messages are trying to get public attention; most will fail.

Increasingly, winning public attention and thus public support is becoming a highly professional activity. Groups that can afford to hire or that can recruit public relations and advertising experts have a considerable advantage over other groups in getting a public hearing for their grievances. It is interesting to note that, regardless of the expertise available to them, all groups share the problem of developing an effective strategy to attract attention in a way that will not, at the same time, provoke outrage and opposition.

Public Interest Groups

Lawmakers are fully cognizant of the fact that private interests are much better represented than public interests (see, for example, Maloney et al., 1994). There are literally hundreds of organizations and individuals who represent one or more private interests on a full- or part-time basis (Mahood, 2000). They range from extremely well-financed organizations, involved in worldwide affairs and supported by lawyers and public relations experts, to small, single-issue groups. Some, such as oil companies, regulate refinery output to maintain prices, and they lobby government representatives for favourable tax policies. There are over 20 000 entries in the most current *Directory of Associations in Canada*. Most of them represent specific private interests.

By contrast, the number of groups that claim to represent public interests is quite small. Among these are the Sierra Club, the Canadian Environmental Law Association, and the Public Interest Research Groups (PIRGs) (Reske, 1994; Toffolon-Weiss and Roberts, 2004). These groups have been instrumental in the initiation of a series of changes in the law designed to benefit and protect the public.

Spurred by the belief that the world faces an ultimate ecocatastrophe unless immediate and successful efforts are made to halt the abuse and deterioration of the environment, Sierra Club members "are no longer the outdoor recreationists of yesterday, but rather today's environmental politicos, in the vanguard of society's newest social movement" (Faich and Gale, 1971:282). The Sierra Club and similar organizations have been active in recent years in providing the impetus for a series of laws dealing with the protection of the environment.

PIRGs were originally launched in the 1970s by activist Ralph Nader as a means of harnessing the energy and talent of students in solving social problems. Today there are over 200 PIRG chapters in the United States and 19 in Canada, funded through voluntary student fees. The goals of PIRGs are to motivate civic participation and responsibility by encouraging individuals to become informed, concerned, and active in their communities; to recognize and pursue integrative analyses of societal and environmental issues; to respect and encourage local and global ecosystem integrity; to encourage diversity and social equality for all people by opposing all forms of oppression; to work in a co-operative way, employing a consensual decision-making process; and to work in solidarity with other like-minded environmental and social justice movements. PIRGs in Canada have produced a variety of issue-oriented publications and audio-visual materials on such topics as the food industry, acid rain, nuclear power, tenant rights, Ontario Hydro, freedom of information, and the management of toxic waste.

Impetus for law may also come from the various quasi-public specialized interest groups. They may represent certain economic interests, such as consumer groups or organized labour. Or they may represent certain occupational interests, such as the Canadian Medical Association, which not only exercises considerable control over the practice of medicine in this country, but also takes stands, raises money, and lobbies in favour of specific positions on such issues as euthanasia, drugs, and alcohol. The same can be said for the Canadian Association of University Teachers (though not on the same issues). Still others include groups representing what may be called moral interests, such as temperance, various types of anti-drug concerns, various forms of "child saving" (for example, delinquency control), sexual deviance, the "work ethic," and anti-pornography. The important point to remember is that all these organizations can agitate for changes in the law and can provide the needed impetus for it.

For a group to effectively promote its interests and to provide an impetus for lawmaking, it naturally must have access to lawmakers. But access to lawmakers depends, at least in part, on the socioeconomic status of the group. Groups with the most financial resources, the most prestigious membership, and the best organization are likely to have the greatest access to legislators. Moreover, lawmakers, on the local as well as the higher levels, may be more sympathetic to groups that represent interests of the middle and upper classes than to groups representing poor people, welfare recipients, and the like. Generally, groups with "mainstream" views, seeking only small changes in the status quo, may be given a more sympathetic hearing than those advocating large-scale radical changes.

The Mass Media

The mass media (newspapers, magazines, and radio and television stations) function in part as an interest group. Each component of the mass media is a business, and like other businesses, it has a direct interest in various areas of public policy. For example, the media have had a general objective of securing legislation, such as access to information laws that facilitate their access to the news, and legislation or court decisions that affect the confidentiality of news sources.

The mass media also function as conduits, although not altogether impartial ones, for others who would shape policy. Wealthier groups, for example, purchase media time or space in an effort to align public opinion behind their causes. Through the media, these groups may reach the ear of legislators and administrators by publicly exposing problems and proposals about which they might not otherwise hear, or in some instances, about which they might not want to hear.

The mass media, especially the news media, are able to generate widespread awareness and concern about events and conditions—to bring matters before the public so that they become problematic issues. The Watergate case is arguably *the* classic demonstration of the number of ways in which the mass media influence current events. Without dogged investigations by the mass media, the scandal probably would have remained buried. Without the blitz of mass-media coverage, the issues probably would not have achieved as rapid, widespread, or deep an impact on the public. Many of the most scandalous incidents of the Watergate affair involved the improper solicitation and employment of campaign funds. Outraged segments of public opinion demanded the prevention of future "Watergates." The legislative response to this outcry in the United States was the passage of a bill in April 1974 that drastically altered the way in which presidential and congressional campaigns are funded. This is illustrative of situations in which, as a result of investigative reporting, the mass media provide a direct impetus for legislation. However, there are numerous other examples of how journalists have impacted on law and social policy. Indeed, one might consider that, in addition to being a father of Confederation, George Brown, the founder of the Toronto *Globe*, "is perhaps best known as one of Canada's most prominent opponents of American slavery. . . [and who] expressed his views on this subject in issue after issue" of this newspaper (Morton and Weinfeld, 1998:29).

Since public opinion is an important precursor of change, the mass media can set the stage by making undesirable conditions visible to a sizable segment of the public with unparalleled rapidity. Through the exposure of perceived injustices, the mass media play a crucial role in the formation of public opinion. Ralph Turner and Lewis M. Killian (1987) discuss six processes considered essential in understanding how the mass media can influence public opinion. First, the mass media *authenticate* the factual nature of events, which is decisive in the formation of public opinion. Second, the mass media *validate* opinions, sentiments, and preferences. It is reassuring to hear one's views confirmed by a well-known commentator. It also enables a person to express his or her views more effectively by borrowing the commentator's words. A third effect of the mass media is to *legitimize* certain behaviours and viewpoints considered to be taboo. Issues that were discussed only in private can now be expressed publicly, since they have already been discussed on television (for example, legal rights of homosexuals). Fourth, the mass media often *symbolize* the diffuse anxieties, preferences, discontents, and prejudices that individuals experience. By giving an acceptable identification for these perplexing feelings, the mass media often aid their translation into specific opinions and actions. By providing symbols—terrorists, separatists, feminists, law and order, the new morality—the mass media create a number of objects toward which specific sentiments can be directed. Fifth, the mass media *focus* the preferences, discontents, and prejudices into lines of action. Finally, the mass media *classify into hierarchies* persons, objects, activities, and issues. As a result of the amount of consideration, preferential programming, and placement of items, they indicate relative importance and prestige.

The generalization that the views of individuals whose prestige and influence are established carry more weight than the views of others applies to public opinion. As a result, the "influences stemming from the mass media first reach 'opinion leaders,' who in turn, pass on what they read or hear to those of their everyday associates for whom they are influential" (Katz, 1957:61). Opinion leaders are usually leaders in only one sphere of activity. They tend to be different from the rest of the public in that they are more highly educated and are engaged in more prestigious occupations. They are also more powerful, active, and influential in specific community, interest-group, or political affairs. Consequently, their opinions are considered much more influential and, therefore, are targeted by much of the media efforts.

In addition to investigative reporting and the shaping of public opinion, the mass media can pressure or challenge lawmakers into taking action on an issue or into changing their stand on a question. Influential newspapers such as the *Globe and Mail* and the *National Post* can make or break legislators by the use of the editorial pages (Sauvageau, Schneiderman, and Taras, 2006). Endorsement by a major newspaper can greatly facilitate a candidate's chances for being elected. Conversely, opposition to a candidate on the editorial page can influence the outcome of an election. Legislators are quite aware of the power of the press, and as a result, editorial recommendations are given serious consideration. Similarly, articles in various influential weekly or monthly publications and the diverse specialized professional and legal journals can agitate for change.

Finally, an indirect way by which the mass media can furnish an impetus for lawmaking is through the provision of a forum for citizens' concerns. The "letters to the editor" page in newspapers is a traditional outlet for publicizing undesirable conditions. Such letters can accomplish several objectives. First, the letter can alert the community that an issue is before a lawmaking body; second, it can persuade the reader to take a position; third, it can make clear that there are responsible and articulate people in the community who are concerned with the issue; and fourth, it can enlist the active support of others. Similarly, many radio and television stations have local talk shows and public-affairs programs that can be used to air grievances and to seek redress.

SUMMARY

- Although various theories attempt to account for lawmaking, including the rationalistic model, the functional view, conflict theory, and the "moral entrepreneur" thesis, none of these theories can account for the creation of all laws. At best, they explain in part how laws are made.

- Three general types of lawmaking process—legislative, administrative, and judicial—were analyzed. Legislative lawmaking basically consists of finding major and minor compromises to ideas advanced for legislation by administrative agencies, interest groups, and various party agencies and spokespersons. Administrative lawmaking consists of rulemaking and adjudication. Rulemaking is essentially legislation by administrative agencies. Adjudication differs from rulemaking in that it applies only to a specific, limited number of parties involved in an individual case and controversy before the agency. Judicial lawmaking is generally directed at other government agencies rather than at private individuals.

- Interest groups, public opinion, and social science all exert an influence on the law-making process.
- Demands for lawmaking come from a multitude of sources including scholarly investigations, and novels, institutionalized forces, such as lobbying activities and public-interest groups, as well as from organized protest activities or social movements. The mass media can also set the stage for lawmaking by calling attention to an issue.

CRITICAL THINKING QUESTIONS

1. In the early 1990s, a Somali woman, Khadra Hassan Farah, sought refugee status for herself and her 10-year-old daughter, Hodan, with the plea that, in Somalia, Hodan would be forced to undergo female genital mutilation (FGM). In response, Canadian immigration officials ruled in 1993 that Hodan's "right to personal security would be greatly infringed" if forced to return to Somalia, and granted Farah and her daughter refugee status in this country (Amnesty International, 1998). Later in that decade, the United States (1996), Sweden (1997), and Australia (1997) would also rule that women, at risk of FGM if returned to their country, qualified as refugees under the 1951 UN Convention relating to the Status of Refugees (Amnesty International, 2004). The World Health Organization (2000) defines female genital mutilation as "all procedures involving partial or total removal of the external female genitalia or other injury to the female genital organs whether for cultural, religious or other non-therapeutic reasons." It is estimated that, worldwide, between 100 and 140 million girls and women have undergone FGM and that an additional 2 million girls "are at risk of undergoing FGM" each year (Amnesty International, 2004). FGM is reported to be extensively practised in Africa, in some countries in the Middle East, and among immigrant communities in parts of Asia, the Pacific, North and Latin America, and Europe. According to Brym et al. (2003:79), FGM is generally performed as a "rite of passage" on young girls (i.e., between the age of 4 and 14). They observe that, "[i]n some cultures, it is believed to enhance female fertility. However, it is most commonly based on the assumption that women are naturally 'unclean' and 'masculine' inasmuch as they possess a vestige of a 'male' sex organ, the clitoris." Within countries that practise FGM, women who have not undergone FGM are thought more likely to demonstrate a "masculine" (i.e., voracious) sexual appetite. As such, they are considered more likely than women who have undergone FGM to engage in both premarital and extramarital sex.

   The UN Convention on the Elimination of All Forms of Discrimination Against Women, which took effect in 1981, requires all member countries to work toward the elimination of customs and practices which are based "on the idea of the inferiority or the superiority of either of the sexes." The Committee on the Elimination of Discrimination Against Women has also issued various general recommendations that relate specifically to FGM and that are designed to eradicate its practice. In 1993, the UN Declaration on the Elimination of Violence Against Women also specifically identified FGM as a practice that constituted violence against women. The 1995 UN Beijing Declaration and Platform for Action condemned FGM and reaffirmed that it was the duty of states to take action against this practice. Canada's Criminal Code was amended in 1997 to criminalize FGM; in Canada, FGM is defined as aggravated assault, an indictable offence that carries a maximum term of 14 years imprisonment.

In addition, section 273.3 of the Criminal Code prohibits any person from taking a child who is normally resident in Canada outside of the country for the purposes of subjecting that child to FGM.

It has been argued that the prohibition of FGM attests, most fundamentally, to the ability of the powerful to translate their vantage point into law. Some charge that the practice of FGM is no more intrinsically abhorrent than practices that our own culture ostensibly views as acceptable—such as male circumcision, body piercings, and the myriad forms of "cosmetic surgery" (e.g., breast and penile implants, liposuction, botox injections) that are legal in Canada. The prohibition of FGM, critics maintain, simply demonstrates ethnocentricism and cultural imperialism: the criminalization of FGM, along with "all talk of 'universal human rights' denies cultural sovereignty to less powerful peoples," and may function to "undermine tolerance and multicultural-ism while reinforcing racist attitudes" (Brym et al., 2003:79). Accordingly, it has been suggested that, in Canada, the ethos of multiculturalism should result in legal accom-modations made for the cultural practices of minorities (see, for example, Howard-Hassman, 2000).

For others, however, the pursuit of multicultural accommodation is problematic. Thus, in posing the rhetorical question, "Is multiculturalism bad for women?" Okin's (1999) analysis of arranged marriages among Iraqi immigrants in the United States, the Hmong practice of "marriage by capture," and female genital mutilation implicitly directs readers toward an affirmative responsive. She maintains that the practice of multicultural accommodation often proves repressive for minority women, and that allowing these practices to exist may revitalize and further entrench sexism in both the dominant and minority cultures. Echoing this sentiment, a 1996 joint statement by the World Health Organization, the UN Children's Fund (UNICEF), and the UN Population Fund affirmed that "the rights of women and girls to physical and mental integrity, to freedom from discrimination and to the highest standard of health are uni-versal" and emphasized that "[c]ultural claims cannot be invoked to justify their viola-tion" (quoted in Amnesty International, 2005). How should democratic societies respond to incidents of culture-clash? How should democratic countries respond to the tension that may exist between rights and the protection of vulnerable persons—or of a culture, values, and/or personal interests?

2. How has the role of the judiciary changed in Canada with the entrenchment of the *Charter of Rights and Freedoms* in the Constitution?

chapter five

Law and Social Control

Over the years, a great deal has been written on social control, and the topic continues to occupy a central position in the sociological literature (see, for example, Bernard, Vold, and Snipes, 2002; Hil and Tait, 2004). Social control refers to the methods used by members of a society to maintain order and promote predictability of behaviour. There are many different forms of social control, and law is only one of them. The emphasis in this chapter is on social control through laws that are activated when other control mechanisms are ineffective or unavailable. The chapter examines the processes of informal and formal social control, the use of criminal sanctions, the effectiveness of the death penalty, and civil commitment to regulate behaviour. Part of the chapter is concerned with crimes without victims (drug addiction, prostitution, and gambling), white-collar crime, and the control of dissent. The chapter concludes with a consideration of administrative law as a means of control in the context of licensing, inspection, and the threat of publicity.

There are two basic processes of social control: the internalization of group norms and control through external pressures (Clinard and Meier, 2004). In the first instance, social control is the consequence of socialization, the process of learning the rules of behaviour for a given social group. Individuals develop self-control by being taught early what is appropriate, expected, or desirable in specific situations. People acquire a motivation to conform to the norms, regardless of external pressures. Most students do not cheat because of the fear of being caught, and most people pay their taxes, most of the time. There is conformity to norms because individuals have been socialized to believe that they should conform, regardless of and independent of any anticipated reactions of other persons.

Mechanisms of social control through external pressures include both negative and positive sanctions. Negative sanctions are penalties imposed on those who violate norms. Positive sanctions, such as a promotion, a bonus, and encouragement, are intended to reward conformity. These positive and negative sanctions are forms of social control. Some types of social control are formal or official, and others are informal or unofficial in character. Typical reactions to deviance and rule breaking may generate both informal and formal sanctions. Although there is a considerable amount of overlap between informal and formal mechanisms of social control, for analytical purposes they will be discussed separately.

INFORMAL SOCIAL CONTROLS

Methods of informal social controls are best exemplified by **folkways** (established norms of common practices such as those that specify modes of dress, etiquette, and language use) and **mores** (societal norms associated with intense feelings of right or wrong and definite rules of conduct that are simply not to be violated—for example, incest). These informal controls consist of techniques whereby individuals who know each other on a personal basis accord praise to those who comply with their expectations and show displeasure to those who do not (Shibutani, 1961:426). These techniques may be observed in specific behaviours such as ridicule, gossip, praise, reprimands, criticisms, ostracism, and verbal rationalizations and expressions of opinion. Gossip, or the fear of gossip, is one of the more effective devices employed by members of a society to bring individuals into conformity with norms. Unlike formal social controls, these informal controls are not exercised through official group mechanisms, and there are no specially designated persons in charge of enforcement.

Informal mechanisms of social control tend to be more effective in groups and societies where relations are face-to-face and intimate and where the division of labour is relatively simple. For example, Emile Durkheim argues that in simple societies, such as tribal villages or small towns, legal norms more closely accord with social norms than in larger and more complex societies. Moral disapproval of deviance is nearly unanimous in such communities (Shilling and Mellor, 1998); and as Daniel Glaser (1971:32) notes: "Tolerance of behavioural diversity varies directly with the division of labour in a society." In simple societies, laws are often unwritten, necessitating the direct teaching of social norms to children. Socialization in such simple societies does not present children with contradictory norms that create confusion or inner conflict. Intense face-to-face interaction in such societies produces a moral consensus that is well-known to all members; it also brings deviant acts to everyone's attention quickly.

There is substantial evidence in the sociological literature to support the contention that informal social control is stronger in smaller, traditional, more homogeneous communities than in larger, more modern and heterogeneous communities (Hanawalt, 1998). In a classic and influential study of deviance in the 17th-century Massachusetts Bay Colony, Kai T. Erikson found that the small size and the cultural homogeneity of the community helped control behaviour, since everyone in the community pressured potential deviants to conform to dominant norms. There was a substantial amount of surveillance by neighbours in the community watching for acts of deviance. Moral censure immediately followed any observed act of deviance (Erikson, 1966:169). Even today, reaction to certain crimes (for example, incest or murder) in a small, homogeneous, and close-knit community may be so intense and immediate that justice for a defendant in a criminal case may be difficult, since public pressure on the legal system to exact harsh and immediate punishment may make the provision of due process rights doubtful. In such instances, it may be necessary to change the location of the trial to minimize public pressure. Such a change of venue order is more likely to take place in small communities than in larger ones where the court would not assume that the defendant cannot receive a fair trial because of prejudice (Vidmar and Schuller, 2001:139).

Undoubtedly, informal social controls operate more effectively in smaller communities where people know each other and regularly interact. In such communities, law enforcement agents can probably expect better co-operation. As the President's Commission on Law Enforcement and Administration of Justice (1967:6) points out: "A man who lives in the country or in a small town is likely to be conspicuous, under surveillance by his community so to speak, and therefore under its control. A city man is often almost invisible, socially isolated from his neighbourhood and therefore incapable of being controlled by it. He has more opportunities for crime."

The greater effectiveness of informal social control mechanisms in small communities is demonstrated by Sarah L. Boggs' often-cited study of formal and informal social controls in central cities, suburbs, and small towns. Boggs found that residents of large cities were more apt than suburban or small-town residents to feel that crime was likely to occur in their community. City residents were also more likely to think that their neighbours would not report a burglary that they observed, and more urban residents knew of a crime or a suspicious incident in their community within the previous year. Most people in all areas felt that their own neighbourhood was safe, but fewer felt that way in the cities. When they were asked what it was that made their neighbourhood safe, 83 percent of those in rural areas and small towns said that it was informal controls; 70 percent in suburbs and 68 percent of those in the cities attributed safety to informal controls. When they said that their neighbourhood was kept safe by informal social controls, the people meant that they felt secure because of the character of the community and its residents—"good, decent, law-abiding, middle-class citizens" (Boggs, 1971:323). Safety in a neighbourhood was also attributed to the social network in the community that might lead to bystander intervention in a crime. Respondents who lived in suburbs and large cities were more likely than those who lived in rural areas and small towns to attribute safety to such formal control agents as the police (Boggs, 1971:234). Boggs concluded that people in cities were most inclined to expect crime but least likely to feel that they could rely on their neighbours rather than the police to protect their community. As a result, they were more likely to take precautions, such as purchasing weapons or a watchdog, than their counterparts who lived in suburbs, small towns, and rural areas.

Similar conclusions about the role of informal social-control mechanisms can be drawn from studies dealing with developing nations. For example, in comparing a low-crime-rate community and a high-crime-rate community in Kampala, Uganda, Marshall B. Clinard and Daniel J. Abbott found that the areas with less crime showed greater social solidarity, more social interaction among neighbours, more participation in local organizations, less geographical mobility, and more stability in family relationships. There was also greater cultural homogeneity and more emphasis on tribal and kinship ties in the low-crime community, helping to counteract the anonymity of recent migrants to the city. The stronger primary group ties among residents of the low-crime area made it more difficult for strangers in the community to escape public notice. To prevent theft, residents of an area must feel that it is wrong, share some responsibility for protecting their neighbours' property, be able to identify strangers in the area, and be willing to take action if they observe a theft (Clinard and Abbott, 1973:149).

These and other studies (see, for example, Garofalo and McLeod, 1989) show that if there is intense social interaction on an intimate face-to-face basis, normative consensus, and surveillance of the behaviour of members of the community, informal social control will be strong to the extent that legal or formal controls may be unnecessary. This contention is reinforced by Roberto Mangabeira Unger's (1976) argument, which was discussed in Chapter 2. To reiterate, Unger contends that bureaucratic law emerges when state and society become differentiated and there is a felt need for an institution standing above conflicting groups. This occurs when the community disintegrates; that is, when individuals may no longer be counted on to act in set ways without overt guidance. Such a disintegration comes about as the division of labour creates new opportunities for power and wealth, which, in turn, undercut old hierarchies determined by birth. This process is accompanied by an increased reliance on formal social controls.

Finally, the role of neighbourhood committees (for example, little old ladies employed by the state to monitor their neighbours), such as those found in China, should be considered. The Chinese call them "KGB with little feet" (Ignatius, 1989). The "old lady" network, established in the 1950s as a bridge between the party and the people, remains China's most effective means of grass-roots social control (Diamant, Lubman, and O'Brien, 2005). In the mid-2000s, there were an estimated one million neighbourhood committees in cities and villages around the country, employing 6.4 million retirees, virtually all women. In Beijing, there is, on the average, one old lady keeping watch on every 20 families. Their primary task is to seek out and resolve squabbles among neighbours. They report everything they see to higher-ups, investigate disturbances, routinely stop strangers, and pry into couples' plans for having children. In the summer of 1989, they were active in circulating photos of fugitive prodemocracy activists and helped to mobilize residents to attend mass rallies and public executions. This technique of community-based surveillance is modelled after the one introduced in the former Soviet Union in the 1920s, which was based on the principle of denouncement. People were encouraged, and rewarded, to report on friends and relatives who were suspected of engaging in activities contrary to the interests of the government. Various versions of this technique were subsequently used in Nazi Germany and other totalitarian regimes.

FORMAL SOCIAL CONTROLS

Although there is no clear-cut dividing line, formal social controls are usually characteristic of more complex societies with a greater division of labour, heterogeneity of population, and subgroups with competing values and different sets of mores and ideologies. Formal controls arise when informal controls alone are insufficient to maintain conformity to certain norms. Formal controls are characterized by systems of specialized agencies, standard techniques, and general predictability of universal sanctions. The two main types are those instituted by the state and authorized to use force, and those imposed by agencies other than the state, such as churches, business and labour groups, universities, and clubs.

Formal social controls are incorporated in the institutions in society and are characterized by the explicit establishment of procedures and the delegation of specific bodies to enforce them (laws, decrees, regulations, codes). Since they are incorporated in the institutions of society, they are administered by individuals who occupy positions in those institutions. Generally, anyone who attempts to manipulate the behaviour of others through the use of formal sanctions may be considered an agent of social control (Clinard and Meier, 2004).

Social institutions are organized for securing conformity to established modes of behaviour and consist of established procedures for satisfying human needs. These procedures carry a certain degree of compulsion. They involve mechanisms of imposing conformity. Non-political institutions may resort to a variety of penalties and rewards to ensure compliance (see, for example, Vaughan, 1998). For example, an organization may fire an employee; a church may withhold religious services at a wedding or a burial, or even excommunicate a member; a league owner may fine or suspend a professional athlete for infractions of rules. These same organizations may also use formal rewards to ensure conformity. To illustrate, through bonuses and promotions, an organization often rewards those who make an outstanding contribution. Dedicated church members may be commended for exemplary service, and professional athletes are often enticed by financial rewards.

It should be noted at the outset that control through law is seldom exercised by the use of positive sanctions or rewards. A person who, throughout his or her life, obeys the law and meets its requirements seldom receives rewards or commendations. State control is exercised primarily, but not exclusively, through the use or threat of punishment to regulate the behaviour of citizens. The next two sections focus on the use of criminal sanctions, with particular emphasis on the death penalty debate and civil commitment to control certain types of behaviour.

Criminal Sanctions

The social control of criminal and delinquent behaviour exemplifies the most highly structured formal system (the criminal justice system) used by society (see, for example, McBarnet, 2004). At the start of the new millennium, no fewer than 2 600 994 men and 681 199 women in Canada had a criminal record (including young offenders); the total population of Canada in that year was 30 750 087 (15 232 909 men and 15 517 178 women). Stated somewhat differently, in 2000, about 1 in 10 persons living in Canada (17 percent of men and 4 percent of women) had a criminal record. Moreover, although Canada's incarceration rate (including individuals held in federal, provincial, and territorial correctional systems) has declined in recent years, in 2003–04, for every 100 000 adults in the population, 130 were incarcerated (Statistics Canada, 2005). The average count of adults incarcerated in Canada's federal, provincial, and territorial prisons during that time period was 32 007 (Statistics Canada, 2005). When the incarceration rate is calculated to include both adults and youths, Canada's 2003 incarceration rate (108 per 100 000 population) is notably lower than that of the United States (714 per 100 000), New Zealand (168), England/Wales (142), Scotland (132), and Australia (117); however, it is nevertheless higher than the rates found in many Western European countries including Austria (106), Italy (98), Germany (96), France (91), Switzerland (81), Sweden (75), Finland (71), Denmark (70), and Norway (65) (Public Safety and Emergency Preparedness Canada, 2005).

The laws, enacted by legislators and modified by court decisions, define criminal behaviour and specify the sanctions imposed for violations (see, for example, Beckett and Sasson, 2004). Over time, there has been an increasing reliance on law to regulate the activities and, thus, the lives of people. As the law has proliferated to incorporate more types of behaviour, many changes in penalties for certain crimes have also occurred. These increases inevitably result in more social control and in further changes in the control methods. As more behaviours are defined as criminal, more acts become the interest of the police, the courts, and the prison system.

The term **legalization** is used to describe the process by which norms are moved from the social to the legal level. Not all social norms become laws; in fact, only certain norms are translated into legal norms. Why is it that the violation of certain norms, but not others, is chosen to be incorporated into the criminal code? Austin T. Turk (1972) suggests that there are certain social forces involved in the legalization and creation of legal norms: moral indignation, a high value on order, response to threat, and political tactics.

As discussed in Chapter 4, laws may be created by the actions of "moral entrepreneurs" who become outraged over some practice they regard as reprehensible (for example, smoking marijuana). Others prefer order and insist on provisions to regulate life and to make society as orderly as possible. They promulgate laws to ensure order and uniformity, as in the case of traffic regulation. Some people react to real or imaginary threats and advocate legal-control measures. For instance, some people may assume that the availability of pornographic material is not only morally wrong but also directly contributes to the increase of sex crimes (although acts of sexual violence, including child molestation, undoubtedly predate erotic books, pornographic magazines, videocassettes, and websites). In this instance, it would appear certain that these people would attempt to legally prohibit the sale of pornographic material (Trebilcock, 2006). The final source of legalization of norms is political, where criminal laws are created in the interest of powerful groups in

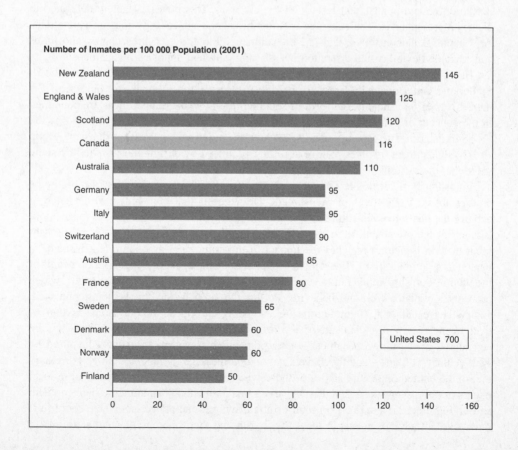

Number of Inmates per 100 000 Population (2001)

New Zealand	145
England & Wales	125
Scotland	120
Canada	116
Australia	110
Germany	95
Italy	95
Switzerland	90
Austria	85
France	80
Sweden	65
Denmark	60
Norway	60
Finland	50

United States 700

society. This source is identified with the conflict perspective that we have considered in the preceding chapters.

The process of legalization of social norms also entails the incorporation of specific punishments for specific kinds of criminal law violators. Rusche and Kirchheimer note: "Every system of production tends to discover punishments which correspond to its productive relationships" (1968:5). Michel Foucault (1977) tells us that before the Industrial Revolution, life was considered cheap and individuals had neither the utility nor the commercial value that is conferred on them in an industrial economy. Under those circumstances, punishment was severe and often unrelated to the nature of the crime (for example, death for stealing a chicken). When more and more factories appeared, the value of individual lives, even criminal ones, began to be stressed. Beginning in the last years of the 18th century and the early years of the 19th century, efforts were made to connect the nature of a given punishment to the nature of the crime.

Fitting the punishment to the crime is a difficult and at times controversial and politically sensitive task. The definition of crime and the penalty for it and the components of the culture of control (Garland, 2001) vary over time and from one society to another. For example, in rural areas in Communist China, it is not uncommon to burn down the houses or to confiscate the property of those who violate birth control laws. In the words of a villager: "If you have more than one child, they will come and rip the engine out of your boat or destroy your house on the land" (Tyler, 1995:6). By contrast, in a democracy the power to define crime and punishment rests with the citizenry. This power is largely delegated to elected representatives. Their statutes are often broad and subject to various interpretations. As Chapter 3 demonstrated, legislative enactments allow judges, prosecutors, and juries considerable flexibility and discretion in assessing guilt and imposing punishment.

But what does it mean to punish an individual who violates a criminal law? Edwin H. Sutherland and Donald R. Cressey (1974:298) provide the following definition of the ingredients of punishment as a form of social control: "Two essential ideas are contained in the concept of punishment as an instrument of public justice. (a) It is inflicted by the group in its corporate capacity upon one who is regarded as a member of the same group . . . (b) Punishment involves pain or suffering produced by design and justified by some value that the suffering is assumed to have."

Punishment of lawbreakers has several purposes. Paul W. Tappan (1960:241) offers the now established objectives of punishment. He suggests that punishment is designed to achieve the goal of **retribution** or social retaliation against the offender. This means punishment of the offender for the crime that has been committed and, to an extent, punishment that (in principle) matches the impact of the crime upon its victim (for instance, a person or an organization). The state is expected to be the agent of vengeance on behalf of the victim. Punishment also involves **incapacitation** (for example, a prison term), which prevents a violator from misbehaving during the time he or she is being punished. Judicially created public humiliations are also being introduced in courtrooms as alternatives to incarceration and to satisfy a "retributive impulse" (Karp, 1998:277). They are considered as "shaming penalties"—after punishments such as the stocks favoured by 17th-century Puritans—and they take a *mea culpa* message to the community. For example, in the United States the names of those who solicit prostitutes are identified in local papers or radio shows; drunken drivers carry signs on their cars announcing their problem and urging other drivers to report their erratic driving to the police; convicted shoplifters must take out advertisements in local papers running their photographs and stating their crimes; and the courts have ordered people convicted of assault or child molestation to put signs in their yards announcing their transgression (Belluck, 1998). Shaming and embarrassment are potent forces in social control, and various techniques are being more and more widely used nowadays (Allyn, 2004).

Further, punishment is supposed to have a **deterrent effect**, both on the lawbreaker and on potential deviants. **Individual** or **specific deterrence** may be achieved by intimidation of the person, frightening him or her against further deviance, or it may be affected through reformation, in that the lawbreaker changes his or her deviant behaviour. **General deterrence** results from the warning offered to potential criminals by the example of punishment directed at a specific wrongdoer. It aims to discourage others from criminal behaviour by making an example of the offender being punished.

The theory of **deterrence** is predicated on the assumption that individuals weigh the costs and rewards associated with alternative actions, and select behaviours that maximize gains and minimize costs. Thus, crime takes place when lawbreaking is perceived as either more profitable (rewarding) or less costly (painful) than conventional activities. In this context, the purpose of punishment is to prevent crime (Bailey and Peterson, 1994). The concept of deterrence is often used to designate punishment in the form of threats directed at offenders or potential offenders so as to frighten them into law-abiding conduct. The effectiveness of these threats is conditioned by the operation of three variables: (1) the severity of the punishment for an offence, (2) the certainty that it would be applied, and (3) the speed with which it would be applied (Friedland, 1989). Research generally supports the view that certainty of punishment is more important than severity for achieving deterrence, but there is little research data as yet on the swiftness of punishment. For example, in a study of a series of criminal offences, Charles R. Tittle (1969) found strong and consistent negative relationships between certainty of punishment and crime rates. On the other hand, severity of punishment bore no marked relationship to crime rates. Tittle's findings led him to conclude that measures to improve the efficiency of police work probably would have significant effects on crime rates but that increasing the severity of punishment would be of limited effectiveness.

However, sociologists have recognized that punishment may deter only some crimes and some offenders. For example, William J. Chambliss (1975) makes a distinction between crimes that are instrumental acts and those that are expressive. Illustrations of instrumental offences include burglary, tax evasion, embezzlement, motor vehicle theft, identity theft (which became of increasing concern in the early part of the 21st century) and other illegal activities directed toward some material end. Examples of expressive acts are murder, assault, and sex offences, where the behaviour is an end in itself. Chambliss hypothesizes that the deterrent impact of severe and certain punishment may be greater on instrumental crimes because they generally involve some planning and weighing of risks. Expressive crimes, by contrast, are often impulsive and emotional acts. Perpetrators of such crimes are unlikely to be concerned with the future consequences of their actions.

Chambliss further contends that an important distinction can be made between individuals who have a relatively high commitment to crime as a way of life and those with a relatively low commitment. The former would include individuals who engage in crime on a professional or regular basis. They often receive group support for their activities, and crime for them is an important aspect of their way of life (such as prostitutes or participants in organized crime). For them, the likelihood of punishment is a constant feature of their life, something they have learned to live with, and the threat of punishment may be offset by the supportive role played by their peers. On the other hand, a tax evader, an embezzler, or an occasional shoplifter does not view this behaviour as criminal and receives little, if any, group support for these acts. Fear of punishment may well be a deterrent for such low-commitment persons, particularly if they have already experienced punishment (for example, a tax evader who has been audited and then subjected to legal sanctions).

On the basis of these two distinctions—instrumental and expressive acts, and high- and low-commitment offenders—Chambliss contends that the greatest deterrent effect of punishment will be in situations that involve low-commitment individuals who engage in instrumental crimes. Deterrence is least likely in cases involving high-commitment persons who engage in expressive crimes. The role of deterrence remains questionable in situations that involve low-commitment individuals who commit expressive crimes (such as murder), which can be illustrated by the arguments used for or against the death penalty.

Discord over the Death Penalty

As the most severe form of punishment, the death penalty is the most obvious, controversial, and emotional issue in the concept of deterrence (see, for example, Bedau and Cassell, 2004; Christianson, 2004; Ruddell, 2005). Historically, property offences rather than violent crimes accounted for the majority of executions. In the 18th century, the death penalty was imposed in England for more than 200 offences, including poaching and smuggling. Executions were performed in public. They were a popular spectacle. The public applauded a skillful execution of a criminal much as aficionados today cheer the matador who skillfully slays a bull (Foucault, 1977). The standard methods of execution included hanging, beheading, disemboweling, and quartering. The increased severity and frequency of executions during this period were associated with the growth of urbanization and wealth. Notes Loh: "Capital statutes 'served the interests of private property and commerce' against those who might seek to undermine them" (1984:194). Although the colonies inherited many of the capital punishments from England, by the middle of the 19th century most of them were repealed and the death sentence was imposed primarily for murder and, to a lesser extent, rape.

While the precise number of people hanged in early Canada remains unknown, inasmuch as accurate records date only from 1867, the first person executed for a crime is reputed to have been a young girl in the early 1600s who was hanged at the age of 16 for the crime of petty theft. The last hangings in Canada occurred in 1935 in Nova Scotia, 1941 in Prince Edward Island, 1942 in Newfoundland, 1946 in Saskatchewan, 1951 in Manitoba, 1957 in Quebec, 1959 in British Columbia, and 1960 in Alberta. The last execution in Canada was a double execution in 1962 at Toronto's Don Jail (Engel, 1996:157). Although capital punishment was formally abolished in this country in 1976, surveys conducted throughout the 1980s and 1990s consistently reported widespread support for its reintroduction. For example, in 1995, approximately 82 percent of a national, random sample of Canadians expressed the belief that the death penalty should be exercised in some instances (Bibby, 1995). In 2000, the Project Canada survey found that, even though support for the use of capital punishment had fallen somewhat, almost three in four (74 percent) of Canadian adults and about six in ten (59 percent) of Canadian teens agreed that "the death penalty should sometimes be used to punish criminals" (Bibby, 2001:244). More recently, however, polls suggest that support for the reintroduction of the death penalty in Canada "has been dying off dramatically over the years," with a 2004 IPSOS-Reid survey noting that just 42 percent of Canadians agreed that capital punishment should be reintroduced while 56 percent opposed its reintroduction (Bricker and Wright, 2005:9). In 2001, the Supreme Court of Canada also demonstrated its opposition to the use of capital punishment in its unanimous 9–0 decision in *United States v. Burns*. In this case, the Supreme Court ruled that "[i]n the absence of exceptional circumstances" Canada is constitutionally required, prior to extraditing any fugitive—Canadian or otherwise—to another country, to seek assurances that the death penalty will not be imposed (Religious Tolerance.org, 2001).

According to Amnesty International, as of February 2006, over half of the world's countries had abolished capital punishment in law or practice. More specifically, 86 countries and territories had abolished the use of the death penalty for all crimes, 11 had abolished the death penalty for all but exceptional crimes (e.g., crimes committed in times of war), and 25 were "abolitionist in practice: they retain the death penalty in law but have not carried out any executions for the past 10 years and are believed to have a policy or established practice of not carrying out executions." Once the death penalty is abolished, its reintroduction is rare; of the more than 50 countries worldwide that have abolished the death penalty since 1985, only four reintroduced it; of these four countries, one (Nepal) has subsequently re-abolished it, another (the Philippines) has ceased to carry out executions, and in the remaining two (Gambia, Papua New Guinea) no executions had occurred up until the time that this book went to press.

While 74 countries and territories still retain and employ the death penalty, the number of countries that execute prisoners in any given year is much smaller. Nevertheless, in 2004, "at least 3797 people were executed in 25 countries and at least 7935 people were sentenced to death in 64 countries. These were only minimum figures; the true figures were certainly higher" (Amnesty International, 2006). Currently, the United States, India, and Japan are the only democracies that retain capital punishment; however, indicative of the worldwide trend toward the abolition of the death penalty, in October of 2005, President Kalam of India called for the discussion of the death penalty in Parliament and the construction of a comprehensive policy of reform. In Japan, Minister of Justice Sugiura Seiken announced in his inaugural address that he would not sign execution warrants and told reporters that: "From the standpoint of the theory of civilization, I believe that the general trend from a long-term perspective will be to move toward abolition." Shortly after, however, Seiken retracted his comments, stating that they simply represented his "feelings as an individual."

In 2004, 97 percent of the world's known executions took place in China, Iran, Vietnam, and the United States (Amnesty International, 2006). In China, for example, where the death penalty applies to approximately 68 crimes, including such non-violent offences as tax fraud, embezzlement of state property, and accepting a bribe, at least 3400 people were executed in 2004 alone; some estimates suggest that China executes approximately 10 000 people per year (Amnesty International, 2006; Li, Zhang and Deng, 2005; Lu and Zhang, 2005). In 2004, at least 159 individuals were executed in Iran and, in Vietnam, no fewer than 64.

In the United States, capital punishment was declared unconstitutional by the US Supreme Court in the case of *Furman v. Georgia* (1972). The Court held that the discretionary application of the death penalty to only a small fraction of those eligible to be executed was capricious and arbitrary and hence unconstitutional. However, a number of states responded to the ruling by legislating modifications in state laws that make the death penalty mandatory for certain offences, such as multiple killings; killing in connection with a robbery, rape, kidnapping, or hostage situation; murder for hire; killing a police officer or prison guard; and treason. Some of these revised statutes were held to be constitutional by the Supreme Court in 1976 when it voted 7–2 in *Gregg v. Georgia* to reinstate the death penalty. Since that time, 38 states have passed capital punishment laws, and "more than 1000 men and women have been judicially executed in the United States, an average of one execution every 10 days" (Amnesty International, 2006). In that country, a 54-page Execution Protocol, prepared by the US Bureau of Prisons, spells out with minute-by-minute precision every detail of an execution ranging from the length of the last meal to the surrender of the body to the coroner. It also deals with detailed contingency plans for handling disturbances that might be caused by protesters and sympathizers both within and outside of the facility.

Between 1930 (when national reporting began) and 2005, 4863 executions were carried out in the United States (Bureau of Justice Statistics, 2006). In 2005, 60 persons in 16 US states were executed—all by lethal injection. Between 1976 and 2006, the state of Texas carried out the most executions (357), followed by Virginia (94) and Oklahoma (79). As of October 1, 2005, the state of California held the largest number of death row inmates (648), followed by Texas (413) and Florida (385). The youngest death row inmate in the United States in that year was 18, the oldest, 89 years of age. Although 22 Americans have been executed since 1976 for crimes that they had committed as juveniles, in *Roper v. Simmons* (2005) the Supreme Court struck down the death penalty for juveniles.

Since 1976, 11 women have been executed in the United States. As of December 31, 2005, women represented 1.5 percent of death-row inmates; of those executed in 2005, 59 were men and 1 was a woman (Bureau of Justice Statistics, 2006). Of the 3383 prisoners who resided on death row on October 1, 2005, 46 percent were white, 42 percent were Black, 10 percent were Hispanic, and 2 percent were American Indians, Asians, or of unknown race; of those executed in 2005, 68.3 percent were white and 31.6 percent were Black.

Studies show that other things being equal, killers of white people are more likely to receive death sentences than killers of blacks. According to one American study, "[o]ver 80 percent of the murder victims resulting in an execution were white, even though nationally only 50 percent of murder victims generally are white" (Death Penalty Information Center, 2006). A comprehensive study of the use of the death penalty in North Carolina reported that the odds that a defendant would receive a death sentence rose 3.5 times among those whose victims were white (Boger and Unah, 2001); in California, those who killed whites were more than three times more likely to be sentenced to death than those who killed Blacks, and over four times more likely to receive the death penalty than those who killed Latinos (Pierce and Radelet, 2005). Empirical studies of the death penalty find that the race and gender of victims are associated with the severity of legal responses in homicide cases even after controlling for legally relevant factors. For example, Holcomb, Williams, and Demuth (2004) report that defendants convicted of killing white females were significantly more likely to receive death sentences than killers of victims with other race-gender characteristics.

In the United States, the dilemma of whether to kill the killers comes up only in a small fraction of homicides (see, for example, Smith and Zahn, 1998). The criteria for capital murder vary from state to state and from case to case. However, in general, there must be "aggravating circumstances." These can be as specific as the murder of a police officer or a prison guard; as common as homicide committed along with a lesser felony such as burglary; or as vague as Florida's law citing "especially heinous, atrocious or cruel" killing. Some 10 percent of homicides qualify. Those killings are the ones the threat of capital punishment is meant to prevent.

What are the preventive effects of capital punishment? The arguments for the death penalty are mostly anecdotal but, at times, can become visceral. Proponents of the death penalty contend that it is a deterrent to others and that it protects society. It constitutes retribution for society and the victim's family and serves to protect police officers and prison guards. It also removes the possibility that the offenders will repeat the act. However, there is little empirical evidence in support of the death penalty as a deterrent. Were it not for the work of Isaac Ehrlich, the deterrence debate would be very much one-sided. Using econometric modelling techniques to construct a "supply-and-demand" theory of murder, Ehrlich (1975), in a now classic and frequently cited article subtitled "A Question of Life and Death," argued that the death penalty prevents more murders than do prison sentences. He speculates that because of the 3411 executions carried out from 1933 to 1967, enough murderers were discouraged so that some 27 000 victims' lives were saved. As might be expected, his conclusions drew immediate criticisms.

An assortment of concerns were raised. Among others, Ehrlich did not compare the effectiveness of capital punishment with that of particular prison terms. When data from 1965 to 1969 are omitted, the relationship between murder rates and executions is not statistically significant (Loh, 1984:258). While considering the increases in homicides in the United States during the 1960s, he failed to account for the possible influences of rising racial tensions, the Vietnam War, and increased ownership of handguns. Moreover, for deterrence to be effective, murderers need to take into consideration the probable costs of their action. Emotions and passions at play can make a cost-benefit analysis unlikely. Most murderers, in Chambliss's words, are low-commitment individuals, often under the influence of drugs or alcohol, who are unlikely to assess rationally the consequences of their action. For them, the death penalty remains a highly questionable deterrent.

Aside from ethical and moral considerations, there are many arguments against the death penalty. For serial killers and particularly for female serial killers, capital punishment is not a deterrent (Fisher, 1997; Kelleher and Kelleher, 1998). Various studies have found that there is no material difference in the rate of homicides in American states that have capital punishment and those that do not (see, for example, Decker and Kohfeld, 1990). Some find that American states with the death penalty have higher homicide rates than states without the death penalty (Harries and Cheatwood, 1997; Harris, 1999) and suggest a possible "**brutalization effect**"—with executions increasing violent crime rather than serving as a deterrent. One might consider, in this context, that while more than 80 percent of American executions to date have been carried out in the South, 2004 FBI Uniform Crime Report data indicate that it was this region of the country that had the highest murder rate (6.6 per 100 000); the Northeast United States, which accounts for less than 1 percent of all executions, had the lowest murder rate (4.2 per 100 000) in 2004 (Death Penalty Research Center, 2006). In addition, a survey of research findings on the relationship between the death penalty and homicide rates that was originally conducted for the United Nations in 1988 and updated in 2002 concluded that "it is not prudent to accept the hypothesis that capital punishment deters murder to a marginally greater extent than does the threat and application of the supposedly lesser punishment of life imprisonment" (in

Hood, 2002:230). A study of different types of police killings for 1976 to 1989 involving 1204 officers also found no evidence that police are afforded an added measure of protection against death by capital punishment (Bailey and Peterson, 1994).

Studies in Canada, England, and other abolitionist countries have found nothing to suggest that the death penalty is a more effective deterrent than long prison sentences (Cheatwood, 1993). For example, in Canada, while the homicide rate per 100 000 population was 3.09 in 1975 (the year before the abolition of the death penalty for murder), by 1980 it had fallen to 2.4, and by 2003 (27 years after abolition) had plummeted to its lowest level in 36 years—1.73—a rate that was 44 percent lower than it had been in 1975 (Statistics Canada, 2005; Amnesty International, 2006). As a United Nations survey pointedly noted, "The fact that the statistics continue to point in the same direction is persuasive evidence that countries need not fear sudden and serious changes in the curve of crime if they reduce their reliance upon the death penalty" (in Hood, 2002:214). While a cause-and-effect relationship cannot be inferred between capital punishment and murder rates, Lawrence M. Friedman (1998:214) speculates that while capital punishment may work efficiently in some societies "which use it quickly, mercilessly, and frequently," in democratic countries that have elaborate due-process safeguards, its use will inevitably be "rare, slow, and controversial."

Opponents of the death penalty argue that prison terms without parole deter as many potential murderers as capital punishment. US data indicate that the certainty of being punished is negated by the fact that the death penalty is seldom imposed and that juries are less willing to convict when the penalty is death. Trials of capital cases are also more costly and time-consuming than trials for other cases; the 2003 Kansas Performance Audit Report pointedly observed that the costs of capital cases are no less than 70 percent more expensive than comparable non-capital cases, including the costs of incarceration (Death Penalty Information Center, 2006). Maintenance costs for inmates on death row are higher than for inmates in the rest of the prison. An exhaustive system of judicial review is required in American capital cases. Today, no death-row inmate in the United States will be executed until his or her case has been brought to the attention of the state's highest court, a federal district court of appeals, and the US Supreme Court. There are 20 federally funded centres for death-row appeals at an annual cost of around $30 million, and it would not be surprising if their numbers declined in the foreseeable future because of budget considerations. Almost two decades ago, the total costs for trials and appeals were estimated to range between $3 million and $5 million (*Economist*, 1990). By one study, each execution in North Carolina cost $2.16 million more than life imprisonment, with the majority of these costs incurred at the trial level. California spent over $1 billion between 1977 and 1996 on its death penalty—but executed only five men during this period (Costanzo, 1997:61). Tempest (2005) reports that, by 2004, "with 11 executions spread over 27 years, on a per execution basis, California and federal taxpayers have paid more than $250 million for each execution." Excluding the court-related costs of post-conviction hearings in state and federal courts, California's death penalty system was reported to cost taxpayers "more than $114 million a year beyond the cost of simply keeping the convicts locked up for life." In like fashion, "[e]nforcing the death penalty costs Florida $51 million a year above what it would cost to punish all first-degree murderers with life in prison without parole" (Death Penalty Information Center, 2006).

In addition, there is always the possibility that an innocent person will be executed. Wrongful convictions do occur (Auditor General of Canada, 2002; Kennedy, 2004). In rendering its decision in *United States v. Burns*, the Supreme Court of Canada referred to various cases in which Canadians have been wrongfully convicted of murder. These included the wrongful convictions of Donald Marshall, convicted of stabbing a teenager to death in a Sydney, Nova Scotia park, and who spent 11 years in some of Canada's toughest prisons before he was exonerated; Guy Paul Morin, convicted in the sex slaying of a young Ontario girl, and incarcerated for 17 months before DNA tests proved him innocent; and David Milgaard, convicted of the sex slaying of a Saskatoon nursing aide and who spent 23 years in various prisons, including the Oak Ridge institution for dangerous mentally ill offenders, before being exonerated on the basis of DNA evidence. In each of these cases of wrongful conviction, compensation of a sort was possible; each fought for, and eventually obtained, financial settlements from the federal and provincial governments. After a nine-year battle, Marshall received a $1.2 million settlement; Morin also received $1.2 million to cover his legal fees for two first-degree murder trials and as compensation for the months he had spent in custody (Tibbetts, 2001). David Milgaard received the largest settlement to date in Canada for a wrongfully convicted person: $9.25 million, to cover pain and suffering, lost income, out-of-pocket expenses, and legal fees (which amounted to $1.5 million) (Bourrie, 1999). However, it is evident that post-execution vindication can, at best, only result in a symbolic victory for the wrongfully convicted.

According to Amnesty International (2006), "[s]ince 1973, 122 prisoners have been released in the USA after evidence emerged of their innocence of the crimes for which they were sentenced to death. There were six such cases in 2004 and three up to December of 2005. Some prisoners had come close to execution after spending many years under sentence of death." The most common reasons for wrongful conviction are mistaken eyewitness testimony, the false testimony of informants and "incentivized witnesses," incompetent lawyers, defective or fraudulent scientific evidence, prosecutorial and police misconduct, and false confessions.

Although DNA evidence has played an increasing role in overturning wrongful death convictions, some death row inmates "have gone to their deaths despite serious doubts over their guilt" (Amnesty International, 2006). One study reports that some 139 innocent people were sentenced to death between 1900 and 1985 in the United States. Of those, 29 were actually executed (Haines, 1992:130). Other studies show that one innocent person has been convicted for every 20 executions carried out since the turn of the century (Radelet et al., 1992). The 2000 report of Equal Justice USA directed attention to 16 instances in which individuals were executed despite their probable innocence and asserted that these cases represented "only a small number of the actual cases in which people have been executed for crimes they probably did not commit." According to this study, these cases demonstrated "patterns and practices in the administration of justice. . . that violate constitutionally and internationally protected rights," including the failure of defence attorneys to provide their clients with competent legal counsel, prosecutorial and police misconduct, racial bias, and the unwillingness of state and federal appellate courts to intervene in even those cases in which there existed "compelling evidence of innocence and evidence of rights violations" (cited in Religious Tolerance.org). A second study, conducted by the Justice Project and entitled "A Broken System," also reported "serious, reversible error in nearly 7 of every 10 of the thousands of capital sentences" that were reviewed over the 23-year study period (Liebman, Fagan, and West, 2000; see also Hoffman, 2005). Nevertheless, some remain unmoved by such evidence. For example, Marquis (2005) emphasizes that "wrongful convictions are episodic rather than endemic," maintains that "claiming the accused as true innocents caught up by a corrupt and uncaring system discredits the abolitionist movement," and insists that "nothing justifies making the victims nameless and faceless, making martyrs out of murderers, and turning killers into victims."

The death penalty is also more likely to affect the poor and minority group members than more affluent whites (Berlow, 2001; Jones and Connelly, 2001). This has to do in part with the quality of legal help available to murder defendants. Those with court-appointed lawyers are more likely to be sentenced to death than those represented by private lawyers. Court-appointed lawyers in most US states are not required to stay on a homicide case after a conviction. Defendants with more money get better legal defence. In a study carried out in Texas in 2000, it was found that people represented by court-appointed lawyers were 28 percent more likely to be convicted than those who hired their own lawyers. If convicted, they were 44 percent more likely to be sentenced to death (*New York Times*, 2001b). As Franklin Zimring concludes, "no one on either side can defend the current system, which is hypocritical and unprincipled" (Zimring quoted by Kaplan, 1995:29).

The debate on the penological effectiveness of capital punishment continues despite the paucity of empirical evidence in support of its alleged deterrent effect. Aside from the moral need for eliminating the death penalty, the evidence shows that capital punishment does not deter murder. The threat of the death penalty raises the stakes of getting caught, and anyone who is subject to the death penalty has little to lose by killing again and again. Criminals who already face death for a previous crime are more likely to kill in order to avoid being captured or to silence possible witnesses. Police officers voice skepticism as to the efficacy of the death penalty and purportedly view it as "the enemy of law enforcement" (Morgenthau, 1995). When a Hart Research Poll asked American police chiefs what they felt should be a primary focus of efforts to reduce violent crime, these highly ranked officers were far more likely to identify "reducing drug abuse" (31 percent), "better economy, jobs" (16 percent), "simplifying court rules" (16 percent), "longer prison sentences" (15 percent), "more police officers" (10 percent), and "reducing guns" (3 percent) than to recommend the expanded use of the death penalty (1 percent) (Death Penalty Information Center 2006). Similarly, a survey of former and current presidents of America's top academic criminological societies (i.e., the American Society of Criminology; the Academy of Criminal Justice Sciences; the Law and Society Association) reported that, when asked, "Do you feel that the death penalty acts as a deterrent to the commitment of murder—that it lowers the murder rate?", 57 of the 64 presidents (87.5 percent) believed that the death penalty does not have deterrent effects (Radelet and Akers, 1996).

At this point, it should be noted that the majority of murders in both Canada and the United States are committed by acquaintances or family members of the victim rather than coldly calculating "contract killers" (Gannon, 2001:5). In 2000, acquaintances committed over half of homicides in Canada (51 percent) and the United States (54 percent). In that year, about one in three (32 percent) victims of homicide in Canada and one in four (23 percent) victims of homicide in the United States were killed by a family member (Gannon, 2001:5). However, two in three American homicides in 2000 involved the use of firearms, compared with one in three in Canada. Over the past decade, the proportion of Canadian homicides involving a firearm has remained fairly stable, ranging from 26 to 34 percent; in 2004, firearms were used in 28 percent of homicides in Canada. "In contrast, in the United States, two-thirds of all homicide victims were killed with a firearm in 2003, more than double the proportion seen in Canada" (Statistics Canada, 2005a; see also Fox and Zawitz, 2004). Noting that the homicide rate in the United States is three times higher than that of Canada, four times higher than western Europe's, six times higher than Great Britain's, and seven times higher than Japan's (Doyle, 2000; Gannon, 2001), some researchers emphasize that the greater availability of firearms in the United States may explain the difference in levels of homicide (Zimring and Hawkins, 1997). In the United States, where some 36 states permitted adults to carry a concealed handgun in 2001 (Henderson, 2005), controlling handguns might be a more effective method of reducing homicide rates than capital punishment. However, some would undoubtedly bristle at this suggestion.

For example, in two highly controversial books, *More Guns, Less Crime: Understanding Crime* and *Gun Control Laws and the Bias Against Guns: Why Almost Everything You've Heard About Gun Control is Wrong*, economist John Lott (2000, 2003) claims that if more law-abiding citizens were allowed to carry guns, murder rates and crime would go down. In his first book, based on data from all 3054 counties in the United States from 1977 to 1994, Lott argues that, for each year that a concealed-handgun law was in effect, the local murder rate declined by 3 percent, robberies by over 2 percent, and rape by 2 percent. In addition, it is his contention that the two groups most vulnerable to violent crime in the United States—women and blacks—benefit the most from concealed-weapon laws. Lott's second book reiterates these conclusions and attempts to demonstrate how various gun-related regulations, bans, and registration procedures are counterproductive. It is, perhaps, predictable enough that these books have inspired furious protests from gun-control lobbyists and criminologists who question the methodologies used and view the conclusions drawn as suspect at best (*Focus on Law Studies*, 2003; Henderson, 2005). Gun control, in the United States and elsewhere, continues to be a topic of contentious debate among social scientists and policy makers (see, for example, Harcourt, 2003; Stolzenberg and D'Alessio, 2000).

Civil Commitment

The formal control of deviant behaviour is not limited to criminal sanctions (see, for example, Arrigo, 2002; Diesfeld and Freckelton, 2003). There is another form of social control through laws that operates through the medicalization of deviance (Conrad, 1996:69). "Medicalization" refers to the process of defining behaviour as a medical problem or illness and mandating the medical profession to provide treatment for it. Examples of this would include drug abuse, alcoholism, and viewing violence as a genetic or psychological disorder.

According to John Goodman (1999:1469), "[m]ental illness is the most pervasive health problem in Canada." Although definitional problems abound, one cross-national study reports a 12 percent lifetime prevalence of "any mental disorder" in Turkey, a 20 percent lifetime prevalence in Mexico, a 37.5 percent lifetime prevalence in Canada, and a 40 percent lifetime prevalence in the Netherlands and the United States (World Health Organization International Consortium on Psychiatric Epidemiology, 2000a). Other estimates suggest that one in five Canadians will be affected by a mental illness at some time in their lives (Canadian Mental Health Association, 2002) or that 3 million Canadians are currently living with some kind of mental illness (Simmie and Nunes, 2001). The most common mental disorder, both in Canada and worldwide—depression—affects one in four Canadian women and one in ten Canadian men at some point in their lives (Canadian Psychiatric Association, 2002).

Research suggests that only one-quarter of Canadians with a mental disorder seek help and that those who do often find themselves frustrated by long waiting lists; while there are three times as many psychologists as psychiatrists in Canada, provincial health plans do not cover the costs of psychologists working in private practices (Butters and Erickson, 2003; Simmie and Nunes, 2001:246). Although persons who perceive themselves as needing the assistance of mental health professionals may voluntarily seek admission at a psychiatric or general hospital, others may be hospitalized against their will. Every Canadian jurisdiction allows authorities to detain for a limited time a person who has been certified as mentally incompetent by one or more physicians. Civil commitment is a non-criminal process that commits disabled or otherwise dependent individuals, without their consent, to an institution for care, treatment, or custody, rather than punishment. Although all individuals have the right to accept or refuse any form of psychiatric or medical treatment as long as they are mentally competent (i.e., able to understand what they are doing and their consent informed and voluntary), in only some jurisdictions do those who are involuntarily committed retain the legal right to refuse treatment.

Although mental health acts vary substantially across Canada, legislation in relation to involuntary hospitalization of the mentally incompetent has historically reflected one of two dominant models. The first of these models makes dangerousness—the assessed potential of individuals to pose a danger to themselves or to others—the predominant test for involuntary hospitalization. For example, prior to the proclamation of Bill 68 ("Brian's Law") in June of 2000, legislation in Ontario reflected this model. It allowed for the involuntary hospitalization of an individual who "apparently" had a mental disorder "of a nature or quality" that would likely result in "(i) serious bodily harm to self, or (ii) such harm to others, or (iii) serious physical impairment of the person" and who had threatened or attempted to cause bodily harm to him or herself, behaved violently toward another, or caused another to fear bodily harm. Accordingly, a person who was perceived to be acting in an irrational manner but was not believed to be at "imminent" risk (i.e., within several weeks) of serious bodily harm would not have satisfied the criteria for involuntary admission. Since that time, however, Ontario has shifted to the second model of mental health, which emphasizes a "best interests" approach. The best interests model builds on the legal principle that the state has the right and responsibility to assume guardianship over individuals suffering from some disability. The basic premise is that, whether or not individuals are at "imminent" risk of danger to themselves or others, they should nevertheless be held involuntarily if they require treatment, are likely to suffer mental or physical deterioration without treatment, and are currently unable to understand their need for treatment.

Ontario's *Mental Health Act* governs how people in that province are admitted to psychiatric facilities, their mental health records kept and assessed, their financial affairs handled, and when and how they are to be released into the community. The *Health Care Consent Act* outlines how persons are to be cared for and treated within various facilities. The *Substitute Decisions Act* addresses legal guardianship and power of attorney issues in relation to those who are judged to be permanently, or temporarily, "mentally incompetent." Ontario's *Mental Health Act* has expanded the criteria for involuntary admission to include those who are "apparently incapable" of making treatment decisions for themselves; have previously been treated for a disorder of an "ongoing and recurring" nature that will likely result in either substantial mental or physical deterioration, physical impairment, violence, or harm to self; "apparently" suffer from the same or a similar disorder; and have shown "clinical improvement" with treatment in the past (Queen Street Outreach Society, 2002).

Several features of Bill 68 have precipitated concern. For example, a police officer can bring anyone into a facility for an examination if the officer has "reasonable and probable grounds" to believe that the individual has acted in a "disorderly manner" (meaning irrational but not necessarily criminal) as long as the person "apparently" suffers from a mental disorder and has threatened or attempted to harm themselves, behaved violently, or caused someone else to fear bodily harm, or is perceived by the officer to lack the competence to care for him- or herself. Those who are involuntarily detained for "observation and assessment" are subject to a type of preventive detention without appeal for a 72-hour period. Moreover, a "community treatment order" (CTO) can be imposed on any individual who has been treated (voluntarily or not) in a "mental health facility" for a minimum of 30 days or twice within the past three years. A CTO authorizes a health professional to forcibly treat (e.g., drug or electroshock) those who are identified as needing treatment. Those who refuse treatment, fail to follow a treatment plan, or miss scheduled appointments with their health professional can be apprehended by police and involuntarily returned to a mental health centre for treatment. Critics charge that such provisions target and criminalize the conduct of vulnerable people, such as the homeless, exacerbate the stigma associated with seeking help for mental health problems, and impose potentially severe penalties upon those who fail to comply with the treatment plan (PACT, 2002). In essence and effect, a CTO imposes a type of parole upon psychiatric patients after they are discharged from hospital.

Procedurally, the civil commitment is different from criminal commitment. Douglas and Koch (2001:355) note that "in comparison to criminal procedures, there are fewer safeguards protecting the rights of persons confined under civil commitment legislation." In civil commitment, certain procedural safeguards are not available, such as a right to trial by jury, which involves confronting witnesses against the defendant, and the right to avoid testifying against oneself. Moreover, the formal moral condemnation of the community is not an issue in involuntary commitment. Forst notes: "This situation may arise if the behaviour is intentional but not morally blameworthy, as in a civil suit for damages, or if the behaviour would have been morally blameworthy, but because of mental impairment, criminal culpability is either mitigated or negated. In the latter instance, the. . . issue is not the person's behaviour but his status" (1978:3). In this view, a heroin addict, a mentally incompetent person, or a sex offender is not held morally responsible for their actions. The general consensus is that the individual deserves treatment, not punishment, even though the treatment may entail the deprivation of his or her liberty in a mental institution without due process.

Civil commitments can be controversial. For example, in 1996, a Winnipeg judge attempted to protect the fetus of a pregnant, glue-sniffing 22-year-old woman by ordering the woman into the custody of the Director of Child and Family Services and permitting the Director to have the woman committed under mental health legislation if she failed to take treatment during her pregnancy for her addiction. In this case, the judge based his ruling on the "parens patriae" jurisdiction of judges "to act beyond the scope of the statute or interpretive law to protect the weak, vulnerable, and mentally incompetent" (Dranoff, 2001:12). He emphasized the risk the woman's conduct posed to herself and her unborn child, and noted that the woman's glue-sniffing had already resulted in damage to three other children (all of whom had become Crown wards). Nevertheless, the judge's decision was reversed by the Manitoba Court of Appeal on the grounds that (i) a fetus was not a "legal person" under Canadian law with all the rights and privileges that legal personhood confers; (ii) the courts should not be placed in the position of choosing between the rights of a mother and her fetus; and (iii) the lower court had no jurisdiction to force the woman into treatment since psychiatric testimony had established that the woman was not mentally ill as defined by law. Therefore, as a mentally competent person, the woman was entitled to consent to or refuse treatment as she saw fit. In 1997, the Supreme Court of Canada affirmed the decision of the Manitoba Court of Appeal.

Civil commitment for mental illness and incompetence is only one of the many types of civil commitments used to control deviant behaviour. However, critics have argued that the medicalization of deviance and psychiatry's immersion into the legal process is neither therapeutic nor benevolent in intent and simply "widens the net" by creating more intensive, intrusive, and prolonged measures of social control (Lowman, Menzies, and Palys, 1987). For example, because of the movement to treat teenage deviance with medicine, teenagers are increasingly being diagnosed as sufferers of "conduct disorder," "oppositional defiant disorder," and the popular "adolescent adjustment reaction." These terms sound impressive, but they cover a variety of fairly commonplace teenage activities: running away, aggression, persistent opposition to parental values and rules, and engaging in "excessive" sexual activity (usually as defined by the parent). Not surprisingly, many adolescents who are defined as requiring treatment may be less troubled than troubling to someone else.

In the legal arena, the causes of criminal behaviour and the responsibility for such behaviour lie within the individual. But in a legal system that posits individual causation, complications arise in attempts to control individuals who are threatening yet have broken no law (see, for example, Peay, 1998). One way to control such individuals is to define their conduct as a mental disorder. Greenaway and Brickey state: "This definition has the combined effect of imputing irrationality to the behaviour and providing for the control of the individual through ostensibly benign, but coercive psychiatric intervention" (1978:139). Thus, it is not surprising to find that many mental hospitals include people who have committed trivial offences or who have not been convicted of any crime at all.

There are diverse explanations for the increased use of civil commitment as a mechanism of social control. Forst states:

> There are those (the positive criminologists) who view the increase as a beneficial shift from the traditional emphasis on punishing people to rehabilitating them . . . Another explanation for the increased use of civil commitments (the divestment of the criminal law) is that the civil commitment serves as a substitute for, or a supplement to, the criminal law in order to socially control undesirable forms of behavior. (1978:9)

As we have noted, the use of civil commitment is not without criticisms. Some critics advocate the abolition of all civil commitment laws because the rights of the individuals subjected to them are violated, in spite of the number of recent laws designed to protect the rights of the mentally ill. Others oppose it and allied measures (e.g., the transfer of mentally ill prisoners to psychiatric facilities) because it allows people to avoid the punishment they deserve. Although the issue remains controversial, the use of civil commitment as a form of social control is on the increase.

CRIMES WITHOUT VICTIMS

Canada invests enormous resources in controlling victimless crimes where harm occurs primarily to the participating individuals. For 2004, there were about 2.6 million criminal incidents (excluding traffic offences) reported to Canadian police agencies. Many of these incidents involved crimes without victims. For example, of the 97 135 drug incidents known to police in that year, no less than half (48 052) were for possession of cannabis (Statistics Canada, 2005b).

The criminalization of some acts that have no victims stems from the fact that society regards those acts as morally repugnant or vexatious and wishes to restrain individuals from engaging in them. There is an extensive victimless crime literature dealing with drug addiction, prostitution, gambling, euthanasia, suicide, and public nudity. These are crimes *mala prohibita* (that is, behaviours made criminal by statute, but there is no consensus as to whether these acts are criminal of themselves). They are acts against public interest or morality and appear in criminal codes as crimes against public decency, order, or justice. Crimes like sexual assault or homicide are *mala in se* (that is, evils in themselves, with public agreement on the dangers they pose).

Victimless crimes are also differentiated from other crimes by the element of consensual transaction or exchange. These crimes are also differentiated from other kinds of crimes by the lack of apparent harm to others and by the difficulty in enforcing the laws against them as a result of low visibility and the absence of complainants. In other words, they are plaintiffless crimes—that is, those involved are willing participants who, as a rule, do not complain to the police that a crime has been committed. Although many people do not consider these activities "criminal," the police and the courts continue to apply laws against such groups as drug users, prostitutes, gamblers, and pornography distributors— laws that large sections of the community do not recognize as legitimate and simply refuse to obey. This situation is further compounded (and muddied) by recent technological breakthroughs such as the use of computers to create pornographic images. Is there a line between "fake" pornography, where digital simulations are used to create images, and "real" pornography with "live" subjects? The two are virtually indistinguishable from each other, and the criminalization of foul figments of cyber technology that do not involve human subjects raises some interesting legal questions (Liptak, 2001).

The formal controls exerted on these types of behaviour are expensive and generally ineffective. Still, they serve certain functions. Robert M. Rich (1978:28) notes that persons who are labelled as criminals serve as an example to community members. When the laws are enforced against lower-class and minority-group members, it allows those who occupy relatively more powerful positions (i.e., middle- and upper-class people) to feel that the law is serving a useful purpose because it preserves and reinforces the myth that low-status individuals account for most of the deviance in society. Finally, the control of victimless crimes, in the forms of arrests and convictions, strengthens the notion in the community that the police and the criminal justice system are doing a good job of protecting community moral standards. Let us now consider law as a means of social control for certain victimless crimes such as drug addiction, prostitution, and gambling.

Drug Addiction

Although there have been several major periods of anti-drug sentiments, crusades, and drug scares, the non-medical use of drugs, such as opium and heroin, only relatively recently became a criminal act in Canada. Before 1908, there had been only sporadic attempts to regulate the use of drugs. "While there were instances of prior restrictive and regulative legislation deriving from medical concern about the free availability of 'poisons' and consumer protection interest in product purity, it appears that no Western nation used the criminal law to prohibit the distribution of narcotics for recreational purposes until Canada's pioneering effort of 1908" (Green, 1986:24). In 1908, Canada's first criminal narcotics legislation, *An Act to Prohibit the Importation, Manufacture and Sale of Opium for Other than Medicinal Purposes*, a simple two-paragraph statute, was passed (without discussion in the House of Commons and with an absence of effective opposition in the Senate) within a period of three weeks. Although some maintain that the real statutory beginning of narcotic control in Canada occurred with the 1911 passage of the *Opium and Drug Act* (Giffen, Endicott, and Lambert, 1991:13), there is little doubt that racism directed against the Chinese played a critical role in the history of Canadian narcotics legislation (Backhouse, 1999:142).

Hostility to the use of opium emerged in part because of a labour surplus that followed the completion of railway construction and the diminished intensity of the Gold Rush. Green (1986:25) notes that before this time, in the midst of a labour shortage, "the Chinese were regarded as industrious, sober, economical and law-abiding individuals." As jobs became scarce and the Chinese were viewed as competitors for the positions that existed, "the earlier friendly feelings toward the Chinese changed." Simultaneously, opium use, which had been previously viewed, at worst, as "an individual medical misfortune or personal vice, free of severe moral opprobrium," became defined as a significant social "evil." Morgan (1978:59) observes, "The first opium laws. . . were not the result of a moral crusade against the drug itself. Instead, it represented a coercive action directed against a vice that was merely an appendage of the real menace—the Chinese—and not the Chinese per se, but the labouring 'Chinamen' who threatened the economic security of the white working class." The criminalization of other drugs, including cocaine, heroin, and marijuana, have followed similar patterns of social control of the powerless, political opponents, and/or minorities (see, for example, Carstairs, 2002).

As James Hackler (2003:213) has emphasized, "the societal demand to punish, stigmatize, and exclude users of certain substances is not based on pharmacological evidence" and evidence of such damage "plays a secondary role in drug policy." Consider the irony: Of the $18.5 billion cost of substance abuse to the Canadian economy in 1992, tobacco accounted for $9.6 billion, alcohol $7.5 billion, and illicit drugs $1.4 billion (Canadian Centre on Substance Abuse, 1999:25).

Although a common tendency is to presume that Canada's "drug problem" is largely attributable to illegal or illicit drugs, in reality, two of the most widely used and dangerous drugs in Canada—alcohol and tobacco—are legal. According to Health Canada (2002), one Canadian dies every 12 minutes of a tobacco-related disease, with deaths due to tobacco killing over 45 000 Canadians each year—more than the combined totals of all murders, alcohol-related deaths, car accidents, and suicides. Moreover, an estimated four to five million Canadians engage in high-risk drinking, "which is linked to motor vehicle accidents, Fetal Alcohol Syndrome Disorder and other health issues, family problems, crime and violence" (Health Canada, 2005). Statistics Canada's 2002 Community Mental Health Survey found that of the approximately three-quarters of a million Canadians who reported symptoms consistent with drug dependence at some time during the year prior to the survey, the majority suffered from alcohol dependence (about 2.6 percent of the population aged 15 or older) rather than from dependence on an illicit drug (0.7 percent [Statistics Canada, 2003]).

In May 1997, the *Controlled Drugs and Substances Act* (CDSA) became law in Canada, consolidating most of the illicit drug legislation and outlining the six federal criminal offences of possession, trafficking, possession for the purpose of trafficking, production, importing or exporting, and "prescription shopping." While the penalties for possession vary depending on the type of drug, the maximum penalties under this act for the majority of offences are severe. For example, for "Schedule 1" drugs (i.e., cocaine, heroin, opium, phencyclidine, and those drugs that, prior to May 1997, were dealt with under the *Narcotics Control Act*), the maximum penalty for trafficking, possession for the purpose of trafficking, producing, and importing or exporting is life imprisonment. Life imprisonment is also the maximum penalty for importing or exporting any amount of any form of cannabis (Solomon, 1999).

According to Statistic Canada (2004), between 1977 and 2002, the police-reported drug crime rate rose approximately 42 percent to reach a 20 year high, with the increases largely driven by increases in cannabis offences. In 2004, almost 100 000 people were charged with Criminal Code offences under the *Controlled Drugs and Substances Act*; offences involving cannabis accounted for more than two-thirds (69.8 percent) of these charges, and approximately half (49.5 percent) of the charges laid were for possession (Statistics Canada, 2005).

Although drug addiction ranks among the top concerns of many Canadians (Bibby, 2001), surveys indicate that illegal drug use of all kinds is far less common than alcohol and tobacco use (Statistics Canada, 2004). The most commonly used and most heavily trafficked illicit drug in Canada and in the world is marijuana (Reitox, 2001). It is estimated that over 40 million Europeans have tried cannabis at least once in their lifetime and that there are 200 to 250 million marijuana users worldwide, predominantly in Africa and Asia (Francis, 2000). The 2002 Canadian Community Health Survey reports that over 10 million Canadians—just over 41 percent of Canada's population— have used cannabis on at least one occasion and that almost one-third (32 percent) have used it more than once (Statistics Canada, 2004). In addition, this survey notes that cannabis use is increasing in this country and that "[t]he proportion of Canadians aged 15 and older who admit to using cannabis nearly doubled between 1989 (7.4 percent) and 2002 (12.2 percent). With the exception of Canadians aged 15 to 17 (where men and women are equally likely to report cannabis use), men are more likely than women to use cannabis (Statistics Canada, 2004). Young Canadians are more likely to use cannabis than those who are older, with use of this drug peaking in the late teens and declining notably after age 24. Moreover, the number of young people who believe marijuana is dangerous has steadily declined over the past decade and marijuana use among young people has steadily increased. The 2000 Project Canada national survey of youth also finds that 50 percent of Canadian teens (58 percent of males and 42 percent of females) favour the legalization of marijuana use—up from 27 percent in 1992 (Bibby, 2001:188).

"While estimates vary, the United Nations believes that the annual global sales of illicit drugs are between $450 billion and $750 billion. In Canada, the government's estimates of sales range from $7 billion to $18 billion" (Auditor General, 2001; see also Auditor General, 2002). The illegal drug industry is simple and profitable. Its simplicity makes it fairly easy to organize and its profitability makes it hard to stop. At every level, its pricing is determined by the level of risk of enforcement: the risk of seizure and jail, and the uncertainty that arises because traders cannot rely on the laws to enforce the bargains. For example, while a Pakistani farmer may receive $90 for a kilo of opium, the wholesale price in Pakistan approaches $3000; in Canada, the wholesale price may exceed $80 000 and, on the street at 40 percent purity, soar to $290 000 a kilogram. As for cocaine, the leaf needed to produce a kilo costs between $400 and $600. By the time it leaves Colombia, the price has gone up to about $1800. On the streets in Canada, after a kilo of cocaine has changed hands a few times, the retail price may reach $110 000 and, in Europe, substantially more. The vast gap between the cost of production and the price paid by the end users obviously plays a role in the failure of drug policies. The producers see a modest return; the real profit is embedded mainly in the distribution chain, which is very hard to control effectively (see, for example, Marez, 2004).

Since 1987, Canada's Drug Strategy has emphasized the need for a "balanced" approach that combines prevention and education with law enforcement. Among its stated objectives: "reducing the demand for drugs; reducing drug-related mortality and morbidity by reducing high-risk behaviours, such as spreading HIV/AIDS through needle sharing; improving the effectiveness of and accessibility to substance abuse information and interventions; restricting the supply of illicit drugs; reducing the profitability of illicit trafficking; and reducing the costs of substance abuse to Canadian society" (Auditor General, 2001). In recent years, the majority of the federal government's changes to legislation in relation to illicit drugs have targeted the issue of supply rather than demand. These efforts have included the amendment of the Canadian Criminal Code to include organized crime offences and the creation of the Financial Transactions and Reports Analysis Centre of Canada. The latter attempts to detect money laundering by monitoring financial transactions. The federal Integrated Proceeds of Crime initiative, whose mandate involves investigating organized crime groups and seizing assets gained through criminal activities, is acknowledged as largely a drug-related initiative, with an estimated 90 percent of seizures related to drugs. Since the enactment of this legislation in 1989, the RCMP has seized or restrained assets of more than $400 million; in Ontario alone, during the first nine months of 2004, police seized over $44 million in goods and $5 million in cash under this legislation (RCMP, 2006).

Although Canadian federal agencies spend approximately $500 million each year to fight drugs (Rodrique, 2002), the lack of a complainant, the sheer volume of available drugs, and the extreme profitability of the illicit drug trade make enforcement efforts difficult (see, for example, Beare, 2002). Some of the by-products of the tremendous legal efforts to control drugs have resulted in the formation of elaborate illegal organizations for the supply of illicit drugs. Consider here that since 1994, over 150 deaths in Quebec have been attributed to "biker" wars over the control of the illicit drug trade (Auditor General, 2001; *Economist*, 2002a). Many users turn to other criminal activities to support their habit; in Vancouver, for example, it is estimated that 70 percent of criminal activity is associated with illicit drugs (Auditor General, 2001; see also Braitstein, Li, and Tyndall, 2003; Erickson, Butters, and McGillicuddy, 2000). Among those serving criminal sentences of over two years in length, almost two-thirds (63 percent) have drug abuse problems (Auditor General, 2001; see Kitchin, 2005, for a discussion of the links between crime and substance abuse among provincial inmates in Nova Scotia).

Drug laws have also contributed to a situation in which politicians and police may ignore drug traffic—because of payoffs. In addition, a federal government report on organized crime concluded that "with drugs as its primary source of revenue, organized crime has intimidated police officers, judges, juries, and correctional officers" (Auditor General, 2001). Efforts at enforcement may encourage the police to resort to entrapment and illegal search and seizure tactics. Furthermore, there is obvious potential for conflict and recrimination in the control of the flow of illegal drugs. The principal consumer countries are affluent and industrialized; the principal drug-producing countries are poor and basically agricultural. Cocaine and heroin traffic in the Western Hemisphere is a particularly serious example of how this conflict of interests plays out (Martin and Romano, 1992:51). Consuming and producing countries vehemently accuse and blame each other and, depending on which side they are on, advocate either demand-side or supply-side solutions—controlling the demand of users as opposed to controlling the supply. Elites in drug-producing countries view anti-drug campaigns with hostility because they impose significant new burdens and create formidable new challenges. There are powerful vested economic interests profiting from drugs; during the 1990s, Colombia alone lost 23 judges, 63 journalists, 4 presidential candidates, and more than 3000 soldiers and police officers in its attempt to moderate drug production (Samper, 1995).

In short, there is little prospect of effective control of drugs through the criminal law. Some even argue that the so-called "war on drugs" has corrupted the government institutions and that no law enforcement agency has escaped the effects of the profit and racism that drive the drug trade and its criminalization (Baggins, 1998; Marez, 2004). Duke and Gross (1994) maintain that the war on drugs has also served to intensify other social problems such as overcrowded prisons, the diversion of police from other serious crime, unemployment, and the spread of AIDS. For Duster (1995), the "war on drugs" is better seen as a war on the poor—an argument that is also reinforced by a 1998 book by Michael Massing, *The Fix*. Massing contends that the hard-core users of heroin and cocaine are disproportionately poor, unemployed, and members of minority groups. Although hard-core users represent only one-fifth of total users, they consume three-fourths of the cocaine and heroin used and are responsible for most of the pathological behaviour that elicits public and governmental responses. If society could provide appropriate treatment to anyone in this population who wanted it, Massing maintains, the whole drug problem would diminish, as would the crime and illness associated with it. It has been shown that every $1 invested in drug treatment saved $7 in future costs of crime and incarceration (Treaster, 1995). Many would concur that the various punitive approaches—attacking drug production abroad, interdiction (seizing drugs in transit), and domestic law enforcement (arresting and incarcerating sellers and buyers)—have failed and that the "war on drugs" should be abandoned.

There are two controversial alternatives. The first is a consideration of drug addiction and drug use as more a medical than a legal problem, with an emphasis on comprehensive treatment, as is done, to some extent, in Great Britain and the Scandinavian countries (De Kort and Korf, 1992). The Netherlands, for example, has had an official government policy of treating the use of such drugs as marijuana, hashish, and heroin as a health issue rather than a crime issue since the mid-1970s. However, while drug use did not appear to increase during the first decade of this policy, increases in marijuana use were reported in the early 1990s with the advent of "cannabis cafes"—coffee shops which sell small amounts of marijuana for personal use (MacCoun and Reuter, 2001). More recently, marijuana use among Dutch youth is reported to be on the decline (Sheldon, 2000). Beginning in the 1960s, Great Britain also adopted a medical model, particularly in relation to heroin and cocaine. British doctors prescribed opiates and cocaine for patients whom they judged to be unlikely to quit using drugs on their own and, as well, for the treatment of withdrawal symptoms. However, since the 1970s, British laws have become increasingly more restrictive, and current government policy only provides for limited distribution of drugs by licensed drug treatment specialists to addicts who might otherwise resort to crime in order to support their drug habits. Reported increases in drug use in Great Britain have also resulted in calls for the adoption of a "zero-tolerance" policy in relation to drugs (Francis, 2000).

Despite the variable success that this alternative has enjoyed elsewhere, some Canadians continue to view its premise as appealing—as suggested by the 2003 Vancouver opening of Insite, North America's first supervised drug-injection clinic. This facility, modelled on 27 similar injection sites in Europe and Australia, furnishes a safe place for up to 800 drug addicts a day "to inject their own drugs with clean needles, supervised by a nurse and without fear of arrest" (*Economist*, 2003; see also Green, Kankins, and Palmer, 2003). Similarly, the opening of "drug treatment courts" (DTCs) in Canada would seem congruent with this approach.

Beginning in this country with the 1998 establishment of a DTC in Toronto as a pilot program (Evans, 2001), and followed by the establishment of a second DTC in Vancouver in 2001, these federally run courts impose court-supervised treatment, rehabilitation (including group and individual counselling), random drug testing, and job training rather than jail time for non-violent drug addicts who have committed a crime to support their addiction. Offenders are given one year to graduate from the program, with those who fail or are expelled returning to the regular court system. Some preliminary data suggest that DTCs may offer an innovative way to combine two systems—justice and health—in responding to the problem of drug-related crime. For example, it is noted that, "[i]n Toronto, only 11.6 percent of offenders who graduated from the program ended up getting into trouble with the law again, compared to 63.4 percent who were expelled" (Rabson, 2005). Reportedly, in its first three years of operation, 85 percent of Toronto's DTC graduates did not re-offend. Moreover, when compared to the costs of incarceration, DTCs strike some as a good investment: "the Toronto court spends an average of $8000 a year for each offender, compared to $50 000 a year to keep them in jail" (*Edmonton Journal*, 2005). Buoyed by such reports, by January 2006, DTCs had been introduced in Regina, Edmonton, and Ottawa, and eight other Canadian cities had applied to Ottawa for their establishment.

In the United States, where the first drug court was established in Dade County, Florida, in 1989, DTCs have flourished (with more than 1000 drug courts in existence in 2006) (see, for a discussion of the US experience, Deschenes et al., 2003; Goldkamp and White, 2002). In that country, a study which explored the perspectives of participants in six US drug courts (Goldkamp, White and Robinson, 2001) found that, even though participants largely enrolled in drug court to avoid the adverse consequences of their criminal charges, they came to believe that drug court offered them an "honest chance" and that the drug court model was a more effective vehicle for encouraging behavioural change than other approaches.

Relatively few studies on the efficacy of DTCs have been conducted to date. However, this limited body of research suggests that while many offenders are able to redress their substance abuse problems through court-mandated treatment (Goldkamp, White, and Robinson, 2001a; Wolfe et al., 2004), others are not (Gudish et al., 2001; Miller and Schutt, 2001). A recent study which sought to identify predictors of treatment outcome in a drug court program, based on a review of the records of 99 individuals who had been enrolled in a one-year-long drug court program in California, found that 49 successfully completed the drug court treatment program while 50 did not (Roll et al., 2005). According to this study, the best predictor for completing the drug court program was the presence of employment at the time of initial participation in the drug court program, with those who were employed about 14 times more likely than unemployed participants to graduate. The second best predictor of completing the program successfully was the absence of a history of needle use, with those "who did not have a history of injecting illicit drugs at the time of enrollment in the drug court program almost five-and-a-half times more likely to graduate than participants who had used needles to inject illicit drugs" (Roll et al., 2005). Due to the finite number of openings available for individuals in drug court programs, however, Klieman, Gottfredson, and Goldkamp (2003) caution against the assumption that DTCs will result in large-scale cost reductions. As such, DTCs may constitute a palliative rather than the panacea that some may envisage.

The second alternative is the legalization or decriminalization of drugs. For example, in April 1999, noting that about 2000 Canadians go to jail each year for cannabis possession at a cost of approximately $150 a day per offender, the board of directors of the Association of Canadian Chiefs of Police made a recommendation to the federal government that simple possession of marijuana and hashish be decriminalized. Decriminalization, they argued, would clear a backlog of drug cases in the courts and allow Canadian police services to focus their resources on more serious crimes like drug trafficking (Fife, 1999). Canada has already amended its law to allow those who require marijuana for medical purposes (e.g., to relieve symptoms associated with such conditions as HIV, cancer, and multiple sclerosis) to apply for an exemption under section 56 of the Controlled Drugs and Substances Act (*Economist*, 2001a). In 2002, over 800 Canadians were permitted by Health Canada to possess marijuana for medical purposes. In addition, the Marijuana Medical Access Regulations permit people with authorizations to possess and cultivate marijuana for medical purposes (McLellan, 2002). However, even these regulations can pose enforcement problems. For example, as of February 2006, almost half of those authorized to purchase government-certified marijuana or seeds for various medical problems were officially in arrears for bills that had been left unpaid for more than 90 days; collectively, they owed almost $170 000 to Health Canada for their medical marijuana. Reportedly, "[t]he arrears amount has swollen by more than $100,000 over the last year alone, as department officials realized that their medical marijuana policy never indicated to patients the consequences of not paying their drug bills" (Beeby, 2006).

Hathaway and Erickson's (2003) analysis of the official harm reduction aims of Canada's national drug strategy with the actual evolution of the Controlled Drugs and Substances Act reports "little evidence of harm reduction, and much of sustained and punitive prohibition." They note that the criminal sanctions that are currently imposed upon those who are convicted of cannabis possession reveal "the limits of what can be achieved in reducing the impact of criminalization when the fundamental ban on personal use and access is restrained." As the *Economist* (2001) argues, drugs are dangerous, but so is the illegality that surrounds them. Because it is illegal, it cannot be regulated. Governments cannot insist on minimum quality standards for cocaine; or warn asthma sufferers to avoid ecstasy; or demand that distributors take responsibility for the way their products are sold. With alcohol and tobacco, such restrictions are possible; with illicit drugs, they are not. In legitimate commerce, the sale of drugs would be controlled, taxed, and supervised. Educational campaigns would proclaim their dangers. Through legalization, drugs would poison fewer customers, kill fewer dealers and bystanders, bribe fewer enforcement people, and raise more public revenue. Initially, there may be more users and more addicts. The recommendation of the *Economist* (2001:16) is simply "to set it free." The article contends that governments allow their citizens to engage in a variety of self-destructive things: to go bungee-jumping, to ride motorcycles and jet skis, to own guns, to drink alcohol to excess, and to smoke cigarettes. Some of them are far more dangerous than taking drugs. It concludes that trade in drugs may be immoral or irresponsible, but it should no longer be illegal. The same theme is echoed in Jacob Sullum's (2003) book *Saying Yes: In Defense of Drug Use*. He highlights the injustice of punishing people for their choice of intoxicants and argues that government agencies, anti-drug activists, and a naive national media have exaggerated the public's fear of the harmful effects of recreational drugs—a nice controversial position to debate.

Before moving to the next topic, there is a novel form of drug control that is worth noting for its unique cultural component. Because of the practically unchecked methamphetamine production in Myanmar, close to the Thai border, it became the drug of choice in the hills of northern Thailand. Many farmers became drug smugglers and dealers (earning more in a day than they could in a month on rice fields) and drug use spread in the area, fueling theft to pay for the little orange pills. One village seriously afflicted with the drug problem came up with an indigenous—and perhaps ingenious—way to combat the drug epidemic. The village elders threatened drug dealers and users with a terrifying fate for a Thai: if they died, no one would attend their funerals and no monk would say prayers for their souls. Thai Buddhists believe the soul will be consigned to hell if funeral rights are not performed properly. A well-attended funeral—a major affair with relatives and musicians—is a principal requirement for a proper cremation. When dealers and users in the village were told that they would be cut off from the community, the drug problem ceased to exist. The 53 known drug dealers in the village of 1500 people gave up the trade and the addicts were weaned from the habit (Tang, 2003).

Prostitution

If there is one area in the criminal law that arouses the most anxiety concerning public morals, it is sexual conduct. The range of sexual conduct that has historically been covered by the law is so great and extensive that these laws, if re-enacted, would undoubtedly make criminals of most Canadian teenagers and adults. One of the justifications for such a complete control of sexual behaviour has been to protect the family system. Only two decades ago, a number of laws within Canada's Criminal Code were designed to control acts that would otherwise endanger the chastity of women before marriage. These included laws prohibiting rape as well as the seduction of a female between the ages of 16 and 18 years of age of "previously chaste character"; the seduction under promise of marriage of an unmarried female person, under the age of 21 and of previously chaste character; and the seduction of female passengers on vessels. Criminal laws prohibiting adultery were also designed to protect the family by preventing sexual relations outside of marriage (Quinney, 1975:83). In addition, a complex set of laws have historically surrounded the advertising, sale, distribution, and availability of contraceptives; the performance of abortion; voluntary sterilization; and artificial insemination (Childless by Choice Trust, 2000; Dranoff, 2005). Because of the complexity and extensiveness of legal control on sexual conduct and related matters, this section will be limited to a discussion of the legal controls of prostitution.

It is now recognized that laws throughout the world against prostitution discriminate against women (see, for example, Maticka-Tyndale, Lewis, and Street, 2005; Matthew and

O'Neill, 2003; Rabinovitch and Strega, 2004). Although a definitional amendment in 1983 provided that the term prostitute in Canada referred to "a person of either sex engaging in prostitution" and extended liability for engaging in prostitution to men, both as prostitutes and as purchasers, prostitution remains "the only area of criminal activity for which women are charged more often than men" (Shaver, 1993:154). Shaver (1999:1918) points out that "contemporary enforcement practices penalize women more often and more severely than men; penalize prostitutes more than customers, procurers, or pimps; and penalize street prostitutes more than off-street prostitutes." For example, while men (mostly clients) accounted for slightly more than half (56 percent) of those convicted for prostitution-related offences in 1996, they were much less likely to receive jail sentences than women convicted of prostitution-related offences (3 percent versus 39 percent) (Duchesne, 1999). Many prostitutes' rights groups and some feminist groups here and abroad maintain that a prostitute should have the right to engage in sexual relations for pay if she or he so desires (Poel, 1995; Rabinovitch and Strega, 2004). Moreover, they note that although prostitution has never been a crime in Canada, the prohibition of acts surrounding prostitution make it practically impossible to legally engage in prostitution.

At present, Canadian law prohibits four types of prostitution-related activities: "(1) procuring or living on the avails of prostitution; (2) owning, operating, or occupying a bawdy house; (3) all forms of public communication for the purpose of prostitution; and (4) knowingly transporting another to a bawdy house" (Shaver, 1999:1918). A 1985 amendment to the Criminal Code made it an offence for a person in a public place to stop or try to stop a car, impede the free flow of pedestrians or traffic or access to premises, or stop or try to stop a person or "in any manner communicate" or try to communicate with a person for the purpose of engaging in prostitution or of obtaining the sexual services of a prostitute. Although a Nova Scotia man challenged the constitutionality of this law, claiming that it violated the Charter guarantees of freedom of expression—a claim supported by Nova Scotia's Court of Appeal—the Supreme Court of Canada later ruled that even though Charter protections of freedom of expression extended to the activity of communication for the purposes of engaging in prostitution, it was reasonable to infringe on that freedom under the circumstances (Dranoff, 2005:162).

"On April 12, 2005, for the first time ever, charges were laid under a new piece of federal legislation designed to combat human trafficking. An 11-month investigation into an acupuncture therapy centre resulted in a series of charges being filed against one individual alleging that he had brought women into Canada under false pretences and forced them into prostitution" (Treasury Board of Canada, 2006). Current law additionally provides that those who profit from or participate in juvenile prostitution face more severe punishment than those who profit from or participate in adult prostitution. Since 1988, those who live on the avails of a prostitute under the age of 18 are liable for a maximum period of incarceration of 14 years; a customer who purchases the sexual services of a prostitute under the age of 18 is liable to a maximum sentence of five years. Amendments to the Criminal Code in 1997 made it illegal to attempt to procure the sexual services of someone under the age of 18. The offence of "aggravated procuring" imposes a five-year minimum sentence for individuals who, for their own personal profit while living on the avails of child prostitution, use violence or intimidation to force a child to engage in prostitution. Amendments made to the Criminal Code extends the jurisdiction of Canadian courts, allows for proceedings to be instituted in Canada against Canadian citizens who engage in child prostitution outside of the country ("sex tourism"), and permits police to charge tour operators or travel agents who arrange for such services (Criminal Intelligence Service Canada, 2002). The first case to make use of these changes occurred in 2004 when a married father from British Columbia was charged with sexual interference, sexual touching, and soliciting the services of a girl under the age of 18; all of these activities were alleged to have occurred in Asian countries (Dranoff, 2005:173). The majority of the evidence against the man consisted of videotapes that he had himself made and which, in part, showed him having sex with girls (the oldest of whom was 12) in Cambodia. At trial, the man originally entered a plea of not guilty, maintaining that Canada could not lawfully prosecute individuals for activities that were committed beyond its borders. However, in June 2005, he changed his stance, pled guilty to ten counts of sexual assault, and received a 10-year prison sentence (CBC Canada, 2004).

Other attempts to forestall the sexual exploitation of children have proven less successful. In 1998, for example, the province of Alberta passed the *Protection of Children Involved in Prostitution Act*, which classified prostitutes under the age of 18 as victims of child sexual abuse and those who purchased their services as child abusers. This act, which came into effect in February 1999, authorized police to enter a building without a search warrant if they believed that child prostitutes were inside and allowed officers to place those that the police suspected of being prostitutes in a "safe house" for 72 hours. Between February and October of 1999, 108 young people, almost all girls, were taken into custody, many more than once. However, in November of that year, lawyers representing two 17-year-old prostitutes challenged the law on the grounds that it was beyond the province's legal powers and that it violated four sections of the Constitution (Canadian Press, 1999). In 2000, this law was struck down by an Alberta provincial court as an unconstitutional violation of the rights against unreasonable search and seizure (Dranoff, 2005:173).

Laws against prostitution represent the attempt to control private moral behaviour through punitive social control measures. However, as the influential Wolfenden Report noted, as long as there is a demand for the services of prostitutes and there remain those individuals who choose this form of livelihood, "no amount of legislation directed towards its abolition will abolish it" (1963:132). Still, from time to time, community leaders and law enforcement agents would like to "clean up" some areas of the cities, and through these efforts, they persist in trying to suppress prostitution through the law (Larsen, 1999; Van Brunschot, 2003).

Various critics argue that the criminal statutes improperly and unwisely extend the coverage of criminal law to harmless matters of private morality, such as commercial sex between consenting adults. In many European countries in 2006, prostitutes ply their trade legally, pay taxes, and receive health and retirement benefits. The Netherlands, where the sex industry is now a $1 billion business or 5 percent of the economy, has legalized brothels, and the 30 000 or so sex workers now have a chance to get the basic labour rights, insurance policies, and disability payments enjoyed by other citizens (Daley, 2001). In Germany, the law has required for years that cities with populations of 500 000 or more designate 10 percent of their area as an "amusement" zone, with prostitution included among the amusements. In stark contrast, in Sweden, following years of public debate spearheaded by the Swedish women's movement, a law which prohibits the purchase of sexual services came into force on January 1, 1999. This law, which establishes a zero tolerance policy for prostitution and trafficking in human beings, has been described as "the first attempt by a country to address the root cause of prostitution and trafficking in beings: the demand, the men who assume the right to purchase persons for prostitution purposes" and to represent a "cornerstone of Swedish efforts to create a contemporary, democratic society where women and girls can live lives free of all forms of male violence" (Ekberg, 2004). The argument is that "[w]hen the buyers risk punishment, the number of men who buy prostituted persons decreases, and the local prostitution markets become less lucrative. Traffickers will then choose other and more profitable destinations."

Some writers (see, for example, Matthews and O'Neill, 2003) suggest that the law should only prohibit those acts that are clearly harmful to society and argue that prostitution does not meet this criterion. The decriminalization of prostitution would, in essence, extend the practice of official tolerance already operative in many places. It would allow the police to deal with more important matters, and it would possibly help lower the number of sex crimes. Lowman's (2000) investigation of murders against sex workers in British Columbia between 1964 to 1998 directs pointed attention to the "outlaw status" of street prostitutes in Canada and suggests how a "discourse of disposal"—as exemplified by media descriptions of ongoing attempts by police, politicians, and groups of residents to banish street prostitution from residential areas—may have contributed to the steep increase that has occurred in the murder of street prostitutes in that province after 1980. Opponents of decriminalization argue for increased legal control of prostitution, since they believe it leads to other crimes, such as drug addiction, blackmail, assault, and even murder.

Gambling

In 2002, just over three-quarters (76 percent) of adult Canadians had spent money on some form of gambling in the previous year, with four in ten having done so on a weekly basis. Since the 1990s, when provincial governments began to legalize permanent casinos and video lottery terminals (VLTs), a surge has occurred in the Canadian gambling industry and, in 2002, "an estimated 18.9 million adult Canadians wagered $11.3 billion on everything from VLTs, lottery tickets and bingos to blackjack and slot machines in casinos. This amount was more than a four-fold increase from $2.7 billion a decade earlier" (Statistics Canada, 2003).

Since its enactment in 1892, Canada's Criminal Code has always allowed gambling under certain conditions. A 1910 amendment permitted "pari-mutuel" betting (gambling on horse races with a cut of the bet going to the track, to the horsemen, and to the state), certain games at agricultural fairs, and occasional games of chance that profited charitable or religious organizations. Similarly, while section 189 of the Criminal Code specifies that it is an indictable offence to conduct any of a variety of activities related to "any proposal, scheme or plan for advancing, lending, giving, selling or in any way disposing of any property, by lots, cards, tickets, or any mode of chance whatever," a 1969 amendment (rewritten in 1985) allowed for exceptions to be made.

In 1970, amendments to the Criminal Code provided provinces with the right to license and regulate gambling—a situation that has made legal gambling a multibillion-dollar industry in Canada. All of Canada's provinces and territories are now involved in conducting and managing lotteries. Lotteries are managed and conducted in Alberta, Saskatchewan, and Manitoba by the Western Canada Lottery Corporation; in New Brunswick, Newfoundland, Nova Scotia, and Prince Edward Island by the Atlantic Lottery Corporation; in British Columbia by the British Columbia Lottery Corporation; and in Quebec by the Société des loteries et courses du Québec ("Loto-Québec"). Canada's provincial governments are shareholders within the Interprovincial Lottery Corporation, which conducts three national lottery schemes: Loto 6/49, Super- Loto, and the Provincial.

In 1989, Canada's first commercial casino opened in Winnipeg. Since that time, commercial casinos have opened in Quebec, Ontario, Nova Scotia, and Saskatchewan.

The question of whether the right to control gambling on Indian reserves is an Aboriginal right similar to the rights to hunt and fish was raised in the case of *Pamajewon* (1996). In this case, the First Nations of Shawanaga and Eagle Lake asserted the right to authorize and regulate games of bingo involving high stakes on their respective reserves. However, the Supreme Court of Canada ruled that such gaming was not protected as an Aboriginal right. Assuming that the right to self-government was included in section 35(1) of the *Constitution Act, 1982*—an issue that the court did not address—Chief Justice Lamer held that gaming for high stakes was not a distinctive and defining feature of the culture and traditions of Aboriginal societies prior to their contact with Europeans. Noting that the evidence presented before the court did not demonstrate that part of their territory had ever been used for that purpose, the court rejected the claim that the right to self-government included the right to control gambling on Indian reserves (Beaudoin, 1999). As a result, First Nations gambling operates under permission of provincial governments. By 1999, First Nations in Canada had negotiated the right to operate on-reserve video lottery terminal gambling in Manitoba and Nova Scotia, casinos in Saskatchewan and British Columbia, and to share in profits from Ontario's on-reserve casino, Casino Rama (*Casino Gambling*, 1999; *Gaming Magazine*, 2002).

Excluding gambling revenue generated by and for charities and on Indian reserves, legal gambling revenue increased from $2.7 billion in 1992 to $10.7 billion in 2001. During this same period, gambling profit (the net income of provincial governments from total gambling revenue, less operating and other expenses) rose from approximately $1.7 billion to $5.6 billion (Statistics Canada, 2002b:2). Since that time, the profits have only increased: "For 2003–04, the gross profit from government-run gambling activity in Canada was $12.742 billion—an increase of $700 million from 2002–03 reported figures" (Azmier, 2005). Once again, these figures only include those activities "in which governments directly participate as gambling providers" and exclude gambling activities run by charities or First Nations, and horse races (Azmier, 2005). However, the liberalization of legal gambling in Canada since 1970 does not appear to have had any effect on illegal gambling in Canada (Sheppard and Smith, 1999). Currently, legal and illegal gambling exist practically side-by-side, with participants often crossing the line.

In the victimless-crime literature, illegal gambling, just like drug use and prostitution, is considered a consensual transaction and a plaintiffless crime (see, for example, Beare, 1996; Cozic and Winters, 1995). The players are willing participants who generally do not notify the police that a crime has been committed. Enforcement activity therefore must be initiated by the police, who then act as the complainant on the behalf of the community. By contrast, enforcement activity for other crimes, such as thefts or muggings, usually occurs in response to citizen complaints. Although the most popular form of illegal gambling in Canada—betting on individual sporting events—generates huge profits for book-makers and is reported to be "the largest source of gambling revenue of organized crime," it is tolerated "and there is no public pressure exerted to control it" (Sheppard and Smith, 1999:946). Similarly, although illegal private gaming houses are located in every major Canadian city, complaints are infrequent and control efforts sporadic.

The Commission on the Review of the National Policy Toward Gambling (1976:44) identified a number of control techniques used by law enforcement agencies to control illegal gambling. The most frequent source of gambling arrests stems from the direct observation of illegal gambling activity and is primarily " nonserious," involving individual street players or low-level employees of gambling organizations. Arrests at higher levels—for example, large bookmakers or numbers offices—are rarely, if ever, made in this manner. They require investigation leading to a probable cause for search and arrest warrants. The use of informants in gambling control is widespread. Most police departments rely on this technique, as well as on undercover investigators who can often accumulate evidence against individuals and on operations by placing bets. Electronic surveillance is often useful for investigations of gambling because of the dependence of gambling operations on telephones. One of the devices that has been used with some success is the pen register, which records phone numbers dialled from a particular telephone. By attaching a pen register to the telephone line of a gambling location, police can often identify additional locations and individuals involved in illegal gambling operations.

Nevertheless, the criminal law is ineffective in controlling and preventing people from engaging in illegal gambling. The parties involved in gambling do not complain about it, and a typical gambling transaction is probably more easily, rapidly, and privately consummated than is any other kind of illegal consensual transaction. It is much easier to place a bet with a bookie than to buy cocaine or have an encounter with a prostitute. Moreover, public opinion does not consider gambling as particularly wrongful, a sentiment both affected by and reflected in the lenience with which gambling offenders are treated. This, perhaps, is to be expected in a country that now boasts over "87 000 gambling machines (slot machines and video lottery terminals), 33 000 lottery ticket centres, 6050 permanent casinos, 250 race tracks and teletheatres, and 25 000 licenses to run various bingo, temporary casinos, raffles, pull tickets and other activities"; in addition, estimates suggest that "Canadian Internet addresses make up anywhere from 5–15 percent of a multi-billion worldwide online gambling activity in spite of the questionable legitimacy of offshore gambling providers" (Azmier, 2005). Attempts to police the "next generation of gambling products (e.g., home-based Internet gambling, interactive television and video game gambling, and cell phone gambling)" (Azmier, 2005) may prove especially difficult and troublesome.

Illegal gambling continues to supply organized crime with one source of income (Lyman and Potter, 2004). In most urban areas, bookmakers associated with crime syndicates specialize in bets on horse racing, professional football and basketball, boxing, hockey, and baseball. Syndicates have also run "numbers games," which involve placing a bet on the possible occurrence of certain numbers (Light, 1977). However, as Rodney Stamler (2000:452) wryly points out, to appreciate how fully the government now competes with organized crime in relation to gambling activities, one need only consider the Pick 3 lottery, in which winners must choose a three-digit number that matches the one drawn by a government lottery agency. The most notable difference between the Pick 3 Lotto and the "numbers racket," he concludes, "is that criminals paid out a higher share of the take than the government does." Gambling syndicates also operate illegal casinos, "sponsor" backgammon tournaments, and provide on- and off-line opportunities for wagers to be made on a variety of activities.

Ostensibly, control of gambling activities also includes fighting organized crime, maintaining a favourable public image of the police department, keeping undesirable activities or persons out of a city, and maintaining public order. The objective of controlling organized crime is reflected both in the intent of some gambling searches and in the view of the police that illegal gambling is related to organized crime. However, enforcement efforts may result in the corruption of those involved. Few police officers are willing to accept bribes from murderers, burglars, or other criminals whose acts are blatantly harmful and have identifiable victims. However, many police officers tend to feel that gambling is not particularly serious and that, in any case, it is impossible to eradicate (see Klockars, Ivkovic, and Haberfeld, 2004; Kraus, 2004).

One response to the difficulty and wastefulness in trying to enforce laws against gambling is to completely remove the criminal label. As the Knapp Commission recommended: "The criminal law against gambling should be repealed. To the extent that the legislature deems that some control over gambling is appropriate, such regulation should be by civil rather than criminal process. The police should in any event be relieved from any responsibility for the enforcement of gambling laws or regulations" (Wynn and Goldman, 1974:67). Although a number of similar suggestions have been made, the question of the decriminalization of gambling still remains a hotly debated and controversial issue (see, for example, Bernhard and Preston, 2004). Among the concerns fuelling this controversy are estimates that some 5 percent of the adult population are pathological gamblers (people who chronically fail to resist impulses to gamble and for whom gambling interferes with other aspects of life) and that the rate of problem gambling among adolescents is three times higher than the adult rate (Sheppard and Smith, 1999; Lesieur, 1992:49).

According to the 2002 Canadian Community Health Survey, about 1.2 million adult Canadians are either problem gamblers or at risk of becoming so; within this study, a "problem gambler" was defined as an individual who suffers adverse effects from their gambling behaviour, such as financial or social problems, anxiety or depression, or dependence on alcohol. Reportedly, men, Aboriginal people, those with less education, individuals who played VLTs (often considered the "crack cocaine" of gambling), and people who gambled frequently were the groups most likely to be in the at-risk or problem categories. This survey found that, when compared with non-problem gamblers, problem gamblers were more likely to report that they had spent over $1000 in the past year on gambling (62 percent versus 4 percent). In addition, problem gamblers were more likely to report that their gambling had caused difficulties in their relationships with family and/or friends, that they experienced high levels of stress (42 percent versus 23 percent), and that, in the year prior to the survey, they had contemplated suicide (18 percent versus 3 percent). Almost two-thirds of problem gamblers (versus 27 percent of moderate gamblers) desired to stop gambling but believed they could not; another 56 percent had. This study notes that the provinces of Manitoba and Saskatchewan had "considerably higher proportions of at-risk gamblers than other provinces" and suggests that may be attributable to the fact that these two provinces "have the highest VLT participation rates in the country, above-average Aboriginal populations, and, along with Ontario, the highest attendance rates at casinos" (Statistics Canada, 2003). In consequence, while First Nations continue to lobby the federal and provincial governments for a direct Criminal Code exemption that would allow them to enter the gambling arena more fully, opponents argue that doing so would only serve to exacerbate "dependency on gambling revenues within reserves, high rates of problem gambling among First Nations peoples and the over-saturation of the gambling market" (*Casino Gambling*, 1999; see also Cramer, 2005).

While research conducted in Alberta by gerontologist Sandy Cousins concluded that bingo offers seniors many social and recreational benefits (*Edmonton Journal*, 2002), other researchers emphasize that there are risks. For example, a 2001 survey of 315 senior citizens who frequented riverboat casinos and bingo parlours to escape boredom suggested that they were particularly prone to develop gambling problems, and 11 percent showed signs of being pathological or compulsive gamblers (Young and Stern, 2001). Elder adults remain a prime target for the industry. Casinos, in particular, court those over 65 with cheap buffets, free transportation, money-back coupons, and other discounts. There are also risks for the young. O'Brien (1998) cautions that "Compulsive gambling disorders may be for Generation X what cocaine and crack were for their parents' generation" (O'Brien, 1998). A study by the International Centre for Youth Gambling at McGill University reported that, among Canadian teens aged 12 to 17, more than half were recreational gamblers, 10 to 15 percent were at risk of developing a severe gambling problem, and 4 to 6 percent qualified as "pathological gamblers." According to this study, young adults aged 18 to 24 were also two to four times more likely to develop a problem with gambling than the general adult population (Schmidt, 2003). With further liberalization and legalization of gambling, activities thought to be associated with pathological and problem gambling (excessive borrowing, family problems, difficulties at work, psychiatric disorders, crime, and so on) would probably increase (Single, 2003).

WHITE-COLLAR CRIME

White-collar crimes are essentially crimes of privilege (Friedrichs, 2004; Salinger, 2005; Shover and Wright, 2001), being of the suite rather than of the street. The term "white-collar crime" was coined by Edwin H. Sutherland (1949:9) and first used in an address to the American Sociological Association in 1939. He criticized proponents of social disorganization and social pathology theories of crime and introduced class and power dimensions. "White-collar crime" he proposed, "may be defined approximately as a crime committed by a person of respectability and high status in the course of his [sic] occupation." He documented the existence of this form of crime with a study of the careers of 70 large, reputable corporations which together had amassed 980 violations of the criminal law, or an average of 14 convictions apiece. Behind the offences of false advertising, unfair labour practices, restraint of trade, price-fixing agreements, stock manipulation, copyright infringement, and outright swindles were perfectly respectable middle- and upper-middle-class executives.

Gilbert Geis (1978:279; 1994) argues that "white-collar crimes constitute a more serious threat to the well-being and integrity of our society than more traditional kinds of crime" and that workplace injuries, unnecessary surgeries, and illegal pollution consign far more people to the cemeteries than the offences of traditional criminals. According to Moore and Mills (1990:414), the effects of white-collar crime include "(a) diminished faith in a free economy and in business leaders, (b) loss of confidence in political institutions, processes and leaders, and (c) erosion of public morality." Society's response to white-collar crime also raises questions about the equity of law and provides justification for other types of law violations.

The now classic textbook case of the $23 million "unauthorized loan" in the United States illustrates the inequities of laws dealing with white-collar crime. The defendants were charged with setting up a cheque-kiting operation: the art of repeatedly taking cheques written on one account and quickly depositing them into another, and vice versa, staying a step ahead of the clearing system and thus creating a false impression of the balances in the accounts. Once false balances have been created, a kiter can take out money against them, and that is just what perpetrators of this scheme did, leaving Marine Midland Bank holding the bag for a loss in excess of $23 million. The two already wealthy individuals found themselves indicted for the felony of grand larceny and the misdemeanour of scheming to defraud. However, because larceny requires an intent to deprive an owner of his or her property permanently, the defendants' repayment—as well as their ability to repay—played an important role in their defence. Their attorneys argued that it was a temporary borrowing; they never intended to deprive the bank permanently of the funds. They insisted that they had no intention of keeping the money—so that what they were doing did not qualify as larceny. The jurors apparently agreed. The defendants were found innocent of the felony charge of grand larceny, which carries a possible seven-year prison sentence, because they claimed they intended to return the money and had the ability to pay. They were convicted only of a misdemeanour count of scheming to defraud, for which the maximum sentence is one year. The defendants unsuccessfully appealed the conviction (Cony and Penn, 1986).

Canadian counterparts are not hard to come by. For example, Augustine Brannigan (1984:130) highlights the case of *Regina v. McNamara et al.*, in which nine corporations and 11 corporate executives had "rigged" the bids for government dredging and construction works for a minimum of five years and possibly up to a 14-year period. The companies conspired among themselves to artificially inflate their closed bids for dredging contracts with the government, on the understanding that the successful lowest bidder would compensate the others through cash and the payment of false invoices for work never performed. Brannigan notes that "[e]ven before the trial started, the accused appeared to have been given the benefit of a less severe charge" (130). Rather than being charged with bid-rigging under the *Anti-Combines Act*, McNamara and company were charged with a section of the Criminal Code which made it illegal to defraud—an offence carrying a lighter maximum penalty. While five persons and eight corporations were initially found guilty of conspiracy to defraud, upon appeal, this number was later reduced to two executive convictions. Moreover, although one executive received a sentence of five years' incarceration and the other a jail sentence of three years, they "ended up free on the streets in ten months and six months respectively" (131).

More recently, consider the fate of Senator Michel Cogger, convicted of pocketing $323 000 while in office for assisting a businessman who was attempting to obtain a $45 million government grant. "His sentence? No prison time, a $3000 fine and 240 hours of community service. Nor did his sins cost him his seat in the Senate" (MacDonald, 1999:147). One may also contemplate the $94 million fraud against financial institutions committed by Ron and Loren Koval, a couple who systematically falsified leases for medical and industrial equipment for many years and, as a result of their criminal activities, were able to boast to their friends and acquaintances of being "not millionaires but billionaires" (Gadd, 2001). Although the couple's actions left "scores of people" without jobs at King's Health Centre in Toronto and millions of dollars unaccounted for at their private leasing company, BACC Capital Corp, Ontario Superior Court Justice David ruled out a prosecution request for a restitution order for the $94 million. In a "sometimes lyrical speech that lauded the couple's tight-knit family and formerly sterling reputation," Justice Watt emphasized that although the Kovals had been dishonest in their dealings with lenders, they had committed no breach of trust, nor had they placed the lives or health of any patients at the health centre in jeopardy. "The victims [chiefly the Royal Bank of Canada and Société-Générale (Canada)] were not without resources to protect themselves from this fraud" (as quoted in Gadd, 2001). While the Kovals did receive a prison sentence, in general, those who commit suite crimes are far less likely to be incarcerated than those who commit street crimes. In 2000 to 2001, 61 percent of adult offenders convicted of break and enter but only 35 percent of those convicted of fraud received a prison sentence (Thomas, 2002:9).

The full extent of white-collar crime is difficult to assess. Many illegal corporate activities go undetected, and many wealthy individuals are able to evade taxes for years without being found out. White-collar crimes ("crimes in the suites") that are often dubbed crimes of the middle class (Weisburd et al., 1991) are generally considered less serious than the crimes of the lower class ("crimes of the streets"), and there is often strong pressure on the police and the courts not to prosecute at all in these cases—to take account of the offenders' "standing in the community" and to settle the matter out of court. For example, a bank that finds its safe burglarized at night will immediately summon the police, but it may be more circumspect if it finds that one of its executives has embezzled a sum of money. To avoid unwelcome publicity, the bank may simply allow the offender to resign after making an arrangement for him or her to pay back whatever possible.

The concept of white-collar crime generally incorporates both occupational and corporate crimes (Coleman, 2001:5; Salinger, 2005). Some individuals commit crimes in connection with their occupations. For example, physicians may give out illegal prescriptions for narcotics, give false testimony in court cases, or make fraudulent reports for health insurance payments. Indeed, James Hackler (2003:11) estimates the cost of medical fraud in Canada to be around $600 million a year. According to 2006 estimates provided by the anti-corruption organization Transparency International, "at least 5 percent of the $3.6 trillion spent globally every year of medical care is lost to corruption," with medical corruption including such practices as overcharging hospital patients and the dispensing of counterfeit (and potentially lethal) drugs (*Maclean's*, 2006). Lawyers may also engage in various illegalities, such as securing false testimony from witnesses, misappropriating funds in receivership, and various forms of ambulance chasing to collect fraudulent damage claims arising from accidents. Consider lawyer Gerald Lavoie's 1999 conviction for laundering $1.7 million as part of a scheme that also led to the conviction of a former Quebec Superior Court justice (*Canadian Lawyer*, 1999). Corporate crimes are considered those illegal activities that are committed in the furtherance of business operations but are not the central purpose of business. A convenient distinction between occupational and corporate crimes may be in the context of immediate and direct benefit to the perpetrator. In occupational crimes, generally the benefit is for the individual who commits a particular illegal activity—for example, the physician who receives money for giving out illegal prescriptions. In corporate crime, the benefit is usually for the organization (see, for example, Pearce and Tombs, 1998). For example, an executive bribes a public official to secure favours for his or her corporation. In this instance, the benefit would be for the corporation and not directly for the individual. The desire to increase profits is a crucial factor in a wide range of corporate crimes. Bre-X, reputedly one of the world's largest stock frauds, cost investors $6 billion. In this case, the Calgary-based company's geologist had sought to make worthless mining property seem valuable by salting core samples with gold. After his actions became known, the market for Bre-X stock collapsed and the company's shares became worthless (Hagan, 2000).

The remainder of this section will focus on what is strictly called **corporate crime**. It is distinguished from ordinary crime in two respects: the nature of the violation and the fact that administrative and civil law are more likely to be used as punishment than criminal law.

In Canada, corporate crime did not exist until the 19th century because there were no laws against dangerous or unethical corporate practices. Corporations were free to sell unsafe products, keep workers in unsafe conditions, pollute the atmosphere, engage in monopolistic practices, overcharge customers, and make outrageously false advertising claims for their products. By the end of the 19th century and the beginning of the 20th, laws were passed that attempted to regulate some of the more flagrant business practices. Examples include the *Patent and Propriety Medicines Act* (1908), the first anti-combines law, introduced to the Criminal Code in 1889, and the *Customs Tariffs Act* (1897). Since that time, a vast array of federal, provincial, and municipal laws have been passed to regulate potentially harmful corporate activities, including the *Food and Drugs Act*, the *Weights and Measures Act,* and environmental protection laws. The *Competition Act*, a federal statute, prohibits misleading advertising and deceptive marketing practices, sets parameters between what Parliament defines as acceptable and unacceptable, or unlawful, business practices in promoting the supply or use of a product or service, or any business interest. In addition, it prohibits certain mergers and monopolies that are believed to be contrary to the public interest; price fixing that would eliminate normal competition among businesses in the marketplace (e.g., bid-rigging); and such practices as "predatory pricing" (selling products or services at an unreasonably low price in order to eliminate competition) and "discriminatory allowances" (offering discounts and rebates that are not offered to competing purchasers) (Auerbach, 2000:267). The Act's criminal offences are prosecuted by the Attorney General of Canada in the criminal court system and can result in such penalties as fines (levied against both corporations and individuals), jail terms, and prohibition orders. Although "deceptive marketing practices" may be dealt with by the courts, the Act's civil "reviewable practices" are generally adjudicated by the Competition Tribunal—a specialized administrative body that consists of judges and lay experts. "The Act's civil reviewable practices relate to abuse of dominance, refusal to deal, exclusive dealing, tied selling, market restrictions and deceptive marketing practices"—prohibited conduct that is not, however, accompanied by either the threat of imprisonment or, except in limited circumstances, monetary penalties (although administrative monetary penalties [AMPs] can be imposed for deceptive marketing practices and for abuse of dominance by a domestic airline service). Instead, the Tribunal may issue a variety of behavioural or structural orders. "In the case of abuse of dominance, for example, the Tribunal may issue an order prohibiting the continuance of activity found to be anti-competitive where that conduct prevents or lessens competition substantially. The Tribunal may also order a person to take . . . additional action including the divestiture of assets or shares, as required to overcome the effects of the anti-competitive conduct" (Addy, Cornwall, and Kearney, 2005).

However, efforts to control corporate crime have been less than wildly successful. Although selling used cars as new ones, making false claims about a product, and advertising special "sales" when, in fact, prices have not been reduced, are all prohibited behaviours, they remain common crimes in Canada. Indeed, the federal department of Industry Canada receives more complaints than it can investigate and, in consequence, only prosecutes the most flagrant cases. In addition, when compared to other Western countries, the fines levied in Canada for such offences are low, with those convicted of false advertising, for example, generally receiving fines of less than $400 per charge (Snider, 1999). This type of modest penalty is not, perhaps, surprising, given that in 1991, in a case involving false advertising by a travel agency named Wholesale Travel, the Chief Justice of the Supreme Court of Canada saw fit to refer to business frauds as not "true crimes" (MacDonald, 1999:148). In similar fashion, even though the maximum fine in Canada for conspiracy offences was raised to $10 million in 1986, "judges traditionally do not assess fines anywhere near the maximum allowable amount for corporate crimes" (Snider, 1999).

Despite the perception that corporate crime is less serious than street crime, "corporate crimes cause far more financial harm, and many more personal injuries (some leading to death) than do traditional crimes such as theft, robbery and assault" (Snider, 1999). Some have argued that the term "corporate murder" (Swartz, 1978) is an appropriate label for deaths resulting from such circumstances. Among the best-known cases are the failures of administrators within the Johns-Manville Corporation to alert workers to the serious health hazards posed by asbestos. Hagan (2000) notes that although these hazards have been recognized "since the turn of the [19th] century, people working with it were not informed, and the government bureaucracy and the medical community ignored the hazard." Currently, almost half of all deaths among asbestos insulation workers are caused by exposure to that substance (Coleman, 1998:70). In addition, Hagan emphasizes that the 1992 explosion at the Westray coal mine in Pictou County, Nova Scotia, which killed 26 miners instantly, "was not an accident, but the result of conscious decisions by those responsible for the safety of the miners." An official inquiry into the disaster resulted in a report tellingly entitled *The Westray Story: A Predictable Path to Disaster*. In it, Justice Richard concludes that the managers at Westray had "displayed a certain disdain for safety and appeared to regard safety-conscious workers as the wimps in the organization" (in Hagan, 2000). More recently, Dussault (2005) has directed attention to the paradoxes of the application of the 1999 Tobacco Law (which is intended to reduce smoking and improve health by banning smoking at work) in factories. She notes that blue-collar plant workers felt that it was "illogical" that this act was being enforced in workplaces that were perceived as taking a "lax approach to the quality of the work environment" as a whole.

Corporate crime is controlled by a variety of regulatory agencies. The control of corporate activities may be prospective, as in licensing, when control is exercised before deviant acts occur; processual, as in inspection where control is continuous; and retrospective, as when a lawsuit is brought for damages after deviance has occurred. These types of controls will be discussed further in the final section of this chapter. In addition, if a business concern defies the law, the government may institute, under civil law, an injunction to "cease and desist" from further violations. If further violations occur, contempt-of-court proceedings may be instituted. As we have already noted, fines and various forms of assessments are also used in attempts to control deleterious corporate activities, as, for example, in cases of levying fines on water and air polluters. At times, the government can also exercise control through its buying power by rewarding firms that comply and withdrawing from or not granting governmental contracts to those that do not (Nagel, 1975:341).

But, as Christopher D. Stone (1978:244) points out: "Whether we are threatening the corporation with private civil actions, criminal prosecutions, or the new hybrid 'civil penalties,' we aim to control the corporation through threats to its profits." Corporate offenders are rarely criminally prosecuted and even more rarely imprisoned. A large proportion of these offenders are handled through administrative and civil sanctions, and the penalty is monetary. In a sense, the penalty imposed for violating the law amounts to little more than a reasonable licensing fee for engaging in illegal activity. Essentially, it is worthwhile for a large corporation to violate the laws regulating business. Brannigan (1984:126) argues, "[i]f we calculate the size of the fine as a proportion of their gross company revenues, and determine what a comparable proportion would be for an individual earning $15 000, we discover that the fines have a relative value of twenty cents to twelve dollars, depending on the size of the company." However, Addy, Cornwall, and Kearney (2005) note that the penalties for violations of the *Competition Act* "have escalated in recent years."

In 1997, five electrical contractors were found guilty of bid-rigging and fined a total of $2.55 million. In 1999, five foreign firms, which comprised what was described as "the world bulk vitamin cartel," were convicted of a conspiracy that rigged Canadian prices and fined a total of $88 million, "the largest criminal fines ever imposed under the *Competition Act*, and the largest in Canadian history" (Auerbach, 2000:267). Record penalties have also been imposed in recent years for those who violate the Act's price maintenance provisions and the deceptive marketing provisions. In October 2004, two individuals who had been involved in a phony invoice scam were sentenced to three years in prison for violating the false or misleading representations provisions of the Act; two others who had been involved in the scheme were given 18-month and 9-month conditional jail sentences. In March of 2005, the president of a firm that had been fined under the deceptive marketing practice provisions of the Act received a conditional prison sentence of two years. In addition, section 36 of the Act allows any individual who has suffered losses as a result of conduct that is contrary to any of the Act's criminal provisions to launch a civil action and recover damages from those who engaged in that criminal conduct—and the amounts awarded can be significant. For example, Addy, Cornwall, and Kearney (2005) point out that participants in a graphite electrodes cartel were not simply required to pay a criminal fine of $11 million, but also $19 million in settlement of a civil suit; according to these authors, "In the past few years, an unprecedented number of these claims have been initiated under provincial class action legislation."

Recent rulings by the federal Competition Tribunal also suggest a growing intolerance for those who engage in deceptive and misleading marketing practices. Although violations of the deceptive marketing provisions of the Act are $50 000 for individuals and $100 000 for corporations, "much larger penalties have been imposed on consent" (Addy, Cornwall and Kearney, 2005). In 2003, clothier Suzy Shier agreed to pay a $1 million penalty to settle allegations that the retailer had held bogus sales. In 2004, Canada's largest sporting goods retailer, Forzani Group Ltd (Sports Chek/Sport Mart), while admitting no fault, agreed to pay $1.7 million as a penalty for having "significantly inflated" regular prices on hockey skates, in-line skates, and 10 other products in order to exaggerate the "savings" offered by their "sale prices." In 2005, the federal Competition Tribunal ruled that Sears Canada Inc had breached federal laws by pitching exaggerated savings on five lines of automobile tires in its ads; although one ad suggested a saving of $248, in reality, consumers saved a mere $12 (Straus and Tuck, 2005). Ultimately, Sears would agree to pay $100 000 —the maximum penalty that the Tribunal can impose on a corporation—as well as $387 000 toward the Competition Bureau's legal costs (Addy, Cornwall, and Kearney, 2005).

Nevertheless, controlling corporations through the law often becomes, as Stone (1978:250) puts it, a "misplaced faith on negative reinforcement." Although there are now sophisticated detection and record-keeping technologies, forensic accountants, and other legal specialists (Lindquist, 1995), the law constitutes only one of the threats that the corporation faces in dealing with the outside world. Often, paying a fine is considered part of doing business. For a businessperson, reducing the profits by a lawsuit does not involve the same loss of face as losses attributable to other causes. For example, being sued may be construed as "messy" but "understandable." It is not a question of improving such behaviour but a realization by businesspeople that it could happen to anyone. In financial reports, losses through lawsuits are generally explained in footnotes as non-recurring losses.

Although there are signs of increased enforcement by federal agencies and local authorities (see, for example, Benson and Cullen, 1998; Addy, Cornwall, and Keaney,

2005), the current legal controls on corporate crime are inefficient. The government's response to corporate violations cannot be compared to its response to ordinary crime. Generally, penalties imposed on corporations are quite lenient, particularly in view of the gravity of the offences committed, as compared with the penalties imposed on ordinary offenders. Few members of corporate management ever go to prison, even if convicted; generally they are placed on probation or requested to carry out some kind of community service (Podgor, 1994). If they go to prison, it is almost always for a very short time period. Gilbert Geis (1994) points out that it is, indeed, ironic that the penalties for corporate crime are the least severe, even though they are given to the very persons who might be the most affected by them, or who might "benefit" the most from them. In other words, if these offenders are potentially the most deterred, an increase in punishment and the intensity of enforcement might result in the greatest benefit to society. As it stands now, however, the penalty for corporate crime is far less than the harm caused.

SOCIAL CONTROL OF DISSENT

A universal, omnipresent, and pervasive governmental activity is the control of dissent. Political trials, surveillance, and suppression of information and free speech are rampant in most countries (see, for example, Sunstein, 2003). Some examples: Ellen Johnson- Sirleaf, the current president of Liberia and Africa's first elected female head of state, was thrown in jail in 1985 and nearly executed for saying that the government of dictator Samuel Doe was run by "many idiots" (*Maclean's*, 2006a:45). In Islamic countries, fundamentalists regularly ban books. In 1989, Ayatollah Ruhollah Khomeini of Iran denounced writer Salman Rushdie's book, *The Satanic Verses*, as a blasphemy against Islam and offered a million-dollar reward for the writer's execution. The offer was raised to $2.8 million by hard-liners in late 1998, although the Iranian government officially rescinded the reward in an attempt to improve relations with the West (*St Louis Post-Dispatch*, 1998). Nevertheless, "Rushdie's Japanese and Italian translators were both stabbed, the former fatally, in 1991. Rushdie's Norwegian publisher was shot outside his home in 1993" (CBC News, 2006). As of 2006, Rushdie is still in hiding—although he has made sporadic public appearances for book tours, talk shows, and award ceremonies under the watchful eyes of security guards. In Islamic countries, also, the press is state-controlled, and dissidents, at best, are jailed. In some African and Asian countries, journalistic fealty to the ruling dictatorship is demanded and the abuse of psychiatry to intimidate and torture dissidents in the former Soviet Union was well documented and loudly deplored by the West.

In China, the democracy movement continues to be suppressed in the aftermath of the 1989 Tiananmen crackdown (Christenson, 1999; Diamant, Lubman, and O'Brien, 2005; Luo, 2000), and the abuse of psychiatry as a form of social control for dissent once again appears to be increasing. For example, the government has forcibly imprisoned members of Falun Gong in psychiatric hospitals. Falun Gong, a popular movement that advocates channelling energy through deep breathing and exercises, has been identified by the Chinese Communist Party as a "heretical cult" and made the target of government crackdowns, with abuses reminiscent of the Cultural Revolution decades earlier (Fu, 2003; Keith and Lin, 2003; Kurlantzick, 2003; Thorton, 2002). Hundreds of Falun Gong members have been taken to psychiatric institutions and drugged, physically restrained, isolated, or given electric shocks (Chan, 2004; *Economist*, 2002). There is also a development of a network of new police psychiatric hospitals—called *Ankangs*, which means "peace and happiness"—built in recent years. Chinese law includes "political harm to society" as legally dangerous mentally ill behaviour. Law enforcement agents are instructed to take into psychiatric custody "political maniacs," defined as people who make anti-government speeches, write reactionary letters, or otherwise express opinions in public on important domestic and international affairs contrary to the official government position. There are 20 Ankangs, with plans to build many more. In a broader context, one might also wish to consider "the capitulation of some of our richest corporations to the repressive political agenda of the Communist government. Google, Yahoo and Microsoft have [as of late February, 2006] abetted the Communist regime's sprawling system of censorship, blocking access to Internet sites and squashing bloggers who dare offend the ruling elite. In the case of Yahoo, it appears the company ratted out at least two dissidents who are now serving hard time for criticizing their government online" (*Maclean's*, 2006b).

Democratic countries such as Canada, which welcome dissent in the abstract, may nevertheless punish it in the concrete. Alison Hatch (1995) notes that while Canadian governments have long shown remarkable tolerance of right-wing extremism and anti-Semitism, they have evidenced considerably less sympathy for those on the left. It was the fear of a communist conspiracy, she argues, that lay behind the violent government reaction to the Winnipeg General Strike in 1919, which resulted in 30 casualties and one death. In its aftermath, she points out, "the federal government passed section 98 of the Criminal Code, prohibiting 'unlawful associations,' and amended the *Immigration Act* to permit the deportation of British-born immigrants, a move clearly aimed at the leaders of the General Strike" (Hatch, 1995:264). From the time that the Communist Party of Canada was founded in 1921, the RCMP used section 98 of the Code to harass its members, break up its meetings, raid its offices, and confiscate its literature (Reilly, 1999). Until 1937, when section 98 of the Criminal Code was declared illegal, "hundreds were deported as suspected communists, without recourse to due process protections" (Hatch, 1995:264). Similarly, while the *Trade Union Act*, assented to in June 1872, implicitly recognized the right of workers to strike, picketing remained a criminal offence in Canada until the Criminal Code was amended in 1934 to allow for information picketing. In addition, in 1937, a Quebec statute known as the "Padlock Act" (*An Act Respecting Communist Propaganda*) allowed the Attorney General to close, for a period of one year, any building used for propagating "communism or bolshevism" and to confiscate and/or destroy any printed matter that propagated such ideas. Those who were convicted of printing, publishing, or distributing such materials could be incarcerated for up to a year without the possibility of appeal. It was only in 1957 that this law was struck down by the Supreme Court of Canada as *ultra vires* ("beyond the powers")—an unconstitutional invasion of the provincial government into the federal field of criminal law.

More recently, concern has been raised in relation to Canada's *Anti-Terrorism Act* (Bill C-36). Drafted in the wake of the September 11, 2001 terrorist attacks on the Pentagon and World Trade Center, Bill C-36 was passed in the Senate with a vote of 45 to 21 and became law in December of 2001. The *Anti-Terrorism Act* begins with a vague, broad definition of terrorism as acts of violence or destruction committed out of religious, ideological, or political motivation that are intended to influence government or intimidate the public. Unlike Britain, where the law provides for a 10-year maximum penalty for simply belonging to a terrorist organization (and, in 2006, passed hate crime legislation that makes the "glorification" of terror illegal [*Maclean's*, 2006b]), Canada has not banned membership (or seen fit to criminalize the "glorification" of terror). However, offences under the *Anti-Terrorist Act* do include "participating, facilitating, instructing, [and] harbouring" terrorist activity.

The *Anti-Terrorism Act*, the recently changed *Privacy Act*, and the *Access to Information Act* give police new investigative powers for search and seizure. For example, police are allowed to exercise "preventative arrest" powers and to detain, without judicial warrant, suspected terrorists for up to 48 hours. The valid period of a wiretap has been extended, while the standard required to obtain a wiretap has been lowered. Compared to the *Emergencies Act, the Anti-Terrorism Act* imposes fewer restrictions upon government and contains fewer provisions for review. For example, the Solicitor General is allowed to act "on the advice of CSIS or the police in branding activities and organizations as 'terrorist,' with virtually no provision for review" (Morden, 2002:47).

Supporters of Bill C-36 have argued that, following the events of 9/11, it was necessary to bolster Canadian security in order to comply with Resolution 1373 of the United Nations Security Council that, on September 28, 2001, "called on all member countries to adopt the necessary measures to prevent any one country from becoming a haven for terrorists" (Chwialkowska, 2001). In the immediate aftermath of 9/11, polls also suggested that many Canadians were fearful, with 64 percent of respondents in the *Maclean's* 2001 year-end poll expressing the belief that Canada could become a terrorist target, and almost 60 percent reporting that they were prepared to give up some personal freedoms to counter terrorism. Although 65 percent of respondents thought it likely that police would abuse the powers they received under the *Anti-Terrorism Act,* about 80 percent indicated acceptance of mandatory fingerprinting and identity cards for all Canadians, while approximately 60 percent endorsed the tapping of their phones or screening of their mail (Gregg, 2001/2002; Macnamara, 2002). A more recent survey, conducted by Ipsos-Reid in 2004, found that 45 percent of Canadians agree that "police and security forces in Canada are now going too far in using anti-terrorism powers" (Bricker and Wright, 2005:16), with individuals in the provinces of British Columbia (51 percent) and Quebec (50 percent) more likely to express this view than those in other provinces, and those 55 years of age more likely to do so than younger Canadians (aged 55+, 50 percent; 35–54, 44 percent; 18–34, 42 percent). This survey additionally found that many Canadians believe that "once you're suspected of terrorism, all bets are off when it comes to being treated fairly. Fully four in ten worry that they would not get a fair hearing if they were to be detained by police or security services in Canada and were wrongly suspected of terrorism activities" (Bricker and Wright, 2005:17). Residents of Quebec, Saskatchewan, and Manitoba (all at 47 percent), and older Canadians were most likely to express this concern (aged 18–34, 37 percent; 35–54, 42 percent; and 55+, 44 percent). It would also seem telling that, when asked if they were prepared to see Canadian police and security forces receive additional powers in their fight against terrorism ("specifically, the power to tap their phones, open their mail, or read personal emails without their ever knowing it"), 75 percent of respondents replied with an "emphatic 'no'" (Bricker and Wright, 2005:17).

Critics of Canada's *Anti-Terrorism Act* maintain that the definition of terrorism it employs is too broad, that the Act contains various measures that are open for abuse, and that there are only limited provisions for oversight (Barkun, 2002; Borovoy, 2002; Tremblay, 2002). Alain Gagnon (2002:18) argues that by employing such vaguely defined terms as "participating in" or "facilitating," it is theoretically possible that "any ideologically driven political or social movement could be held responsible for random acts of terrorism carried out in its name without organizers' direct participation in or even knowledge of the terrorism act." The Honourable Ron Atkey, a former Conservative Solicitor General and first chairperson of the Security Intelligence Review Committee, has recently pointed out some examples of non-terrorist groups and activities that might, nevertheless, be caught under Bill C-36's definition of terrorism:

- Protest activities by Aboriginal people, against development activities on Aboriginal lands that disrupt an essential service or block a road;
- Workers involved in recent nurses' or truckers' strikes or the protestors of the Quebec City Summit or the APEC conference in Vancouver;
- Political activists who may have appeared to be "terrorists" to those in power at the time but who are ultimately remembered as champions of freedom, such as Louis Riel or Nelson Mandela; and
- Community groups that sponsor Muslim immigration into Canada, when an immigrant is alleged to have been involved in terrorist activities in the country of origin, even if some time in the past (Morden, 2002:48).

In consequence, Tony Clarke (2002:49) argues that the new law is best seen as "the recriminalization of dissent" and that it provides law enforcement with "intrusive new powers, and the wherewithal to detain a person as a criminal solely on the basis of ideology." In addition to fears that racial profiling—the practice of targeting suspects based upon their race—will become a prominent feature of investigations conducted under this act, at least some legal experts have suggested that law enforcement authorities may engage in ideological profiling (Borovoy, 2002; Morden, 2002; Tremblay, 2002). Moreover, in observing that "[w]e now live in an area of increased and increasing state surveillance" with "[i]nternational instruments, agreements, protocols, and conventions [that] call for the collection, aggregation and sharing of information on a scale not previously realized," some have suggested that "privacy itself has become a casualty of the war on terrorism" (Cohen, 2005:2; see also Jurgenson, 2004).

The law supports the government as the legitimate holder of power in society. The government in turn is legitimately involved in the control of its citizens. The principal objectives of the government are to provide for the welfare of its citizens, to protect their lives and property, and to maintain order within society. To maintain order, the government is mandated to apprehend and punish criminals. However, in a democratic society, there are questions about the legitimacy of a government that stifles dissent in the interest of preserving order. In principle, in a democratic society, tradition and values affirm that dissent is appropriate. At the same time, for social order to prevail, a society needs to ensure that existing power relationships are maintained over time. Furthermore, those in positions of power who benefit from the existing power arrangement use their influence to encourage the repression of challenges to the government. Consequently, governments generally opt for the control and repression of dissent.

One way of controlling dissent is through the selection processes used to place individuals into desirable social positions (Oberschall, 1973:249). In most political systems, the leaders have ways of controlling the selection and mobility of people through patronage systems, the extension of the government bureaucracy, and co-optation in its many forms. Loyalty and conformity are generally the primary criteria for advancement. Another form of control in this context is the dismissal of individuals who do not comply with the stated expectations and voice "unpopular" opinions. In some instances, the leaders can directly control the supply and demand of certain services and skills. For example, "by exercising influence on budgets, examinations, student stipends, and university expansion, a government can within a couple of years reduce the total number of students in higher education for the purpose of quashing a troublesome student movement and floating population of unemployed graduates that it has brought into being and subsidized" (Oberschall, 1973:250).

Control can also be achieved through the manipulation of the structure of material benefits. For example, Frances Fox Piven and Richard A. Cloward (1993) contend that welfare programs serve as a social-control mechanism in periods of mass unemployment by diffusing social unrest and thus reducing dissent. They argue that public assistance programs are used to regulate the political and economic activity of the poor. In periods of severe economic depression, the legitimacy of the political system is likely to be questioned by the poor. The possibility of upsetting the status quo of power and property relationships in society increases. Demands grow for changing the existing social and economic arrangements. Under this threat, public assistance programs are initiated or expanded by the government. They cite case after case, from 16th-century Europe to mid-20th-century North America, to document their thesis that social welfare has, throughout the ages, been used as a mechanism of social control and a way by the government to diffuse unrest through direct intervention. They note, however, that when economic conditions improve, the relief rolls are cut back in response to pressures from those who employ the poor so as to ensure an adequate supply of low-wage labour.

Another option for the government to use in the control of dissent is its coercive social-control apparatus to deal with crime, enforce the law, and keep social interaction peaceful and orderly. As compared with other mechanisms, "a coercive response to social disturbances is the cheapest and most immediately available means of control to the authorities" (Oberschall, 1973:252). The government is expected by the citizens, and is required by law, to protect life and property and to arrest the perpetrators of illegal activities. In addition to these coercive responses to dissent, the government has in its arsenal a variety of less overt, though equally effective, control mechanisms. For example, the federal Royal Commission of Inquiry into Certain Activities of the RCMP revealed RCMP surveillance of radicals on university campuses, breaches of the confidentiality of the files of the National Revenue Department and Unemployment Insurance Commission, and the use of illegal activities designed to discredit, impede, deter, or undermine political radicals in an effort known as "Operation Checkmate" (Brannigan, 1984:65). In *Whose National Security? Canadian State Surveillance and the Creation of Enemies*, Gary Kinsman (2001) suggests that the government has shown a strong tendency to closely watch the activities of people who threaten it by collecting, concealing, suppressing, and manipulating information.

Obviously, the government has to exert some control over its citizens, but in exerting control, care needs to be exercised to protect individuals' rights as guaranteed by the *Charter of Rights and Freedoms*. There is a thin line between governmental control of dissent and the creation of a police state. The technology is also a new disturbance to the delicate balance between the privacy rights of citizens and the growing power of technology to help government to invade privacy.

This control technology is ubiquitous in the modern state. To illustrate the potential of just one aspect of that technology, consider that the federal, provincial, and municipal governments in Canada are the prime customers of computer and computer services (Statistics Canada, 1998). There are thousands of computers in use in the federal government providing electronic access to millions of records. There is even a monitoring technology which records keystrokes on a personal computer (Schwartz, 2001). Social insurance numbers have become national "identifiers," and privacy has eroded because the information in the database can be used with little notice or recourse. "Computer matches"—the cross-checking of records by one agency against another—are conducted routinely (Havemann, 1986). This is how the government withholds the income tax refunds of student loan and other loan defaulters. Similarly, to trace those who fail to abide by child support, custody, and access orders, various amendments to the *Family Orders and Agreements Enforcement Assistance Act* now provide for various databanks to be searched in order to trace those who fail to comply. These include the Canada Pension Plan's record of earnings; international social security records maintained by Health and Welfare Canada; Canada Employment and Immigration records and social insurance number records; and, most recently, the records of the Canada Revenue Agency (formerly Revenue Canada). Computer matches also form the backbone of the federal licence denial scheme that authorizes the suspension of passports and certain federal transport licences when a payer of child support has persistently breached support obligations. The technology is available now to create an electronic dossier on every citizen in Canada.

This situation is hardly unique to Canada. Flowing from the September 11, 2001, terrorist attacks, the US Department of Homeland Security was created along with demands on the Attorney General for the establishment of a cross-agency, cross-platform electronic system that includes face recognition, electronic finger printing, retinal scan technology, hand geometry assayers, face recognition software, and smart cards with custom identification chips that will be fully implemented around the mid-2010s (see, for example, Martin, 2004). Moreover, in that country, horror stories already abound. For example, for almost 30 years, a state legislative committee spied on 20 000 Californians, documenting their personal habits, social lives, and political and professional relationships, and the committee has yet to release the 80 cartons of information gathered (Kennedy, 1998). From time to time, target groups are even required to pay a fee for being tracked. For example, the United States Immigration and Naturalization Services (INS) instituted a $90 fee for international students during the summer of 2001 to help pay for the technology to track them. They too will have a nationwide computer database. The rationale is to try to minimize the risk of terrorism by keeping close surveillance on foreign students. Perhaps it is time to start thinking about some effective controls and checks to be devised and imposed upon the users of this technology so they do not overstep the boundaries (Kerr, 2004).

ADMINISTRATIVE LAW AND SOCIAL CONTROL

A broadly and popularly held misconception about the law is that it consists almost entirely of criminal law, with its apparatus of crime, police, prosecutors, judges, juries, sentences, and prisons. Another misconception is that all law can be divided into criminal law and civil law. But the resources of legal systems are far richer and more extensive than either of these views implies. This section is concerned with how distinctive legal ways can be used to control what Robert S. Summers and George G. Howard (1972:199) call "private primary activity." They use this concept to describe various pursuits, such as production and marketing of electricity and natural gas; provision and operation of rail, air, and other transport facilities; food processing and distribution; construction of buildings, bridges, and other public facilities; and radio and television broadcasting. But these activities are not confined to large-scale affairs such as electrical production and provision of air transport. The list can be expanded to include provision of medical services by physicians, ownership and operation of motor vehicles by ordinary citizens, construction of residences by local carpenters, and the sale and purchase of stocks and bonds by private individuals. Private primary activities not only are positively desirable in themselves, but also are essential for the functioning of modern societies. These activities generate legal needs that are met through administrative control mechanisms (see, for example, Beermann, 2003).

Today, all kinds of services are needed, such as those provided by physicians, transport facilities, and electric companies. But an incompetent physician might kill rather than cure a patient. An unqualified airline pilot might crash a plane, killing everyone on board. A food processing plant might poison half a community. In addition to incompetence or carelessness, deliberate abuses are also possible. An individual may lose his or her entire savings through fraudulent stock operations. A utility company might abuse its monopoly position and charge exorbitant rates. An owner of a nuclear waste disposal facility may want to cut corners, thus exposing the public to harmful radiation.

Private primary activities, Summers and Howard (1972:199) note, can cause harm, avoidable harm. At the same time, such activities can have great potential for good. Airplanes can almost be made safe, and stock frauds by fly-by-night operators can be reduced. Legal control of these activities is then justified on two grounds: the prevention of harm and the promotion of good. For example, in the case of radio and television broadcasting, laws can be concerned with both the control of obscenity and the problem of balanced programming, such as covering public affairs, in addition to entertainment and sports. Control is exerted on private primary activity through administrative laws, primarily in the context of licensing, inspection, and the threat of publicity.

Licensing

The power of administrative law goes beyond the setting of standards and the punishing of those who fail to comply. Horack notes: "The belief that law enforcement is better achieved by prevention than by prosecution has contributed to the emergence of administrative regulation as a primary means of government control" (quoted by Summers and Howard, 1972:202). In Canada, three types of regulatory agencies can be distinguished: self-governing bodies which regulate the conduct of their own members (e.g., professions such as law, medicine, accounting, and engineering), independent regulatory agencies (e.g., the Canadian Radio-television and Telecommunications Commission), and departmental regulatory agencies (e.g., an occupational safety branch of a provincial Ministry of Labour that enforces employment safety standards) (Janisch, 1999).

Requiring and granting licences to perform certain activities is a classic control device. Licensing is pervasive, and by one estimate, at least 5000 different licences have been granted to more than 5000 occupations (Simon et al., 1992:542). With so many groups being licensed, licensing as a form of social control affects a substantial portion of the labour force. Nowadays a licence may be required to engage in an occupation, to operate a business, to serve specific customers or areas, or to manufacture certain products (see, for example, Tashbrook, 2004). Physicians and lawyers must obtain specific training and then demonstrate some competence before they can qualify for licences to practice. Here, licensing is used to enforce basic qualifying standards. Airplane companies just cannot fly any route they wish, and broadcasters are not free to pick a frequency at will. Underlying all regulatory licensing is a denial of a right to engage in the contemplated activity except with a licence.

The control of professions and certain activities through licensing is justified as protection for the public against inferior, fraudulent, or dangerous services and products. But, under this rubric, control has been extended to occupations that, at the most, only minimally affect public health and safety, such as licences for cosmetologists, strippers, auctioneers, weather-control practitioners, taxidermists, junkyard operators, and weather-vane installers. In addition to requiring a licence to practise these occupations, control is exerted through the revocation or suspension of the licence. For example, under administrative law, the state may withdraw the right to practise from a lawyer, a physician, or a beautician, and it may suspend a bar or restaurant owner from doing business for a few days, a year, or even permanently. Administrative laws generally specify the conditions under which a license is required, the requirements that must be met by applicants, the duties imposed upon the licensees, the agency authorized to issue such licenses, the procedures in revoking licenses and the grounds that constitute cause for revocation, and the penalties for violations.

Inspection

Administrative law grants broad investigatory and inspection powers to regulatory agencies (Reed, 2005). Periodic inspection is a way of monitoring ongoing activities under the jurisdiction of a particular agency. Such inspections determine whether cars and trains can move, planes fly (see, for example, Wald, 1998), agricultural products can meet quality standards, newspapers can obtain second-class mailing privileges, and so forth. Similar procedures are used to prevent the distribution of unsafe foods and drugs, to prohibit the entry of diseased plants and animals into the country, or to suspend the licence of a pilot pending a disciplinary hearing.

Inspections constitute a primary tool of administrative supervision and control. A housing official may inspect buildings to determine compliance with building codes. In some instances, inspection takes place occasionally, such as when ensuring compliance with building codes. In other instances, inspection is continuous, as in food inspection. Both forms of inspection, sporadic and continuous, also exert pressure for self-regulation and contribute to the maintenance of internal controls specified by the law. At times, these inspections may also lead to proposals for corrective legislation governing regulatory standards.

Threat of Publicity

In small communities where people tend to know each other, adversely publicizing wrongdoers can have a significant effect on changing their behaviour. Such a system of social control normally would not work in an urban industrial society for individual deviance. However, large companies selling widely known brand-name products might be greatly influenced by the threat of well-circulated publicity. For example, the publicity surrounding the Ford Motor Company's internal documents on defective and recalled Pintos, which showed that needed structural fuel tank improvements at a cost of about $11 per car could have prevented 180 fiery deaths a year, resulted in a significant drop in market share for the company (Fisse and Braithwaite, 1993). The public was aghast to realize that Ford had pragmatically calculated that it was preferable to lose $49.5 million in death and injury claims for exploding Pintos rather than retool the assembly line to make the car safer, at a cost of $137 million (Brannigan, 1984:119).

Publicity can serve a highly useful, if not indispensable, control function. For example, in response to negative publicity, companies that make goods for Nike and the Gap have cut back on their use of child and sweatshop labour (Greenhouse, 2000). The International

Programme on the Elimination of Child Labour has also employed publicity in their campaign to remove child labourers from oppressive work conditions and provide them with education and their parents with jobs or income. Since its inception in 1992, it has grown from six participating countries to over 200 in 2000 (Human Rights Watch, 2001). Publicity also provided momentum for the 1999 adoption of the new Convention on the Worst Forms of Child Labour by 174 nations and, by September 2000, for its ratification by 37 countries (Human Rights Watch, 2001). One might also consider here the use of publicity by human rights organizations such as the International Labour Organization, UNICEF, the Bonded Labour Liberation Front, Free the Children, and the Child Labour Coalition, in their campaign against child labour.

Perhaps the most potent tool in any administrator's hands is the power to publicize (Gellhorn and Levin, 1997). A publicity release detailing the character of a suspected offence and the offender involved can inflict immediate damage. Furthermore, in the enforcement of legislation protecting consumers against the manufacture and sale of impure food and drugs, the ability of administrative agencies to inform the public that a product may contain harmful ingredients can play an important role in preventing consumption of the product under investigation until the accuracy of this suspicion can be determined.

In some cases, however, firms that have a monopoly on their products, such as local gas and electric companies, are not likely to be hurt by adverse publicity. Agencies are, at times, also reluctant to stigmatize firms because adverse publicity is considered a form of informal adjudication, although it is often used and justified by the notion that people have a right to know. Moreover, it would be naïve to suppose that the threat of adverse publicity is always sufficient to prevent corporate wrongdoing. Consider that, in 1999, GM was ordered to pay $4.9 billion (US) to six people who were severely burned when their cars exploded in flames after rear-end collisions. In court, lawyers for the plaintiffs produced an internal GM study that acknowledged that the gas tanks in the Chevrolet Malibu and El Camino, the Pontiac Grand Am, and Oldsmobile Cutlass were mounted in unsafe positions—27 centimetres from the rear bumper. However, the GM study also noted that it would be cheaper to settle lawsuits that might arise from accidents in which victims were fatally burned (calculated to be $2.40 per car produced) than to change where the tanks were placed (calculated to be $8.59 per car produced). Here, as in the earlier case involving the Ford Pintos, a profit-motivated decision was made and the placement of the gas tanks in these cars remained unaltered from 1979 to 1983. Moreover, it should be noted that while the amount awarded in this case was both the largest product-liability award and the largest personal injury verdict in US history, legal experts opined that the enormous punitive award was unlikely to stand on appeal. "Even with awards in the tens of millions, it is rare for a plaintiff to actually get anything close to the jury's verdict" (White, 1999).

SUMMARY

- Laws are one type of formal social control. Other types of formal social control rely on both penalties and rewards, whereas control through the law is exercised primarily, but not exclusively, by the use of punishments to regulate behaviour.
- The goals of punishment include retribution or social retaliation, incapacitation, and both specific and general deterrence.
- Formal control of deviant behaviour is not limited to criminal sanctions. The use of civil commitment as a mechanism of legal control is also widespread.

- Canada invests enormous resources in controlling victimless crimes. These are crimes *mala prohibita* and are differentiated from other crimes by the element of consensual transaction or exchange. The legal control of victimless crimes, such as drug addiction, prostitution, and gambling, tends to be expensive and ineffective, and may lead to the corruption of law enforcement agents.

- White-collar crimes constitute a greater threat to the welfare of society than more traditional kinds of crime. The notion of white-collar crime incorporates both occupational and corporate crimes.

- Control through administrative law is exercised in the context of licensing, inspection, and the use of publicity as a threat.

CRITICAL THINKING QUESTIONS

1. Fuelled by the strong belief that pornography incites men to commit sexual and nonsexual violence against women, some notable feminists, such as Andrea Dworkin (1981) and Catherine MacKinnon (1987, 1993) have fought for decades to ban virtually all explicit depictions of sexuality. Although evidence for a causal link between exposure to and use of pornography and sexual violence remains inconclusive, the movement to ban pornography has recently intensified in reaction to cyberporn (Fabi, 2004; Lillie, 2002), child pornography, and the advent of Internet rape sites in which "the pain caused to the victim is a primary selling point" (Gossett and Byrne, 2002:689). Various pro-family organizations in Canada, the United States, and Britain have also campaigned for the enactment of laws that would suppress the production and availability of pornography (Luff, 2001). Others, however, oppose censorship and, in particular, the censorship of sexuality. It is evident that myriad practical difficulties emerge in attempts to distinguish between "art," "erotica," "pornography," and "obscenity" and, equally, to police the Internet. In addition, within democratic societies, constitutional protections to freedom of expression and privacy may be deemed of superordinate importance. Consider here that, in 2002, a US federal court ruled that the *Children's Internet Protection Act* of 2001, which required libraries in that country to filter Internet material that was deemed "unsuitable" for children, "was unconstitutional insofar as it interfered with the First Amendment right of other library patrons" (Friedrichs, 2006:22).

    Investigate what the Canadian Criminal Code currently prohibits in relation to "obscenity" and "pornography." Should such materials be more—or less—strictly controlled? How do the constitutional rights of Canadians, guaranteed by the *Canadian Charter of Rights and Freedoms*, impact upon current determinations of what is, or is not, deemed to be a criminal offence in this regard?

2. Some maintain that "rights" only work in those situations where individuals are in a position to press for them and that, in other cases, the granting of formal rights merely provides for the semblance of justice. Discuss this charge with reference to Aboriginal peoples, LGBT persons, women, or the disabled.

chapter six

Law and Dispute Resolution

One of the major functions of law is the orderly resolution of disputes. The intent of this chapter is to examine the questions of why, how, and under what circumstances laws are used in disagreements between individuals, between individuals and organizations, and between organizations.

A NOTE ON TERMINOLOGY

There are a number of different terms used in the sociological and legal literature to describe the role of law in controversies. Terms such as "conflict resolution," "conflict regulation," "conflict management," "dispute processing," "dispute settlement," "dispute resolution," or simply "disputing" are often used more or less interchangeably (Coltri, 2004; Goldberg et al., 2003; Doak, 2004; Haynes, Haynes, and Fong, 2004; Kriesberg, 2002).

Some scholars contend that disputes are processed in society rather than settled, and conflicts are managed or regulated rather than resolved (Menkel-Meadow, 2003; Palmer and Simon, 1998). Third-party intervention, whether through legal or nonlegal means, represents for them only the settlement of the resolution of the public component of the dispute or conflict, rather than the alleviation of the underlying forces or tensions that have created that conflict. Richard L. Abel (1973:228) epitomizes this position and chides anthropologists and sociologists who "have tended to write as though 'settlement' must be the ultimate outcome of disputes, 'resolution' the inevitable fate of conflicts." Then he adds that "it has recently become almost commonplace to observe that the outcome of most conflicts and disputes are other conflicts and disputes, with at most a temporary respite between them" (Abel, 1973:28).

Other authors point out that the actual dispute is preceded by several stages. For example, Laura Nader and Harry F. Todd (1978:14) contend that there are three distinct phases or stages in the disputing process: the **grievance** or **preconflict stage**, the

conflict stage, and the **dispute stage**. The grievance or preconflict stage refers to situations that an individual or a group perceives to be unjust and considers grounds for resentment or complaint. The situation may be real or imaginary, depending on the aggrieved parties' perception. This condition may erupt into conflict or it may wane. If it is not resolved, it enters into the conflict stage, in which the aggrieved party confronts the offending party and communicates his or her resentment or feelings of injustice to the person or group. The conflict phase is dyadic; that is, it involves only two parties. If it is not de-escalated or resolved at this stage, it enters into the final, dispute stage when the conflict is made public. The dispute stage is characterized by the involvement of a third party in the disagreement. P. H. Gulliver (1969:14) suggests that "no dispute exists unless and until the right-claimant, or someone on his [sic] behalf, actively raises the initial disagreement from the level of dyadic argument into the public arena, with the express intention of doing something about the denied claim." Ideally, then, a grievance is *monadic*, involving one person or a group; a conflict is *dyadic*; and a dispute is *triadic*, since it involves the participation of a third party, who is called upon as an agent of settlement.

The legal approach to dispute resolution entails the transition from a dyad of the conflicting parties to the triad, "where an intermediary who stands outside the original conflict has been added to the dyad" (Aubert, 1963:26). The stages discussed by Nader and Todd are not always clear-cut or sequential. A person may file a lawsuit without ever confronting the offender, or one party may quit or concede at any stage in the disagreement.

When disagreements formally enter the legal arena (that is, trial), from the perspective of the law, disputes are authoritatively settled rather than processed through the intervention of third parties (that is, judges), and conflicts are resolved rather than simply managed or regulated. The use of the terms "conflict resolution" and "dispute settlement" is thus, in this sense, justified. In this chapter, we shall use these concepts interchangeably, and at the same time, we will repeatedly emphasize, in different contexts, that the law resolves or settles only the legal components of conflicts and disputes, rather than ameliorating the underlying causes. The law, in brief, deals with disagreements that have been translated into legal disputes or conflicts. A legal resolution of conflict does not necessarily lead to a reduction of tension or antagonism between the aggrieved parties, as evidenced by many of the approximately 70 000 or so Canadians who annually get divorced.

METHODS OF DISPUTE RESOLUTION

Disputes are ubiquitous in every society at every level, and there is a wide variety of methods for their management (see, for example, Coltri, 2004; Fiss and Resnik, 2003). Most societies use fairly similar methods; the differences among them consist in the preference given to one method over others. Cultural factors and the availability of institutions for settling disputes will usually determine such preferences. There are two principal forms of legal dispute resolution throughout the world. "*Either* the parties to a conflict determine the outcome themselves by negotiations, which does not preclude that a third party acting as a mediator might assist them in their negotiations. *Or*, the conflict is adjudicated, which means that a third, and ideally impartial, party decides which of the disputants has the superior claim" (Ehrmann, 1976:82). These forms are used (and are sometimes intertwined) for the settlement of civil, criminal, and administrative suits. For nonlegal disputes, there are a variety of other means for settlement.

A noted anthropologist, Simon Roberts (1979:57), points out that in some societies, direct interpersonal violence constitutes an approved method of dispute settlement. Such interpersonal violence may be a way of retaliation for violence already suffered or a reaction to some other form of perceived injustice (see, for example, Adinkrah, 2005). Occasionally, physical violence may be channelled into a restricted and conventionalized form, such as *duelling*. In Germany before the Second World War, for example, duelling was a popular form of dispute settlement among university students, members of the officer corps in the military, and the nobility in general. Duels took place under controlled conditions and according to specific rules. The participants wore protective clothing, and usually the first sign of bloodletting marked the end of the dispute. It was often a question of honour to challenge the insulting party to a duel, who was, by convention, compelled to accept it. In the event of an insult or injustice, all the offended party had to do was to slap the offender. This act was a challenge to a duel, and the parties involved promptly settled on the time and place. Duelling scars on one's face represented symbols of courage and high status. More recently, Garkawe (1995) reports that a traditional punishment among Australian Aborigines, which involves the spearing of the offender by one or more members of the victim's family, was incorporated into the sentencing of an Aboriginal man, Wilson Jagamara Walker, from Central Australia, who was convicted of manslaughter in 1994. Although Walker was initially sentenced to three years' incarceration, Chief Justice Martin of the Supreme Court of the Northern Territory released Walker on a bond, "the basis of which being that he [Walker] would be speared in both thighs by the younger brother of the man he had killed. If this did not occur within the allocated time, Walker would have to return to the court and have the sentence reviewed" (Garkawe, 1995:11). According to Garkawe, this decision, which incorporated "genuine customary Aboriginal punishment as a sentencing option available to the Court" may represent a "turning point in Australian law" for its acknowledgment that "western perceptions of human rights should not necessarily predominate over Aboriginal practices."

Another form of physical violence is **feuding** (Gulliver, 1979:1). Feuding is a state of recurring hostilities between families or groups, instigated by a desire to avenge an offence (insult, injury, death, or deprivation of some sort) against a member of the group. The unique feature of a feud is that responsibility to avenge is carried by all members of the group. The killing of any member of the offender's group is viewed as appropriate revenge, since the group as a whole is considered responsible. Nicholas Gubser (1965) describes a feud that lasted for decades within a Nunamiut Inuit community caused by a husband's killing of his wife's lover. When a man is killed, in Gubser's words:

> The closely related members of his kindred do not rest until complete revenge has been achieved. The immediate relatives of the deceased. . . recruit as much support from other relatives as they can. Their first action, if possible, is to kill the murderer, or maybe one of his closest kin. Then, of course, the members of the murderer's kindred are brought into the feud. These two kindreds may snipe at each other for years. (1965:151)

At times, the feud can turn into a full-scale battle when, in addition to the families, the communities are drawn into a dispute.

Disagreement, at times, is channelled into rituals. For example, the parties to the dispute may confront each other before the assembled community and voice their contentions through songs and dances improvised for the occasion. In the form of a song, the accuser states all the abuse he or she can think of; the accused then responds in kind. A number of such exchanges may follow until the contestants are exhausted, and a winner emerges through public acclaim for the greater poetic or vituperative skill.

In some societies, **shaming** is used as a form of public reprimand in the disapproval of disputing behaviour. Ridicule directed at those guilty of anti-social conduct is also used to reduce conflict. At times, the singing of rude and deflating songs to, or about, a troublesome individual is also reported as a means of achieving a similar end. Ridicule, reproach, or public exposure may also take the form of a "public harangue," in which a person's wrongdoings are embarrassingly exposed by being shouted out to the community at large (Roberts, 1979:62). Another form of shaming, however, does not employ shaming as a form of humiliation but rather, as a method of resolving disputes through the "healing" of wounds. For example, the Report of the Aboriginal Justice Inquiry of Manitoba (1991:27) noted that, within traditional Aboriginal societies, the underlying philosophy stressed atonement and the restoration of harmony—not punishment (see also Ross, 1992). In "**reintegrating shaming**," disapproval is expressed toward the rule-violating act but the essential value of the offender, him or herself, is reaffirmed along with the prospect of reacceptance (Braithwaite, 1989; McAlinden, 2005). According to Larry Siegel (1998:121), "A critical element of re-integrative shaming occurs when the offenders begin to understand and recognize their wrongdoing and shame themselves. To be re-integrative, shaming must be brief and controlled and then followed by 'ceremonies' of forgiveness, apology, and repentance."

Recently, in pursuit of a "culturally relevant disposition" in a case involving an Aboriginal man who had pled guilty to sexually assaulting his two daughters and a foster child over the course of several years, Judge Lilles adopted a community-based disposition in lieu of a period of incarceration. In doing so, he implicitly recognized that methods of re-integrative shaming may function as an effective form of social control:

> First one must deal with the shock and then the dismay on your neighbours' faces. One must live with the daily humiliation, and at the same time seek forgiveness not just from the victims, but from the community as a whole. For in a Native culture, a real harm has been done to everyone. A community disposition continues that humiliation, at least until full forgiveness has been achieved. (*R. v. P. [J.A.] 1991, 317* in Razack, 1994:908)

In attempts to resolve disputes, parties may also choose to resort to supernatural agencies. The notion that supernatural beings may intervene to punish wrongdoers is rather widespread. This notion is often accompanied by the belief that harm may be inflicted by witches or through the practice of sorcery. In some societies, witchcraft and sorcery are seen as a possible cause of death and of almost any form of illness or material misfortune. Jane Fishburne Collier (1973:113), for example, identifies a variety of witchcraft beliefs among the Zinacantecos in Mexico. They include witches who send sickness, ask that sickness be sent, perform specific actions (such as causing the victim to rot away), control weather, talk to saints, or cause sickness by an evil eye. Notes Collier: "Witchcraft beliefs underlie all of the reasons given for actions during a hearing" (1973:122). Consequently, in such societies the procedures for identifying witches or sorcerers responsible for particular incidences or misfortunes assume great importance in the handling of conflict.

Of course, not all disputes are handled by violence, rituals, shaming, ostracism, or resorting to supernatural agencies. Some of these methods can be "domesticated" (Cobb, 1997), and most societies have access to a number of alternative methods of dispute resolution. These alternatives differ in several ways, including whether participation is voluntary, the presence or absence of a third party, the criteria used for third-party intervention, the type of outcome and how it may be enforced, and whether the procedures employed are formal or informal. Before considering them, let us look at two other popular ways of coping with disputes: "lumping it" and avoidance.

"**Lumping it**" refers simply to inaction, to not making a claim or a complaint. Galanter says: "This is done all the time by 'claimants' who lack information or access or who knowingly decide gain is too low, cost too high (including psychic cost of litigating where such activity is repugnant)" (1974:124). For example, Mullis's (1995) investigation of doctor-patient conflict found the modal response to medical injury was toleration, with poorer patients less likely to file a malpractice suit against their physician than higher income patients. In "lumping it," the issue or the difficulty that gave rise to the disagreement is simply ignored and the relationship with the offending party continues. For example, a professor may not want to press a particular claim (say, for a higher increment) against the administration and continues his or her relationship with the university. A somewhat different form of withdrawal from conflict situations that seems likely to result in dispute is described by Carol J. Greenhouse (1989:252) in her study of Baptists in a southern US town. The findings indicate that Baptists in the community consider disputing a profoundly un-Christian act because the Bible states clearly that Jesus is the judge of all people. The implication is that to partake in a dispute is to stand as judge over another person. This would be an indication of a lack of faith and a pre-emption of Jesus' power.

Avoidance refers to limiting the relationship with other disputants sufficiently so that the dispute no longer remains salient (Felstiner, 1974:70). Albert O. Hirschman (1970) calls this kind of behaviour "exit," which entails withdrawing from a situation or terminating or curtailing a relationship. For example, a consumer may go to a different store rather than press grievances. In consumer-transaction disputes, "the exit option is widely held to be uniquely powerful: by inflicting revenue losses on delinquent management" (Hirschman, 1970:21). This option can be considered not only expedient in dispute settlement but also a way of imposing sanctions. Avoidance entails a limitation or a break in the relationship between disputants, whereas "lumping it" refers to the lack of resolution of a conflict, grievance, or dispute for the reason that one of the parties prefers to ignore the issue in dispute, generally basing the decision on feelings of relative powerlessness or on the social, economic, or psychological costs involved in seeking a solution. Avoidance is not always an alternative, especially in situations when the relationship must continue— for example, with certain companies that have monopolies, such as gas or electric companies, or with Canada Revenue Agency. An important aspect of avoidance is the reduction of social interaction or its termination. Lumping behaviour entails the ignoring of the issue in dispute while continuing the relationship.

Primary Resolution Processes

The primary dispute resolution mechanisms can be depicted on a continuum ranging from negotiation to adjudication. In negotiation, participation is voluntary and disputants arrange settlements for themselves. Next on the continuum is mediation, in which a third party facilitates a resolution and otherwise assists the parties in reaching a voluntary agreement. At the other end of the continuum is adjudication (both judicial and administrative), in which parties are compelled to participate, the case is decided by a judge, the parties are represented by counsel, the procedures are formal, and the outcomes are enforceable by law. Close to adjudication is arbitration, which is more informal and in which the decision may or may not be binding. Negotiation, mediation, and arbitration are the principal components of what is referred to as "alternative dispute resolution" (ADR) in legal parlance (Barrett and Barrett, 2004; Sargent, 2002). The movement is spreading to other parts of the world. In France, for example, recourse to ADR carries with it a fashionable progressive connotation, and ADR is regularly promoted by the French authorities and legal scholars alike as a means of relieving the burden on the courts, of rendering dispute resolutions that are faster, simpler, and cheaper, and of "de-dramatizing" disputes to render their resolutions more satisfactory to the parties (Gaillard, 2000).

Since dispute resolutions are bread-and-butter issues in the legal profession, not surprisingly there is now mounting evidence that law firms are becoming uneasy about the spreading use of alternative means (France, 1995). Let us now consider these processes and some of their variants in some detail.

Negotiations in disputes take place when disputants seek to resolve their disagreements without the help of neutral third parties. Negotiation is a two-party arrangement in which disputants try to persuade one another, establish a common ground for discussion, and feel their way, by a process of give-and-take, toward a settlement. It involves the use of debate and bargaining (Lewicki, 2004; Raiffa, 1997). A basic requirement for successful negotiation is the desire of both parties to settle a dispute without escalation and without resort to neutral third parties. Aubert states: "The advantage of negotiated solutions is that they need not leave any marks on the normative order of society. Since the solution does not become a precedent for later solutions to similar conflicts, the adversaries need not fear the general consequences of the settlement" (1969:284). When interests are contradictory to the extent that gains and losses must cancel each other out, negotiations are inadequate in resolving the conflict, and in such situations, parties may bring the case to court for legal settlement. In industrialized countries, such as Canada, lumping behaviour, avoidance, and negotiation are the most frequent responses to dispute situations.

Mediation is a dispute resolution method that interposes a disinterested and non-coercive third party, the mediator, between the disputants (Bush and Folger, 2005; Haynes, Haynes and Fong, 2004; McCorkle and Reese, 2005). Unlike litigation, where the ultimate decision is imposed by the judge, the mediator does not make the final decision. Rather, the terms of settlement are worked out solely by and between the disputants. It can be an effective way of resolving a variety of disputes if both parties are interested in a reasonable settlement of their disagreement (Fitzpatrick, 1994). Mediation begins with an agreement. It is non-adversarial, and the basic tenet is co-operation rather than competition. The role of the mediator in the dispute is that of a guide, a facilitator, and a catalyst.

A mediator may be chosen by the disputants or appointed by someone in authority. A mediator may be selected because the person has status, position, respect, power, money, or the alleged power to invoke sanctions on behalf of a deity or some other superhuman force. (There is some empirical evidence that lawyers playing the role of mediators are considered effective by clients in dispute resolutions [Croson and Mnookin, 1997]). A mediator may have none of these but simply be a designated agent of an organization set up to handle specific disputes. Bringing disputes to a mediator may be the choice of both parties or of one but not the other party to a conflict, or it may be the result of private norms or expectations of a group which "require" that disputes be settled as much as possible within the group.

Mediation essentially consists of influencing the parties to come to an agreement by appealing to their own interests. The mediator may use a variety of techniques to accomplish this objective.

He [sic] may work on the parties' ideas of what serves them best. . . in such a way that he [sic] gets them to consider the common interests as more essential than they did previously, or their competing interests as less essential. He [sic] may also look for possibilities of resolution which the parties themselves have not discovered and try to convince them that both will be well served by his [sic] suggestion. The very fact that a suggestion is proposed by an impartial third party may also, in certain cases, be sufficient for the parties to accept it. (Eckhoff, 1978:36)

Ideally, both parties should have confidence in the mediator, be willing to co-operate, listen to his or her advice, and consider the mediator as impartial. A mediator may also use warnings, promises, or flattery in attempts to reconcile differences between the parties. Eckhoff points out:

The conditions for mediation are best in cases where both parties are interested in having the conflict resolved. The stronger the common interest is, the greater reason they have for bringing the conflict before a third party, and the more motivated they will be for cooperating actively with him [sic] in finding a solution, and for adjusting their demands in such a way that a solution can be reached. (1978:36)

Mediation may be "*interest-based*," in which the mediator acts as a facilitator, encouraging the parties to identify their needs and expectations to the other and arrive at a win/win solution, or "*rights-based*." **Rights-based mediation,** which is sometimes referred to as "early neutral evaluation" or "evaluative mediation," involves a mediator's evaluation of the case in the context of formal rules (e.g., the law or accepted principles of accounting). For example, labour mediation, which has been widespread across Canada for decades, is generally rights-based (Bumstead, 2001:513).

Throughout the 1990s, a variety of projects and programs began to explore mediation models for family law disputes. For example, for over a decade, the Unified Family Court in Hamilton, Ontario, operated as a pilot project offering totally subsidized family mediation as an in-house program with staff mediation. In 1999, Nova Scotia introduced voluntary mediation for family cases as part of the then-new Supreme Court (Family Division), with mediation available on matters relating to custody, access, support or maintenance, and property. The use of mediators is increasingly touted as desirable if not, indeed, essential in cases of divorce. Canada's *Divorce Act* requires lawyers to mention mediation to their clients, and divorce mediation has been championed as an alternative, non-adversarial means of dispute resolution by which the couple, with the assistance of a mediator or mediators (frequently a lawyer-therapist team but sometimes social workers, psychologists, psychiatrists, lawyers, or accountants) negotiate the terms of their settlement of custody, support, property, and visitation issues (Beck and Sales, 2000; Picard and Saunders, 2002:230). Mediation can be "*closed*" (in which case, everything said during mediation remains confidential and the mediator cannot prepare a report for the court) or "*open*" (allowing the mediator to quote anything said during mediation in the preparing of a report). In "**collaborative mediation**," which is now used by some lawyers in Ontario, Alberta, and British Columbia, lawyers and clients must all agree in advance not to go to court, reducing the incentive for lawyers to recommend litigation.

Research indicates that couples who use divorce mediation have less re-litigation, feel more satisfied with the process and the results, and report better relationships with ex-spouses (Marlow and Sauber, 1990) and children (Beck and Blank, 1997). Children of mediated divorces also seem to adjust better to the divorce of their parents than do children of litigated divorces (Wallerstein, 1999). However, various women's task groups have noted that mediation as it is currently practised may be biased against women, who report being chastised and labelled as "unladylike" or "vindictive" if they refuse to give in on a point (Woo, 1992). In addition, "[s]pouses who have been bullied or dominated during the marriage may not be capable of holding their own in mediation, while rigid or abusive spouses may not be capable of the necessary flexibility and compromise" (Dranoff, 2005:271).

In 1995, Saskatchewan's Queen's Bench Civil Mediation Program was first launched in Regina and Swift Current. The program, which requires parties involved in non-family civil disputes to meet with a mediator early in the legal process and explore options for settlement, claims a high success rate, with one-fifth to one-quarter of cases being resolved at the initial mediation (Conrod, 1999:59). Beginning with the introduction of the notice-to-mediate process for motor vehicle actions in 1998, British Columbia has pursued mediation options in a number of areas, including residential construction disputes. In 1999, following a two-year pilot project in Ottawa, *mandatory mediation* for non-family civil disputes was implemented in Ontario for the Toronto and Ottawa-Carleton regions. "Mandatory mediation, as its name suggests, is a non-voluntary process that creates significant pressures to settle, and it is incorporated within the physical and ideological confines of the formal justice system" (Sargent, 2002:211). In Alberta, the Civil Claims Mediation Pilot Project, created in 1998, was so successful that it was made a permanent part of the court program in the following year. The Canadian *Environmental Assessment Act* provides for the use of mediation as does the *Youth Criminal Justice Act* (Picard and Saunders, 2002:230).

The use of community-based mediation projects in Canada began in the 1980s as a grass-roots response to such crimes as vandalism. Beginning in Elmira, Ontario, with the attempt to provide restorative justice through a facilitated meeting between a group of boys who had vandalized some homes and the affected homeowners, community mediation programs have spread through many Canadian cities, with trained volunteers working to help resolve a variety of neighbourhood disputes and some criminal matters (Bumstead, 2001).

> Rooted in social activism, proponents of mediation sought to assist individuals and groups to use non-violent and more effective problem-solving strategies. Interest in mediation was also tied to attempts at legal reform based on growing public concerns about fair and effective dispute resolution as well as concerns about court costs and delays. . . . The growth in mediation was also driven by the many practitioners drawn to a field offering the potential of bettering society and serving the public good by restoring harmony to communities and by transforming (or supplanting) legal institutions. (Picard and Saunders, 2002:226)

In the United States, where the experience and development of various forms of alternative dispute resolution are "probably 10 to 20 years ahead of the Canadian experience" (Braniff, 2005:558), the use of mediators is widespread in the more than 300 neighbourhood justice resolution centres. The initial idea for such centres came from Richard Danzig (1973). Using the Liberian example of resolving intratribal disputes by conciliation, Danzig suggested the establishment of neighbourhood community moots. Such moots involve community members with shared values who might be able to resolve more effectively than courts those disputes that affect the disputants and the neighbourhood, such as family and housing disputes and minor criminal charges. Although there is a great variation among centres in the types of cases they handle, almost all tend to concentrate on disputes between persons with an ongoing relationship. Participation in mediation is voluntary. The majority of disputants are referred to the centres by judges, police, prosecutors, and court clerks. Mediators include lawyers, law students, undergraduates, and laypeople. Before acting as mediators, they receive training in mediation techniques (American Bar Association, 2004).

There are many reported advantages of such neighbourhood justice centres. These non-judicial forums can increase access to justice because of their low cost (or no cost), convenient hours, and location. Mediation provides a better process than other forums for handling disputes because participants are able to explore the underlying problems contributing to the dispute without legal formalities, time limits, and lawyers acting as intermediaries in the discussion. The reliance on informal alternatives also frees the courts to attend to more serious cases (Wright and Galaway, 1989) and is being used with increasing frequency in victim-offender mediation for nonviolent offences in attempts to work out a restitution program as an option to a prison sentence (Reske, 1995). However, if "one of the principal attractions of mediation is the potential to *avoid* what law and legal institutions offer and represent: complexity, expense, delay, inaccessibility, formality, alienation, and elitism. . . the professions' power and influence are already being felt within mediation" (Picard and Saunders, 2002:232).

> In addition to the fact that many lawyers are directly involved in the practice, law schools in Canada and the U.S. have moved aggressively over the last decade to establish and promote ADR courses. Lawyers now advertise their "specialty" in mediation services, and the Canadian and American Bar Associations both have subcommittees on ADR as well [as] local committees to oversee the practice. . . . The imposition of the values and direction of a profession that continues to reflect the advantaged and elite of society. . . threatens to leave mediation trapped within the narrow confines of a rights-based, cost-effective, and settlement-focused framework. (Picard and Saunders, 2002:232)

Related to mediation is the **ombudsman process**, which combines mediatory and investigatory functions in dispute resolution. In the classic Scandinavian model, the ombudsman is a public official designated to hear citizen complaints and carry out independent fact-finding investigations to correct abuses of public administration. In a traditional sense, ombudsmen are independent agents of the legislature and they can criticize, publicize, and make recommendations, but they cannot reverse administrative actions (Rosenbloom and Goldman, 1998:474).

The ombudsman system is widely used as an alternative to courts in other countries. In Denmark, for example, courts are very rarely used by the consumer (Blegvad, 1983:207). Instead, the ombudsman negotiates with the firms in disputes on behalf of clients. In Canada, the role of the ombudsman was specifically designed to investigate complaints from individuals who perceived themselves to be unfairly treated by government agencies, officials, or employees. Beginning with Alberta and New Brunswick in 1967, Quebec in 1968 (where the ombudsman is referred to as the "Protecteur du citoyen"), and Manitoba in 1969, the office of ombudsman spread throughout Canada. Currently, almost every Canadian jurisdiction (the exceptions are Prince Edward Island, Newfoundland and Labrador, the Northwest Territories, and Nunavut) has an ombudsman appointed by the provincial or territorial government. The mission statement of Ontario's ombudsman announces the goal that is common of most ombudsmen: "to strive to ensure that people are served justly, equitably, and fairly by. . . governmental organizations." Despite calls for the introduction of a federal ombudsman, Canada has, instead, four federal commissioners who are limited to specialized roles: the privacy commissioner; the correctional investigator; the commissioner of official languages; and the information commissioner under the Access to Information Act.

Dranoff (2005:151) reports that persons selected to be ombudsmen are typically high-level public officials who enjoy the respect of the public for their "independence from outside pressure." She emphasizes that the ombudsman does not act as an advocate, as a lawyer does, but as an impartial investigator and that an ombudsman should not be perceived as an "omnipotent being who can provide perfect justice and right all wrongs"; rather, the ombudsman can only act "within the authority established by Parliament or a provincial legislature, to which she or he is responsible." Reportedly, the most common types of complaint made to ombudsmen in Canada are: "wrong or unreasonable interpretations of criteria, standards, guidelines, regulations, laws, information or evidence; discriminatory consequences of a decision or policy on an individual or group; harassment, bias, mismanagement, or bad faith by a government official; and unreasonable delay" (Dranoff, 2005:151). However, she notes that the growing "trend towards privatization, contracting-out and outsourcing of services could remove certain public services from the ombudsman's jurisdiction" and suggests that the ombudsman's office "is the agency best situated to view and comment on the effect on public services of downsizing within the public service."

In recent years, the role of the ombudsman has been extended with the creation of university ombudsmen to address complaints by students, hospital ombudsmen to address complaints by patients, and others relying on the process to correct organizational abuses and resolve internal disputes. In 1996, for example, the Canadian Bankers Association established an ombudsman as a "court of last resort" to settle customer complaints against member banks (Dranoff, 2001:139). In 2002, the Canadian financial services industry (e.g., banks, life and health insurers, property and casualty insurers, investment and mutual fund dealers) established a Financial Services Ombuds Network to deal with complaints by the public (Dranoff, 2005: 151). Some newspapers and radio stations, through "action lines," also perform the role of ombudsman in disputes. A major criticism against the ombudsman process, however, is that the person acting as mediator often represents the vested interest of a particular agency, which suggests bias in favour of his or her employer.

Arbitration is another way of involving a third party in a dispute. Unlike mediation, in which a third party assists the disputants to reach their own solution, arbitration requires a final and binding decision to be made for the disputants by a third party. Disputants agree beforehand both to the intervention of a neutral third party and to the finality of his or her decision. In general, the rules of evidence and procedure are more relaxed than in the court process. Arbitration is rights-based and has an adversarial process that is structured much like a civil trial. However, the proceedings in arbitration, unlike in courts, can remain private. Arbitration and other nonjudicial methods tend to reduce the cost of dispute resolution because of the lack of opportunity to appeal the arbitrator's decision and especially when lawyers are not hired. It is also faster than adjudication because participants can proceed as soon as they are ready rather than waiting for a trial date to be set.

Nowadays, almost all collective bargaining contracts contain a provision for final and binding arbitration (Warskett, 2002). For example, "under the Canadian Labour Code, which applies to about 10 percent of Canadian workers who are within the regulatory sphere of the federal Parliament, a worker claiming to have been dismissed without just cause can have the claim adjudicated by a neutral arbitrator appointed by the government" (Mac Neil, 2002:184). Arbitration clauses are also showing up more often in business contracts and even in executive employment letters. Many private organizations, professional groups, and trade associations have their own formal arbitration machinery for the settlement of disputes among members. Similarly, labour–management disputes are often brought before arbiters, designated in advance, whose decisions are binding by mutual consent of the disputants and ultimately enforceable by private sanctions and by the courts. In general, willingness to submit disputes to private but formal arbitration is characteristic of parties who have a commitment to long-term relationships (Sarat, 1989). Although organizations such as the Arbitration and Mediation Institute of Ontario have designations that recognize training and experience, alternative dispute resolution practitioners in Canada are not regulated by the government or by any professional body (Bumstead, 2001:508). However, as Braniff (2005:558) notes, "Many ADR practitioners are professionals qualified and regulated as lawyers, social workers or accountants" and must abide by professional codes of conduct. For example, she notes that in Ontario, the Law Society of Upper Canada, which is the governing body for Ontario's lawyers, "has amended its Code of Ethics to deal with issues facing lawyers in the role of mediator."

Arbitration is increasingly considered as an alternative to judicial and administrative processes. Compulsory arbitration, especially for small claims, can free courts for more substantial disputes, and depending upon the issues involved, it may reduce the cost to litigants and be a more effective way of solving problems. The Ontario Civil Justice Review, conducted in the late 1990s, concluded that an average case that included a three-day trial costs a litigant $38 000 in lawyers' fees and results in an average award of $58 000; similarly, according to figures from the Ministry of the Attorney General, "a typical two-party civil suit that goes to trial in Ontario will take up to five years to resolve and result in a judgment of $55 000—70 percent of which will go to pay legal fees" (Conrod, 1999:57). Systems of compulsory arbitration already exist in England, Germany, the Scandinavian countries, and China, where arbitration is used quite extensively (Tao, 2004). In Philadelphia, a case that is under $10 000 is automatically assigned by the court to arbitration. Three arbitrators are selected by the deputy court administrator from a panel of lawyers. They make their decisions on the pleadings supplemented by oral arguments by the lawyers for the parties. It is estimated that the average arbitrated case costs one-fifth less per day than it would in the Philadelphia court system.

Adjudication is a public and formal method of conflict resolution and is best exemplified by courts (Fiss and Resnick, 2003). Courts have the authority to intervene in disputes whether or not the parties desire it and to render a decision and to enforce compliance with that decision. In adjudication, the emphasis is on the legal rights and duties of disputants, rather than on compromises or on the mutual satisfaction of the parties. Adjudication is also more oriented toward zero-sum decisions than the other mechanisms we have noted. Courts require disputants to narrow their definitions of issues in the identification of the nature of their problems. Felstiner states: "Adjudication as a consequence tends to focus on 'what facts' and 'which norms' rather than on any need for normative shifts" (1974:70). In other words, courts deal with issues and facts. Consequently, they can deal only with disagreements, grievances, or conflicts that have been transformed into legal disputes. For example, in a divorce case, the court may focus on one incident in what is a complex and often not very clear-cut series of problems. This results in a resolution of a legal dispute but not necessarily of the broader issues that have produced that conflict.

Although courts occasionally seek compromise and flexibility, generally the verdict of the court has an either/or character: The decision is based upon a single definite conception of what has actually taken place and upon a single interpretation of legal norms. When a conflict culminates in litigation, one of the parties must be prepared for a total loss. Aubert says: "One aspect of legal decisions that is closely linked to their either/or character is the marked orientation toward the past" (1969:287). The structure of legal thinking is also oriented toward comparisons between actions and sanctions rather than toward utility and effectiveness. Because of this orientation, and because of the use of precedents, there is a fair amount of predictability in how similar cases will be settled by courts. But since the courts are dealing only with the legal issues, they do not take into consideration the possibility that the applicable legal facts and norms may have been influenced by different social conditions and that, in many instances, courts are treating only the symptoms rather than the underlying causes of a problem. With these limitations, the courts work "to clean up all the little social messes (and the occasional big ones) that recurrently arise between the members of the society from day to day" (Hoebel, 1954:280).

Hybrid Resolution Processes

In both the public and private sectors, the intervention of a third party—a person, a government agency, or other institution—can often facilitate dispute resolution among conflicting parties (Ross and Conlon, 2000), and there are currently several "hybrid" dispute-resolution processes in use. The term "hybrid" is employed because these processes incorporate features of the primary processes discussed in the preceding section. The main ones include rent-a-judge, med- arb, and mini-trial.

The *rent-a-judge* process is basically a form of arbitration (Goldberg et al., 2003: 310). In the process, the disputants, in an attempt to avoid the use of a regular court, select a retired judge to hear and decide a pending case as an arbitrator would. The same procedure is used as in court, and the decision of the judge is legally binding. Unlike in arbitration, the "referee's" decision can be appealed for errors of law or on the ground that the judgment was against evidence, though such appeals are rare.

There are other hybrid processes of dispute resolution that have been used with considerable success (Goldberg et al., 2003). One is **med-arb**, in which the issues that were not solved by mediation are submitted to arbitration, with the same person serving first as mediator, then as arbitrator. Med-arb has been used often in contract negotiation disputes between public employers and their unionized employees. Another is the **mini-trial**, which has been repeatedly utilized in a number of big intercorporate disputes. In this method, lawyers for each disputant are given a short time (not more than a day) in which to present the basic elements of their case to senior executives of both parties. After the presentation, the senior executives try to negotiate a settlement of the case, usually with the aid of a neutral adviser. If there is no settlement, the adviser gives the parties his or her opinion of the likely outcome if the dispute were litigated. This dose of reality at times helps to break the deadlock.

In this section, we have distinguished among a number of procedures used for settling disputes. Some are public, some private. Some are official, some unofficial. Some are formal, some informal. These procedures overlap, and each has its limitations and advantages. They are related in different ways to outcomes and consequences. A number of procedures may also be used for the settlement of a single dispute. Table 6.1 summarizes the salient features of the more widely used procedures.

TABLE 6.1   Partial List of Characteristics of the Major Primary and Hybrid Dispute Resolution Processes

Negotiation	Mediation	Arbitration	Adjudication	Rent-a-judge	Mini-trial
Voluntary	Voluntary	Voluntary unless contractual or court-ordered	Nonvoluntary	Voluntary	Voluntary
Nonbinding	Nonbinding	Binding, usually no appeal	Binding, subject to appeal	Binding but subject to appeal and possibly review by trial court	Nonbinding
No third-party facilitator	Party-selected facilitator	Party-selected third-party decision-maker,	Imposed third-party neutral decision-maker	Party-selected third-party decision-maker, usually a former judge or lawyer	Third-party neutral adviser
Informal and unstructured	Informal and unstructured	Procedurally less formal than adjudication	Highly procedural; formalized and structured by predetermined, rigid rules	Flexible as to timing, place, and procedures	Less formal than adjudication and arbitration
Presentation of proofs usually indirect or nonexistent	Presentation of proofs less important than attitudes of each party	Opportunity for each party to present proofs supporting decisions in its favour	Opportunity for each party to present proofs supporting decisions in its favour	Opportunity for each party to present proofs supporting decisions in its favour	Opportunity and responsibility for each party to present proofs supporting decisions in its favour
Mutually acceptable agreement sought	Mutually acceptable agreement sought	Compromise result possible	Win/lose outcome	Win/lose outcome (judgment of court)	Mutually acceptable agreement sought
Agreement usually included in contract or release sought	Agreement usually embodied in contract or release	Reason for result not usually required	Expectation of reasoned statement	Findings of fact and conclusion of law possible but not required	Agreement usually embodied in contract or release
Emphasis on disputants' relationship	Emphasis on disputants' relationship	Consistency and predictability balanced against concerns for disputants' relationship	Process emphasizes attaining substantive consistency and predictability results	Adherence to norms, laws, and precedent	Emphasis on sound, cost-effective, and fair resolution satisfactory to both parties
Highly private process	Private process	Private process unless judicial enforcement sought	Public process; lack of privacy of submissions	Private process unless judicial enforcement sought	Highly private process

Obviously, no single procedure is applicable to every kind of problem. A number of considerations appear relevant in the selection of a particular method. One is the relationship between the disputants; that is, is there an ongoing relationship between the disputants, such as business partners, or is the dispute the result of a single encounter, such as an automobile accident? When an ongoing relationship is involved, is it more productive for the parties to work out their difficulties through negotiation or mediation, if necessary? An advantage of mediation is that it encourages the restructuring of the underlying relationship so as to eliminate the source of conflict rather than dealing only with the manifestation of conflict (Bush and Folger, 2005). Another consideration is the nature of the dispute. If a precedent is required, such as in civil rights cases, litigation in the form of class action may be appropriate. The amount at stake in a dispute also plays a role in deciding on the type of dispute-resolution procedure. Small, simple cases might end up in small-claims courts, whereas more complex issues might require court-ordered arbitration, such as in contract negotiation disputes between public employers and unions. Speed and cost are other relevant factors. For example, arbitration may be speedier and less costly than a court trial. Finally, consideration must be given also to the power relationship between the parties. When one party in a dispute has much less bargaining strength than the other, as in the case of a pollution victim faced by a powerful corporation, an adjudicatory forum in which principle, not power, will determine the outcome may be desirable. In the remainder of this chapter, we shall consider why some disputants turn to legal mechanisms of conflict resolution, under what circumstances they choose the law rather than some other procedures, and the limitations of the law in resolving conflicts.

DEMANDS FOR COURT SERVICES IN DISPUTE RESOLUTION

William Bogart (2002:5) observes that "[a] survey of the last five decades of Western industrialized society would highlight, as a defining element, the insinuation of law into all manner of human endeavour." He acknowledges that the United States, "more than any other industrialized nation, is the land of law," observing that:

> [T]he United States is the society of detailed legal rules, deterrence-oriented enforcement practices, intensely adversarial procedures, and frequent judicial review of administrative orders and legislative enactments. It is the country of rights, most obviously in the courts, but also in the legislatures, in the media, and on the streets. It is the society that most invokes the heaviest machinery of the law, the criminal process culminating in litigation (prosecutions), as a primary response to crime. America leads Western industrialized nations, by a wide margin, in rates of imprisonment; the United States, alone among nations of a similar tradition, retains and imposes the most severe of sanctions: capital punishment. (2002:5)

Yet, he points out that in some areas—most notably in relation to health care, education, and social assistance—other nations, including Canada, actually surpass the United States in the level of regulations they impose through law. The "lure of law," he maintains, is strong and is attested to in Canada by the increased number of lawyers, statutes, regulations, law reports, administrative tribunals and agencies, and litigation (Bogart, 2002:24). He additionally notes that "turning to litigation in Canada has been accelerated by the advent of the *Charter of Rights and Freedoms* (the approximate Canadian equivalent to the U.S. Bill of Rights)" and maintains that, with the incorporation of the *Charter of Rights and Freedoms* into the Canadian Constitution, it is possible that Canadian society may increasingly come to "mimic America's approach to law" (Bogart, 2002:33, 7).

Whether or not Bogart's prediction comes to fruition, there can be little doubt that, increasingly, our lives are bound up in laws and legalisms (Rosen, 2001). Indeed, "if Canada's degree of civility were to be measured in reams alone, Canadian law would already have much to commend itself on for there are no fewer than 40 000 federal and provincial statutes and a broad range of municipal bylaws in force in Canada today comprising literally tens of thousands of pages which govern subjects as diverse as the activities of lobbyists and the standards of purity of precious metals" (Statistics Canada, 1998:499). More generally, Galanter (1992) suggests that in Canada, the United States, and Great Britain, there is now "law abounding" within areas that, in the past, were not viewed as in need of legal structuring.

In industrialized countries worldwide, the legal profession has been flourishing. Boyd (2002:176) observes that while Canada's population increased by approximately 50 percent between the 1960s and the 1990s, the number of lawyers increased by about 300 percent over this same time period. While in 1962 there were 10 000 lawyers practising in Canada, by 1995 there were over 65 000 lawyers registered with Canada's provincial law associations (Statistics Canada, 1998:517). A recent report by the Canadian Bar Association (2005:9, 13) also notes that "the Canadian legal profession has grown almost ten-fold in the past 50 years (there were 9000 lawyers in 1951, and 85 863 lawyers in 2002)" and suggests that, by 2015, "we can expect 125 000 practicing lawyers in Canada." In Canada, the rate of growth of the legal profession has far exceeded that of physicians and surgeons; in the 1970s, for example, the population of lawyers grew by 109 percent while the population of physicians and surgeons grew by a more modest 42 percent. Recent estimates by the Canadian Bar Association (2005) suggest a "net increase of 15 000 lawyers every five years" in this country.

Statistics compiled by Federation of Law Societies of Canada indicate that, as of December 31, 2004, its 14 Law Societies included no fewer than 91 187 members, "of which 87 646 were lawyers in one of the 10 provinces or three territories and 3541 were *notaires* in the provinces of Quebec" (Federation of Law Societies of Canada, 2006). Nevertheless, the increase in lawyers within Western industrialized societies has been most marked in the United States where, at the start of the new millennium, there were over one million lawyers (one lawyer for every 260 Americans). At present, the United States, which has about 5 percent of the world's population, now accounts for more than two-thirds of all the lawyers.

Not surprisingly, perhaps, this growth in the number of lawyers has been accompanied by societies' growing dependence on lawyers. "In the United States the portion of the national income and gross national product derived from legal services almost doubled from the early 1960s to the mid-1980s, and of these increasing expenditures a larger portion is spent by businesses than by individuals. It has been suggested that there have been parallel occurrences in Canada and the United Kingdom as evidenced by the growth in the number and size of law firms that focus on business" (Bogart, 2002:21). Between 1973 and 1993, total spending on civil legal services in Canada soared from $1.9 billion to $11 billion (Bogart, 2002:28). As previously noted in Chapter 3, tort litigation, which primarily involves claims or damages related to personal injury, has also increased in Canada, Great Britain, and, in particular, the United States. For example, despite substantial differences in their health care systems, Canada, England, and the United States all experienced an increase in medical malpractice litigation during the 1970s and 1980s (Dewees et al., 1991). According to the Canadian Medical Protective Association, this trend has continued, with the cumulative cost of medical malpractice claims in 2000 estimated at $3 million per Canadian doctor. In that year, average settlements in closed cases ranged from a high of $172 000 in Ontario to a low of $67 000 in Quebec (Bueckert, 2000).

In the United States, tort costs "reached a record $260 billion in 2004, or approximately $886 per person" (Tillinghast, 2006); in that country, about 47 percent of all torts involve lawsuits between individuals, with 37 percent between individuals and businesses, and the rest between individuals and government agencies or hospitals (Haltom and McCann, 2004). The most recent edition of the periodic Tillinghast-Towers Perrin studies (which began in 1985) compared tort costs in the US with those of several other industrialized nations and noted that US tort costs exceed other countries, "by a sizeable margin, when measured as a ratio to economic output (measured by GDP). The U.S. had a 2.2 percent ratio of tort costs to GDP, compared with Germany (1.1 percent), Japan (0.8 percent), and the U.K. (0.7 percent)" (Towers Perrin, 2006). This report pointedly suggests that "[t]he higher ratio of tort costs to GDP in the US may be partly explained by differences in health care systems. Injured parties in countries with national health care may have less of a need to sue to recover the medical costs of injuries" (Towers Perrin, 2006a). Similarly, a study that used data from 21 countries over 12 years to investigate the relationship between the size of government programs and the size of private tort liability also finds a "strong negative relationship between government social program expenditures and national liability costs" (Kerr, Ma, and Schmit, 2006). The investigators suggest that "in nations where government programs are far more readily available to pay for health care and lost income [than they are in the United States], the compensation objective [of the tort liability system] has far less purpose." However, while most researchers seem to agree "that a large divide exists between the U.S. and the 'Rest of the World'" (Kerr, Ma, and Schmit, 2006:5), the specific reasons they advance vary (see, for example, La Porta et al., 1998; Pfennigstorf, 1993).

There are several explanations for the increase in litigation over time. It has been suggested that in some countries, most notably the United States, there is increased acceptance of litigation as a viable option. Miethe's (1995) national US survey of 1004 adults, for example, finds that legal remedies are widely endorsed by the American public. Some, pointing to the enormous onslaught and popularity of law-related programming, go as far as to suggest that litigation has come to be seen as a form of entertainment (Rapping, 2004; Zobel, 1994; Young, 2005). Sauvageau, Schneiderman, and Taras (2006:17) observe that "films, TV programs, and novels about law and justice have become a mainstay of popular culture. From *To Kill a Mockingbird* to *CSI*, from *Law and Order* to the Michael Jackson trial, from *Judge Judy* to Court TV, a 24-hour cable channel in the United States (now available in Canada) devoted exclusively to showing ongoing trials, crime and its punishment are deeply embedded in the public imagination." These authors stress that this "is not just an American phenomenon" and note the wide variety of law-related programs that have enjoyed massive popularity in both French- and English-speaking Canada (e.g., *Da Vinci's Inquest*, *Street Legal*, *The Docket*, *History's Courtroom*, *Dossiers Justice*, and Radio-Canada's *Justice*).

It has also been argued that lawsuits are good for a nation and can usher in progressive reforms (Bogus, 2001; Howard, 2002). For instance, product liability litigation has undoubtedly saved countless lives, brought critical information to light (along with labels that warn us about most everything that could be potentially harmful), forced manufacturers to make products safer, and driven off the market unreasonably dangerous products when regulatory agencies lacked the political will to do so (Koenig and Rustad, 2004). Class action suits in Canada have resulted in compensation for such disparate groups as those who have contracted hepatitis C from tainted blood, received faulty cardiac pacemakers or leaky breast implants, suffered in train and subway crashes, experienced sexual abuse as children at the hands of authority figures within such settings as church-run orphanages and residential schools, or have lost their jobs as a result of large-scale corporate restructuring. Court decisions can also redefine the limits of the law's reach. Some examples: In 1992, a powerful obstacle for pursuing claims for compensation for childhood assault in civil court was removed with a Supreme Court decision that confirmed that an adult who experienced childhood sexual abuse can sue for compensation even though the limitation period has expired. Prior to this decision, provincial legislation required that a victim of childhood assault launch legal action within a specified period of time (in Ontario, four years; in the majority of other provinces, two years) after reaching the age of majority. In 2005, Alberta became the first Canadian province to enact legislation that allowed children to sue their mothers for injuries they had sustained in the womb. In that year, another legal first occurred when a psychiatrist was held civilly responsible for a murder committed by a psychotic patient that she allowed to be released from hospital (Mandel, 2005). In 2006, the Supreme Court of Canada ruled that financial support could be awarded to a wife for "her inability to work due to ongoing trauma from her ex-husband's infidelity years earlier" (Makin, 2006). Reportedly, after her husband had left her for another woman, the woman had become "bitter to the point of obsession with [her husband's] misconduct" and, in consequence, unable to enter the labour force (Cheadle, 2006). Following the Court's decision, various legal experts publicly mused that this ruling could "encourage litigation from other estranged spouses who may want to mount similar arguments based on their emotionally fragile state. . . [and] argue that they cannot become self-sufficient" (Makin, 2006).

At times, however, litigations appear to get out of control. For example, toothbrushes seem like innocent little things. Inexpensive and simple to use, they make life a lot more pleasant for everybody. But in 1999, a couple of US lawyers filed a class action suit against several manufacturers, arguing that toothbrushes are dangerous. When used improperly, the lawyers said, they can lead to discomfort, receding gums, and sensitive teeth—conditions that could, in extreme cases, cost a few thousand dollars to repair. If the plaintiffs' lawyers had been able to convince a jury that they were right, the defendants could have been hit with a judgment of $1 billion or more (France, 2001:122). (Lest our readers be misled, compared to the United States, personal injury awards in Canada have always been far more modest [Olson, 2004]. Consider, for example, that in 1995, an Ontario class action on behalf of all Ontario and Quebec women who had received silicone breast implants manufactured by Bristol-Myers Squibb resulted in a $29 million settlement; however, three years earlier, in a similar product-liability case, a Texas jury awarded a single implant victim $25 million [Dranoff, 2005:203]).

Some economists contend that litigation is related to the proportion of lawyers in the population and the relative expenditure on civil justice (Chinloy, 1989:8, 88; Olson, 2003). Basically, the more lawyers there are, the greater the quantity of litigation. It has been argued that the increase in the supply of lawyers results in more litigation, increasing the demand for lawyers. Lawyers are better informed about the legal system than the client, and as a result, there is an asymmetric exchange of information between them. Thus, an increase in the supply of lawyers can increase the demand for legal services and litigation. Simply stated, there is an economic incentive for lawyers to suggest intervention. The increase in the number of lawyers also increases competition and reduces a variety of costs, such as the cost of retaining a lawyer and lower contingency fees. **Contingency fees**, which originated in the United States and were once illegal in Canada, may in themselves represent a "ticket to the courthouse" for individuals of modest means who cannot afford to pay hourly legal fees. When a lawyer agrees to be paid for his or her services only if he or she wins an award or settlement in the case, any money the lawyer gets is called a contingency fee. Although contingency fee arrangements are generally not available in family law cases, they are now legal everywhere in Canada and most useful in cases where the litigant hopes to receive a sizable sum at the end of his or her case. While British Columbia has set a maximum of one-third for legal fees in personal injury and wrongful death arising from motor vehicle accidents and 40 percent on any other personal injury or wrongful death claims, contingency fees in Canada usually range from 25 to 50 percent of the proceeds of litigation. Contingency fees are especially common in class action suits, where the cost to the individual litigant decreases even though the total cost of tort action goes up.

In addition to the hypothesis that the supply of lawyers accounts for the increase in court cases, it is possible that there has been an increase in the number of individuals who have, at one time or another, been involved in litigation. An expansion in the volume of litigation may result even from a small increase in the total number of litigants. Such an expansion may be attributed to changes in the social and political conditions that facilitate the translation of conflicts and disputes into lawsuits. Although litigation requires a substantial investment of time and money, in recent years a number of attempts have been made to reduce or redistribute such costs through, for example, prepaid legal insurance (available through some unions and employers) and the provision of legal aid. During 2004–05, Canada's legal aid plans spent $608 million on delivering legal services; during that time period, cases involving civil matters accounted for just over half (52 percent) of direct legal aid expenditures (Statistics Canada, 2006). It is undoubtedly true, however, that the slashing of legal aid budgets over the past decade has left many vulnerable and unable to afford to bring disputes to court.

Another explanation for the increase in the number of cases reaching the courts may be that although the number of litigants has not increased, the relatively few individuals or organizations (that is, repeat players) who typically use courts to settle disputes have in recent years simply found more occasion to do so. This has resulted in a kind of assembly-line litigation aided by all-but-automated computerized litigation packets that are now available for products (France, 2001).

The increase in litigation is also related to the increase in the range and variety of legally actionable or resolvable problems.

> As the scope of law expands, as more legal rights and remedies are created, the amount of litigation increases as a result of the new opportunities for court action. As new rights are created, litigation may be necessary to clarify the way in which those rights will be defined and understood by the courts. Furthermore, the creation of new rights may direct the attention of organized interest groups to the judiciary. Interest groups may come to perceive litigation as a viable strategy for stimulating group mobilization to achieve the group's political goals. (Goldman and Sarat, 1989:41)

At the same time, it is also plausible that litigation is not viewed by the parties as an effort to settle a conflict; "instead it is a tactical engagement in a sustained war" (Barton, 1975:575). In such a situation, resolving the legal issue or the conflict becomes secondary to creating publicity for a cause or to obtaining a delay of decision through procedural grounds (see, for example, Skerry, 1998). An example of this is a situation in which general minority rights have priority over the resolution of a specific disagreement, such as alleged discrimination in hiring or promotion. It is also part of what has been termed the "entitlement mentality" evidenced by general demands rather than specific claims and epitomized by what one author refers to as the "rights talk" (Glendon, 1991). It is perhaps most pronounced in instances of prisoners' lawsuits where inmates claim that prisons have violated their rights to: wear sunglasses; own Soap on a Rope; have *Rolling Stone* magazine delivered to isolation cells; receive a low-cholesterol diet and prescription dandruff shampoo (filed by a death-row inmate in California); wear silky women's lingerie, make-up, and jewellery (filed by a 47-year-old male inmate); partake of unlimited refills of Kool-Aid; and watch recent videos (Manning, 1995; Smith, 1999).

In the United States, prisoners' lawsuits make up around 20 percent of all civil cases before the federal courts (*Newsweek,* 1995:6). This kind of court use has been dubbed by some as "recreational litigation," and fewer than 1 percent of such suits result in a verdict for the prisoner; most are dismissed for causes that counsel would have foreseen. Note that, in the United States, the constitutional right to an attorney does not apply to such civil cases (Dilworth, 1995). Because of the huge price tag, some US states have already passed laws that penalize inmates if a judge rules their lawsuits "frivolous" (to be sure, a value-laden term). The state can delay a parole hearing by two months or raid half of the inmate's prison bank account (Bell, 1995). But care must be exercised that "frivolous" lawsuits are not turned into a serious denial of rights.

Sheldon Goldman and Austin Sarat (1989:41) identify three generic factors that may explain litigation. The first they call *social development*. Variation in the frequency of litigation is a function of changes in the level of complexity, differentiation, and skill of the society in which courts operate. Social development and changes in the structure of society bring about increased reliance on courts to process disputes. In less developed societies, as a result of stable and enduring contacts among individuals, disputes are easier to resolve informally. Consequently, courts play a less important role in disputes. In more complex societies, on the other hand, relationships are typically more transitory in nature, disputes often take place between strangers, and under such circumstances, informal dispute processing is impractical. Furthermore, in developed societies, there is no longer a single dominant ethos or a set of customs that, resulting from heterogeneity, secularization, and the closer interaction among different subgroups with specific norms. For example, corporate executives and environmentalists offer radically different ethical norms for the same activities, such as potentially hazardous waste disposal. In consequence, some interpret increases in litigation as evidence of a breakdown in the forms of community that traditionally held a society together and warn that, at best, law is only capable of creating a tenuous and fractious social bond. As one commentator has cynically observed, "The better the society, the less law there will be. . . . The worse the society, the more law there will be. In Hell there will be nothing but law, and due process will be meticulously observed" (Gilmore, 1977:111).

The second generic factor that explains why disputes are translated into demands for court services is subjective cost-benefit calculations on the part of disputants. For some disputants, the decision to use courts is a relatively objective, well-thought-out decision, since they must calculate a "risk" factor and weigh what they may lose against the possible benefits of doing nothing or of using different methods of conflict resolution. For others, however, resorting to courts may be an act "that has value because of its cathartic effect, even though it may not produce tangible, material benefits" (Goldman and Sarat, 1989:42). In such a situation, vindictiveness, spite, or the desire for a "moral" victory outweighs the financial considerations. Moreover, the disputants' decision to use the court decreases the pressure on them to resolve disputes by using nonlegal resources that they can mobilize. Informal and private settlements seem less likely where the parties have the option for legal recourse (Turk, 1978:224).

The third generic factor in litigation is the creation of more legally actionable rights and remedies by legislatures and courts. Goldman and Sarat state: "The greater the reach and scope of the legal system, the higher its litigation rate will be" (1989:42). To some extent, the expanded use of courts is attributable to the expansion of rights. As William Bogart observes:

> [T]he "rights revolution," especially in America, focused on giving recognition to interests, individuals, and groups mainly through litigation. It was primarily courts, not politicians, that would confer entitlements, often constitutionalized. There were many ambitions for this revolution, but a primary one was to gain recognition legally that had not been obtained politically. (2002:43)

The growing scope of law increases litigation implicitly or explicitly by expanding the jurisdiction of the courts. The creation of new rights is likely to stimulate litigation designed to vindicate or protect those rights. Thus, with the creation of new norms, courts actually (although unintentionally) promote disputing, since these new norms may lead to claims that otherwise would not have been asserted. Consider here that the newly entrenched right to free speech in Canada led to the launching of litigation by tobacco companies—and the striking down of legislated curbs on cigarette advertising (Bogart, 2002:323). Moreover, in clarifying certain norms, courts may make other normative conflicts salient and thus more likely to be disputed. For example, in 1988 the Supreme Court ruled in *R. v. Morgentaler* that the law on abortion was unconstitutional because it restricted a woman's right to control her own reproductive life, and as such violated her constitutionally protected guarantees to security of the person, liberty, and freedom of conscience. This ruling invalidated the consent requirements in the Criminal Code, decriminalized abortion, and also led to a series of disputes concerning such issues as access and whether the provinces would pay for abortions and whether abortions would be permitted outside of hospitals in clinics. In addition, the *R. v. Morgentaler* decision has led to disputes over whether parents must consent to a minor's abortion and whether the prospective father of the fetus can veto the woman's decision to terminate a pregnancy (the answer, delivered in the 1989 Supreme Court's decision in the case of *Tremblay v. Daigle*, is no. In this case, the Supreme Court held that the woman's right to control her own body overrode the man's interest in the fetus and declared that a fetus had no rights until it was born alive).

Rights, protections, and entitlements for whole groups of people can generate potentially conflict-laden situations conducive to further litigation. For example, in 2002, a fluently bilingual federal government employee launched a suit against Air Canada for $525 000 and an apology because he was unable to order a 7-Up in French. "I am not asking for a right here; I am exercising a right I already have," the man said shortly after filing his lawsuit (Corbett, 2002). The entrenchment of the *Canadian Charter of Rights and*

Freedoms, for example, has impacted litigation, with Canadian courts, "after some hesitation," involving themselves in myriad questions relating to "abortion, mercy killing, assisted suicide, language rights, and an array of issues relating to the administration of criminal justice, to name but a few" (Bogart, 2002:151). In addition, the Court Challenges Program of Canada, a national non-profit organization, has made funding available to launch certain Charter challenges that focused on equality issues (Court Challenges Program, 2006). "This organization was created by an unprecedented amalgam of official language groups, organizations working in the field of equality rights, universities (primarily law schools) and various jurists' associations in this country" (CCP Annual Report, 1994–95). The stated objective of the CCP is the clarification of certain constitutional provisions related to equality and language rights. This objective is "to be achieved through the provision of financial assistance for test cases of national significance" put forward by or on behalf of individuals or non-profit groups that represent "official language minority groups" (i.e., anglophones in Quebec and francophones in the rest of the country) and/or "disadvantaged groups or individuals," an evolving concept but one which would logically include, for example, racial and religious minorities, women, and individuals with disabilities (Canada Heritage, 2006). However, questions are increasingly being raised by critics and others about the "rights industry" and its impact on major institutions (Borovoy, 1999).

Variations in Litigation Rates

There are two general ways of measuring judicial involvement in dispute settlement (Galanter, 1988). It can be measured by the percentage of disputes that courts play some part in resolving, and by the percentage of the adult population who take disputes to courts. With both measures, there are some difficulties. As Richard Lempert (1978:99) points out, there are several ways in which courts contribute to dispute settlement:

1. Courts establish norms that influence or control the private settlement of disputes. For example, norms established in an appellate opinion resolving one dispute can lead other disputants to resolve their conflict without legal intervention.

2. Courts ratify private settlements and provide guarantees of compliance. For example, in divorce cases where the parties have already reached an agreement, courts ratify that agreement, which carries with it the probability of sanctions should it be breached.

3. Courts can escalate the cost of disputing, thereby increasing the likelihood of private settlement.

4. Courts provide opportunities to disputants to learn about each other's cases, thus increasing the probability of private settlement by decreasing mutual uncertainty.

5. Court staff act as mediators to encourage consensual private settlement.

6. Courts resolve certain issues in the case, leading disputants to agree on others.

7. Courts authoritatively resolve disputes.

Thus, at times, it is difficult to determine the extent to which courts contribute to dispute settlement. The clearest case is when disputes are adjudicated and a settlement is imposed after a full trial. But many cases do not end up at trials. A settlement may be reached during a pretrial conference or through informal negotiations where the judge is a participant. Judges also exert informal pressure, even after litigation has commenced, and lawyers usually listen to the recommended solutions. Settlement may also be encouraged by the mounting financial costs. Defendants may calculate that it is cheaper and less time-consuming to settle than to try a case. Under the so-called English rule (Polinsky and Rubinfeld, 1998) that is used in England, Canada, and Japan, the defendant recovers costs against an unsuccessful plaintiff; in contrast, in the United States, each side pays his or her own way, win or lose. In consequence, a person contemplating litigation in Canada must consider if he or she can absorb the potential of both their own and the other's legal expenses in the event that their lawsuit is unsuccessful. Thus, attempts to explore the dispute-settlement functions of courts over time must consider the different roles courts play and the influences they exert. Lempert notes: "Exploration is complicated by difficulties in measuring the various ways that courts contribute to dispute settlement, and these difficulties are compounded if the measures must allow comparisons over time" (1978:100).

It should also be noted that, in contrast to the United States or England and Wales, "[d]ata on courts are not highly developed in Canada" (Bogart, 2002:31) and precise longitudinal data on litigation is not available. More generally, however, it has been noted that there are a variety of difficulties that may frustrate attempts to measure longitudinally the percentage of the adult population who use court services in disputes. For example, the figures may be inaccurate to the extent that certain individuals or organizations are "repeat players" (Galanter, 1974). Many courts do not keep adequate records for long periods of time and, where records are kept, the record-keeping procedures vary. Historically, a number of minor courts, such as justice of the peace and magistrate courts, did not keep records. Over time, the court systems had changed through reorganization, with new courts established and others eliminated. There were also changes in the jurisdiction of many courts. Consequently, there are a variety of questions that can be asked about the validity and reliability of longitudinal studies that deal with rates of litigation over time. In view of these precautions, let us turn briefly to some studies that have challenged the idea that the dispute-processing function of the courts has increased in recent years as a result of social and economic changes.

In modern societies, the use of courts as a forum for conflict resolution is on the increase as a result of societal developments toward increased complexity, heterogeneity, and the prevalence of impersonal and contractual relations. For example, some maintain that increasing urbanization, which results in greater social distance between community members, leads to higher litigation rates. Simply put, "[s]uing a friend is considered far more costly than suing a stranger" (Kerr, Ma, and Schmit, 2006:6). It is also evident that urbanization may result in greater availability of and access to legal services. Gerson (1994) suggests that computers have made a major contribution to increases in litigation by making it feasible to engage in protracted and occasionally frivolous litigation. Although data are available to support both of these contentions, others observe that social, economic, and technological developments do not necessarily lead to higher rates of litigation. For example, it has been noted that the litigation rate in Spain over time "has remained remarkably constant and at a relatively low rate. . . . [In Spain,] the process of economic change does not seem to have affected the rate of litigation" (Jose Toharia, in Goldman and Sarat, 1978:59). Lawrence M. Friedman (1973:338) argues that there is no evidence that 19th-century America witnessed proportionately less interpersonal litigation than mid-20th-century America, despite more cohesive kin and residential systems. Similarly, Van Loon and Langerwerf's (1990) investigation of socioeconomic development and litigation rates in the civil courts in Belgium between 1835 and 1980 finds that while "under some conditions and in some periods the effect of socioeconomic factors is important, in others it is insignificant" (see also Clark, 1990, and Wollschlager, 1990).

A comparable conclusion was reached by Vilhelm Aubert (1969) in his study of the Norwegian legal system. He notes that the demand for dispute resolution during the last 100 years has remained stable or has even decreased throughout a period characterized by vast social changes and great economic progress, whereas the demand for most other kinds of services has multiplied at a very rapid rate. Aubert concludes that "the pure legal model plays a modest part in actual instances of conflict resolution in Norway today" (1969:302). Joel B. Grossman and Austin Sarat also conclude that "industrialization is a useful predictor of levels of legal activity but not litigation rates; legal activity but not litigation rates appears to be greater in more industrialized areas" (1975:343). Their study was based on litigation rates in federal courts in the United States from 1902 to 1972.

In a study of the civil load of two trial courts in California between 1890 and 1970, Friedman and Percival sampled civil case files of the superior courts in two counties. They found that highly developed economic systems do not show growth in their litigation. On the contrary, rates tend to decline in the face of rapid economic growth. Although they are careful about the generalizability of their data, they conclude that "the dispute settlement function in the courts is declining" (1976:296). They attempt to explain the decline in litigation by suggesting that uncertainty—a prime breeder of litigation—has declined in the law and that rules are more "settled" now than in 1890. The routine administrative function has replaced the dispute settlement functions in these courts. It is plausible that the court itself—its style, its mode of operation—discourages its use for dispute settlement. In reanalyzing the data used by Friedman and Percival, Richard Lempert comes to the opposite conclusion: Although "the mix of judicial business has changed over the years," there is "little reason to believe that courts today are functionally less important as dispute settlers than they were in 1890. . . . [O]ver all, I do not believe that we can conclude from the Friedman and Percival data that the dispute settlement function of courts. . . has diminished over time" (1978:133). Lempert further comments that the conclusion about the diminution in the dispute settlement activity of trial courts is overstated because Friedman and Percival neglect the mediative activity of trial judges and court personnel (1978:131). This neglect is attributable, in part, to the difficulty of measuring activities of courts over time.

In addition to these studies contending that social and economic developments, with their concomitant increases in the complexity and impersonality in social relations, do not lead to higher rates of litigation, there is also a substantial amount of differentiation in the use of courts in disputes among other nations. Henry W. Ehrmann (1976:83) points out that litigiousness, the propensity to settle disputes through the judicial process, is a cultural factor of some importance. Studies that have compared such attitudes cross-culturally have used as a measure the index of civil cases initiated per unit of population. This research concludes that Americans are more likely to turn to the civil court system than are people in similar situations in other countries (Kritzer, 1991:407). In contrast, people in India do not exhibit a propensity for litigation and never resort to legal measures when alternative means to resolve a dispute are available. There has been a decrease in India in court cases since the pre-independence period (Moog, 1993). Similarly, Chen's (2000) exploration of the impact of social development in the postwar period reports that Taiwanese litigation rates did not increase along with social development even though its litigation volume greatly increased. He reports that, in Taiwan "[p]eople did not prefer litigation to mediation, even after radical social change" and that mediation remained popular among the Taiwanese in both urban and rural areas.

Despite the suggestions that "in England 'the law' plays a less important role than in almost any other western country" and that "Nobody in England would regard tort law as playing more than a very peripheral role in the life of the society" (Atiyah in Bogart, 1994:166), Ehrmann (1976:84) provides figures to show an extraordinarily high litigation rate for Great Britain, "higher than that for Western Germany, whose population is frequently described as being addicted to solving conflicts by lawsuits." The litigation rate per 100 000 population in Great Britain was 3605 in 1969, and 2085 in the former West Germany during the same year. Enormous differences exist also in the rate of litigation between Denmark and other Scandinavian countries. Resort to the judiciary in disputes is about 10 times higher in Denmark than in Norway, Sweden, or Finland. Ehrmann finds it difficult to explain the differences between these countries, especially in view of the fact that Norway has about three times as many lawyers per 100 000 population as Denmark.

It is also difficult to explain the relatively high litigation rates for Japan in relation to some Western European countries and in view of the contention that the courts are still not a highly valued site for conflict resolution (see, for example, Hirowatari, 2000; West, 2003). The litigation rate for Japan was 980 per 100 000 population in 1986—but still 10 times lower than in California (Tanase, 1995:58). Comparable rates for Scandinavian countries for the same year were 683 for Sweden, 493 for Finland, and 307 for Norway. In an often-quoted article, "Dispute Resolution in Japan," Takeyoshi Kawashima (1969) discusses specific social attitudes toward disputes that are reflected in the judicial process. Traditionally, the Japanese prefer extrajudicial, informal means of settling a controversy. Litigation in Japan presupposes and admits the existence of a dispute and leads to a decision that makes clear who is right and wrong in accordance with legal standards. This is contrary to the attitude in favour of a compromise that does not assign a moral fault to disputants. This attitude is related to the nature of social groups in Japan, which are hierarchical in the sense that differences in social status are reflected in degrees of deference and authority; the relations among individuals in social groups are intimate and diffuse. Legal intervention in disputes would upset the harmonious social relationships. As a result, Kawashima contends, the Japanese not only hesitate to resort to a lawsuit but also are quite ready to settle a dispute through informal means of dispute resolution, such as mediation and conciliation. Supporting this view of Japanese regulation as informal and co-operative, Kagan's (2000) comparison of "national styles of regulation" in Japan and the United States reports that, in regulating pollution and occupational safety in larger firms, Japan's regulatory style is as effective—and more economically efficient than America's adversarial and legalistic approach. (However, he notes that Japan's style is less effective when regulation requires that changes be made in elite attitudes [e.g., attaining workplace equality for women] and that, within the financial sector, informal regulation may result in undue deference being shown to business and political interests).

In Japan, the use of law is further discouraged by the lack of easy availability of lawyers and judges. Donald Black (1989:84) notes that the number of judges and lawyers per capita has declined in Japan since the 1920s. In fact, the total number of judges has not increased since 1890. Today, there is only one judge for every 60 000 persons, compared with one for every 22 000 a century ago. This is due to Japan's decision to place statutory limitations on the number of judges and prosecutors in its system (Westermann and

Burfeind, 1991:162). (Consider here that while the population of Japan is roughly half that of the United States, there were some 12 000 lawyers in Japan in the late 1990s compared to a very conservative estimate of about 950 000 lawyers in the United States.) A typical, uncomplicated civil case can take five or ten years to be heard (*Economist,* 1993:62).

Moreover, in Japan the individual who asserts legal rights and insists on judicial intervention

> is thought to be "inflexible" and selfish. . . . Introduction of a lawyer into a business conference is thought to be an unfriendly act. . . equal to an explicit threat of litigation. . . . When acts such as drafting a contract or the bringing of a suit are unavoidable, the contract is made as short and flexible as possible, or the act of suit is viewed as deplorable, even by the plaintiff. . . . The law. . . goes directly contrary to the Japanese feeling that their relations (even business relations) should be based upon a warm subjective relationship which can solve every practical problem by mutual compromise and accommodation, regardless of formal rights and obligations. The most notable practical result of this attitude is a paucity of litigation in Japan. (Strick, 1977:209)

Undoubtedly, it is difficult to reconcile the differences between these arguments and the relatively high rate of litigation in Japan today. It is possible that the attitudes toward the law as a means of conflict resolution are changing and that in urban areas there is a greater reliance on the judiciary to settle disputes. However, the puzzle has yet to be solved empirically.

Complete and reliable data are lacking for the United States as well. However, the differences that exist between two neighbouring states, Massachusetts and New Hampshire, are startling. In Massachusetts, the litigation rate for 1971 per 100 000 was 1814, and in New Hampshire for the same year 345. The differences point to the likely fact that the socioeconomic characteristics of a state or the particularities of its historic court system will have an effect on people's inclination to take their disputes to the courts (Ehrmann, 1976:84). But why the difference in litigation rates between two neighbouring New England states should be that enormous remains unexplained. A more recent study (Yates, Davis, and Glick, 2001), which examined tort filings in 10 representative US states over a 20-year period, also cautions against the assumption of a general litigiousness among Americans. It found that filing rates could vary substantially over time within individual states and suggests that social complexity, opportunities for political participation, and social policy are important in explaining variation in filing rates. According to the authors of this study, "The tendency of Americans to use the courts to resolve disputes is related to the milieu in which they live and how the political system responds to demands for participation and social support."

Even within a single US state, differences in litigation rates exist among cities of comparable size and characteristics. In a study of four Wisconsin cities, Herbert Jacob (1969:92) suggests that "political culture may be a significant explanatory device for accounting for the differences in litigation rates." A traditional political culture is characterized by a relatively low level of bureaucratization in government and a reluctance to invoke governmental processes. There is a greater reliance on private dispute-settling processes in a traditional culture than in a more modern one with a more highly bureaucratized government. In traditional political cultures, people make greater efforts to settle disputes between themselves as neighbours and friends, and they have greater opportunities to settle conflicts within the confines of established private relationships. In a modern political culture, personal relationships are more strained, individuals deal with each other more on a contractual basis, and they have, as a result, less confidence in using private dispute-settling procedures. At the same time, they are more willing "to invoke the public processes of government for solving their problems, be they a neighbourhood development programme needing a city council decision or a creditor-debtor conflict which requires the services of a court" (Jacob, 1969:92). Jacob provides some evidence for his contention that the use of courts will be greater in more modern political cultures. In his study on debtors, he found that the process of taking a debtor to court to collect a loan occurs more frequently in modern political cultures. But, beyond that, available data do not permit one to make further generalizations concerning the impact of political culture on the "propensity to sue" (Kritzer, 1988) although it may play a role in encouraging excess consumption and the subsequent inability to pay for the goods and services (see, for example, Ritzer, 2005).

Finally, in the past few years the term **litigation explosion** has received considerable publicity in the wake of the publication of Walter Olson's controversial book by the same title (1991). He contends that there is a "revolution" in civil litigation which he views as a "civil war in very, very slow motion." But is there really such an "explosion," or is it a myth? It depends on whom one asks. In the United States, for example, the estimated number of lawsuits filed each year varies from 18 to 30 million, but no one really knows the precise numbers (Jacob, 1995; *Newsweek*, 2005).

Traditionally, one of the more important uses of the administrative state in Canada has been as a "direct alternative to tort litigation" (Bogart, 1994:177) in areas such as human right discrimination, collective organizing and bargaining, compensation for victims of crime, and workplace injuries.

> What in fact has evolved in Canada is a three-level system of compensation. At the base are social welfare schemes that provide hospital and medical care and some income replacement for injury or illness. At the second level are several schemes that provide fuller compensation on a no-fault basis for special groups in society, such as workers or victims of crime and, in some jurisdictions, auto accidents. At the third level is tort litigation, which provides the fullest compensation for those who are willing to sue and who can establish that their injury is the fault of the person they seek to hold responsible. (Bogart, 1994:169)

However, with the entrenchment of the Charter, there is some evidence that Canada is moving in the same direction as the United States—specifically, toward an enhanced role for the judiciary, the dominance of the courts and, perhaps, to the development of a political and legal culture that is more individualistic and less amenable "to collective solutions to problems agreed to through legislative processes and implemented through governmental programs" (Bogart, 2002:152).

PREREQUISITES FOR THE USE OF COURTS IN DISPUTE RESOLUTION

Courts provide a forum for the settlement of a variety of private and public disputes. The courts are considered a neutral and impartial place for dispute processing. Other than criminal cases, legal disputes are processed in civil courts. Individuals and organizations who want to use the courts for dispute processing must meet certain legal requirements. At the minimum, plaintiffs must be able to demonstrate justiciability and standing (Jacob, 1969:17).

Justiciability means that the conflict is viable to trial and courts. The court must be mandated to provide a remedy. In Canada, most disputes are justiciable in one court or another, although the jurisdiction of particular courts varies. For example, family courts, which are provincially constituted, are responsible for hearing cases involving custody or access to children, support obligations, and adoptions. Provincial small-claims courts handle civil cases involving small amounts of money, although in some jurisdictions provincial courts may hear cases involving up to $15 000. The potential litigant must turn the grievance into a legal dispute and must determine, with or without the aid of a lawyer, whether the complaint is justiciable. Essentially, justiciability refers to real and substantial controversy that is appropriate for judicial determination, as differentiated from disputes or differences of a hypothetical or an abstract character. Furthermore, in some instances, the courts may not be authorized to intervene in certain types of disputes.

Until relatively recently, **standing** has posed a more severe limitation to litigation than justiciability. The traditional view of standing was that individuals should only be able to bring lawsuits if their personal legal rights have been violated. For example, a mother-in-law cannot sue for a divorce: such proceedings must be initiated by the husband or wife. It should be noted, though, that there are a number of examples where standing rules have been liberalized by legislation. For example, since 1975, the issue of standing has been examined by the Supreme Court of Canada five times and, on four of these occasions, the court "relaxed the requirement that the ability to sue must be based on a traditional legal interest, i.e., a pecuniary, proprietary, or economic claim or one to personal liberty" (Bogart, 1994:80). In doing so, the court established the vague requirement that a plaintiff must simply have a "'genuine interest,' meaning that a traditional legal interest is no longer the boundary between those who are and those who are not entitled to litigate" (Bogart, 1994:80). Moreover, Brisbin (2004) points out that "standing to appeal some government actions is often more difficult to achieve in Canada than in the U.S. For example, there are rules restricting appeals to the judiciary of aspects of the determinations of uniquely Canadian adjudicatory institutions such as the Ontario Municipal Board, Manitoba Municipal Board, and Nova Scotia Utility and Review Board. These bodies possess broad powers to define property rights, evaluate challenges to local and provincial environmental initiatives, and even—in Nova Scotia—establish the age-group rating of movies."

However, justiciability and standing are not the only limitations to the use of courts in disputes. There is also the old legal axiom *de minimus non curatlex*: the law will not concern itself with trifles. Trivial matters may not be litigated. For example, a court may refuse to hear a suit to recover a $10 overcharge even if the cause appears just (Lempert and Sanders, 1986:137). There are also statutes which limit the period of time in which lawsuits for various causes of action must be commenced in every Canadian province and territory. Depending upon the manner in which the injury arose and the identity of the defendant (e.g., a case alleging malpractice versus actions against government bodies), there are many different limitation periods in the area of tort law. In addition, untold numbers of disputes arise over which the courts have clear jurisdiction and someone has standing to sue. But using the court is dependent on a number of considerations. These considerations are superimposed on the legal barriers to litigation.

Resort to court services in disputes is voluntary for the plaintiffs; for defendants, participation is involuntary. The plaintiffs approach the courts with different expectations and often through different circumstances from those of the defendants. Jacob (1969:19) notes: "Whereas the initiation of court action may promise relief to the plaintiff, it threatens deprivation for the defendant. Since the plaintiff initiates court action he [sic] can exert a certain degree of control over it, but the action often descends without warning upon defendants."

Economic resources for both plaintiffs and defendants are important in their decision to pursue a suit through trial and appeal. With the exception of magistrate courts and individuals who qualify for legal aid services, plaintiffs are unlikely to use the courts unless they have sufficient funds to hire a lawyer and bear the costs of litigation. Disputants must also be able to afford the costs of delay, which occur when disputes are submitted to the courts. Often the cost of waiting must be calculated against the benefits of a quick settlement for only part of the claim. Obviously, for many people economic resources play an important role in the use of court services and may be decisive in out-of-court settlements.

Before initiating a lawsuit, individuals must recognize the relevance of court services to their problems. Jacob (1969:20) notes that the use of the judiciary varies with education, for better-educated individuals are more likely to differentiate between the courts and other agencies and to be aware of their various services. Perception of the courts also varies with other factors, such as integration into a social group in which court usage has previously occurred or where it is relatively prevalent. Says Jacob: "Thus it may be that certain ethnic groups or communities are more litigious than others. Members of such groups are more likely to perceive court action as relevant to their problems and consequently they become more frequent consumers of court services" (1969:20). Posner's (1996) more recent research also finds a positive relationship between litigation rates and educational levels, suggesting that those with greater levels of education may have greater knowledge of the law and/or more skill in obtaining legal assistance.

Socioeconomic status is also related to the use of the judiciary in disputes. Those who cannot afford a lawyer and the necessary court fees are less likely to litigate than those who have sufficient funds. Moreover, social status is related to the kind of court services that are used. In general, the poor are more likely to be defendants and recipients of court-ordered sanctions. Middle-class litigants are less likely to be subjected to court sanctions and more likely to benefit from the use of court services in their own behalf from the legitimization of their private agreements or from out-of-court negotiations. However, as Kerr, Ma, and Schmit (2006:6) observe, "income. . . also can represent time costs, with higher income suggesting that undertaking litigation itself is costly." They note that some research has reported a negative relationship between income and litigation and suggest that the liability system may act "as a lottery with great potential payoff at low probabilities. Low-income individuals often have little to lose in this lottery, and perhaps value their time at lower levels, leading to the negative relationship."

TYPOLOGY OF LITIGANTS

Practically an unlimited variety of economic and non-economic disputes take place between individuals and end up before a judge for decision. Some examples:

- In Windsor, Ontario, a couple who discovered a fly in a bottle of Culligan bottled water before opening it launched a lawsuit against the manufacturer. Although the couple did not drink any of the water, the husband maintained that simply seeing the fly in the bottled water had caused him to experience a host of problems including nightmares, difficulty sleeping, and the tendency to become argumentative and edgy. (The lawsuit was successful and a Canadian court awarded the couple $340 000 [Thompson, 2005]).

- In 2004, a Vancouver woman who dropped her 17-month-old daughter from the Capilano Suspension Bridge sued the owners of the bridge; although the child miraculously survived, the woman claimed that the experience and media speculation on whether she had deliberately or accidentally dropped her child had caused her to experience stress (Canadian Press/AZ Central, 2004).

- In 2002, a 37-year-old woman and her husband filed a $1 million lawsuit against the Ontario Lottery and Gaming Corporation for failing to exclude the wife, a compulsive gambler, from the casinos where she gambled away her savings. The lawsuit maintained that, although the woman had entered a voluntary, casino self-exclusion program, "the casinos did little or nothing to enforce the exclusion" (Malarek, 2002).

- In Rimouski, Quebec, a hockey mother sued the Rimouski Minor Hockey Association for $1000 over a lack of ice time for her 14-year-old goalie son (Basu, 2000).

- A Toronto family claimed its nine-year-old daughter discovered a severed rat's head in her Big Mac and sued McDonald's Canada for $17.5 million. According to the family's lawyer, the child, "having been enticed by McDonald's pervasive child-focused advertising," ordered the burger which was "served in a paper wrapper bearing the Disney 'Tarzan' logo," and began to "partially ingest" the bewhiskered rodent head. The suit alleged that as a result of the experience, the child suffered extensive psychiatric damage, that the mother was so shocked by the experience that she could no longer carry on routine daily activities or earn a living, and that it was likely that the child's sister would be similarly afflicted with psychiatric difficulties when she grows up. The complaint additionally charged that "customers should be warned to inspect sandwiches prior to consumption" and that McDonald's Canada was negligent for not issuing such a warning (CBC News, 2001).

- A Coquitlam, BC man who was a front-row spectator at a strip bar sued a "reckless" exotic dancer and the bar where she was employed. The man claimed that, while swinging around a pole, the stripper put her foot in his face, breaking his nose and causing him to experience blurred vision, headaches, and difficulty in breathing (Nordlinger, 2002).

- An assistant professor of political science at the University of Manitoba fought a $40 traffic ticket in provincial court by launching a constitutional challenge of stop signs claiming the message was too vague (Yellon, 2002).

- A Haileybury, Ontario woman who, in 1990, smothered her nine-year-old daughter as she slept and served five years in mental institutions after being found not guilty by reason of insanity, sued her two psychiatrists and family doctors for over $20 million, maintaining that they should have prevented her from killing her daughter. Her doctors, in turn, described the woman as "an uncooperative, recalcitrant patient who didn't take her medication as prescribed, often cancelled appointments, would not let those treating her share critical medical information and either minimized or lied about both her symptoms and state of mind" (Blatchford, 2000).

As we noted in Chapter 3, the use of courts varies also by the types of litigants. Marc Galanter advances a typology of litigants by the frequency of the utilization of courts. Those who have only occasional recourse to the courts are called one-shotters, and those who are engaged in many similar litigations over time are designated as repeat players. Illustrations for the former include the wife in a divorce case while the latter is exemplified by insurance or finance companies. Based on this typology, Galanter proposes a taxonomy of litigation by the configuration of parties. He comes up with four types of litigation—one-shotter versus one-shotter, repeat player versus one-shotter, one-shotter versus repeat player, and repeat player versus repeat player.

A large number of cases involving disputes between one-shotters are divorces and custody battles. Disputes between one-shotters are "often between parties who have some intimate tie with one another, fighting over some unsharable good, often with overtones of 'spite' and 'irrationality'" (Galanter, 1974:108). The courts are used when an ongoing relationship is ruptured and the law is invoked *ad hoc* and instrumentally by the parties. When such disputes take place between neighbours or business partners, there may be a strong interest in vindication, and the court decisions are seldom appealed.

The second type of litigation, repeat players versus one-shotters, is exemplified by suits initiated by finance companies against debtors and landlords against tenants. Except for personal injury cases and divorces, the great bulk of litigation is found in disputes between repeat players and one-shotters. Here, the law is used for routine processing of claims by parties for whom the making of such claims is a regular business activity. In many instances, courts authorize repeat players to borrow the government's power for their private purposes. Repeat players may use that power to achieve many objectives, such as to collect debts, oust tenants, or prohibit some harmful activity. In such a case, the plaintiff comes to court with a grievance. If the court considers the complaint a legitimate one, it issues a judgment or an injunction. The judgment authorizes the plaintiff to make use of the government's police power to effectuate it. Thus, a real estate agent may, for example, be empowered to oust a tenant, to reclaim some property, to sell property belonging to a defendant, or to seize the defendant's wages or property. When the court issues an injunction on behalf of the plaintiff, it orders the defendant not to engage in the activity about which the plaintiff complained. If the defendant persists, he or she may be fined or imprisoned.

The third combination of litigants is one-shotters versus repeat players. Illustrations of this include tenant versus landlord, injury victim versus insurance company, student versus university, defamed person versus publisher, and client versus welfare agency. Outside of the personal injury area, litigation in this combination is not routine. It usually represents the attempt of some one-shotters to invoke outside help to create leverage on an organization with which the individual has a dispute.

The fourth type of litigation is repeat players versus repeat players. Examples of this include litigation between union and management, purchaser and supplier, regulatory agency and firms of regulated industry, and church/state litigations focusing on value differences (who is right) rather than interest conflicts (who gets what). With these types of litigation in the background, let us now turn to certain types of conflicts between individuals, between individuals and organizations, and between organizations where one of the disputants resorts to the judiciary in an attempt to resolve the conflict.

DISPUTES BETWEEN INDIVIDUALS

Although most controversies between individuals never come to the attention of courts, the handling of interpersonal differences is a traditional function of courts. Most individual disputes involve one-shotters. For those individuals whose disagreements come before a court, the experience is likely to be the most intimate they will have had with the government, and the manner in which the dispute is handled is likely to have a marked effect on their attitudes toward the government. Judicial resolution of individual disputes also affects the distribution of values. Some people gain, others lose; some individuals are honoured, others are stigmatized; and as with all types of disputes, a court decision seldom resolves the underlying conditions for the conflict.

Individual disputes include private litigation as opposed to organizations, criminal defendants, or state agencies. These disputes generally deal with the distribution of economic resources and a variety of non-economic problems. Economic disputes include various claims associated with contests over wills, trusts, and estates, landlord-tenant controversies, and disputes over property, titles, and sales. The greatest distinction between economic and non-economic individual disputes is that the former directly involve a conflict over the control of economic resources, whereas the latter, although often involving money, do not necessarily stem from economic conflicts. Non-economic conflicts include allegations of slander and libel, custody cases, divorce proceedings, involuntary commitments, and malpractice suits.

Courts often make an effort to encourage disputants to settle their differences by agreement, since this is a less costly way to reestablish an equilibrium, which any conflict is likely to disturb. Settlements may even be encouraged after the disputants have brought their complaint to a court. Such efforts may be initiated by the judge in pretrial hearings or in open court. The success of such efforts depends to a great extent on the skills of the judge and on the nature of the disputes. When the parties are unable or unwilling to resolve their disputes by agreement, and when they have decided against letting matters rest, formal adjudication must take over and will normally end in a decision that claims to be binding on the parties.

In the adjudication of individual disputes, one party wins and the other loses. Robert B. Seidman (1978:213) points out that in situations in which parties want to, or must, cooperate after the dispute, both must leave the settlement procedures without too great a sense of grievance. If, however, there are opportunities for avoidance (that is, parties need not live or work together), then the disputants may continue their antagonism. Compromises tend to resolve the disputes in the sense that they reduce any continuing antagonism. Win-or-lose situations, however, will not ameliorate antagonism. Therefore, disputants who wish to maintain an ongoing relationship will generally engage in compromise settlements. Businesspeople do not sue customers whose trade they want to keep. Married couples who want to stay together do not sue each other; instead, they consult marriage counsellors who look for compromises.

The structure of social relationships thus plays a role in the decision as to whether to take a dispute to court. When continuing relations are important to the individuals involved in the dispute, they are generally more predisposed to resolve their differences through nonlegal means. In a now classic paper, Stewart Macaulay describes the avoidance of the law as a way of building and maintaining good business relations. Businesspeople prefer not to use contracts in their dealings with other businesspeople. Says Macaulay: "Disputes are frequently settled without reference to the contract or potential or actual legal sanctions. There is a hesitancy to speak of legal rights or to threaten to sue in these negotiations" (1969:200). Similar sentiments prevail in other countries. For example, "For a Korean, it is not decent or 'nice' to insist on one's legal rights. When a person hauls another person into court, he [sic] is in fact declaring war on [another]. . . lined himself [sic] up on the side of the bureaucrats to use the power of the state to oppress [another]. Thus, a Korean cannot think of law as anything other than oppressive. . . . This reluctance to maintain one's legal right is particularly pronounced in the area of property" (Hahm, quoted by Friedman and Macaulay, 1977:1026).

How the either/or court decision would mitigate against continuing relations is further illustrated by Jane Fishburne Collier in her work on the Zinacanteco Indians of Southern Mexico. She points out that Indians who wish to preserve a valued relationship will seek a settlement procedure that promotes reconciliation.

> Cases end when an appropriate settlement has been found. In Zinacanteco eyes, an ideal settlement involves reconciliation: Both sides agree to forget their differences and drink together, or the guilty person begs pardon and is forgiven through acceptance of a bottle of rum. Settlements often involve agreements to pay money or repair damages, though such agreements are seen as a part of the reconciliation process. A case that ends without reconciliation and drinking is considered less than satisfactory. (Collier, 1973:38)

However, continuing relationships are but part of a broader issue of whether to litigate in individual disputes. Nader and Todd point out: "It is not enough to state that because litigants wish to continue their relation they will seek negotiated or mediated settlement with compromise outcomes" (1978:17). In some instances, ties within the family itself may give rise to disputes over inheritance among brothers or sisters, or arguments between males and females over the males' attempts to control the behaviour of their unmarried sisters. At the same time, social relations may act not as an impetus to conflict but as a constraint on escalation. For example, Barbara B. Yngvesson (1978:59), in her study of a small Scandinavian fishing village, notes that "disputes are focused less on *acts than on people*. What was done *is less important than who did it*. An act considered normal when done by a kinsman or fellow community member may generate an entirely different response when done by an 'outsider.'"

Thus, it is no longer sufficient to generalize that a preference for continuing relations will turn disputants to some kind of compromise or reconciliation mechanism rather than to litigation. In a variety of instances, disputants resort to legal rather than nonlegal ways, with the full awareness of the risks involved in their attempts to settle their disputes.

Reasons for litigation vary. Affluent litigants may want possession of boats, silverware, or family dogs. Married couples want a divorce, and unmarried ones argue over property rights. A client may sue his or her lawyer for legal malpractice, and lawyers' malpractice insurance rates have been going up both directly and indirectly (Hazard, 1994; Karsten, 1998). A patient may institute charges against a physician for medical malpractice, with many suits arising out of problems in surgery. There have also been several "wrongful birth" actions in which women have undergone sterilization but nevertheless became pregnant and gave birth. The growing popularity of alternative medical treatments in both Canada and the United States has also been accompanied by a proportionate increase in lawsuits directed against naturopaths, herbal remedy specialists, massage therapists and, in particular, chiropractors (Cohen, 1999). In the United States, a clergyman was charged with "clerical malpractice" by a plaintiff who alleged that following the cleric's advice to remain married to her husband had caused her "severe trauma, insomnia, and a chronic lower-back problem" (*Saturday Review*, 1979:7). (As a result of this suit, a number of American insurance companies began to offer malpractice coverage for the clergy [*New York Times*, 1986:1F].) Myers (2002) reports that "as a result of fears regarding criminal and civil liability, many child welfare professionals are resorting to defensive practice strategies."

Data on patterns of outcomes in individual disputes are scarce. In adjudication, courts are supposed to decide disputes by reference to the facts of who did what to whom, and by identifying, interpreting, and applying appropriate legal norms. Sheldon Goldman and Austin Sarat (1989:514) suggest that this requires that judges remain neutral with regard to both the issues of the case and its result. They use the notion of result impartiality in referring to the extent that cases are decided independently of the personal attributes of the parties involved. Impartiality is displayed when both parties in a dispute are given the same opportunities and are shown the same considerations. It requires that the judge not be influenced by an interest in the outcome or by attitudes toward the disputants and the situations in which they are involved.

To study the question of impartiality, it is necessary to examine a number of decisions involving similar situations to discover whether over time different kinds of disputants are equally likely to gain favourable results. For impartial results, the pattern of decision should be random and should not consistently favour one type of litigant over another. For example, if courts in custody cases at times rule for the mother and at other times for the father, it may be concluded that they show equal regard for both sexes. However, if they consistently favour mothers over fathers, regardless of the facts or the applicable law, then the results would not be impartial.

Goldman and Sarat point out, however, that the difficulty with this way of determining result impartiality is that it does not take into account other factors responsible for variation from the standard of randomness that go beyond the attitudes and values of the judges. A most obvious factor is that, even if courts are impartial in their procedures, they may still produce biased results if the laws that they apply favour one type of litigant.

The outcome of court decisions may also be influenced by the type of lawyer that disputants are able to retain. Availability of resources to disputants directly affects the quality of legal talent they can hire. Access to a skillful lawyer increases the likelihood of a favourable court decision, since courts assume that in individual disputes both parties can marshal the resources and legal skills needed to present a case effectively.

To an extent, these considerations can be useful in predicting the outcomes of individual disputes. In some instances, however, both parties may be able to afford delays and the services of highly trained lawyers, and to have convincing legal arguments on their side. In such instances, the determination of the outcome of the case will have to wait until the judge hands down the verdict.

DISPUTES BETWEEN INDIVIDUALS AND ORGANIZATIONS

In this section, we will discuss disputes between individuals and organizations. The first part of the section will consider individuals as plaintiffs and organizations as defendants. The second part will deal with legal disputes initiated by organizations against individuals. We will use the term "organization" to cover a broad range of social groups that have been deliberately and consciously constructed to achieve certain specific goals—hospitals, credit agencies, universities, regulatory agencies, and so forth.

Disputes between individuals and organizations may take place over a variety of issues, many of which may be included in four general categories: (1) disputes over property and money (economic disputes); (2) claims for damages and restitution; (3) issues of civil rights; and (4) disputes concerning organizational actions, procedures, and policy. These broad categories of disputes are, of course, not mutually exclusive.

Usually, organizations are plaintiffs in the first category of disputes and defendants in the other three. In general, organizations are more successful as both plaintiffs and defendants than are individuals (Galanter, 1975; Relis, 2002). They enjoy greater success against individual antagonists than against other organizations. Individuals fare less well contending against organizations than against other individuals. Consider, for example, that in 2000 the retail-store chain Wal-Mart was hit with 4851 suits filed by individuals, and currently it has about 9400 cases open. Dozens of lawyers now specialize in suing Wal-Mart; many share documents and other information via the Internet. The allegations range from falls on slippery floors and icy parking lots to claims of being injured in shoppers' stampedes triggered by bargain hunting to employment discrimination practices. However, in the vast majority of cases (no exact numbers are available) Wal-Mart wins by aggressively fighting cases even when it would be cheaper for the company to settle (*Bellingham Herald,* 2001).

Galanter's conclusion is supported by the Wal-Mart example and reinforced by Donald Black's (1976:92, 1989:41) contention that law and organization are inversely related: law is greater toward less organization. Over one-half of the plaintiffs in civil cases in the United States are organizations, and two-thirds of the defendants are individuals. Organizations win more often than individuals. In small-claims courts, as well, more organizations sue individuals than the other way around. In these instances, the plaintiffs nearly always win. For example, David Caplovitz (1974:222) found that legal actions against debtors in his sample of 1331 cases, drawn from four cities, resulted in creditor victories in all but 3 percent of the cases. Moreover, if an organization loses its case against an individual, it is more likely to appeal, and, if it does, it is more likely to win a reversal.

Black also points out that "although any group is more likely to bring a lawsuit against an individual than vice versa, then, the likelihood of a lawsuit by a group increases with its organization. On the other hand, the likelihood of a lawsuit by an individual against a group decreases with the organization of the group" (1976:93). In other words, a large organization is more likely to sue an individual than the reverse. Organization, as Black notes, provides an immunity from law and "an offense committed by an organization or its representatives is less serious than an offense by an individual on his [sic] own, and the more organized the organization, the less serious it is" (Black, 1976:94).

Although organizations have a greater chance of winning and a higher frequency of initiating lawsuits, it does not mean that individuals do not sue organizations (see, for example, Hellman, 2004). On the contrary, individuals are increasingly taking their disputes with organizations to courts. For example, when the Toronto-Dominion Bank introduced a mandatory drug-testing policy for both newly hired and returning employees in 1990, the screening of employees for drug use was presented as an attempt to "maintain a safe, healthy and productive workforce, to safeguard bank and customer funds and information and to protect the bank's policy" (Schmidt, 2001). Nevertheless, a complaint was filed with the Canadian Human Rights Tribunal that alleged that the policy constituted discrimination on the basis of disability (defined as "any previous or existing mental or physical disability and includes disfigurement and previous or existing dependence on alcohol or a drug"). Although a Canadian Human Rights tribunal initially issued a finding of nondiscrimination, a federal Court of Appeal ruled in 1998 that the policy *did* constitute "adverse-effect discrimination." As defined then by Supreme Court of Canada Justice Bertha Wilson, adverse-effect discrimination refers to "a rule that is neutral on its face but has an adverse discriminatory effect on certain members of the group to whom it applies" (in Dranoff 2005:40). In consequence, the policy was found to be in violation of the *Canadian Human Rights Act* because it could discriminate against certain employees and because it was not sufficiently related to job performance.

A similar decision was reached in relation to Imperial Oil's drug and alcohol testing policy for "safety-sensitive" positions within that company. In 1992, four employees of Imperial Oil filed complaints of discrimination with the Ontario Human Rights Commission. One of the complainants maintained that, despite giving up alcohol eight years earlier and participating in a company-sponsored substance-abuse program, he had been demoted as a result of the policy. The Ontario Human Rights Commission later ruled that, under the Ontario Human Rights Code, alcoholism is a handicap protected from discrimination and that the employer has the duty to accommodate the employee. The Commission ordered Imperial Oil to reinstate the employee in his "safety-sensitive" position and awarded the complainant $21 241 in damages. When Imperial Oil appealed this decision, the Ontario Court of Appeal ruled in July 2000 that Imperial Oil's use of both a pre-employment drug testing screening test and random drug testing for employees was discriminatory and in violation of the province's human rights code. The court held that a breathalyzer is permissible for people in high-risk jobs such as oil refinery workers, pilots, and train engineers because it determines whether someone is impaired at the moment the test is administered. However, because drug testing only measures past use, not present impairment or future impairment on the job, the court ruled that Imperial Oil could not justify pre-employment testing or random drug testing for employees.

Under the *Canadian Human Rights Act*, which applies to federal government employees, Crown corporations and companies in the federal jurisdiction (e.g., banks and airlines), discrimination based on alcohol or drug dependency is prohibited. In 1999, the Canadian Human Rights Commission instituted a policy on drug testing which specified that, unless safety is an issue, drug testing cannot be justified as a bona fide occupational requirement. However, while drug test requirements by employers in the federal jurisdiction are normally considered to be discriminatory, "[n]o law in Canada states that it is illegal for an employer to insist, before or after hiring, that an employee take a test to confirm the absence of drug use. . . . There is also no constitutional protection against drug testing" (Dranoff, 2001:37). In consequence, if a prospective employee is asked to take a drug test and refuses, he or she cannot later complain if s/he is not hired. Similarly, if the job applicant consents to take the test and it reveals drug use, the applicant may have no legal remedy if s/he is not hired. "It all depends on whether freedom from drug use is a reasonable requirement of the job, and therefore whether human rights protections are infringed" (Dranoff, 2005:39). It is, perhaps, inevitable that there will be disagreements about whether or not freedom from drug use is or is not a "reasonable requirement" of the job— and that some of these disagreements will be resolved in courtroom settings.

For the remainder of this section, we shall consider disputes initiated by individuals and organizations separately. For the former, we shall illustrate the use of law as a method of dispute resolution in academe, and for the latter, we shall discuss the use of courts as collection agencies in the field of consumer credit.

Law as a Method of Dispute Resolution in Academe

In the new millennium, law remains a potent force in institutions of higher learning (Gerstein and Gerstein, 2004). More and more, disputes that develop on campuses are resolved outside the groves of academe. Students, faculty members, academic administrators, and their institutions are becoming litigants in steadily growing numbers. Over the years, a substantial amount of literature has emerged on legal guidelines in institutions of

higher learning (see, for example, O'Reilly and Green, 1992), about the offences committed in academe in the name of what is disparagingly referred to as "political correctness"
(Kors and Silverglate, 1998), and law's pronounced presence on the campus reverberates
on most activities (Kaplin and Lee, 1995:1). Some have charged that as an unintended
consequence of growing legalism on campus, some faculty members are now reluctant
to fail a student or to assign a D or even a C+ due to concerns with probable complications, adverse administrative reactions, lengthy justifications, a myriad of memos,
grievance committees, and even the possibility of litigation. Although acknowledging
intellectual diversity and divergent performance on the grade sheet is a pedagogical fact
of life, Johnson (2003) contends that fewer professors do so because of the fear of consequences; instead of distinguishing between superior, average, and inferior student
performance, he argues, professors are giving in to administrative and student intimidation. The result is **grade inflation**: the assignment of higher grades than the work
warrants.

We will briefly consider law as a method of dispute resolution in academe in the context of faculty-administration, student-faculty, and student-administration relations.

The faculty-administration relationship in post-secondary institutions is defined by an
increasingly complex web of legal principles and authorities. The essence of this relationship is contract law, but "that core is encircled by expanding layers of labour relations law,
employment law, human rights law and, in public institutions, constitutional law and public employment statutes and regulations" (Kaplin and Lee, 1995:150). The growth in the
number and variety of laws and regulations governing faculty-administration relations provides a fertile ground for grievances and coincides with an increase in the number of lawsuits stemming from that relationship.

Many legal disputes centre on the meaning and interpretation of the faculty-institution
contract. Depending on the institution, a contract may vary from a basic notice of appointment to a complex collective bargaining agreement negotiated under labour laws. In some
instances, the formal document does not encompass all the terms of the contract, and other
terms are included through "incorporation by reference"—that is, by referring to other
documents, such as the faculty handbook, or even to past custom and usage at an institution. In the context of contract interpretation, legal disputes arise most often in the context
of contract termination and due notice for such termination.

A number of suits instituted by faculty members to redress their grievances against university administrations have focused on faculty-personnel decisions, such as appointment,
retention, promotion, and tenure policies; pecuniary matters affecting women and minority
groups; and sex discrimination. Termination procedures must also follow specific guidelines
and deadlines, and in recent years faculty members have increasingly resorted to lawsuits on
the grounds of procedural matters.

Other potentially conflict-laden situations in academe arise from student-faculty relations. Students are increasingly considering themselves consumers of education, treating
education like other consumer items; concomitantly, there is a growing emphasis on the
proper return for their educational dollars (see, for example, Johnson, 2003). Well over a
generation ago, Ladd and Lipset (1973:93) observed: "students are the 'consumers,' the
buyers, the patrons of a product sold by the faculty through a middle-man, the university
system. In economic class terms, the relationship of student to teacher is that of buyer to
seller, or of client to professional. In this context, the buyer or client seeks to get the most
for his [sic] money at the lowest possible price" (1973:93).

Because students are purchasers of education, they expect "delivery" of a product. In this context, the question of academic malpractice becomes important. Although the legal definition of academic malpractice is yet to be codified, it is generally considered as improper, injurious, or negligent instruction or action that has a "negative effect" on the student's academic standing, professional licensing, or employment (Vago, 1979:39). Although the concept of academic malpractice is rather amorphous, several patterns have emerged. A faculty member may be charged with malpractice by a student who perceives a particular course as "worthless," or by a student who contends that he or she did not obtain any "relevant" information or that for some reason it did not fit into the student's general educational outlook, requirement, or area of concentration. In such instances, individual professors are charged, and the object of the lawsuit is usually the recovery of tuition monies, and occasionally an intent to seek punitive damages, since the legal doctrine of *respondeat superior* (that is, the sins of the employee are imputed to the employer) is usually invoked. Several cases have been also litigated in the United States in which students have claimed contract damages for an institution's failure to provide bargained-for services. In a most extraordinary case, the defendant-student alleged that Columbia University:

> had represented that it would teach the defendant wisdom, truth, character, enlightenment, understanding, justice, liberty, honesty, courage, beauty, and similar virtues and qualities; that it would develop the whole man [sic], maturity, well-roundedness, objective thinking and the like; and that because it failed to do so it was guilty of misrepresentation, to the defendant's pecuniary damage. (Vago, 1979:41)

In this case, the trial court granted the university's motion for summary judgment, which was sustained on appeal.

Disputes resulting from a student's failure to pass an internal examination may also culminate in attempts to involve the courts. In such a situation, a student may question the expertise and competency of professors to evaluate examinations, or a department may be accused of following improper procedures during examinations. Questions of expertise and competency usually arise in the area of alleged academic overspecialization. (That is, is someone qualified to evaluate an examination in methods when his or her professed specialty is the sociology of law?) Issues of improper procedures often arise in the context of due process involving the department's or the university's failure to list specific guidelines for examination procedures, or to live up to those guidelines, or to provide clearly written guidelines and appeal procedures. But when it comes to strictly academic decisions made by faculty members about a student's academic career, the right of judges to overturn such decisions is limited.

Student-administration relations provide a third area for potential conflict in academe. Increasingly, suspension and dismissal procedures, the rights of students to organize, alleged censorship activities over student publications, and discrimination on the basis of factors such as sex, for example, are being challenged by students in courts.

Although institutions of higher learning have the right to dismiss, suspend, or otherwise sanction students for misconduct or academic deficiency, this right is determined by a body of procedural requirements that must be observed in such actions. Under the due process clause, students are entitled to a hearing and notice before disciplinary action is taken. In general, there is a trend toward increased protection of student rights, in both public and private institutions, in suspension and dismissal cases (Gerstein and Gerstein, 2004; Kaplin and Lee, 1995:371).

In some instances, however, post-secondary institutions retain the authority to revoke or withhold recognition, and to regulate the organizational use of campus facilities. When a mutually acceptable and satisfactory balance between the organization's rights and the institution's authority cannot be attained, the organizing students may turn to the courts to settle their dispute with the administration. The contents of student publications have also promoted controversy and disputes. Current controversies include questions of obscenity and libel in the context of student publications.

The need for universities to develop and maintain effective mechanisms of internal conflict management is obvious. The following section will consider disputes initiated by organizations against individuals in the domain of consumer credit.

The Courts as Collection Agencies

Disputes between individuals and organizations, where organizations are the plaintiffs, are most often triggered by disagreements over property and money. Such disputes are most prevalent in the creditor-debtor relationship, where the creditor is usually an organization such as a finance and loan company, car dealership, or department store. In such situations, there is a gross power disparity between the debtor and the organization, the debtor is relatively ignorant of the technical aspects of the product, and the stakes are small in dollars but large in their impact on the debtor (Goldberg et al., 2003).

Kagan (1984:324) comments: "If the extension of credit is the lifeblood of a dynamic commercial society, the forcible collection of unpaid debts is its backbone." When a debtor defaults on his or her contractual obligation to make payments, the standard legal remedy is to pursue collection of the debt through court action. The purpose is to establish the legality of the debt and its amount. Of course, creditors "hope to collect the debt by invoking the power of the court, but even if they do not collect, a judgment against the debtor is still of value for income tax purposes" as a deduction (Caplovitz, 1974:191).

If the creditor is successful in the suit, he or she obtains a judgment against the debtor. Once it is obtained, there are a variety of legal remedies available for collecting the judgment, including garnishment, liens, and the forced sale of the debtor's property. A **garnishment** is a court order directing someone who owes or possesses money due to the debtor (such as an employer) to pay all or some of that money to the court, which then turns it over to the creditor (Bryant, 2004). A **lien** establishes a creditor's claim on property (such as a house or a car). A **writ of seizure and sale** results in a forced sale involving the seizure and sale at an auction of the debtor's property. The proceeds then are turned over to the creditor to satisfy the judgment.

Before going to court, a creditor may resort to a number of social pressures and sanctions of varying severity, ranging from impersonal routine "reminders" and dunning letters or telephone appeals to get the debtor "in" to make some kind of "arrangement" and to remind or threaten him or her, to personal visits to the debtor's home from a "skip tracer" (investigator) in an attempt to elicit payments or at least promises (Hobbs, 2004). At times, creditors resort to unusual extrajudicial methods of collection. For example, a London firm is using a rather unconventional method of extracting money from debtors—smell: "Smelly Tramps, Ltd. is just what it sounds like: a motley crew of ragged, foul-smelling tramps, who specialize in dunning particularly evasive debtors. The tramps are really otherwise respectable chaps, dressed in disgusting clothes and treated with a special stomach churning chemical" (*Economist*, 1979:104). Their technique is simply to sit around the victim's office or home until he or she signs a cheque. Not to be outdone, a debt-collecting firm in Bombay, India, is employing six eunuchs who threaten to remove their saris if the defaulters do not pay up. The eunuchs' arrival at a debtor's home or office usually ensures the debtor pays his or her debt rather than be embarrassed in front of colleagues or neighbours (*Vancouver Sun,* 1999:E3).

When such dunning efforts fail and creditors have exhausted nonlitigation alternatives, they are likely to sue. A characteristic of most civil suits for debt is that the plaintiff usually wins by default. Most defendants are not represented by counsel. In fact, many of them are not present when their cases are heard. Their absence is treated as an admission of the validity of the claim, and a default judgment is entered against them. Such judgments are rendered in the vast majority of consumer cases.

There are a number of reasons why defendants fail to respond to summonses and to appear in court. Some recognize the validity of the creditor's claim and see no point in attempting to contest it or cannot afford a lawyer to do so (Hobbs, 2004). Others may simply find it impossible to leave work (with consequent loss of pay), travel to court, and spend most of the day waiting for their cases to be called. At times, the wording of a summons is so complicated and obtuse that many debtors cannot grasp what is at stake, or that they must appear if they are to avoid a default judgment. Others simply do not know that they are being sued. These individuals learn the hard way about suits against them—when a garnishment or eviction notice is served.

A similar situation but with much greater consequences existed in South Africa until late 1995. A creditor would go to court complaining that he had not been paid. A judge would then issue a judgment against the debtor and a request for payment. If the debtor did not pay within 10 days, the judge would hold the debtor in contempt of the court and send him or her to jail for up to three months. But many debtors were never even aware of the court proceedings. In some cases, debtors were illiterate and did not comprehend what was going on. Often, the first sign of trouble was when the police van showed up to take them to prison. The imprisonment of debtors has been very common, almost always involving the poor. In the late 1980s, for example, one-tenth of South Africa's prison population had been incarcerated because of debt. It should be noted, however, that by one criterion—payment of outstanding obligations—the system of imprisoning debtors was rather effective. Most people paid off their creditors within days. Studies showed that while the average contempt sentence was 31 days, the average debtor spent only 9 days in jail. Most of the time, the incarceration of the debtor set off a family-wide scramble to come up with the money (Daley, 1995).

Although we have focused on suits for debts, there are a number of other important types of actions initiated by organizations against individuals. Real estate companies regularly initiate legal action in the form of evictions against unknown numbers of tenants. Revenue Canada continuously files suits against individuals (and at times organizations) for back taxes or for tax evasion. Radio and television stations regularly use the courts to settle disputes with former announcers or disc jockeys who have decided to join competing stations, contrary to the desires of their former employers. In the final section, we shall consider disputes between organizations.

DISPUTES BETWEEN ORGANIZATIONS

There are two general types of organizational conflicts: (1) conflict between groups within the organization; and (2) conflict between organizations. For example, intraorganizational conflict within a university includes disputes between the faculty and administration over issues of collective bargaining, unionization, faculty freedom, and staff reduction based on alleged financial exigencies (Kaplin and Lee, 1995). Interorganizational conflict is exemplified by disputes between the university and the community over such matters as zoning and land use, or between the university and the federal government concerning compliance with federal regulations, such as occupational safety, pollution, and human rights.

Although the emphasis in this section is on interorganizational disputes, the generalizations that will be made are, of course, applicable to intraorganizational disputes. Such disputes may arise between private firms, between private firms and government, between government agencies, and between public-interest groups and private firms or government, or both. After a brief consideration of the various types of interorganizational disputes, we will examine in greater depth the activities of public-interest law firms in environmental disputes. At this point it should be noted that although most environmental offences are processed by regulatory agencies and corrected by civil and administrative remedies, there is an increased "criminalization" of environmental wrongs (see, for example, Situ and Emmons, 2001), and the trend is likely to continue.

Disputes between organizations cover a wide spectrum of participants and controversies. Businesspeople may take their disagreements to court over contract interpretation, trademarks, or alleged patent infringements. The federal government is involved as a plaintiff in suits to acquire land needed for federal projects (highways, dams, parks, buildings) which the acquiring agency is unable to purchase through negotiation, and in actions to force private companies to comply with contracts with federal agencies. Disputes between the government and private firms arise over matters of licensing and regulation, labour relations, and governmental contracts. The government is often the defendant in cases involving zoning and land use, location of public housing projects, and tax reassessment.

Social-policy disputes develop when the government pursues broad national objectives that may involve or impinge upon many interests and groups, such as equality and economic opportunity, environmental protection, income security, and public health and safety. In fact, all large-scale social welfare programs generate similar complex public-policy disputes (Mink and Solinger, 2004).

Regulatory disputes frequently involve difficult technical questions, whereas social-policy disputes raise difficult political and value questions. In both types of disputes, information about important variables is often incomplete or inaccurate, effects of alternative choices are hard to ascertain, and often there are no easy answers to cost-benefit questions or to questions of trade-offs among various interests. The various regulatory agencies discussed in Chapter 3 also process large numbers of routine disputes.

In many instances, the formal quasi-adjudicative procedures used by regulatory agencies are ill-suited to resolving large and complex disputes. Delays in settling disputes are frequent, and the situation is further compounded by the fact that some agencies traditionally engaged in economic regulations are now being asked to consider environmental claims as well. The regulatory process, in a sense, encourages conflict, rather than acting to reconcile opposing interests.

Public-Interest Law Firms in Environmental Disputes

Since the mid-1960s, there has been a proliferation of the types of activities associated with Ralph Nader and his consumer organizations (Reske, 1994), with the Sierra Club and its environmental programs, and with a new institutional form embodied in law firms that characterize their activities as partly or wholly "public interest" law and "cause lawyering" (Sarat and Scheingold, 1998).

Public-interest law is the term frequently used to describe the activities of law firms that represent environmentalists, consumers, and like groups, as well as test-case litigation in civil rights and poverty controversies. It is generally oriented toward causes and interests of groups, classes, or organizations, rather than individuals. Although public-interest law firms engage in activities such as lobbying, reporting, public relations, and counselling, litigation is by far their most important activity.

Private groups may use the courts to pursue better environmental quality (Naysnerski and Tietenberg, 1992). For example, in various countries, environmental lawyers are exploring novel legal strategies to adopt against global warming (Seelye, 2001; Anand, 2004). Public environmental enforcement can occur at the federal level through administrative proceedings, or through either civil or criminal judicial action. Public-interest lawyers have been active in a variety of environmental domains. They have challenged dams and other water resource projects, raised questions about nuclear power plants and bio-engineered food, attacked the pricing policies of electric utilities, attacked the use of dangerous pesticides, and recommended various changes to regulatory systems. For example, in recent years the Canadian Environmental Law Association (CELA) has campaigned for changes to the *Pest Control Products Act* to ensure a precautionary approach when the weight of evidence suggests a potentially unacceptable risk of harm; argued for the implementation of a federal toxic substances management policy to allow for immediate bans on pesticides that stay in the environment for a long time or accumulate in fat cells; proposed revision of the registration process for new products to ensure that their impact on children is taken into account; lobbied for improved inspection and enforcement by the Pest Management Regulatory Agency to ensure appropriate pesticide use; and sought improvements to public access to information that is essential to understanding the risks posed by pesticide exposure (CELA, 1999). Accounts of environmental policy disputes regularly fill the daily press (see, for example, Almeida and Stearns, 1998). Disputes include such questions as "Shall we expand or contract our programmes for flood control and stream channelization ? Should we relax or tighten the rules governing air pollution? Should we build a dam on a scenic stream, or allow nuclear energy plants to damage aquatic life in the natural bodies of water they use for cooling?" (Trubek, 1978:152).

Environmental disputes typically fall into two broad categories—enforcement and permitting cases. Enforcement disputes come about when a public-interest group raises questions about a party's compliance with a law or laws setting specific environmental standards, such as air or water quality. Permitting cases involve disputes over the planned construction of new facilities, such as a dam or an airport. Environmental disputes are also different from more traditional disputes in several ways: Irreversible ecological damages may be involved; at least one party to the dispute may claim to represent broader public interest—including the interests of inanimate objects, wildlife, and unborn generations; and the instrumentation of a court decision may pose special problems (what will happen to the community if the major employer is forced to close a factory responsible for water pollution) (Goldberg et al., 2003:419).

The background of the actors in environmental disputes may also be different. Unlike those involved in many other disputes, environmentalists, by and large, do not come from oppressed groups. In fact, they tend to draw most of their support from the white middle class. More often than not, their commitment is born of ideology rather than of pressing social or economic need. Consequently, environmental disputes seem to lack the immediacy of disputes in other areas. Often, they go on for years. Unlike in other disputes, delay favours the dissidents, and environmentalists prefer to postpone as long as possible decisions involving, for example, permits to construct new facilities.

Over the years, there has been a steady growth in the number of environmental disputes in all advanced industrialized countries (see, for example, Applegate, 2004; Heidenheimer et al., 1990:308). This phenomenon can be attributed to the significant increase in public awareness that our civilization causes substantial and possibly irreparable damage to the natural environment and to the growing significance of public action affecting the environment. Consequently, the recognition of the costs society pays for environmental damage and the failure of companies to internalize environmental costs has led to a proliferation of regulatory laws designed to protect the natural environment. Many environmental controversies are about the extent to which the government should regulate private-sector decisions that are considered contributive factors in environmental degradation (Rabe, 1991). At the same time, the government itself is also a potential cause of environmental damages. Public programs of many types, from flood control to mineral leasing, have a potential for environmental damage.

Environmental disputes are further complicated by the establishment of a number of mission-oriented government agencies. These agencies are set up to carry out programs: for example, to build dams, construct highways, or develop nuclear power. Such activities may cause environmental harm, but if an agency recognizes this harm, it will be forced to curtail its own activities and thus undermine, at least in part, the justification for its existence. At the same time, since these activities are perfectly lawful, they tend to magnify the advantages of those organized groups that favour development and to increase the obstacles facing environmental groups that set out to challenge agency decisions. Much environmental advocacy occurs in complex policy disputes. In many such disputes, the resources available to environmental advocates may be insufficient to ensure that their concerns receive the degree of attention from decision-makers that they would if the full extent of their demands were reflected in their representational resources.

SUMMARY

- Disagreements are ubiquitous in social relationships. Nonlegal methods of dispute resolution include violence, rituals, shaming and ostracism, supernatural agencies, "lumping it," avoidance, negotiation, mediation, and arbitration.

- As a result of social developments, the increased availability of legal mechanisms for conflict resolution, and the creation of legally actionable rights and remedies, there is a growing demand for court services in dispute resolution.

- Courts provide a forum for the settlement of a variety of private and public disputes. To qualify for the use of court services, plaintiffs must be able to demonstrate justiciability and standing, at the minimum. Those who have only occasional recourse to the courts are called one-shotters, and those who are engaged in many similar litigations over time are termed repeat players.

- Disputes between individuals and organizations may take place over economic issues, claims for damages and restitution, issues of rights, and issues concerning organizational actions, procedures, and policy. In general, more organizations are plaintiffs and more individuals are defendants, and organizations tend to be uniformly more successful than individuals in the courts.

- Disputes between organizations cover a wide spectrum of participants and controversies. In general, the party that is better organized, with greater resources and greater capacity to generate data, will have a higher probability of influencing the outcome of the dispute.

CRITICAL THINKING QUESTIONS

1. A primary intent behind the passage of the *Arbitration Act* in Ontario in 1991 was to reduce the backlog within the court system by allowing individuals to settle their disputes outside of that system. To this end, the *Arbitration Act* allowed for both mediation and arbitration, including faith-based arbitration. Only civil matters could be arbitrated and the rulings arrived at through arbitration were subject to Canadian law.

    As a result of this Act, from 1991 to 2005, Jews, Catholics, and members of other faiths in Ontario were afforded the right to use the guiding principles of their religion to settle divorce, custody, inheritance, and other civil disputes outside of the court system. Following its passage, it was possible for Catholics, for example, to annul religious marriage according to Canon Law (although it took a secular court to legally dissolve a civil marriage). Similarly, although the Orthodox Jewish community in Ontario had, since 1889, been using a "millennia-old rabbinical court system—called Beit Din (House of Law)—to settle marriage, custody and business disputes," the 1991 Act made Beit Din rulings, as well as those of other private arbitrations, "legally enforceable in a secular court, provided the parties consented beforehand" (CTV, 2005; Csillag, 2007).

    In 2003, the Toronto-based Canadian Society for Muslims proposed the creation of a formalized tribunal: the Islamic Institute of Civil Justice. "There, Muslim arbitrators would be allowed to make legally-binding decisions for Ontario Muslims when it comes to family and personal law" (CTV, 2005). Although the process already existed informally, the announcement generated heated opposition. Opponents charged that such tribunals would disadvantage women by forcing them to participate in a male-dominated process. In the months that followed, Amnesty International, along with dozens of other international groups and some 80 national organizations, voiced concern that these tribunals would discriminate against women and fail to fully comply with international human rights standards, and demonstrations were held in various Canadian and European cities (McIlroy, 2006; *Globe and Mail*, 2005). It was claimed that Sharia law "runs counter to the *Charter of Rights and Freedoms*"; that under "most interpretations of Islamic law, women's rights to divorce are strictly limited and they only receive half the inheritance of men"; and that this system of law "allows for polygamy and often permits marriage of girls at a younger age than does secular law" (Duff-Brown, 2006).

    In June 2004, the Ontario government announced that a review of the entire *Arbitration Act* would be conducted. The report, conducted by former Ontario Attorney-General Marion Boyd, ultimately recommended that the province's existing arbitration system be strengthened and concluded that Muslims should enjoy the same rights as other religions to use faith-based arbitration to settle family disputes. To many, it appeared that Ontario was well on its way to becoming the first Western jurisdiction to allow Sharia tribunals to settle marital and other family disputes according to the tenets of Islamic law. However, in September 2005, Ontario premier Dalton

McGuinty announced, "I've come to the conclusion that the debate has gone on long enough. There will be no Sharia law in Ontario. . . There will be no religious arbitration in Ontario. There will be one law for all Canadians" (in McIlroy, 2006). McGuinty maintained that religious arbitrations "threatened our common good" and pledged to move quickly to introduce legislation that would outlaw all religious arbitrations. "Ontarians will always have the right to seek advice from anyone in matters of family law, including religious advice," he commented. "But no longer will religious arbitration be deciding matters of family law" (in Duff-Brown, 2005).

Some applauded this move. The head of the Muslim Canadian Congress described McGuinty's announcement as not simply "a great victory for all Canadians" but "particularly Muslims. . . and a defeat for Islamic fundamentalists and those who are preaching it in Canada" (CTV, 2005). Others were markedly less impressed. The founder of the Islamic Institute of Civil Justice in Ontario noted that, for religious Muslims, it's a religious duty to settle their disputes in Muslim courts. The head of the Canadian Islamic Congress maintained that "Arbitration will continue anyway, because it is part of our social fabric" (in McIlroy, 2006). The regional chairman of the Canadian Jewish Congress described his reaction as "stunned" and commented that, "[a]t the very least, we would have thought the government would have consulted with us before taking away what we've had for so many years. . . . If there have been any problems flowing from any rabbinical court decision, I'm not aware of them" (CTV, 2006).

In the summer of 2006, the Ontario government passed Bill 27, the *Family Statute Amendment Act*. This new provincial law prohibits all forms of binding arbitration in family matters (e.g., divorce, child custody, and division of property). The new law states that resolutions "based on other laws and principles—including religious principles—will have no legal effect and will not be enforced by the courts." In addition, it specifies that family arbitrators must be trained and hold membership within a professional arbitration organization. In response, a lawyer who had represented several groups of Orthodox Jews in the process that led up to the law's passage, announced that he would be taking steps "to challenge the measure under the religious freedom provisions of the Charter of Rights and Freedoms" (Csillag, 2006).

The 2005 Portraits of Canada survey, conducted by the Centre for Research and Information on Canada, found that almost two-thirds of Canadians were opposed to giving any religious group the right to use faith-based arbitration to settle family disputes: 63 percent were opposed to the idea, with 48 percent "strongly opposed" and 15 percent "somewhat opposed"; only 30 percent reported some or strong approval (CRIC, 2006). Opposition to faith-based arbitration was highest in Ontario, where more than two-thirds (68 percent) opposed the idea. When asked specifically about giving the Muslim community the right to faith-based arbitration, 67 percent voiced opposition (51 percent strongly opposed, 16 percent somewhat opposed). The region with the strongest opposition to religious tribunals for Muslims was Quebec, where three out of four (61 percent strongly, 14 percent somewhat) voiced opposition. "The strongest support for faith-based arbitration in general, and for Muslims in particular. . . [exists] in the North. There, 44 percent agreed with the concept of faith-based arbitration, and fully 55 percent believed that if other communities had the right to use faith-based arbitration, then Muslims should be given that right, too" (CRIC, 2006).

Ontario's *Family Statute Amendment Act* would seem consistent with the views expressed by the majority of respondents in the CRIC survey. However, do *you* support or oppose this Act? Should the new law contain a transitional or grandparenting clause or should past rulings, arrived at through faith-based arbitration rulings but not incorporated into secular divorce settlements, become void? Is faith-based arbitration inherently more likely to privilege men and disadvantage women than other forms of ADR?

2. It is common that Canadian universities and colleges have student grievance policies that describe the procedural steps a student may take to seek remedies for both academic grievances (which allege errors in academic judgement) and procedural/other grievances (which may include, for example, allegations of bias or prejudice, abuse of supervisory authority, or sexual harassment). The grievance process is typically divided into a series of stages, with each successive stage becoming increasingly formal.

   Grievance policies provide a mechanism for students to challenge a decision of a university/college authority or the action of a university/college member that they believe has been unreasonable, unjust, or unfair. However, it is evident that not all students who perceive that they have been unfairly treated will initiate a grievance or appeal. What factors might limit the effectiveness of student grievance policies and make them more rhetorically appealing than practically potent?

chapter seven

Law and Social Change

Law and society theorists have long been preoccupied with attempts to explain the relationship between legal and social change in the context of development of legal institutions (see, for example, Anleu, 2000). These theorists, some of whom were discussed in Chapter 2, view the law as both an independent and a dependent variable in society and emphasize the interdependence of the law with other social systems. In light of the theoretical concerns raised earlier in the book, this chapter will further examine the interplay between law and social change. The law will again be considered as both a dependent and an independent variable—that is, as both an effect and a cause of social change. The chapter will also analyze the advantages and the limitations of the law as an instrument of social change, and will discuss a series of social, psychological, cultural, and economic factors that have an influence on the efficacy of law as an agent of change.

The initial step in understanding the relationship between law and social change is conceptual. What is social change? The term *change*, in everyday usage, is often employed loosely—as demonstrated in the rhetoric of the 2006 political campaigns at various levels—to refer to something that exists that did not exist previously, or to the demise or absence of something that formerly existed. But not all change is social change. Many changes in life are small enough to be dismissed as trivial, although at times they may add up to something more substantial and consequential. In its most concrete sense, social change means that large numbers of people are engaging in group activities and relationships that are different from those that they or their parents engaged in previously. Society is a complex network of patterns of relationships in which all the members participate in varying degrees. These relationships change, and behaviour changes at the same time. Individuals are faced with new situations to which they must respond. These situations reflect such factors as new technologies, new ways of making a living, changes in place of residence, and innovations, new ideas, and new social values. Thus, social change means modifications in the way people work, rear a family, educate their children, govern themselves, and seek ultimate meaning in life. It also refers to a restructuring of the basic ways people in a society relate to each other with regard to government, economics, education, religion, family life, recreation, language, and other activities (McCarthy, 2005; Vago, 2004).

Social change is a product of a multitude of factors and, in many cases, the interrelationships among them. In addition to law and legal cultures (Gibson and Caldeira, 1996), there are many other mechanisms of change, such as technology, ideology, competition, conflict, political and economic factors, and structural strains (see, for example, McMichael, 2004). All the mechanisms are in many ways interrelated. One should be very careful not to assign undue weight to any one of these "causes" in isolation. Admittedly, it is always tempting and convenient to single out one "prime mover," one factor, one cause, one explanation, and use it for a number of situations. This is also the case with legal change; it is extremely difficult, perhaps impossible, to set forth a cause-and-effect relationship in the creation of new laws, administrative rulings, or judicial decisions. Although there are exceptions, as will be alluded to in this chapter, one should be somewhat skeptical and cautious concerning one-factor causal explanations in general, and in particular about such explanations for large-scale social changes.

RECIPROCITY BETWEEN LAW AND SOCIAL CHANGE

The question of whether law can and should lead, or whether it should never do more than cautiously follow changes in society, has been and remains controversial. The conflicting approaches of the British social reformer Jeremy Bentham and the German legal scholar Friedrich Karl von Savigny have provided the contrasting classical paradigms for these propositions. At the beginning of industrialization and urbanization in Europe, Bentham expected legal reforms to respond quickly to new social needs and to restructure society. He freely gave advice to the leaders of the French Revolution, since he believed that countries at a similar stage of economic development needed similar remedies for their common problems. In fact, it was Bentham's philosophy, and that of his disciples, that turned the British Parliament—and similar institutions in other countries—into active legislative instruments bringing about social reforms partly in response to and partly in stimulation of felt social needs. Writing at about the same period, Savigny condemned the sweeping legal reforms brought about by the French Revolution that were threatening to invade Western Europe. He believed that only fully developed popular customs could form the basis of legal change. Since customs grow out of the habits and beliefs of specific people, rather than expressing those of an abstract humanity, legal changes are codifications of customs, and they can only be national, never universal.

Well over six generations later, the relationship between law and social change remains controversial. Still, "there exist two contrasting views on the relationship between legal precepts and public attitudes and behaviour. According to the one, law is determined by the sense of justice and the moral sentiments of the population, and legislation can only achieve results by staying relatively close to prevailing social norms. According to the other view, law, and especially legislation, is a vehicle through which a programmed social evolution can be brought about" (Aubert, 1969:69). At one extreme, then, is the view that law is a dependent variable, determined and shaped by current mores and opinions of society. According to this position, legal changes would be impossible unless preceded by social change; law reform could do nothing except codify custom. This is clearly not so, and ignores the fact that throughout history, legal institutions have been found to "have a definite role, rather poorly understood, as instruments that set off, monitor, or otherwise regulate the fact or pace of social change" (Friedman, 1969:29). The other extreme is exemplified by jurists in the former Soviet Union, such as P. P. Gureyev and P. I. Sedugin (1977), who saw the law as an instrument for social engineering. Accordingly, "during the period of the transition from capitalism to socialism, the Soviet state made extensive use of legislation to guide society, establish and develop social economic forms, abolish each and every form of exploitation, and regulate the measure of labour and the measure of the consumption of the products of social labour. It used legislation to create and improve the institutions of socialist democracy, to establish firm law and order, safeguard the social system and state security, and build socialism" (Gureyev and Sedugin, 1977:12).

These views represent the two extremes of a continuum representing the relationship between law and social change. The problem of the interplay between law and social change is obviously not a simple one. As Olivo (2001:10) emphasizes, in some cases, the law leads; in others, the law may been seen to follow social change. However, he acknowledges that "[i]n many cases it is hard to say whether the law is bringing about social change or social change is transforming the law. The process of lawmaking is a dynamic process."

Consider, for example, that prior to the liberating reform of the *1968 Divorce Act* (the first Canada-wide divorce act), Canada had one of the lowest divorce rates of all industrialized countries. This should not be surprising given that, until Parliament passed this Act, divorce was available only in certain provinces. In Quebec, for example, provincial courts could not grant divorce and residents seeking divorce were forced to apply to Parliament to dissolve their marriage.

Between 1867 and 1968, adultery was the only legally recognized ground for divorce in most of Canada; Nova Scotia also recognized cruelty as grounds, and New Brunswick recognized frigidity, impotence, and consanguinity. New Brunswick was the only province to ever acknowledge sexual and reproductive "failure" on the part of either spouse as a "fault" or "offence" against the marriage. Nevertheless, "[b]reaking the bonds of matrimony used to be almost impossible until 1967" (Dranoff, 2005:263). The *1968 Divorce Act* expanded the list of fault-grounds that entitled a petitioner to an immediate divorce; these included mental or physical cruelty, addiction to alcohol or other drugs, sodomy, bestiality, or homosexual acts. This Act also took a first step toward "no-fault divorce." Divorce was permitted on the grounds of unspecified "marital breakdown" if the couple had lived "separate and apart" for a three-year period and jointly consented to being divorced. In the event that one party did not wish to be divorced, the court required that five years pass from the time of separation before application be made for divorce. However, this Act continued to place strong emphasis on the virtues of marriage; lawyers for each spouse were legally obliged to discuss reconciliation with their clients. Divorce-trial judges were also required to determine whether reconciliation was possible, and a judge who felt that there was insufficient evidence of matrimonial fault or marital breakdown could deny a divorce.

The *1985 Divorce Act* (effective in 1986) simplified the divorce process even further. Under this Act, only one ground is available for divorce: marital breakdown. This simplification of divorce procedures was intended to reflect our society's endorsement of individualism and gender egalitarianism. Essentially, the power to decide if a marriage should be terminated has been placed in the hands of the spouses themselves, with the courts relegated mainly to an administrative role, ensuring that proper form is followed in legally dissolving the relationship, as well as an adjudicative role in cases where there are contested issues. For purposes of divorce, a couple's having lived separate and apart for a period of not less than one year, or one partner's having committed adultery, or one partner's having treated the other with mental or physical cruelty are viewed as sufficient evidence of marital breakdown. Over 80 percent of Canadian divorces are currently based on evidence of a one-year separation.

The number of divorces per 100 000 population in Canada (known as the "crude divorce rate") rose from 36.0 in 1961 to 271.0 in 1981, reached a peak of 362.3 in 1987, then declined to 282.0 in 1991 and, by 2003, to 223.7 (Statistics Canada, 2005). Olivo (2001:10) asserts that, "While attitudes toward divorce were changing anyway. . . [the *1968 Divorce Act*] brought about an increase in the number of divorces in the country, with various cultural and social changes following the change in the law. There were suddenly more single-parent families, divorce was not seen as a social stigma or disgrace, and a new phenomenon, the "combined family" made its appearance, composed of two remarried spouses and the children of both their previous marriages" (Olivo, 2001:10). Yet, while Olivo (2001) suggests that the passage of the *1968 Divorce Act* played a catalytic and causal role in the social changes that followed, the relationship between law and social change is complex. Various social changes—such as the diminished influence of religious ideologies concerning the sanctity of marriage vows, the growing acceptance of singlehood and cohabitation as alternatives to marriage, the significant rise of women's labour-force participation (which enables greater economic self-sufficiency), and the ideology of feminism have also clearly impacted upon both the incidence of divorce in Canada and the provisions that are contained within the federal Act. Most recently, for example, Canada's recognition of the right to same-sex marriage has led to the recognition of the right to same-sex divorce. In what is believed to be a world first, an Ontario court granted a same-sex divorce in 2004 and declared that the opposite-sex definition of "spouse" within the *Divorce Act* was "unconstitutional, inoperative and of no force and effect" because it contravened the Charter's guarantees of equality (Dranoff, 2005:145).

Essentially, the question is not, "Does law change society?" or "Does social change alter law?" Both contentions are likely to be correct. Instead, it is more appropriate to ask under what specific circumstances law can bring about social change, at what level, and to what extent. Similarly, the conditions under which social change alters law need to be specified.

In general, in a highly urbanized and industrialized society like Canada, law does play a large part in social change, and vice versa, at least much more so than is the case in traditional societies or in traditional sociological thinking (Nagel, 1970:10). There are several ways of illustrating this reciprocal relationship. For example, in the domain of intrafamily relations, urbanization, with its small apartments, has lessened the desirability of three-generation families in a single household. This social change helped to establish social security laws that in turn helped generate changes in the labour force and in social institutions for the aged. Changes in landlord-tenant relations brought about changes in housing codes, resulting in changes in tenancy relations. As a result of technological change, the relation of personal property owners to other individuals has become more impersonal and frequently more likely to lead to injury. As a result, there have been alterations in the legal definition of *fault*, which in turn has changed the insurance system. Finally, in the context of employer-employee relations, much of Canadian labour history pointed toward the enactment of precedents and statutes guaranteeing the right to unionize, and once the legislation permitting union certification and forcing employers to accept collective bargaining with employee representatives was passed in 1944, with the federal government establishing a full national system of collective labour relations law, the percentage of the labour force in unions did drastically increase, with the level of unionization rising from 20 percent to 30 percent during the 1940s. By 1977, the unionization rate in Canada was 32.6 percent; in 1987, 34.2 percent. However, while Canada's union ranks swelled from 2.8 million in 1977 to just over 4 million in 2003, "this 43 percent growth did not keep pace with increases in employment, resulting in a unionization rate that has slowly declined" (Statistics Canada, 2004). As the result of changing labour laws, workforce demographics, and economic structures, dramatic shifts have occurred in Canada's labour movement over the past several decades, including, most notably, "the increasing feminization of the movement, the growing prominence of unions in the public service and services sectors, and the declining influence of international unions" (Statistics Canada, 2004).

Although there is an obvious and empirically demonstrable reciprocal relationship between law and social change, for analytical purposes we will briefly consider this relationship as unilateral. To this end, in the next section we will examine the conditions under which social change induces legal change; then, in the following section, we will discuss law as an instrument of social change.

SOCIAL CHANGES AS CAUSES OF LEGAL CHANGES

In a broad historical context, social change has been slow enough to make custom the principal source of law. Law could respond to social change over decades or even centuries (see, for example, Edgeworth, 2003). Even during the early stages of the Industrial Revolution, changes induced by the invention of the steam engine or the advent of electricity were gradual enough to make legal responses valid for a generation. Notes Friedmann : "But today the tempo of social change has accelerated to a point where today's assumptions may not be valid even in a few years from now" (1972:513). In the often-quoted dramatic words of Alvin Toffler (1970:11), "Change sweeps through the highly industrialized countries with waves of ever accelerating speed and unprecedented impact." In a sense, people in modern society are caught in a maelstrom of social change, living through a series of contrary and interacting revolutions in demography, urbanization, bureaucratization, industrialization, science, transportation, agriculture, communication, biomedical research, education, and civil rights. Each of these revolutions has brought spectacular changes in a string of tumultuous consequences, and transformed people's values, attitudes, behaviour, and institutions.

These changes further transformed the social and economic order of society. Contemporary society is characterized by a great division of labour and specialization in function. In modern society,

> interpersonal relations have changed; social institutions, including the family, have become greatly modified; social control previously largely informal has become formalized; bureaucracy, that is, large-scale formal organizations, has proliferated both in the private and public sectors;

and new risks to the individual have emerged including the risk of disrupted income flow through unemployment, of industrial accidents, and of consumer exploitation; and increased chronic illness and physical impairments have accompanied the extension of life. (Hauser, 1976:23)

The emergence of new risks to the individual as a result of the attenuation of the various family functions, including the protective function, has led to the creation of legal innovations to protect the individual in modern society. Illustrations of such innovations include provisions for workers' compensation, unemployment insurance, old-age pensions, Medicare, and various forms of categoric and general provisions for "welfare" (Doran, 2002; Hauser, 1976:24; Machum, 2002; Quaile, 2002).

Many sociologists and legal scholars assert that technology is one of the great moving forces for change in law (see, for example, Volti, 2001). Law is influenced by technology in at least three ways:

> The most obvious. . . is technology's contribution to the refinement of legal technique by providing instruments to be used in applying law (e.g., fingerprinting or the use of a lie detector). A second, no less significant, is technology's effect on the process of formulating and applying law as a result of the changes technology fosters in the social and intellectual climate in which the legal process is executed (e.g., televised hearings). Finally, technology affects the substance of law by presenting new problems and new conditions with which law must deal. (Stover, quoted by Miller, 1979:14)

Illustrations of technological changes leading to legal changes abound. The advent of the automobile and air travel brought along new regulations. The automobile, for example, has been responsible for an immense amount of law: traffic rules, rules about drunk driving, rules about auto safety, drivers' licence laws, rules about pollution control, registration, and so on. New devices in crime detection (fingerprinting and electronic snooping, among a host of others) resulted in changes in the law, such as the kinds of evidence admissible in court. The computer makes possible our present systems of credit, merchandising, manufacturing, transportation, research, education, dissemination of information, government, and politics. The computer and easy access to cyberspace, especially the Internet, have also inspired legislation to safeguard privacy, to protect against abuse of credit information and computer crime (although not too efficiently, as evidenced by the phenomenal increase in identity thefts [see, for example, Huey and Rosenberg, 2004; May and Headley, 2004]). It has also prompted discussion of how the absence of certain extra-linguistic cues and established cultural conventions within cyberspace may result in misperceptions and miscommunications—and make it necessary to re-examine the law of defamation and consider critically whether a libel published on the Internet should be dealt with in the same way as, for example, a libel published in a newspaper (Burkell and Kerr, 2000). The success of the 2004 Mars Rover explorations renewed interest in space law, which was initially modelled on maritime law. The once remote possibility of space tourism, for example, is now just around the corner, but liability questions abound. The helium 3 isotope, abundant on the moon, could make a fortune for anyone who mines it. And space's zero gravity promises attractive manufacturing opportunities. There are now businesses that sell rights to name stars, and there is an entrepreneur in Nevada who claims that a loophole in international law allows him to assert ownership of the moon (Weir, 2004). New regulations and treatises dealing with various facets of space exploration and rights are ground out daily; not surprisingly, space law is "in," and more and more law schools (see, for example, McGill and the University of Mississippi) are offering courses and programs on the new legal frontier of outer space.

Change in law may be induced by a voluntary and gradual shift in community values and attitudes. People may come to think that poverty is bad and laws should be created to reduce it in some way. People may come to condemn the use of laws to further racially discriminatory practices in voting, housing, employment, education, and the like, and may support changes that forbid the use of laws for these purposes. People may come to think that businesspeople should not be free to put just any kind of foodstuff on the market without proper governmental inspection, or fly any plane without having to meet governmental safety standards, or show anything on television that they wish. So laws may be enacted as appropriate, and regulatory bodies may be brought into being as necessary. And people may come to think that the practice of abortion is not evil, or that the practice of contraception is desirable, or that divorce and remarriage are not immoral. Hence, laws governing these practices may undergo repeal or revision.

Changes in social conditions, technology, knowledge, values, and attitudes, then, may induce legal change. In such instances, the law is reactive and follows social change. It should be noted, however, that changing the law is one of many types of response to social change. But the legal response in some respects is important, since it represents the authority of the state and its sanctioning power. A new law in response to a new social or technological problem may aggravate that problem—or alleviate and help to solve it. Often, the legal response to social change, which inevitably comes after a time lag, induces new social changes. For example, laws created in response to air and water pollution brought about by technological changes may result in unemployment in some areas, where polluting firms are unwilling or unable to install the required pollution-abatement controls. Thus, law can be considered as both reactive and proactive in social change. In the next section, the proactive aspect of law as an initiator of social change will be considered.

LAW AS AN INSTRUMENT OF SOCIAL CHANGE

There are numerous historical and cross-cultural illustrations in which the enactment and instrumentation of laws have been used deliberately to induce broad social changes in society (see, for example, Fernandes and Varley, 1998). With the advent of Roman jurists, the notion of law as an instrument of social change became clearly conceptualized. Says Nisbet: "The conversion of Rome from republic to empire could not have been accomplished except by means of explicit legal decree buttressed by the doctrine of imperial sovereignty" (2000:184). Since Roman times, great ages of social change and mobility almost always involved great use of law and of litigation. There are several illustrations of the idea that law, far from being simply a reflection of social reality, is a powerful means of *accomplishing* reality—that is, of fashioning it or making it. Although Marx, Engels, and Lenin maintained that law is an epiphenomenon of bourgeois class society doomed to vanish with the advent of the Revolution, the former Soviet Union did, notably, succeed in making enormous changes in society by the use of laws (Dror, 1968). In Spain, during the 1930s, law was used to reform agrarian labour and employment relations (Collier, 1989:201). More recently, the attempts by Eastern European countries to make wholesale social changes through the use of laws— such as nationalization of industry, land reform and introduction of collective farms, provision of free education and health care, and elimination of social inequities—are illustrative of the effectiveness of law to induce change (Eorsi and Harmathy, 1971). Another example is provided by China. China managed to moderate through law its population growth and, as a result, devote more of its resources to economic development and modernization (Diamant, Lubman, and O'Brien, 2005; Tyler, 1995). The Chinese established an effective women's health system that discourages large families through patient education, contraceptive choice, and heavy taxes for couples who choose to have an additional child (Rosenthal, 1998).

Recognition of the role of law as an instrument of social change is becoming more pronounced in contemporary society. Says Friedmann: "The law—through legislative or administrative responses to new social conditions and ideas, as well as through judicial reinterpretations of constitutions, statutes or precedents—increasingly not only articulates but sets the course for major social changes" (1972:513). Thus, "attempted social change, through law, is a basic trait of the modern world" (Friedman, 1975:277). In the same vein, Yehezkel Dror (1968:673) contends that "the growing use of law as a device of organized social action directed toward achieving social change seems to be one of the characteristics of modern society." Many authors, such as Joel B. Grossman and Mary H. Grossman (1971:2), consider law as a desirable, necessary, and highly efficient means of inducing change, preferable to other instruments of change.

In present-day societies, the role of law in social change is of more than theoretical interest. In many areas of social life, such as education, race relations, housing, transportation, energy utilization, the protection of the environment, and crime prevention, the law and litigation are important instruments of change (Reed, 1998; Potvin, 2005). In Canada, the law has been used as the principal mechanism for improving the political and social position of minorities, for dismantling a discriminatory system embedded in the law and in practice for generations, and for entrenching the concept of **human rights.** In contrast to **civil liberties**, which, in general, refer to a narrower class of fundamental freedoms such as freedom of religion, expression, assembly, and association, human rights also include such rights as the right to education, accommodation, and employment.

In the past, the law functioned as an instrument of discrimination, depriving minority groups of civil, political, and economic rights (Hall, 2000). For example, prior to the *British Emancipation Act* of 1833, slavery was legal in the colonies. Discriminatory laws were also passed to discourage or entirely prohibit the immigration of nonwhites. Canada's 1910 *Immigration Act* gave the government the formal power "to prohibit for a stated period of time, or permanently, the landing in Canada . . . of immigrants belonging to any race unsuited to the climate or requirements of Canada" (Sher, 1983:33). Canada's *Chinese Immigration Act* of 1923 completely barred the Chinese from entering Canada, and Chinese persons already in Canada were not allowed to sponsor family or relatives. From 1952 to 1977, immigration laws prohibited homosexuals from entering Canada and subjected those who were homosexual to the threat of deportation if their sexual orientation became known (Kinsman, 1996).

Consider as well that, in 1868, when the first federal general election was held, only men who owned a specified amount of property were allowed to vote; in 1885, the *Electoral Franchise Act* defined a "person" who was eligible to vote as a male who was of other than Mongolian or Chinese origin. While the *1917 Wartime Election Act* granted wives, sisters, and mothers of servicemen the right to vote, it was not until 1918 that Canadian women won the right to vote in federal elections (Frank, 1994). Women over the age of 21 were granted the right to vote in provincial elections in 1916 in Manitoba, Saskatchewan, and Alberta; in 1917, in British Columbia and Ontario; in 1918 in Nova Scotia; in 1919 in New Brunswick; in 1922 in Prince Edward Island; in 1925 in Newfoundland (where initially this right was limited to women over the age of 25); and in

1940 in Quebec (Whitla, 1995:320). These rights were first granted to white women; women from certain other ethnic groups did not receive the franchise until later years (Mossman, 1998).

Laws also imposed **segregation**—the separation of groups in residence, workplace, and social functions. Sher (1983:33) observes that, in British Columbia, "where anti-Asian sentiment was endemic from the 1850s to the 1950s, Chinese, Japanese and South Asians could not vote, practice law or pharmacy, be elected to public office, serve on juries, or work in public works, education or the civil service." Nelson and Fleras (1995:246) report that, during the 1920s and 1930s, Jews were automatically excluded from employment in major institutions such as banks, universities set limits on Jewish enrollment, and "signs warning that 'Jews and dogs not allowed' were posted along Lake Ontario beachfronts in Toronto." They note that African-Canadians were treated as inferior in this country from the time they began to settle here and "routinely excluded from restaurants and other public venues by laws as discriminatory as those in the southern United States. Segregated schools, for example, were not taken off the books in Ontario or Nova Scotia until the early 1960s." While the last segregated school in southwestern Ontario closed in 1956, it was not until 1975 that Windsor desegregated its public facilities. Borovoy (1999:35) additionally observes that

> [i]n the mid-1940s, a black woman in New Glasgow, Nova Scotia was jailed overnight because she refused to sit in the theatre balcony that had been allocated for blacks (whites sat downstairs). In the mid-1950s, the prime minister of Barbados was denied a room in a Montreal hotel. As late as 1968, a dead black child in Nova Scotia was denied burial in what was then an all-white cemetery.

Beginning with the introduction of Ontario's 1944 *Racial Discrimination Act* and Saskatchewan's 1947 *Bill of Rights*, the first acts dealing with human rights in this country, a variety of legislation has attempted to counter the problem of discrimination in Canada. In 1960, Parliament adopted the *Canadian Bill of Rights* and currently every Canadian province and territory, as well as the federal government, has adopted antidiscrimination legislation and established human rights commissions. Since 1982, the Constitution has contained an entrenched *Canadian Charter of Rights and Freedoms,* which applies to federal and provincial jurisdiction.

In general, human rights codes prohibit discrimination in employment, accommodation, and the provision of goods, services, and facilities based on race or colour, religion or creed, sex (including pregnancy or childbirth), age, disability, marital status ("civil status" in Quebec), sexual orientation, family status, ancestry or place of origin, and, in some places, language (Quebec only), gender identity (the Northwest Territories only), political belief, dependence on alcohol or drugs, criminal conviction for which a pardon has been obtained, source of income (e.g., Ontario prohibits discrimination in accommodation on the grounds of receipt of public assistance), and poverty (e.g., since 1996, Alberta recipients of welfare can complain to their province's human rights commission if they are turned down for housing or bank accounts because of their financial status). In addition, section 718.2 of the Criminal Code provides that "evidence that [an offence] was motivated by bias, prejudice or hate based on race, national or ethnic origin, colour, religion, sex, age, mental or physical disability, sexual orientation or any other similar factor" is to be considered an aggravating circumstance in sentencing convicted offenders. For example, in the case of *R. v. Ingram and Grimsdale* (1977), it was held that "An assault which is racially motivated renders the offence more heinous. Such assaults, unfortunately, invite imitation and repetition by others and incite retaliation. The danger is even greater in a multicultural, pluralistic urban society." Section 319 of the Criminal Code defines the willful promotion of hatred against any identifiable group (i.e., "any section of the public distinguished by colour, race, religion, ethnic origin or sexual orientation") and advocating genocide as criminal offences, punishable by up to two years' imprisonment. Perhaps the best-known prosecution under this section of the code is that of James Keegstra, a former Alberta high school teacher who was accused of fomenting hatred against Jews in his classroom lectures. In 1996, the Supreme Court ruled that while freedom of expression is guaranteed within subsection 2(b) of the *Charter of Rights and Freedoms,* the prohibition of hate propaganda was a reasonable limitation of that freedom and supported by international documents to which Canada is a party and by sections 15 (equality) and 27 (multiculturalism) of the Charter.

Canada is also a signatory to numerous international treaties and has ratified various international conventions that make the promotion and protection of human rights focal concerns. These include, for example, the United Nations' Convention on the Rights of the Child—a treaty which has been described as "the most comprehensive human rights document ever adopted by the international community" (Mooney et al., 2004:182). However, as Olivo (2001a:85) points out, international public law typically lacks effective enforcement mechanisms and countries "often ignore it when it suits a state's interests to do so"; for this reason, he observes, public international law has been variously described as "not really law" or, even less charitably, "as more wishful thinking than law" (91). In consequence, while both national and international law have attempted to curb the most egregious examples of discrimination, it would be both erroneous and naïve to conclude that the human rights and interests of historically disadvantaged minority groups are now automatically protected (Hunt, 2002).

Another example of law as an instrument of social change is provided in the former Eastern-bloc countries, where the law was a principal instrument in transforming society after the Second World War from a bourgeois to a socialist one. Legal enactments initiated and legitimized rearrangements in property and power relations, transformed basic social institutions such as education and health care, and opened up new avenues of social mobility for large segments of the population. Legislation guided the reorganization of agricultural production from private ownership to collective farms, the creation of new towns, and the development of a socialist mode of economic production, distribution, and consumption. These changes, in turn, affected values, beliefs, socialization patterns, and the structure of social relationships.

There are several ways of considering the role of law in social change. In an influential article, "Law and Social Change," Dror (1968) distinguishes between the indirect and direct aspects of law in social change. Dror (1968:673) contends that "law plays an important indirect role in social change by shaping various social institutions, which in turn have a direct impact on society." He uses the illustration of the compulsory education system, which performed an important indirect role in regard to change. Mandatory school attendance upgraded the quality of the labour force, which, in turn, played a direct role in social change by contributing to an increased rate of industrialization and modernization. He emphasizes that law interacts in many cases directly with basic social institutions, constituting a direct relationship between law and social change. He warns, however, that "the distinction is not an absolute but a relative one: in some cases the emphasis is more on the direct and less on the indirect impact of social change, while in other cases the opposite is true" (Dror, 1968:674).

Dror argues that law exerts an indirect influence on social change in general by influencing the possibilities of change in various social institutions. For example, the existence of a patent law protecting the rights of inventors encourages inventions and furthers change in the technological institutions, which, in turn, may bring about other types of social change.

For all modern societies, every collection of statutes and delegated legislation is "full of illustrations of the direct use of law as a device for directed social change" (Dror, 1968:676). A good example of social change directly induced by law was the enactment of Prohibition in both Canada and the United States to shape social behaviour. (It was also a conspicuous failure in both countries, showing that there are limits to the efficacy of law to bring about social change, as we will discuss later.)

Another way of considering the role of law in social change is in the context of Leon H. Mayhew's (1971:195) notion of the possibility of either redefining the normative order or creating new procedural opportunities within the legal apparatus. The former, which he designates as an "extension of formal rights," is illustrated by the unanimous pronouncement of the Supreme Court of Canada in 1999 that the New Brunswick government was under a constitutional obligation to provide an indigent mother with state-funded counsel so that she could respond to a custody application by the government in child protection proceedings. The mother, who was receiving social assistance when she applied for legal aid, was told that custody applications were not covered by New Brunswick's legal aid plan. However, the court ruled that the principles of fundamental justice contained in section 7 of the *Canadian Charter of Rights and Freedoms* required that the mother have legal representation at the custody hearing. The court noted that section 7 provides every parent with the right to a fair hearing and that fairness required the parent to have the opportunity to present her case effectively and to be represented by a lawyer. The desire of the New Brunswick government to limit the costs of legal-aid spending was not, according to the court, justification for breaching the parents' charter rights to a fair hearing (Dranoff, 2005:367). The creation of new procedural opportunities, which is termed the "extension of formal facilities," is exemplified by the development of small-claims courts, which were established in a number of provinces in the 1970s in an attempt to make justice accessible to citizens, as well as in the creation of publicly funded legal aid with services provided by either salaried or fee-for-service lawyers. The extension of formal rights and of formal facilities has definite implications for the criminal justice system in the form of greater protection of individual rights.

A rather different perspective on law in social change is presented by Lawrence M. Friedman. He describes two types of change through law: "planning" and "disruption." *Planning* "refers to architectural construction of new forms of social order and social interaction. *Disruption* refers to the blocking or amelioration of existing social forms and relations" (Friedman, 1973:25). Planning through law is an omnipresent feature of the modern world. Although it is most pronounced in socialist countries (for example, five-year plans of social and economic development), all nations are committed to planning to a greater or lesser extent. Both planning and disruption operate within the existing legal system and can bring about "positive" or "negative" social change, depending on one's perspective.

Although revolution is the most distinct and obvious form of disruption, milder forms are everywhere. Judicial review is frequently disruptive. . . . Activist reformers have [also] played a sensational role. . . in the last decade. Ralph Nader is the most well-known example. . . He stimulates use of legal process as a lever of social change. Much of his work is technically disruptive; it focuses on litigation and injunctions, on stopping government dead in its tracks, when it fails to meet his ethical and policies standards. Legal disruption can. . . include lawsuits;. . . reformers have frequently gone to court to upset many old and established arrangements. (Friedman, 1975:277)

Whether the change produced by such action is considered "destructive" or "constructive," the fact remains that law can be a highly effective device for producing social change.

Although Friedman considers social change through litigation an American phenomenon, he raises the question, will this spread to other countries? His own response is that creative disruption of the judicial type presupposes a number of conditions that include an activist legal profession, financial resources, activist judges, a genuine social movement, and what he describes as "the strongest condition": that "elites—the power holders—must accept the results of disruptive litigation, like it or not" (Friedman, 1975:278). Clearly, the legal structures of socialist or authoritarian countries are not designed to accommodate these patterns.

The Efficacy of Law as an Instrument of Social Change

As an instrument of social change, law entails two interrelated processes: the institutionalization and the internalization of patterns of behaviour. Institutionalization of a pattern of behaviour refers to the establishment of a norm with provisions for its enforcement (such as nondiscrimination in employment), and internalization of a pattern of behaviour means the incorporation of the value or values implicit in a law (for example, discrimination is "wrong"). William M. Evan notes: "Law. . . can affect behaviour directly only through the process of institutionalization; if, however, the institutionalization process is successful, it, in turn, facilitates the internalization of attitudes or beliefs" (1965:287).

Law is often an effective mechanism in the promotion or reinforcement of social change. However, the extent to which law can provide an effective impetus for social change varies according to the conditions present in a particular situation. Evan (1965:288) suggests that a law is likely to be successful to induce change if it meets the following seven conditions: (1) the law must emanate from an authoritative and prestigious source; (2) the law must introduce its rationale in terms that are understandable and compatible with existing values; (3) the advocates of the change should make reference to other communities or countries with which the population identifies and where the law is already in effect; (4) the enforcement of the law must be aimed at making the change in a relatively short time; (5) those enforcing the law must themselves be very much committed to the change intended by the law; (6) the instrumentation of the law should include positive as well as negative sanctions; and (7) the enforcement of the law should be reasonable, not only in the sanctions used but also in the protection of the rights of those who stand to lose by violation of the law.

The efficacy of law as a mechanism of social change is conditioned by a number of factors. One is the amount of information available about a given piece of legislation, decision, or ruling. When there is insufficient transmission of information about these matters, the law will not produce its intended effect. Ignorance of the law is not considered an excuse for disobedience, but ignorance obviously limits the law's effectiveness. In the same vein, law is limited to the extent that rules are not stated precisely, and not only because people are uncertain about what the rules mean. Vague rules permit multiple perceptions and interpretations. What do expressions such as "undue exploitation of sex" mean and how is the "undue exploitation of sex" to be distinguished from a "due" exploitation of sex? What do phrases such as "wilfully promote" or "unreasonable delay" mean?

Gudgeon (2003:133) observes that, in this country, "[p]erhaps no area of law is vaguer than the rules and regulations that oversee sex for hire. . . . Lap dancing, for example, which blurs the line between prostitution and performance (if such a line really exists), is either legal or illegal, depending on your interpretation. Body rubs are fine. . . unless the rubber is compelled by the business' owner to provide full service to the rubbee. Even prostitution is technically legal in this country, though conducting the business of prostitution by and large isn't. Got it?" As one can appreciate, there is an obvious need for the language of the law to be free of ambiguity, with care exercised to prevent multiple interpretations and loopholes (Carter, 1998; Carter and Burke, 2005; Durand, 2002).

Legal regulations and the required behaviour of people to whom the law is addressed must be clearly known, and the sanctions for noncompliance need to be enunciated precisely. The effectiveness of the law is directly related to the extent and nature of perception of officially and clearly stated and sanctioned rules. Perceptions of rules, in turn, vary with their sources. Rules are more likely to be accepted if they reflect a notion of fairness and justice that is prevalent in society and when their source is considered legitimate (Jacob, 1995). It should be noted, however, that the contrast between legitimacy and legality can remain, at times, confusing. As Carl J. Friedrich (1985:202) observes: "Law must not be seen as operating only in one dimension of the state, but in the many dimensions of the community if we are to comprehend legitimacy as an objective pattern. Legitimacy is related to right and justice; without a clarification of what is to be understood by the rightness and justice of law, legitimacy cannot be comprehended either. Hitler's rule was legal but it was not legitimate. It had a basis in law but not in right and justice."

The responsiveness of enforcement agencies to a law also has an impact on its effectiveness (see, for example, Kerley, 2005). Law enforcement agents not only communicate rules, but also show that the rules are taken seriously and that punishment for their violation is likely. But for a law to be enforceable, the behaviour to be changed must be observable. For example, it is more difficult to enforce a law against incest than a law against communicating for the purposes of prostitution. Moreover, law enforcement agents need to be fully committed to enforcing a new law. One reason for the failure of Prohibition, for example, was the unwillingness of law enforcement agents to instrument the law. Selective enforcement of a law also hinders its effectiveness. The more high-status individuals are arrested and punished, the greater will be the likelihood that a particular law will achieve its intended objective (Zimring and Hawkins, 1975:337). Laws regularly and uniformly enforced across class and group lines tend to be perceived as more binding than they would have been if they were seldom and selectively enforced, because enforcement establishes behavioural norms, and in time, as E. Adamson Hoebel (1954:15) puts it: "The *norm* takes on the quality of the *normative*. What the most do, others should do."

As a strategy of social change, law has certain unique advantages and limitations as compared with other agents of change. Although these advantages and limitations go hand in hand and represent the opposite sides of the same coin, for analytical purposes we will examine them separately. The following discussion will focus on some of the more obvious reasons why law can facilitate change in society.

ADVANTAGES OF LAW IN CREATING SOCIAL CHANGE

As emphasized earlier, identifying the perimeters of change and attributing change to a particular causal variable or a set of variables should always be undertaken with prudence. In many instances, the state of the art of social-change endeavours is not methodologically sophisticated enough to distinguish clearly among causal, necessary, sufficient, and contributory conditions to produce desired effects in society. Social change is a complex, multi-faceted phenomenon brought about by a host of social forces. At times, change is slow and uneven and can be brought about by different factors to differing degrees. Change in society may be initiated by a number of means. Of these, the most drastic is revolution, aimed at fundamental changes in the power relation of classes within society. Others include rebellion, riot, *coup d'état*, various forms of violent protest movements, sit-ins, boycotts, strikes, demonstrations, social movements, education, mass media, technological innovations, ideology, and various forms of planned but nonlegal social-change efforts dealing with various behaviours and practices at different levels in society.

Compared with this incomplete list of change-inducing forces, the law has certain advantages. Change efforts through law tend to be more focused and specific. Change through law is a deliberate, rational, and conscious effort to alter a specific behaviour or practice. The intentions of legal norms are clearly stated, with a concomitant outline of the means of instrumentation and enforcement and sanction provisions. Essentially, change through law aims at rectifying, improving, ameliorating, or controlling behaviours and practices in precisely defined social situations—as identified by the proponents of a particular change. The advantages of law as an instrument of social change are attributed to the fact that law in society is seen as legitimate, more or less rational, authoritative, institutionalized, generally not disruptive, and backed by mechanisms of enforcement and sanctions.

Legitimate Authority

A principal advantage of law as an instrument of social change is the general feeling in society that legal commands or prohibitions ought to be observed even by those critical of the law in question. To a great extent, this feeling of obligation depends on respect for legitimate authority (Andenaes, 1977:52) and the perception of power (Ewick and Silbey, 2003).

The classic treatment of **legitimate authority** is that of Max Weber (1947). Weber defines "imperative coordination" as the probability that specific commands from a given source would be obeyed by given groups of persons. Obedience to commands can rest on a variety of considerations, from simple habituation to a purely rational calculation of advantage. But there is always a minimum of voluntary submission based on an interest in obedience. In extreme cases, this interest in obedience can be seen in the tendency for people to commit illegal acts when so ordered by authority (and for others to excuse such acts as not subject to ordinary morality). Perhaps the most notable example of the "only following a superior's orders" defence appeared at the Nuremberg trials, where 22 major Nazi war criminals were brought before the International Military Tribunal at Nuremberg, Germany. However, anticipating this response and recognizing that the use of this defence would undermine the entire case for the prosecution (and make only Hitler responsible for the atrocities committed), the court decided, in advance of the proceedings, that it would only consider this defence as an aid for establishing degrees of guilt.

Obedience to authority can be based on custom, affectual ties, or a purely material complex of interests—what Weber calls "ideal motives." These purely material interests result in a relatively unstable situation and must therefore be supplemented by other elements, both affectual and ideal. But even this complex of motives does not form a sufficiently reliable basis for a system of imperative co-operation, so that another important element must be added: the belief in legitimacy.

Following Max Weber, there are three types of legitimate authority—traditional, charismatic, and rational-legal. **Traditional authority** bases its claims to legitimacy on an established belief in the sanctity of traditions and the legitimacy of the status of those exercising authority. The obligation of obedience is not a matter of acceptance of the legality of an impersonal order but, rather, a matter of personal loyalty. The "rule of elders" is illustrative of traditional authority. **Charismatic authority** bases its claim to legitimacy on devotion to the specific and unusual sanctity, heroism, or exemplary character of an individual and the normative patterns that are revealed or ordained. The charismatic leader is obeyed by virtue of personal trust in his or her revelations, or in his or her exemplary qualities. Illustrations of individuals with charismatic authority include Moses, Christ, Mohammed, and Gandhi.

Rational-legal authority bases its claims to legitimacy on a belief in the legality of normative rules and in the right of those elevated to authority to issue commands under such rules. In such authority, obedience is owed to a legally established impersonal order. The individuals who exercise authority of office are shown obedience only by virtue of the formal legality of their commands, and only within the scope of authority of their office. Legal authority is not entirely conceptually distinct from traditional authority, although the distinction is nonetheless worth having. In modern society, "legality" suggests a component of rationality that traditional authority seems to lack (see also Berg and Meadwell, 2004). Indeed, during the transition to modernity, especially in the 16th and 17th centuries, authority tends more and more to be rationalized in distinctively legalistic and voluntaristic terms. "Rational" people "voluntarily" make a "contract," which generates the impersonal legal order.

Theory and research show that legitimate authority can wield considerable influence over both actions and attitudes (see, for example, Tyler et al., 1988). It can be the result of both the coercive processes involved and the individual's internalized values regarding legitimate authority. There is a tendency on the part of individuals to assume that the law has the right to regulate behaviour and then to justify conformity to the law. To an extent, obedience to the law stems from respect for the underlying process: "People obey the law, 'because it is the law.' This means they have general respect for procedures and for the system. They feel, for some reason, that they should obey [if a law is passed by parliament]. . . , if a judge makes a decision, if the city council passes an ordinance. If they were forced to explain why, they might refer to some concept of democracy, or the rule of law, or some other popular theory sustaining the political system" (Friedman, 1975:114).

Acceptance of legitimate authority can also minimize the possibility of cognitive dissonance (discrepancies between action and cognition) by interpreting or construing legally prohibited action as "wrong" or morally bad. The law, consequently, not only represents accepted modes of behaviour but also enforces and reinforces those accepted modes of behaviour (Vining, 1986). Further, it defines the "correct" way of behaving in our daily lives. This effect is ingrained and institutionalized and is present even without the sanctions that are part of the enforcement machinery. In fact, most people in most situations tend to comply with the law without consciously assessing the possibility of legal sanctions

statute that commits the central government to funding a large portion of the health-care system [despite a sharply curtailed constitutional competence over health care] *so long as these governments maintain systems that adhere to a set of requirements* designed to achieve universal access" (Bogart, 2002:65, emphasis added). Rewards are also frequently part of regulatory statutes attempting to change established patterns of economic behaviour. Those who violate such laws not only lose prospective rewards but also may be liable for fines or criminal penalties. Grossman and Grossman point out: "Laws or statutes which seek positive societal changes of major proportion must rely as much on education and persuasion as on negative sanctions. For the carrot and stick approach to be successful, the latter must be visible and occasionally used" (1971:70).

The circumstances are different where the changes sought through the law are the reduction or the elimination of deviant behaviour. In such instances, the law does not provide rewards or incentives to dissuade individuals from committing such acts—only the possibility, if not the certainty, of detection and punishment. In such instances, the emphasis is on deterrence, punishment, and vengeance, and the objective is the elimination or the reduction of a particular type of behaviour considered harmful.

There are, of course, additional discernible advantages of the law in creating social change. For example, the law as an instrument of change can effectively be involved in the context of John Stuart Mill's notion of the law:

> (i) to achieve common purposes which cannot be left to the forces of supply and demand—such as education; (ii) to protect the immature and helpless; (iii) to control the power of associations, managed not only by the persons directly interested but by delegated agencies; (iv) to protect individuals acting in concert in cases where such action cannot be effective without legal sanctions; (v) to achieve objects of importance to society, present and future, which are beyond the powers of individuals or voluntary associations or which, if within their powers, would not normally be undertaken by them. (Ginsberg, 1965:230)

The list of conceivable advantages of the law as an instrument of social change is indeed incomplete. What has been said so far is intended simply to demonstrate that the law has a peculiar and unparalleled position among agents of social change. At the same time, it has certain limitations. Knowledge and an awareness of the limitations will help us to understand more fully the role of the law in social change, and they need to be taken into account for the use of the law in change efforts.

LIMITATIONS OF LAW IN CREATING SOCIAL CHANGE

In a period when alienation from virtually all social institutions proceeds swiftly, when there is widespread demoralization brought on by uncontrollable economic conditions, when people are suffering from a "crisis of confidence," it would seem a bit absurd to advance the idea that the law is an expression of the will of the people. For the great majority of individuals, the law originates externally to them and is imposed upon them in a manner that can be considered coercive. In reality, very few individuals actually participate in the formation of new laws and legislation. Consequently, one of the limitations of the law as an instrument of social change is the possibility of prevailing conflict of interest, which tends to determine which laws are promulgated and which alternatives are rejected. Other limitations bearing on the efficacy of the law as an instrument of social change include the divergent views on the law as a tool of directed social change and the prevailing morality and values. In the following pages, we will consider these limitations separately and then examine a number of conditions conducive to resistance to change from sociological, psychological, cultural, and economic perspectives.

In every society, access to scarce resources and highly cherished objects is limited. In the struggle to achieve them, some individuals and groups win; others lose. Several decades ago, Max Weber recognized, as did Karl Marx before him, that many laws are created to serve special economic interests. Individuals with the control of ownership of material goods are generally favoured by laws since "economic interests are among the strongest factors influencing the creation of law" (Weber, 1968:334). Weber further recognized that other special interests, in addition to the economic ones, influence the formation of law. Says Weber: "Law guarantees by no means only economic interest, but rather the most diverse interests ranging from the most elementary ones of protection of personal security to such purely ideal goods as personal honour or the honour of the divine powers. Above all, it guarantees political, ecclesiastical, familial, and other positions of authority as well as positions of social pre-eminence of any kind" (1968:333).

There are two important insights contained in Weber's points. The first is that conflict of interest provides the framework in which laws are framed and change is brought about. Consequently, social stratification in a society will determine to a large extent the part laws will play in bringing about change based on the selectiveness and preferences exercised by those who promulgate those changes. The second point concerns the significance of the use of power to back up those changes. Studies of the legislative, judicial, and administrative processes in a society could lead very quickly to a discovery of not only who wields the power in society but also what interests are significant and influential in that group. Thus, the law as an instrument of a change can be viewed in the context of the organization of power and the processes by which interests are established in everyday social life; the resulting changes might very well be evaluated in those terms.

In a sense it is obvious, understandable, and even tautological that the powerful make and administer the laws in society. If anything gets done, it is because somebody had the power to do it. At the same time, those who are powerful and influential tend to use the law to protect their advantageous position in society, and for them "the law in effect structures the power (superordinate, subordinate) relationships in a society; it maintains the status quo and protects the various strata against each other" (Hertzler, 1961:421).

One might consider, in this context, the uncommon latitude that has traditionally been shown in Canada to those corporations who pollute the environment. Dranoff (2005:8) charges that both the provincial and federal governments "have been abandoning or reducing their role as guardians of public health and safety" by their failure to sanction environmental polluters. In Ontario, she argues, this move can be discerned in the government's elimination of "many environmental regulations without public consultation, moving toward privatization of such essentials as drinking water, and slashing funds for environmental programs, including tests of drinking water." She notes that charges against environmental polluters fell by about 50 percent from 1992 to 1997— a situation that "resulted in a number of public tragedies, including, in 2000, an outbreak of E. Coli bacteria in Walkerton, Ontario, that caused seven fatalities." More recently, she notes, a 2002 Sierra Legal Defence Fund report found that, while Ontario experienced over 1900 water protection law violations in 2000, only four of the approximately 200 violators were charged. The response to environmental pollution on a federal level, she notes, has been unequally uninspired:

> Federal environmental charges against polluters dropped 78 percent between 1992 and 1998. No one was jailed in the ten-year period between 1988 and 1998 under Canada's *Environmental Protection Act* or *Fisheries Act*. And statistics released in 2000 reveal that Canadian imports of hazardous waste are rising sharply and a growing proportion of it is being dumped without treatment rather than being recycled. The volume of hazardous waste imported in 1999 exceeded all hazardous waste produced within Canada that year. The budget for Environment Canada has been reduced by about 40 percent over the past few year. (Dranoff, 2005:9)

In addition, Dranoff observes that even though the 1988 *Canadian Environmental Protection Act* was intended to eliminate toxic pollution, it only assessed 31 out of 32 000 chemicals in the 11 years that it was in force. Moreover, while this legislation was revised (and purportedly strengthened) in both 1999 and 2003, "a 2004 report by the Canadian Environmental Law Association. . . shows that the amount of toxic pollutants reportedly released and transferred had increased by 49 percent over a seven-year period. Ninety percent of companies report no change projected for 2003 to 2005. Fines remain low, and even those who do face fines deduct them as a business expense" (Dranoff, 2005:9).

Many legislative enactments, administrative rulings, and judicial decisions reflect the power configurations in society. Some groups and associations are more powerful than others, and by virtue of being at the centre of power, they are better able to reinforce their interests than those at the periphery. Even members of the legal profession are considered "professional go-betweens" for the principal political, corporate, and other interest groups, and hence serve to "unify the power elite" (Mills, 1957:289; Porter, 1965). Furthermore, as we noted in Chapter 3, many people are often apathetic about or unaware of an issue, but even when they are concerned, they are frequently unable to organize and thus successfully impose their preference on the legislature.

Curiously, however, those who are supposed to be coerced or oppressed by a system of laws imposed upon them by a ruling minority often seem unaware of their coercion or oppression. Indeed, they are frequently among the strongest partisans of the existing legal system. It may be argued that they have been "indoctrinated" by the ruling establishment, which uses its power to confuse them as to their true interests. But this requires that we distinguish between what people define as their interests and what their "true interests" are, a distinction that has given rise to a great deal of complex, subtle, and inconclusive polemics.

There are numerous instances of racial, ethnic, and sexual orientation minorities, women, and workers organizing to promote what they perceive to be in their best interests (see, for example, Cowan, 2005; Scholes, 2002). For example, labour was instrumental in the enactment of a series of legislations dealing with occupational safety and health, flextime work schedules, collective bargaining, and unemployment compensation. Activists in the first and second wave of the women's movement in Canada have seen their efforts result in such changes as the right to vote, the entrance of women into higher education, reforms in the direction of greater equality between spouses within family law, equal pay legislation, the striking down of Canada's abortion law, and legislation providing redress for victims of discrimination, domestic violence, and sexual harassment (Backhouse, 2004; Morton and Allen, 2001). The recent research of Margaret Walton-Robert (2004) highlights the civic participation of immigrant women in advancing the rights of women within the development of the *Immigration and Refugee Protection Act*, which came into effect in Canada in June 2002. Activists in the LGBT (lesbian, gay, bisexual, and trans-gendered) community have also lobbied aggressively for more equitable laws for LGBT people and achieved considerable success (EGALE, 2004).

As evidence of how profound the changes incurred by law may be, consider that from Confederation until 1969, homosexual acts were punishable by up to 14 years in prison under Canadian criminal law. From 1946 to 1977, a practising homosexual faced the possibility of life in prison if decreed a "criminal sexual psychopath" (Kinsman, 1996). It was not until 1969 that homosexual acts, taking place in private between two consenting adults over the age of 21 (later reduced to 18), were decriminalized in this country. Moreover, when Quebec included sexual orientation in its *Charter of Human Rights and Freedom*, it became the first province in Canada to support homosexual civil rights (Gudgeon, 2003:198); until 1986, Quebec would remain the only jurisdiction in Canada in which "sexual orientation" was a prohibited ground of discrimination under statute law (Yogis et al., 1996:1).

In the decades that followed, all provincial and territorial human rights acts have been amended to include sexual orientation as a prohibited basis for discrimination (with Alberta forced to do so by a Supreme Court of Canada decision [*Vriend v Alberta* (1998)]) (Filax, 2004). In 1996, the federal *Human Rights Act* was amended to include "sexual orientation" as a prohibited ground of discrimination. With general human rights protection enshrined in federal as well as provincial/territorial legislation, the focus of activists shifted to issues falling under the rubric of the "family" (e.g., marriage, spousal benefits, adoption).

Throughout the 1990s, and with growing momentum in the new millennium, many of the rights and obligations that were once exclusively associated with marriage (e.g., the right to spousal support; the right to benefit from a partner's job benefits plan) were extended to couples living in marriage-like relationships. In 1990, the Ontario government extended full coverage of supplementary health, hospital, and dental benefits to the same-sex partners of provincial government employees. In 1995, the federal government amended its policies, extending leave-related benefits (e.g., bereavement leave, leave for family-related responsibilities) to the same-sex partners of federal civil servants. In that same year, an Ontario provincial court judge ruled that, under the *Child and Family Services Act*, homosexual couples have the right to adopt a child. In the 1996 case of *M. v. H.*, the opposite-sex definition of "spouse" in Ontario's *Family Law Act* was struck down when, both at trial and on appeal, the courts ruled that M. was entitled to sue H. for support following the breakdown of their lesbian relationship.

In 1998, the province of British Columbia enacted changes to its *Adoption Act* and *Family Relations Act* that gave same-sex couples who had cohabited for a period of two years the same rights and responsibilities as their opposite-sex counterparts, including pension and inheritance rights. Other changes in that year were prompted by an Ontario Court of Appeal ruling that declared the federal government's definition of "spouse" in the *Income Tax Act*, which excluded same-sex survivor benefits from employers' pension plans, was unconstitutional. A year later, the Supreme Court of Canada dismissed an appeal by Ontario's Attorney General of the 1996 *M. v. H*. Decision, upholding the right of same-sex couples to seek and obtain spousal support in the same way as opposite-sex common-law couples and informing the Ontario government that it had six months to ensure that its legislation in this area was constitutional. Although the Ontario government, in response, passed an omnibus bill in 1999 that amended 67 of its laws to include same-sex couples, it did so by creating a separate class of "same-sex partners" rather than providing same-sex couples with all of the rights of opposite-sex common-law couples.

When the Quebec National Assembly unanimously passed Bill 32 in June 1999, the Quebec government became the first Canadian province to ensure that same-sex couples would receive all the benefits and responsibilities of opposite-sex couples, excluding the right to marriage. Other notable changes in that year occurred when the Alberta government joined with Ontario and British Columbia in allowing same-sex couples to jointly adopt a child and when the British Columbia government introduced the "Definition of Spouse Amendment," which expanded the definition of a spouse in that province to ensure that "persons of the same gender" would be treated the same as opposite-sex couples in relation to such matters as wills, estates, and inheritance. Although that year also witnessed the federal Parliament's voting to preserve the opposite-sex definition of marriage, the tides of change were clearly moving in the opposite direction.

In 2000, for example, the federal government of Canada enacted the *Modernization of Benefits and Obligations Act,* which equalized the treatment of same-sex and opposite-sex common-law couples under 68 federal laws (EGALE, 2001b). In separate legislation that year, the *Immigration Act*'s "family class" provisions were expanded to include same-sex couples. Also in that year, Nova Scotia introduced legislation that revised the definition of "spouse" in family law to include common-law and same-sex partners who had cohabited for a period of one year. The following year, Nova Scotia's same-sex couples became the first Canadians to be able to register their unions under registered domestic partnership legislation. In 2001, Quebec extended the definition of spouse to same-sex couples in a "de facto" union in 39 of its laws.

Perhaps the most noteworthy legal change, however, has occurred in relation to the definition of marriage itself. Under the *Constitution Act*, the federal Parliament of Canada controls who may marry (i.e., the capacity of persons to marry), while the provinces regulate the technical aspects of the "solemnization of marriage" (e.g., who can perform the ceremony, how the deed is registered) (EGALE, 2004). In July 2002, three Ontario Superior Court judges made Canadian legal history when they ruled that the opposite-sex limitation in common law (which restricted marriage to the union of one man and one woman) was unconstitutional. This decision was echoed in 2003 by courts in British Columbia, Quebec, the Yukon and, in 2004, in Manitoba, Nova Scotia, Saskatchewan, Quebec, and Newfoundland and Labrador. In the fall of 2004, the federal government of Canada presented a "Reference re Same-Sex Marriage" to the Supreme Court of Canada, requesting that the Court clarify whether the opposite-sex requirement for marriage was consistent with Charter guarantees of equality. In response, the Supreme Court stated that the federal government had the power to change the definition of marriage to include same-sex couples and that their doing so would be constitutional. The Supreme Court of Canada likened our systems of laws to a "living tree which by way of progressive interpretation, accommodates and addresses the realities of modern life," noting that the definition of marriage in Canada's constitution "does not exclude same-sex marriage." The Court also observed that clergy could, as an expression of freedom of religion, refuse to conduct marriage ceremonies involving same-sex couples. With the passage of Bill C-38, Parliament changed the definition of marriage to comply with the Charter and, on July 20, 2005, the *Civil Marriage Act* received Royal Assent.

Aboriginal peoples have also engaged with the law, seeking recognition of their sovereign status as the ancestral occupants of Canada. They have laboured to reclaim their historic land and contractual rights from the government and sought the right to make and interpret laws in relation to their own people. As Fleras (2005:314, 320) observes,

"Aboriginal peoples increasingly claim to be relatively autonomous political communities with an inherent right to self-determining autonomy" and seek "to construct Aboriginal models of self-determining autonomy over jurisdiction, identity and political voice."

As early as five years prior to the Northwest Rebellion of 1885, the Plains Cree began to forge a political alliance to force the federal government to honour what they viewed as treaty commitments. In the 1880s, the Nishga (Nisga'a) in British Columbia began their long campaign to obtain government recognition of their Aboriginal land rights and became, in 1912, the first native group to initiate a legally constituted land claim action against the Canadian government. On February 15, 1996, the Nisga'a Tribal Council and representatives of both the British Columbia and federal governments initialled a historic agreement in principle which called for the creation of Nisga'a government with communal ownership of and self-government over approximately 1900 square kilometres of land in the Nass River valley. In 1999, the agreement was signed and provincial legislation passed which ratified the treaty—the first treaty in British Columbia since 1899. "This landmark 'treaty' in which enabling legislation embraces a kind of Aboriginal sovereignty has finally put to rest an historical fiction: namely, that Aboriginal claims to self-government were extinguished at Confederation when all legislative powers were divided between federal and provincial authorities" (Fleras, 2005:317).

Although the Nisga'a Final Settlement (which took effect in May 2000) protects federal jurisdiction over criminal law, Canadian citizenship, and the Charter, it "secures a degree of exclusive and paramount jurisdiction over [Nisga'a] tribal land and citizens that virtually amounted to a third tier of governance alongside the federal and provincial" (Fleras, 2005:318). In addition to a land base, the Final Settlement provides band members with "control of forest and fishery resources; $200 million in cash (but much more wealth if timber and mining rights are included); release from *Indian Act* provisions; a municipal level of government including control over policing, education, community services, and taxes; . . . the eventual elimination of on-reserve tax exemptions (including sales and income tax); . . . forest and timber cutting rights; access to oil and mineral resources; a 26 percent share of the salmon fishery, plus $21.5 million to purchase boats and equipment; . . . a fishery-conservation trust . . . [and] exclusive jurisdiction in matters related to language and culture in addition to membership and property—even when these conflict with federal/ provincial laws" (Fleras, 2005:318).

Fleras (2005:318–319) acknowledges that Nisga'a powers remain "considerably less than those implied by federal recognition of Canada's Aboriginal tribes as 'peoples' with an 'inherent right to self-government.' . . . The Nisga'a do not have absolute or sovereign authority since federal laws will generally prevail when key jurisdictions collide. The Nisga'a will have full policing services on Nisga'a land, but provincial standards will continue to apply to police training, conduct and qualifications. . . . And while the Nisga'a have the right to fish, they must adhere to conservation measures contained in the Agreement." Nevertheless, he emphasizes that the Nisga'a Final Settlement represents the enduring efforts of "six generations of Nisga'a who since 1887 have tried to achieve self-government by establishing native title to ancestral land that had never been surrendered to European powers" (p. 320).

Aboriginal efforts were also responsible for three provisions within the *Constitution Act*, 1982, specifically: (i) section 25 of the Charter, which provides that guarantees of rights and freedoms does not detract "from any Aboriginal, treaty or other rights or freedoms" that Aboriginal people possess as the result of the Royal Proclamation, 1763, or any then-existent or future land-claims agreements; (2) section 35 (in Part II) of the act, which recognizes and affirms "the existing Aboriginal and treaty rights of Aboriginal peoples"— a significant phrase which acknowledges Aboriginal rights as inherent rather than delegated rights; and (3) section 37, which guarantees the convening of a constitutional conference which would include "an item respecting constitutional matters that directly affect the Aboriginal peoples of Canada, including the identification and definition of the rights of those peoples to be included in the Constitution of Canada" within one year of the act coming into force (Carson, 1999). After being largely ignored by government until 1939, the Inuit negotiated the dramatic land claim settlement which resulted in the creation of the new territory of Nunavut ("Our Land") in April of 1999 and a factual situation of Aboriginal self-government.

Do these types of developments not mean that minorities can also become a part of the power structure? And if they are, does this not mean that the distribution of power in society is more widespread and complicated than is suggested by writers who speak of a simple division of society into "the powerful" and "the powerless" or who suggest, for example, that Aboriginal peoples are destined to remain in "helpless bondage to fundamental principles firmly established in the common law" (Bell and Asch, 1997:45)?

It is debatable whether the existence of conflicting interests could really be construed as pointing to a serious limitation of the law as an instrument of change. The points raised concerning the power of certain interest groups are valid, but the actual mechanics of change through the law would in any case preclude inclusion of large segments of the population. Large-scale participation of the citizenry in legal change, even in a democratic society, is seldom feasible. But lack of participation does not necessarily mean lack of representation. In Canada, the United States, and most parts of Europe, people do have access (albeit of varying degrees) to lawmakers and to the legal apparatus, and their aspirations for change through the law have, at least on occasion, been partially realized (Cairns, 2000; Delgado and Stefancic, 2000; Fournier and Grey, 1997; Monture-Agnes, 1999; Singh, 2002).

Law as a Policy Instrument

A different school of thought on the limits of the law as an instrument of social change is epitomized by Yehezkel Dror. He contends that "law by itself is only one component of a large set of policy instruments and usually cannot and is not used by itself. Therefore, focusing exclusive attention on law as a tool of directed social change is a case of tunnel vision, which lacks the minimum perspective necessary for making sense from the observed phenomena" (Dror, 1970:554). He suggests that it is necessary to redefine the subject of "law as a tool of directed social change" and to consider it as part of other social policy instruments, since the law is but one of many policy instruments that must be used in combination. In the context of social problems such as race relations, public safety, drug abuse, and pollution, "the necessity to use law as a policy instrument should be quite convincing" (Dror, 1970:555). This view certainly has merits. At times, change through the law can and should be construed as an ingredient of a larger policy. However, the law is often used as an instrument of change outside of the context of a broad policymaking framework. This is typically the situation in reform-oriented litigation, where the object is to alter a particular institutionalized practice. For example, the 1988 Supreme Court decision to strike down the abortion sections of the Criminal Code as unconstitutional was not carried out within specific policy considerations, and yet it obviously had a tremendous impact on women seeking to terminate pregnancy legally. Although judicial decisions are generally not rendered a policy instrument, because of the adversarial nature of litigation, legislative and administrative reforms dealing with larger social issues should take place in a broader social policymaking framework such as environmental and natural resource management activities (Sterner, 2003). Such an approach would greatly enhance the efficacy of the law as an instrument of change. To this end, Dror advocates the establishment of interdisciplinary teams of lawyers, social scientists, and policy analysts to engage in relevant studies and prepare policy recommendations. Increasingly, this seemingly common-sense advice is being translated into practical applications, and policy preparatory and advisory teams are becoming interdisciplinary.

Morality and Values

The sociological literature recognizes, as James P. Levine (1970:592) notes, that the ability of the law to produce social change is probabilistic, contingent, and sequential. If a law is enacted or a court decision is rendered, it is probable that certain changes will follow, but the degree of change is contingent on certain prevailing circumstances. The law is sequential to the degree that it must precede certain desired changes, but because a large number of factors influence change, the time lag is not obvious. Moreover, a number of factors other than the law may have an effect on change in a particular area, which means that the cause-and-effect relationship between the law and change is very difficult to identify. Some of these factors are related to the prevailing morality and values in society (see, for example, Sterba, 2004).

Patrick Devlin (1965) argues that a society owes its existence less to its institutions than to the shared morality that binds it together. Although his thesis is only partly true, morality and values affect the efficacy of the law in social change. Obviously, society could not exist without accepting certain basic values, principles, and standards. On certain issues, such as violence, truth, individual liberty, and human dignity, a shared morality is essential. This does not mean, however, that all the values in our shared morality are basic and essential, or that decline in one value spells decline in all the rest. Moreover, not all our values are essential. Rules about property, for example, are not; some principles about property are essential, but no society needs to have those very property principles that are characteristic of, for example, Canada—the principle of private ownership. A society could own all property in common without ceasing to count as a society.

In general, when the law is used as an instrument of social change, it needs the support of society. Says Schur: "A good illustration of the systematic ineffectiveness of unsupported law is provided by the utter failure of legislation designed to enforce private morality" (1968:132). Thus, an obvious limitation of the law in social change appears when it tries to deal with what may be called moral issues in society. The well-known failure of the prohibition of alcohol through legislation to produce a truly "dry" society, or to keep most people from drinking, is a potent example of the limitation of the law to bring about social change in public "morals."

A comparable situation exists with regard to the prohibition of several kinds of drugs, especially marijuana. Interestingly, the marijuana laws have been called the "new prohibition," to underline the similarity to alcohol prohibition and the futility of legal control of consumption of those substances (Nadelmann, 2006). Clearly, "behaviour that is perceived of as satisfying important drives is more difficult to extinguish than behaviour that satisfies less compelling drives" (Zimring and Hawkins, 1975:332). In fact, some argue that mari-juana at least should be a source of pleasure, not pain or shame:

> We should be free to cultivate and sell and buy this "euphoriant." The only controls should be those imposed to protect [us] from bogus or polluted merchandise. With the dreadful example of Prohibition before us, it seems nearly unthinkable that we should have done it again. . . . When will we learn that in a democracy it is for the people to tell the government, not for the govern-ment to tell the people, what makes them happy? (Goldman, quoted in *Behavior Today*, 1979:8)

The link between law and morality in the making and unmaking of law raises two ques-tions: (1) What needs to be done in considering a change in the law when moral opinion is divided? Are there criteria other than individual likes and dislikes to which appeal can be made? (2) How can the line be drawn between that part of morality or immorality which needs legal enforcement and that which the law ought to leave alone (Ginsberg, 1965:232)? In response to these questions, Morris Ginsberg suggests that the law ought to deal only with what can be ascertained on reliable evidence and with acts that can be pre-cisely defined, and primarily with overt or external observable acts; and the law must, as far as possible, respect privacy. He contends that these are "principles of demarcation aris-ing from the limitations inherent in the machinery of the law" (Ginsberg, 1965:238).

Thus, laws are more likely to bring about changes in what may be called external behav-iour. However, changes in external behaviour are after a while usually followed by changes in values, morals, and attitudes. As Morroe Berger (1952:172) emphasizes: "While it is true that the province of law is 'external' behaviour, it is also true that in an urban, secular soci-ety an increasing number of relations fall within this province. Thus the range of behaviour that can be called 'external' is enlarged. At the same time, law can influence 'external' acts which affect or constitute the conditions for the exercise of the private inclinations and tastes that are said to be beyond the realm of law." The fact that a change in attitude is only partial at first does not make it any the less of a change. This is contrary to the arguments advanced decades ago by William Graham Sumner (1906), which since have been echoed by many, that "stateways cannot change folkways."

Sumner contended that the law is limited to the regulation of individual behaviour, and it cannot be used to alter attitudes, values, and morality. There are many examples both to support and to refute this contention (see, for example, Peach, 2002). There are several instances where the promulgation of laws did not result in widespread acceptance by the population. For example, the Constitution of India purportedly outlawed discrimination against untouchables, but that has not significantly changed the values and attitudes of most Indians (Seidman, 1978:156). Similarly, one may consider the fate of Ontario's employment equity law, where "the Ontario New Democratic Party's (NDP) approach to employment equity gave rise to the complete annihilation of this law at the hands of the Ontario Tories. . . . The public had become overwhelmingly fed up with the whole idea of employment equity" (Borovoy, 1999:xv).

On the other side of the debate regarding the power of law to change attitudes, there are several studies suggesting that law can, indeed, alter values and attitudes. For example, stud-ies on the effects of anti-discrimination laws in situations such as "armed forces units, hous-ing projects, and employment situations indicate that change required by law has lessened prejudice" (Greenberg, 1959:26). Essentially, the purpose of the law is to change behaviour, and in some measure the laws requiring changed behaviour have changed attitudes.

However, although there has been an enormous shift toward more favourable attitudes toward, for example, racial and sexual orientation minorities, resistance to change is still widespread (Bricker and Greenspon, 2001:267).

If the law can change morality and values only under some conditions, those conditions need to be specified. As Robert B. Seidman (1978:156) notes, "The literature contains little more than speculations," and there is a great lack of empirical studies. In general, the law will more readily change morality and values where it first changes behaviour. Such a change is usually followed by a justification of the new activity. To a great extent, however, the efficacy of the law depends much upon its adaptation to morality and values if it is intended to induce change (Fuller, 1969:38).

There is still much to be learned about when and under what conditions the law cannot "only *codify* existing customs, morals, or mores, but also. . . *modify* the behaviour and values presently existing in a particular society" (Evan, 1965:286). In change efforts through the law, the prevalence and intensity of moral feelings and values need to be taken into account in both preserving and altering the status quo.

RESISTANCE TO CHANGE

In addition to the limitations of law as an instrument of social change discussed in the preceding section, the efficacy of the law (as well as other mechanisms of change) is further hindered by a variety of forces. In the modern world, situations of resistance to change are much more numerous than situations of acceptance. Members of a society can always find a justification in some more or less practical and rational terms for active resistance to change. Often change is resisted because it conflicts with traditional values and beliefs and/or prevailing customs (Banks, 1998), or a particular change may simply cost too much money, and sometimes people resist change because it interferes with their habits or makes them feel frightened or threatened. Although the law has certain advantages over other agents of change, for a greater appreciation of the role of law in change, it is helpful to identify some general conditions of resistance that have a bearing on the law. The awareness of these conditions is a major, but often overlooked or underutilized, prerequisite for a more efficient use of law as a method of social engineering.

The sociological literature recognizes a variety of tendencies to ward off change that directly or indirectly have an effect on law as an instrument of change. The intent of this section is to discuss briefly, rather than to analyze in depth, a series of forces that act as barriers to change. For the sake of clarity, we shall consider resistance to change through law in the context of social, psychological, cultural, and economic factors. The categories are only illustrative, and this distinction is made only for analytical purposes, for many of these factors operate in various combinations and intensities, depending on the magnitude and scope of a particular change effort. As may be expected, there is a substantial amount of overlapping among these factors. They are not mutually exclusive; in fact, they are often interrelated and interdependent, and many of them, depending on the purpose or rationale of the investigation, may be subsumed under different categories.

Social Factors

There are several factors that may be construed as potential barriers to change. They include vested interests, social class, ideological resistance, and organized opposition.

Vested Interests

Change may be resisted by individuals or groups who fear a loss of power, prestige, or wealth should a new proposal gain acceptance. There are many different types of vested interests for whom the status quo is profitable or preferable. Most British lawyers and judges insist on wearing the arcane court uniform of wigs and ceremonial robes that became fashionable and subsequently mandatory under King Charles II in the late 17th century (Schmidt, 1992), although there is a move led by the Lord Chancellor, head of Britain's judiciary, to wear business attire for every day and save the knee breeches, silk stockings, and buckled shoes for special occasions (*St. Louis Post-Dispatch,* 1998). Residents in a community often develop vested interests in their neighbourhood. They often organize to resist zoning changes or the construction of correctional facilities nearby. In fact, nearly everyone has some vested interests.

The acceptance of almost any change through law will adversely affect the status of some individuals or groups in society, and to the degree that those whose status is threatened consciously recognize the danger, they will oppose the change. For example, Gregory Massell (1973) reports that Soviet efforts in the early 1920s in central Asia to induce Muslim women to assert their independence from male domination were perceived by men as threatening to traditional status interests. The men reacted by forming counter-revolutionary bands and murdering some of the women who obeyed the new laws.

Social Class

Rigid class and caste patterns in general tend to hinder the acceptance of change. In highly stratified societies, people are expected to obey and take orders from those in superior positions of authority or power. The prerogatives of the upper strata are jealously guarded, and attempts to infringe upon them by members of lower socioeconomic groups are often resented and repulsed. For instance, under the traditional Indian and Pakistani rigid caste system, members of different castes could not draw water from the same well, go to the same schools, eat together, or otherwise mingle. In most cases, for the upper classes there is a tendency to cherish the old ways of doing things and to adhere to the status quo.

In Canada, those who identify themselves as working-class people tend more readily to agree that legal intervention is necessary to rectify deleterious social conditions and that the government should intervene in the economy. However, while the working class is more liberal on economic issues (i.e., favours government spending), it is more conservative on social issues (such as the rights of homosexuals and the teaching of religion in schools) (Lambert and Curtis, 1993).

Ideological Resistance

Resistance to change through law on ideological grounds is quite prevalent. An example of resistance to change through law on ideological grounds is evidenced by the reaction of religious fundamentalists and other conservative groups to legislation that has sought to equalize the rights of same-sex and opposite-sex couples. Although Canada's first widely publicized, unofficial gay "marriage" took place in 1977, when two gay men were married by a Unitarian-Universalist minister in Winnipeg (Jackson and Persky, 1982), Canada has not been historically guided by a concept of "different, but equal" when it comes to same-sex relationships (Kinsman, 1996; Bourassa, 2004). In 1993, when Gallup Canada first attempted to gauge public attitudes toward same-sex marriages, 76 percent of Canadians expressed opposition. It was only in February 2000 that less than half (48 percent) opposed homosexual marriages. Another polling milestone was reached in June 2001, when a Leger marketing poll found majority support for gay adoption. Yet as recently as 1988 only 25 percent of Canadians agreed that gays should be allowed to adopt children (Bricker and Greenspon, 2001:267).

Although a November 2005 survey conducted by CBC and Environics found that two-thirds of Canadians feel that the issue of same-sex marriage has now been settled in this country and should not be revisited (EGALE, 2006), it is apparent that others hold a different opinion. For example, on the very first day of the 2006 federal election campaign, Conservative Party leader Stephen Harper declared that, if elected Prime Minister, he would re-open the equal marriage issue and ask Parliament to approve an amendment that would limit the definition of marriage to opposite-sex couples. In December 2005, 135 law professors from across Canada issued an open letter to Harper challenging his remarks and his desire "to enact clearly unconstitutional legislation" and accused him of "playing politics with the Supreme Court and the Charter" (Choudhry et al., 2005).

For some Canadians, objections to same-sex marriage are anchored in the belief that the rights of same-sex couples to marry under the equality provisions of the *Canadian Charter of Rights and Freedoms* are secondary to the "main purpose of marriage, which is to provide a structure within which to raise children"—a view expressed in a 2001 Supreme Court of British Columbia decision (quoted in Arnold, 2001). Earlier, in 1995, the Supreme Court of Canada had expressed a similar view and identified procreation as the "ultimate purpose of marriage" in the case of *Egan v. Canada*. The flaw in this argument is that, while opposite-sex partners are uniquely able to procreate, infertile heterosexual couples or those who simply do not wish to have children are not legally prohibited from marrying. Moreover, "extending marital rights and obligations, or even marital status, to same-sex couples will not derail the state objective of encouraging procreation" (Bailey, 2000:20). Nevertheless, for some, the changed status of same-sex couples in Canada is unwelcome and hotly resisted. In June 1999, for example, a Baptist preacher announced that he and a group of his followers would be leading a demonstration on the steps of the Supreme Court of Canada to protest its decision to extend the definition of "spouse" to same-sex couples and scathingly referred to Canada as the "sperm bank of Satan" (Anderssen, 1999). On other occasions, like-minded others saw fit to wield posters that proclaimed, "God made Adam and Eve, not Adam and Steve" (Smolowe, 1996). Opposition to same-sex marriage is more marked in the United States, where 32 states have passed laws opposing same-sex marriage.

A second illustration of ideological resistance (which goes hand in hand with vested interests) was the fierce opposition of the medical profession to the launching of medical-services insurance in Saskatchewan in 1962 and later, toward "medicare." It was feared that medicare would result in "state medicine" and the role and status of physicians would be reduced to that of civil servants. In general, the basic intellectual and religious assumptions and interpretations concerning existing power, morality, welfare, and security tend to be rather consistent and adversely disposed to change (Vago, 2004:232).

Organized Opposition

Occasionally, widespread individual resistance to change may become mobilized into organized opposition, which can assume formal organizational structures, or it may be channelled through a social movement or political action committees or lobbyists. In modern societies, with the multiplicity of informal and formal organizations often in conflict with each other, a variety of new organizations have developed to combat specific threats to the status quo. For example, members of REAL Women of Canada decry a whole range of social changes from liberalized divorce laws to the acceptance and legal protection of homosexuals.

The emergence of groups such as the Aryan Nations, Heritage Front, Canadian Liberty Net, Church of the Creator, and the Identity Church Movement are based on public opposition to social change but focus mainly on changing race relations. These and similar organizations elsewhere have resisted change that was underway, and although most of them have fought a losing battle, their delaying effects have often been considerable. For example, even though the birth-control pill has been available in most countries in the West for more than three decades, it was only in the summer of 1999 that Japan's national pharmaceutical regulatory board recommended approval of the pill to the government's ministry of health. Critics of the birth-control pill in Japan had long claimed that its use would damage the nation's morals and cause a variety of social ills, including environmental harm from the hormones in the urine of women who took it. Nevertheless, women's groups in Japan intensified their campaign for the pill's approval after the Japanese government gave their swift approval to Viagra, the male anti-impotence pill (*Maclean's*, 1999). At other times, however, when organized opposition to change through law has *not* been forthcoming, the consequences have been disastrous. For instance, more than six million Jews were slaughtered in concentration camps during the Second World War in part because there was no well-organized and effective resistance to the heinous activities that began in the early 1930s in Nazi Germany (Vago, 2004:259).

Psychological Factors

Goodwin Watson (1969:488) remarks that "all of the forces which contribute to stability in personality or in social systems can be perceived as resisting change." Any detailed discussion of these forces is obviously beyond the scope of this book (see, for example, Matsumoto and Juang, 2004). For the present purpose, we shall consider only habit, motivation, ignorance, selective perception, and moral development.

Habit

From a psychological perspective, habit is a barrier to change. Once a habit is established, its operation often becomes satisfying to the individual. People become accustomed to behaving or acting in a certain manner, and they feel comfortable with it. Once a particular form of behaviour becomes routinized and habitual, it will resist change. Meyer F. Nimkoff (1957:62) suggests that the customs of a society are collective habits; in particular, where sentiment pervades custom, custom is slow to change when challenged by new ideas and practices. To cite but a single illustration, attempts to introduce the metric system in Canada originally met with considerable resistance. Canadians were accustomed to thinking about distance in terms of miles, measuring height in feet and inches, and shopping for a quart of something. When the law is used as an instrument of social change to alter established customs, it is more likely that the achievement of acceptable rates of compliance will require an active reorientation of the values and behaviours of a significant part of the target population (Zimring and Hawkins, 1975:331).

Motivation

The acceptance of change through law is also conditioned by motivational forces (see, for example, Ginsberg and Fiene, 2004). Some motivations are culture-bound, in the sense that their presence or absence is characteristic of a particular culture. For instance, religious beliefs in some cultures offer motivations to certain kinds of change, whereas in other cultures these motivations centre on the preservation of the status quo. Other kinds of motivations tend to be universal, or nearly universal, in that they cut across societies and cultures (Foster, 1973:152). Examples of these motivations include the desire for prestige or for economic gain and the wish to comply with friendship obligations. Changes that may threaten the desire for economic gain or the attraction of prestige and high status will in general be considered threatening and likely resisted.

Ignorance

Ignorance is another psychological factor generally associated with resistance to change. At times, ignorance goes hand in hand with fear of the new—a fear that was clearly on display when, in the 1950s, Canada Customs "added a new enemy to its most wanted list: the comic book, that latest organ of American pop culture, with its appalling graphic nature and limitless ability to undermine literacy and encourage juvenile delinquency" (Gudgeon, 2003:169). At the time, many moral alarmists were convinced that comics in general and, in particular, so-called "crime comics" (pulp rags bearing titles such as *Crime Fighters*, *Detective Comics*, and *True Police*) posed significant risks to naive and impressionable youths; like rap music more recently, crime comics were considered "the corrupters of youth and a direct cause of the wave of juvenile delinquency and teen pregnancy that was washing through the country." Although these charges were (and remain) of dubious merit, they convinced Canada's federal minister of justice to introduce legislation in the early 1950s to restrict crime comics. And, as Gudgeon (2005:169) points out, "comics in general are still the only form of media with their own special obscenity sub-section in Canada's Criminal Code."

Ignorance can also be a factor in noncompliance with laws designed to reduce discriminatory practices. For example, employers often make observations about nonwhites as a group relative to whites and then on that basis hesitate to hire individual nonwhites (Beeghley, 2005). Ignorance is obviously an important factor in prejudice when a pre-existing attitude is so strong and inflexible that it seriously distorts perception and judgment.

Selective Perception

Law, by design and intent, tends to be universal. The perception of the intent of the law, however, is selective and varies with socioeconomic, cultural, and demographic variables. The unique pattern of people's needs, attitudes, habits, and values derived through socialization determines what they will selectively attend to, what they will selectively interpret, and what they will selectively act upon. For example, a few weeks after the Supreme Court of Canada upheld the constitutionality of the Criminal Code section on obscenity, "the obscenity provisions were invoked, not against material designed to arouse men, but against material designed to interest lesbians. . . . In short, the law that was supposed to protect women was being used against women and against the constituency of women that has long been a 'repressed voice'" (Borovoy, 1999:8). People in general will be more receptive to new ideas if they are related to their interests, consistent with their attitudes, congruent with their beliefs, and supportive of their values (Baker, 2005). Differing perceptions of the purpose of a law may hinder change. For example, in India the law provides for widespread distribution of family planning information and supplies. But the use of contraceptive devices has been rejected by many Indian villagers because they perceive the law's intent is to stop birth completely. In the United States, the early attempts to fluoridate city water supplies met with perceptions that a "communist conspiracy" was behind these efforts, and as a result they were resisted in many communities.

The way a law is written, as we noted earlier, also affects perception. For example, in their early stages, most of Canada's antidiscrimination laws have been ambiguous and weak. Section 281 of the Criminal Code, which concerns hate literature, is a good example. This section specifies that "everyone who by communicating statements in any public place, incites hatred against any identifiable group where such incitement is likely to lead to a breach of the peace" has committed an indictable offence. Yet:

1. Most of our criminal law is nowhere nearly as vague as the anti-hate provision. Murder, kidnapping, arson, robbery, and theft, for example, are defined with much more precision.

2. Where there is comparable vagueness, the values put at risk involve matters such as driving a car (it requires "reasonable care"), not values like freedom of speech, which engage the very grievance procedure of the democratic system. Those who seek to control dangerous instruments such as automobiles *should* be chilled into being exceptionally careful. Those who seek to speak their minds in order to redress grievances should not be commensurately chilled. (Borovoy, 1999:43)

Moreover, the language used makes this law a "cumbersome weapon against racism" (Sher, 1983:192) for it allows an accused to use the defence that his or her statements "were relevant to any subject of public interest." "This 'wilfully' caveat of the law has been ably exploited by the [Ku Klux] Klan. *The Spokesman* [a KKK newspaper] publishes a disclaimer in every issue stating that it 'does not wilfully promote hatred against any identifiable group. . . *The Statesman* believes all statements made on its pages to be true with respect to any that would be prosecutable under Section 281.2 of the Criminal Code'" (Sher, 1983:192).

As Rodgers and Bullock (1972:199) have remarked, "Ambiguity always lends itself to individualized perceptions," and individuals will interpret and perceive the meaning of the law in a way they consider most advantageous.

Moral Development

To a great extent, obedience to the law stems from a sense of moral obligation, which is the product of socialization. Only relatively recently, however, has there been some awareness of moral codes that are not necessarily linked to conventional external standards of right and wrong behaviour, but represent internally consistent principles by which people govern their lives.

Perhaps the most extensive work on moral development was carried out by Lawrence Kohlberg (1964, 1967; Gibbs, 2003). He defines six stages in moral development. The first stage is described as an "obedience and punishment" orientation. This stage involves a "deference to superior power or prestige" and an orientation toward avoiding trouble. The second stage, "instrumental relativism," is characterized by naive notions of reciprocity. With this orientation, people will attempt to satisfy their own needs by simple negotiation with others or by a primitive form of equalitarianism. Kohlberg calls these two stages "pre-moral." The third stage, "personal concordance," is an orientation based on approval and pleasing others. It is characterized by conformity to perceived majority beliefs. Such people adhere to what they consider to be prevailing norms. Stage four is the "law and order" stage. People with such orientations are committed to "doing their duty," and being respectful to those in authority. Stages three and four combine to form a conventional moral orientation.

Stages five and six indicate the internalized-principle orientation. Kohlberg calls stage five the "social contract" stage; it involves a legalistic orientation. Commitments are viewed in contractual terms, and people at this stage will avoid efforts to break implicit or explicit agreements. The final and highest stage of moral development is "individual principles." This emphasizes conscience, mutual trust, and respect as the guiding principles of behaviour.

If the development theory proposed by Kohlberg is correct, the law is more or less limited depending on the stage of moral development of members of a society. In this context, David J. Danelski (1974:14) suggests that both qualitative and quantitative considerations are important. We would need to know the modal stage of the moral development of elites, of "average" citizens, and of deprived groups. If most members of a society were at the first and second stages, institutional enforcement would be essential to maintain order and security. Law would be least limited in a society in which most people were at the third and fourth stages of development. Law at the last two stages is probably more limited than at stages three and four, "but it might be otherwise if it is perceived as democratically agreed upon and consistent with individual principles of conscience. If it is not, it is likely to be more limited" (Danelski, 1974:15). The limits of law, in other words, appear to be curvilinear with respect to moral development.

Cultural Factors

When long-established practices or behaviours are threatened, resistance to change is usually strong, often on the basis of traditional beliefs and values. The status quo is protected and change resisted. For example, the Mormons, on the basis of traditional religious beliefs, opposed laws threatening their polygamous marriages. Similarly, in India, where malnutrition is a problem of considerable magnitude, millions of cows sacred to Hindus are not only exempt from being slaughtered for food but also are allowed to roam through villages and farm lands, often causing extensive damage to crops. Eating beef runs counter to long-held religious beliefs, and as a result it is unlikely that the raising of cattle for food will be acceptable in India. Other cultural factors also act often as obstacles to change. They include fatalism, ethnocentrism, notions of incompatibility, and superstition.

Fatalism

States Mead: "In many parts of the world we find cultures adhering to the belief that man [sic] has no causal effect upon his [sic] future or the future of the land; God, not man [sic], can improve man's [sic] lot. . . . It is difficult to persuade such people to use fertilizers, or to save the best seed for planting, since man [sic] is responsible only for the performance, and the divine for the success of the act" (1953:201). Basically, fatalism entails a feeling of a lack of mastery over nature. People have no control over their lives and everything that happens to them is caused by God or evil spirits. Such a fatalistic outlook undoubtedly results in resistance to change, for change is seen as human-initiated rather than having a divine origin.

Ethnocentrism

Some groups in society consider themselves "superior," possessing the only "right" way of thinking about the world and of coping with the environment. Feelings of superiority about one's group are likely to make people unreceptive to the ideas and methods used in other groups. As a result, ethnocentrism often constitutes a bulwark against change (Asante, 2003).

Incompatibility

Resistance to change is often due to the presence in the target group of material and systems that are, or considered to be, irreconcilable with the new proposal. When such incompatibility exists in a culture, change comes about with difficulty. An illustration is the marriage-age law enacted in Israel in an attempt to induce changes in the immigrant population through legal norms. The law sets 17 as the minimum age for marriage, with the exception of pregnancy, and imposes a criminal sanction on anyone who marries a girl below the age of 17 without permission of the district court. By setting the minimum age at 17, the law attempted to impose a rule of behaviour that was incompatible with the customs and habits of some of the sections of the Jewish population of Israel that came from Arab and Oriental countries, where marriage was usually contracted at a lower age. The act had only limited effect, and communities that formerly permitted marriage of females at an early age continued to do so (Dror, 1968:678).

Superstition

Superstition is defined as an uncritical acceptance of a belief that is not substantiated by facts (Ambrose, 1998). Nevertheless, people may act on the basis of these beliefs. For example, a 2006 news report noted that "[w]hen the upper teeth of a 17-month-old girl in eastern India appeared before her lower teeth, her family, members of the Santhal tribe, took it as a bad omen. To remove the 'evil eye' that had fallen upon her, the girl married a stray dog to confuse and thwart evil spirits. Her father. . . led three days of ceremonies to mark the girl's marriage to the dog" (*Maclean's*, 2006). Superstitions can act as barriers to change. For example, in one situation in Zimbabwe (formerly Rhodesia), nutrition-education efforts were hampered because many women would not eat eggs. According to widespread belief, eggs cause infertility, make babies bald, and cause women to be promiscuous. Similarly, in the Philippines, it is a widely accepted idea that squash and chicken eaten at the same time produce leprosy. In some places, women are not given milk during late pregnancy because of the belief that it produces a fetus too large for easy delivery, and in other places, a baby may not be given water for several months after birth because water's "cold" quality will upset the infant's heat equilibrium. Obviously, where such superstitious beliefs prevail, change efforts through law or other agents will meet some resistance.

Economic Factors

Even in affluent societies, limited economic resources constitute a barrier to changes that might otherwise be readily adopted. For instance, in Canada, almost everyone would readily accept the desirability of more effective controls on pollution, cheaper and more convenient systems of public transportation, effective welfare programs, and improvements in our systems of health care and education. The fact that changes in these areas come very slowly is a matter not only of priorities but also of cost. Cost and limited economic resources in a society do in effect provide a source of resistance to change.

It is a truism that, like everything else, change through law has its costs. In most instances, the instrumentation of legislation, administrative ruling, or court decision carries a price tag. In addition to the direct cost of a particular change effort, the way costs and benefits are distributed also affects resistance. For example, when costs and benefits are widely distributed (as in social security), there is minimal resistance to programs. The cost to each taxpayer is relatively small, and the benefits are so widely distributed "that they are almost like collective goods; beneficiaries will enjoy the benefits, but only make small contributions to their retention or growth" (Handler, 1978:15). Resistance will be forthcoming in situations where benefits are distributed while costs are concentrated. For example, automakers still resist (although not too successfully) legal attempts to impose more sophisticated pollution-control measures on cars.

Although a particular change through the law may be desirable, limited economic resources often act as barriers to such change efforts. Of the four sources of resistance to change, the economic factors are perhaps the most decisive. Regardless of the desirability of a proposed change, its compatibility with the values and beliefs of the recipients, and many other considerations, it will be resisted if the economic sacrifice is too great. Simply stated, regardless of how much people in a society want something, if they cannot afford it, chances are they will not be able to get it. As George M. Foster (1973:78) suggests: "Cultural, social and psychological barriers and stimulants to change exist in an economic setting. . . (and) economic factors. . . seem to set the absolute limits to change."

SUMMARY

- Law is both a dependent and an independent variable in social change.
- Increasingly, law is being considered an instrument of social change. In many areas of social life, such as education, race relations, housing, transportation, energy utilization, and the protection of the environment, the law has been relied on as an important instrument of change.
- The advantages of law as an agent of change are attributed to the perception that the law in society is legitimate, more or less rational, authoritative, institutionalized, generally not disruptive, and backed by mechanisms of enforcement and sanctions.
- The law has certain limitations in creating social change. It is not always able to resolve conflicting interests, and generally the powerful in society fare better than the less privileged and the unorganized. The law is further limited by the divergencies in values and moral codes, the difficulty in enforcing some laws, the occasional lack of clarity of law, and the questionable diligence in enforcing certain laws.
- A variety of social, psychological, cultural, and economic forces may provide direct or indirect resistance to change efforts. The social factors include vested interests, social class, moral sentiments, and organized opposition. Psychological resistance may be triggered by habit, motivation, ignorance, selective perception, and the complexities inherent in moral development. Cultural barriers to change include fatalism, ethnocentrism, notions of incompatibility, and superstition. Cost and limited economic resources effectively set a limit to change.

CRITICAL THINKING QUESTIONS

1. On September 30, 2005, a Danish newspaper, *Jullands-Posten*, published a dozen cartoons depicting the prophet Mohammed; for those who adhere to the Islamic religion, depicting Mohammed in any form is blasphemy. In October of that year, ambassadors from 10 Muslim countries and the Palestinian representative in Denmark co-signed a letter to the Danish Prime Minister Anders Fogh Rasmussen that requested a meeting and urged him to take action against the newspaper; he declined to do both. Although on January 1, 2006, Rasmussen would publicly condemn "attempts to demonize groups of people on the basis of their religion," he maintained that Denmark was committed to freedom of speech; later that month, after receiving bomb threats and facing thousands of demonstrators, *Jullands-Posten* would post an apology on its website, saying that it regretted offending Muslims—but that it was standing by its decision to publish the cartoons. In the month that followed, protest reactions against the publication of the cartoons continued: Saudi Arabia withdrew its ambassador to Denmark; masked gunmen stormed an EU office in Gaza City, firing into the air; Saudi Arabian imams denounced the Danish newspaper and urged the Islamic world to react; several hundred protestors, some armed, stormed a NATO base in Maymana, which housed a reconstruction team of Norwegian and Finnish troops—an act that led to three deaths; four people were killed in Afghanistan and two in Pakistan during demonstrations attended by thousands; in Beirut, thousands of protestors gathered and went on a rampage that culminated in setting fire to the Danish embassy; in Damascus, Syria, the Danish and Norwegian embassies were also set ablaze; and in various cities, protestors pointedly burned the Danish (and, on occasion, the American) flag. Demonstrations, some peaceful, others not, also occurred in Bangladesh, Malaysia, Kenya, Russia, Pakistan, and Canada. On February 7, 2006, Denmark's Prime Minister referred to the unrest that had followed the publication of the cartoons as a "growing global crisis" (in CBC, 2006). Although UN Secretary-General Kofi Annan urged newspaper editors to not republish the cartoons—maintaining that, "It is insensitive. It is offensive. It is provocative, and they should see what has happened around the world" (in CBC, 2006)— by February of 2006, they had appeared in newspapers in the US, France, Germany, Spain, Italy, the UK, Belgium, Switzerland, Hungary, Greenland, Bulgaria, Portugal, Norway, and Jordan. The only Canadian newspaper to publish the cartoons was *Le Devoir* (on February 3, 2006). In addition, eight of the twelve cartoons would appear in the Alberta-based *Western Standard* magazine (with its publisher maintaining, "I'm doing something completely normal. I'm publishing the centre of a controversy. That's what news magazines do" [in CBC, 2006]) and in the University of Prince Edward Island's student newspaper, *The Cadre*. *Maclean's* magazine, while opting not to republish the cartoons, featured a blistering editorial, bearing the headline "What it means to be free," in its February 27 edition, that proclaimed: "We do not believe it necessary to give offence in order to champion the rights of others to be offensive. But freedom of expression must be vigorously defended. . . . [I]t is unacceptable for the progress of international human rights to be held to ransom by the demands of a handful of countries with suspect records on human rights. It is appalling to see precious freedoms, won over centuries at great human cost, bargained away for commercial profit, short-term political gain, and the false hope of appeasing incorrigibles" (*Maclean's,* 2006b). Echoing these sentiments, Canadian lawyer and leading human rights advocate Julius Grey publicly advocated the publication of the cartoons, "arguing that by not printing them, the media jeopardizes Canada's

culture of freedom of expression and fails to properly inform its citizens" (CBC, 2006). Others, however, viewed the situation in a much different light. Prime Minister Stephen Harper issued a statement announcing his "regret" that the cartoons had been published in this country. The Canadian Council on American-Islamic Relations warned that the publication of the cartoons in this country could endanger the lives and well-being of Canadian soldiers. On an international level, the Organization of the Islamic Conference demanded that the new UN Human Rights Council include a ban on "blasphemy." Freedom of expression is considered one of the key freedoms in a democracy. Section 2(b) of the Charter guarantees Canadians the freedom to think and believe what we will and to publicly express these opinions through writing, speech, artwork, photography, and other means. Freedom of the press and other media is included with section 2(b) because the media plays an undeniably important role as both a forum for speaking out on issues and in the communication of information to the public. Freedom of speech, however, is not an absolute right—as noted in our earlier discussion of Canada's "hate laws." As a response to the furor provoked by the publication of the cartoons, some suggest that Canada's hate laws be expanded to criminalize speech that exposes "identifiable groups" to ridicule, mockery, or contempt and/or recommend the establishment of a new media code of conduct that would prevent the media from publishing words or images that may give offence to such groups—an idea that, at the time of writing, is being entertained by the European Justice and Security Commission (*Maclean's*, 2006b). Others, however, would view acquiescence to any further restrictions (formal or informal) upon our speech as simply evidence of Canada's "anemic cowardice" in the face of "political correctness" (Amiel, 2006). What limits (if any) do you believe should be placed on your right to freedom of expression? Should the Canadian media have narrower—or more expansive—rights to freedom of expression than private citizens?

2. Examine the editorials in local and/or campus newspapers and within news magazines. What changes to law are proposed? What arguments and types of evidence are used to justify arguments that such change is necessary? If the editorial suggests that Canada will be ill-served by proposed or pending legislation, what justifications are offered in defence of the status quo?

chapter eight

The Legal Profession

An examination of the legal profession and its role in society touches on key issues in sociological theory—issues involving power, social control, stratification, socialization, and the social organization of law work. This chapter analyzes the character of the legal profession and the social forces shaping it. It begins with a historical background of law, with an emphasis on the professionalization of lawyers and the evolution of the legal profession in Canada. Next, the chapter focuses on the legal profession today: what lawyers do and where, their income, and how they compete for business. The emphasis is then placed on the accessibility of legal services to the poor and the not-so-poor, followed by a discussion of law schools and the training and socialization of lawyers into the profession. The section concludes with some comments on bar admission, bar associations as interest groups, and professional discipline.

BACKGROUND

The cultural history and emergence of the legal profession and the legal professional have long fascinated scholars in history, law, and sociology (see, for example, Pue and Sugarman, 2003). In traditional societies, as noted in Chapter 2, custom and law coincide. The laws of a traditional legal system are unwritten and comparatively undifferentiated. Such societies have courts and judges but no lawyers. The courts are temporary, and when a violation of a law has occurred, the defendant is not represented by a "lawyer." Each individual is his or her own "lawyer" and everyone more or less knows the law. Although some individuals may be wiser than others and more skilled in social affairs, this skill is not considered a *legal* skill.

The development of the legal profession has been intimately connected with the rise and development of legal systems. The origins of the legal profession can be traced back to Rome (Friedman, 1977:21). Initially, Roman law allowed individuals to argue cases on behalf of others; however, those persons were trained not in law but in rhetoric. They were called orators and were not allowed to take fees. Later on, by Cicero's time (106–43 B.C.), there were jurists as well—individuals who were knowledgeable about the law and to whom people went for legal opinions. They were called *jurisprudentes,* but these men learned in the law did not yet constitute a profession. Only during the Imperial Period did lawyers begin to practise law for a living and schools of law emerge. By this time, the law had become exceedingly complex in Rome. The occupation of lawyers arose together with a sophisticated legal system, and the complexity of that system made the Roman lawyer indispensable.

C. Ray Jeffery (1962:314) points out that by the Middle Ages, the lawyer had three functions—agent, advocate, and jurisconsult. The word "attorney" originally meant "an agent, a person who acts or appears on behalf of someone else." In this role of agent, the lawyer appeared in court to handle legal matters in place of his client. In ancient Athens and Rome, an agent was allowed to appear in the place of another person. In France, however, a person had to appear in court himself, and in England, he needed special permission from the king to be represented in court by an agent. In France, by 1356, there were 105 *légistes* (men of law) representing clients in court (Jacoby, 1973:14).

The distinction between an agent and an advocate appeared when the lawyer went to court with his client to assist the client in presenting his case. In addition to law, the advocate was trained in the art of oratory and persuasion. In England, the function of the agent was taken over by solicitors and attorneys; the advocate became the barrister (trial lawyer). The function of a lawyer as a jurisconsult was both as a legal adviser and as a writer and teacher. Although contemporary lawyers perform essentially the same functions, the modern legal profession is fundamentally different. Friedman notes: "It is organized. It is lucrative. It is closed except to those who have undergone training or apprenticeship. It holds a monopoly of courtroom work and the giving of 'legal' advice" (1977:21).

THE PROFESSIONALIZATION OF LAWYERS

Law is considered one of the three archetypical "learned" professions—the clergy and medicine are the other two (Kritzer, 1990:5). But what is a profession, and what does the process of professionalization entail? In the sociological literature, professionalization implies the transformation of some nonprofessional occupation into a vocation with the attributes of a profession, and the specification of these could be discussed in great detail (see, for example, Macdonald, 1995). Foote captures the essential ingredients: "As a modicum, the possession (1) of a specialized technique supported by a body of theory, (2) of a career supported by an association of colleagues, and (3) of a status supported by community recognition may be mentioned as constituting an occupation as a profession" (1953:371). Also usually included in the discussion of professions are the ideas of a client-practitioner relationship and a high degree of autonomy in the execution of one's work tasks. Harold L. Wilensky (1964:143) has studied those occupations that are now viewed as professions, such as law, medicine, and the Church, and notes that they have passed through the following general stages in their professionalization:

1. Became full-time occupations
2. Training schools established
   University affiliation of training schools
3. Local professional associations started
   National professional associations evolved

4. State licensing laws established
5. Formal codes of ethics established

Magali Sarfatti Larson (1977) provides additional insights into professionalization as the process by which producers of special services seek to constitute and to *control* a market for their expertise. Because marketable expertise is an important element in the structure of inequality, professionalization also appears as a collective assertion of special social status and as a collective process of upward mobility. She considers professionalization an attempt to translate one type of scarce resources—special knowledge and skills—into another—social and economic rewards. The attempt by professions to maintain scarcity implies a tendency toward monopoly: monopoly of expertise in the market and monopoly of status in a system of stratification. She contends: "Viewed in the larger perspective of the occupational and class structures, it would appear that the model of professional passes from a predominantly economic function—organizing the linkage between education and the marketplace—to a predominantly ideological one—justifying inequality of status and closure of access in the occupational order" (Larson, 1977:xviii). For Larson, the following elements in the professionalization process are inseparably related: differentiation and standardization of professional services; formalization of the conditions for entry; persuasion of the public that they need services only professionals can provide; and state protection (in the form of licensing) of the professional market against those who lack formal qualifications and against competing occupations. She argues that educational institutions and professional associations play a central role in attaining each of these goals.

A crucial element in the professionalization process is market control—the successful assertion of unchallenged authority over some area of knowledge and its professional instrumentation (Abel, 2003). Until the body of legal knowledge, including procedure, became too much for the ordinary person to handle, there was no need for a legal profession. Before the 13th century, it was possible for a litigant to appoint someone to do his or her technical pleading. This person was not a member of a separate profession, for apparently anyone could act in that capacity. The person who did the technical pleading eventually developed into, or was superseded by, the attorney who was appointed in court and had the power to bind his employer to a plea.

"The profession of advocate," writes Michael E. Tigar (1977:157), "in the sense of a regulated group of (law) practitioners with some formal training, emerged in the late 1200s." Both the English and the French sovereigns legislated with respect to the profession, limiting the practice of law to those who had been approved by judicial officers. The profession of full-time specialists in the law and in legal procedures appeared initially as officers of the king's court. The first professional lawyers were judges who trained their successors by apprenticeship. The apprentices took on functions in the courtroom and gradually came to monopolize pleading before the royal judges. In England, training moved out of the courtroom and into the Inns of Court, which were the residences of the judges and practising attorneys. The attorneys, after several reorganizations of their own ranks, finally became a group known as barristers. Members of the Inns became organized and came to monopolize training in the law as well as control of official access to the government. Signs of the professionalization of lawyers began to appear.

In England, the complexity of court procedures required technical pleading with the aid of an attorney, and oral argument eventually required special skills. By the time of Henry III (1216–1272), judges had become professionals, and the courts started to create a body of substantive legal knowledge as well as technical procedure. The king needed individuals to represent his interests in the courts. In the early 14th century, he appointed sergeants of the king to take care of his legal business. When not engaged in the king's business, these fabled sergeants-at-law of the Common Pleas Court could serve individuals in the capacity of lawyers.

A crucial event in the beginning of the legal profession was an edict issued in 1292 by Edward I. During this period, legal business had increased enormously; yet, there were no schools of common law, and the universities considered law too vulgar a subject for scholarly investigation. The universities were, at that time, agencies of the church, and the civil law taught there was essentially codified Roman law, the instrument of bureaucratic centralization. Edward's order, which directed Common Pleas to choose certain "attorneys and learners" who alone would be allowed to follow the court and to take part in court business, created a monopoly of the legal profession.

The effect of placing the education of lawyers into the hands of the court cannot be overestimated. It resulted in the relative isolation of English lawyers from continental, Roman, and ecclesiastical influences. Lawyer taught lawyer, and each learned from the processes of the courts, so that the law had to grow by drawing on its own resources and not by borrowing from others. But the court itself was no place for the training of these attorneys and learners. It did, however, provide aid in the form of an observation post, called the crib, in which students could sit and take notes, and from which occasionally they might ask questions during the course of a trial.

Training for lawyers was provided by the Inns of Court. A small self-selecting group of barristers gave informal training and monopolized practice before the government courts of London, as well as judgeships in those courts. Barristers evolved into court lawyers (that is, lawyers who acted as the mouthpiece of their clients in court proceedings). Originally they were called "story-tellers" (Latin *narrators*); they told their client's story in courts, and this is their essential function to this day. The barristers' monopoly of court activities helped create a second group within the legal profession, named the "solicitors" (or "fixers"), who advised clients, prepared cases for trial, and handled matters outside the courtroom (Simpson, 1988:148). This group arose to meet the needs of clients because barristers were too involved as officers of the court to be very responsible to outsiders. The barristers outranked solicitors, both by virtue of their monopoly of access to the court and through their control of training. Originally, solicitors were drawn from the ranks of those who attended the Inns of Court, and later they came to be trained almost entirely by apprenticeships or through schools of their own. At first, in the Inns of Court, lawyers lived together during the terms of court, and for them the Inns represented law school, a professional organization, and a tightly knit social club, all in one.

Initially, universities such as Oxford and Cambridge saw little reason to include training such as it was practised in the Inns in their teaching programs. (Until fairly recently, law was not regarded highly as a university subject. The number of law professors was small, and their prestige was rather low, since "law school was treated as the appropriate home for rowing men of limited intellect" [Simpson, 1988:158].) Only subjects such as legal history, jurisprudence, and Roman and ecclesiastical law were considered part of a liberal education to be provided by the universities (Kearney, 1970). University education was sought by "gentlemen," whereas legal training at the Inns of Court became the cheapest and the easiest route of social mobility for those who aspired to become gentlemen. Many sons of prosperous yeomen and merchants chose legal apprenticeship in an attempt to adopt a lifestyle associated with a gentleman. The appointment in 1758 of Sir William Blackstone to the Vinerian chair of jurisprudence at Cambridge marked the first effort to make English law a university subject. Blackstone thought it would help both would-be lawyers and educated people generally to have a "system of legal education" (as he called it), which would be far broader than the practical legal training offered in the Inns of Court. Blackstone may thus be considered the founder of the modern English system of university education in law (Berman, Greiner, and Saliba, 1996:6; see also Carrese, 2003).

By the end of the 18th century, law in England had become a full-fledged profession. Members of the profession considered the law a full-time occupation, training schools were established, universities began to offer degrees in law, and a professional association evolved in the form of a lawyers' guild. The practice of law required licensing, and formal codes of ethics were established. Knowledge of law and skills of legal procedures became a marketable commodity, and lawyers had a monopoly on them. The practice of law in royal courts was limited to members of the lawyers' guild, which in turn enhanced their political power, their monopoly of expertise in the market, and their monopoly of status in a system of stratification. Access to the profession became controlled, and social mobility for those admitted assured. By the end of the 18th century, the name "attorney" had been dropped in favour of the term "solicitor," with the formation of the Society of Gentlemen Practicers in the Courts of Law and Equity, which was their professional society until 1903, when the Law Society came into being. In the following section, we shall examine the rise of the legal profession in Canada.

THE EVOLUTION OF THE CANADIAN LEGAL PROFESSION

The Canadian legal profession, like Canada more generally, reflects the influence of the "charter groups"—the English and French. Guillaume Audouart, who began practice as a "notaire public" in 1649, was the first legal professional to settle in New France. By 1663, there were 26 meagerly trained *notaires* practising in New France. During this early time period, *avocats* (barristers) were not allowed, for Louis XIV desired to maintain tight control over the legal and political affairs of the colony and "[t]he authorities feared that 'avocats' would not only slow down the judicial process with lengthy arguments, but that their presence would also promote additional disputes and litigation" (Thompson, 1979:18). In 1733, Louis-Guillaume Verrier, an expatriate *Parisien*, launched Canada's earliest structured program of legal education. This led, in 1744, to the development of a system of licensing those who had obtained Verrier's certificate as "assessors" before the Sovereign Council and the lower courts of New France. The *notaires* enjoyed a monopoly of legal practice until after the British conquest.

Following the British conquest and the Treaty of Paris in 1763, the French judicial institutions were replaced by the English courts of King's Bench and Common Pleas. A hybrid legal system developed, with certain concessions made to traditional French practices. For example, while would-be lawyers in "proudly Protestant Britain" during this time period were required to declare, under oath, that they rejected the Catholic doctrine of transubstantiation, British governors granted Roman Catholics the right to practise law (Moore, 1997:18). As the need for trained courtroom lawyers became increasingly evident, *avocats* were authorized to appear before the Court of Common Pleas in 1765 and, in the following year, to practise in all the province's civil courts. However, it would not be until 1835 that *avocats* were permitted to represent accused persons in criminal courts.

Following the reintroduction of French civil law by the *Quebec Act* of 1774, Lieutenant Governor Henry Hamilton proclaimed the earliest operative regulation on the training of Canadian lawyers: the 1785 "Ordinance Concerning Advocates, Attorneys, Solicitors and Notaries." Until that year, a lawyer of the British colony was any person that the governor declared as such. While the granting of licence remained exclusively within the governor's discretion, the 1785 ordinance affirmed the right of any qualified English or colonial to practise in the province's courts and stipulated that those who wished to practise law in old Quebec were required to serve a minimum five years' apprenticeship *(la cléricature)* and successfully pass a bar admission examination. The Ordinance additionally prohibited the double commissioning of advocates and notaries, forbidding one person to simultaneously occupy both roles. Although this forced separation of the profession led to protests to both the colonial government and to the King of England, neither were moved, "thinking perhaps that by having a single individual act in both capacities it would be easier to bring an action in court, and would encourage litigation" (Thompson, 1979:18). The Ordinance was to survive the 1791 division of old Quebec into the provinces of Upper and Lower Canada and continue to govern the profession well into the 19th century.

In 1847, the Chambre des Notaires du Québec was established to control entry into the profession of a *notaire*. Two years later, the Communauté des Avocats, a voluntary association of *avocats*, was transformed by a legislative enactment that created the Barreau du Québec. The 1849 Act for the Incorporation of the Barreau of Lower Canada granted the province-wide corporation the power to regulate admission to practice. Canada's first university faculty of law was established in 1853 at McGill and, in 1854, at Laval. Additional law schools were later established at what are now the Université de Montréal and the Université de Sherbrooke.

In Quebec, the division of the profession into two mutually exclusive branches has endured with the passage of time. "Like branches on a tree, both have a common trunk, source or base. . . . But after the basic education in the law they go their separate directions" (Thompson, 1979:18). In that province, the principal function of the *notaire* is to draft or receive acts and contracts (e.g., marriage covenants, mortgages on immovables, trust deeds, and deeds of sale involving mortgages) that parties wish to have authenticated. *Notaires* specialize in non-litigious matters and have exclusive rights "where there is no question between the parties as to the law or the facts" (Thompson, 1979:19). In consequence, they often act for parties on both sides of a transaction. While both *notaires* and *avocats* may deal with a variety of non-litigious matters such as "tax, intellectual property and trade marks, and all areas of non-litigious commercial and business law" (Gill, 1988:7), the role of the *avocat*, like that of the barrister in England, focuses upon areas of contention. In Quebec, *avocats* have the exclusive right to plead cases in court that involve a conflict between the parties. Every practising *avocat* in Quebec must be a member of the Barreau.

Those pursuing a degree in law in Quebec must declare their intention to become *notaires* by December 1 in the last year of their three-year program. After graduation, those who wish to become *notaires* are required to spend an additional year in notarial practice at a civil law school and to pass a notarial examination. Those who intend to work as *avocats* must complete an eight-month *formation professionelle*, roughly similar to a bar admission course, followed by a six-month *stagiarie* or skills-training course, and pass a bar examination.

In Upper Canada, the introduction of the 1797 *Law Society Act* appears to have stemmed from dual motives. First, "to provide a means for the existing bar to organize and improve itself, but also to shelter its members from being superseded by better-qualified newcomers who might find the incumbents' credentials inadequate" (Moore, 1997:31). The Act established the Law Society of Upper Canada as a self-governing body with exclusive authority over the admission of barristers and solicitors and the control of their education. Under the Act, immigrant lawyers were allowed to practise—provided that they joined the Society and agreed to conform to its rules. The Law Society was additionally empowered to assume a wide range of functions including the establishment and maintenance of professional standards and dispensing discipline when those standards were breached.

As in the two other Loyalist-populated provinces, Nova Scotia and New Brunswick, the bar in Upper Canada was grounded in the English model, with a "rigid, functional division between solicitor and barrister. . . with different periods of clerkship, or articles, specified for each. Carrying over the traditional labels from the Inns of Court, the law society was to be composed of elected 'benchers' and the governing body was to be called 'convocation.'" However, because there were relatively few practitioners of the law during this early period (a few dozen at most), the English-style, divided distinction between barrister and solicitor was always a "legal fiction" and, by 1822, it had "effectively disappeared" (Buckingham et al., 1996:2).

To obtain a licence to practise law from the Law Society required five years' study as a legal apprentice. However, beginning in 1854, the apprenticeship period was shortened for those who earned the University of Toronto's "Bachelor of Civil Law" degree. The Law Society would later create, in 1862, its own law school, Osgoode Hall, named after the first chief justice of Upper Canada, William Osgoode (1754–1824). In Upper Canada, legal education would remain "exclusively or principally the prerogative of the Law Society of Upper Canada for almost two centuries" (Baker, 1983:49). In 1889, the Law Society adopted a recommendation that reaffirmed its control over education and asserted that this function would not be shared with the province's universities. It was not until 1957 that the Law Society of Upper Canada would relinquish its statutory monopoly over legal education and grant recognition to other Ontario schools.

In the first half-century of its existence, the Law Society of Upper Canada had declared itself open to applicants of little wealth and little or no social prominence. During this early period, the parents of entrants included blacksmiths, farmers, stonemasons, and labourers, along with lawyers and other professionals. In consequence, "the construction of Upper Canada's legal elite was neither an exclusively English, metropolitan, nor family enterprise" (Baker, 1983:56). As long as applicants could pass the entrance exams, exist for several years on a fairly meagre income, and find a lawyer who was willing to accept them as an articling student, they could aspire to the gentlemanly status that the profession offered. However, legal education for most law students remained anchored in apprenticeship, and finding articles often made it difficult, if not impossible, for cultural and racial minorities to gain entrance into the profession. While the act of 1797 had authorized each legal practitioner to have one student, the vast majority of Ontario's 19th-century lawyers were English, Scottish, Irish, and Protestant and "they tended to take in students of their own class and kind" (Moore, 1997:176). While the first black Ontarian, Robert Sutherland, was called to the bar in 1855, the second black lawyer to practise in Ontario, Delos Rogest Davis, was forced to petition the Ontario legislature declaring that, as a result of prejudice and bigotry, he had been unable to locate a single lawyer, over a period of 11 years, who was willing to accept him as an articling student. As the result of his petition, Davis was allowed to sign the solicitors' roll—without serving articles in the usual fashion—after passing the Law Society's exams in 1885 and paying his fees. (Davis's son, who articled with his father and later entered into partnership with him, became Ontario's third black lawyer when he was called to the bar in 1900. It would not be until 1926, however, that another black Ontarian would become a lawyer.)

Over time, entrance into the legal profession in Ontario became progressively more exclusionary. "As it began to promulgate rules for entry, the Law Society wanted to identify gentlemen far more than to test for any specific legal skill or aptitude" (Moore, 1997:43). As Archdeacon John Strachan emphasized in an 1826 letter written to Lieutenant-Governor Sir Peregrine Maitland, "Lawyers must, from the very nature of our political institutions— from there being no great landed proprietors—no privileged orders—become the most powerful profession, and must in time possess more influence and authority than any other. They are emphatically our men of business, and will gradually engross all the colonial offices of profit and honour " (in Baker, 1983:55).

Toward this end, the practice of admitting talented but impoverished students was increasingly criticized as misguided. Admission standards were raised and increasingly, an unlevel playing field was created. The benchers had demanded "proofs of a liberal" education and begun to test would-be students for their competence in Latin and English as early as 1820; the test was stiffened in 1825 and, "by the 1830s, the entrance exam covered Latin and English composition, history, geography, and the elements of Euclid. . . . [M]astery of such a curriculum indicated that one had a disciplined mind, a certain breath of culture, and *the time and means for thought and study*" (Moore, 1997:89, emphasis added). Intermarriage among families already ensconced in the legal elite became more common during the second half of the 19th century, and successful applicants to Ontario's legal fraternity were increasingly likely to bear the surnames of earlier Society members. "[T]he caste was beginning to close ranks and. . . the occupational status of lawyers was becoming hereditary" (Baker, 1983:56). The linkages between legal professionals, elite economic interests, and the Canadian political system have been emphasized by John Porter (1965) in his now-classic analysis of the structure of the Canadian economic elite.

"In the maritime provinces of Nova Scotia and New Brunswick, the bar, such as it was at the end of the 18th century, tended to follow the professional practices of the lawyers in American states, from whose ranks these Loyalist lawyers came." Gaining admission to the bar entailed articling for a period of three to five years and then convincing a Superior Court justice of one's competence. Professional organizations such as the Nova Scotia Law Society and the Law Society of New Brunswick, both of which were incorporated in 1825, "were loosely structured gentlemen's clubs brought together for mutually advantageous projects, such as accumulating a library for the use of the local bench and bar" (Buckingham et al., 1996:3). However, in contrast to the experience in Upper Canada, the task of educating lawyers in the Maritime provinces was quickly transferred to the universities. Dalhousie University founded its law school and a full-time, three-year course in 1883 and became the first law school to teach common law in the British Empire. The Saint John Law School (which was to become the University of New Brunswick Faculty of Law) later followed.

From its inception, Dalhousie Law School had links to Harvard Law School. It is therefore not surprising that the teaching method adopted reflected the "case method" model developed by Harvard Law Dean Christopher Columbus Langdell. Instead of using the older system of text reading and lectures, the instructor carried on a discussion of assigned cases designed to bring out their general principles. Langdell believed that law was a general science and that its principles could be experimentally induced from the examination of case materials. He rejected the use of textbooks and instead used casebooks as teaching materials; these were collections of reports of actual cases, carefully selected and arranged to illustrate the meaning and development of principles of law. The teacher became a Socratic guide, leading the student to an understanding of concepts and principles hidden as essences among the cases. While common-law schools in Canada typically adopted teaching methods based on the case method model, this method of teaching has been increasingly challenged (Olivo, 2004:147).

Beginning in the colony of New Caledonia (renamed British Columbia in 1858), practising lawyers (primarily English-trained) in western colonies approaching provincial status began to lobby for formal recognition of their professional status and for the creation of standards regulating training and admission to the profession. The *Legal Professions Act* of 1863 gave formal recognition to the professions of barrister and solicitor and "gave the Supreme Court the power to examine and admit new members, and administer discipline to existing members" (Buckingham et al., 1996:3). Following the 1866 union of Victoria and British Columbia and the granting of provincial status upon that territory, the expanding bar demanded and was granted increasing professional autonomy. "In 1874 the Law Society of British Columbia was incorporated under the *Legal Professions Act* and benchers were ceded full authority over legal training, admission, and discipline. The self-governing status of the law society was made permanent in 1895, by which time the society had put into place a course of mandatory lectures in its Vancouver Law School" (Buckingham et al., 1996:3). It was not until the 1930s that the responsibility for education would be transferred to provincial universities.

In 1877, the Law Society of Manitoba was incorporated by provincial law and, over time, achieved the power to control entry into the profession, specify education, and dispense discipline. By the time Alberta and Saskatchewan attained provincial status in 1905, there were substantial numbers of legal practitioners living in the major centres of these provinces, and legislation which created law societies was quickly passed. Fledlging law schools in these provinces represented the joint efforts of the bar and the universities.

The increased emphasis on professionalization and monopoly of the practice of law brought about concerted efforts to improve the quality of legal education, to raise admission standards, and to intensify the power of bar associations. By the 1920s and 1930s, the legal profession in Canada, when compared to its counterpart in the United States, revealed several distinctive features:

> First, admission to the profession was far more difficult, demanding, time-consuming and expensive in Canada. In the United States a considerably more casual, laissez-faire approach obtained; the only entrance requirement for the Indiana bar, for example, was "good moral character," and only a few states had mandatory exams or prescribed periods of study of clerkship. . . .

> Second, admission to the bar in Canada was controlled (except, anomalously, in Manitoba) exclusively by the law society of the province. This was the practice in Great Britain as well, but the common practice in the United States put control of admission fully into the hands of the bench. . . .

> [Third], the law societies in Canada acquired piecemeal, or simply assumed, far more powers of self-governance and control over the profession than equivalent associations in the United States. . . .

> [Fourth], [t]he autonomy of the Canadian legal profession created a smaller, more highly trained, more cohesive, and, as a result, more elitist profession than that in the United States. (From Buckingham, Donald E., Jerome E. Bickenbach, Richard Bronaugh and The Honourable Bertha Wilson. 1996. *Legal Ethics in Canada: Theory and Practice*. Toronto: Nelson Thomson Learning. Reprinted with permission of Nelson.)

However, some similarities between the two systems can be noted. For example, in both countries, the profession has been historically dominated by white males. Women, particularly married women, were not considered suitable for the practice of law. They were seen as delicate creatures and, just like children and lunatics, lacked full legal rights. It was argued that allowing women to practise law would derail the traditional order of the family. In a notorious opinion of a justice of the US Supreme Court in 1873, "the natural and proper timidity and delicacy which belongs to the female sex evidently unfits it for many of the occupations of civil life . . . . The paramount destiny and mission of women are to fulfil the noble and benign offices of wife and mother. This is the law of the Creator" (Stevens, 1983:82). When Mabel Penery French petitioned to be admitted to the legal profession in New Brunswick in 1905 after completing all the necessary training, the Canadian judge approvingly quoted from the decision in this earlier case and ruled that it was not possible for women to be lawyers. Echoing this viewpoint, when Anne Macdonald Langstaff applied to become a lawyer in Quebec in 1915 after graduating from McGill University, Judge Saint-Pierre ruled that "to admit a woman and more particularly a married woman as a barrister, that is to say, as a person who pleads cases at the bar before judges or juries in open court, and in the presence of the public, would be nothing short of a direct infringement upon public order and a manifest violation of the law of good morals and public decency" (in Mossman, 1994:214). Assuredly, this situation was not unique to Canada and the United States. In exploring the struggles European women faced in attempting to gain access to the legal profession, James Albisetti (2000:825) argues that access to law "universally trailed access to medicine not because of issues related to the study or practice of law, but because the arguments put forward to justify admission to the bar appeared to many opponents to lead directly to women's suffrage and equality in other areas."

When Clara Brett Martin was admitted to practise law by the Law Society of Upper Canada in 1897, she became the first woman lawyer in the British Empire. A trailblazer, Martin had confronted hostility at each step of her professional path. In 1891, when she had first applied to the Law Society of Upper Canada for admission as a student, she had been refused; it was only with the support of such influential persons as Premier Sir Oliver Mowat and Dr Emily Stowe and the passage of a provincial act that admitted women as solicitors that she was finally admitted in 1893 (Backhouse, 1991). Between 1898 and 1923, the overwhelming majority of European countries also allowed women to become lawyers. However, it was not until 1941 that Quebec granted women the right to be admitted to the practice of law, with access delayed even longer to women of racialized minorities. In 1946, Greta Wong Grant became Canada's first Chinese-Canadian lawyer. In 1979, Delia Opekokew became the first Native woman to be admitted to the bar in Saskatchewan and also, four years later, the first Native woman to be admitted to the bar in Ontario. In 1984, when Marva Jemmott was appointed as a Queen's Counsel, she became the first Black woman in Canada to receive this honour. The first woman president of the Canadian Bar Association, Paule Gauthier, was appointed in 1997 (Dawson and Quaile, 1998:119). As late as 1971, women accounted for only a very small proportion of the legal profession (5 percent). In July of 1993, the Canadian Bar Association reported that of 59 310 lawyers in Canada, 16 043 (27.1 percent) were women (Canadian Bar Association, 1993:19). However, the proportion of women who are law students at Canadian universities has grown rapidly in recent decades, from 6 percent in 1965 to 11 percent in 1969, 20 percent in 1973, 30 percent in 1976, and about 42 percent in 1986 (Mazer, 1989). By the early 1990s, women accounted for approximately half of Canada's law school students (Canadian Bar Association,

1993:9). This trend has continued in the new millennium. For example, statistics prepared by the Law Society of Upper Canada indicate that, in Ontario, women represented 57 percent of those called to the bar in 2005 (Law Society of Upper Canada, 2006). Similarly, a recent report by the Canadian Bar Association (2005:14) points out that in 1990–91, "female law students outnumbered males for the first time" in Canada and, that in 2003, 60 percent of law school enrollees were women. In addition, this report notes that while "in 1970, only one in 20 lawyers in Canada was female. . . [t]oday, one of every three lawyers is a woman, with the majority under age 35." (Bearing witness to the dynamics of past practices, it can be noted that, in Canada, only one in ten lawyers over the age of 50 is female.)

The profession in both Canada and the United States also historically discriminated against ethnic and racial minorities. This was particularly overt in the United States where the legal profession explicitly discriminated against Blacks (Abel, 1986), and where Blacks were excluded from the American Bar Association and many law schools until the 1950s. As recently as 1965, African Americans made up 11 percent of the US population but less than 2 percent of lawyers and only 1.3 percent of law students, half of them in all-Black law schools. Even in 1977, only 5 percent of the country's law students were Black (Friedman, 1998, 2002). By the 1990–91 academic year, this figure had risen slightly to 5.6 percent. Although American law schools claim that they recruit aggressively for minorities, in 1992 African Americans accounted for merely 3.4 percent of lawyers in the United States (Pollock and Adler, 1992:4). In 2004, only 29.2 percent of American lawyers were women, 4.8 percent were African American, 2.8 percent were Hispanic, and 92.6 percent were white (*U.S. News & World Report*, 2004).

During the past two decades, Canadian lawyers have become a more diverse group; the proportion of lawyers born in Canada has decreased slightly while "the proportion of different ethnicities, genders, nationalities, and religious affiliations has changed significantly" (Hutchinson, 1999:36). For example, while about 55 percent of lawyers were of British ethnicity in 1961, this decreased to just over 50 percent in 1971 and about 44 percent in 1981. The percentage of lawyers who were of neither British nor French ethnicity increased from 20 percent in 1961 to almost 30 percent in 1981. Nevertheless, Henry et al. (2000:150) report that, in the early 1990s, fewer than 3 percent of lawyers were members of a visible minority and fewer than 1 percent were Native Canadians.

At its 1994 meeting, the Canadian Bar Association adopted a recommendation to conduct a full inquiry into racial equality in the legal profession. The results of this inquiry into the position of racialized groups within the Canadian legal community were reported in 1999 and resulted in Resolution 99-04-A-Revised, *Racial Equality in the Legal Profession*. Among its recommendations it encouraged law schools to: review their admission criteria for possible systemic barriers; create an internal results-based monitoring process to ensure that Aboriginal students and students from racialized communities were fairly treated in admission decisions; diversify perspectives of admission committees by including third-year students from equality-seeking communities; ensure student exposure to human rights principles and ethics, critical race theory, and Aboriginal law; develop a strategic hiring plan to diversify the faculty at all levels; and develop bursaries and scholarships to increase and encourage representation of students from racialized communities at the undergraduate and graduate levels. It additionally urged the federal Department of Justice to conduct a feasibility study to design and establish an Aboriginal law school (Canadian Bar Association, 1999).

Although the 2005 Report of the Canadian Bar Association's Futures Committee (CBA, 2005:16) observes that "[r]ace data for the Canadian legal profession are sketchy

and even misleading, particularly since most depend on self-identification," it acknowledges that visible minorities remain under-represented, relative to their proportion of the
population, in the legal profession. While the 2001 Census found that 13.4 percent of the
Canadian population were members of a visible minority, simply 6.8 percent of Canadian
lawyers identified themselves as such—a situation that compares unfavourably with many
other professions. For example, in 2001, more than one-fifth (21.3 percent) of Canadian
dentists and 17.5 percent of specialized physicians self-identified as members of a visible
minority group. An earlier study conducted in Canada's most populous province also noted
that while 17.5 percent of Ontario's population self-identified as non-white in 1996, only
7.3 percent of lawyers did so (compared with 24.5 percent of Ontario's physicians and 22.1
percent of its engineers). It is evident that, despite "important inroads across various fields
of law and across different practice settings, including law firms of all sizes, . . . people of
racialized communities are under-represented relative to their numbers in the Canadian
population" (Kay, Masuch, and Curry, 2004). This is particularly true in relation to
Aboriginal peoples. As the Canadian Bar Association (2005:18) remarks, "Equity programs at law schools may slowly change the demographics of the profession, but numbers
of Aboriginal students. . . are so low that such programs are unlikely to have much impact
over the next decade unless special measures are introduced."

In the past, law firms in both Canada and the United States were about as exclusionary as law schools. Many excluded Jews, Catholics, visible minorities, Aboriginal people,
and women. Through the 1950s, most firms were solidly and resolutely WASP (white
Anglo-Saxon Protestant) (Stevens, 1983:100). Since then, discriminatory practices have
decreased but, assuredly, have not fully disappeared. For example, one might consider that,
in 1995, among lawyers aged 50–54, the earnings of non-white lawyers in Ontario were
less than 50 percent of their white counterparts (Canadian Bar Association, 2005:16). As
Hutchinson observes:

> From its elite status at Confederation, the legal profession has become increasingly fragmented,
> both in terms of diversity (different people and forms of organization) and stratification (a
> hierarchical order to such diversity). Unfortunately, there has been a marked tendency for the
> benefits of diversity to be neutralized by the imposition of stratification: the new and diverse
> personnel are relegated to the marginalized periphery of the legal profession. While the pro-
> fession has diversified, the typical lawyer remains male, white, English-speaking, early middle-
> aged, and Christian; lawyers who deviate from this norm are greater in number, but still less
> powerful in prestige and influence. (1999:35)

There are still signs of tokenism, and women and racialized groups remain marginalized within high-prestige fields (Hagan and Kay, 1995, 1999; Heinz and Laumann, 1994;
Kay and Brockman, 2000). For example, Mary Anne Mossman (1994) has pointed to the
predominance of women lawyers in the lower-status family law profession. Within the
legal profession in Toronto, observe Hagan et al. (1988:9), women lawyers tend to compose a "legal working class." A recent longitudinal study of women lawyers in Ontario
(Kay, Masuch, and Curry, 2004) found that "more women lawyers than ever are working
part-time; that male lawyers are still more highly represented in partnership positions and
are more likely to be solo practitioners; . . . that women are under-represented in the over
$200 000 income bracket and most highly represented in the under $40 000 bracket;
that, of sole practitioners, male lawyers earn on average $126 000 annually compared
to $86 000 for women; that women lawyers are more likely to have several legal posi-
tions over the course of their careers, and more likely to make lateral professional moves;

and that there are very high attrition rates for women" (in CBA, 2005:14). A second study, "Equity and Diversity in Alberta's Legal Profession" (Cooper et al., 2004) similarly reports that women "remain under-represented in authority and leadership positions in large law firms, perhaps out of choice, but perhaps not" (CBA, 2005: 14).

Only 14 percent of the partners in the top 250 law firms in the United States are women (Nossel and Westfall, 1998), and a 2001 survey of the 12 highest-grossing law firms in the US found that minority lawyers accounted for about 5 percent of the new partners in recent years at the seven firms that supplied such data (Glater, 2001). Gorman (2005) suggests that the gender stereotypicality of selection criteria used by law firms as well as decision-makers' same-gender preferences may combine and intensify gender inequality in hiring. While law schools and many law firms have aggressively recruited visible minorities and women, promotions and partnerships for traditionally marginalized groups remain elusive (O'Donovan-Polten, 2001). Based on a sample of Canadian lawyers, Kay (1997) reports that women continue to be under-represented in law firm partnerships, advance to these positions more slowly than do men, and exit law firm practice at a much higher rate than their male counterparts (see also Brockman, 2001).

Income disparities and more subtle forms of gender bias in promotion to top positions also persist (Hagan, 1990; Keeva, 1995). Robson and Wallace's (2001) examination of the earnings of 261 male and 251 female lawyers in Canada found that while the sex of lawyers does not have a direct impact on earnings, pay discrimination may operate in a variety of subtle ways. They argue that women lawyers are disadvantaged in relation to many factors that significantly influence earnings and report that, when compared to their male counterparts, women lawyers have less job autonomy. Investigators using survey data to compare the experience of male and female lawyers in Canada (Hagan and Kay, 1999, 1995), interviews of 100 women lawyers in Australia (Thornton, 1996), and in-depth interviews and participation observation among male and female lawyers at a large law firm and corporate legal department in San Francisco (Pierce, 1995) all find that women lawyers are disadvantaged by social structures operating on multiple levels. Leiper (1998, 2006) finds that Canadian women lawyers report heightened time-crunch stress, particularly if they are mothers and assume the major responsibility for child care.

One reason lawyers offer is that minority lawyers are less likely to have relationships with important clients or to have landed a significant amount of business for the firm. But some minority-group lawyers say that they are not given the same opportunities as white male lawyers to work with important clients, often because they do not have mentors who ensure that they have access to the best work. Jean Wallace (2001) finds that, among women lawyers, the experience of being mentored is typically positive—regardless of whether the mentor is male or female—with protégés reporting greater career satisfaction that non-protégés. Although female protégés with male mentors earned significantly more than protégés with female mentors, those mentored by women were more likely to indicate that their professional expectations were being met, reported greater career satisfaction and less work-nonwork conflict, and were more likely to declare their intent to continue practising law. However, it is evident that not all minority-group members receive the positive career and emotional outcomes that can accrue from the experience of mentoring.

Minority lawyers also identify what they perceive to be a lack of opportunity for advancement within firms and as a result they opt for career opportunities in business, consulting firms, government jobs or corporate legal departments. In addition, there are complaints about alleged disparate treatment of male and female lawyers in court in demeanour and language (Curriden, 1995). Minority female lawyers report that they lack support by white female and minority male lawyers, face both race and sex discrimination, and have difficulties establishing networks (Quade, 1995). Sexual harassment continues to be a problem. In one survey, 60 percent of female lawyers alleged that they had been sexually harassed by males involved in the court system (Woo, 1992).

In addition to changes over time in the composition of its membership, there have also been noticeable changes in the practice of law. Lawyers were instrumental in the growth of corporations, devising new forms of charters, and assisting companies to organize national business, while taking maximum advantage of variable laws concerning incorporation and taxation. The emergence and proliferation of firms specializing in corporation law provided those lawyers who possessed appropriate social, religious, and ethnic credentials with an opportunity to secure personal power and to shape the future of their profession. But only lawyers who possessed what Gerald S. Auerbach (1976:21) calls "considerable social capital" could inhabit the world of the corporate-law firm. In addition, "large firms have become larger and these larger firms have, in turn, merged with other large firms. As a result, some major law firms are now national and international with branch offices around the world" (Gill, 1990:ix). It should be noted, however, that such large firms were, and are today, an exception. The preponderance of firms are small, with the vast majority of Canadian law firms composed of 10 or fewer lawyers. Generally, individual practitioners of law use the legal profession more as an avenue of social mobility than do their counterparts in large firms.

THE PROFESSION TODAY

As noted in Chapter 3, law has become one of the fastest-growing of all professions in Canada. The number of lawyers in Canada has risen from 9000 in 1951 to 27 100 in 1986; 53 570 in 1991; 65 000 in 1995; 85 863 in 2002; and 91 187 in 2004 (Canadian Bar Association, 2006; Federation of Law Societies of Canada, 2006; Hutchinson, 1999:36; Statistics Canada, 1998a).

The number of lawyers in any society is a function of the social role assigned to lawyers (Halliday, 1986). The role of lawyers in society is conditioned by a variety of factors, such as the degree of industrialization, bureaucratization, complexity of business transactions, expansion of legal entitlements, the growth of regulation, crime rates, and attitudes toward and availability of nonlegal methods of conflict resolution.

Lawyers have never been popular, and "on the whole, have a terrible image" (Friedman, 2002). Plato spoke of their "small and unrighteous" souls, and Keats said, "I think we may class the lawyer in the natural history of monsters." Thomas More left lawyers out of his Utopia, and Shakespeare made his feelings known in that famous line from *Henry VI, Part II:* "The first thing we do, let's kill all the lawyers." Undoubtedly, the adversarial system is costly not only in money but also in trust. Polls show that the public has limited confidence in the profession. A Gallup poll found that only 41 percent of Canadians ranked the honesty/ethical standards of lawyers as "very high" or "high," while 16 percent ranked the honesty/ethical standards of lawyers as "low" or "very low." By way of comparison, 69 percent ranked doctors as having "very high" or "high" standards, while merely 3 percent ranked doctors as "low" or "very low." For police officers, the percentages were, respectively, 55 percent and 7 percent (Gill, 1988:9). In a more recent Gallup poll, 46 percent of the respondents rated lawyers as "low" or "very low" in honesty and ethical standards—just slightly above car salesmen (Gross, 1998:26). Although the results

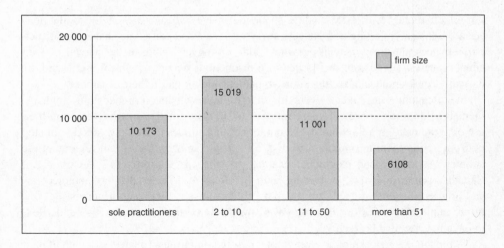

of a 2003 Gallup poll found some improvement, with only 36 percent of respondents rating lawyers as "low" or "very low" on these measures, Harris International reported that, in 2006, "lawyers ranked second-to-last on its annual list of most trusted professions. Only actors were deemed less trustworthy" (*Maclean's*, 2006:14).

Headlines in professional and popular publications and book titles are anything but flattering. In *Why Lawyers Behave As They Do,* Paul G. Haskell (1998) actually claims that the public is justified in its low opinion of the legal profession and explains the professional rules that govern how lawyers behave and that allow—or require—conduct that laypersons may find unethical. Richard Zitrin and Carol M. Langford (1999) argue that the delivery of legal and adjudicative services should not be governed solely by market forces and human acquisitiveness. Catherine Crier (2002) in *The Case Against Lawyers: How Lawyers, Politicians and Bureaucrats Have Turned the Law into an Instrument of Tyranny, and What We as Citizens Have to Do About It,* decries a system of laws so complex that even the enforcers cannot understand them and excoriates lawyers who profit from inefficiency, injustice, and abuse. Given this landscape, it is probably not surprising that a 2004 Ipsos-Reid survey found that "image is a burning preoccupation of the legal profession" or that the Canadian Bar Association (2005:20) observes that "[p]erhaps the biggest threat" to the legal profession "on the demand side is the current *poor image* of lawyers held by the public." Whether these negative opinions stem from "weaknesses, inequities or failings in the current legal systems (delays, appeal processes, filing costs, etc.) or from public misconceptions about the role of the legal profession vis-a-vis the justice system" or are based upon stereotypical and unflattering presentations of lawyers in the media, "all lawyers are affected, especially when there is an actual case of impropriety or unprofessional behaviour" (Canadian Bar Association, 2005:20).

Negative attitudes have prevailed toward lawyers in other countries as well. For example, in the former Soviet Union (even though Lenin himself was trained as a lawyer and actually practised for a short time), lawyers were considered one of the most unnecessary, parasitic, and exploitative groups, ranking in esteem with priests and capitalists (Cameron, 1978:50). Oleinik (2003) suggests that this lowly opinion of lawyers endures today in Russia. In India, the profession "has lost the social and moral prestige," and lawyers "go all out for money with little qualms about the image and morality of the profession" (Gandhi, 1982:33). In England, lawyers always have had bad press. They have been depicted as hypocrites, greedy social parasites, and pettifoggers, who, in the pursuit of their clients' interests, obfuscate real issues, use distinctions devoid of ethical merit, and are basically contemptuous of truth and unsympathetic and brutal in their behaviour.

We frequently criticize lawyers for their reliance on incomprehensible language, their unwillingness to provide legal services to the poor, their excessive fees, and their use of technicalities. Yet, consider the paradox: our attitudes toward lawyers do not stop us from voting them into public office at all levels of government in all regions of the country. As simply one example, consider that the vast majority (17 out of 22) of Canada's prime ministers, beginning with Sir John A. Macdonald, have studied law and/or been lawyers; indeed, our current prime minister, Stephen Harper, is the first prime minister since Lester Pearson (who was prime minister between 1963 and 1967) to have not attended law school.

Although lawyer-bashing is a venerable tradition, in fairness to lawyers, much of their negative image is exaggerated, and they are probably not much worse than members of other professions. Some of the charges are due to guilt by association. They often deal with people in trouble: criminals, politicians, and businesspeople threatened with disgrace, and those seeking divorce. At times, they articulate strong partisan interests, and it is no surprise that they are the object of strong sentiments. Although lawyers play a useful role and are sometimes admired, they are rarely loved. Probably no other legitimate profession has been as subjected to extremes of homage and vilification as lawyers (Bonsignore et al., 1989:241). Moreover, while lawyers are often presumed to be richly rewarded for their work and to enjoy enviable work conditions, these assumptions may be more apparent than real. The Canadian Bar Association (2006:17) reports that "[m]any first- and second-year lawyers are frustrated with being 'out of the loop' for stimulating work, instead finding themselves relegated to a form of 'hazing' (long hours, high volumes of routine work, relatively low pay)." Key stressors identified included excessive demands on their time, heavy workloads, and diminished opportunities for a personal life. These feelings of dissatisfaction were also common among more experienced lawyers. "In fact, even among lawyers with seven to eight years of practice, almost 70 percent are still thinking of leaving the profession" (CBA, 2006:17). A 2004 Ipsos-Reid online survey of Canadian lawyers within 10 large firms also reports that the majority of lawyers (62 percent of female lawyers and 50 percent of male lawyers) planned to change their jobs within five years' time; this was also true of lawyers who had practised for at least 15 years (in CBA, 2006:18).

It should be evident that lawyers are an increasingly heterogeneous group. Indeed, those who practise law now comprise "such a horizontally and vertically differentiated set of people and organizations engaging in different sorts of legal practice that generalizations are as unfounded as they are misleading" (Hutchinson, 1999:35). Consider that, at the start of the new millennium, the legal profession in Canada "is differentiated into megafirms, smaller partnerships, and single practitioners, not to mention government lawyers and the like; there is little shared experience, little interaction among them, and each operates in line with different cultures and norms" (Hutchinson, 1999:35). Nevertheless, for the sake of analytic simplicity, we can identify four principal subgroups within the legal profession: lawyers in private practice, lawyers in government service, lawyers in private employment, and the judiciary.

WHERE THE LAWYERS ARE

Each year, growing numbers of young adults graduate from law school, pass the bar, and enter an increasingly competitive marketplace. Some go into private practice, some find jobs in government, private industry, and in the teaching professions and others decide not to stay in law. Indeed, David Cohen (1998), who was then Dean of the University of Victoria's Law School, asserted that "a substantial proportion of law graduates do not plan to have a career in law."

As of December 31, 2004, the majority of lawyers, male and female, in every Canadian province and territory, were either sole practitioners or practised in small firms composed of 10 or fewer lawyers. For example, just over 40 percent of British Columbia's lawyers were solo practitioners (49.8 percent of female lawyers and 37.3 percent of male lawyers) while roughly one-third (33.6 percent) worked in firms with two to ten lawyers (30.3 percent of female lawyers and 34.8 percent of male lawyers). In Ontario, 30.9 percent of lawyers were solo practitioners (25.7 percent of female lawyers and 32.9 percent of male lawyers), while 31.7 percent worked in firms with two to ten lawyers (30.7 percent of female lawyers and 32 percent of male lawyers). In Nova Scotia, 24.5 percent of lawyers were solo practitioners (22.6 percent of female lawyers and 34.0 percent of male lawyers), while over one-third worked in firms with two to ten lawyers (37.1 percent of female lawyers and 52.9 percent of male lawyers). The percentage of lawyers who worked in that year in large firms, composed of 51 or more lawyers, varied from a low of 0 percent in Saskatchewan, PEI, Newfoundland and Labrador, and all three territories, to a high of 28.0 percent in Manitoba; nationally, roughly 16 percent of Canada's lawyers worked in firms of this size (Federation of Law Societies of Canada, 2005).

Private Practice

The majority of lawyers in Canada are in private practice. Contrary to the popular image that is reinforced by television (Rapping, 2004), only a small proportion of lawyers engage in litigation. In private practice, lawyers perform a number of significant roles. One is **counselling**. Lawyers spend about one-third of their time advising their clients about the proper course of action in anticipation of the reactions of courts, agencies, or third parties. Another is **negotiating**, both in criminal and in civil cases. Plea bargaining is an example of negotiation and is widely used in criminal cases (Palermo et al., 1998). Pretrial hearings and conferences in attempts to reach a settlement and thus avoid a costly trial are illustrative of the negotiating role of lawyers in civil cases. **Drafting**, the writing and revision of legal documents such as contracts, wills, deeds, and leases, is the "most legal" of a lawyer's role, although the availability of standardized forms for many kinds of legal problems often limits the lawyer to filling in the blanks. **Litigating** is a specialty, and relatively few lawyers engage in actual trial work. Much of the litigation in Canada is generally uncontested in cases such as debt, divorce, civil commitment, and criminal charges. Some lawyers also engage in **investigating**. In a criminal case, for example, the defence lawyer may search for the facts and gather background information in support of the client's plea. Finally, lawyers take part in **researching**—searching, for example, for precedents, adapting legal doctrine to specific cases, and anticipating court or agency rulings in particular situations. Much of such research activity is carried out by lawyers in large firms and appellate specialists. Experienced lawyers working in their specialty (or those working for a small fee) usually do little research (Klein, 1984:74).

The two extremes in private practice are represented by solo practitioners and big law firms. In between, there are partnerships and small law firms of relatively modest size. There is now a growing trend of female lawyers setting up their own firms (Graham, 1995). Solo practitioners are generalists; they operate in small offices and are "the jacks-of-all-trades of the legal profession" (Jacob, 1995). Many of these lawyers engage in marginal areas of law, such as collections, personal injury cases, rent cases, and evictions. They face competition from other professionals, such as accountants and real estate brokers, who are increasingly handling the tax and real estate work traditionally carried out by the solo practitioner. Jerome E. Carlin's (1962:209) classic work emphasized how the pressures to make a living could force individual practitioners to submit to pressures to violate legal ethics; in a later study, he suggested that this, indeed, was the case (Carlin, 1966). Lawyers in solo practice often act, he found, as intermediaries between clients and other lawyers to receive referral fees. In such an instance, the individual practitioner could become a businessperson rather than a lawyer, often defeating his or her original purpose in becoming a professional. Carlin (1962:206) observed that the individual lawyer was "rarely called upon to exercise a high level of professional skill" due, in large measure, "to the character of the demands placed upon him by the kinds of work and clients he is likely to encounter." He elaborates:

> Most matters that reach the individual practitioner—the small residential closing, the simple uncontested divorce, drawing up a will or probating a small estate, routing filings for a small business, negotiating a personal injury claim, or collecting on a debt—do not require very much technical knowledge, and what technical problems there are, are generally simplified by use of standardized forms and procedures. (1962:206)

Carlin notes that these lawyers attempt to justify their low status in the profession by emphasizing their independence and pointing out that they are general practitioners and thus knowledgeable about all facets of the law. This notion of autonomy, however, does not compensate for their feeling of insignificance in the overall legal structure and their frustration over not realizing their initial high ambitions, although they are professionals. Carlin (1962:206) suggests that these individual practitioners, like their counterparts in general practice in medicine, are "most likely to be found at the margin of (their) profession, enjoying little freedom in choice of clients, type of work, or conditions of practice."

Jack Ladinsky (1963), in a study of a sample of 207 lawyers, of whom 100 were solo and 107 were medium- to large-firm practitioners, reinforced Carlin's findings on individual practitioners. Ladinsky also found that individual practitioners come from minority religious and ethnic backgrounds, have parents of entrepreneurial or small-business status, and receive qualitatively and quantitatively inferior education more often than the lawyers in the law firm practice he included in the study (1963:49). Ladinsky suggests that social background (religious preference of mother and occupation of father) is the strongest determinant of whether a lawyer goes into firm or solo practice. The quality of the law school is an important intervening variable. Ladinsky notes: "Social background describes two major career contingencies: level of technical skill and access to clients" (1963:53). Ladinsky further points out that after graduation, relatively poor training and discrimination in firm recruitment make it difficult to get a prestigious firm job, and so solo lawyers end up doing low-paying, low-status work—that is, injury suits, divorce, petty criminal, and debt collection. They often develop a clientele of people of similar class, ethnic, and religious background.

There are also differences between individual and firm practitioners in acceptance of and compliance with ethical norms. Jerome Carlin (1966) found that the individual practitioner was the most likely to violate ethical norms (for example, soliciting kick-backs), with the nature of the client and the type of case being important contributing factors in the violations. Since solo practitioners often represent individuals, as contrasted with corporations that are represented by larger firms, the quality of the lawyers involved adversely affects the legal representation that many individuals receive. Because these lawyers are often from minority groups, minority clients are the ones who are adversely affected. Moreover, many of the larger, more prestigious, and more ethical firms will not accept the kinds of cases the individual practitioner confronts, and in fact refer those cases to him or her, so that the organization of the bar is such that ethical violations and ineffective practice are almost built into certain situations.

In a survey of lawyers' attitudes toward a specific problem in professional ethics (ambulance chasing), Kenneth F. Reichstein (1965) documents essentially the same relationship between professional status and notions of professional ethics reported by Carlin. Even though selecting personal injury cases is prohibited by the canons of ethics, an elaborate social structure (that is, legitimating values, specialist practitioners, techniques, and so on) exists around this type of practice. Reichstein found that high-status lawyers (high income, corporate practice, large firm, and the like) were almost unanimous in strongly disapproving of personal injury practice (and those lawyers engaged in it), on the grounds that "it brings disrepute on the profession." On the other hand, low-status lawyers (low income, solo practitioners, lack of established clientele) were more likely to give qualified approval of personal injury practice. Low-status lawyers based their attitudes on the rationale that "it is necessary to make a living," or "it prevents poor people from being taken advantage of." Reichstein also notes that "deviance" in this case is in no small part a product of elite control of the rulemaking and enforcement machinery of the organized bar, which will be discussed later in this chapter.

Practising in large law firms is very different from solo practice. These firms employ legions of supporting staff, including paralegals, business-trained administrators, librarians, and technicians (*Lawyer's Almanac,* 2004). As noted earlier, many of these large firms are becoming national and international in scope. These firms shy away from less profitable business—individual legal problems such as wills and divorces—in favour of corporate clients. Unlike solo practitioners, firms maintain long-term relationships with their clients, and many are on retainers by large corporations. Large firms offer a variety of specialized services, with departments specializing in a number of fields such as tax law, mergers, antitrust suits, and certain types of government regulations. These firms deal generally with repeat players and provide the best possible information and legal remedies to their clients along with creative and innovative solutions for the clients' problems (Jacob, 1995).

Large firms have a pronounced hierarchical organization structure (Hagan, Huxter, and Parker, 1988). Young lawyers are hired as associates. Beginning associates are seen as having limited skills, in spite of their elite education, and are assigned the task of preparing briefs and engaging in legal research under the supervision of a partner or a senior associate. In seven or eight years, they either become junior partners or leave the firm. For a new associate who has a strong desire to move into a partnership position, the competition with cohorts is very strong.

Associates are on a fixed salary, whereas partners' incomes are based on profits. In most firms, law partners earn profits largely on hourly billings of associates: the more associates per partner, the higher the profits. How profits are divided among partners is usually decided by a small committee that looks at such factors as work brought in, hours billed, and seniority. The traditional rule is that associates should produce billings of about three times that of their salaries—a third goes to the associate, a third to overhead, and a third to the firm's profit. At most firms, lawyers' time is billed in 6-minute or 15-minute units, with each nonbusiness conversation, personal phone call, and vacation day cutting into billable hours. No wonder many associates are labelled "workaholics" and spend evenings and weekends in their offices.

One of the most complete analyses of elite law firms is Erwin O. Smigel's (1964) *Wall Street Lawyer*. Although the Wall Street law firm is not typical of the majority of law firms in either the United States or Canada because of its size and type of practice, the contrast between this type of law practice and that of the individual practitioner illustrates the immense diversity within the legal profession.

The law firms investigated by Smigel perform a variety of functions. They are spokespersons for much of big business in the United States. But they not only represent business; many members of the firms also serve as members of the boards of directors of corporations they represent. These law firms also act as recruiting centres for high-level government service. Members of the firm are appointed to important government positions and seek national political offices. Many of their members are also active in various capacities in national, state, and local governmental agencies and participate in civic and philanthropic activities.

The Wall Street law firms are large, ranging from 50 to several hundred lawyers on the staff. Over 70 percent of the lawyers attended Harvard, Yale, or Columbia Law School—the elite schools of the nation—and were top students. The Wall Street law firms actively recruit these top individuals, and would prefer all their lawyers to have these credentials. In addition, the firms also look for the "correct" family background, which is considered important in making contacts that will bring business in the future. As might be expected, Smigel found very few visible minority or women attorneys in the Wall Street firms. Similarly, relatively few Catholic lawyers were found in the Wall Street firms because of what are considered to be lower-class origins, poorer education, and immigrant parents. As compared with individual practitioners, the Wall Street lawyers have a superior education, both quantitatively and qualitatively. It should be noted, however, that not every graduate of prestigious law schools desires the kind of law practised by the Wall Street lawyers. Smigel notes that many students feel that the specialization in the large law office is so great that they would soon become limited in their abilities. Others feel that they would be lost in such a setting, and their mobility opportunities impaired. Some law school graduates look upon a Wall Street firm as a postgraduate training period, using it as a springboard for future positions in industry and government.

The observations of Carlin and Ladinsky on solo practitioners and Smigel on large law firms are supplemented by the conclusions of John P. Heinz and Edward O. Laumann (1994), who note that much of the "differentiation within the legal profession is secondary to one fundamental distinction—the distinction between lawyers who represent large organizations (corporations, labour unions, or government) and those who represent individuals. The two kinds of law practice are the two hemispheres of the profession." Most lawyers, they add, "reside exclusively in one hemisphere or the other and seldom, if ever, cross the equator" (1994:319). The two sectors of the profession are separated by the social origins of lawyers, the schools where they were trained, the types of clients they serve, office environment, frequency and type of litigation, values, and different circles of acquaintance; the two sectors "rest their claims to professionalism on different sorts of social power" (1994:384). Large cities, Heinz and Laumann conclude, have two legal professions—one that is recruited from more privileged social origins where lawyers serve wealthy and powerful corporate clients, and the other from less prestigious backgrounds where lawyers serve individuals and small businesses. Thus, "the hierarchy of lawyers suggests a corresponding stratification of law into two systems of justice, separate and unequal" (1994:385).

Government

"Many lawyers are employed in government service at both the provincial and federal levels, acting as government advisors, conducting legal research, drafting legislation and serving as counsel in litigation matters involving the government" (Gill, 1990:189). Malcolm Spector (1972) suggests that taking positions in government agencies may be a strategy used by young lawyers for upward professional mobility. He considers employment with the government a mobility route into a more prestigious practice for the young lawyer handicapped by mediocre education or stigmatized by sex, religion, or ethnic background. It is notable that a recent study of 100 lawyers called to the bar in British Columbia finds that women are more likely to practise as government lawyers than men (Brockman, 2001).

Spector maintains that by pursuing a short-term career in a government agency, the young lawyer not able to initially break into "big league" firms gains valuable trial experience, specialized knowledge of regulatory law, and government contacts that eventually might be parlayed into a move to elite firms. Many of those entering public service are recent law school graduates who find government salaries sufficiently attractive at this stage of their careers, and seek the training that such service may offer as a prelude to private practice. Limitations on top salaries discourage some from continuing with the government, although in recent years, public service has become more attractive as a career.

The majority of lawyers serve by appointment in legal departments of a variety of federal and provincial agencies. Those who find legal research stimulating may pursue employment with either the federal or provincial law reform commissions which conduct research into various areas of law. Various governmental departments and regulatory agencies employ lawyers. Still others are engaged as crown attorneys, agents of either the Attorney General of Canada or the attorneys general for the provinces and territories who respectively serve as the chief legal officers for Canada's federal, provincial, and territorial governments. Included among the most important responsibilities of crown attorneys are preparing and conducting criminal prosecutions. With the exception of prosecutions conducted in the Northwest Territories, the Yukon Territory, and Nunavut, which are the responsibilities of the Federal Prosecution Service (FPS), provincial crown attorneys are responsible for the majority of Criminal Code prosecutions. The FPS, "staffed by full-time prosecutors and agents recruited from the private bar, conducts prosecutions across Canada on behalf of the Attorney General of Canada. These prosecutions are carried out under a wide range of federal statutes, including the *Controlled Drugs and Substances Act*, the *Customs Act*, the *Excise Act* and the *Income Tax Act*" (Griffiths and Cunningham, 2003:6).

As a rule, lawyers in government are directly engaged in legal work, since law training is infrequently sought as preparation for general government service. However, a small but important minority, which is considered an exception to this rule, consists of those who have been appointed to high executive positions and those who have been elected to political office.

Private Employment

Lawyers are also engaged in private employment. These lawyers (often referred to as house counsels) are salaried employees of private business concerns, usually industrial corporations, insurance companies, and banks. Large corporations typically have huge legal departments with almost 500 lawyers (*Lawyer's Almanac,* 2004).

The growth of corporations, the complexity of business, and the multitude of problems posed by government regulation make it desirable, if not imperative, for some firms to have lawyers and legal departments familiar with the particular problems and conditions of the firm. In view of the increased complexity of business transactions and the growth of federal regulations, the proportion of the profession engaged in this kind of activity can be expected to increase in coming years. In addition to legal work, lawyers often serve as officers of the company, and may serve on important policymaking committees, perhaps even on the board of directors. Although lawyers in legal departments are members of the bar and are entitled to appear in court, their lack of trial experience means that a firm will usually hire an outside lawyer for litigation and for court appearances. Lawyers in legal departments of business firms do not tend to move to other branches of legal work after a number of years. Many of these lawyers have been in private practice or in government service. There is some horizontal mobility between government work and private employment, but not to the same extent as between government and law firms (Jenkins, 1977).

Judiciary

A very small proportion of lawyers are members of the judiciary. The *Constitution Act* and the federal *Judges Act* govern the appointment, removal, retirement, and remuneration of federally appointed judges. Judges of the Supreme Court and Federal Court are appointed by the federal government through the Office of the Commissioner for Federal Judicial Affairs. Under section 96 of the *Constitution* Act, the federal government also appoints judges to some provincial courts. "Sometimes referred to as 'section 96 judges,' they sit in the provincial Supreme Court or Court of Appeal or in equivalent courts such as the Court of Queen's Bench, the Superior Court (in Quebec) or the General Division of the Courts of Justice (in Ontario)" (Gill, 1999:1225).

In Canada, federally appointed judges must be lawyers who have been members of a provincial bar for a minimum of 10 years. According to Neil Boyd (1998:186), Canada's federally appointed judiciary continues to be drawn "almost exclusively from the ranks of men and women who support the Conservative and Liberal parties." As well, while "efforts are being made to address the failure of the judiciary to reflect Canada's diversity," there continues to be an "overrepresentation of elderly, white Anglo males" in Canada's judiciary (Griffiths and Cunningham, 2003:174).

Provincial appointments in most provinces occur after the applicant has been considered by a judicial advisory committee that is composed of representatives of the legal profession, the judiciary, and the public. While in some provinces prospective judges must be lawyers who have been members of the bar for five years, eligibility rules vary across provinces. However, while "many so-called police magistrates are retired members of national or local police forces. . . even in provinces where judges need not be lawyers, only lawyers are now appointed" (Gill, 1999:1225). Provincial court judges, who hear less serious criminal matters and civil cases involving relatively small amounts of money, are appointed and paid by the province in which they serve.

The Supreme Court of Canada, which is Canada's highest court of law, is composed of a Chief Justice and eight puisne judges. Three of the judges must be appointed from Quebec and, by convention rather than legal requirement, three judges have generally been appointed from Ontario, two from the western provinces and one from Atlantic Canada. Sauvageau, Schneirman, and Taras (2006:21) pointedly note that "even though the federal government and provinces share jurisdiction in many areas of Canadian life over which the [Supreme] court has jurisdiction," the prime minister does not always consult with provincial premiers prior to appointing members to the Supreme Court. While law societies, legal experts, and the federal justices are typically consulted prior to a prime minister's appointing a judge from a short list of qualified candidates, those appointed "do not have to be approved by Parliament nor are nominees made to appear before a parliamentary committee," nor are they obliged to "undergo the intense scrutiny, the ordeal of public exhibition, which is required of judges in the United States."

In recent years, some additional levels have added to the appointment process. In August 2004, the Paul Martin government added an ad hoc Committee of the House of Commons, along with a representative from the Canadian Bar Association and Canadian Judicial Council, being afforded the opportunity to question the Justice Minister about the prime minister's appointment (the proceedings were broadcast live on the Canadian Parliamentary Affairs Channel [CPAC]). With the defeat of the Liberal government, Prime Minister Harper announced further refinements to the process, maintaining that the process introduced by the Liberals "was not sufficiently open" (CBC News, 2006). With the retirement of Justice John Mayor, an advisory committee of MPs from all parties, along with a variety of people from within and outside the justice community, were asked to compile a list of three candidates and Harper publicly stated that he would select the nominee from that list. In February of 2006, Harper announced that the next person he nominated to the Supreme Court would be required to appear at a televised hearing before a committee composed of 12 members of Parliament, selected from each of the four parties represented in the House of Commons in a way that ensured no party held a minority. However, he also stated that the committee would not have the power to either confirm or quash the nomination of the prospective judge, and that he would reserve that right for himself as prime minister.

Supreme Court judges are appointed and paid by the federal government and may continue to hold office until they reach the age of 75. (While federally appointed judges serving on the Federal Court or a provincial superior court are also able to hold office until their mandatory retirement at age 75, provincially appointed judges are generally required to retire at age 70). As of August 2006, there were four women among the Supreme Court Justices of Canada. The average age of Supreme Court judges in that year was 62, with the youngest judges 54 years of age (the Hon Madam Justice Marie Deschamps) and the oldest, 68 (the Hon Mr Justice Morris J. Fish). The Rt Hon Madam Justice Beverley McLachlin became the first woman to be the Chief Justice of the Supreme Court of Canada when she was appointed on January 7, 2000; the first woman appointed to the Supreme Court of Canada, Justice Bertha Wilson, was appointed in 1982.

Supreme Court judges earn the highest salaries among judges in Canada. In 2006, the annual salary of the Chief Justice of the Supreme Court was $278 400, while puisne justices earned $257 800 (CBC News, 2006). In general, the average earnings of Canadian judges placed them at the top of the 25 highest-paying occupations. In 1995, the average earnings of both male and female judges was $126 246, with the average earnings of male judges ($128 791) surpassing those of female judges ($117 707) (Statistics Canada, 1998b). In 2003, the salary of a federally appointed judge (other than a chief justice or a judge of the Supreme Court of Canada), was $216 600 (Canadian Judicial Council, 2006). In 2004, a federal commission recommended a salary increase of roughly 19 percent over four years (reasoning that the federal judiciary must be paid generously to attract meritorious candidates and to offset the increasing stresses and difficulties that their work poses). However, a Liberal bill granting this increase died with the fall of the Liberal Party from power. In June of 2006, the federal government introduced legislation to raise the salaries of 1100 federally appointed judges by simply 7.25 percent; under the proposed bill, the salary of the chief justice of the Supreme Court would increase to $298 500 while her eight colleagues would earn $276 400; chief justices and associate chief justices on the Federal Court, Tax Court of Canada, and superior courts in each province would earn $254 600; and all other federally appointed judges would receive $232 300.

While horizontal appointments from bar to bench have been common in Canada and, frequently, judges have been elevated from a lower to a high court, there is no prescribed route for the young law graduate who aspires to be a judge—no apprenticeship that he or she must serve, no service that he or she must necessarily enter (Carp and Stidham, 2001:209). This is in contrast to some other countries, such as Japan and France, where there are special schools for training judges. In Scandinavian countries, judicial training is acquired during a practical internship period following law school. In the former Soviet Union, judges often lacked formal legal training and were appointed on the basis of loyalty and Communist Party affiliation (Glendon et al., 1994). In the United States, yet another system is employed. In that country there is no career judiciary, and in over two-thirds of American states, judges are elected, usually by popular vote and occasionally by the legislature. Since 1937, the American Bar Association has advocated a system (the Missouri Plan) under which the governor appoints judges from a list submitted by a special nominating board, and the judge then periodically stands unopposed for re-election by popular vote on the basis of his or her record. Such a system is now in effect in several states. In a small group of states, judges are appointed by the governor, subject to legislative confirmation. This is also the method of selection of federal judges, who are appointed by the president, subject to confirmation by the Senate. Although some Canadians clamour for American-style judicial elections, the selection of judges in the United States has not been immune from political influence, pressure, and controversy (Davison, 2002; Shuman and Champagne, 1997). Moreover, it has not resulted in a judiciary reflective of the racial and ethnic composition of the population. To illustrate: In 1992, of the 356 judges sitting on the states' highest courts, only 4.2 percent were Black, and there was only one Hispanic. Of the 837 judges on the federal bench, 5.2 percent were African American (Pollock and Adler, 1992:4). In the ensuing 10 years, the situation has not changed noticeably in the United States, and the progress of minorities on the bench has been very slow at all levels.

LAWYERS AND MONEY

The fiscal position of lawyers is often assumed to be enviable. However, contrary to conventional wisdom, the results of the 2001 Canadian census reveal that "[t]here are more sales managers and advertising executives earning at least $100 000 a year than lawyers" (Vallis, 2003). According to this census, lawyers and Quebec notaries were the most common occupations of Canadian women working full-year, full-time who earned $100 000 or more in 2000. However, among high-income earning men, these occupations were the fifth most common, accounting for 4.2 percent of all men who worked full-year, full-time. Canadian men earning $100 000 or more were more likely to be employed as sales, marketing, and advertising managers (5.1 percent), as senior managers in goods production, utilities, transportation, or construction (5.0 percent), as senior managers in finance, communications, carriers, and other business services (4.9 percent), or in computer and information systems occupations (4.8 percent) (Statistics Canada, 2003).

There is an unusually large range of income among lawyers. The income of a partner in a corporate law practice on Bay Street in Toronto and a solo practitioner on Selkirk Avenue in North-End Winnipeg who battles in the legal aid trenches are scarcely interchangeable. There are several factors that account for the variation in lawyers' incomes. They include the type of practice (firm or solo); the type of clientele (corporations or individuals with "minor" problems); the reputation of the law school attended; achievement in law school; the age and length of practice; the degree of specialization; and the region and population of the place of practice (generally, the larger the community, the greater the average income). On the whole, lawyers in private employment do not fare as well as their corporate colleagues. For large corporations, it is not unusual for chief legal officers to have a total compensation package (salary, bonus, profit sharing, insurance, company car, and various perks) well in excess of $1 million (Mansnerus, 1995:F7).

In private practice, there are several ways lawyers generate income. Although hourly rates "appear to be on the way out, with clients pressing for capped fees, flat fees, and other billing alternatives," some lawyers continue to charge by the hour for services rendered—a practice that "can too easily reward inefficiency, incompetence and even encourage duplicity" (Hutchinson, 1999:79). While hourly billing has been the traditional norm, the cost of legal services is not dependent upon the complexity of the work involved or the amount of time that is actually expended.

While law firm billing practices have come under closer scrutiny, there remains a "thick fog" around the issues of legal fees (Hutchinson, 1999:77). In addition to the amount, there are legal and ethical questions concerning billing practices. Such practices include "using a heavy pen," which means rounding up to the next time unit in measuring fractions of hours worked on a client's case. There is also "late time," adding to the bill extra hours that lawyers did not work. Another questionable practice is the "smell test," a crude way lawyers can tell whether a padded bill will seem exorbitant to the client. Of course, there is not a clear-cut line between aggressive billing practices and fraud. Ideally, legal billing would be as simple as paying for a housecall by a plumber. Both charge by the hour, and they expect to be reimbursed for expenses incurred. However, it is not as simple as it sounds. Since lawyers may charge hundreds of dollars per hour and incur thousands in expenses, any imprecision can be costly to the client. Associates, for example, who are expected to bill from 1800 to 2400 hours (the latter means 6.57 hours of *actual* work 365 days a year), often introduce a modest multiplier in the charges (rounding off phone calls so a 1-minute call costs the client a full time unit of 6 or 15 minutes on the bill, or charging a full hour of work that includes lunch and a visit to the bathroom) (Moses and Schmitt, 1992). Through a process of legal alchemy known as double billing, lawyers can make two into four (take two hours of research spent on Client A's legal problem, which turns out to be the same as Client B's problem). Associates may even be encouraged to believe that any time spent thinking about a client's legal woes, even while eating or jogging, should be billed (Stracher, 2001).

Unfortunately, the professional rules governing Canadian lawyers "have little to say about the actual prices charged, other than that they be 'fair and reasonable,' and are more concerned with ensuring that lawyers do not engage in dubious practices, such as charging for hidden fees, splitting fees with non-lawyers, or not giving full disclosure to clients of the basis for fees charges. . . . [Moreover] [t]he incidence of discipline for charging unfair or excessive fees is extremely rare; action is taken only when there is evidence that the lawyer has actually cheated or duped the client" (Hutchinson, 1999:80; see also Fleming, 1997).

As we noted in Chapter 6, Canadian lawyers now also take cases on a contingency-fee basis. This is an arrangement whereby a lawyer receives a percentage of any damages collected. Such fees are used primarily in medical malpractice, personal injury, and some product liability and wrongful death cases. If the plaintiff loses, there is no payment required for legal services; if he or she wins, the lawyer takes his or her expenses off the top, then gets a percentage of the remainder. Nowadays, it is not unusual to hear of lawyers receiving multimillion-dollar fees, especially in large class-action suits. For example, in June of 2000, following the federal government's announcement of a $1.2-billion compensation package for Canadians who had become infected with hepatitis C after receiving tainted blood from the public blood services system from January 1986 to July 1990, the lawyers who had represented the victims were granted $52.5 million. This amount was divided among the lawyers who had been involved in three separate class-action suits in British Columbia, Quebec, and Ontario. Although lawyers representing the federal, territorial, and provincial governments (with the exception of Quebec and BC) later argued before the Ontario Court of Appeal that the amount awarded was excessive, the three-judge panel dismissed the motion to appeal (Pacienza, 2001). In May 2006, a draft copy of the final resolution agreement for the settlement of claims by residential school abuse survivors indicated that the lawyers who represented the survivors would receive the largest payment ever recorded for a Canadian class action: $80 million. While individual survivors of residential abuse would receive, on average, $30 000, the Regina-based Merchant Law Group was expected to receive $40 million with an additional $40 million paid to a national consortium of lawyers. Moreover, it was expected that the ultimate "legal fee payout. . . [would] be higher because more than a dozen other lawyers. . . [were] involved who. . . [were] not part of the class action lawsuits" (CBC News, 2006a).

The contingency-fee system undoubtedly has its merits. Among them: the contingency-fee system allows those who ordinarily could not afford legal representation to retain the services of a lawyer. However, at the same time, it has been noted that contingency fees may actually exacerbate rather than eradicate the problem of unequal access to justice. Specifically, "[t]he scope for abuse in such arrangements is great: lawyers might easily be tempted to exaggerate the difficulty of the case to boost their fees, or they might engage in unsuitable tactics to inflate the amount that a case is worth" (Hutchinson, 1999:81). It may additionally encourage lawyers to screen out weak cases because they share the risk of litigation—if they do not win, they do not collect. Although the oath taken on call to the bar in Canada customarily contains a commitment to "refuse no man's [sic] just cause," Canadian lawyers are not prohibited from refusing to represent particular clients or causes (even though some provinces have declared that lawyers must not discriminate against clients on the basis of their race, gender, or similar distinctions).

It should be noted that, in addition to actual damages, **punitive damages**, an extra amount over and above the victim's proven losses, further increase the dollar amount involved in litigation. Punitive damages are not intended to compensate plaintiffs but rather to punish defendants where their conduct has been outrageous, grossly negligent, and close to criminal. Although punitive damages are not ordered if the perpetrator has been punished as a criminal, punitives may be awarded in many types of tort litigation, including medical malpractice, product liability, and exceptional cases of libel and slander. Lawyers have little to lose by pressing a punitive-damages claim, and, if they win, it can be a pleasant surprise for the plaintiff. For example, in a 1996 British Columbia case, a lawyer was awarded damages of $20 000 plus $10 000 in punitive damages after the court found that the lawyer's reputation had been defamed by a real estate agent who had falsely and maliciously accused the lawyer of unethical conduct (Dranoff, 2001:200). Although only a fraction of civil cases end with punitive damages (*New York Times,* 1995a:B12), the threat of punitive damages has become an effective bargaining chip in settlement negotiations.

COMPETITION FOR BUSINESS

Historically, bar associations have strongly opposed advertising by lawyers (Cebula, 1998). In the common-law tradition, a lawsuit was considered an evil, albeit a necessary one. Lawmakers and judges considered litigation wasteful, expensive, time-consuming, and an invasion of privacy. It was considered acrimonious, increasing hostility and resentment among people who could otherwise find an opportunity to co-operate. It hindered productive enterprise, and society discouraged litigation where it was not absolutely imperative. Lawyers were forbidden to "stir up" litigation. Any attempt to drum up business as ordinary tradesmen did was discouraged. Lawyers were expected to wait passively for clients and to temper any entrepreneurial urge to solicit them (Olson, 1991b:27).

The demise of opposition to advertising began with a simple idea. Lawsuits came to be considered an effective way to deter misconduct and to compensate wronged persons. There was also a need to increase the demand for legal services, in part because law schools kept turning out large numbers of newly minted lawyers. Many lawyers and law firms began to view law as a business which requires the use of business marketing strategies (Savell, 1994). Of course, lawsuits are not the only products of lawyers. Much of their work can be seen as preventive, non-adversarial, or defensive, such as tax planning, contract negotiation, adoption, or document drafting. But all these activities can lead to a cycle of new demands and suspicions, for much of lawyering work contains an element of adversariness and assertiveness. Thus, an uncontested divorce can turn into a contested one, and advertising can entice aggrieved parties to seek out a lawyer to help them "to drop the spouse but keep the house." Moreover, Charter decisions on the freedom of communication of other professional groups have led to a softening of earlier attitudes on advertising, and "it is now common for lawyers to use some form of advertising" (Yates et al., 2000:114). Although the exact content of regulations enacted by provincial law societies vary, in the main, Canadian lawyers are allowed to advertise—provided the content of the advertising is truthful, largely informational, non-competitive, and not "in bad taste or otherwise offensive as to be prejudicial to the interests of the public or the legal profession" (Hutchinson, 1999:87).

When compared to their counterparts in the United States, Canadian lawyers are far less likely to advertise their services in a serious or substantial way. In the United States, the number of lawyers advertising has risen sharply over the years and late-night American television routinely airs a steady drumbeat of messages inviting the audience to "dump their hubbies, stiff their creditors, and take their bosses to the cleaners" (Olson, 1991b:31). Nowadays, there are even manuals and how-to books for lawyers on how to advertise on their own (see, for example, Randall, 2002). Nevertheless, members of the legal profession in both the United States as well as Canada have not unanimously welcomed these developments. There is concern that lawyer advertising has contributed to the low public image of attorneys (Podgers, 1995). Some believe that increased competition leads to a decreased quality of service. In addition, most bar associations still regard advertising as something that is vaguely unseemly. As a result, while some Canadian lawyers may advertise their services in bold full-page ads within telephone directories, legal directories, referral services, and websites such as CanLaw.com, others restrict themselves to a modest and more traditional one-line listing in the yellow pages.

After advertising, the next step in competition for business is solicitation. While dignified and comparatively unobtrusive tactics of soliciting for business—such as schmoozing and purposeful elbow-rubbing among the elite at society functions and private clubs—have been long-accepted ways of attracting clients, bar associations frowned upon lawyers drumming up litigation against a particular opponent, such as the Catholic Church or Xerox. However, while "it is accepted that activities designed to stimulate legal work where none exists, to harass or mislead potential clients, or to offer referral incentives are of ethically dubious provenance. . . the problem remains how lawyers who are driven as much by public spiritedness as commercial gain can take effective steps to ensure that the least advantaged in society are made aware of their legal rights and the means to enforce them" (Hutchinson, 1999:87). For example, while it may appear unseemly for lawyers to send letters to solicit the business of individuals known to have legal problems, there are few actual restrictions on lawyers from making their services known. Even in-person solicitation is no longer a taboo. The scenes of airplane disasters and mine accidents may precipitate a " ravenlike descent" of tort lawyers anxious to contact the victims or their relatives. One of the most egregious examples of this occurred in the wake of the 1989 Exxon oil spill in the Alaskan town of Valdez. One commentator described the "tanker chasing" of the time with the following wry observation: "Liability lawyers and prostitutes fresh from nearby Anchorage are said to prowl the dark, smoky bars in search of clients. Townspeople aren't as concerned about the prostitutes as they are about the lawyers" (Olson, 1991b:32).

Some large law firms are becoming more competitive by adopting modern cost-management techniques and strategic planning. Others are starting to experiment with public relations firms to handle new contacts. It is routine that major law firms have a partner for whom management has become a primary preoccupation. Many firms are also increasing the number and size of specialized departments, and there is a growth of "specialty firms," such as the type that specializes in labour law work on the side of management (Heinz and Laumann, 1994). The business of law in large firms, in fact, is turning out to be much like business in any field. Some even provide written service guarantees promising to resolve issues to the clients' satisfaction.

The Canadian Bar Association (2005:21) reports that "[c]hanges in supply and demand for legal services have created a number of important new trends" within the Canadian legal marketplace. For example, the demand for specific legal services has enhanced the trend toward *commoditization* or *unbundling* of services—a development that "demands a greater level of rigour in defining, pricing, delivering, and charging for services" and "opens the door for the potential use of paralegal suppliers for the more routine actions on some files." It also notes that Canadian lawyers are increasingly being asked to provide consumers with *alternative pricing models* that include, for example, fixed-price contracts and/or quantity discounts. Moreover, the CBA points out that, as firms experience continuing pressure to decrease their costs, "they may opt for mergers or alliances or, at the other end of the scale, move towards specialization or 'boutique' status. General or sole practitioners will find it increasingly difficult to survive amidst large or highly specialized competitors. Because of the changing nature of demand, firms are moving from local to regional to national to global practices." Other trends and developments that are expected to continue into the future include: a "widening compensation gap, particularly between lawyers in large firms and those in sole practice or small firms; the growing trend to contract or part-time work; and, the challenges of meeting increased client expectations in a faster, interconnected world in which competitors will be prepared to offer more for less" (CBA, 2005: 22).

Competition for law business is not limited to Canada or the United States. In India, for example, the legal profession is "extremely crowded" (Nagpaul, 1994:66), and there is excessive and unrestrained competition among lawyers for clients. India has the longest written Constitution incorporating ideas of basic rights, equalities, and social justice. Citizens are becoming more aware of their legal rights, the number of statutes enacted annually is staggering, and the courts are increasingly used as a forum for dispute resolution. In this legal environment, the author of an excellent study on lawyers bitterly complains that the profession has turned into a commercial business "bereft of all ideals, principles. . . there are no sacrosanct ground rules" and "the ruling passion of the Bar is greed and maximization of economic gains" (Gandhi, 1982:153). Many lawyers rely on "touts" or brokers to get business, and "touting" is a widely used, albeit highly unprofessional, activity. A tout may be a government clerk, a typist in the courtroom, a police officer, a village headman, or anyone with some prestige and visibility in the community. A tout befriends a potential client and refers the individual to a lawyer. The tout gets a commission from the lawyer, the seller of legal services, to whom the tout brings business. A tout may get up to 50 percent of the fee the lawyer collects from the client but receives no commission from the client. A tout works for only one lawyer, and good touts are sought after by lawyers. Successful lawyers have several touts "procuring" for them, and about two-thirds of criminal and one-third of civil cases are obtained through touts (Gandhi, 1982:108). In another study, it was noted that young lawyers were acting as touts for older, well-established lawyers primarily because they were unable to obtain professional work on their own (Nagpaul, 1994:69).

In this highly competitive climate, the clients are often cheated by unscrupulous touts and lawyers, who know they are vulnerable and expendable. The clients are helpless because they are ignorant of the law and unfamiliar with the legal arena. In rural areas in particular, most litigants are either illiterate or have a low level of formal education. They do not know where to find adequate and reasonable legal services and welcome the advances of touts with the promise of professional help. Once entrapped, they are passed on "among the various actors of the drama as a nutritious morsel and each has his [sic] mouthful of bite." Clients have no recourse, or even a chance to protest, because lawyers do not give them receipts for services rendered. Lawyers view clients as exclusive trading commodities and non-repeat business and extract whatever they can from them the first time. They are even reluctant to be seen with clients unless they have a formal business arrangement. The touts associated with lawyers are equally ruthless and exploitative and, like lawyers, do not develop continuing relationships with the clients.

LEGAL SERVICES FOR THE POOR AND THE NOT-SO-POOR

Although about one Canadian in two has consulted a lawyer in the purchase of a house and one in three has used the services of a lawyer in preparing a will, about one in four (26.3 percent) has never consulted a lawyer. Utilization of lawyers varies with income, with utilization being greatest in the highest income class (Gill, 1988:9; Blohm, 2004). In general, low- and moderate-income families do not seek legal help for their problems. One survey reports that although 41 percent of the poor and 52 percent of moderate-income families encountered at least one legal problem in the 1990s, 71 percent of the poor and 61 percent of moderate-income families did not turn to lawyers for help with their legal problem. The legal problems faced by these people were mainly consumer issues and personal finance (Hansen, 1994; Kritzer and Silbey, 2003).

There are many reasons why people do not use a lawyer. One Ontario survey found that almost two-thirds of respondents (64.7 percent) agreed that "a person should not call a lawyer until he [sic] has exhausted every other possible way of solving his [sic] problem." In addition, individuals may not label the difficulties they confront as "legal problems" per se. Within this survey, over seven out of ten respondents (72.4 percent) agreed with the statement that "many people do not go to lawyers because they do not recognize the legal nature of the problem." As well, people may perceive that consulting a lawyer is a costly undertaking. Within the Ontario survey, two-thirds of respondents (66.6 percent) agreed that "most people cannot afford the money to see a lawyer" (Gill, 1988:11).

Enforcing one's legal rights and engaging the services of lawyers are expensive. For some individuals, the costs involved are simply prohibitive. For others who need or want a lawyer, paying the price will be difficult. Allan Hutchinson observes:

> Urban lawyers cost on average about $200 per hour; the average piece of divorce litigation carries a price tag of about $8000. Bear in mind that these bills usually come at a time when things are going badly for clients; the price of justice is well out of the reach of most ordinary Canadians. Many are obliged to forgo warranted legal action or must act for themselves—which is like asking people to perform much-needed surgery on their own bodies. (2002:A17)

Since 1967, the main option for those Canadians who are unable to pay full legal fees has been legal aid. Legal aid plans, under which lawyers accept a significant reduction in their customary fees, are generally funded through a combination of government funds, lawyers' subsidy, and client contributions. In 1966, Ontario became the first province to enact legislation establishing a comprehensive legal aid system. By the mid-1970s, all Canadian provinces and territories had established some system of legal aid to help low-income persons obtain legal representation in criminal, family law, and other matters. Legal aid services fall within the provinces' constitutional responsibility for the administration of justice. However, since legal aid services in criminal law are a matter within federal constitutional responsibility, the federal Department of Justice became involved in legal aid programs with federal-provincial cost-sharing agreements (Mossman, 1999:1318).

> Legal aid, we should note, is not entirely "free" to clients. All plans require the legal aid client to repay at least part of the legal fees (depending on income), and/or to give the plan a lien on any real property the client may own (the legal fees remain as a debt registered against the property,

to be repaid when and if the property is sold), and/or to repay fees from any money awarded in the lawsuit. (Dranoff, 2001:347)

In 2004–05, as in previous years, governments were the major source of revenue for legal aid plans, contributing $545 million or 90 percent of the $599 million total revenues. Client contributions and cost recoveries provided 3 percent of the revenue for legal aid plans, while legal profession contributions accounted for 1 percent and other sources accounted for 5 percent (Statistics Canada, 2006).

Unlike Canada's system of " medicare " or universal health care, the current legal aid system does *not* provide all Canadians with basic legal services. For example, while Canada's legal aid plans received 755 000 applications for assistance in 2004–05, only 469 000 of these applications were approved for full legal aid (Statistics Canada, 2006). Obtaining legal aid funding is contingent upon an individual's financial status, and it is only available to those whose household income falls within low income eligibility limits established by provincial aid plan administrators. Canadians who are on welfare, for example, can generally expect legal aid—as long as their provincial or territorial legal aid plan covers their specific type of legal problem. In some provinces, for example, only criminal actions are covered. However, in all areas of the country, legal aid officers will use their discretion in evaluating the merits of the proposed lawsuit or the validity of a defence. In 2004–05, civil cases accounted for just over half (52 percent) of the cases funded through legal aid while criminal cases made up the remainder (Statistics Canada, 2006).

> Notwithstanding the idea of legal aid as a right, provincial legislation. . . generally provides for discretion in granting legal aid to clients who are charged with less serious offenses, or who must appear in lower courts in family law disputes, or where the client's case is heard in a small claims court or before a tribunal. In addition, the provision of legal advice, the preparation of documents, and negotiation on behalf of a client are all usually discretionary matters under legal aid legislation. (Mossman, 1999:1318)

Two major types of legal aid exist in Canada. In the "judicare model" of legal aid, which is widely used in Alberta, for example, individuals who require a lawyer's services apply to their provincial/territorial legal aid plan for a certificate that will grant them the right to be funded according to the provincial legal aid tariff. If this certificate is granted, the individual selects a private lawyer of his or her choice who is on the legal aid panel. In the second system of legal aid, referred to as the "public defender model," staff-salaried lawyers provide virtually all legal services. In Saskatchewan, Quebec, Nova Scotia, Prince Edward Island, and Newfoundland and Labrador, staff lawyers provide most or all services. In other jurisdictions, such as Ontario, Manitoba, and British Columbia, a hybrid legal aid situation exists. For example, while private lawyers on certificates feature prominently in legal aid services in British Columbia, there are also salaried lawyers in certain communities. In Ontario, the legal aid landscape is also mixed. In 2002, the cost to the province of Ontario for all legal aid certificates, including family, criminal, and immigration, was $111 million (Tyler, 2002). However, beginning in 1999, Legal Aid Ontario, the agency created to run the system independent of government, established pilot projects in Toronto, Ottawa, and Thunder Bay in order to compare family law services performed by government lawyers with the more traditional methods of issuing certificates to clients so that they could hire their lawyer of choice. In September 2002, the agency's board decided to make these three family law clinics permanent.

Although legal aid is designed to assist those who would be otherwise unable to afford legal representation, the current system falls short in many ways. First, it is notable that many provincial governments began slashing their legal aid budgets in the 1990s. Reductions in transfer payments to the provinces for social assistance have also adversely affected the funding available for legal aid. For example, Dranoff (2005:366) points out that, in response to the federal government's promise of subsidies, immigration and refugee law was initially paid for by some provincial plans. However, these subsidies have been cut back "and left the provinces to cope with the expectation that provincial plans will pay for legal aid in these areas." She grimly notes that these expectations are not always met. For example, in Ontario, the number of legal aid certificates for immigration and refugee issues rose from 1610 in 1989 to 15 247 in 1991; however, "for the 2003–04 fiscal year of the plan, only 10 191 certificates were granted for immigration and refugee cases" (Dranoff, 2005:366). Second, while the Canadian Bar Association's Code of Professional Conduct exhorts lawyers "to reduce or waive a fee in cases of hardship or poverty," this does not create an enforceable obligation that obliges lawyers to serve all sectors of society equally. Rather, it merely states that lawyers "*may* assist in making legal services available by participating in legal aid plans and referral services." Hutchinson (1999:84) charges that: "If the profession is to have any real chance of matching its rhetoric of service to the reality of social need, lawyers must begin to take seriously the obligation to provide their services at reduced rates. This obligation must be built into the basic ethical fabric of professional responsibility."

Canadian courts have acknowledged that attaining justice may be forestalled by lack of adequate counsel, particularly in cases where individuals face criminal charges. For example, in 1996, an Alberta court stayed proceedings against an individual facing criminal charges and ruled that persons charged with criminal offences possessed a constitutional right to a lawyer. According to Mr Justice Alexander Andrekson, an individual who cannot afford to engage the services of a lawyer and cannot adequately defend himself or herself must be provided with a government-funded lawyer or the case will be stayed. However, this decision was reversed in 1997 by the Alberta Court of Appeal. In 1996, an Ontario judge also stayed charges against a man who could neither afford a lawyer nor an expert witness and ruled that "to proceed. . . would adversely affect the fairness of the trial" (Dranoff, 2001:348). In that year, a second Ontario judge extended the right to counsel to include a case of child custody. In this case, a father, who was seeking sole custody of the couple's child, was represented by counsel. However, the child's mother, who was living on social assistance, had been denied a legal aid certificate. Relying on the Charter right to equal protection and benefit of the law, Justice Stong ordered the Attorney General to provide counsel for the mother in this case.

Canada's Criminal Code contains provisions empowering judges to appoint counsel for an accused who is not represented by a lawyer *if* the accused person is mentally unfit or is an appellant before an appeal court or the Supreme Court of Canada. As well, since persons accused of committing a sexual offence are prohibited from personally cross-examining witnesses under the age of 18, judges must appoint legal counsel in such cases to cross-examine any child witness. The *Youth Criminal Justice Act* also provides for appointment of counsel to represent a young person at any stage of proceedings if the young person was unable to retain counsel. However, this Act permits the provinces and territories to require youth or their parents to pay for their legal costs if they are fully capable of paying. In addition, in the case of *British Columbia v. Okanagan Indian Band*, the Supreme Court of Canada ruled in

2004 that trial judges could award costs before a trial is held and identified three criteria that would justify such an award: "the litigation could not proceed otherwise; the claim must obviously have merit; the issues raised transcend the individual litigant's interests, are of public importance, and have not been resolved in previous cases" (Dranoff, 2005:368).

Although legal aid undoubtedly helps some of the most disadvantaged members of society, legal assistance continues to fall beyond the means of many. Without access to affordable legal services, many people will remain unaware of what, exactly, their legal rights are and how to protect and enforce them. Those who face criminal charges may be especially vulnerable. While most Canadian provinces and territories also maintain "duty counsel"—"lawyers paid by legal aid who assist unrepresented litigants with urgent legal questions 'at the courthouse door,' usually on a temporary basis" (Dranoff, 2001:347)—the counsel provided here cannot hope to rival the breadth of services enjoyed by the affluent. In general, most lawyers appointed to represent the poor do not hire private investigators to look for witnesses or evidence. Most do not get expert witnesses, like psychiatrists or pathologists, to help challenge the prosecution's case. Most do not take the time to go to the scene of the crime, and some do not even make a jail or prison visit to discuss the case with their clients. A study of 137 New York homicide cases completed by appointed lawyers in 2000 showed that in 42 of them—nearly one-third—the lawyers did less than a week of preparation, raising questions about their effort and thoroughness. Only 12 spent at least 200 hours—five weeks or more—investigating and preparing their cases, a sign of "appropriate diligence, according to legal experts" (Fritsch and Rohde, 2001:27). The median for all cases was 72 hours—not quite two weeks' work.

The legal profession has almost always taken an adversarial stance to initiatives that would make legal services less costly. "The main thrust of the law societies' position is that attaching terms and conditions on lawyer availability infringes on the societies' regulatory role and is an unfair limitation on individual lawyers' freedom to deploy their services as and how they see fit." At times, in part to maintain public confidence in the legal system (Podgers, 1994), lawyers do provide legal services *pro bono publico* (for the public good) for indigents. However, *pro bono* work is often seen by the legal profession "as a virtuous act of *noblesse oblige* rather than [as] a basic responsibility that comes with being a lawyer" (Hutchinson, 1999:85). In consequences, organizations such as Pro Bono Law Ontario and *Pro Bono* Law of British Columbia are attempting to encourage law firms to make *pro bono* work a part of their firm's culture. Some Canadian law firms are considered exemplary in this regard. For example, Toronto-based Osler Hoskin & Harcourt LLP has operated a Community Law Program for over a quarter of a century. Its *pro bono* policy states that "our free legal assistance to these clients strengthens our community" and identifies various benefits of the program, including "great personal and professional satisfaction to the lawyers involved"; enhancement of the firm's image within the community; improved recruitment of top associates who are "interested in the social contribution of law"; superior training opportunities for young lawyers; enhanced associate morale; involvement of young lawyers in "socially meaningful cases"; and opportunities for seasoned lawyers who are near retirement to become involved with community groups and organizations that provide assistance to the disadvantaged (CBA, 2004). "The firm requires lawyers to record time spent on a *pro bono* file and credits them for it in the same they would a chargeable file. *Pro bono* hours are assigned to a 'phantom partner,' and lawyers are not penalized for providing legal services on a *pro bono* basis, so long as prior approval has been obtained" (CBA, 2004).

From time to time, various bar associations have recommended that all lawyers engage in such endeavours. But many cannot afford it, and others, particularly those who work for large firms, are discouraged from doing so. Many large firms are reluctant to take on *pro bono* criminal-law work, divorce, housing disputes, and consumer problems because doing so would be regarded as unseemly by their corporate clients. A principal reason for the reluctance of large firms to represent "the poor, downtrodden, friendless, and despised" or to engage in public-interest causes is that this sort of legal work "would give offense to their regular clientele" (Heinz and Laumann, 1994:371). Standard arguments against making *pro bono* work compulsory include that it would infringe upon the professional autonomy of lawyers, devalue the altruistic nature of the work, operate in an inequitable way with the burden felt most acutely by economically marginal members of the legal profession, and result in lawyers representing clients in matters that are outside of their areas of particular competence or expertise.

A second way of providing low-cost legal services is through prepaid legal plans (Cotterman, 2004). In some countries, the idea of legal insurance has already caught on. In Germany, for example, prepaid legal plans are widely accepted, and about 40 percent of households carry legal-expense insurance. In recent years, unions have been the prime movers in organizing prepaid plans in Canada and elsewhere. For example, probably the largest prepaid legal insurance plan in the United States was set up by the United Auto Workers and covers over 150 000 Chrysler employees, retired workers, and their immediate families.

LAW SCHOOLS

Similar to the United States and unlike the situation in England, students entering Canadian law schools do not enter directly from high school. In both Canada and the United States, the usual minimum requirement for entrance into law school is two years of university education, although the majority of successful applicants in both countries possess an undergraduate degree upon admission.

Admission to law school is determined to a great extent by the combined scores of grade point averages at university and Law School Admission Test (LSAT) scores. Although they do not like to publicize the fact, law schools are also not above admitting students based on non-academic criteria such as alumni or substantial family donations. This process is referred to as "institutional interest," and is in part justified by suggesting that it helps poorer students by bringing in extra money from donations (Myers, 1994). The LSAT is an American-designed, standardized test taken by all law school applicants in both Canada and the United States.

The LSAT has been used in various forms since 1948. The current version was administered for the first time in June 1991. The LSAT is a one-half-day standardized test. It consists of five 35-minute sections of multiple-choice questions designed to measure the ability to read with understanding and insight, the ability to structure relationships and to make deductions from them, the ability to evaluate reading, the ability to apply reasoning to rules and facts, and the ability to think analytically. There is also a 30-minute writing sample that is sent directly to the applicant's law school. The score is reported on a scale of 120 to 180, with 180 as the highest possible score (*Official Guide,* 2004). For tests administered before 1991, the scores ranged from 10 to 48. Applicants are advised not to take the LSAT for practice since all scores will be reported to every law school that one applies to for admission.

Most people take the test only once; only about 18 percent take it twice, and about 4 percent more than twice.

The use of the LSAT has repeatedly drawn criticism, and questions have been raised concerning the extent to which the LSAT can predict success in law school. Performance criteria of success in law school have traditionally been, and continue to be, grades obtained in formal course work. More and more studies conclude that the LSAT, or a combination of LSAT and grade point average, does not predict law school grades for practical purposes of selection, placement, or advisement for candidates seeking entrance into law school. There have also been accusations that its content is biased against women and non-whites and favours those who have middle-class or higher-class backgrounds. A task force report of the Canadian Bar Association (1993:27) reported that "Aboriginal students suggested that LSAT questions were not geared for Aboriginal understanding and were not culturally relevant." Even though there are questions about the validity and reliability of the LSAT to predict success in law school, all law schools require it as part of the admission process even though individual universities may assign less weight to LSAT scores than to grade point averages achieved in previous university work.

In order to reduce barriers to entry for groups that have traditionally been marginalized, some law schools have developed admission policies with special criteria for under-represented groups. For example, in the mid-1970s, the University of Calgary opted to reserve 15 of the 60 places in its first-year law class for "mature and Native students." While these two groups of students "had to demonstrate some ability, as reflected in undergraduate grades and LSAT scores. . . they were not required to possess standards" (Boyd, 1998:167). Although Aboriginal students were not required to possess the qualifications generally demanded for law school admission, they were expected to have completed the University of Saskatchewan's legal studies program for Aboriginal Canadians, "an intensive summer course developed in order to prepare Native students for the unfamiliar pedagogy and routines of law school" (Boyd, 1998:167). Other law faculties have also developed pre-law admission programs for groups targeted by equity programs (e.g., the indigenous Black and Micmac program at Dalhousie Law School). Several Canadian law schools have also attempted to employ more "holistic" criteria in selecting among applicants. For example, since 1978, the University of Windsor has employed an admission policy that aims "not only to select from among the many applicants those students who would excel in the study of law, but also to select those students who, while doing well in the study of law, would have the potential to contribute creatively and meaningfully to the law school and to the community" (Canadian Bar Association, 1993:26).

In Canada, law schools have a monopoly on the training of lawyers and are the gatekeepers for the legal profession. Entry into law schools is intensely competitive and continues to be conditioned by socioeconomic status and academic standing. Robert Stevens (1973), in a sample of eight law schools studied in 1960, 1970, and 1972, concluded that law schools tend to draw students from more affluent families. Students in general come from better-educated and richer families than the general population. In addition, obtaining a law school education has become a progressively more expensive endeavour in recent years. For example, in 1999, Queen's Law School voted to raise its tuition costs from $4800 a year to $10 000 in 2003. At York University's Osgoode Hall, tuition was $3900 in 1998, $4650 in 1999, and $8000 in 2000 for incoming students. While at some Canadian universities, the tuition hikes have been relatively modest (e.g., at Dalhousie, the cost for one year of the LL.B. increased from $5625 in 1999 to $6000 in 2000), at the University of Toronto, tuition fees rose 380 percent between 1995 and 2001, with the increases particularly steep since 1998, when the Ontario government deregulated tuition fees for professional and graduate programs and allowed institutions to establish tuition fee levels. While in 1997–98, law school tuition at the University of Toronto was a comparatively modest $3808, in 2001, the University of Toronto Law School announced a five-year plan that would more than double its tuition fees from $12 000 to $25 000 a year (Schmidt, 2001). The 2004 Study of Accessibility to Ontario Law Schools found that "[b]etween 1997 and 2004 law school tuition fees have more than doubled at four of the five schools and more than tripled at the other" (Queen's News Centre, 2004). It noted that while one-fifth of current students antic-ipated that they would graduate from law school with no debt, 27 percent expected to have debts of $40 000–$70 000 and 13 percent believed that they would have a debt in excess of $70 000 by the time that they graduated. In addition, the researchers observed a change in who is attending law school based on family income. Specifically, it found "an increase of 4.7 percent in the proportion of students' parents who earn incomes in the top 40 percent of the average Canadian family income distribution, and a decrease in the proportion of stu-dents whose parents earn incomes in the middle 20 percent of the distribution."

Although tuition fees at the majority of Canadian law schools are still far less than the costs involved in attending such leading American law schools as Harvard (where, for the 2003–04 academic year, tuition fees exceeded $30 500 US per year), Yale ($31 400) or Stanford ($31 230), the costs remain significant. According to Jamie Cassels, dean of law at the University of Victoria Law School, while rising tuition fees are unlikely to reduce substantially the number of applicants or law students, "it will affect the socio-economic diversity of the student body, and threatens to make law schools a preserve for the rich" (in Eggleston, 2000:8). After adding food, housing, books, and personal expenses, the costs involved in obtaining a law degree may be prohibitive for some and entail significant dif-ficulties for many. As we earlier noted, law schools generally admit only those with an undergraduate degree—which itself restricts the profession to those who can afford about seven years of education beyond high school.

Socialization into the Profession

The purpose of law school is to change people; to turn them into novice lawyers and to instill "in them a nascent self-concept as a professional, a commitment to the value of the calling, and a claim to that elusive and esoteric style of reasoning called 'thinking like a lawyer'" (Bonsignore et al., 1989:271). Chambliss and Seidman sardonically but correctly note that "law school education is a classic example of an education in which the subject matter for-mally studied is ridiculously simple, but the process of socialization into the profession is very difficult" (1971:97). The study of law is a tedious although not a challenging undertak-ing. After the first year, the workload in law schools tends to be light. The popular con-ception of law students' life as a mixture of long hours, poring over casebooks, and endless discussions of the contents of those books is more myth than reality. For many students, law school is a part-time commitment, and by the fifth semester, they have the equivalent of a two-day work week and discuss their studies rarely, if at all. Says Stevens: "At least intellec-tually law school appears to be a part-time operation" (1973:653).

The key to an understanding of the socialization of law students is best found through an exam-ination of the case or Socratic method (see, for example, Gee, 2005). This method of education "generally involves an intensive interrogation by the teacher of individual students concerning the facts and principles presumed to be operative" in a particular case. The method is intended to accomplish two objectives. The first is informational: instruction in the substantive rules of law. The second is to develop in the student a cognitive restructuring for the style analysis generally called "thinking like a lawyer." In that analysis, a student is trained to account for the factual "details" as well as legal issues determined by the court to be at the core of the dispute which may allow an intelligent prediction of what another court would do with a similar set of facts. The technique is learner-centred: students are closely questioned and their responses are often taken to direct the dialogue. (Bonsignore et al., 1989:275)

This method of learning the law through court decisions, appellate opinions, and attempts to justify those opinions still predominates, despite growing criticism, at virtually every law school in the country during at least the first year of law school. Historically, as well as today, the first year of legal education is the most dramatic of the law school's three years. It is during the first year that law students learn to read a case, frame a legal argument, and distinguish between seemingly indistinguishable ideas; then they start absorbing the mysterious language of the law, full of words like *estoppel* and *replevin*. It is during the first year that a law student learns "to think like a lawyer," to develop the habits and perspectives that will stay with him or her throughout a legal career (Turow, 1977:60).

Many students deplore the Socratic method's inconclusiveness, its failure to encourage creativity, and its lack of intellectual stimulation (Stevens, 1973:636). The class atmosphere is considered to be a hostile one, with the hostility directed from the icily distant law professor toward the student on the spot. Law professors often ignore the emotional level of communication. The impersonal nature of education and mistrustful relations between faculty and students culminate in an intense emotional climate in the classroom, which can pose a threat to the students' self-esteem, self-respect, and identity. Elevated levels of depression and anxiety are ubiquitous among law students (Carney, 1990). Many complain of a high level of stress which will stay with them during their professional careers (*New York Times*, 1995b:B15).

These unintended results of the Socratic method of teaching are generally rationalized by explaining that the method is meant to acclimate the students to "real life," "legal reasoning," or "thinking like a lawyer." But it is difficult to see the relationship between the psychic damage and those stated goals, "and one often gets the feeling that the recitation of 'thinking like a lawyer' has become more a talismanic justification for what is going on than an articulated educational program" (Packer and Ehrlich, 1972:30). In addition to the tendency of the Socratic method to provoke anxiety, hostility, and aggression in the classroom, the domination by the law professor as an authority figure suggests that another aspect of law school training is to enforce a respect for authoritative power (Bonsignore et al., 1989:277).

Essentially, the objective of law school education is to indoctrinate students into the legal profession. Questions that challenge the basis of the system are seldom raised, and law students define the problems presented to them within the framework of the existing system. "Thinking like a lawyer" has traditionally meant ignoring the experiences of marginalization and exclusion and failing to consider the influence of social locations and social identities.

For example, the Canadian Bar Association observes that:

[While] Aboriginal students begin from a different legal perspective, little or no effort is made in most law schools to incorporate Aboriginal law or Aboriginal perceptions of law into the school curricula. For example, tax law is taught with no concern for Aboriginal tax law in Canada. However, the problem is also more fundamental. Law professors need to recognize that everything learned by Natives presents them with new perspectives. In particular, property law is foreign to the Aboriginal concept of land and land ownership. From the Aboriginal perspective, there is a false premise to property law because it is based on private ownership.

The socialization of law students tends to make them intellectually independent, but at the same time it restrains them from looking for radical solutions, "for throughout their law school education they are taught to define problems in the way they have always been defined" (Chambliss and Seidman, 1971:99). During law school, students often change their political orientation in a conservative direction (Erlanger and Klegon, 1978). For example, Michelle Fine (1997) has suggested how professional socialization of law students impacts upon their critical awareness of race and gender. Fine observes that women law students who enter their first year of legal studies with concerns about social justice (e.g., the need for inclusive language, an intolerance for sexist or racist remarks, and awareness of the differential participation by race and gender) have patterned their political attitudes on those of white men by the third year of their schooling. She remarks, "Social critique by race/gender does not age very well within educational institutions" (1997:61). By graduation, she writes, "the vast difference in visions for the future by race and gender" had disappeared. In addition, it is not, perhaps, surprising that "legal education seems to socialize students toward an entrepreneurial value position in which the law is presumed to be primarily a conflict-resolving mechanism and the lawyer a facilitator of client interests. The experience seems to move students away from the social welfarist value in which the law is seen as a social change mechanism, and the lawyer a facilitator of group or societal interests" (Kay, 1978:347).

Political values are often fused with the learning of law, and "students are conditioned to react to questions and issues which they have no role in forming or stimulating. Such teaching *forms* have been crucial in perpetuating the status quo in teaching *content*. For decades, the law school curriculum reflected with remarkable fidelity the commercial demands of law firm practice" (Nader, 1969:21). Students anticipate and law professors reinforce the notion that successful lawyers tend to be conservative and use conservative solutions. A financially successful lawyer needs clients who are able to pay fees. Businesspeople and rich people in general pay larger fees than wage earners and poor people. Successful lawyers represent successful clients, and such a lawyer, "if not already attuned to the value-sets of his [sic] client, tends to adopt them" (Chambliss and Seidman, 1971:99).

In response to the escalating criticism of the socialization process of law students, there is a growing emphasis on interdisciplinary work in law schools, and on joint degrees such as law and psychology, and law and business. For example, the Law Department at Carleton University now houses the largest Bachelor of Arts program and the only Master of Arts program in Legal Studies. Carleton, Dalhousie University, Queen's University, Simon Fraser University, and the University of British Columbia offer undergraduate and graduate programs in law and psychology. The University of British Columbia, in co-operation with Simon Fraser University, also offers a joint degree in which students may earn both a law degree and a Ph.D. in psychology. Since the patriation of the Constitution, Canadian law schools have placed increasing emphasis on cases interpreting the *Charter of Rights and Freedoms* and how Charter cases have impacted upon such areas as administrative, constitutional, and criminal law. In response to criticism that the curriculum has failed to address pressing social needs, courses in poverty law, women and the law, and civil liberties have emerged along with those which expose students to alternative methods of resolving disputes. Feminism and critical legal studies have also served to invigorate debates within law schools, although their introduction has been marred, on occasion, by belligerence and hostility on the part of some students and faculty (McIntyre, 1995). There are also calls for the globalization of legal education (Arthurs, 1996, 1997; Collier, 2005) and increased emphasis on "clinical" training (e.g., drafting documents, writing opinions, preparing for trial and cross-examination, interviewing, and negotiating) (Schrag and Meltsner, 1998). However, some universities look with disdain on innovations that seek to provide courses that are snobbishly referred to as "vocational training."

BAR ADMISSION

The legal profession has defined the perimeters of the practice of law and carefully excluded all who cannot utter the password of bar membership. In Canada, the possession of a law degree (LL.B.) does not entitle one to practise law. The system of articles, which aims at providing "practical" training, has endured. After completing a law degree, there remains a period of articling or apprenticeship with a lawyer and some combination of course work and examination. All provinces require a period of articles, although the exact length demanded of students varies. However, the rising numbers of law school graduates have made obtaining good articles difficult and forced provincial law societies to re-evaluate their post-LL.B. entrance requirements. Some have charged that articling, at best, is a "rite of passage" during which "students are supposed to learn more by osmosis than education" (Hutchinson, 1999:59). Most law societies in Canada have established a Bar Admission Course to supplement articles. These courses vary greatly in content, timing, and length. Ontario's Bar Admission Course is among the most ambitious and requires students to attend a six-month course after they have completed the year of article and study such topics as real estate transaction, handling estates, forming companies, etc. In other parts of the country, however, the length of the Bar Admission Course may be as short as one week. Beginning in the mid-1980s, British Columbia replaced its Bar Admission Program with a Professional Legal Training Course that is 10 weeks in length. While continuing legal education and assessment is not currently mandated by professional associations, it has been suggested that requiring lawyers to attend annual professional courses which would offer substantive updates and skills training would be preferable to a once-and-for-all initiation into the legal profession.

In addition to educational qualifications of would-be lawyers, bar associations restrict admission procedures to those who are morally fit to become lawyers. Applicants for admission to the legal profession must be certified as being of "good moral character" and to swear on oath that they will uphold the highest standards of moral integrity. But the definition of this standard is weak, and the first recorded case in which an applicant in Ontario was denied admission to the bar for lack of good character did not occur until 1989 (Hutchinson, 1999:61). Basically, it means that no one who has a serious criminal record (e.g., sexual offences against children) can be admitted to the practice of law. The standards are vague, and some have argued that the inquiry into moral character arises too soon in the overall professional process and before the ethical and moral sensibilities of applicants have really been put to the test.

BAR ASSOCIATIONS AS INTEREST GROUPS

In addition to restricting entry into the profession and seeking to control the activity of their members, bar associations are interest groups actively engaged in the promotion of activities that the bar considers vital to its interests, such as taking a leading part in shaping laws (especially on criminal and regulatory matters), structuring the legal system, and making recommendations for judicial positions. Bar associations have also turned to politics to promote their professional and economic interests.

For example, the spread of legal self-help materials and the growth of the legal self-help industry has alarmed some bar associations. Such materials dispense step-by-step guidance for solving common legal problems and translate legalese into plain English. Not surprisingly, publishers of self-help legal books and software are reporting brisk sales (Benjamin, 2001). These popular legal resources are useful for some matters such as simple wills, no-fault divorces, landlord-tenant disputes, bankruptcies, and other bread-and-butter issues that were previously the exclusive domain of lawyers. Even though many lawyers invoke the old maxim that a person who represents himself or herself "has a fool for a client," Nolo Press, one of the more successful publishers of legal self-help material, produces hundreds of titles annually and sells thousands of books. Self-Counsel Press, which advertises itself as "Canada's original and leading publisher for the layperson since 1971," offers an assortment of titles such as the *The Living Together Contract* (complete with an accompanying CD-ROM).

The Canadian Bar Association (CBA, 2005:19) recently acknowledged that lawyers increasingly face competition from a host of new service providers: "Accounting firms, management consultants, paralegals, service bureaus, infomediaries and dispute resolution consultants are providing new choices of service providers to the public." In a remarkably blunt admission of the threat that these new service providers pose to the legal profession, the CBA warns that "If uncontested and unregulated, these alternative choices could provide significant competition to traditional legal suppliers" and expresses chagrin over "the increased sophistication of the legal services consumer, especially in accessing information, simple forms or regulations directly online or through intermediaries. This trend will continue to have an impact on certain areas of practice (e.g., wills, real estate, insurance, traffic offences, and small claims disputes)." The CBA observes that some traditional areas of legal practice may also become "'de-legalized' as simple language and simple process alternatives become available (especially online)" (CBA, 2005:121) and predicts that the increasing use of Alternative Dispute Resolution procedures (see Chapter 6) will also impact the legal marketplace. It additionally warns that, "In a price-driven market, loyalty to a single lawyer or firm could become a thing of the past. . . . Clients will be limiting their actual needs to specific items and negotiating price on a distinct set of services. Perceived benefits of a single source of 'legal memory' might also disappear" (CBA, 2005: 20). It grimly notes that while "[t]here may. . . be increased calls for regulation of non-legal service providers, such as immigration consultants. . . this trend might also lead to calls for greater regulation of lawyers."

Of course, the bar associations, like all professional associations (and unions), have as one of their primary functions the promotion of the social, political, and economic interests of their members. Ideally, at least, however, there is a fundamental difference between the legal profession and other professions. Fred Rodell of Yale is quoted as stating that "while law is supposed to be a device to serve society. . . it is pretty hard to find a group less concerned with serving society and more concerned with serving themselves than lawyers" (Green, 1976:19). In his research on legal advocacy, Kritzer (1998) describes lawyers and nonlawyer advocates at work in four different legal situations: unemployment compensation claim appeals; social security disability appeals; tax appeals; and labour grievance arbitrations. Somewhat ironically, he concludes that nonlawyers can be effective advocates and, in some legal settings, more effective than many lawyers. However, some charge that the most discernible common cause of bar associations is to represent the needs of their lawyers and those clients whose interests they regularly attend. Bar associations, in the final analysis, have been rather successful in preserving lawyers' monopoly on legal practice and the profession's lucrative role in society.

PROFESSIONAL DISCIPLINE

One of the characteristics of a profession is a code of ethics. A profession involves, among other things, a sense of service and responsibility to the community, and the conduct required of a professional is delineated in a code of ethics for that profession. A lawyer's code of ethics deals with his or her relations with clients, other lawyers, the court, and the public. In Canada, the first attempt to establish legal ethics occurred in 1915. In 1921, the Canadian Bar Association's Canons of Legal Ethics were accepted as a template for professional discipline by CBA members and largely adopted by provincial law societies. A review of the original canons launched in 1969 by a committee of the Canadian Bar Association resulted in the introduction of a new Code of Professional Conduct in 1974 and its adoption by the provincial law societies. In 1984, another committee of the CBA was struck to review and reform the Code. The 1987 code made only modest changes to its 1974 counterpart and continues to serve as the basis of almost all the provincial rules of professional conduct for lawyers (Hutchinson, 1999:13).

The Rules set out the duties, obligations, and responsibility that lawyers have as (i) a representative of clients; (ii) an officer of the legal system; and (iii) a public citizen. It contains a series of guidelines on matters such as fees, confidentiality of information, certain types of conflict of interest, safekeeping property, unauthorized practice of law, advertising, and reporting professional misconduct. Types of conduct that would be contrary to the code include:

a. committing any personally disgraceful or morally reprehensible offence that reflects upon the lawyer's integrity (whereof a conviction by a competent court would be *prima facie* evidence);

b. committing, whether professionally or in the lawyer's personal capacity, any act of fraud or dishonesty, e.g., by knowingly making a false tax return or falsifying a document, even without fraudulent intent, and whether or not prosecuted therefor;

c. making untrue representations or concealing material facts from a client with dishonest or improper motives;

d. taking improper advantage of the youth, experience, lack of education or sophistication, ill health, or unbusinesslike habits of a client;

e. misappropriating or dealing dishonestly with the client's monies;

f. receiving monies from or on behalf of a client expressly for a specific purpose and failing, without the client's consent, to pay them over for that purpose;

g. knowingly assisting, enabling, or permitting any person to act fraudulently, dishonestly, or illegally toward the lawyer's client;

h. failing to be absolutely frank and candid in all dealings with the Court, fellow lawyers, and other parties to proceedings, subject always to not betraying the client's cause, abandoning the client's legal rights, or disclosing the client's confidences;

i. failing, when dealing with a person not legally represented, to disclose material facts, e.g., the existence of a mortgage on a property being sold, or supplying false information, whether the lawyer is professionally representing a client or is concerned personally;

j. failure to honour the lawyer's word when pledged even though, under technical rules, the absence of writing might afford a legal defence. (From Boyd, Neil. 2002. *Canadian Law: An Introduction.* 3rd ed. Toronto: Nelson Thomson Learning. Reprinted with permission of Nelson.)

In 2000–01, the CBA Standing Committee on Ethics and Professional Issues identified further possible changes to CBA's Code of Professional Conduct and, in 2002–03, sought input from members on these issues and considered the suggestions they made. In 2004, the CBA Council unanimously adopted an amended CBA Code; however, as of the time that this book went to press, the amended code was still in the process of production (CBA, 2006).

Some have charged that codes developed by lawyers function as little more than "ethical window-dressing" and represent, "at best, a stylized form of professional regulation and, at worst, a self-serving paean to professional prestige" (Hutchinson, 1999:12). Disciplinary authorities are supposed to make sure that only honest and competent people are licensed to practise law. However, in practice, "[t]he enforcement of the various ethical responsibilities is selective and seldom . . . with money-related offenses, serious addiction, and lack of cooperation with the law society at the top of the list . . . [and] directives to act in the public interest, to strive to reform the law, and to ensure that the administration of justice is available to all are almost entirely ignored by regulatory agencies, even though they are consistently overlooked by many lawyers" (Hutchinson, 1999:15). Based on an examination of the records of the Law Society Disciplinary Committee of Canada, Bruce Arnold and Fiona Kay (1995) argue that the social networks in which lawyers reside and the social capital that accrues from such relationships actually encourage rule violation while buffering lawyers from being detected or sanctioned by the disciplinary boards of law societies (see also Arnold and Hagan, 1992).

For example, although lawyers have an obligation to report known or suspected ethical violations by other lawyers according to the ethics rules and standards of the governing bodies, only seven out of ten lawyers say that they would report a lawyer outside of their firm who acted unethically, and six out of ten would report a colleague in their own firm. Because 71 percent say they have occasionally encountered dishonest opposing counsel, it is obvious that lawyers should be doing much more reporting. But they are not (Pitulla, 1995). Most complaints against lawyers are filed by clients or initiated by the bar council. It is rare that lawyers or judges report lawyer or judicial misconduct. The reasons for not reporting vary from "no use" because nothing would happen and it is not their responsibility to not wanting to ruin someone's career. About 40 percent of the lawyers who do not report misconduct fear that too much time would be taken up testifying in a disciplinary proceeding, do not know where to report the misconduct, or are afraid of being subjected to a lawsuit. Although lawyers claim that ethical conduct is important and the majority are willing to report violation of professional norms, in reality, they are reluctant to do it—which raises serious concerns about the efficacy of the internal modes of control of the profession.

In general, disciplinary sanctions, such as reprimands, suspensions, or disbarments, are imposed only for serious instances of misconduct, such as criminal acts, mishandling of a client's property, and flagrant violation of certain rules of professional conduct, such as breach of confidentiality. Some of these sanctions are in addition to possible criminal proceedings, which are handled separately by law-enforcement authorities, and they may be publicized as a form of "risk prevention" (Davis, 1995). Of course, unhappy clients can always sue their lawyers, and an indirect form of punishment is the very high cost of lawyers' malpractice insurance (Hazard, 1994). Other rule violations rarely evoke formal disciplinary action, although there is informal discipline in the form of expressed disapproval, which carries its own practical penalties, such as questions about one's professional reputation.

Research suggests that not all lawyers are equally vulnerable to disciplinary action. For example, Arnold and Hagan (1992) report that it is inexperienced solo practitioners who face a "heightened risk of sanctioning during a recessionary period. . . [and] it is regulatory attention more than pre-existing behavioural differences that structures these deviant careers" (see also Arnold and Hagan, 1994). Similarly, Hutchinson (1999:15) notes that while, on occasion, headlines direct attention to the wrongdoings of elite lawyers, "the (small) bulk of disciplinary activity occurs at the margins of the profession, even though there is no evidence that lawyers who work for wealthy clients are any more (or less) ethical than those who have disadvantaged clients."

How serious are lawyers about professional responsibility? It has been suggested that lawyers "have been collectively long on righteous celebration of the importance of maintaining ethical standards, but short on any action and debate" (Hutchinson, 1999:39). Evidence of this is suggested (Arthurs, 1998; 2001) by the lack of institutional vigour in disciplining lawyers for breaches of ethical rules, the reactive stance taken by law societies, and the fact that at the beginning of the new millennium only four Canadian law schools had compulsory courses on legal ethics and professional responsibility. There are, however, some hopeful signs. There is a growing body of Canadian literature on the issue of legal ethics that includes Beverley Smith's *Professional Conduct for Canadian Lawyers*, Gavin MacKenzie's (1999) comprehensive *Lawyers and Ethics: Professional Responsibility and Discipline*, Donald E. Buckingham et al.'s (1996) *Legal Ethics in Canada: Theory and Practice*, and Allan C. Hutchinson's (1999) *Legal Ethics and Professional Ethics*. In addition, various provincial law societies are initiating an overhaul of their professional conduct codes and disciplinary structures. Finally, as Harry W. Arthurs (1999:xiv) observes:

> The rapidly changing demographics, market conditions, sources of intellectual capital, and professional ideologies among Canadian lawyers have created crises of professional governance, which to some extent manifest themselves in a critique of the whole apparatus of professional discipline. And, of course, changes in Canada's political economy, and in public attitudes towards elites and regulatory institutions, are bound to generate pressures for a change in how lawyers behave both individually and collectively. It would be surprising indeed if these and other important developments did not soon lead to a top-to-bottom rethinking of the style, content, and practice of professional ethics in Canada.

SUMMARY

- The origins of the legal profession can be traced back to Rome. Lawyers, in the sense of a regulated group of practitioners, emerged in the late 1200s. By that time, the body of legal knowledge, including procedure, had become too much for the ordinary person to handle alone.

- Legal education in Canada was initially modelled after the British system. University-based law schools are a fairly recent method of obtaining a legal education in Canada. It was not until 1960 that a law degree was required for admission to the bar of each province.
- Lawyers have established a monopoly on legal business, and the profession of law has become the fastest-growing of all professions in Canada.
- The legal profession is highly stratified. There is substantial variation in income by types of lawyers. Income is related to such factors as the type of practice, the type of clientele, the degree of specialization, the size of the firm, age and length of practice, and the size and location of the place of practice.
- Although Canada graduates about 2000 lawyers each year, the cost of legal services is still beyond the reach of many people. Law and lawyers are expensive and legal aid is not available to all Canadians facing all types of legal difficulties.
- In addition to setting standards for admission and practice, law societies are also responsible for disciplining those among their members who fail to meet professional standards. Although violation of legal ethics may be punished by reprimand, suspension from the bar, or disbarment, only a very small proportion of lawyers who violate the ethical standards are ever subjected to disciplinary action.

CRITICAL THINKING QUESTIONS

1. In its 2005 report, the Canadian Bar Association's Futures Committee identified the following factors as likely providing the "greatest challenges, risks and opportunities" to both the Canadian legal profession and to the CBA itself: the changing demographics of the profession, especially the greater presence of women; inter-generational variance in the expectations, attitudes, work habits, and career intention of lawyers; the desire among lawyers for an improved work and family balance; the growing fragmentation of the profession; new forms of marketplace competition; the proliferation of sub-groups that define the mission of their profession differently (e.g., a calling, a business, a job); the negative imagery of lawyers and its impact upon societal respect, consumer demand, and career satisfaction; globalization; technology; the commercialization of the profession and the introduction of business concepts into legal practice; and shifts in the volume and nature of legal work. From this list, select the one factor that you feel will pose the greatest challenge to the legal profession and/or the CBA and suggest strategies to address it.

2. A recent survey by Ipsos Reid reported that the most common motivations among current Canadian law students for entering into the profession were, in order, "the desire to help society (35 percent), the range and flexibility of professional opportunities that a legal career provides (32 percent), and the intellectual stimulation and challenge of the law (29 percent). Far down the list was the motivation of income potential or financial stability (21 percent)" (CBA, 2006:17). Yet, it has been noted that professional experience has an impact upon the attitudes, expectations, and intentions of lawyers. Identify factors within the practice of law that you feel might result in altered opinions of the mission of this profession.

chapter nine

Researching Law in Society

Empirical studies provide the background for many of the generalizations and conclusions reached about law and society in the previous chapters. The purpose of this chapter is to show how sociologists carry out such studies by describing some of the ways they research law and the methods they use to arrive at their findings. The chapter also demonstrates the significance and applicability of sociological research to the formulation, instrumentation, and evaluation of social policy. The general comments on methodological tools for research on law are not intended to replace the more detailed technical discussions found in books on methods of social research (see, for example, McIntrye, 2005; Schutt, 2004; Yates, 2001). They are intended merely to provide an exposure to the strategies used in the study of the interplay between law and society and to highlight the methodological concerns and complexities inherent in such endeavours.

METHODS OF INQUIRY

Several methods can be applied in researching law in society, and more than a single method is usually involved in such a study. However, there are four commonly used methods of data collection in sociology. All other methods are variations and combinations of these four methods. The four methods that will be considered are the historical, the observational, the experimental, and the survey methods.

Actual research is much more complicated than these methods indicate. All research is essentially a process in which choices are made at many stages. There are several methods and they are combined in various ways in the actual research. Methodological decisions are made on such diverse matters as the kind of research design to be used, the type of research population and sample, the sources of data collection, the techniques of gathering data, and the methods of analyzing the research findings. The differences among the four methods are more a matter of emphasis on a particular data-collection strategy for a particular research purpose than a clear-cut "either/or" distinction. For example, in the observational method, although the emphasis is on the researcher's ability to observe and record social activities as they occur, the researcher may interview the participants—a technique associated with the survey and experimental methods. Similarly, in the experimental method, the subjects are usually under the observation of the researcher and his or her collaborators. The information gained in such observations also plays a crucial role in the final analysis and interpretation of the data. Furthermore, historical evidence is often used in observational, survey, and experimental studies.

At all stages of sociological research, there is an interplay between theory and method (Morse and Field, 1995). In fact, it is often the theory chosen by the researcher that determines which methods will be used in the research. The selection of the method is to a great extent dependent on the type of information desired. **Observation** (especially participant observation) seems to be the best data collection method for studying a sequence of events and their meaning as interpreted by the participants and other observers before, during, and after the events. The researcher directly observes and participates in the study system with which he or she has established a meaningful and durable relationship, as did, for example, Jerome H. Skolnick (1994) in his study of police officers. More recently, Ralph Peeples (2000) and his colleagues used this technique to compare the perspectives of three parties involved in medical malpractice lawsuits: physicians who had been sued for medical malpractice; their defence counsel; and counsel for the plaintiff. Although the observer may or may not play an active role in the events, he or she observes them firsthand and can record the events and the participants' experiences as they unfold. No other data-collection method can provide such a detailed description of social events. Thus, observation is best suited for studies of a particular group and certain social processes within that group. When these events are not available for observation (for example, if they occurred in the past), the historical approach is the logical choice of method for collecting data.

If an investigator wishes to study norms, rules, and status in a particular group, intensive interviewing of "key" persons and informants in or outside the group is the best method of data collection. For example, in a well-known study, Jerome E. Carlin (1966) interviewed approximately 800 lawyers for his study of legal ethics and their enforcement. Those who set and enforce norms, rules, and status, because of their position in the group or relations with persons in the group, are the ones who are the most knowledgeable about the information the researcher wishes to obtain. Intensive interviews (especially with open-ended questioning) with these persons allow the researcher to probe for such information. Similarly, in conducting detailed analysis of the political consciousness and commitment of six individuals who served as gender equity coordinators in the same American public agency over a 20-year period, Taylor (2005) sought to understand the diverse ways in which people who are charged with instituting movement-inspired laws come to perceive their mandates and the organizational/political milieus in which they work (see also Kenney, 2000; Owens, 2000).

When an investigator wishes to determine the numbers, the proportions, the ratios, and other quantitative information about the subjects in his or her study possessing certain characteristics, opinions, beliefs, and other categories of various variables, then the best method of data collection is the survey. The survey relies on a representative sample of the population to which a standardized instrument can be administered.

Finally, the experiment is the best method of data collection when the researcher wants to measure the effect of certain independent variables on some dependent variables. The experimental situation provides control over the responses and the variables, and gives the researcher the opportunity to manipulate the independent variables. In the following pages, we will examine and illustrate these methods in greater detail.

Historical Methods

Sociologists generally are accustomed to studying social phenomena at one time—the present. But social phenomena do not appear spontaneously and autonomously. Historical analysis can indicate the possibility that certain consequences can issue from events that are comparable to other events of the past: history as something more than a simple compilation of facts. It can generate an understanding of the processes of social change and document how a multitude of factors have served to shape the present (see, for example, Cramer, 2005). The study of history also has an existential function. It informs us who we are, and reminds us that we are links that connect the past with the present and the future (Inciardi et al., 1977:27).

Historical research carried out by sociologists is a critical investigation of events, developments, and experiences of the past; a careful weighing of evidence of the validity of sources of information on the past; and the interpretation of the evidence. Historical research is important and valuable in sociology because the origins of the discipline have to be understood if contemporary theories and research are to be understood. As a substitute for direct data from the participants, contents from documents and historical materials are used as a method of data collection. These documents and materials can range from census data, archives of various types, official files such as court records, records of property transactions, tax records, and business accounts to personal diaries, witness accounts, judicial rhetoric in appellate court opinions (Phillips and Grattet, 2000), propaganda literature, and numerous other personal accounts and letters (Simonds, 1996). The researcher uses these available data sources to carry out what is generally referred to as secondary analysis; that is, the data were not generated or collected for the specific purpose of the study formulated by the researcher. For example, Sandy Dennis, Myrna Dawson, and Annette Nierobisz (2002) examined 267 sexual harassment complaints against corporate respondents or employing organizations that were dealt with by the Canadian Human Rights Commission between 1978 and 1993 in an attempt to discover what types of factors (legal, extra-legal, and case-processing) resulted in a complaint being dismissed or settled. Davis and Davidson (2005) employed a range of legal, medical, and governmental files to explore the medical experience of the 1967 *Abortion Act* in Scotland. Of course, the usefulness of the historical method depends to a large extent on the accuracy and thoroughness of the documents and materials. With accurate and thorough data, the researcher may be able to gain insights, generate hypotheses, and even test hypotheses (see, for example, Boyle and Preve, 2000, and Petrunik, 2003).

Official records and public documents have provided the data for sociological analyses attempting to establish long-term legal trends. For example, as we mentioned in Chapter 1, William J. Chambliss (1964) has shown how the vagrancy statutes changed in England according to emerging social interests. The first full-fledged vagrancy law, enacted in 1349, regulated the giving of alms to able-bodied, unemployed people. After the Black Death and the flight of workers from landowners, the law was reformulated to force labourers to accept employment at a low wage. By the 16th century, with an increased emphasis on commerce and industry, the vagrancy statutes were revived and strengthened. Eventually, vagrancy laws came to serve, as they do today, the purpose of controlling people and activities regarded as undesirable to the community. Similarly, Jerome Hall (1952) has shown, on the basis of historical records, how changing social conditions and emerging social interests brought about the formulation of trespass laws in 15th-century England. More recent investigations include Banner's (2000) analysis of how British colonizers in colonial New Zealand modified the structure of the land market in New Zealand over the course of the 19th century in order to transfer wealth from the Maori to themselves, and Asbridge's (2004) examination of the antecedents of the enactment of municipal smoking bylaws in Canada between 1970 and 1995 (see also Scott, 2003).

The historical method is also used to test theories (Brenner, 1992). For example, Mary P. Baumgartner (1978) was interested in the relationship between the social status of the defendant and the litigant and the verdicts and sanctions awarded them. She analyzed data based on 389 cases (148 civil and 241 criminal) heard in the colony of New Haven (in what is now Connecticut) between 1639 and 1665. She found, not unexpectedly, that in both the civil and the criminal cases, individuals who enjoyed high status were more likely to receive favourable treatment by the court than their lower-status counterparts. In addition to relying on official documents, the historical method may also be based on narrations of personal experiences, generally known as the **life-histories method**. This technique requires that the researcher rely solely on a person's reporting of life experiences relevant to the research interest with minimal commentary. Often life histories are part of ethnographic reports. In such instances, they are referred to as "memory cases" (Nader and Todd, 1978:7). This method is useful to learn about events such as conflict or dispute that occurred in the past, particularly when there are no written records available. Obviously, this method has certain pitfalls, for life histories tend to be tainted by selective recall. That is, subjects tend to remember events that have impressed them in some way and tend to forget others. Although the life-history method has been little used in recent years, it serves several functions. First, it provides insights into a world usually overlooked by the objective methods of data collection. Second, life histories can serve as the basis for making assumptions necessary for more systematic data collection. Third, life histories, because of their details, provide insights into new or different perspectives for research. When an area has been studied extensively and has grown "sterile," life histories may break new ground for research studies. Finally, they offer an opportunity to view and study the dynamic process of social interactions and events not available with many other kinds of data (McGillivray and Comaskey, 1999; Weibe and Johnson, 1998).

A notable difficulty of the historical method lies in the limited accuracy and thoroughness of the documents and materials involved. Because the data are "compiled" by others with no supervision or control by the researcher, the researcher is, in fact, at the mercy of those who record the information. The recorders use their own definitions of situations, define and select events as important for recording, and introduce subjective perceptions, interpretations, and insights into their recordings. For example, how do the recorders define a dispute? In many instances, a dispute enters officially into the court records when it is adjudicated, and a settlement is imposed after full trial. But as we noted in Chapter 6, not all disputes are adjudicated. Many are settled informally in pretrial conferences, or judges may intervene in other less formal ways as well. Therefore, a researcher must ascertain the reliability and validity of documents. They should be verified for internal consistency (consistency between each portion of the document and other portions) and external consistency (consistency with empirical evidence, other documents, or both). Although the historical method provides details, and in certain cases presents a processual view of events often unmatched by other methods of data collection, it is desirable (when possible, of course) to combine this method with other data-collection methods.

Observational Methods

Observational methods can be divided into two types: those utilizing either human observers (participant observers or judges) or mechanical observers (cameras, tape recorders, and the like) and those directly eliciting responses from subjects by questioning (questionnaires, schedules, and interview guides). Observational methods can be carried out both in laboratory or controlled situations and in field or natural settings.

Participant observation has a long history of use in anthropological research. Thus, there is justification if the term conjures up the image of a social scientist living with some preliterate tribe, perhaps for several years. Indeed, much of our knowledge of primitive law comes from anthropologists who lived in traditional societies, such as Bronislaw Malinowski and E. Adamson Hoebel. Of course, for anthropologists, the opportunity to observe ongoing legal phenomena (outside of an institutional setting such as a court) depends on a combination of circumstances and luck. It means that the anthropologists have to be in the right place at the right time. Anthropological (and sociological) field researchers generally proceed by way of a kind of methodological eclecticism, choosing the method that suits the purpose and circumstances at any given time. In summary: "Hence, unobtrusive measurement, life history studies, documentary and historical analysis, statistical enumeration, in-depth interviewing, imaginative role-taking, and personal introspection are all important complements of direct observation in the field worker's repertoire" (Williamson et al., 1982:200).

Many of the observational techniques are used in laboratory or controlled situations. For example, comparatively little empirical research has been performed with actual juries because of the legal requirements of private deliberations. Consequently, mock trials in which jurors or juries respond to simulated case materials have become a primary research vehicle. The mock trial permits both manipulation of important variables and replication of cases. Many of the laboratory jury studies deal with the deliberation processes preceding the verdict and how the verdict is reached by juries of diverse composition, deliberating under various conditions. One method of analyzing deliberations is to audiotape or videotape the deliberations and then analyze their content.

Observational methods have been used by sociologists extensively in field settings that involve direct contact with subjects and take place in relatively natural social situations. They are often part of what is called "action research," the way to integrate knowledge with action (Reason and Bradbury, 2001). For example, in attempts to find out and understand how the law typically works on a day-to-day basis, sociologists have focused on various aspects of the criminal justice system. Classic studies of the police by Richard V. Ericson (1989) and Jerome H. Skolnick (1994), among others, have noted the role of discretion in the application or nonapplication of the law in legally equivocal and unequivocal situations. At each step in the criminal justice system, from the citizen's decision to lodge a complaint or to define the situation as one in which it is necessary to summon the police, to the judge's decision as to what sentence a convicted person should receive, decisions are made that are not prescribed by statutory law. Fairman and Yapp's (2005) recent examination of the ways that small and medium-sized enterprises made compliance decisions when confronted with self-regulatory and prescriptive demands suggests the important insights of research that allows for attention to be directed to social processes. They report that compliance is best conceptualized as a "negotiated outcome" of the regulatory encounter. Rosseau et al.'s (2002) analysis of the decision-making process of the Canadian Immigration and Refugee Board (see also Barsky, 2000) as well as John Hagan and Ron Levi's (2005) recent investigation of prosecutorial and court practices at The Hague Tribunal for the former Yugoslavia also suggest the utility and potential richness of observational research methods.

There are both advantages and limitations to observational methods. The advantages include the opportunity to record information as the event unfolds or shortly thereafter. Thus, the validity of the recorded information can be high. Often observations are made and information is recorded independently of the observed person's abilities to record events. At times, when verbal or written communication between the researcher and the subjects is difficult—for example, in studying traditional societies—observation is the only method by which the researcher can obtain information. Finally, the observer need not rely on the willingness of the observed persons to report events.

There are also several limitations of observational research. The method is not applicable to the investigation of large social settings. The context investigated must be small enough to be dealt with exhaustively by one or a few researchers. In the case of fieldwork, there is the omnipresent possibility that the researcher's selective perception and selective memory will bias the results of the study (Khan, 2005). There is also the problem of selectivity in data collection. In any social situation, there are literally thousands of possible pieces of data. No one researcher, in other words, can account for every aspect of a situation. The researcher inevitably pulls out only a segment of the data that exist, and the question inevitably arises as to whether the selected data are really representative of the situation. There is also no way to easily assess the reliability and validity of the interpretations made by the researcher. As long as data are collected and presented by one or a few researchers with their own distinctive talents, faults, and idiosyncrasies, suspicion will arise about the validity of their rendering of the phenomena studied. Researchers often respond to these criticisms by suggesting that the cost of imprecision is more than compensated for by the in-depth quality of the data produced. Finally, Palys and Lowman (2002) note that even though researchers have an ethical duty to protect the confidentiality of their respondents, their doing so may be challenged when third parties employ subpoenas in the context of criminal proceedings and civil litigation. Elsewhere (2000) they describe the controversy that erupted at Simon Fraser University when a graduate student in SFU's School of Criminology who was conducting research on the assisted suicide and euthanasia of persons with AIDS, and who had pledged to keep the identity of his respondents "absolutely confidential," was subpoenaed to testify at an inquest by Vancouver's Coroner.

Experimental Methods

The prevailing method for testing causal relations by social scientists, especially psychologists, is the experiment. An **experiment** may be carried out in a laboratory or a field setting, and it ideally begins with two or more equivalent groups, with an experimental variable introduced into only the experimental group. The researcher measures the phenomenon under study before the introduction of the experimental variable and after, thus getting a measure of the change presumably caused by the variable.

There are two common ways of setting up experimental and control groups. One is the matched-pair technique. For each person in the experimental group, another person similar in all important variables (age, religion, education, occupation, or anything important to the research) is found and placed in the control group. Another technique is the random-assignment technique, in which statistically random assignments of persons to experimental and control groups are made—such as assigning the first person to the experimental group and the next to the control group, and so on.

Experiments in sociology face certain difficulties (see, for example, Orr, 1998). An experiment involving thousands of people may be prohibitively expensive. It may take years to complete a study. Ethical and legal considerations prohibit the use of people in any experiments that may injure them. The scientific community reacts strongly in those infrequent instances where human subjects have been used in a hazardous or harmful manner. When people are unwilling to co-operate in an experiment, they cannot be forced to do so (although occasionally they are tricked into unconscious co-operation). Moreover, when individuals realize that they are experimental subjects, they begin to act differently and the experiment may be spoiled. Almost any kind of experimental or observational study upon people who know they are being studied will give some interesting findings, which may vanish soon after the study is terminated. Experiments with human subjects are most reliable when the subjects do not know the true object of the experiment. But the use of deception in social research poses the ethical question of distinguishing between harmless deception and intellectual dishonesty.

Moreover, there would be legal and ethical questions involved in the use of experimental methods in the study of legal services, welfare payments, or incarcerations. There are exceptions, however, such as the Wisconsin Welfare Experiment (DeParle, 1998), the controversial New Jersey Guaranteed Income Experiments (US Office of Economic Opportunity, 1970), and "Mincome," a large-scale negative income tax experiment conducted in Manitoba (Hum and Simpson, 2001). These experiments involve the systematic selection of experimental and control groups, the application of the policy under study to the experimental groups only, and a careful comparison of differences between the experimental and the control group after the application of the policy.

The New Jersey Guaranteed Income Experiments were designed to resolve some serious questions about the impact of welfare payments on the incentives for poor people to work. Debates over welfare reform have generated certain questions that social science could presumably answer with careful, controlled experimentation. Would a guaranteed family income reduce the incentive to work? If payments were made to poor families with employable male heads, would the men drop out of the labour force? Would the level of the income guarantee, or the steepness of the reductions of payments with increases in earnings, make any difference in working behaviour? Since existent welfare programs did not provide a guaranteed minimum family income, or make payments to families with employable males, or graduate payments in relation to earnings, these questions could be answered only through experimentation.

To assess the impact of guaranteed incomes on families with able-bodied men, the Office of Economic Opportunity sponsored a three-year social experiment involving 1350 families in New Jersey and Pennsylvania. The research was undertaken by the University of Wisconsin's Institute of Research on Poverty and began in 1968. To ascertain the effects of different levels of guaranteed income, four guarantee levels were established. Some families were chosen to receive 50 percent of the Social Security Administration's poverty-line income, others 75 percent, others 100 percent, and still others 125 percent. To ascertain the effects of graduated payments in relation to earnings, some families had their payments reduced by 30 percent of their outside earnings, others 50 percent, and still others 70 percent. Finally, a control sample was observed—families who received no payments at all in the experiment but were matched in every way with families who were receiving payments. A preliminary report issued by the US Office of Economic Opportunity (1970) showed that there were no differences between the outside earnings of families who were receiving guaranteed incomes (experimental groups) and those who were not (control group). In the United States, a total of four large-scale social experiments were conducted to test a guaranteed income plan and investigate the size of the work disincentive effect.

Derek Hum and Wayne Simpson (2001) observe that such large-scale social experiments to test a guaranteed income plan did not go unnoticed in Canada. "In November 1970, the Department of National Health and Welfare emphasized the potential of a guaranteed income as an anti-poverty measure but called for more study of the experiments under way in the United States, correctly pointing out that fear of the impact on productivity would be the main deterrent to the introduction of a general guaranteed income plan" (p. 79). In the midst of a federal-provincial social policy review, the Manitoba government announced its interest in participating in a demonstration project of the guaranteed income approach and, in 1974, Canada and Manitoba agreed to conduct Mincome, as the experiment was subsequently termed (Hum and Simpson, 1991).

Mincome was based on a sample of Manitoban families (the majority from Winnipeg) that were randomly assigned for a period of three years to different guaranteed annual income (GAI) plans. The sampling method took into account type of family structure and the normal income received. Those families who earned above a set amount ($13 000 for a two-adult, two-child family) were excluded. Three different levels of GAI support were used, with support levels adjusted for differing family size and structure (due to inflation, support levels were also increased annually). The experiment employed three tax-back rates: 35 percent, 50 percent, and 75 percent. However, the most generous and least generous combinations of support levels and tax-back rates were not tested. A control group was also used, allowing strong inferences to be made.

Overall, the results of the Mincome experiment were favourable to those who support a guaranteed annual income. They suggested that a guaranteed annual income did not function as an "excessive" work disincentive. "The reduction in work effort was modest: about 1 percent for men, 3 percent for wives, and 5 percent for unmarried women" (Hum and Simpson, 2001:80). These effects were not only small in absolute terms but also smaller than those observed in the four American experiments. While the researchers discovered that administering a guaranteed annual income was more complex than they had originally anticipated, they concluded that doing so was certainly feasible. However, the Mincome project "died a quiet death in 1979. The social security review had ended by then, and with the onset of post-OPEC stagflation, there was no political support in the country for sweeping reforms of the type promised by a guaranteed income" (Hum and Simpson, 2001:80).

These experiments raise a series of questions. Do researchers have the right to withhold public services from some individuals simply to provide a control for experimentation? In the medical area, where the giving or withholding of treatment may result in death or injury, the problem is obvious, and many attempts have been made to formulate a code of ethics (see, for example, Bravo et al.'s [2000] examination of the new provisions for consent to experimentation enacted by the 1994 Quebec Civil Code and its implications for research on the elderly and disabled). In the area of social experimentation, what can be said to control groups who are chosen to be similar to experimental groups but are denied benefits so that they may serve as a basis for comparison (see, for example, Tomossy and Weisstub, 2003)?

Setting aside the legal and moral issues, it would be politically difficult to provide services for some people and not for others. Moreover, as noted earlier, people behave differently when they know they are being watched. Students, for example, generally perform at a higher level when something—anything new and different—is introduced into the classroom routine. This "Hawthorne effect" may cause a new program or reform to appear more successful than the old, but it is the newness itself that produces improvement rather than the program or the reform. Another problem in such experimentation is that results obtained with small-scale experiments may differ substantially from what would occur if a large-scale nationwide program were adopted. In the New Jersey and Mincome experiments, if only one family receives income-maintenance payments in a neighbourhood, its members may continue to behave as the neighbours do. But if everyone in the nation is guaranteed a minimum income, community standards may change and affect the behaviour of all recipient families.

On a smaller scale, experimental methods have also been used in the study of jury deliberation, the evaluation of objections in the courtroom (Koehler, 1992), allocation of scarce criminal resources, the impact of increasing or decreasing police patrol on crime, and the determination of the effectiveness of pretrial hearings (Hans, 1992; Horowitz and Bordens, 2002; Jonakait, 2003). Many experiments, such as those dealing with juror and jury behaviour (Burnett and Badzinski, 2000; Diamond, 1997) or with violence, are conducted in a laboratory situation. However, laboratory experiments achieve rigorous and controlled observation at the price of unreality. The subjects are isolated from the outside and from their normal environment. In consequence, the laboratory experiment has been criticized for its unnaturalness and questioned as to its generalizability. By contrast, experimental methods that are used in nonlaboratory settings increase the generalizability of results and lend greater credence to the findings, but concomitantly increase the difficulty of controlling relevant variables.

Survey Methods

Survey research aims for a systematic and comprehensive collection of information about the attitudes, beliefs, and behaviour of people. The most common means of data collection are face-to-face interviews, self-administered questionnaires (for example, mail questionnaires), and telephone interviews. Typically, the questionnaire or the interview schedule is set up so that the same questions are asked of each respondent in the same order with exactly the same wording, and the validity of surveys is dependent on the design of the questions asked (see, for example, Fink and Kosecoff, 1998; Groves, 2004). A survey deals with a representative sample of a population. Probabilistic sampling is essential to survey studies. Survey studies tend to be larger than is typically the case in observational or experimental studies. Usually, data are collected at one time, although a survey approach can be used to study trends in opinion and behaviour over time. Because of its ability to cover large areas and many respondents, the survey method has become the dominant method of data collection in sociology.

Survey methods, like other research methods, have their pitfalls. Probably foremost among them is the response rate or the non-response rate. Because one of the important reasons for conducting a survey is that it deals with a large representative sample from a population and thus permits inference from the sampled data to the population, it is essential that the sample maintain its representativeness, which may be affected severely when a substantial number of the respondents fail to participate in the study. The return rate for mail questionnaires is generally low; a 60 percent or higher return rate is considered rather good (see, for example, Mangione, 1995). Of course, for the interview survey, the expected response rate is higher than that of the questionnaire survey. In both cases, in addition to the subject's refusal to participate, other factors affect the response rate. They include the inability of the subject to understand the question, the possibility that the subject may have moved or died, and the physical or mental incapacitation of the participants. Although questionnaire and interview studies have a margin of error, they are still useful. For example, public officials seldom take a position on a public issue without first reviewing public opinion polls, and legislators may delay casting a vote on an important bill until they receive the latest survey of voter opinion.

An illustration of the use of survey methods can be seen in the efforts of Statistics Canada to gain a more accurate measure of the extent of crime in Canada. For years both law enforcement agencies and sociologists have had to rely on official records compiled by police agencies to measure the amount of crime. However, there have been concerns about the accuracy of these reports, and many sociologists have suggested that officially recorded crime statistics are a far better indicator of police activity than they are of criminal activity. In consequence, victimization surveys represent an attempt to supplement official crime records and to overcome some of the problems of accuracy therein.

In victimization surveys, subjects in a large sample of the population are systematically interviewed to determine how many crimes have been committed against them (see, for example, Gomes et al., 2003). In addition to determining the volume of crime, the surveys are also used in developing a variety of information on crime characteristics and the effects of crime on the victims: victim injury and medical care, economic losses, time lost from work, victim self-protection, and reporting of crime to the police. There are three advantages of victimization surveys that make them superior to self-report studies and *Uniform Crime Reports*. First, people are more willing to discuss crimes committed against them than the ones they have committed. Second, victimization surveys by design seek out information about crimes rather than waiting for victims to report them as is the case with the *Uniform Crime Reports*. Third, victimization surveys rely on more representative samples than the other sources of crime data. There are also some disadvantages to these surveys. They are rather expensive and, while they provide detailed information about crime victims, they furnish less reliable data about offenders. In addition, it is evident that victimization surveys cannot provide us with information on all forms of crime; as John Evans (2004:106) laconically observes, "One need not be a methodologist to recognize that murder cannot be included in such a survey. Nor can consensual crimes for which there are not direct victims—drug use, gambling and the like . . . . Similarly, those crimes designed to keep victims unaware that they have been victimized [such as fraud, embezzlement, employee theft, price fixing, and other forms of white collar/consumer/corporate crime] cannot be captured accurately in victimization surveys."

Although the first victimization surveys were carried out in the United States in 1966 for the President's Commission on Law Enforcement and Administration of

Justice, victimization surveys in Canada have a much shorter history. Fattah (1991) reports that, "[n]o truly national victimization survey was done in Canada until the General Social Survey was carried out by Statistics Canada in 1988." Since that time, Statistics Canada has conducted a victimization survey every five years as part of its General Social Survey. For Statistics Canada's 2004 General Social Survey on Victimization, roughly 24 000 people, aged 15 and older, were interviewed by telephone and asked if they had been victimized by crime and, if so, where and when the crime had occurred and whether or not it had been reported to the police. Eight types of offences (based on Criminal Code definitions) were included in this survey: sexual assault, robbery, physical assault, theft of personal property, breaking and entering, motor vehicle/parts theft, theft of household property, and vandalism. The 2004 GSS also measured spousal harassment and criminal harassment ("stalking"). In addition, respondents were queried on their perceptions of the level of crime in their neighbourhood, their personal fear of crime, and their views on the criminal justice system (Statistics Canada, 2005). Among this survey's findings: violent victimization was highest among young Canadians aged 15 to 24, single people, those who frequently engaged in evening activities, and those who lived in an urban area; sexual assault was the type of victimization least likely to be reported to police (8 percent) compared with almost half of break-ins (54 percent), thefts of motor vehicle/parts (49 percent), and robberies (46 percent); injury, the presence/use of a weapon, and the need to take time off from activities such as work increased the likelihood that a violent incident would be reported to police; the self-reported rate of violent victimization was about 2.5 times higher for those who identified themselves as gay or lesbian; approximately 4 percent of all self-reported victimization incidents and 8 percent of self-reported violent offences were believed to be motivated by hatred for an identifiable group, most often a group distinguishable by their "race" or ethnicity.

In addition to national surveys, the International Crime Victim Survey collected victimization data using the same questionnaire in many countries, including Canada, in 1989, 1992, 1996–97, and 2000 (Besserer, 2002). This survey examines householders' experience with crime, policing, crime prevention, and feelings of being unsafe. According to this survey, only 55 percent of victimization incidents are reported to police on average, with property crimes more likely to be reported than crimes against persons. In part, this reflects the general requirement by insurance companies that individuals seeking compensation for property stolen or damaged as the result of a criminal act file a police report.

Survey methods have also been widely used in a variety of cross-cultural studies dealing with knowledge and opinions about law, evaluation of the effectiveness of the law, prestige of the law, and legal and moral attitudes. For example, a European study asked people in Poland, the Netherlands, and Germany whether they thought people should obey the law. They found significant national variations; more Germans (66 percent) than Poles (45 percent) or Netherlanders (47 percent) answered yes to this general question (Friedman and Macaulay, 1977:216). Several surveys have also found that public knowledge in a number of European countries on legal topics is considerably less than assumed by the legal authorities and by many scholars. But lack of knowledge about the law is not limited to European countries. For example, many respondents in an Oregon study did not know that Oregon law provides minors with the right to treatment for venereal disease, birth control information, and medical treatment without parental knowledge (Friedman and Macaulay, 1977:607). Similarly, Julian Roberts (2000) points out that Canadians tend to underestimate the severity of sentencing practices, the harshness of prison life, and the costs of incarceration and are generally ill-informed on the functioning of the parole system and the success and failure rates of offenders released on parole. He additionally observes that almost a decade after the *Young Offenders Act* became law, almost half the sample in a nationwide survey "admitted that they were 'not at all' or 'not very' familiar with the act" (2000:10). Consider as well the results of an Environics poll, commissioned by the Canadian Safety Council, that found that 65 percent of Canadians—56 percent of men and 74 percent of women—think Canada's impaired driving laws are not strict enough. However, only one in ten respondents realized that a first-time impaired driving conviction brings a minimum $600 fine and one-year driving prohibition while only two in ten correctly believed that life in prison is the maximum penalty for impaired driving causing death. As Canadian Safety Council president Emile Therien observed, "We doubt Canadians want the death penalty for impaired driving. A lot of people don't realize the law is already very strict" (Canadian Safety Council, 2000). According to this survey, better-educated individuals were less likely to know the penalties than those with lower levels of education.

THE IMPACT OF SOCIOLOGY ON SOCIAL POLICY

In every scientific field there is a distinction between pure and applied science. *Pure* science is a search for knowledge, without primary concern for its practical use. *Applied* science is the search for ways of using scientific knowledge to solve practical problems. For example, a sociologist making a study of the social structure of a lower-class neighbourhood is working as a pure scientist. If this is followed by a study of how to prevent crime in a lower-class neighbourhood, the latter study is applied science.

Essentially, however, sociology is both a pure and an applied science, for unless a science is constantly searching for more basic knowledge, its applications of knowledge are not likely to be very practical. This explains, in part, why a substantial amount of sociological work is still generated for academic purposes and executed with disciplinary concerns in mind. Much of sociological knowledge remains within the boundaries of the discipline. Often, the consumers of this knowledge are other sociologists and their students. But, simultaneously with the continuing development of scientific knowledge, social scientists are also concerned with the generation and dissemination of knowledge and information with potential applied or policy-relevant implications (Anderson, 2003; Calavita, 2001; Meenaghan, Kilty, and McNutt, 2004). Social science research has long been used to help resolve empirical issues that arise in litigation, and sociological knowledge and methodology can be useful in the formulation and instrumentation of social policy and in the evaluation of current policies or proposed policy alternatives (Monahan and Walker, 1991, 1998). Contemporary sociologists are attempting to contribute toward improving conditions of life in society by providing policymakers with the information that is needed to make informed decisions (D'Antonio, 1992:4). Other fields, such as economics, are already playing a significant role in policy matters. There are attempts to reformulate legal concepts in the language and equations of the marketplace. Many law schools now employ at least one economist, and policy reforms in fields as diverse as antitrust law, environmental regulation, and criminal sentencing bear the distinctive imprint of economic analysis (see, for example, Posner, 2001).

Theoretical knowledge can and should be translated into practical applications, and the purpose of this section is to demonstrate how sociological knowledge and expertise can have an impact on social policy. But what is "social policy"? Although there is no consensus in the sociological literature on the term **social policy** (Cochran and Malone,1999; Lavalette and Pratt, 1997), it generally refers to purposive legal measures that are adopted and pursued by representatives of government who are responsible for dealing with particular social conditions in society. The term "policymaking" refers to the process of identifying alternative courses of action that may be followed and choosing among them. Following Robert A. Scott and Arnold R. Shore (1979:13), the impact of sociology on social policy can be ascertained by looking at sociology's contributions to policy recommendations and sociology's contributions to enacted policy. The former deals with specific sociological research endeavours carried out on social problems that have been used for the development of specific policy recommendations for governmental programs, to diminish and ameliorate those conditions, and the latter has had a direct impact on enacted policy.

Contributions of Sociology to Policy Recommendations

The proposition that law should be seen in a broad social context is now almost a truism. "Widespread acceptance of the view that law is at least in part concerned with policy making, coupled with realistic enthusiasm for empiricism has resulted in increasing use of social science materials in resolving many legal problems" (Monahan and Walker, quoted by Freeman and Roesch, 1992:571). Over the years, there have been many instances in which sociological knowledge, perspectives, concepts, theories, and methods have been useful in connection with the development of policy recommendations (see, for example, Meenaghan, Kilty, and McNutt, 2004; Mink and Solinger, 2004; Mullard and Spicker, 1998). Canadian sociologists contributed to research that resulted in the social security and medicare systems, as well as to *La Commission d'enquête sur l'enseignement au Québec* (1963–66), which resulted in massive changes to the educational system in the province of Quebec. Sociological research also informed the recommendations of the Royal Commission on Health Services (1964–65), the Royal Commission on Bilingualism and Biculturalism (1963–69), the Royal Commission on the Status of Women in Canada (1967–70), and the Royal Commission on New Reproductive Technologies (1993).

Sociologists have also provided sensitizing concepts and theories that oriented the search for solutions to the crime problem. For example, studies of the correctional system and the operation of law enforcement in the courts have raised doubts about the effectiveness of existing criminal justice policies and of rehabilitation and treatment efforts. On the basis of sociological data, attention has been directed to such issues as accessibility of justice, alternative systems of social control, child custody in the context of parental violence, racial profiling, the need for specialized courts to deal with criminal charges of domestic violence and drug addiction, and a reconsideration of consensual crimes, or "crimes without victims" (Basemore and Schiff, 2001; Greenwood and Boissery, 2000; Jaffe and Crooks, 2004; Murdocca, 2004; Wortley and Tanner, 2005). Sociologists have examined subjects as diverse as the relative effectiveness of promotions, anonymity, and rewards in Canadian Crime Stoppers programs (Lippert, 2003) and the extent to which the Canadian media have complied with a relatively new law (passed shortly before the 2000 Canadian electoral campaign), which seeks to regulate the publication of polls in the media during electoral campaigns (Durand, 2002).

Feminist legal theorizing, which defines obscenity as that which subordinates or degrades women rather than that which offends some notion of sexuality, clearly influenced the Supreme Court's decision in the 1992 case of *R. v. Butler*. This case was a constitutional challenge that alleged that Canada's obscenity laws violated freedom-of-expression guarantees in the *Canadian Charter of Rights and Freedoms*. The ruling of the Supreme Court emphasized that the purpose of obscenity provisions, which prohibit "the undue exploitation of sex or of sex and one or more of the following subjects: namely, crime, horror, cruelty and violence" were to avoid harm rather than to express moral opprobrium. Determining whether "undue" exploitation occurred "must be made on the basis of the degree of harm that may flow from such exposure, harm of the type which predisposes persons to act in an anti-social manner." This decision, which explicitly found the obscenity provisions necessary in order to avoid harm—specifically, women's rights to equality, their sense of self-worth, and their physical safety—was lauded by the Women's Legal Education and Action Fund (LEAF), which had been granted intervener status in this case, and had argued that pornographic representations of sex combined with violence are discriminatory to women (Busby, 1999; see also Lo and Wei, 2002). However, the relationship between pornography and anti-social behaviour continues to inspire investigation and debate (see, for example, Hickey, 2006; Malamuth, Addison, and Koss, 2000).

Although the findings of social science research are not always viewed as compelling, Scott and Shore conclude that sociology has made a contribution to recommendations for policy in three ways:

> The first is through the use of sociological concepts that are said to provide new or unique perspectives on social conditions—perspectives that are based upon more than common sense and that may in fact be inconsistent with basic notions upon which existing policies are based . . . . Second, prescriptions for policy are sometimes suggested by the findings of sociological research undertaken primarily to advance scientific understanding of society . . . . The third is the use of sociological methods and techniques of research to obtain information about specific questions. (1979:20)

Of these three uses of sociology, the third is by far the most common (see, for example, Deutscher, 1999; Howard-Hassman, 2000). However, it should be noted that there is no way of precisely determining the extent to which sociology can or does contribute to policy recommendations. For example, in many instances the methods of empirical research, not the knowledge and concepts of sociology, have been directly responsible for policy prescriptions. Obviously, conducting research is not a skill possessed exclusively by sociologists. Moreover, there is no way of distinguishing between the contributions of intelligent and insightful individuals who happen to be trained as sociologists and the contributions of sociological knowledge and perspective as such. Consequently, care needs to be exercised in crediting the discipline's knowledge in all cases in which sociology has had an impact on policy.

Despite these qualifications, it is fair to state that sociological knowledge can and at times does have an impact on developing recommendations for social policy. "For this reason," as Scott and Shore observe (1979:23), "sociologists can legitimately claim that their discipline has been and is relevant to the development of policy recommendations."

Contributions of Sociology to Enacted Policy

Although there is a growing influence of social science in law, measuring the impact of social science research is a fairly difficult endeavour (see, for example, Anderson, 2003; Kraft and Furlong, 2004; Meenaghan, Kilty, and McNutt, 2004; Mink and Solinger, 2004).

Impact studies rely predominantly on citations for an indication of whether policymakers have used such research (Roesch et al., 1991:2). Counts of social science publications and findings cited in legal decisions could possibly under-represent the influence of research because policymakers are reluctant to cite them even when they have influenced their decisions. Because of their training in law, they have a preference for legal scholarship and precedent rather than for social science methodology and statistics. Consequently, the extent of impact in some instances remains controversial. However, sociologists have assuredly contributed research and conceptual skills toward the "formulation of programs and policies that were eventually enacted to ameliorate social conditions deemed harmful to society" (Scott and Shore, 1979:24; see also Bernhard and Preston, 2004; Doms, 2004; Dussault, 2005; Lippert, 2003).

In social-policy research, sociologists doing scientific work are often confronted with problems and issues that have an impact on many people whose lives may be substantially altered or changed. To illustrate, environmental sociologists have pointed out that governments are increasingly abandoning their role as the guardians of public health and welfare in relation to the environment. It is noted that: federal environmental charges against polluters decreased by 78 percent between 1992 and 1998; that no one was jailed under Canada's *Environmental Protection Act* or *Fisheries Act* for the entirety of the 1988 to 1998 period; that Canadian imports of hazardous waste are rising significantly (with the volume of hazardous wastes imported into Canada in 1999 exceeding all hazardous waste produced within Canada that year); that an increasing proportion of hazardous waste is simply dumped without treatment; that the infamous tar ponds of Sydney, Nova Scotia, where for more than 50 years the effluent from the provincially owned steel mills and coke ovens was dumped without the slightest attempt at containment, are the largest toxic waste dump in North America; and that Environment Canada's budget has shrunk by approximately 40 percent in the past few years (Suzuki and Dressel, 2002). Sociologists have additionally directed attention to environmental injustice (also referred to as environmental racism), and the tendency for socially and politically marginalized groups to bear the brunt of environmental ills from polluting industries, industrial and waste facilities, and transportation arteries (which generate vehicle emissions pollution) (Bullard, 2000; Bullard and Johnson, 1997). Not only are minority communities more likely to be polluted than others are, but environmental regulations are also less likely to be enforced in these areas (Stephens 1998). Renner warns that "minority populations and Indigenous peoples around the globe are facing massive degradation of their environments that threatens to irreversibly alter, indeed destroy, their ways of life and cultures" (1996:59).

The preceding illustrations show some of the contributions sociology can make toward enacted policy. However, a great deal of applied sociological research has no discernible policy implications of any kind. Many of the recommendations are considered to be pragmatically useless (that is, too expensive to instrument) or are considered politically unrealistic or implausible by policymakers. Furthermore, policy questions are fundamentally political and not sociological questions (Kraft and Furlong, 2004). Often, policies are formulated and *then* relevant research is sought to support, legitimize, and dramatize (or even propagandize) these policies. Thus, it would be erroneous to assume that research generally precedes and determines policy actions (see, for example, Girard, 2001). Furthermore, some sociologists feel that they should not be directly involved through research in the development and instrumentation of social policy, and this position is epitomized by Daniel P. Moynihan (1969:193), who contends that "the role of social sciences lies not in the formation of social policy but in the measurement of its results." In the next section, we shall consider evaluation research and impact studies.

EVALUATION RESEARCH AND IMPACT STUDIES

Evaluation of enacted policy is as old as policy itself. Policymakers always have made judgments regarding the benefits, costs, or effects of particular policies, programs, and projects (Mathison, 2005; Nathan, 2000; Rossi, Lipsey, and Freeman, 2004). Many of these judgments have been impressionistic, often influenced by ideological, partisan self-interest and evaluational criteria. For example, a tax cut may be considered necessary and desirable because it enhances the electoral chances of the evaluator's political party, or employment insurance may be deemed "bad" because the evaluator "knows a lot of people" who improperly receive benefits. Undoubtedly, much conflict may result from this sort of evaluation because different evaluators, employing different value criteria, reach different conclusions concerning the merits of the same policy (see, for example, Betcherman, 2000; Wiber, 2000).

Another type of evaluation has centred on the operation of specific policies or programs, such as a juvenile correctional reform (McGarrell, 1988), boot camp (Zhang, 1998), educational diversion program or "john school" designed to change the attitudes of men arrested for soliciting sex (Kennedy, Klein, and Gorzalka, 2004), or welfare program. Questions asked may include: Is the program honestly run? What are its financial costs? Who receives benefits (payments or services) and in what amounts? Is there any overlap or duplication with other programs? What is the level of community reintegration of participants? What is the degree of staff commitment? Were legal standards and procedures followed? This kind of evaluation may provide information about the honesty or efficiency in the conduct of a program but, like the impressionistic kind of evaluation, it will probably yield little if anything in the way of hard information on the societal effects of a program. A welfare program, for instance, may be carried out honestly and efficiently, and it may be politically and ideologically satisfying to a given evaluator. However, such an evaluation will tell us very little about the impact of the program on the poor, or whether it is achieving its officially stated objective.

Since the late 1960s, a third type of policy evaluation has been receiving increasing attention among policymakers. It is the systematic evaluation of programs to measure their societal impact and the extent to which they are achieving stated objectives. Consider, for example, the introduction of "no fault" compensation schemes for harm done in auto accidents. The no-fault system was originally established to ensure that accident victims were compensated for their injuries without delay. Quebec was the first jurisdiction to adopt a no-fault system, in 1978. It allows no separate lawsuits for compensation, apart from the compensation provided by the government. Since that time, the Saskatchewan and Manitoba systems have been modelled on the Quebec plan, and many other jurisdictions have some version of no-fault coverage. However, while the no-fault system has been shown to provide more victims with compensation more quickly than the tort system (Bogart, 2002:106), it has also been subject to criticisms for its inadequacy in addressing the claims of those individuals who have serious and permanent injuries and unusual pain and suffering. In addition, research conducted in Australia, New Zealand, and Quebec has discerned "some troubling, unexpected implications regarding the loss of deterrence effects on dangerous driving when tort actions are abolished and no-fault schemes are substituted" (Bogart, 2002:106). For example, in an assessment of the Quebec scheme, Gaudry (1988) reports that bodily injuries grew by 26.3 percent a year and fatalities by 6.8 percent after the introduction of the no-fault system, and suggests that these increases stem, at least in part, from two factors: "first, compulsory insurance requirements that cause previously uninsured motorists to drive less carefully and, second, flat premiums that significantly decrease insurance for high-risk drivers, resulting in more accidents, when before the differential rates would have priced them off the highway" (Bogart, 2002:106). Findings that indicate that no-fault schemes are associated with elevated rates of automobile accidents, injuries, and fatalities "are clearly at odds with the avowed purposes of such regimes" (Bogart, 2002:107).

For many, evaluation research has become a proper use of sociology in policy-related work (Babbie, 2004:333). This use of social research in policy analysis has become widespread, and an entire field of specialization has developed about methods and procedures for conducting evaluation research. Technically speaking, however, there are no formal methodological differences between evaluation and non-evaluation research. They have in common the same techniques and the same basic steps that must be followed in the research process. The difference lies in the following: (1) evaluation research uses deliberately planned intervention of some independent variable; (2) the programs it assesses assume some objective or goal as desirable; and (3) it attempts to determine the extent to which this desired goal has been reached. As Edward A. Suchman (1967:15) puts it, evaluation research "asks about the *kind* of change the program views as desirable, the *means* by which this change is to be brought about, and the *signs* according to which such change can be recognized." Thus, the greatest distinction between evaluation and non-evaluation research is one of objectives.

Carol Weiss (1998:6) proposes several additional criteria that distinguish evaluation research from other types of research:

1. Evaluation research is generally conducted for a client who intends to use the research as a basis for decision-making.

2. The investigator deals with his or her client's questions as to whether the client's program is accomplishing what the client wishes it to accomplish.

3. The objective of evaluation research is to ascertain whether the program goals are being reached.

4. The investigator works in a situation where priority goes to the program as opposed to the evaluation.

5. There is always a possibility of conflicts between the researcher and the program staff because of the divergences of loyalties and objectives.

6. In evaluation research there is an emphasis on results that are useful for policy decisions.

Social policy evaluation is essentially concerned with attempts to determine the impact of policy on real-life conditions. As a minimum, policy evaluation requires a specification of policy objectives (what we want to accomplish with a given policy), the means of realizing it (programs), and what has been accomplished toward the attainment of the objectives (impacts or outcomes). In measuring objectives, there is a need to determine not only that some change in real-life conditions has occurred, such as a reduction in the unemployment rate, but also that it was due to policy actions and not to other factors, such as private economic decisions.

Thomas R. Dye (2002:337) suggests that the impact of a policy has several dimensions, all of which must be taken into account in the course of evaluation. These include the impact on the social problem at which a policy is directed and on the people involved. Those whom the policy is intended to affect must be clearly defined—that is, the poor, the disadvantaged, schoolchildren, or unwed mothers. The intended effect of the policy must then be determined. If, for example, it is an antipoverty program, is its purpose to raise the income of the poor, to increase the opportunities for employment, or to change their attitudes and behaviour? If some combination of such objectives is intended, the evaluation of impact becomes more complicated, since priorities must be assigned to the various intended effects.

At times, as Friedman and Macaulay (1977:501) note, it is difficult to determine the purpose of a law or a program of regulation. They suggest that the determination of intent is complicated because many individuals with diverse purposes participate in the policy-making. Will consideration be given to the intention or intentions of the persons who drafted the statute or the judge who wrote the opinion creating the rule? To that of the majority of the legislature or court who voted for it? To that of the lobbyists who worked for the bill? To that purpose openly discussed or to the purpose that is implicit but never mentioned? They add that sometimes one can only conclude that a law has multiple and perhaps even conflicting purposes, but this is not to say that one can never be sure of the purpose of a law. However, one must be aware of the complexities of determining "purpose."

It should also be noted that a law may have intended or unintended consequences or even both. A guaranteed-income program, for example, may improve the income situation of the benefitted groups, as intended. But what impact does it also have on their initiative to seek employment? Does it decrease this, as some have contended? Similarly, an agricultural price support program intended to improve farmers' incomes may lead to over-production of the supported commodities.

The difficulties of measurement of impact are most acute for those areas of conduct where the behaviour in question is hard to quantify and where it is hard to tell what the behaviour *would* have been without the intervention of the law. The laws against murder illustrate the difficulties here. There is a fairly good idea about the murder rate in most countries, but no information at all exists about the contribution that the *law* makes to this rate. In other words, there is no way of determining how high the murder rate would be if there were, for example, no punishment assigned for murder.

Knowledge of a new law by members of the legal profession also plays a role in the study of impact. For example, one fairly new area of law permits Canadians to either individually or in class actions sue governments who fail to adequately enforce their own regulations and procedures for "regulatory negligence." For example, homeowners who have not been advised by health authorities that their homes have been constructed on radioactive soil can sue the government, as can those who become ill from polluted drinking water (Dranoff, 2001:8). However, to the degree that lawyers fail to keep abreast of new laws intended to protect consumers, the effectiveness of such laws will obviously be impaired. Consider here as well a survey of 564 Alberta lawyers and 141 psychiatrists that attempted to investigate their knowledge of, attitudes toward, and experiences with the Criminal Code provisions regarding mentally disordered offenders to better understand the lack of impact in practice patterns (Crisanti et al., 2000). The researchers found that psychiatrists had significantly more correct responses to the survey items assessing knowledge; with a highest possible knowledge score of 27, the average score for psychiatrists was 16 and, for lawyers, merely 13. The investigators concluded that the lack of knowledge demonstrated by both lawyers and psychiatrists of many of the key Criminal Code provisions governing mentally disordered offenders is disconcerting. Similarly, a study conducted in the wake of the Supreme Court of Canada decision (in *Reibl v. Hughes*) on informed consent to medical treatment found that 70 percent of Canadian surgeons were unaware of what the decision was and that "a majority of those who were aware expressed views inconsistent with it" (Bogart, 2002:119). Moreover, while the General Counsel to the Canadian Medical Protective Association confidently opined that "No legal event in the last fifty years has so disturbed the practice of medicine as did the decision of the Supreme Court of Canada in *Reibl v. Hughes*" (quoted in Bogart, 2002:350), a second follow-up study conducted a decade after the decision by the Supreme Court concluded that, in actuality, the decision "had had small significance for the severity and frequency of malpractice claims . . . [and] little impact on developments in other areas of health law or in jurisdictions outside Canada" (Bogart, 2002:119, 350).

The study of impact is further complicated by the fact that policies may have effects on groups or situations other than those at which they are directed. These are called spillover effects (Wade, 1972). These spillover effects may be positive or negative. An illustration of the negative effects is the testing of nuclear devices, which may provide data for the design of nuclear power plants but may also generate hazards for the population. An illustration of a positive spillover effect is that when tariffs are lowered at the request of Canadian exporters to increase their sales abroad, consumers in Canada may benefit from lower prices caused by increased imports that lower tariffs stimulate. Obviously, in the evaluation of impact, attention must also be paid to the spillover effects.

A given legislation may also have impact on future as well as current conditions. Is a particular policy designed to improve an immediate short-term situation, or is it intended to have effects over a longer time period? For example, is the Head Start program supposed to improve the cognitive abilities of disadvantaged children in the short run, or is it to have an impact on their long-range development and earning capacity? The determination of long-term effects stemming from a policy is much more difficult than the assessment of short-term impacts (see, for example, Beare, 2002).

A fairly rich literature of evaluation of actual and proposed programs of law has developed, using criteria derived from economics as its standard. This literature takes certain economic goals as its basic values and assesses legal programs as good or bad depending upon whether they most efficiently or rationally achieve the economic goals or make use of theoretically correct economic means. Of course, it is fairly easy to calculate the dollar costs of a particular policy when it is stated as the actual number of dollars spent on a program, its share of total government expenditures, how efficiently the funds are allocated, and so on. Other economic costs are, however, difficult to measure. For example, it is difficult to discover the expenditures by the private sector for pollution-control devices that are necessitated by air pollution control policy. Moreover, economic standards are hardly applicable to the measurement of social costs of inconvenience, dislocation, and social disruption resulting from, for instance, an urban renewal project (see, for example, Clairmont and Magill, 1999).

In addition to the difficulties inherent in the measurement of indirect costs and benefits, other complexities arise because the effects of a particular law may be symbolic (intangible) as well as material (tangible). Intended symbolic effects capitalize on popular beliefs, attitudes, and aspirations for their effectiveness. For example, taken at face value, Canada's "hate laws" are a symbol of equality and progressiveness in combating racism and combating the promotion of genocide. These laws define the willful promotion of hatred against any "identifiable group" as a crime. However, as we noted in Chapter 7, their discernible impact may be substantially lower than many believe. Other laws as well appear to promise more symbolically than their instrumentation actually yields in material benefits. They include antitrust activity, regulation of public utility rates, and various antipoverty efforts. These endeavours attempt to assure people that policymakers are concerned with their welfare, although the tangible benefits are often limited.

These are some of the difficulties that need to be taken into consideration in measuring the impact of a particular law. There are several possible research approaches that can be used for measuring impact. One approach is the study of a group of individuals from the target population after it has been exposed to a program developed to cause change. This approach is referred to as the **one-shot** study. Another possible approach is to study a group of individuals both **before and after** exposure to a particular program. Still another possibility would be the use of some kind of **controlled** experiment. But as we noted earlier in this chapter, in measuring the impact of law, one serious problem is the absence of control groups. As a result, one is rarely able to say with confidence what behaviour would have been had a law not been passed or had a different law been passed. Outside of a laboratory setting, it is difficult to apply an experimental treatment to a group that one has matched in all significant respects to another group that does not receive the treatment, so as to control for all possible sources of distortion or error. This difficulty is further accentuated by ethical problems that often arise from such research methods as the random assignment of persons to different legal remedies.

The final consideration of evaluation research involves the utilization of results. As James S. Coleman (1972:6) states, "The ultimate product is not a 'contribution to existing knowledge' in the literature, but a social policy modified by the research result." In many instances, however, those who mandate and request evaluation research fail to utilize the results of that research. These people may feel committed to particular ways of doing things despite evidence that a program is ineffective. This is particularly true in instances where programs were instigated by political pressures such as the various endeavours in relation to urban renewal, corrections, and drug and alcohol rehabilitation. As public interest waned in the later stages of these programs, there was no real pressure to incorporate the results of evaluation studies into the ongoing activities (Vago, 1999:388). There are, of course, a number of other ways initiators of evaluation research can respond to the results. They include the manipulation of research outcomes for their own interests, rationalization of negative results, and, in some instances where the findings are negative, dismissal of results.

It is evident that sociological expertise can be made relevant to social policy. Of course, it is a question of choice whether one would want to pursue primarily disciplinary or a policy-oriented applied sociology, although the two are not mutually exclusive. Sociology undoubtedly has a good potential to play an active, creative, and practical role in the formulation, instrumentation, and evaluation of social policy (Rogers, 1988). At the same time, as sociological knowledge and methods become relevant to and influential on policy, they become part of politics by definition. In such a situation, the contributions of sociology can become a tool for immediate political ends and propaganda purposes by justifying and legitimizing a particular position. Ideally, the objective should be to insulate, but not isolate, sociological contributions from the immediate vagaries of day-to-day politics, and to strike some sort of balance between political and sociological considerations, permitting neither to dominate.

SUMMARY

- Several methods can be applied in studying law in society, and more than a single method is usually involved in an investigation. The methods of sociological research include the historical, observational, experimental, and survey studies.

- Sociology, like all sciences, may be either pure or applied. Pure sociology searches for new knowledge, whereas applied sociology tries to apply sociological knowledge to practical problems.

- There is an increasing involvement of sociologists in evaluation research and impact studies. The object of evaluation research is to determine how successful a particular change effort is in achieving its goals. Impact studies are concerned with the intent of those who formulated a legal rule or policy, whether or not a legal rule was responsible for the change, knowledge of a law by its interpreters, and spillover effects.

CRITICAL THINKING QUESTIONS

1. Chapter 1 noted that sociologists interested in the law are frequently asked, "What are you doing studying law?" It also suggested that the complexity of legal terminology as well as differences in professional cultures may impede interaction between sociologists and lawyers. After reading this chapter, can you identify any additional factors that might complicate or frustrate the attempts of lawyers and sociologists to collaborate on research endeavours?

2. The subject of gender bias in the law, courts, and the legal profession has attracted significant discussion in both Canada and the United States for at least two decades (see, for example, Brockman, 2000; Brockman and Chunn, 1993; Jaimes-Guerrero, 2003; Lamarche, 2000). Design a study to investigate gender bias in an area of law that is of particular interest to you. What method would you employ? What difficulties do you anticipate? How might these problems be redressed?

References

Abel, Richard L. 1973. "A Comparative Theory of Dispute Institutions in Society." *Law and Society Review* 8 (2) (Winter): 217–347. 1986. "The Transformation of the American Legal Profession." *Law and Society Review* 20 (1): 7–17. 1995a. "What We Talk About When We Talk About Law" in Richard L. Abel (ed.), *The Law and Society Reader*, pp. 1–10. New York: New York University Press. (ed.). 1995b. *The Law and Society Reader*. New York: New York University Press 2003. *English Lawyers Between Market and State: The Politics of Professionalism*. Oxford, UK: Oxford University Press.

Abel, Richard L., and Philip S. C. Lewis (eds.). 1988. *Lawyers in Society: The Common Law World*. Vol. 1. Berkeley and Los Angeles: University of California Press. 1988. *Lawyers in Society: The Civil Law World*. Vol. 2. Berkeley and Los Angeles: University of California Press.

Abraham, Henry J. 1998. *The Judicial Process: An Introductory Analysis of the Courts of the United States, England, and France*. 7th ed. New York: Oxford University Press. 1994. *The Judiciary: The Supreme Court in the Governmental Process*. 9th ed. Madison, WI: Brown and Benchmark.

Abrams, Kathryn. 1995. "Sex War Redux: Agency and Coercion in Feminist Legal Theory." *Columbia Law Review* 95 (2) (March): 304–376.

Abramson, Jeffrey. 2000. *We, the Jury: The Jury System and the Ideal of Democracy*. Cambridge, MA: Harvard University Press.

Abramson, Jill. 1998. "The Business of Persuasion Thrives in Nation's Capital." *New York Times* (September 29): A1, A22–23.

Adams, Bert N., and Rosalind A. Sydie. 2002. *Contemporary Sociological Theory*. Thousand Oaks, CA: Pine Forge Press.

Addy, George, Lori A. Cornwall, and Elisa K. Kearney. 2005. "Canada: Competition Law Compliance Strategies: The Increasingly Complex and Challenging Mandate Facing Compliance Managers." July 15. Retrieved from www.mondaq.com/ i_article.asp_Q_articleid_E_33729.

Adinkrah, Mensah. 2005. "Vigilante Homicides in Contemporary Ghana." *Journal of Criminal Justice* 33 (5) (September–October): 413–427.

Agger, Ben. 1979. *Western Marxism: An Introduction*. Santa Monica, CA: Goodyear.

Ahmed, Ali. 2001. *Cosmopolitan Orientation of the Process of International Environmental Lawmaking: An Islamic Law Genre*. Lanham, MD: University Press of America.

Akers, Ronald L. 1965. "Toward a Comparative Definition of Law." *Journal of Criminal Law, Criminology, and Police Science* 56 (September): 301–306.

Akers, Ronald L., and Richard Hawkins (eds.). 1975. *Law and Control in Society*. Englewood Cliffs, NJ: Prentice Hall.

Al-Azmeh, Aziz. (ed.). 1988. *Islamic Law: Social and Historical Contexts*. London: Routledge.

Albisetti, James C. 2000. "Portia Ante Portas: Women and the Legal Profession in Europe, ca. 1870–1925." *Journal of Social History* 33 (4) (Summer): 825–857.

Albonetti, Celesta A. 1992. "An Integration of Theories to Explain Judicial Discretion." *Social Problems* 38 (2) (May): 247–266.

Alexander, Gregory S., and Grazyna Skapska (eds.). 1994. *A Fourth Way? Privatization, Property, and the Emergence of New Market Economies*. New York: Routledge.

Alford, Robert R. 1998. *The Craft of Inquiry, Methods, Evidence*. New York: Oxford University Press.

Allyn, David. 2004. *I Can't Believe I Just Did That: How Seemingly Small Embarrassments Can Wreak Havoc in Your Life—And What You Can Do To Put a Stop to Them*. New York: Jeremy P. Tarcher/Penguin.

Almeida, Paul, and Linda Brewster Stearns. 1998. "Political Opportunities and Local Grassroots Environmental Movements: The Case of

Minamata." *Social Problems* 45 (1) (February): 37–57.

Althus, Scott L. 2003. Collective *Preferences in Democratic Politics: Opinion Surveys and the Will of the People*. Cambridge, UK: Cambridge University Press.

Ambrose, David. 1998. *Superstition*. New York: Warner Books.

American Bar Association. 2001. *Section of Legal Education and Admission to the Bar: A Review of Legal Education in the United States, Fall, 2001*. Chicago: Author. 2002. *Dispute Resolution Program Directory*. Washington, DC: Author. 2004. *Dispute Resolution Program Directory*. Washington, DC: American Bar Association.

American Tort Reform Association. 1992. "Scapegoat Litigation Will Drain U.S. Economy an Average of $17.8 Billion Annually." Press release (August 5).

Amiel, Barbara. 2006. "A Twilight Zone of Insanity." *Maclean's* (February 13): 7.

Amnesty International. 2005. Female Genital Mutilation: A Human Rights Information Pack." Retrieved from www.amnesty.org/ailib/intcam/femgen/fgm1. htm. 2006. "Facts and Figures on the Death Penalty." Retrieved from web.amnesty.org/web/web.nsf/print/ deathpenalty-facts-eng. 2006a. "Death Penalty News, January 2006." Retrieved from web.amnesty.org/library/print/ ENGACT530012006. 2006b. "Facts and Figures on the Death Penalty." Retrieved from web.amnesty.org/web/web.nsf/ print/deathpenalty-facts-eng. 2006c. "Death Penalty News, January 2006." Retrieved from web.amnesty.org/library/print/ ENGACT530012006.

Amos v. New Brunswick (Electric Power Commission). New Brunswick Court of Queen's Bench, 1976/1977, 1 S.C.R. 500, 13 N.B.R. (2d).

Anand, Ruchi. 2004. *International Environmental Justice: A North-South Dimension*. Burlington, VT: Ashgate.

Andenaes, Johannes. 1977. "The Moral or Educative Influence of Criminal Law," in June Louis Tapp and Felice J. Levine (eds.), *Law, Justice, and the Individual in Society: Psychological and Legal Issues*, pp. 50–59. New York: Holt, Rinehart and Winston.

Anderssen, Erin. 1999. "Gay-Bashing Preacher Calls Off Protest." *Globe and Mail* (June 29). Retrieved from www.egale.ca/archives/ press/9906299gm.htm.

Anderson, Lisa. 2003. *Pursuing Truth, Exercising Power: Social Science and Public Policy in the Twenty-First Century*. New York: Columbia University Press.

Andrews, Lori B. 1982. "Mind Control in the Courtroom." *Psychology Today* (March): 66–73.

Anleu, Sharyn I. Roach. 2000. *Law and Social Change*. Thousand Oaks, CA: Sage.

Applegate, John S. (Ed.) 2004. *Environmental Risk, Volumes I and II*. Burlington, VT: Ashgate.

Arndt, Susan. 2000. "African Gender Trouble and African Womanism: An Interview with Chikwenye Ogynyemi and Wanjira Muthoni." *Signs* 25 (3) (Spring): 709–726.

Arnold, Bruce L., and John Hagan. 1992. "Careers of Misconduct: The Structure of Prosecuted Professional Deviance Among Lawyers." *American Sociological Review* 57 (6): 771–779. 1994. "Self-Regulatory Responses to Professional Misconduct Within the Legal Profession." *Canadian Review of Sociology and Anthropology* 31 (2): 168–183.

Arnold, Bruce L., and Fiona M. Kay. 1995. "Social Capital, Violations of Trust and the Vulnerability of Isolates: The Social Organization of Law Practice and Professional Self-Regulation." *International Journal of the Sociology of Law* 23 (4) (December): 321–346.

Arnold, Thurman. 1935. *The Symbols of Government*. New Haven, CT: Yale University Press.

Arrigo, Bruce A. (ed.). 1999. *Social Justice/Criminal Justice: The Maturation of*

Critical Theory in Law, Crime, and Deviance. Belmont, CA: West/Wadsworth. 2002. *Punishing the Mentally Ill: A Critical Analysis of Law and Psychiatry.* Albany: State University of New York Press.

Arthurs, H. W. 1980. "Jonah and the Whale: The Appearance, Disappearance and Reappearance of Administrative Law." *University of Toronto Law Journal* 30: 225–239. 1996. "Lawyering in Canada in the 21st Century." *Windsor Yearbook of Access to Justice* 12: 202–225. 1997. "Globalization of the Mind: Canadian Elites and the Restructuring of Legal Fields." *Canadian Journal of Law and Society* 12 (2) (Fall): 219–246. 1998. "Why Canadian Law Schools Do Not Teach Legal Ethics," in K. Economides (ed.), *Ethical Challenges to Legal Education and Conduct,* pp. 105–118. Oxford: Hart. 1999. "Introduction," in Allan C. Hutchinson, *Legal Ethics and Professional Ethics,* pp. x–xiv. Toronto: Irwin Law. 2001. "Poor Canadian Legal Education: So Near to Wall Street, So Far from God." *Osgoode Hall Law Journal* 38 (3): 381–408.

Asante, Molefi Kete. 2003. *Afrocentricity: The Theory of Social Change.* Revised and expanded. Chicago, IL: African American Images.

Asbridge, Mark. 2004. "Public Place Restrictions on Smoking in Canada: Assessing the Role of the State, Media, Science and Public Health Advocacy." *Social Science and Medicine* 58 (1) (January): 13–24.

Ash, Russell. 2001. *The Top 10 of Everything 2002.* Canadian Edition. Toronto: Dorling Kindersley.

Ashe, Marie. 1989. "Zig-Zag Stitching and the Seamless Web: Thoughts on 'Reproduction' and the Law." *Nova Law Review* 13: 355–383.

Atiyah, Patrick. 1970. *Accidents, Compensation, and the Law.* London, UK: Weidenfeld and Nicolson. 1997. *The Damages Lottery.* Oxford, UK: Hart.

Aubert, Vilhelm. 1963. "Competition and Dissensus: Two Types of Conflict and Conflict Resolution." *Journal of Conflict Resolution* 7 (1): 26–42. ed. 1969a. *Sociology of Law.* Harmondsworth, UK: Penguin. 1969b. "Law as a Way of Resolving Conflicts: The Case of a Small Industrialized Society," in Laura Nader (ed.), *Law in Culture and Society,* pp. 282–303. Chicago: Aldine. 1973. "Researches in the Sociology of Law," in Michael Barkun (ed.), *Law and the Social System,* pp. 48–62. New York: Lieber-Atherton.

Auditor General of Canada. 2001. Report of the Auditor General of Canada, 2001. Retrieved from www.oag-bvg.gc.ca/ domino/reports.nsf/html/0111xe06.html. 2002. *Report of the Auditor General of Canada.* Retrieved from www.oag-bvg.gc.ca/ domino/reports.nsf/html/0204ce.html.

Auerbach, Alan. 2000. "Consumer Law," in Laurence M. Olivo (ed.), *Introduction to Law in Canada,* pp. 257–294. Toronto: Captus Press.

Auerbach, Jerold S. 1976. *Unequal Justice: Lawyers and Social Change in Modern America.* New York: Oxford University Press.

Ayres, Ian. 2003. Book Review Symposium: "Prevention Perspectives on 'Different' Kinds of Discrimination: From Attacking 'Isms' to Promoting Acceptance in Critical Race Theory, Law and Economics, and Empirical Research: Pervasive Prejudice? Unconventional Evidence of Race and Gender Discrimination." *Stanford Law Review* 55 (June): 2293–2364.

Azmier, Jason J. 2005. *Gambling in Canada 2005: Statistics and Context.* Canada West Foundation, June. Retrieved from www.cwf.ca/abca/cwfl.doc.nsf/ (Publications)/6C89CD3AB8C28DD7872502 7004652791/$file/GamblingInCanada. pdf. *B. (R.) v. Children's Aid Society of Metropolitan Toronto* (1995) 1 S.C.R. 315, 176 N.R. 161, 26 C.R.R. (2d) 202, 78 O.A.C. 1, 122 D.L.R. (4th) 1.

Babbie, Earl. 2004. *The Practice of Social Research.* 10th ed. Belmont, CA: Wadsworth.

Backhouse, Constance. 1991. *Petticoats and Prejudice: Women and Law in Nineteenth-Century Canada*. Toronto: The Women's Press. 1999a. "White Female Help and Chinese Canadian Employers: Race, Class, Gender, and Law in the Case of Yee Chun, 1924," in Nick Larsen and Brian Burtch (eds.), *Law in Society: Canadian Readings*, pp. 3–22. Toronto: Harcourt. 1999b. Colour-Coded: A Legal History of Racism in Canada, 1900–1950. Toronto: University of Toronto Press. 2004. "The Doctrine of Corroboration in Sexual Assault Trials in Early 20th Century Canada and Australia," in Pierre Boyer, Linda Cardinal, and David Headon (eds.), *From Subjects to Citizens: A Hundred Years of Citizenship in Australia and Canada*, pp. 123–159. Ottawa, ON: University of Ottawa Press.

Baggins, David Sadofsky. 1998. *Drug Hate and the Corruption of American Justice*. Westport, CT: Praeger/Greenwood.

Bailey, William C., and Ruth D. Peterson. 1994. "Murder, Capital Punishment, and Deterrence: A Review of the Evidence and an Examination of Police Killings." *Journal of Social Issues* 50 (2) (Summer): 53–75.

Baker, G. Blaine. 1983. "Legal Education in Upper Canada 1895–1889: The Law Society as Educator," in David H. Flaherty (ed.), *Essays in the History of Canadian Law, Vol. 11*, pp. 49–142. Toronto: University of Toronto Press.

Baker, Wayne. 2005. *America's Crisis of Values: Reality and Perception*. Princeton, NJ: Princeton University Press.

Ball, Howard. 2004. The *Supreme Court in the Intimate Lives of Americans: Birth, Sex, Marriage, Childbearing, and Death*. New York: New York University Press.

Banakar, Reza. 2003. *Merging Law and Sociology: Beyond the Dichotomies in Socio-Legal Research*. Madison, WI: Galda Wilch Verlag.

Banakar, Reza, and Max Travers (eds.). 2002. *An Introduction to Law and Social Theory*. Portland, OR: Hart.

Banks, Cindy. 1998. "Custom in the Courts." *British Journal of Criminology* 38 (2) (Spring): 299–316.

Banner, Stuart. 2000. "Conquest by Contract: Wealth Transfer and Land Market Structure in Colonial New Zealand." *Law and Society Review* 34 (1): 47–96. *Barclay v. Fournier*, New Brunswick Court of Queen's Bench, 1991, 112 N.B.R., (2d) 424.

Barkun, Michael. 2002. "Defending Against the Global Apocalypse: The Limits of Homeland Security." *Policy Options* 23 (6) (September): 27–32.

Barlow, Maude, and Bruce Campbell. 1995. *Straight Through the Heart*. Toronto: HarperCollins.

Barrett, Jerome T., and Joseph P. Barrett. 2004. *A History of Alternative Dispute Resolution: From the Wisdom of Solomon to U.S. v. Microsoft and Beyond*. San Francisco, CA: Jossey-Bass.

Barsky, Edward F. 2000. *Arguing and Justifying: Assessing the Convention Refugees' Choice of Moment, Motive and Host Country*. Aldershot, UK: Ashgate.

Bartlett, Katharine T. 1991. "Feminist Legal Methods," in Katharine T. Bartlett and Rosanne Kennedy (eds.), *Feminist Legal Theory: Readings in Law and Gender*, pp. 370–403. Boulder, CO: Westview Press.

Bartlett, Katharine T., and Rosanne Kennedy (eds.). 1991. *Feminist Legal Theory: Readings in Law and Gender*. Boulder, CO: Westview Press.

Bartlett, Katharine T., Angela P. Harris, and Deborah L. Rhode. 2002. *Gender and Law: Theory, Doctrine, Commentary*. 3rd ed. New York: Aspen Law and Business.

Basu, Arpon. 2000. "Mother Sues over Lack of Ice Time for Goalie Son." *National Post* (August 24). Retrieved from http://overlawyered.com/archives/00sept2.html.

Baumgartner, M. P. 1978. "Law and Social Status in Colonial New Haven, 1639–1665," in Rita J. Simon (ed.), *Research in Law and Sociology*,

Vol. 1, pp. 153–174. Greenwich, CT: Jai Press. 2001. "The Sociology of Law in the United States." *American Sociologist* 32 (2) (Summer): 99–113. 1999. *The Social Organization of Law.* 2nd ed. San Diego, CA: Academic Press.

Beare, Margaret E. 1996. *Criminal Conspiracies: Organized Crime in Canada.* Toronto: ITP Nelson. 2002. "Organized Corporate Criminality: Tobacco Smuggling Between Canada and the US." *Crime, Law and Social Change* 37 (3) (April): 225–243.

Beaudoin, Gerald A. 1999. "Pamajewon Case," in James H. Marsh (ed.), *The Canadian Encyclopedia: Year 2000 Edition*, p. 1753. Toronto: McClelland and Stewart.

Beck, Connie J. A., and Bruce D. Sales. 2000. "A Critical Reappraisal of Divorce Mediation Research and Policy." *Psychology, Public Policy and Law* 6 (4) (December): 989–1056.

Beck, Peggy, and Nancee Blank. 1997. "Broadening the Scope of Divorce Mediation to Meet the Needs of Children." *Mediation Quarterly: Journal of the Academy of Family Mediators* 14 (3): 179–185.

Becker, Howard S. 1963. *Outsiders.* New York: Free Press.

Beckett, Katherine, and Theodore Sasson. 2004. *The Politics of Injustice: Crime and Punishment in America.* 2nd ed. Thousand Oaks, CA: Sage.

Bedau, Hugo Adam, and Paul G. Cassell (eds.). 2004. *Debating the Death Penalty: Should America Have Capital Punishment?: The Experts on Both Sides Make Their Best Case.* New York: Oxford University Press.

Beerman, Jack M. 2003. *Administrative Law.* New York: Aspen.

Beeby, Dean. 2006. "Health Canada Going After Medical Pot Users." *Canoe Network: The CNews*, February 6. Retrieved from www.cnews.canoe.ca/CNEWS/LAW/Marijuana/2006/02/05/1427232-cp.html.

Beeghley, Leonard. 2005. *The Structure of Social Stratification in the United States.* 4th ed. Boston: Allyn and Bacon.

Beerman, Jack M. 2003. *Administrative Law.* New York: Aspen.

Behar, Cem. 2004. "Neighborhood Nuptials: Islamic Personal Law and Local Customs— Marriage Records in a Mahalle of Traditional Istanbul (1864–1907)." *International Journal of Middle East Studies* 36 (4) (November): 537–559. *Behavior Today.* 1979. "New Roundup" 10 (26) (July 9): 8.

Bell, C., and M. Asch. 1997. "Challenging Assumptions: The Impact of Precedent in Aboriginal Rights Litigation," in M. Asch (ed.), *Aboriginal and Treaty Rights in Canada: Essays on Law, Equality, and Respect for Difference*, pp. 38–74. Vancouver: UBC Press.

Bell, Kim. 1995. "Prisoners Can Now Lose More Than Their Lawsuits." *St. Louis Post-Dispatch* (July 6): 1, 9. *Bellingham Herald, The.* 2001. "Lawsuits a Volume Business at Wal-Mart" (August 19): E1, E3.

Belliotti, Raymond A. 1992. *Justifying Law: The Debate over Foundations, Goals, and Methods.* Philadelphia: Temple University Press.

Belluck, Pam. 1998. "Forget Prisons, Americans Cry Out for the Pillory." *New York Times* (October 4): WK5.

Bender, Leslie. 2003. "A Lawyer's Primer on Feminist Theory and Tort," in T. Brettel Dawson (ed.), *Women, Law and Social Change: Core Readings and Current Issues*, pp. 186–187. Concord, ON: Captus Press.

Bender, Steven W. 2004. *Greasers and Gringos: Latinos, Law and the American Imagination.* New York: New York University Press.

Benjamin, Matthew. 2001. "Legal Self-Help: Cheap Counsel for Simple Cases." *U.S. News and World Report* (February 12): 54–56.

Bennett, Belinda (Ed.). 2004. *Abortion.* Burlington, VT: Ashgate.

Bennis, Warren G. 1966. *Changing Organizations.* New York: McGraw-Hill.

Benson, Michael L., and Francis T. Cullen. 1998. *Combating Corporate Crime: Local*

Prosecutors at Work. Boston: Northeastern University Press.

Bercal, T. E. 1970. "Calls for Police Assistance: Consumer Demands for Governmental Service." *American Behavioral Scientist* 13 (5–6) (May–August): 681–691.

Berg, Axel van den, and Hudson Meadwell (eds.). 2004. *The Social Sciences and Rationality: Promise, Limits and Problems*. New Brunswick, NJ: Transaction.

Berger, Morroe. 1952. *Equality by Statute*. New York: Columbia University Press.

Berk, Richard A., and Jerrold Oppenheim. 1979. "Doing Good Well: The Use of Quantitative Social Science Data in Adversary Proceedings." *Law and Policy Quarterly* 1 (2) (April): 123–146.

Berk, Richard A., and Phyllis A. Newton. 1995. "Does Arrest Really Deter Wife Battery? An Effort to Replicate the Findings of the Minneapolis Spouse Abuse Experiment." *American Sociological Review* 50: 253–262.

Berlow, Alan. 2001. "The Broken Machinery of Death." *American Prospect* (July 30): 16–17.

Berman, Harold J., William R. Greiner, and Samir N. Saliba. 1996. *The Nature and Functions of Law*. 5th ed. Westbury, NY: Foundation Press.

Bernard, Thomas J., George B. Vold, and Jeffrey B. Snipes. 2002. *Theoretical Criminology*. 5th ed. New York: Oxford University Press.

Bernhard, Bo J., and Frederick W. Preston. 2004. "On the Shoulders of Merton: Potentially Sobering Consequences of Problem Gambling Policy." *The American Behavioral Scientist* 47 (11) (July): 1395–1405.

Besserer, Sandra. 2002. "Criminal Victimization: An International Perspective: Results of the 2000 International Crime Victimization Survey." *Juristat*, Catalogue no. 85–002–XPE, 22 (4) (May).

Betcherman, Gordon. 2000. "Structural Unemployment: How Important Are Labour Market Policies and Institutions?" *Canadian Public Policy* 26 (supplement) (July): S131–S140.

Bibby, Reginald W. 1995. *The Bibby Report: Social Trends Canadian Style*. Toronto: Stoddart. 2001. *Canada's Teens: Today, Yesterday, and Tomorrow*. Toronto: Stoddart.

Bittner, Egon. 1970. *The Functions of the Police in Modern Society*. Chevy Chase, MD: National Institute of Mental Health.

Black, Donald. 1973. "The Mobilization of Law." *Journal of Legal Studies* 2 (1) (January): 125–149. 1976. *The Behavior of Law*. New York: Academic Press. 1980. *The Manners and Customs of the Police*. New York: Academic Press. 1989. *Sociological Justice*. New York: Oxford University Press. 1998. *The Social Structure of Right and Wrong*. Rev. ed. San Diego, CA: Academic Press. 2002. "The Geometry of Law: An Interview with Donald Black." *International Review of the Sociology of Law* 30 (2): 101–130. 2004a. "The Geometry of Terrorism." *Sociological Theory* 22 (1) (March): 14–25. 2004b. "Terrorism as Social Control." *Sociology of Crime, Law and Deviance* 5: 9–18.

Black, Donald J., and Albert J. Reiss, Jr. 1970. "Police Control of Juveniles." *American Sociological Review* 35 (1) (February): 63–77.

Blatchford, Christie. 2000. "Woman Sues Doctors for Not Stopping Her from Killing." *National Post* (May 16). Retrieved from http://over-lawyered.com/archives/00may2.html.

Blegvad, Britt-Mari. 1983. "Accessibility and Dispute Treatment: The Case of the Consumer in Denmark," in Maureen Cain and Kalman Kulcsar (eds.), *Disputes and the Law*, pp. 203–219. Budapest: Akademiai Kiado.

Blomley, Nicholas. 2003. "Law, Property, and the Geography of Violence: The Frontier, the Survey, and the Grid." *Annals of the Association of American Geographers* 93 (1) (March): 121–141.

Blumberg, Abraham S. 1979. *Criminal Justice: Issues and Ironies*. 2nd ed. New York: New Viewpoints.

Bodenheimer, Edgar. 1974. *Jurisprudence: The Philosophy and Method of the Law*. Rev. ed. Cambridge, MA: Harvard University Press.

Bogart, William A. (Bogart, W. A.).1994. *Courts and Country: The Limits of Litigation and the Social and Political Life of Canada*. Toronto: Oxford University Press. 2002. *Consequences: The Impact of Law and Its Complexity*. Toronto: University of Toronto Press.

Boggs, Sarah L. 1971. "Formal and Informal Crime Control: An Exploratory Study of Urban, Suburban, and Rural Orientations." *Sociological Quarterly* 12 (1) (Summer): 319–327.

Bogus, Carl T. 2001. *Why Law Suits Are Good for America: Disciplined Democracy, Big Business, and the Common Law*. New York: New York University Press. 2004a. "Fear-Mongering Torts and the Exaggerated Death of Diving." *Harvard Journal of Law and Public Policy* 28 (1): 17–37. 2004b. "Research Counters Furor over Malpractice Lawsuits." *USA Today* (March 24): 13A.

Bohannan, Paul. 1973. "The Differing Realms of the Law," in Donald Black and Maureen Mileski (eds.), *The Social Organization of the Law*, pp. 306–317. New York: Seminar Press.

Bonnor, Raymond. 2001. "Push Is On for Larger Jury in Military Capital Cases." *New York Times* (September 4): A1, A9.

Bonnycastle, Kevin. 2000. "Rape Uncodified: Reconsidering Bill C-49 Amendments to Canadian Sexual Assault Laws," in Dorothy E. Chunn and Dany Lacombe (eds.), *Law as a Gendering Practice*, pp. 60–78. Don Mills, ON: Oxford University Press.

Bonsignore, John J., Ethan Katsh, Peter d'Errico, Ronald M. Pipkin, Stephen Arons, and Janet Rifkin. 1989. *Before the Law: An Introduction to the Legal Process*. 4th ed. Boston: Houghton Mifflin.

Bordua, David J., and Albert J. Reiss, Jr. 1966. "Command, Control, and Charisma: Reflections on Police Bureaucracy." *American Journal of Sociology* 72 (1) (July): 68–76.

Borg, Marian J., and Karen F. Parker. 2001. "Mobilizing Law in Urban Areas: The Social Structure of Homicide Clearance Rates." *Law and Society Review* 35 (2) (June): 435–466.

Borovoy, A. Alan. 1999. *The New Anti-Liberals*. Toronto: Canadian Scholar's Press. 2002. "Protest Movements and Democracy." *Policy Options* 23 (6) (September): 54–56.

Boulding, Kenneth E. 1956. *The Image*. Ann Arbor: University of Michigan Press.

Bourassa, Kevin. 2004. "Love and the Lexicon of Marriage." *Feminism and Psychology* 14 (1) (February): 57–62.

Bourrie, Mark. 1999. "Compensating the Innocent." *Canadian Lawyer* (November/December): 29–32.

Boyd, Neil. 1998. *Canadian Law: An Introduction*. 2nd ed. Toronto: Harcourt. 2002. *Canadian Law: An Introduction*. 3rd ed. Toronto: Nelson Thomson Learning.

Boyd, Susan B. 2000. "Custody, Access, and Relocation in a Mobile Society: (En)Gendering the Best Interests Principle," in Dorothy E. Chunn and Dany Lacombe (eds.), *Law as a Gendering Practice*, pp. 158–180. Don Mills, ON: Oxford University Press.

Boyle, Elizabeth Heger, and Sharon E. Preves. 2000. "National Politics as International Process: The Case of Anti-Female-Genital-Cutting Laws." *Law and Society Review* 34 (3): 703–737.

Brady, James P. 1981. "A Season of Startling Alliance: Chinese Law and Justice in the New Order." *International Journal of the Sociology of Law* 9: 41–67.

Braithwaite, John. 1989. *Crime, Shame and Reintegration*. Melbourne, Australia: Cambridge University Press.

Braitstein, Paula, Kathy Li, and Mark Tyndall. 2003. "Sexual Violence Among a Cohort of Injection Drug Users." *Social Science and Medicine* 57 (3) (August): 561–569.

Braniff, Michele. 2004. "Alternative Dispute Resolution," in Laurence M. Olivo (ed.), *Introduction to Law in Canada*, pp. 555–584. Concord, ON: Captus Press.

Brannigan, Augustine. 1984. *Crimes, Courts and Corrections: An Introduction to Crime and Social Control in Canada*. Toronto: Holt, Rinehart and Winston.

Bravo, Gina, Michele Charpentier, Marie-France Dubois, and Philippe De Wals. 2000. "Article 21 of the Quebec Civil Code: Implications for Research in Gerontology." *Canadian Journal on Aging* 19 (1) Spring: 1–17.

Bredemeier, Harry C. 1962. "Law as an Integrative Mechanism," in William J. Evan (ed.), *Law and Sociology: Exploratory Essays*, pp. 73–90. New York: Free Press.

Brenner, Susan W. 1992. *Precedent Inflation*. New Brunswick, NJ: Transaction.

Breyer, Stephen G., and Richard B. Stewart. 1998. *Administrative Law and Regulatory Policy*. 4th ed. New York: Aspen Law and Business.

Bricker, Darrell, and Edward Greenspon. 2001. *Searching for Certainty: Inside the New Canadian Mindset*. Toronto: Random House.

Bricker, Darrell, and John Wright. 2005. *What Canadians Think*. Toronto: Doubleday Canada.

Brisbin, Richard A. Jr. 2004. "Book Review: Tournament of Appeals." Retrieved from www.bsos.umd.edu/gvpt/lpbr/subpages/reviews/flemming704.htm.

Brockman, Joan. 2000. "'A Wild Feminist at Her Raving Best': Reflections on Studying Gender Bias in the Legal Profession." *Resources for Feminist Research* 28 (1–2) (Spring/Summer): 61–79. 2001. *Gender in the Legal Profession: Fitting or Breaking the Mould*. Vancouver: UBC Press.

Brockman, Joan, and Dorothy E. Chunn. 1993. "Gender Bias in Law and the Social Sciences," in Joan Brockman and Dorothy Chunn (eds.), *Investigating Gender Bias: Law, Courts, and the Legal Profession*, pp. 3–18. Toronto: Thompson.

Brodsky, Stanley L. 1991. *Testifying in Court*. Washington, DC: American Psychological Association. 2004. *Coping with Cross-Examination and Other Pathways to Effective Testimony*. Washington, DC: American Psychological Association.

Brooks, Richard O., and James Bernard Murphy (eds.). 2003. *Aristotle and Modern Law*. Burlington, VT: Ashgate.

Broughton, Jonathan, Brian Gravelsons, Colm Hensman, James Rakow, Julian Lowe, Mark Malone, Grant Mitchell, and Shreyas Shah. 2004. *The Cost of Compensation Culture*. London, UK: Faculty and Institute of Actuaries.

Brown, Desmond H. 2002. "'They Punish Murderers, Thieves, Traitors and Sorcerers': Aboriginal Criminal Justice as Reported by Early French Observers." *Social History* 35 (70) (November): 363–391.

Bryant, Amorette Nelson. 2004. *Complete Guide to Federal and State Garnishment*. 3rd ed. New York: Aspen.

Bryant, Christopher, and Edmund Mokrzycki (eds.). 1994. *The Great Transformation? Change and Continuity in East-Central Europe*. New York: Routledge.

Brym, Robert J. 2001. "Politics and Social Movements," in Robert J. Brym (ed.), *New Society: Sociology for the 21st Century*, pp. 475–494. 3rd ed. Toronto: Harcourt.

Brym, Robert, John Lie, Adie Nelson, Neil Guppy, and Chris McCormick. 2003. *Sociology: Your Compass for a New World*. Scarborough, ON: Nelson Thomson.

Buckhorn, Robert F. 1972. *Nader, The People's Lawyer*. Englewood Cliffs, NJ: Prentice Hall.

Buckingham, Donald E., Jerome E. Bickenbach, Richard Bronaugh, and The Honourable Bertha Wilson. 1996. *Legal Ethics in Canada: Theory and Practice*. Toronto: Nelson Thomson Learning.

Bueckert, Dennis. 2000. "Malpractice awards averaging $3 million per doctor are a major cost to taxpayers." *St. Catharines Standard* (October 1). Retrieved from http://overlawyered.com/archives/00oct1.html.

Bullard, Robert D. 2000. *Dumping in Dixie: Race, Class and Environmental Quality*. 3rd ed. Boulder, CO: Westview Press.

Bullard, Robert D., and Glenn S. Johnson. 1997. "Just Transportation," in Robert D. Bullard and Glenn S. Johnson (eds.), *Just Transportation: Dismantling Race and Class*

Barriers to Mobility, pp. 1–21. Stony Creek, CT: New Society.

Bumstead, Michele. 2001. "Alternative Dispute Resolution," in Laurence M. Olivo (ed.), *Introduction to Law in Canada*, pp. 505–532. Toronto: Captus Press.

Burbidge, Scott. 2005. "The Governance Deficit: Reflections on the Future of Public and Private Policing in Canada." Canadian *Journal of Criminology and Criminal Justice* 47 (1) (January): 63–86.

Burkell, Jacquelyn, and Ian R. Kerr. 2000. "Electronic Miscommunication and the Defamatory Sense." *Canadian Journal of Law and Society* 15 (1) (Spring): 81–110.

Burnett, Ann, and Diane M. Badzinski. 2000. "An Exploratory Study of Argument in the Jury Decision-Making Process." *Communication Quarterly* 48 (4) (Fall): 380–396.

Busby, Karen. 1999. "LEAF and Pornography: Litigation on Equality and Sexual Representations," in Nick Larsen and Brian Burch (eds.), *Law in Society: Canadian Perspectives*, pp. 42–59. Toronto: Harcourt.

Bush, Robert A., and Joseph P. Folger. 2005. *The Promise of Mediation: The Transformative Model for Conflict Resolution*. Rev. ed. San Francisco: CA: Jossey-Bass.

Butterfield, Fox. 2001. "States Easing Stringent Laws on Prison Time." *New York Times* (September 2): A1, A5.

Butters, Jennifer, and Patricia G. Erickson. 2003. "Meeting The Health Care Needs of Female Crack Users: A Canadian Example." *Women and Health* 37 (3): 1–17.

Cain, Maureen, and Christine B. Harrington (eds.). 1994. *Lawyers in a Postmodern World: Translation and Transgression*. New York: New York University Press.

Cain, Patricia A. 1993. "Feminism and the Limits of Equality," in D. Kelly Weisberg (ed.), *Feminist Legal Theory: Foundations*, pp. 237–247. Philadelphia: Temple University Press.

Cairns, A. 2000. *Citizen Plus: Aboriginal Peoples and the Canadian State*. Vancouver: UBC Press.

Calavita, Kitty. 2001. "Blue Jeans, Rape, and the 'De-Constitutive' Power of Law." *Law and Society Review* 35 (1): 89–115.

Calvi, James V., and Susan Coleman. 2004. *American Law and Legal Systems*. 5th ed. Upper Saddle River, NJ: Prentice Hall.

Cameron, George Dana, III. 1978. *The Soviet Lawyer and His System*. Ann Arbor: Division of Research, Graduate School of Business Administration, University of Michigan.

Camic, Charles, Philip S. Gorski, and David M. Trubek (eds.). *Max Weber's* Economy and Society: *A Critical Companion*. Stanford, CA: Stanford University Press.

Campbell, Elaine. 1999. "Toward a Sociological Theory of Discretion." *International Journal of the Sociology of Law* 27: 79–101.

Campos, Paul F. 1998. *Jurismania: The Madness of American Law*. New York: Oxford University Press.

Canada Heritage. 2006. "The Court Challenges Program: Profile." Retrieved from www.pch.g.ca/progs/em-cr/eval/2003/2003_02/4_e.cfm.

Canadian Bar Association. 1993. *Touchstones for Change: Equality, Diversity and Accountability: The Report on Gender Equality in the Legal Profession*. Ottawa: Author. 1999. Racial Equality in the Legal Profession. Resolution 99-04-A-Revised. 1999 Annual Meeting, Edmonton, Alberta (August 21–22). 2004. "Pro Bono Rising." Retrieved from www.cba.org/cba/ Nationa/augsep04/html. 2005. Crystal Clear: New Perspectives for the Canadian Bar Association. Report of the CBA Futures Committee. Retrieved from www.cba.org/CBA/futures/pdf/crystalclear. pdf. 2006. "CBA Code of Professional Conduct." Retrieved from www.cba.org/CBA/activities/code.

Canadian Centre on Substance Abuse and Centre for Addiction and Mental Health. 1999. *Canadian Profile 1999: Alcohol, Tobacco and Other Drugs*. Ottawa.

Canadian Judicial Council. 2002. Annual Report 2000–2001. Retrieved from www. cjc-ccm.

gc.ca. 2005a. "FAQS." Retrieved from www.chc-ccm.gc.ca/article.asp?id=2201. 2005b. 2004–05 Annual Report. Retrieved from www.cjc-ccm.gc.ca. 2006. "Frequently Asked Questions." Retrieved from www.cjc-ccm.gc.ca/article.asp?id=2291.

Canadian Labour Congress. 2005. Aboriginal Rights Resource Tool Kit, rev. ed. Retrieved from canadianlabour.ca/updir.pdf.

Canadian Lawyer. 1999. "Flahiff, Partner Convicted." 23 (11) (November/ December): 7. 2000. "An Ontario First" 24 (8) (August): 6–7.

Canadian Mental Health Association. 2002. "Depression and Manic Depression." Retrieved from www.cmha.ca/english/ info_centre/mh_pamphlets/ mh_pamphlet_15.htm.

Canadian Press. 1999. "Teen Hookers Oppose Child Protection Law." *Kitchener-Waterloo Record* (November 17): B11.

Canadian Psychiatric Association. 2002. "Anxiety, Depression and Manic Depression." Retrieved from http://cpa-apc.org/MIAW/pamphlets/Anxiety.asp.

Canadian Safety Council. 2000. "Reality Check: Knowledge and Perceptions of Canada's Impaired Driving Law." Retrieved from www.safety-council.org/info/traffic/ impaired/reality.htm.

CanLaw. 2002. "Salaries of Judges in Ontario Courts." Retrieved from www. canlaw.com/judges/salaries.htm.

Cann, Steven J. 2001. *Administrative Law*. 2nd ed. Thousand Oaks, CA: Sage.

Canon, Bradley C., and Charles A. Johnson. 1999. *Judicial Policies: Instrumentation and Impact*. 2nd ed. Washington, DC: CQ Press.

Caplovitz, David. 1963. *The Poor Pay More*. New York: Free Press. 1974. *Consumers in Trouble: A Study of Debtors in Default*. New York: Free Press.

Caputo, T., M. Kennedy, C. Reasons, and A. Brannigan (eds.). 1989. *Law and Society: A Critical Perspective*. Toronto: Harcourt.

Cardozo, Benjamin Nathan. 1924. *The Growth of the Law*. New Haven, CT: Yale University Press.

Carlin, Jerome E. 1962. *Lawyers on Their Own*. New Brunswick, NJ: Rutgers University Press. 1966. *Lawyers' Ethics: A Survey of the New York City Bar*. New York: Russell Sage Foundation.

Carney, Michael E. 1990. "Narcissistic Concerns in the Educational Experience of Law Students." *The Journal of Psychiatry and Law* 18 (1) (Spring/Summer): 9–34.

Carp, Robert A., and Ronald Stidham,. 2001. *Judicial Process in America*. 5th ed. Washington, DC: CQ Press.

Carp, Robert A., Ronald Stidham, and Kenneth L. Manning. 2004. *Judicial Process in America*. 6th ed. Washington, DC: CQ Press.

Carrese, Paul O. 2003. *The Cloaking of Power: Montesquieu, Blackstone and the Rise of Judicial Activism*. Chicago, IL: University of Chicago Press.

Carrington, Paul D. 1984. "Of Law and the River." *Journal of Legal Education* 34 (2) (June): 222–236.

Carson, Rachel L. 1962. *Silent Spring*. Boston: Houghton Mifflin.

Carson, Robert B. 1999. "The Constitution and the Charter of Rights and Freedoms," in Laurence M. Olivo (ed.), *Introduction to Law in Canada*, pp. 361–383. Toronto: Captus Press.

Carstairs, Catherine. 2002. "Becoming a 'Hype': Heroin Consumption, Subcultural Formation and Resistance in Canada, 1945–1961." *Contemporary Drug Problems* 29 (1) (Spring): 91–115.

Carter, David L. 2002. *The Police and the Community*. 7th ed. Upper Saddle River, NJ: Prentice Hall.

Carter, David L., and Louis A. Radelet. 1999. *The Police and the Community*. 6th ed. Upper Saddle River, NJ: Prentice Hall.

Carter, Lief H. 1998. *Reason in Law*. 5th ed. New York: Longman.

Carter, Lief H., and Thomas F. Burke. 2005. *Reason in Law*. 7th ed. New York: Longman.

Casino Gambling. 1999. Canadian Gambling Behaviour and Attitudes: Summary Report. Retrieved from www.casino-gambling-reports.com.

Casper, Jonathan. 1972. *Lawyers Before the Warren Court*. Urbana, IL: University of Illinois Press.

Caudill, D., and S. Gold (eds.). 1997. *Radical Philosophy of Law: Contemporary Challenges to Mainstream Legal Theory and Practice*. Atlantic Highlands, NJ: Humanities Press.

Caufield, T., L. Knowles, and E. M. Meslin. 2004. "Law and Policy in the Era of Reproductive Genetics." *Journal of Medical Ethics* 30 (4) (August): 414–417.

CBC.ca. 2005. "Vancouver Man Pleads Guilty to Overseas Sex Charges." (June 1). Retrieved from www.vancouver.cbc.ca/story/canada/national/2005/06/01/bakker-050601.html.

CBC News. 2000. "Circle Sentencing System Criticized in Carcross." (November 15). Retrieved from www.cbc.ca/story/news/national/2000/11/15/15circle.html. 2001. "Alleged Rat's Head in Big Mac Triggers Lawsuit." (March 27). Retrieved from http://overlawyered.com/archives/01/mar3.html. 2004a. "Indepth: Steven Truscott, The Search for Justice." (October 28). Retrieved from www.cbc.ca/news/background/truscott/ 2004b. "Aboriginal Sentencing Circle Ruling Upheld." (December 16). Retrieved from www.cbc.ca/story/canada/national/2004/12/16/jerome-jack041216.html. 2004c. "Albertan Ordered to Pay Ex-Wife $200 a Month for Pet Support." (August 10). Retrieved from www.cbc.ca/story/canada/national/2004/08/09/dogsupport_040809.html. 2005. "Ontario Premier Rejects Use of Shariah Law." (September 11). Retrieved from www.cbc.ca/Story/canada/national/2005/09/09/sharia-protest-20050909.html. 2006. "MPs to Question New Supreme Court Pick." (February 20). Retrieved from www.cbc.ca/story/canada/national/2006/02/06/supreme-court0606220.html. 2006a. "School Abuse Deal Includes $80M for Lawyers." (May 8). Retrieved from www.cbc.ca/story/canada/national/2006/05/08/residential-legal-fees.html.

CBC News Online. 2006. "Muhammad Cartoons: A Timeline." (February 17). Retrieved from www.cbc.ca/news/background/islam/muhammad_cartoons_timeline.html.

CBC-Sympatico-MSN. 2005. "New Alberta Law Will Permit Some Lawsuits Against Mothers." (December 3). Retrieved from www.cbc.ca/story/canada/national/2005/12/02/albertasuit05/01202.html.

CCP (Court Challenges Program). 1994/1995. Annual Report. Retrieved from www.ccppcj.ca/documents/annrep9495.html.

Cebula, Mark A. 1998. "Does Lawyer Advertising Adversely Influence the Image of Lawyers in the United States? An Alternative Perspective and New Empirical Evidence." *The Journal of Legal Studies* 27 (2) (June): 503–518.

CELA (Canadian Environmental Law Association). 1999. "New Study Warns of Children's Health Risks from Pesticides and Calls for Urgent Changes to Pesticide Regulatory Systems." (December 1). Retrieved from www.web.net/-cela/mr991201.htm.

Chafetz, Janet Saltzman. 1997. "Feminist Theory and Sociology: Underutilized Contributions for Mainstream Theory." *Annual Review of Sociology* 23: 97–121.

Chambliss, William J. 1964. "A Sociological Analysis of the Law of Vagrancy." *Social Problems* 12 (1) (Summer): 67–77. 1975. "Types of Deviance and the Effectiveness of Legal Sanctions," in William J. Chambliss (ed.), *Criminal Law in Action*, pp. 398–407. Santa Barbara, CA: Hamilton. 1976a. "Functional and Conflict Theories of Crime: The Heritage of Emile Durkheim and Karl Marx," in William J. Chambliss and Milton Mankoff (eds.), *Whose Law? What Order? A Conflict Approach to Criminology*, pp. 1–28.

New York: John Wiley. 1976b. "The State and Criminal Law," in William J. Chambliss and Milton Mankoff (eds.), *Whose Law, What Order? A Conflict Approach to Criminology*, pp. 66–106. New York: John Wiley. 1978a. "Toward a Political Economy of Crime," in Charles E. Reasons and Robert M. Rich (eds.), *The Sociology of Law: A Conflict Perspective*, pp. 191–211. Toronto: Butterworths. 1978b. *On the Take: From Petty Crooks to Presidents.* Bloomington: Indiana University Press.

Chambliss, William J., and Robert B. Seidman. 1971. *Law, Order, and Power*. Reading, MA: Addison-Wesley. 1982. *Law, Order, and Power*. 2nd ed. Reading, MA: Addison-Wesley.

Chambliss, William J., and Marjorie S. Zatz (eds.). 1993. *Making Law: The State, the Law, and Structural Contradictions.* Bloomington: Indiana University Press.

Chan, Cheris Shun-Ching. 2004. "The Falun Gong in China: A Sociological Perspective." *The China Quarterly* 179 (September): 665–683.

Chang, Robert S. 1993. "Toward an Asian American Legal Scholarship: Critical Race Theory, Post-Structuralism and Narrative Space. *California Law Review* 81 (5) (October): 1241–1323.

Chaytor et al. v. London, New York and Paris Association of Fashion Ltd. and Price, Supreme Court of Newfoundland, 1961, 30 D.L.R. (2d) 527, 46 M.P.R. 151 (cited in Linden, Allen M., Lewis N. Klar, and Bruce Feldthusen, [2004] *Canadian Tort Law: Cases, Notes and Materials. –* 12th ed. Toronto: LexisNexis and Butterworths).

Cheadle, Bruce. 2006. "Supreme Court Set to Rule on Whether a Cheating Spouse is Debilitating." CP/*Maclean's*, June 20. Retrieved from www.macleans.ca/topstories/news/shownews.jsp?content=n062033A.

Cheatwood, David. 1993. "Capital Punishment and the Deterrence of Violence Crime in Comparable Counties." *Criminal Justice Review* 18: 165–181.

Chen, Tsung-Fu. 2000. "Litigation and Social Development." *Proceedings of the National Science Council. Republic of China, Part C: Humanities and Social Sciences* 10 (4) (October): 435–469.

Cheney, Timothy D. 1998. *Who Makes the Law; The Supreme Court, Congress, the States, and Society*. Upper Saddle River, NJ: Prentice Hall.

Chesney-Lind, Meda, and Lisa Pasko. 2004a. *The Female Offender: Girls, Women and Crime*. 2nd ed. Thousand Oaks, CA: Sage. 2004b. *Girls, Women and Crime: Selected Readings*. Thousand Oaks, CA: Sage.

Childbirth by Choice Trust. 2000. "History of Birth Control in Canada." Retrieved from www.cbctrust.com.

Childs, Scott, and Paul Ceyssens. 1998/2005. "Doe v. Metropolitan Toronto Board of Commissioners of Police and the Status of Public Oversight of the Police in Canada" *Alberta Law Review* (1998) 36, 1000, reprinted (2005). Retrieved from www.pocc.bc.ca.

Chimerine, Lawrence, and Ross Eisenbrey. 2005. "The Frivolous Case for Tort Law Change." Briefing Paper — Economic Policy Institute. Washington, DC.

Chinloy, Peter. 1989. *The Cost of Doing Business: Legal and Regulatory Issues in the United States and Abroad*. New York: Praeger.

Christenson, Ron. 1999. *Political Trials: Gordian Knots in the Law*. 2nd ed. Somerset, NJ: Transaction.

Christianson, Scott. 2004. *Innocent: Inside Wrongful Conviction Cases*. New York: New York University Press.

Christie, R. 1976. "Probability v. Precedence: The Social Psychology of Jury Selection," in G. Bermant, C. Nemeth, and N. Vidmar (eds.), *Psychology and the Law: Research Frontiers*, pp. 265–281. Lexington, MA: Lexington Books.

Chunn, Dorothy E., and Dany Lacombe. 2000. "Introduction," in Dorothy E. Chunn and Dany Lacombe (eds.), *Law as a Gendering*

Practice, pp. 2–18. Don Mills, ON: Oxford University Press.

Chwialkowska, Luiza. 2001. "Anti-Terrorism Bill Becomes Law." *National Post* (December 19): A6.

Clairmont, Donald H., and Dennis W. Magill. 1999. *Africville: The Life and Death of a Canadian Black Community*. Toronto: Canadian Scholars' Press.

Clark, David S. 1990. "Civil Litigation Trends in Europe and Latin America Since 1945: The Advantage of Intracountry Comparisons." *Law and Society Review* 24 (2): 549–569.

Clark, Robert S. 1979. *Police and the Community: An Analytic Perspective*. New York: New Viewpoints.

Clarke, Tony. 2002. "The Recriminalization of Dissent." *Policy Options* 23 (6) (September): 49–50.

Clifford, Robert A. 1995. "Mock Trials Offer Virtual Reality: Simulated Juries Can Be Used Most Effectively Early in the Litigation Process to Develop the Theory of the Case." *The National Law Journal* 17 (26) (February 27): 88.

Clinard, Marshall B., and Daniel J. Abbott. 1973. *Crime in Developing Countries: A Comparative Perspective*. New York: John Wiley.

Clinard, Marshall B., and Robert F. Meier. 2004. *Sociology of Deviant Behavior*. 12th ed. Fort Worth, TX: Harcourt.

Cobb, Sara. 1997. "The Domestication of Violence in Mediation." *Law and Society Review* 31 (3): 397–440.

Cochran, Charles L., and Eloise F. Malone. 1999. *Public Policy: Perspectives and Choices*. 2nd ed. New York: McGraw-Hill, Inc.

Cohen, Felix. 1959. *Ethical Systems and Legal Ideals*. New York: Cornell University Press.

Cohen, Lynne. 1999. "Suing the Alternative Health-Care Provider." *Canadian Lawyer* 23 (11) (November/December): 47–50.

Cohen, Stanley A. 2005. *Privacy, Crime and Terror: Legal Rights and Security in a Time of Peril*. Markham, ON: LexisNexis.

Cohn, Alvin W. 1976. *Crime and Justice Administration*. Philadelphia: Lippincott.

Coleman, James W. 1972. *Policy Research in Social Science*. Morristown, NJ: General Learning Press. 1998. *The Criminal Elite: The Sociology of White Collar Crime*. 4th ed. New York: St. Martin's Press.

Collier, George. 1989. "The Impact of Second Republic Labor Reforms in Spain," in June Starr and Jane F. Collier (eds.), *History and Power in the Study of Law: New Directions in Legal Anthropology*, pp. 201–222. Ithaca, NY: Cornell University Press.

Collier, Jane Fishburne. 1973. *Law and Social Change in Zinacantan*. Stanford, CA: Stanford University Press.

Collier, Richard. 1995. *Masculinity, Law and the Family*. New York: Routledge. 2005. "The Law School, the Legal Academy and the 'Global Knowledge Economy' — Reflections on a Growing Debate." *Social and Legal Studies* 14 (2) (June): 259–265.

Collins, Hugh. 1996. *Marxism and Law*. New York: Oxford University Press.

Collins, Randall. 1995. "Prediction in Macrosociology: The Case of the Soviet Collapse." *American Journal of Sociology* 100 (6) (May): 1552–1593.

Coltri, Laurie S. 2004. *Conflict Diagnosis and Alternative Dispute Resolution*. Upper Saddle River, NJ: Prentice Hall.

Comack, Elizabeth. 1996. *Women in Trouble: Connecting Women's Law Violations to Their Histories of Abuse*. Halifax: Fernwood.

Comack, Elizabeth, and Gillian Balfour. 2004. *The Power to Criminalize: Violence, Inequality and the Law*. Halifax: Fernwood.

Comack, Elizabeth, Vanessa Chopyk, and Linda Wood. 2000. "Mean Streets? The Social Locations, Gender Dynamics and Patterns of Violence Crime in Winnipeg." Winnipeg Canadian Centre for Policy Alternatives (Manitoba).

Commission on the Review of the National Policy Toward Gambling. 1976. *Gambling in*

America. Washington, DC: U.S. Government Printing Office.

Condon, Mary. 2000. "Limited by Law? Corporate Law and the Family Firm," in Dorothy E. Chunn and Dany Lacombe (eds.), *Law as a Gendering Practic*, pp. 181–198. Don Mills, ON: Oxford University Press.

Conley, John, and William O'Barr. 1990. *Rules Versus Relationships*. Chicago: University of Chicago Press. 1998. *Just Words: Law, Language, and Power*. Chicago: University of Chicago Press.

Conrad, Peter. 1996. "The Medicalization of Deviance in American Culture," in Earl Rubington and Martin S. Weinberg (eds.), *Deviance: The Interactionist Perspective*, pp. 69–77. 6th ed. Boston: Allyn and Bacon.

Cooney, Mark. 1994. "Evidence of Partisanship." *Law and Society Review* 28 (4) (October): 833–858. 1997a. "The Decline of Elite Homicide." *Criminology 35* (3) (August): 381–401. 1997b. "Hunting Among Police and Predators: The Enforcement of Traffic Law." *Studies in Law, Politics and Society* 16: 165–188. 2003. "Missing the Mark: Reflections on Greenberg's Comment." *Criminology* 41 (4): 1419–1426.

Conrod, Monique. 1999. "Alternative Dispute Resolution." *Canadian Lawyer* 23 (11) (November/December): 57–68.

Conway, John. 1990. *The Canadian Family in Crisis*. Toronto: James Lorimer.

Cony, Ed, and Stanley Penn. 1986. "Tale of a Kite." *Wall Street Journal* (August 11):1, 10.

Cook, Philip J. 1989. "The Economics of Criminal Sanctions," in Martin Lawrence Friedland (ed.), *Sanctions and Rewards in the Legal System: A Multidisciplinary Approach*, pp. 50–78. Toronto: University of Toronto Press.

Cooney, Mark, and Scott Phillips. 2002. "Typologizing Violence: A Blackian Perspective." *International Journal of Sociology and Social Policy* 22 (7–8): 75–108.

Cooper, John, Ronald L. Nettler, and Mohamed Mahmoud (eds.). 2000. *Islam and Modernity*. New York: I. B. Tauris.

Cooper, Merrill, Joan Brockman, and Irene Hoffart. 2004. *Final Report on Equality and Diversity in Alberta's Legal Profession*. Report prepared for the Joint Committee on Equality, Equity and Diversity of the Law Society of Alberta; Canada Bar Association, Alberta Branch; Faculty of Law, University of Calgary; and Faculty of Law, University of Alberta.

Corbett, Ron. 2002. "Air Canada Sued over Language Dispute." *Ottawa Citizen* (March 2). Retrieved from http://overlawyered.com/archives/02/mar2.html.

Corboy, Philip H. 1975. "From the Bar," in Rita James Simon (ed.), *The Jury System in America: A Critical Overview*, pp. 179–195. Beverly Hills, CA: Sage.

Correctional Services Canada. 2002. "Basic Facts about Canadian Corrections." Retrieved from www.csc scc.gc.ca/text/faits/facts/07 content02_e.shtml. 2005. "Basic Facts About the Correctional Service of Canada." Retrieved from www.csc-scc.gc.ca/text/pblct/basicfacts/BasicFacts_e.shtml.

Costanzo, Mark. 1997. *Just Revenge: Costs and Consequences of the Death Penalty*. New York: St. Martin's Press.

Cotterman, James D. (ed.). 2004. *Compensation Plans for Law Firms*. 4th ed. Chicago, IL: American Bar Association, Law Practice Management Section.

Cotterrell, Roger (ed.). 1994. *Law and Society*. New York: New York University Press.

Couch, Cullen. 2002. "Teaching the Narrative Power of Law." UVA Lawyer, February 5. Retrieved from www.law.virginia.edu/home2002/html/alumni/uvalawyer/f05.humanities.htm.

Court Challenges Program. 2006. "Who We Are." Retrieved from www.ccoocj.ca/e/about/about.shtml.

Cowan, Sharon. 2005. "'Gender Is No Substitute for Sex': A Comparative Human Rights Analysis of the Legal Resolution of Sexual Identity." *Feminist Legal Studies* 13 (1): 67–96.

Cownie, Fiona, and Anthony Bradney. 2005. "Gothic Horror? A Response to Margaret Thornton." *Social and Legal Studies* 14 (2) (June): 277–285.

Cox, S. M., and J. E. Wade. 1985. *The Criminal Justice Network: An Introduction.* Dubuque, IA: W. C. Brown.

Cozic, Charles P., and Paul A. Winters (eds.). 1995. *Gambling.* San Diego, CA: Greenhaven Press.

Cramer, Renee Ann. 2005. "Perceptions of the Process: Indian Gaming as It Affects Federal Tribal Acknowledgment: Law and Practices." *Law and Policy* 27 (4) (October): 578–605.

Crank, John P. 1994. "Watchman and Community: Myth and Institutionalization in Policing." *Law and Society* Review 28 (2) (May): 325–351.

Crenshaw, Kimberle Williams. 1998. "Demarginalizing the Intersection of Rae and Sex: A Black Feminist Critique of Antidiscrimination Doctrine, Feminist Theory and Antiracist Doctrine." *University of Chicago Legal Forum* 189: 139–142.

Crespi, Irving. 1979. "Modern Marketing Techniques: They Could Work in Washington, Too." *Public Opinion* 2 (3) (June–July): 16–19, 58–59.

CRIC (Centre for Research and Information on Canada). 2004. "Facing the Future: Relations Between Aboriginal and Non-Aboriginal Canadians." June. Retrieved from www.cric.ca/pdf/cahiers/cricpapers_june2004. pdf. 2006a. "Legislation, Treaties and Claims." Retrieved from www.cric.ca/ en_html/guide/aboriginal/aboriginal_treaties. html. 2006b. "Backgrounder: Keep Any Religion out of Family Arbitration." (October 25). Retrieved from www.cric.ca/ pdf/cric_poll/portraits/portraits_2005/ eng_religion?arbitrage_2005.pdf.

Criminal Intelligence Service Canada. 2002. Annual Report 2002. Retrieved from www.cisc.gc.ca/AnnualReport2002/Cisc2002/ exploit2002.html.

Crisanti, Annette S., Julio Arboleda-Florez, and Heather Stuart. 2000. "The Canadian Criminal Code Provisions for Mentally Disordered Offenders: A Survey of Experiences, Attitudes and Knowledge." *Canadian Journal of Psychiatry* 45 (9) (November): 816–821.

Cristol, Hope. 2002. "U.S. Jury System on Trial." *The Futurist* 36 (6) (November/ December): 6.

Croall, Hazel. 1989. "Who Is the White-Collar Criminal?" *British Journal of Criminology* 29 (2): 157–174.

Croson, Rachel, and Robert H. Mnookin. 1997. "Does Disputing Through Agents Enhance Cooperation? Experimental Evidence." *Journal of Legal Studies* 26 (June): 331–348.

Crozier, Michel. 1984. *The Trouble with America.* Trans. Peter Heinegg. Berkeley and Los Angeles: University of California Press.

Csillag, Ron. 2006. "Ont. Law Passed to Ban Faith-Based Arbitration." *The Canadian Jewish News* (July 6). Retrieved from www.cjnews.com/view/article.asp?id+8601.

CTV. 2006. "Faith-Based Arbitration." September 12. Retrieved from www.ctv.ca/servlet/ArticleNews/print/CTV/ News/0050912.

Culp, Jerome McCristal, Jr. 1994. "Colorblind Remedies and the Intersectionality of Oppression: Policy Arguments Masquerading as Moral Claims." *New York Law Review* 69 (1) (April): 162–196.

Curriden, Mark. 1995. "Female Lawyers See Bias in Their Arrests: Cursing and Culottes Were Unacceptable to Authorities in Texas, Florida." *ABA Journal* 81 (March): 28–29.

Currie, Dawn H., and Marlee Kline. 1991. "Challenging Privilege: Women, Knowledge and Feminist Struggles." *Journal of Human Justice* 2 (2): 1–36.

Dahrendorf, Ralf. 1958. "Toward a Theory of Social Conflict." Journal of Conflict Resolution 2 (June): 170–183. 1990. *The Modern Social Conflict: An Essay on the*

Politics of Liberty. Berkeley: University of California Press.

Daley, Suzanne. 1995. "Court Tells South Africa to Stop Imprisoning Debtors." *New York Times* (October 1): A4. 2001a. "France's Most Courted: Women to Join the Ticket." *New York Times* (February 8): 1, 8. 2001b. "New Rights for Dutch Prostitutes, But No Gain." *New York Times* (August 12): 1.

Danelski, David J. 1974. "The Limits of Law," in J. Roland Pennock and John W. Chapman (eds.), *The Limits of Law*, pp. 8–27. New York: Lieber-Atherton.

D'Antonio, William V. 1992. "Sociology's Lonely Crowd—Indeed!" *Footnotes* (May): 3–4.

Danzig, Richard. 1973. "Toward the Creation of a Complementary, Decentralized System of Criminal Justice." *Stanford Law Review* 26 (1): 1–54.

Danzig, Richard, and M. Lowry. 1975. "Everyday Disputes and Mediation in the United States: A Reply to Professor Felstiner." *Law and Society Review* 9 (4): 675–694.

Das Gupta, Tanis. 1999. "The Politics of Multiculturalism: 'Immigrant Women' and the Canadian State," in Enakshi Dua and Angela Robertson (eds.), *Scratching the Surface: Canadian Anti-Racist Feminist Thought*, pp. 187–206. Toronto: Women's Press.

David, Rene, and John E. Brierley. 1985. *Major Legal Systems in the World Today*. 3rd ed. London: Stevens and Sons.

Davis, Ann. 1995. "Title Insurers Eye N.J. Lawyers Under Ethics Cloud: Newly Opened Disciplinary Process Lets Them Keep Tabs." *The National Law Journal* 17 (30) (March 27): A7.

Davis, F. James. 1962. "Law as a Type of Social Control," in F. James Davis et al. (eds.), *Society and the Law: New Meanings for an Old Profession,* pp. 39–63. New York: Free Press.

Davis, Gayle, and Roger Davidson. 2005. "'Big White Chief,' 'Pontius Pilate,' and the 'Plumber': The Impact of the 1967 Abortion Act on the Scottish Medical Community, *c.*

1967–1980." *Social History of Medicine* 18 (2) (August): 283–306.

Davis, James H., Robert M. Bray, and Robert W. Holt. 1977. "The Empirical Study of Decision Processes in Juries: A Critical Review," in June Louin Tapp and Felice J. Levine (eds.), *Law, Justice, and the Individual in Society: Psychological and Legal Issues*, pp. 326–361. New York: Holt, Rinehart and Winston.

Davis, Kenneth Culp. 1975a. *Administrative Law and Government*. 2nd ed. St. Paul, MN: West. 1975b. *Police Discretion*. St. Paul, MN: West.

Davison, Charles. 2002. "Wheel of Fortune? Not! Choosing Judges." *LawNow* 27 (2) (October/November): 17–18.

Dawson, Myrna. 2003. "The Cost of 'Lost' Intimacy: The Effect of Relationship State on Criminal Justice Decision Making." *British Journal of Criminology* 43 (3) (Autumn): 689–709.

Dawson, T. Brettel (ed). 2003. *Women, Law and Social Change: Core Readings and Current Issues*. 4th ed. Concord, ON: Captus Press.

Dawson, T. Brettel, and Jennifer Quaile, 1998. "A Collage of Firsts," in T. Brettel Dawson (ed.), *Women, Law and Social Change: Core Readings and Current Issues*, pp. 119–120. North York, ON: Captus Press.

Dawson, T. Brettel, Jennifer Quaile, and Grant Holly. 2002. "A Collage of Firsts," in T. Brettel Dawson (ed.), *Women, Law and Social Change: Core Readings and Current Issues*, pp. 103–105. 4th ed. A Special Prepublication Printing for Carleton University 51.301— Women and the Legal Process (Part 1). Concord, ON: Captus Press.

Daynes, Kathryn M. 2001. *More Wives Than One: Transformation of the Mormon Marriage System, 1840–1910*. Urbana: University of Illinois Press.

Death Penalty Information Center (DPIC). 2006. "Facts About the Death Penalty, February 1, 2006." Retrieved from www.deathpenaltyin-fo.org.

Decker, S., and C. Kohfeld. 1990. "Deterrent Effect of Capital Punishment in the Five

Most Active Execution States: A Time-Series Analysis." *Criminal Justice Review* 15 (2): 173–191.

De Kort, Marcel, and Dirk J. Korf. 1992. "The Development of Drug Control in the Netherlands: A Historical Perspective." *Crime, Law, and Social Change* 17 (2) (March): 123–144.

Delamont, Sara. 2003. *Feminist Sociology*. London: Sage.

Delgado, Richard. 1989. "Storytelling for Oppositionists and Others: A Plea for Narrative. *Michigan Law Review* 87: 2411–2441. 1994. "Rodrigo's Ninth Chronicle: Race, Legal Instrumentalism, and the Rule of Law." *University of Pennsylvania Law Review* 143 (2) (December): 379–416. 2004. *Justice at War: Civil Liberties and Civil Rights During Times of Crisis*. New York: New York University Press.

Delgado, Richard, and Jean Stefancic (eds.). 2000. *Critical Race Theory: The Cutting Edge*. Philadelphia: Temple University Press.

Demerson, Velma. 2004. *Incorrigible*. Waterloo, ON: Wilfred Laurier University Press.

Denvir, John. 1987. "William Shakespeare and the Jurisprudence of Comedy." *Stanford Law Review* 39: 825–849.

Deosaran, Ramesh. 1993. "The Social Psychology of Selecting Jury Forepersons." *British Journal of Criminology* 33 (1) (Winter): 70–80.

DeParle, Jason. 1998. "Wisconsin Welfare Experiment: Easy to Say, Not So Easy to Do." *New York Times* (October 18): Y1, Y20.

Department of Justice Canada. 2005. "Reference to the Supreme Court of Canada." Retrieved from www.justice.gc.ca/en/news/nr/2003/doc_30946.html.

Deschenes, Elizabeth Piper, Roger H. Peters, John S. Goldkamp, and Steven Belenko. 2003. "Drug Abuse Treatment Through Collaboration: Practice and Research Findings That Work," in James L. Sorensen, Richard A. Rawson, Joseph Guydish, and Joan E. Zweben (eds.), *Drug Abuse Treatment Through Collaboration: Practice and*

Research Partnerships That Work, pp. 85–102. Washington, DC: American Psychological Association.

de Soto, Hernando. 2001. *The Mystery of Capital, Why Capitalism Triumphs in the West and Fails Everywhere Else*. New York: Basic Books.

de Tocqueville, Alexis. 1835/1961. *Democracy in America: Volume I*. New York: Schocken.

Deutscher, Irwin. 1999. *Making a Difference: The Practice of Sociology*. Somerset, NJ: Transaction.

Devlin, Patrick. 1965. *The Enforcement of Morals*. New York: Oxford University Press.

Dewees, D., M. Trebilcock, and P. Coyte. 1991. "The Medical Malpractice Crisis: Comparative Empirical Perspective." *New England Journal of Medicine* 324: 89–93.

Diamant, Neil J., Stanley B. Lubman, and Kevin J. O'Brien (eds.). 2005. *Engaging the Law in China: State, Society and Possibilities for Justice*. Stanford, CA: Stanford University Press.

Diamond, Arthur S. 1971. *Primitive Law, Past and Present*. London: Methuen.

Diamond, Shari Seidman. 1997. "Illuminations and Shadows from Jury Simulations." *Law and Human Behavior* 21 (5) (October): 561–573.

Dicey, Albert Venn. 1905. *Lectures on the Relation Between the Law and Public Opinion in England During the Nineteenth Century*. London: MacMillan.

Diesfeld, Kate, and Ian Freckelton (eds.). 2003. *Involuntary Detention and Therapeutic Jurisprudence: International Perspectives on Civil Commitment*. Burlington, VT: Ashgate/Darmouth.

Dilworth, Donald C. 1995. "Prisoners' Lawsuits Burden Federal Civil Courts." *Trial* 31 (5) (May): 98–100.

Dimetrius, JoEllan, and Mark Mazzarella. 1998. *Reading People: How to Understand People and Predict Their Behavior, Anytime, Anyplace*. New York: Random House.

Dines, Gail, Robert Jensen, and Ann Russo. 1997. *Pornography: The Production and Consumption of Inequality*. New York: Routledge.

Doak, Robin. 2004. *Conflict Resolution*. Chicago, IL: Raintree. *Dobson (Litigation Guardian of) v. Dobson,* Supreme Court of Canada, 1999, 2 S.C.R., 753, 214 N.B.R. (2d) 201.

Doerr, Audrey. 1999. "Royal Commission on Aboriginal Peoples," in James H. Marsh (ed.), *The Canadian Encyclopedia: Year 2000 Edition*, pp. 3–4. Toronto: McClelland and Stewart.

Domnarski, William. 2003. "Law and Literature." *Legal Studies Forum* 27 (1): 109–129.

Doms, Kurt. 2004. "Cultural Emergence, Legal Polycentricity and Same-Sex Couples' Right to Marry." *Journal of Gender Studies* 13 (3) (November): 271–274.

Donner, Ted A., and Richard K. Gabriel. 2000. Jury Selection: Strategy and Science. 3rd ed. St. Paul, MN: West Group. *Donoghue v. Stevenson* (cited in Allen M. Linden, Lewis N. Klar and Bruce Feldthusen, [2004]. *Canadian Tort Law: Cases, Notes and Materials.* 12th ed. Toronto: LexisNexis and Butterworths., p. 283).

Doran, Chris "Nob." 2002. "Medico-Legal Expertise and Industrial Disease Compensation: Discipline, Surveillance and Disqualification in the Era of the 'Social,'" in Gayle M. MacDonald (ed.), *Social Context and Social Location in the Sociology of Law*, pp. 159–180. Peterborough, ON: Broadview Press.

Dossa, Parin. 2000. "On Law and Hegemonic Movements: Looking Beyond the Law Towards Subjectivities of Subaltern Women," in Dorothy E. Chunn and Dany Lacombe (eds.), *Law as a Gendering Practice*, pp. 138–156. Don Mills, ON: Oxford University Press.

Douglas, Kevin S., and William J. Koch. 2001. "Civil Commitment and Civil Competence," in Regina A. Schuller and James R. P. Ogloff (eds.), *Introduction to Psychology and Law: Canadian Perspectives,* pp. 353–374. Toronto, ON: University of Toronto Press.

Doyle, Daniel P., and David F. Luckenbill. 1991. "Mobilizing Law in Response to Collective Problems: A Test of Black's Theory of Law." *Law and Society Review* 25 (1): 103–116.

Doyle, Roger. 2000. "The Roots of Homicide." *Scientific American* (October). Retrieved from www.sciam.com/2000.

Dranoff, Linda Silver. 2001. *Everyone's Guide to the Law: A Handbook for Canadians*. Rev. ed. Toronto: HarperCollins. 2005. *Every Canadian's Guide to The Law*. 3rd ed. Toronto, Ontario: HarperCollins.

Dror, Yehezkel. 1968. "Law and Social Change," in Rita James Simon (ed.), *The Sociology of Law*, pp. 663–680. San Francisco: Chandler. 1970. "Law as a Tool of Directed Social Change." *American Behavioral Scientist* 13: 553–559.

Dua, Enakshi. 1999. "Canadian Anti-Racist Feminist Thought: Scratching the Surface of Racism," in Enakshi Dua and Angela Robertson (eds.), *Scratching the Surface: Canadian Anti-Racist Feminist Thought*, pp. 7–31. Toronto: Women's Press.

Duchesne, Doreen. 1999. "Street Prostitution in Canada," in *The Canadian Centre for Justice Statistics, The Juristat Reader: A Statistical Overview of the Canadian Justice System*, pp. 241–252. Toronto: Thompson.

Duff, P., and M. Findlay. 1997. "Jury Reform: Of Myths and Moral Panics." *International Journal of the Sociology of Law* 25 (4) (December): 363–384.

Duff-Brown, Beth. 2006. "Jews, Muslims to Seek Tribunals in Canada." ABC News. Retrieved from www.abcnews.go.com/International/print?id=1126490.

Duke, Steven, and Albert C. Gross. 1994. *America's Longest War: Rethinking Our Tragic Crusade Against Drugs*. New York: G. P. Putnam and Sons.

Durand, Claire. 2002. "The 2000 Canadian Election and Poll Reporting Under the New Elections Act." *Canadian Public Policy* 28 (4) (December): 539–545.

Durkheim, Emile. 1893/1964. *The Division of Labor in Society*. Trans. George Simpson.

New York: Free Press. 1912/1965. *The Elementary Forms of Religious Life*. New York: Free Press.

Dussault, Julie. 2005. "The Tobacco Law (of December 1999) and the Paradoxes of Its Application in Factory Workplaces." *PISTES: Perspectives Interdisciplinaires sur le Travail et la Santé* 7 (2) (May).

Duster, Troy. 1995. "The New Crisis of Legitimacy in Controls, Prisons, and Legal Structures." *American Sociologist* 26: 20–29.

Dworkin, Andrea. 1981. *Pornography: Men Possessing Women*. New York: Penguin. *Dwyer v. Staunton*, Alberta District Court, 1947, 4 D.L.R., 393.

Dyck v. Manitoba Snowmobile Assn. Inc., Supreme Court of Canada, 1985, S.C.R. 589, 18 D.L.R. (4th) 635, cited in Osborne, Philip H. (2003). *The Law of Torts*. 2nd ed. Toronto: Irwin Law.

Dye, Thomas. 2002. *Understanding Public Policy*. 10th ed. Upper Saddle River, NJ: Prentice Hall.

Eckhoff, Torstein. 1978. "The Mediator: The Judge and the Administrator in Conflict-Resolution," in Sheldon Goldman and Austin Sarat (eds.), *American Court Systems: Readings in Judicial Process and Behavior*, pp. 31–41. San Francisco: W. H. Freeman.

Eckholm, Erik. 1995. "Studies Find Death Penalty Often Tied to Victim's Race." *New York Times* (February 24): A1, A11.

Economist. 1979. "The Odour of Solvency." 273 (7101) (October 6): 104. 1993. "Paper Stockade: Lawyers in Japan." 328 (7823) (August 7): 60–62. 2000. "Dead Man Walking Out." (June 10): 21–23. 2001. "The Waiting Game" (April 1): 19–21. 2002. "A Jail by Another Name." (December 21): 52–53. 2002. "Mom's Boys" (May 11): 36. 2003. "Canadian Drug Policy: Needling the Neighbours." (September 20): 36–37. 2001. "A Survey of Russia—Putin's Choice." (July 21): 1–16. 2004a. "How to Reform Brazil's Justice System." (March 25): 66–67. 2004b. "London's Cops Look to New York." (February 21): 53–54. 2004c. "Justice in Japan: The People Come to Court." (March 6): 35–36. 2001. "Mind the Gap." (March 17): 29.

Eder, Klaus. 1977. "Rationalist and Normative Approaches to the Sociological Study of Law." *Law and Society Review* 12 (1) (Fall): 133–144.

Edgeworth, Brendan. 2003. *Law, Modernity, Postmodernity: Legal Change in the Contracting State*. Burlington, VT: Ashgate.

Edley, Christopher R. 1990. *Administrative Law: Rethinking Judicial Control of Bureaucracy*. New Haven: Yale University Press. *Edmonton Journal*. 2002. "Under the B, Bingo Is Good for Health" (September 5): A1, A13. 2005. "Action on Crystal Meth." (October 26): A18.

EGALE. 2004. EGALE Fact Sheet: Who We Are and What We Do. www.egale.ca/index/asp?lang=Eandmenu=2anditem=762.

Eggleston, David. 2000. "Raising the Bar: The Ever-Higher Cost of a Legal Education." *Canadian Lawyer* 24 (8) (August): 8–12.

Ehrlich, Eugen. 1975. *Fundamental Principles of the Sociology of Law*. Foreword. New York: Arno Press. Trans. Walter L. Mall. Originally published by Harvard University Press, 1936.

Ehrlich, Isaac. 1975. "The Deterrent Effect of Capital Punishment: A Question of Life or Death." *American Economic Review* 65: 397–417.

Eisenstadt, S. N. 1972. "Intellectuals and Tradition." *Daedelus* 101 (2): 1–19.

Ekberg, Gunilla. 2004. "The Swedish Law That Prohibits the Purchase of Sexual Services: Best Practices for Prevention of Prostitution and Trafficking in Human Beings." *Violence Against Women* 10 (10) (October): 1187–1218.

Elkins, James R. 2001. "A Law Culture Diagnostic." *Journal of Criminal Justice and Popular Culture* 8 (1): 48–57. 2002. "Narrative Jurisprudence." October 13. Retrieved from www.wvu.edu/~lawfac/jelkins/jruis02/juris02/intro.html. 1993. "Writing Our Lives: Making Introspective Writing a Part of Legal Education," *Willamette Law Review* 29: 41–68. 1988.

"The Quest for Meaning: Narrative Accounts of Legal Education." *Journal of Legal Education* 38: 577–598. 1985. "On the Emergence of Narrative Jurisprudence: The Humanistic Perspective Finds a New Path." *Legal Studies Forum* 9 (2): 123–155.

Ellickson, Robert. 1991. *Order Without Law: How Neighbors Settle Disputes*. Cambridge, MA: Harvard University Press.

Elliott, David W. 2005. *Law and Aboriginal Peoples in Canada*. 5th ed. Concord, ON: Captus Press.

Elster, Jon. 1995. "Transition Constitution-making and Separation in Czechoslovakia." *Archives Européenes de Sociologie* 36 (1): 105–134.

Engel, Howard. 1996. *Lord High Executioner: An Unashamed Look at Hangmen, Headsmen, and Their Kind*. Toronto: Key Porter Books.

Eorsi, Gyula, and Attila Harmathy. 1971. *Law and Economic Reform in Socialistic Countries*. Budapest: Akademiai Kiado.

Epp, Charles R. 1992. "'Honey, They Shrunk the Economy!' An Empirical Examination of the Claim that Lawyers Impair Economic Growth." Institute for Legal Studies, Working Paper DPRP 11–2 (March). Madison: University of Wisconsin.

Ericson, Richard V. 1989. "Patrolling the Facts: Secrecy and Publicity in Policework." *British Journal of Sociology* 40 (2): 205–226.

Ericson, Richard, and Patricia Baranek. 1982. *The Ordering of Justice: A Study of Accused Persons as Dependents in the Criminal Process*. Toronto: University of Toronto Press.

Erickson, Patricia G., Jennifer Butters, and Patti McGillicuddy. 2000. "Crack and Prostitution: Gender, Myths and Experiences." *Journal of Drug Issues* 30 (4) (Fall): 767–788.

Erikson, Kai T. 1966. *Wayward Puritans: A Study in the Sociology of Deviance*. New York: John Wiley.

Erlanger, Howard S., and Douglas A. Klegon. 1978. "Socialization Effects of Professional School: The Law School Experience and Student Orientations to Public Interest Concerns." *Law and Society Review* 13 (1) (Fall): 11–35.

Erlanger, Steven. 1992. "Two Novelties in Russian Courts: Defense Lawyers and Jury Trial." *New York Times* (May 11): A1, A4. 1995. "A Corrupt Tide in Russia from State—Business" (July 3): A1, A5.

Eskridge, William N. Jr., and Nan D. Hunter. 1997. *Sexuality, Gender, and the Law*. Westbury, NY: Foundation Press.

Etzioni, Amitai. 1973. *The Genetic Fix*. New York: Macmillan. 2000. "Social Norms: Internalization, Persuasion and History." *Law and Society Review* 34 (1): 158–178.

Evan, William M. 1965. "Law as an Instrument of Social Change," in Alvin W. Gouldner and S. M. Miller (eds.), *Applied Sociology: Opportunities and Problems*, pp. 285–293. New York: Free Press. 1990. *Social Structure and Law: Theoretical and Empirical Perspectives*. Newbury Park, CA: Sage.

Evans, Donald G. 2001. "Canada's First Drug Treatment Court." *Corrections Today* 63 (3) (June): 30–31.

Evans, John. 2000. "Counting Crime," in Rick Linden (ed.), *Criminology: A Canadian Perspective*. 5th ed., pp. 60–93. Scarborough, ON: Nelson.

Ewick, Patricia, and Susan Silbey. 2003. "Narrating Social Structure: Stories of Resistance to Legal Authority." *The American Journal of Sociology* 108 (6) (May): 1328–1375.

Fabi, M. 2004. "Cybersex: The Dark Side of the Force." *International Journal of Applied Psychoanalytic Studies* 1 (2): 208–209.

Faich, Ronald G., and Richard P. Gale. 1971. "The Environmental Movement from Recreation to Politics." *Pacific Sociological Review* 14 (July): 270–287.

Fairman, Robyn, and Charlotte Yapps. 2005. "Enforced Self-Regulation, Prescription, and Conceptions of Compliance within Small Businesses: The Impact of Enforcement." *Law and Policy* 27 (4) (October): 491–519.

Falk, Richard. 1971. *This Endangered Planet*. New York: Random House.

Farber, Daniel A. 1994. "The Outmoded Debate over Affirmative Action." *California Law Review* 82 (4) (July): 893–934.

Farber, Daniel A., and Suzanna Sherry. 1997. *Beyond All Reason: The Radical Assault on Truth in American Law*. New York: Oxford University Press.

Fattah, Ezzat A. 1991. *Understanding Criminal Victimization: An Introduction to Theoretical Victimology*. Scarborough, ON: Prentice Hall.

Federation of Law Societies of Canada. 2006. "2005 Law Societies Statistics." Retrieved from www.flsc.ca/en/lawSocieties/statisticsLinks.asp.

Feinberg, Joel, and Hyman Gross (eds.). 2003. *Philosophy of Law*. 7th ed. Belmont, CA: Wadsworth.

Feldthusen, Bruce. (1993). "If This Is Torts, Negligence Must Be Dead," in K. Cooper-Stephenson and E. Gibson (eds.), *Tort Theory*, pp. 407–413. Toronto: Captus Press.

Felstiner, William L. F. 1974. "Influences of Social Organization on Dispute Processing." *Law and Society Review* 9 (1) (Fall): 63–94.

Fernandes, Edesio, and Ann Varley (eds.) 1998. *Illegal Cities: Law and Urban Change in Developing Countries*. New York: St. Martin's Press.

Fife, Robert. 1999. "Police Chiefs Get Through to the Top." *National Post* (April 22): A14.

Fine, Michelle. 1997. "Witnessing Whiteness," in M. Fine, L. Weiss, L. Powell, and L. Mun Wong (eds.), *Off White: Readings on Race, Power, and Society*, pp. 57–65. London: Routledge.

Fink, Arlene, and Jacqueline Kosecoff. 1998. *How to Conduct Surveys, A Step-by-Step Guide*. Thousand Oaks, CA: Sage.

Fisher, George. 2003. *Plea Bargaining's Triumph: A History of Plea Bargaining in America*. Stanford, CA: Stanford University Press.

Fisher, Joseph C. 1997. *Killer Among Us*. Westport, CT: Praeger/Greenwood.

Fiss, Owen. 2004. *The Law As It Could Be*. New York: New York University Press.

Fiss, Owen M., and Judith Resnik. 2003. *Adjudication and Its Alternatives: An Introduction to Procedure*. New York: Foundation Press, Thomson/West.

Fisse, Brent, and John Braithwaite. 1993. "The Impact of Publicity on Corporate Offenders: The Ford Motor Company and the Pinto Papers," in Delos H. Kelly (ed.), *Deviant Behavior: A Text-Reader in the Sociology of Deviance*, pp. 627–640. New York: St. Martin's Press.

Fitzgerald, Joseph M. 2000. "Younger and Older Jurors: The Influence of Environmental Supports on Memory Performance and Decision Making in Complex Trials." *Journals of Gerontology Series B: Psychological Sciences and Social Sciences* 55 (6) (November): 323–331.

Fitzpatrick, Robert B. 1994. "Nonbinding Mediation of Employment Disputes." *Trial* 30 (6) (June): 40–44.

Fleming, John G. 1998. *The Law of Torts*. 9th ed. Sydney: LBC Information Services.

Fleming, Macklin. 1997. *Lawyers, Money, and Success: The Consequences of Dollar Obsessions*. Westport, CT: Quorum.

Fleming, Thomas (ed.). 1985. *The New Criminologies: State, Crime, and Control*. Toronto: Oxford University Press.

Flemming, Roy B. 2004. *Tournament of Appeals: Granting Judicial Review in Canada*. Vancouver, BC: UBC Press.

Flemming, Roy B., and Glen S. Krutz. 2002. "Repeat Litigators and Agenda Setting on the Supreme Court of Canada." *Canadian Journal of Political Science* 35 (4) (December): 811–833. 2002a, "Selecting Appeals for Judicial Review in Canada: A Replication and Multivariate Test of American Hypotheses." *Journal of Politics* 64: 232–248.

Fleras, Augie. 2005. *Social Problems in Canada: Conditions, Constructions and Challenges*. 4th ed. Toronto: Pearson. *Focus on Law*

Studies. 2003. "Gun Laws and Policies: A Dialogue." 18 (2) (Spring): 1–20.

Foote, Nelson N. 1953. "The Professionalization of Labor in Detroit." *American Journal of Sociology* 58 (4) (January): 371–380.

Forcese, Craig, and Aaron Freeman. 2005. *The Laws of Government: The Legal Foundations of Canadian Democracy.* Toronto: Irwin Law.

Forman, James, Jr. 2004. "Juries and Race in the Nineteenth Century." *Yale Law Journal* 113 (4) (January): 895–939.

Forst, Martin L. 1978. *Civil Commitment and Social Control.* Lexington, MA: Heath.

Foster, George M. 1973. *Traditional Societies and Technological Change.* 2nd ed. New York: Harper and Row.

Foucault, Michel. 1977. *Discipline and Punish: The Birth of the Prison.* Trans. Alan Sheridan. New York: Pantheon.

Fournier, S., and E. Grey. 1997. *Stolen from Our Embrace: The Abduction of First Nation Children and the Restoration of Aboriginal Communities.* Vancouver: Douglas and McIntyre.

Fox, J. A., and M. W. Zawitz. 2004. Homicide Trends in the United States. Washington, DC: Department of Justice. Retrieved from www.ojp.usdoj.gov/bjs/homicide/homtrnd.htm.

France, Mike. 1995. "More Businesses Ask: Can We Talk, Not Sue?" *National Law Journal* 17 (28) (March 13): B1. 2001. "The Litigation Machine." *Business Week* (January 29): 116–123.

Francis, Craig. 2000. "Europe mellows out over Cannabis." CNN.com (October 9). Retrieved from www.cnn.com/2000/world/europe/10/09/drugs.law.

Frank, Jeffrey. 1994. "Voting and Contributing: Political Participation in Canada," in *Canadian Social Trends: A Canadian Studies Reader,* Vol. 2, pp. 333–337. Toronto: Thompson.

Frank, Jerome. 1930. *Law and the Modern Mind.* New York: Coward-McCann.

Franke, Katherine M. 2001. "Theorizing Yes: An Essay on Feminism, Law, and Desire." *Columbia Law Review* (January): 101–181.

Frankford, David M. 1995. "Social Structure of Right and Wrong: Normativity Without Agents." *Law and Social Inquiry* 20 (3) (Summer): 787–803.

Franklin, Daniel. 1994. "The Right Three Strikes." *Washington Monthly* 26 (9) (September): 25–30.

Frazier, Patricia A., and Jennifer S. Hunt. 1998. "Research on Gender and the Law: Where Are We Going, Where Have We Been?" *Law and Human Behavior* 22 (1) (February): 1–16.

Freeman, Michael, and Andrew Lewis (eds.). 1999. *Law and Literature.* Oxford, UK: Oxford University Press.

Freeman, Richard J., and Ronald Roesch. 1992. "Psycholegal Education: Training for Forum and Function," in Dorothy K. Kagehiro and William S. Laufer (eds.), *Handbook of Psychology and Law,* pp. 567–576. New York: Springer-Verlag.

Friedland, M. L. (ed.). 1989. *Sanctions and Rewards in the Legal System: A Multidisciplinary Approach.* Toronto: University of Toronto Press.

Fridman, G. H. L. 1978. *Introduction to the Law of Torts.* Toronto: Butterworths 2002. *The Law of Torts in Canada.* Toronto: Carswell and Thomson.

Friedman, Lawrence M. 1969. "Legal Culture and Social Development." *Law and Society Review* 4 (1): 29–44. 1973. "General Theory of Law and Social Change," in J. S. Ziegel (ed.), *Law and Social Change,* pp. 17–33. Toronto: Osgoode Hall Law School, York University. 1973a. *A History of American Law.* New York: Simon and Schuster. 1975. *The Legal System: A Social Science Perspective.* New York: Russell Sage Foundation. 1977. *Law and Society: An Introduction.* Englewood Cliffs, NJ: Prentice Hall. 1998. *American Law: An Introduction.* 2nd ed. New York: W. W. Norton. 2002. *American Law in the Twentieth Century.* New Haven, CT: Yale University Press.

Friedman, Lawrence M., and Stewart Macaulay. 1977. *Law and the Behavioral Sciences*. 2nd ed. Indianapolis, IN: Bobbs-Merrill.

Friedman, Lawrence M., and Robert V. Percival. 1976. "A Tale of Two Courts: Litigation in Alameda and San Benito Counties." *Law and Society Review* 10 (1 and 2): 267–302.

Friedman, Robert L. 2000. *Red Mafiya: How the Russian Mob Has Invaded America*. Boston: Little, Brown.

Friedmann, Wolfgang. 1972. *Law in a Changing Society*. 2nd ed. New York: Columbia University Press.

Friedrich, Carl J. 1958. *The Philosophy of Law in Historical Perspective*. Chicago: University of Chicago Press.

Friedrichs, David O. 1990. "Narrative Jurisprudence and Other Heresies: Legal Education at the Margin." *Journal of Legal Education* 40 (1–2) (March–June): 3–18. 2001. *Law in Our Lives, An Introduction*. Los Angeles: Roxbury. 2004. *Trusted Criminals: White Collar Crime in Contemporary Society*. 2nd ed. Belmont, CA: Wadsworth/Thomson Learning. 2006. *Law in Our Lives: An Introduction*. 2nd ed. Los Angeles: Roxbury.

Friendly, Alfred, and Ronald L. Goldfarb. 1967. *Crime and Publicity: The Impact of News on the Administration of Justice*. New York: The Twentieth Century Fund.

Fritsch, Jane, and David Rohde. 2001. "Legal Help Often Fails New York's Poor." *New York Times* (April 8): 1, 27.

Frug, Mary Joe. 1992. *Postmodern Legal Feminism*. New York: Routledge.

Fu, Ziqiu. 2003. "Guest Editor's Introduction." *Chinese Law and Government* 36 (3) (May/June): 3–6.

Fuente, Leticia de la, E. Inmaculada de la Fuente, and Juan Garcia. 2004. "Effects of Pretrial Juror Bias, Strength of Evidence and Deliberation Process on Juror Decisions: New Validity Evidence of the Juror Bias Scale Scores." *Psychology, Crime and Law* 9 (2): 197–209.

Fuller, Lon. 1968. *Anatomy of the Law*. New York: Praeger. 1969. *The Morality of Law*. Rev. ed. New Haven, CT: Yale University Press.

Gadd, Jane. 2001. "Kovals Jailed for 7 Years in Huge Fraud." *Globe and Mail* (March 31): 2001: A17.

Gaddy, Clifford, Jim Leitzel, and Michael Alexeev. 1995. "Mafiosi and Matrioshki: Organized Crime and Russian Reform." *Brookings Review* 13 (1) (Winter): 26–30.

Gagnon, Alain G. 2002. "A Dangerously Shrinking Public Sphere." *Policy Options* 23 (6) (September): 18–19.

Gaillard, Emmanual. 2000. "Alternative Dispute Resolution (ADR) à la Française." *New York Law Journal* (June 1): 1–3.

Galanter, Marc. 1974. "Why the 'Haves' Come Out Ahead: Speculations on the Limits of Legal Change." *Law and Society Review* 9 (1): 95–160. 1975. "Afterword: Explaining Litigation." *Law and Society Review* 9 (2): 347–368. 1977. "The Modernization of Law," in Lawrence M. Friedman and Stewart Macaulay (eds.), *Law and the Behavioral Sciences*, pp. 1046–1060. 2nd ed. Indianapolis, IN: Bobbs-Merrill. 1988. "Beyond the Litigation Panic," in Walter Olson (ed.), *New Directions in Liability Law*, pp. 18–30. New York: Academy of Political Science. 1992. "The Debased Debate on Civil Justice." Working Paper DPRP (May). Institute for Legal Studies. Madison: University of Wisconsin.

Gall, Gerald, and Rebecca Sober. 2000. "The Supreme Court of Canada: Judges Speak Out!" *Canadian Issues* (Spring): 26–29.

Gaming Magazine. 2001. "Winners and Losers: Millions at Stake in Native Dispute over Casino Profits." Retrieved from gaming-magazine.com/managearticle.asp?c=620anda=138.

Gamson, William. 1990. *The Strategy of Social Protest*. 2nd ed. Belmont, CA: Wadsworth.

Gandhi, J. S. 1982. *Lawyers and Touts: A Study in the Sociology of the Legal Profession*. Delhi, India: Hindustan Publishing Corp.

Gannon, Maire. 2001. "Crime Comparisons Between Canada and the United States."

Juristat 21 (11) (December). Cat. No. 85–002–XPE.

Garkawe, Sam. 1995. "The Impact of the Doctrine of Cultural Relativism on the Australian Legal System." Retrieved from www.murdoch.edu.au/elaw/issues/v2n1/garkawe.txt.

Garland, David. 2001. *The Culture of Control: Crime and Social Order in Contemporary Society*. Chicago: University of Chicago Press.

Garner, Bryan A. 2001. *Legal Writing in Plain English: A Text with Exercises*. Chicago: University of Chicago Press.

Garofalo, James, and Maureen McLeod. 1989. "The Structure and Operations of Neighborhood Watch Programs in the United States." *Crime and Delinquency* 35 (3): 326–344.

Gaudry, M. 1988. "The Effects on Road Safety of the Compulsory Insurance, Flat Premium Rating and No-Fault Features of the 1978 Quebec Automobile Act," appendix to Report of the Inquiry into Motor Vehicle Accident Compensation in Ontario (Osborne Report). Ontario: Queen's Printer.

Gaurav, Desai, Felipe Smith, and Supriya Nair. 2003. "Introduction: Law, Literature and Ethnic Subjects: Critical Essay." MELUS (Spring).

Gavigan, Shelley A. M. 2000. "Mothers, Other Mothers, and Others: The Legal Challenges and Contradictions of Lesbian Parents," in Dorothy Chunn and Dany Lacombe (eds.), *Law as a Gendering Practice*, pp. 100–118. Don Mills, ON: Oxford University Press.

Gazette. 2001. "Court Rejects O. J. Simpson's Appeal of $33.5 Million Judgment." January 27: B8.

Geel, Tyll R. van. 2005. *Understanding Supreme Court Opinions*. 4th ed. New York: Longman.

Geiger-Oneto, Stephanie, and Scott Phillips. 2003. "Driving While Black: The Role of Race, Sex, and Social Status." *Journal of Ethnicity in Criminal Justice* 1 (2): 1–25.

Geis, Gilbert. 1994. "Corporate Crime: 'Three Strikes You're Out?'" *Multinational Monitor* 15 (6) (June): 30–31.

Gellhorn, Ernest, and Ronald M. Levin. 1997. *Administrative Law and Process in a Nutshell*. 4th ed. St. Paul, MN: West.

George, Robert P. (ed.) 2003. *Natural Law*. Burlington, VT: Ashgate.

Gerson, Stuart M. 1994. "Computers Generate Litigation Explosion." *National Law Journal* 16 (31) (April 4): A17.

Gerstein, Ralph M., and Lois Gerstein. 2004. *Education Law: A Practical Guide for Attorneys, Teachers, Administrators and Student Advocates*. Tucson, AZ: Lawyers and Judges Publishing.

Gest, Ted. 1995. "Combating Legalese: Law Schools Are Finally Learning That Good English Makes Sense." *U.S. News and World Report* (March 20): 78–81.

Ghanea, Nazila. 2004. "Human Rights of Religious Minorities and of Women in the Middle East." *Human Rights Quarterly* 26 (3) (August): 705–729.

Gibbs, John C. 2003. *Moral Development and Reality: Beyond the Theories of Kohlberg and Hoffman*. Thousand Oaks, CA: Sage.

Gibson, James L., and Gregory A. Caldeira. 1996. "The Legal Cultures of Europe." *Law and Society Review* 30 (1) (February): 55–85.

Giffen, P. J., Shirley Endicott, and Sylvia Lambert. 1991. *Panic and Indifference: The Politics of Canada's Drug Laws*. Toronto: Canadian Centre on Substance Abuse.

Gilbert, Michael J. 1997. "The Illusion of Structure: A Critique of the Classical Model of Organization and the Discretionary Power of Correctional Officers." *Criminal Justice Review* 22 (1) (Spring): 49–64.

Gilgoff, Dan. 2004. "Law Schools Go International." *U.S. News and World Report* (April 12): 58–62.

Gill, David. 1988. *The Market for Legal Services*. Vancouver: The Fraser Institute.

Gill, Gerald L. 1990. *The Canadian Legal System*. 3rd ed. Toronto: Carswell. 1999.

"Judiciary," in James H. Marsh (ed.), *The Canadian Encyclopedia: Year 2000 Edition*, pp. 1224–1225. Toronto: McClelland and Stewart.

Gillespie, Kerry. 2002. "Law and Disorder: Private Security Industry Under Fire." *Toronto Star* (December 1): A1.

Gilmore, G. 1977. *The Ages of American Law*. New Haven, CT: Yale University Press.

Ginsberg, Margery B., with Pablo Fiene. 2004. *Motivation Matters: A Workbook for School Change*. San Francisco, CA: Jossey-Bass.

Ginsberg, Morris. 1965. *On Justice in Society*. Ithaca, NY: Cornell University Press.

Gioacchino, Debora Di, Sergio Sinebri, and Laura Sabani (eds.). 2004. *The Role of Organized Interest Groups in Policy Making*. New York: Palgrave Macmillan.

Girard, Claude. 2001. "Fiscal Treatment of Social Allocations and Human Rights." *Canadian Journal of Law and Society* 16 (2): 119–135.

Glaberson, William.1992. "With Au Pair Acquitted in Murder, the Focus Turns to the Police." *New York Times* (July 12): 20. 2001. "Legal Citations Are on Trial in Innovation v. Tradition." *New York Times* (July 8): A1.

Glaser, Daniel. 1971. "Criminology and Public Policy." *American Sociologist* 6 (6) (June): 30–37.

Glater, Jonathan D. 2001. "Few Minorities Rising to Law Partner." *New York Times* (August 7): A1, A6.

Glazer, Nathan. 1975. "Towards an Imperial Judiciary?" *Public Interest* 41 (Fall): 104–123.

Glendon, Mary Ann. 1989. *The Transformation of Family Law: State, Law, and Family in the United States and Western Europe*. Chicago: University of Chicago Press. 1991. *The Rights Talk: The Impoverishment of Political Discourse*. New York: Free Press. 1994. *A Nation Under Lawyers: How the Crisis in the Legal Profession Is Transforming American Society*. New York: Farrar, Straus and Giroux.

Glendon, Mary Ann, Michael Wallace Gordon, and Christopher Osakwe. 1994. *Comparative Legal Traditions*. 2nd ed. St. Paul, MN: West.

Globe and Mail. 2005. "Sharia (Islamic Law) Protestors Target Canada." (August 31). Retrieved from www.freemuslims.org/news/article.php?article=876.

Godwin, R. Kenneth. 1988. *One Billion Dollars of Influence: The Direct Marketing of Politics*. Chatham, NJ: Chatham House.

Goff, Colin, and Charles E. Reasons. 1978. *Corporate Crime in Canada.* Scarborough, ON: Prentice Hall.

Goldberg, Stephen B., Frank E. A. Sander, and Nancy H. Rogers. 2003. *Dispute Resolution: Negotiation, Mediation, and Other Processes*. 4th ed. Gaithersburg, MD: Aspen Law and Business.

Goldkamp, John S., and Michael D. White. 2002. *The Nevada Reentry Drug Court Demonstration*. Philadelphia, PA: Crime and Justice Research Institute.

Goldkamp, John S., Michael D. White, and Jennifer B. Robinson. 2001. "Do Drug Courts Work? Getting Inside the Drug Court Black Box." *Journal of Drug Issues* 31 (1): 27–72. 2001. *"An Honest Chance": Perspectives of Drug Court Participants*. Philadelphia, PA: Crime and Justice Research Initiative. 2001a. "Context and Change: The Evolution of Pioneering Drug Courts in Portland and Las Vegas (1991–1998)." *Law and Policy* 23 (2) (April): 141–170.

Goldman, Sheldon, and Austin Sarat (eds.). 1978. *American Court Systems: Readings in Judicial Process and Behavior.* San Francisco: W. H. Freeman. 1989. *American Court Systems: Readings in Judicial Process and Behavior*. 2nd ed. New York: Longman.

Goldstein, Joseph. 1960. "Police Discretion Not to Invoke the Criminal Process: Low Visibility Decisions in the Administration of Criminal Justice." *Yale Law Journal* 69 (March): 543–594.

Goldstein, Philip. 2004. *Post-Marxist Theory*. Albany, NY: State University of New York Press.

Gomes, Jeanette T., Lorne D. Bertrand, Joanne J. Paetsch, and Joseph Hornick. 2003. "Self-Reported Delinquency Among Alberta's Youth: Findings from a Survey of 2,001 Junior and Senior High School Students." *Adolescence* 38 (149) (Spring): 75–91.

Goode, Erich. 2005. *Deviant Behavior*. 7th ed. Upper Saddle River, NJ: Prentice Hall.

Goodman, John T. 1999. "Mental Health," in James H. Marsh (ed.), *The Canadian Encyclopedia*, pp. 1468–1469. Toronto: McClelland and Stewart.

Goodrich, Peter. 1993. "Sleeping with the Enemy: An Essay on the Politics of Critical Legal Studies in America." *New York University Law Review* 68 (2) (May): 389–425.

Goodstein, Laurie. 2004. "Citing Survey, CNN Says 4,450 Priests Were Accused of Abuse." *New York Times* (February 27): A1, A17.

Gordon, R. A. 1990. "Attributions for Blue-Collar Crime: The Effect of Subject and Defendant Race on Simulated Juror Decisions." *Journal of Applied Social Psychology* 20: 971–983. 1993. "The Effect of Strong Versus Weak Evidence on the Assessment of Race Stereotypic and Race Nonstereotypic Crimes." *Journal of Applied Social Psychology* 23: 734–749.

Gordon, R. A., J. L. Michels, and C. L. Nelson. 1996. "Majority Group Perceptions of Criminal Behavior: The Accuracy of Race-Related Crime Stereotypes." *Journal of Applied Social Psychology* 26: 148–159.

Gorman, Elizabeth R. 2005. "Gender Stereotypes, Same-Gender Preferences, and Organizational Variation in the Hiring of Women: Evidence from Law Firms." *American Sociological Review* 70 (4) (August): 702–728.

Gossett, J. L., and S. Byrne. 2002. "'Click Here': A Content Analysis of Internet Rape Sites." *Gender and Society* 16 (5) (October): 689–709.

Gottfredson, Michael R., and Michael J. Hindelang. 1979. "A Study of the Behavior of Law." *American Sociological Review* 44 (1) (February): 3–18.

Government of Canada. 2005. "Amendments of Lobbyists Registration Act to Come into Force." Retrieved from www.faa.lfi.gc.ca/fs-fi/04fs-fi_e.asp. 2006. "Toughening the Lobbyists Registration Act." Retrieved from www.faa.lfi.gc.ca/fs-fi/04fs-fi_e.asp.

Graglia, Lino A. 1994. "Do Judges Have a Policy-making Role in the American System of Government?" *Harvard Journal of Law and Public Policy* 17 (1) (Winter): 119–130.

Graham, Deborah. 1995. "Law's New Entrepreneurs." *ABA Journal* 81 (February): 54–60.

Green, Mark J. 1976. "The ABA as Trade Association," in Ralph Nader and Mark Green (eds.), *Verdicts on Lawyers*, pp. 3–19. New York: Thomas Y. Crowell.

Green, Melvyn. 1986. "A History of Canadian Narcotics Control: The Formative Years," in Neil Boyd (ed.), *The Social Dimensions of Law*, pp. 24–40. Scarborough, ON: Prentice Hall.

Green, Traci, Catherine Hankins, and Darlene Palmer. 2003. "Ascertaining the Need for a Supervised Injecting Facility (SIF): The Burden of Public Injecting in Montreal, Canada." *Journal of Drug Issues* 33 (3) (Summer): 713–731.

Greenaway, William K., and Stephan L. Brickey (eds.). 1978. *Law and Social Control in Canada*. Scarborough, ON: Prentice Hall.

Greenberg, Jack. 1959. *Race Relations and American Law*. New York: Columbia University Press.

Greenberg, Judith G., Martha L. Minow, and Dorothy E. Roberts. 1998. *Women and the Law*. 2nd ed. New York: Foundation Press.

Greene, Edith, and Michael Johns. 2001. "Jurors Use of Instructions on Negligence." *Journal of Applied Social Psychology* 31 (5): 840–859.

Greenhouse, Carol J. 1989. "Interpreting American Litigiousness," in June Starr and Jane F. Collier (eds.), *History and Power in the Study of Law: New Directions in Legal Anthropology*, pp. 252–273. Ithaca, NY: Cornell University Press.

Greenhouse, Steven. 2000. "Anti-Sweatshop Movement Is Achieving Gains Overseas." *New York Times* (January 26). Retrieved from nytimes.com.

Greenwood, F. M., and B. Boissery. 2000. *Uncertain Justice: Canadian Women and Punishment, 1754–1953*. Toronto: Dundurn Press.

Greer, Edward. 2000. "Awaiting Cassandra: The Trojan Mare of Legal Dominance Feminism (Part I)." *Women's Rights Law Reporter* 21 (2) (Spring) 95–116.

Gregg, Alan R. 2001/2002. "Scary New World." *Maclean's* 114 (53) (December 31–January 7): 22–25.

Griffith, Curt T., and Alison Hatch Cunningham. 2003. *Canadian Criminal Justice*. Scarborough, ON: Nelson.

Griffith, Curt T., and Simon N. Verdun-Jones. 1989. *Canadian Criminal Justice*. Toronto: Butterworths.

Griffith, C. T., and J. C. Yerbury. 1995. "Understanding Aboriginal Crime and Criminality: A Case Study," in Margaret A. Jackson and Curt T. Griffiths (eds.), *Canadian Criminology: Perspectives on Crime and Criminality*, pp. 383–398. 2nd ed. Toronto: Harcourt.

Gross, Edward. 1998. "Lawyers and Their Discontents." *Society as Needed* 36 (1) (November–December): 26–31.

Gross, Hyman. 1979. *A Theory of Criminal Justice*. New York: Oxford University Press.

Grossman, Joel B., and Mary H. Grossman (eds.). 1971. *Law and Social Change in Modern America*. Pacific Palisades, CA: Goodyear.

Grossman, Joel B., and Austin Sarat. 1975. "Litigation in Federal Courts: A Comparative Perspective." *Law and Society Review* 9 (2): 321–346.

Groves, Robert M. 2004. *Survey Methodology*. Hoboken, NJ: John Wiley.

Gubser, Nicholas J. 1965. *The Nunamiut Eskimos: Hunters of Caribou*. New Haven, CT: Yale University Press.

Gudgeon, Chris. 2003. *The Naked Truth*. Vancouver: Greystone Books.

Gulliver, P. H. 1969. "Introduction to Case Studies of Law in Non-Western Societies," in Laura Nader (ed.), *Law in Culture and Society*, pp. 11–23. Chicago: Aldine.

Gunnell, Barbara. 2000. "A Tale of the Power of Ordinary Folk." *New Statesman* 129 (4474) (February 21): 30.

Gureyev, P. P., and P. I. Sedugin (eds.). 1977. *Legislation in the USSR*. Trans. Denis Ogden. Moscow: Progress Publishers.

Gurvitch, Georges. 1942. *Sociology of Law*. New York: Philosophical Library.

Gusfield, Joseph R. 1967. "Moral Passage: The Symbolic Process in Public Designations of Deviance." *Social Problems* 15 (2) (Fall): 175–188.

Guydish, J., Ellen Wolfe, Barbara Tajima, and William J. Woods. 2001. "Drug Court Effectiveness: A Review of California Evaluation Reports, 1997–1999." *Journal of Psychoactive Drugs* 33 (4) (October–December): 369–378.

Hackler, James C. 2000. *Canadian Criminology: Strategies and Perspectives*. 2nd ed. Scarborough, ON: Prentice Hall. 2003. *Canadian Criminology: Strategies and Perspectives*. 3rd ed. Toronto: Prentice Hall.

Hagan, John. 1990. "The Gender Stratification of Income Inequality Among Lawyers." *Social Forces* 68: 835–55. 2000. "White-Collar and Corporate Crime," in Rick Linden (ed.), *Criminology: A Canadian Perspective*, pp. 459–482. 4th ed. Toronto: Harcourt.

Hagan, John, Marie Huxter, and Patricia Parker. 1988. "Class Structure and Legal Practice: Inequality and Mobility Among Toronto Lawyers." *Law and Society Review* 22 (1): 9–55.

Hagan, John, and Fiona Kay. 1995. *Gender in Practice: A Study of Lawyer's Lives*. Oxford: Oxford University Press. 1999. "Cultivating Clients in the Competition for Partnership: Gender and the Organizational Restructuring of Law Firms in the 1990s." *Law and Society Review* 33 (3): 517–555.

Hagan, John, and Ron Levi. 2005. "Crimes of War and the Force of Law." *Social Forces* 83 (4) (June): 1499–1534.

Haines, Herb. 1992. "Flawed Executions, the Anti-Death Penalty Movement, and the Politics of Capital Punishment." *Social Problems* 39 (2) (May): 125–138.

Hajnal, Zoltan L., and Terry Nichols Clark. 1998. "The Local Interest-Group System: Who Governs and Why?" *Social Science Quarterly* 79 (1) (March): 227–242.

Hall, Anthony J. 2000. "Racial Discrimination in Legislation, Litigation, Legend and Lore." *Canadian Ethnic Studies* 32 (2): 119–135.

Hall, Jerome. 1952. *Theft, Law and Society*. 2nd ed. Indianapolis, IN: Bobbs-Merrill.

Hallaq, Wael B. (ed.). 2004. *The Formation of Islamic Law*. Burlington, VT: Ashgate.

Halliday, Terence C. 1986. "Six Score Years and Ten: Demographic Transitions in the American Legal Profession, 1850–1980." *Law and Society Review* 20 (1): 53–78.

Halperin, Rick. 2004. "Life on Hold." (June 19) Retrieved from venus.soci.niu.edu/~archives/ABOLISH/rick-halperin/sept04/0771.html.

Haltom, William, and Michael McCann. 2004. *Distorting the Law: Politics, Media and the Litigation Crisis*. Chicago: University of Chicago Press.

Hamilton, Graeme. 2002. "Family Sues Coca-Cola over Son's Death." *National Post* (July 11). Retrieved from http://overlawyered.com/archives/01/july2.html.

Hanawalt, Barbara A. 1998. *'Of Good and Ill Repute'—Gender and Social Control in Medieval England*. New York: Oxford University Press.

Handelman, Stephen. 1995. *Comrade Criminal, Russia's New Mafiya*. New Haven, CT: Yale University Press.

Haney-Lopez, Ian F. 1997. *White by Law: The Legal Construction of Race*. New York: New York University Press.

Hans, Valerie P. 1992. "Jury Decision Making," in Dorothy K. Kagehiro and William S. Laufer (eds.), *Handbook of Psychology and Law*, pp. 56–76. New York: Springer-Verlag.

Hans, Valerie P., and Veil Vidmar. 1986. *Judging the Jury*. New York: Plenum.

Hans, Valerie P., and William S. Lofquist. 1992. "Jurors' Judgments of Business Liability in Tort Cases: Implications for the Litigation Explosion Debate." *Law and Society Review* 26 (1): 85–115.

Hansen, Mark. 1994. "A Shunned Justice System: Most Families Don't Turn to Lawyers or Judges to Solve Legal Problems, Survey Says." *ABA Journal* 80 (April): 18–20.

Harmon, Amy. 1998. "'Hacktivists' of All Persuasions Take Their Struggle to the Web." *New York Times* (October 31): A1, A5.

Harries, K., and D. Cheatwood. 1997. *The Geography of Execution: The Capital Punishment Quagmire in America*. Lanham, MD: Rowman and Littlefield.

Harris v. T. T. C. and Miller, Supreme Court of Canada, 1967, S.C.R. 460, 63 D.L.R., (2d), 450.

Harris, Angel P. 1994. "Forward: The Jurisprudence of Reconstruction. Symposium: Critical Race Theory." *California Law Review* 82 (4) (July): 741–785.

Harris, R. 1999. "Effects on an Execution on Homicides in California." *Homicide Studies* 3: 129–150.

Hart, Henry M., Jr. 1958. "The Aims of the Criminal Law." *Law and Contemporary Problems*, No. 23 (Summer): 401–441.

Harris, Richard A., and Sidney M. Milkis. 1989. *The Politics of Regulatory Change: A Tale of Two Agencies*. New York: Oxford University Press.

Haskell, Paul G. 1998. *Why Lawyers Behave As They Do*. Boulder, CO: Westview Press.

Hatch, Alison. 1995. "Historical Legacies of Crime and Criminal Justice in Canada" in Margaret A. Jackson and Curt T. Griffiths (eds.), *Canadian Criminology: Perspectives on Crime and Criminality*, pp. 247–272. Toronto: Harcourt.

Hathway, Andrew D., and Patricia G. Erickson. 2003. "Drug Reform Principles and Policy Debates: Harm Reduction Prospects for Cannabis in Canada." *Journal of Drug Issues* 33 (2) (Spring): 465–495.

Hauser, Philip M. 1976. "Demographic Changes and the Legal System," in Murray L. Schwartz (ed.), *Law and the American Future*, pp. 15–29. Englewood Cliffs, NJ: Prentice Hall.

Havemann, Judith. 1986. "Federal Computers Are Putting a Glitch into Laws on Privacy." *St. Louis Post-Dispatch* (July 12): B1.

Hayman, Robert L., Jr. 1995. "The Color of Tradition: Critical Race Theory and Postmodern Constitutional Traditionalism." *Harvard Civil Rights-Civil Liberties Law Review* 30 (1) (Winter): 57–108.

Haynes, John Michael, Gretchen L. Haynes, and Larry Sun Fong. 2004. *Medication: Positive Conflict Management*. Albany, NY: State University of New York Press.

Hazard, Geoffrey C. 1994. "Liability Coverage May Become Impossible to Obtain Under Traditional Procedures." *National Law Journal* 16 (28) (March): A17.

Health Canada. 1999. "Statistical Report on the Health of Canadians." Retrieved from www.hc-sc.gc.ca/hpph/phdd/report/stat/eng/over.html. 2002. "The Scoop on Smoking—Health Canada for Youth." Retrieved from www.hc-sc.gc.ca/hecs-sesc/tobacco/youth/scoop.html. 2005. "Alcohol." Retrieved from www.hc-sc.gc.ca/hl-vs/alc/index_e.html.

Heard, Andrew. 2006. "Women and Canadian Elections." Retrieved from www.sfu.ca/~aheard/elections/women.html.

Hearns, Jeff. 1992. *Men in the Public Eye*. London: Routledge.

Heidenheimer, Arnold J., Hugh Helco, and Carolyn Teich Adams. 1990. *Comparative Public Policy: The Politics of Social Choice in America, Europe and Japan*. New York: St. Martin's Press.

Heilbrun, Carolyn, and Judith Resnick. 1990. "Convergences: Law, Literature and Feminism." *Yale Law Journal* 99 (8): 1912–1956.

Heinz, John P., and Edward O. Laumann. 1994. *Chicago Lawyers: The Social Structure of the Bar*. Rev. ed. Evanston, IL: Northwestern University Press.

Hellman, Hal. 2004. *Great Feuds in Technology: Ten of the Liveliest Disputes Ever*. Hoboken, NJ: John Wiley and Sons.

Henderson, Harry. 2005. *Gun Control*. Rev. ed. New York: Facts on File.

Hendley, Kathryn. 2004. "Business Litigation in the Transition: A Portrait of Debt Collection." *Law and Society Review* 38 (2) (June): 305–347.

Henry, Frances, Carol Tator, Winston Mattis, and Tim Rees. 2000. *The Colour of Democracy: Racism in Canadian Society*. 2nd ed. Toronto: Harcourt.

Hertzler, J. O. 1961. *American Social Institutions*. Boston: Allyn and Bacon.

Hickey, Eric W. 2006. *Sex Crimes and Paraphilia*. Upper Saddle River, NJ: Prentice Hall.

Higgins, Tracy E. 1997. "Democracy and Feminism." *Harvard Law Review* 110 (8) (June): 1657–1703.

Hil, Richard, and Gordon Tait. (eds.). 2004. *Hard Lessons: Reflections on Governance and Crime Control in Late Modernity*. Aldershot, UK; Burlington, VT: Ashgate/Dartmouth.

Hirowatari, Seigo. 2000. "Post-War Japan and the Law: Mapping Discourses of Legalization and Modernization." *Social Science Japan Journal* 3 (2) (October): 155–169.

Hirschman, Albert O. 1970. *Exit, Voice, and Loyalty: Responses to Decline in Firms, Organizations, and States*. Cambridge, MA: Harvard University Press.

Hobbs, Robert J. 2004. *Fair Debt Collection*. 5th ed. Boston: National Consumer Law Center.

Hoebel, E. Adamson. 1954. *The Law of Primitive Man: A Study of Comparative Legal Dynamics*. Cambridge, MA: Harvard University Press.

Hoffman, Jan. 2004. "Finding the Ideal Jury, Keeping Fingers Crossed." *New York Times* (March 11): B2.

Hoffmann, Joseph L. 2005. "Protecting the Innocent: The Massachusetts Governor's Council Report." *The Journal of Criminal Law and Criminology* 95 (2) (Winter): 561–585.

Hogg, Peter. 1997. *Constitutional Law of Canada.* 4th ed. Toronto: Carswell.

Holcomb, Jefferson E., Marian R. Williams, and Stephen Demuth. 2004. "White Female Victims and Death Penalty Disparity Research." *Justice Quarterly* 21 (4) (December): 877–902.

Hollis v. Dow Corning, Supreme Court of Canada, 1995, 4, S.C.R. 634.

Holmes, Malcolm D., Howard C. Daudistel, and William A. Taggart. 1992. "Plea Bargaining Policy and State District Court Caseloads: An Interrupted Time Series Analysis." *Law and Society Review* 26 (1): 139–159.

Holmes, Oliver Wendell, Jr. 1897. "The Path of the Law." *Harvard Law Review* 10 (March): 457–461. 1963. *The Common Law.* Cambridge, MA: Harvard University Press. Mark D. Howe (ed.). Originally published in 1881.

Honey, Kim. 1998. "Police Fail Rape Victim, Judge Rules." *Globe and Mail* (July 4): A1.

Honore, Tony. 1987. *Making Law Bind: Essays Legal and Philosophical.* Oxford: Clarendon Press.

Hopper, Kim. 1998. "Negotiating the Right to Housing: Fifteen Years of Advocacy for the Homeless Poor in the United States (1980–1995)." *Societes Contemporaines* 30 (April): 67–93.

Horowitz, Donald L. 1977. *The Courts and Social Policy.* Washington, DC: Brookings Institution.

Horowitz, Irwin A., and Kenneth S. Bordens. 2002. "The Effects of Jury Size, Evidence Complexity and Note Taking on Jury Process and Performance in a Civil Trial." *Journal of Applied Psychology* 87 (1) (February): 121–130.

Howard, A. E. Dick. 1979. "The Road from 'Brown,'" *Wilson Quarterly* 3 (2) (Spring): 96–107.

Howard, Philip K. 1994. *The Death of Common Sense, How Law Is Suffocating America.* New York: Random House. 2001. *The Lost Art of Drawing the Line: How Fairness Went Too Far.* New York: Random House. 2003. *The Collapse of the Common Good: How America's Lawsuit Culture Undermines Our Freedom.* New York: Random House.

Howard, Robert M. 2002. "Litigation, Courts, and Bureaucratic Policy: Equity, Efficiency and the Internal Revenue Service." *American Politics Research* 30 (6): 583–607.

Howard-Hassman, Rhoda E. 2000. "Multiculturalism, Human Rights and Cultural Relativism: Canadian Civic Leaders Discuss Women's Rights and Gay and Lesbian Rights." *Netherlands Quarterly of Human Rights* 18 (4) (December): 493–514.

Huey, Laura, and Richard S. Rosenberg. 2004. "Watching the Web: Thoughts on Expanding Police Surveillance Opportunities Under the Cyber-Crime Convention." *Canadian Journal of Criminology and Criminal Justice* 46 (3) (October): 597–606.

Huff, Toby E., and Wolfgang Schlucter (eds.). 1999. *Max Weber and Islam.* New Brunswick, NJ: Transaction.

Hughes, John C. 1995. *The Federal Courts, Politics, and the Rule of Law.* New York: HarperCollins.

Hum, Derek, and Wayne Simpson. 1991. *Income Maintenance, Work Effort, and the Canadian Mincome Experiment.* Ottawa: Economic Council of Canada. 2001. "A Guaranteed Annual Income? From Mincome to the Millennium." *Policy Options* January–February: 78–82. Retrieved from www.irpp.org/po/archive/jan01/hum.pdf.

Human Rights Watch. 2001. World Report 2001. Retrieved from www.hrw.org.

Hunt, Alan. 1978. *The Sociological Movement in Law.* Philadelphia: Temple University Press. 1993. *Explorations in Law and Society; Toward a Constitutive Theory of Law.* New York: Routledge. 2002. "Legal Governance and Social Relations: Empowering Agents and the Limits of Law," in Michael Mac Neil, Neil Sargent, and Peter Swan (eds.), *Law, Regulation and Governance*, pp. 54–77. Don Mills, ON: Oxford University Press.

Hunt, Morton. 1982. "Putting Juries on the Couch." *New York Times Magazine* (November 28): 70–87.

Hutchinson, Allan C. 1999. *Legal Ethics and Professional Responsibility*. Toronto: Irwin Law. 2002. "Legal Aid or Lawyers' Aid?" *Globe and Mail* (August 13): A17. 2005. *Evolution and the Common Law*. New York: Cambridge University Press.

Ignatius, Adi. 1989. "China's Golden Girls Monitor Neighbors." *Wall Street Journal* (August 1): A10.

Inbau, Fred E., James R. Thompson, James B. Zagel, and James P. Manak. 1997. *Criminal Law and Its Administration*. 6th ed. Westbury, NY: Foundation Press.

Inciardi, James A., Alan A. Block, and Lyle A. Hallowell. 1977. *Historical Approaches to Crime: Research Strategies and Issues*. Beverly Hills, CA: Sage.

Ippolito, Dennis S., Thomas G. Walker, and Kenneth L. Kolson. 1976. *Public Opinion and Responsible Democracy*. Englewood Cliffs, NJ: Prentice Hall.

Israel, Mark. 1998. "Ethnic Bias in Jury Selection in Australia and New Zealand." *International Journal of the Sociology of Law* 26: 35–54.

Jacob, Herbert. 1969. *Debtors in Court: The Consumption of Government Services*. Chicago: Rand McNally. 1984. *Justice in America: Courts, Lawyers, and the Judicial Process*. 4th ed. Boston: Little, Brown. 1988. *Silent Revolution: The Transformation of Divorce Law in the United States*. Chicago: University of Chicago Press. 1995. *Law and Politics in the United States*. 2nd ed. Ft. Washington, PA: HarperCollins. 1997. "The Governance of Trial Judges." *Law and Society Review* 32 (1): 3–30.

Jacob, Margaret A. 1995. "Reliable Data About Lawsuits Are Very Scarce." *Wall Street Journal* (June 9): B1, B2.

Jacoby, Henry. 1973. *The Bureaucratization of the World*. Trans. Eveline L. Kanes. Berkeley and Los Angeles: University of California Press.

Jaffe, Peter G., and Claire V. Crooks. 2004. "Partner Violence and Child Custody Cases: A Cross-National Comparison of Legal Reforms and Issues." *Violence Against Women* 10 (8) (August): 917–934.

Jaimes-Guerrero, M. A. 2003. "'Patriarchal Colonialism' and Indigenism: Implications for Native Feminist Spirituality and Native Womanism." *Hypatia* 18 (2) (Spring): 58–69.

Janisch, Hudson N. 1999. "Regulatory Process," in James H. Marsh (ed.), *The Canadian Encyclopedia: Year 2000 Edition*, p. 1994. Toronto: McClelland and Stewart.

Jarviluoma, Helmi, Pirkko Moisala, and Anni Vilkko. 2003. *Gender and Qualitative Methods*. Thousand Oaks, CA: Sage.

Jeffery, C. Ray. 1957. "The Development of Crime in Early English Society." *Journal of Criminal Law, Criminology and Police Science* 47: 647–666. 1962. "The Legal Profession," in F. James Davis, Henry H. Foster, Jr., C. Ray Jeffery, and E. Eugene Davis, *Society and the Law: New Meanings for an Old Profession*, pp. 313–356. New York: Free Press.

Jenkins, John A. 1977. "The Revolving Door Between Government and the Law Firms." *Washington Monthly* 8 (11) (January): 36–44.

Jewell, Malcolm E., and Samuel C. Patterson. 1986. *The Legislative Process in the United States*. 4th ed. New York: Random House.

Johansen, Bruce Elliott (ed.). 1998. *The Encyclopedia of Native American Legal Tradition*. Westport, CT: Greenwood.

Johnson, Alan V. 1977. "A Definition of the Concept of Law." *Mid-American Review of Sociology* 2 (1) (Spring): 47–71.

Johnson, Alex M., Jr. 1997. "The Underrepresentation of Minorities in the Legal Profession: A Critical Race Theorist's Perspective." *Michigan Law Review* 95 (4) (February): 1005–1062.

Johnson, Rebecca. 2000. "If Choice Is the Answer, What Is the Question? Spelunking in Symes v. Canada," in Dorothy Chunn and Dany Lacombe (eds.), *Law as a Gendering Practice*, pp. 199–222. Don Mills, ON: Oxford University Press.

Johnson, Valen E. 2003. *Grade Inflation: A Crisis in College Education*. New York: Springer.

Jonakait, Randolph N. 2003. *The American Jury System*. New Haven, CT: Yale University Press.

Jones, Greg, and Michael Connelly. 2001. "Research on Death Penalty and Related Topics." Maryland State Commission on Criminal Sentencing Policy. Retrieved from www.msccsp.org/publications/death.html.

Jordan, Tim, and Paul A. Taylor. 2004. *Hacktivism and Cyberwars: Rebels with a Cause?* New York: Routledge.

Jurgensen, Arnd. 2004. "Terrorism, Civil Liberties, and Preventive Approaches to Technology: The Difficult Choices Western Societies Face in the War on Terrorism." *Bulletin of Science, Technology and Society* 24 (1) (February): 55–59.

Kagan, Robert A. 1984. "The Routinization of Debt Collection: An Essay on Social Change and Conflict in Courts." *Law and Society Review* 18 (3): 323–371. 1995. "What Socio-Legal Scholars Should Do When There Is Too Much Law to Study." *Journal of Law and Society* 22 (1) (March): 140–148. 2000. "Introduction: Comparing National Styles of Regulation in Japan and the United States." *Law and Policy* 22 (3–4) (October): 225–244. 2001. *Adversarial Legalism: The American Way of Law.* Cambridge, MA: Harvard University Press.

Kahn, Susan Martha. 2000. *Reproducing Jews: A Cultural Account of Assisted Conception in Israel*. Durham, NC: Duke University Press.

Kallen, Evelyn. 2003. *Ethnicity and Human Rights in Canada*. 3rd ed. Don Mills, ON: Oxford University Press.

Kalven, Harry, Jr., and Hans Zeisel. 1966. *The American Jury*. Boston: Little, Brown.

Kane, Robert J. 1999. "Patterns of Arrest in Domestic Violence Encounters: Identifying a Police Decision-Making Model." *Journal of Criminal Justice* 27 (1): 65–79.

Kapardis, Andreas. 2003. *Psychology and Law: A Critical Introduction*. 2nd ed. New York: Cambridge University Press.

Kaplan, David A. 1995. "Anger and Ambivalence." *Newsweek* (August 7): 24–29.

Kaplin, William A., and Barbara E. Lee. 1995. *The Law of Higher Education*. 3rd ed. San Francisco: Jossey-Bass.

Karp, David R. 1998. "The Judicial and Judicious Use of Shame Penalties." *Crime and Delinquency* 44 (2) (April): 277–294.

Karsten, Peter. 1998. "Cows in the Corn, Pigs in the Garden, and the Problem of Social Costs: High and Low Legal Cultures of the British Diaspora Lands in the 17th, 18th, and 19th Centuries." *Law and Society Review* 32 (1): 63–92.

Kassin, Saul M., and Lawrence S. Wrightsman. 1988. *The American Jury on Trial*. New York: Hemisphere.

Katz, Elihu. 1957. "The Two-Step Flow of Communication: An Up-to-Date Report on a Hypothesis." *Public Opinion Quarterly* 21 (1) (Spring): 61–78.

Kawashima, Takeyoshi. 1969. "Dispute Resolution in Japan," in Vilhelm Aubert (ed.), *Sociology of Law*, pp. 182–193. Harmondsworth, UK: Penguin.

Kay, Fiona M. 1997. "Flight from Law: A Competing Risks Model of Departures from Law Firms." *Law and Society Review* 31 (2): 301–333.

Kay, Fiona M., and Joan Brockman. 2000. "Barriers to Gender Equality in the Legal Establishment." *Feminist Legal Studies* 8 (2): 169–198.

Kay, Fiona M., and John Hagan. 1995. "The Persistent Glass Ceiling: Gendered Inequalities in the Earnings of Lawyers." *British Journal of Sociology* 46 (2): 279–310. 2003. "Building Trust: Social Capital, Distributive Justice, and Loyalty to the Firm."

Law and Social Inquiry 28 (2) (Spring): 483–519.

Kay, F. M., C. Masuch, and P. Curry. 2004. Diversity and Change: The Contemporary Legal Profession in Ontario. Report to the Law Society of Upper Canada (September).

Kay, Susan Ann. 1978. "Socializing the Future Elite: The Nonimpact of a Law School." *Social Science Quarterly* 59 (2) (September): 347–356.

Kearney, Hugh. 1970. *Scholars and Gentlemen: Universities and Society in Pre-Industrial Britain*. Ithaca, NY: Cornell University Press.

Keen, Lisa, and Suzanne B. Goldberg. 1998. *Strangers to the Law: Gay People on Trial*. Ann Arbor: University of Michigan Press.

Keeton, R. E. 1973. *Trial Tactics and Methods*. 2nd ed. Boston: Little, Brown.

Keeva, Steven. 1995. "Standing Up for Women." *ABA Journal* 81 (April): 118–119.

Keith, Ronald C., and Zhiqiu Lin. 2003. "The 'Falun Gong Problem': Politics and the Struggle for the Rule of Law in China." *The China Quarterly* 175 (September): 623–642.

Kelleher, Michael D., and C. L. Kelleher. 1998. *Murder Most Rare: The Female Serial Killer*. Westport, CT: Praeger/Greenwood.

Kelly, Mary Ann. 2004. "The Court System—Ontario," in Laurence M. Olivo (ed.) *Introduction to Law in Canada*, pp. 116–137. Concord, ON: Captus Press.

Kelsen, Hans. 1967. *The Pure Theory of Law*. 2nd ed. Trans. M. Knight. Berkeley and Los Angeles: University of California Press.

Kennedy, Duncan. 2004. *Legal Education and the Reproduction of Hierarchy: A Polemic Against the System: A Critical Edition*. New York: New York University Press.

Kennedy, Jerome P. 2004. "Writing the Wrongs: The Role of the Defence Counsel in Wrongful Convictions—A Commentary." *Canadian Journal of Criminology and Criminal Justice*. Special Issue: Wrongful Conviction: Perspectives, Experiences, and Implications for Justice 46 (2) (January): 197–208.

Kennedy, M. Alexis, Carolin Klein, and Boris B. Gorzalka. 2004. "Attitude Change Following a Diversion Program for Men Who Solicit Sex." *Journal of Offender Rehabilitation* 40: 41–60.

Kennedy, Randall. 1998. *Race, Crime, and the Law*. New York: Random House/Vintage.

Kenney, Sally J. 2000. "Beyond Principals and Agents: Seeing Courts As Organizations by Comparing Referendaires at the European Court of Justice and Law Clerks at the U.S. Supreme Court." *Comparative Political Studies* 33 (4) (June): 593–625.

Kerley, Kent R. (ed.) 2005. *Policing and Program Evaluation*. Upper Saddle River, NJ: Prentice Hall.

Kerr, Dana, Yu-Luen Ma, and Joan T. Schmidt. 2006. "Do Extensive Government Social Programs Reduce Liability Costs?" Proposal to the American Risk and Insurance Association Annual Meeting, Washington, DC. (August). Retrieved from www.terry.uga.edu/insurance/research/documents/KerrMaSchmitARIA006.doc.

Kerr, Ian R. 2000. "Pregnant Women and the 'Born Alive' Rule in Canada." *Tort Law Review* 8: 713–719. 2004. "Look Out: The Eyes Have it." *Globe and Mail* (January 12): A11.

Kerrigan, Laura J. et al. 1993. "Project: The Decriminalization of Administrative Law Penalties: Civil Remedies, Alternatives, Policy and Constitutional Implications." *Administrative Law Review* 45 (4) (Fall): 367–434.

Kerwin, Cornelius M. 1999. *Rulemaking: How Government Agencies Write Law and Make Policies*. 2nd ed. Washington, DC: CQ Press.

Kevelson, Roberta (ed.). 1994. *Codes and Customs; Millennial Perspectives*. New York: Peter Lang.

Khan, Shahnaz. 2005. "Reconfiguring the Native Informant: Positionality in the Global Age." *Signs* 30 (4) (Summer): 2017–2035.

King, Alan J. C., Wendy K. Warren, and Sharon R. Miklas. Study of Accessibility to Ontario Law Schools. Report submitted to the Deans of Law at Osgood Hall, York University, University of Ottawa, Queen's University, University of Western Ontario, and University of Windsor.

King, Lawrence Peter, and Ivan Szelenyi. 2004. *Theories of the New Class: Intellectuals and Power*. Minneapolis, MN: University of Minnesota Press.

Kinsman, Gary. 1996. The *Regulation of Desire: Homo and Hetero Sexualities*. Rev. ed. Montreal: Black Rose Books. 2001. *Whose National Security? Canadian State Surveillance and the Creation of Enemies*. Toronto: Between the Lines.

Kitchin, Heather A. 2005. "Needing Treatment: A Snapshot of Provincially Incarcerated Adult Offenders in Nova Scotia with a View Towards Substance Abuse and Population Health." *Canadian Journal of Criminology and Criminal Justice* 47 (3) (July): 501–525.

Kleiman, Mark A. R., Denise C. Gottfredson, and John S. Goldkamp. 2003. "Drug Treatment Courts." *Criminology and Public Policy* 2 (2): 167–212.

Klingsberg, Ethan. 1992. "Judicial Review and Hungary's Transition from Communism to Democracy: The Constitutional Court, the Continuity of Law, and the Redefinition of Property Rights." *Brigham Young University Law Review* 1992, No. 1: 41–144.

Klockars, Carl B., Sanja Kutnjak Ivkovic, and M. R. Haberfeld. (eds.). 2004. *The Contours of Police Integrity*. Thousand Oaks, CA: Sage.

Koehler, Jonathan J. 1992. "Probabilities in the Courtroom: An Evaluation of the Objections and Policies," in Dorothy J. Kagehiro and William S. Laufer (eds.), *Handbook of Psychology and Law*, pp. 167–184. New York: Springer-Verlag.

Koenig, Thomas, and Michael Rustad. 2004. *In Defense of Tort Law*. New York: New York University Press.

Kohlberg, Lawrence. 1964. "Development of Moral Character and Ideology," in L. Hoffman and M. Hoffman (eds.), *Review of Child Development Research*, Vol. 1, pp. 383–431. New York: Russell Sage Foundation. 1967. "Moral Education, Religious Education, and the Public Schools: A Developmental Approach," in T. Sizer (ed.), *Religion and Public Education*, pp. 164–183. Boston: Houghton Mifflin.

Kolmar, Wendy K., and Frances Bartkowski. (eds.). 2005. *Feminist Theory: A Reader*. 2nd ed. Boston: McGraw-Hill.

Kors, Alan Charles, and Harvey A. Silverglate. 1998. *The Shadow University: The Betrayal of Liberty on America's Campuses*. New York: The Free Press.

Kraft, Michael E., and Scott R. Furlong. 2004. *Public Policy: Politics, Analysis and Alternatives*. Washington, DC: CQ Press.

Kramer, Geoffrey P., and Norbert L. Kerr. 1989. "Laboratory Simulation and Bias in the Study of Juror Behavior: A Methodological Note." *Law and Human Behavior* 13 (1): 89–99.

Kramer, Matthew H. 1995. *Critical Legal Theory and the Challenge of Feminism: A Philosophical Reconception*. Lanham, MD: Rowman and Littlefield.

Krauss, Clifford. 2004. "Canadian Police Image: Taking Hit Thanks to Scandals." *The Seattle Times* (January 25): A13.

Krawietz, Werner. 2001. "The Concept of Law Revised—Directives and Norms in the Perspectives of a New Legal Realism." *Ratio Juris* 14 (1): 34–46.

Kriesberg, Louis. 2002. *Constructive Conflicts: From Escalation to Resolution*. 2nd ed. Lanham, MD: Rowman and Littlefield.

Krisberg, Barry. 1978. "The Sociological Imagination Revisited," in Charles E. Reasons and Robert M. Rich (eds.), *The Sociology of Law: A Conflict Perspective*, pp. 455–470. Toronto: Butterworths.

Kristof, Nicholas D. 1995. "A Neighborly Style of Police State." *New York Times* (June 4): E5.

Kritzer, Herbert M. 1988. "Political Culture and the 'Propensity to Sue,'" Working Papers Series 9. Institute for Legal Studies.

University of Wisconsin 9 (1) (July): 1–50. 1990. *The Justice Broker: Lawyers and Ordinary Litigation*. New York: Oxford University Press. 1991. "Propensity to Sue in England and the United States of America: Blaming and Claiming in Tort Cases." *Journal of Law and Society* 18 (4) (Winter): 400–427. 1998. *Legal Advocacy: Lawyers and Nonlawyers at Work*. Ann Arbor: University of Michigan Press. (ed.). 2002. *Legal Systems of the World: A Political, Social and Cultural Encyclopedia*. Santa Barbara, CA: ABC-CLIO.

Kunz, Jennifer, and Phillip R. Kunz. 2001. "Social Distance of Deviants and Deviant Offenders." *Psychological Reports* 88 (2) (April): 505–513.

Kurlantzick, Joshua. 2003. "The Dragon Still Has Teeth: How the West Winks at Chinese Repression." *World Policy Journal* 20 (1) (Spring): 49–58.

Ladd, Everett C., Jr., and Seymour Martin Lipset. 1973. *Professors, Unions and American Higher Education*. Washington, DC: American Enterprise Institute for Public Policy Research.

Ladd, John. 1970. "Legal and Moral Obligation," in Roland Pennock and John W. Chapman (eds.), *Political and Legal Obligation*, pp. 3–45. New York: Lieber-Atherton.

Ladinsky, Jack. 1963. "Careers of Lawyers, Law Practice, and Legal Institutions." *American Sociological Review* 28 (1) (February): 47–54.

Lahey, Kathleen. 2003. "On Silences, Screams and Scholarship: An Introduction to Feminist Legal Theory," in T. Brettel Dawson (ed.), *Women, Law and Social Change: Core Readings and Current Issues*, pp. 191–192. Concord, ON: Captus Press.

Lamarche, Lucie. 2000. "Quebec Feminism, The Crisis of Rights and Research in the Law: Some Reasons to Worry . . . And Some Reasons to Hope." *Cahiers de recherche sociologique* 34: 99–126.

Lambert, Ronald D., and James E. Curtis. 1993. "Perceived Party Choice and Class Voting." *Canadian Journal of Political Science* 26: 273–286.

Langworthy, Robert H., and Lawrence F. Travis. 2003. *Policing in America, A Balance of Forces*. 3rd ed. Upper Saddle River, NJ: Prentice Hall.

La Porta, Rafael, Florencio Lopez-de-Silanes, Andrei Shleifer, and Robert W. Vishny. 1998. "Law and Finance." *Journal of Political Economy* 107: 1113–1155.

LaPrairie, Carol P. 1996. *Examining Aboriginal Corrections in Canada*. Ottawa: Supply and Services Canada.

Larsen, Nick. 1999. "The Politics of Law Reform: Prostitution Policy in Canada, 1985–1995," in Nick Larsen and Brian Burtch (eds.), *Law in Society: Canadian Readings*, pp. 60–74. Toronto: Harcourt.

Larson, Magali Sarfatti. 1977. *The Rise of Professionalism: A Sociological Analysis*. Berkeley and Los Angeles: University of California Press.

Lauderdale, Pat. 1997. "Indigenous North American Jurisprudence." *International Journal of Comparative Sociology* 38 (1–2) (June): 131–149.

Lavalette, Michael, and Alan Pratt (eds.). 2001. *Social Policy: A Conceptual and Theoretical Introduction*. 2nd ed. Thousand Oaks, CA: Sage.

Law and Society Review. 1995. "From the Editor." 29 (1): 5–9.

Law Reform Commission of Canada. 1975. Fourth Annual Report. Ottawa: Information Canada.

Law Society of Upper Canada. 2006. The Changing Face of the Legal Profession. Retrieved from www.lsuc.on.ca/news/a/fact/changing.

Lawyer's Almanac, 2004. 2004. Englewood Cliffs, NJ: Aspen Law and Business.

Lax, Jeffrey R. 2004. "Certiorari and Compliance in the Judicial Hierarchy: Discretion, Reputation and the Rule of Four." *Journal of Theoretical Politics* 15 (1): 61–79.

Lehrman, Frederica L. 1996. "Uncovering the Hidden Tort." *ABA Journal* 82 (9): 82.

Leiper, Jean MacKenzie. 1998. "Women Lawyers and Their Working Arrangements: Time

Crunch, Stress and Career Paths." *Canadian Journal of Law and Society* 13 (2) (Fall): 117–134. 2006. *Bar Codes: Women in the Legal Profession.* Vancouver: UBC Press.

Lempert, Richard O. 1978. "More Tales of Two Courts: Exploring Changes in the 'Dispute Settlement Function' of Trial Courts." *Law and Society Review* 13 (1) (Fall): 91–138. 1989. "Humility Is a Virtue: On the Publicization of Policy-Relevant Research." *Law and Society Review* 23 (1): 145–161. 2001. "Activist Scholarship." *Law and Society Review* 35 (1): 25–32.

Lempert, Richard, and Joseph Sanders. 1986. *An Invitation to Law and Social Science.* New York: Longman.

Leo, Richard A., and George C. Thomas III (eds.). 1998. *The Miranda Debate: Law, Justice, and Policing.* Boston: Northeastern University Press.

Leonard, Walter J. 1977. *Black Lawyers.* Boston: Senna and Shih.

Lesieur, Henry R. 1992. "Compulsive Gambling." *Society* 29 (4) (May–June): 43–50.

Lessan, Gloria T., and Joseph F. Sheley. 1992. "Does Law Behave? A Macrolevel Test of Black's Propositions on Change in Law." *Social Forces* 70 (3) (March): 655–678.

Levi, Avraham M. 1998. "Are Defendants Guilty If They Were Chosen in a Lineup?" *Law and Human Behavior* 22 (4) (August): 389–408.

Levine, James P. 1970. "Methodological Concerns in Studying Supreme Court Efficacy." *Law and Society Review* 4 (1) (May): 583–592.

Levy, Harold. 2005. "A Balance of Probabilities: A Murder Charge Against Rob Anderson, Laid After His Wife Kerry Was Found Dead, Was Dropped. Now Kerry's Mother Is Turning to the Civil Courts to Have Him Declared Guilty." *Toronto Star* (April 15): A3.

Lewin, Tamar. 1995. "Who Decides Who Will Die? Even Within States, It Varies." *New York Times* (February 23): A1, A13.

Li, Kejie, Jun Zhang, and Jaijian Deng. 2005 "Who Will Benefit from Reducing Capital Punishment? *Beijing Review* 48 (7) (February 17): 30–31.

Liebman, James S., Jeffrey Fagan, and Valerie West. 2000. "A Broken System: Error Rates in Capital Cases, 1973–1995." Retrieved from www.justicepolicy.net/jpreport/. 2002. "A Broken System, Part II: Why There Is So Much Error in Capital Cases and What Can Be Done About It." Retrieved from ccjr.policy.net/cjedfund/dpstudy.

Light, Ivan. 1977. "Numbers Gambling Among Blacks: A Financial Institution." *American Sociological Review* 42 (6) (December): 892–904.

Lilley, Lin S. 1994. "Techniques for Targeting Juror Bias." *Trial* 30 (11) (November): 74–80.

Lillie, J. J. M. 2002. "Sexuality and Cyberporn: Toward a New Agenda for Research." *Sexuality and Culture: An Interdisciplinary Quarterly* 6 (2) (Spring): 25–47.

Linden, Allen M. 2001. *Canadian Tort Law.* 7th ed. Toronto: LexisNexis and Butterworths.

Linden, Allen M., Lewis N. Klar, and Bruce Feldthusen. 2004. *Canadian Tort Law: Cases, Notes and Materials.* 12th ed. Toronto: LexisNexis and Butterworths.

Linden, Rick (ed.) 2004. *Criminology: A Canadian Perspective.* 5th ed. Toronto: Nelson Thomson.

Lindquist, Robert J. 1995. "Private Investigators with Accounting Acumen: Forensic Accountants Can Aid Attorneys in Recognizing and Ferreting Out White-Collar Crime." *National Law Journal* 17 (23) (February 6): B13.

Lippman, Matthew, Sean McConville, and Mordechai Yerushalmi. 1998. *Islamic Criminal Law and Procedure.* New York: Praeger.

Lipset, Seymour Martin. 1976. "The Wavering Polls." *Public Interest* 43 (Spring): 70–89 Liptak, Adam. 2001. "When Is a Fake Too Real? It's Virtually Uncertain." *New York Times* (January 28): WK3.

Llewellyn, Karl N. 1930/1960. *The Bramble Bush.* Dobbs Ferry, NY: Oceana.

Llewellyn, Karl N., and E. Adamson Hoebel. 1941. *The Cheyenne Way: Conflict and Case Law in Primitive Jurisprudence*. Norman, OK: University of Oklahoma Press.

Lo, Ven-hwei, and Ran Wei. 2002. "Third-Person Effect, Gender Pornography on the Internet." *Journal of Broadcasting and Electronic Media* 46 (1) (March): 13–33.

Loewenberg, Gerhard, Peverill Squire, and D. Roderick Kiewiet (eds.). 2002. *Legislatures: Comparative Perspectives on Representative Assemblies*. Ann Arbor: University of Michigan Press.

Loh, Wallace D. 1984. *Social Research in the Judicial Process: Cases, Readings, and Text*. New York: Russell Sage Foundation.

London, Ephraim (ed.). 1960. *The Law in Literature*. New York: Simon and Schuster.

London, Kamala, and Narina Nunez. 2001. "The Effect of Jury Deliberations on Jurors' Propensity to Disregard Inadmissible Evidence." *Journal of Applied Psychology* 85 (6) (December): 932–939.

Longride, Bridget N. 2006. "Introduction." *Roger Williams University Law Review* 11 (2) (Winter): 1.

Lonmo, Charlene. 2001. "Adult Correctional Services in Canada, 1999–00." *Juristat*, Catalogue No. 85-002-XPE, 21 (5), July.

Lott, John. 2000. *More Guns, Less Crime: Understanding Crime and Gun Control Laws*. 2nd ed. Chicago: University of Chicago Press. 2003. *The Bias Against Guns: Why Almost Everything You've Heard About Gun Control Is Wrong*. Washington, DC: Regnery.

Loveday, Barry. 1998. "Improving the Status of Police Patrol." *International Journal of the Sociology of Law* 26: 161–196.

Lowman, John. 2000. "Violence and the Outlaw Status of (Street) Prostitution in Canada." *Violence Against Women* 6 (9) (September): 987–1011.

Lowman, John, Robert J. Menzies, and Ted S. Palys. 1987. *Transcarceration: Essays in the Sociology of Social Control*. Aldershot, UK: Gower.

Lowman, John, and Ted Palys. 2000. "Ethics and Institutional Conflict of Interest: The Research Confidentiality Controversy at Simon Fraser University." *Sociological Practice* 2 (4) (December): 245–264.

Lu, Hong, and Lening Zhang. 2005. "Death Penalty in China: The Law and the Practice." *Journal of Criminal Justice* 33 (4) (July/August): 367–376.

Luff, D. 2001. "'The Downright Torture of Women': Moral Lobby Women, Feminists and Pornography." *The Sociology Review* 49 (1) (February): 78–99.

Luo, Shuze. 2000. "Some Hot Issues in Our Work on Religion." *Chinese Law and Government* 33 (2) (March/April): 101–106.

Luyster, Deborah. 1997. "Crossing the Bar— Lawyering Skills in Law and Literature." The Column of the Legal Education Committee, *Michigan Bar Association Journal*. Retrieved from www.michbar.org/journal/ article.cfm?articleID=376andvolumeID=27.

Lyman, Michael D. 2004. *The Police: An Introduction*. 3rd ed. Upper Saddle River, NJ: Prentice Hall.

Lynch, D. R., and T. D. Evans. 2004. "Attributes of Highly Effective Criminal Defence Negotiators." *Journal of Criminal Justice* 30 (5): 387–396.

Lyons, William T., Jr. 1999. *The Politics of Community Policing: Rearranging the Power to Punish*. Ann Arbor: University of Michigan Press.

Macaulay, Stewart. 1969. "Non-Contractual Relations in Business," in Vilhelm Aubert (ed.), *Sociology of Law*, pp. 194–209. Harmondsworth, UK: Penguin.

MacCoun, Robert K., and Peter Reuter. 2001. "Does Europe Do It Better? Lessons from Holland, Britain and Switzerland," in D. Stanley Eitzen and Craig S. Leedham (eds.), *Solutions to Social Problems*, pp. 260–264. Boston: Allyn and Bacon.

MacDonald, Alex. 1999. *Outrage: Canada's Justice System on Trial*. Vancouver: Raincoast Books.

Macdonald, Keith M. 1995. *The Sociology of Professions*. Thousand Oaks, CA: Sage.

Machado, Nora, and Tom R. Burns. 2000. "The New Genetics: A Social Science and Humanities Research Agenda." *Canadian Journal of Sociology* 25 (4) (Fall): 495–506.

Machum, Susan T. 2002. "The Farmer Takes a Wife and the Wife Takes the Farm: Marriage and Farming," in Gayle M. MacDonald (ed.), *Social Context and Social Location in the Sociology of Law*, pp. 133–158. Peterborough, ON: Broadview Press.

MacKenzie, Gavin. 1999. *Lawyers and Ethics: Professional Responsibility and Discipline*. 2nd ed. Scarborough, ON: Carswell.

MacKinnon, Catherine A. 1987. *Feminism Unmodified: Discourses on Life and Law*. Cambridge, MA: Harvard University Press. 1993. *Only Words*. Cambridge, MA: Harvard University Press.

Macklin, A. 1992. "Symes v. M. N. R.: Where Sex Meets Class." *Canadian Journal of Women and the Law* 5: 498–517.

Maclean's. 1999a. "No Title." (January 11): 16. 2006. "Crooked Doctors." (February 3): 10–11. 1999b. "The Pill, Finally." (June 14): 53. 2006. "Avoiding the Evil Eye." (March 6): 11. 2006a. "What It Means To Be Free." (February 27): 4. 2006b. "Making History in Liberia." (February 6): 44–45. 2006c. "What It Means To Be Free." (February 27): 4.

Macnamara, Don. 2002. "September 11, 2001–September 11, 2002." *Policy Options* 23 (6) (September): 14–17.

Mac Neil, Michael. 2002a. "Governing Employment," in Michael Mac Neil, Neil Sargent, and Peter Swan (eds.), *Law, Regulation, and Governance*, pp. 171–187. Don Mills, ON: Oxford University Press. 2002b. "Cyberspace Governance: Canadian Reflections," in Michael Mac Neil, Neil Sargent, and Peter Swan (eds.), *Law, Regulation, and Governance*, pp. 264–286. Don Mills, ON: Oxford University Press.

Mac Neil, Michael, Neil Sargent, and Peter Swan (eds.). 2002. *Law, Regulation and Governance*. Don Mills, ON: Oxford University Press.

Mahood, H. R. 2000. *Interest Group Politics in America: A New Intensity*. Englewood Cliffs, NJ: Prentice Hall.

Maine, Sir Henry Sumner. 1861. *Ancient Law*. London: J. Murray. 2003. *Ancient Law: Its Connection with the Early History of Society, and Its Relation to Modern Ideas*. 2003 ed., Holmes Beach, FL: Gaunt.

Makin, Kirk. 2006. "Divorce Ruling Threatens to Open Floodgates." *Globe and Mail* (June 22): A1.

Malamuth, Neil M., Tamara Addision, and Mary Koss. 2000. "Pornography and Sexual Aggression: Are There Reliable Effects and Can We Understand Them?" *Annual Review of Sex Research* 11: 26–91.

Malarek. 2003. "A Gambler's Rehab Gone Wrong." *Globe and Mail* (July 30): A1.

Malette v. Shulman, Ontario Court of Appeal, 1990, 2 C.C.L.T. (2d) 1, 67 D.L.R. (4th) 321 (cited in Allen M. Linden, Lewis N. Klar, and Bruce Feldthusen [2004]. *Canadian Tort Law: Cases, Notes and Materials*. 12th ed. Toronto: LexisNexis and Butterworths).

Maloney, William A., Grant Jordan, and Andrew M. McLaughlin. 1994. "Interest Groups and Public Policy: The Insider/Outsider Model Revisited." *Journal of Public Policy* 14 (1) (January-March): 17–39.

Mandel, Michele. 2005. "A Wrong Righted." *Sunday Sun* (April 24): 36.

Mandy, Martha. (ed.) 2002. *Law and Anthropology*. Aldershot, UK; Burlington, VT: Ashgate/Darmouth.

Mangione, Thomas W. 1995. *Mail Surveys*. Thousand Oaks, CA: Sage.

Manning, Carl. 1995. "Legal Party's Over, Inmates Told: Attorney General Clamps Down on Frivolous Suits." *St. Louis Post-Dispatch* (September 6): 1B.

Manning, Peter K. 1975. "Deviance and Dogma." *British Journal of Criminology* 15 (1) (January): 1–20.

Mansnerus, Laura. 1995. "Good Job, Great Pay: Legal Officer for a Company." *New York Times* (February 10): B13.

Marez, Curtis. 2004. *Drug Wars: The Political Economy of Narcotics*. Minneapolis, MN: University of Minnesota Press.

Margolick, David. 1992. "Chorus of Judicial Critics Assail Sentencing Guides." *New York Times* (April 12): A1, A20.

Marlow, Leonard, and S. Richard Sauber. 1990. *The Handbook of Divorce Mediation*. New York: Plenum.

Marquis, Joshua A. 2005. "The Myth of Innocence." *The Journal of Criminal Law and Criminology* 95 (2) (Winter): 501–521.

Marsil, Dorothy F., Jean Montoya, and David Ross. 2002. "Child Witness Policy: Law Interfacing with Social Science." *Law and Contemporary Problems* 65 (1) (Winter): 209–241.

Martin, John M., and Anne T. Romano. 1992. *Multinational Crime: Terrorism, Espionage, Drug and Arms Trafficking*. Newbury Park, CA: Sage.

Martin, Sheilah, and Kathleen Mahoney (eds.). 1987. *Equality and Judicial Neutrality*. Toronto: Carswell.

Marx, Karl. 1959. "A Contribution to the Critique of Political Economy," in L. S. Feuer (ed.), *Marx and Engels: Basic Writing on Politics and Philosophy*, pp. 42–46. Garden City, NY: Doubleday.

Marx, Karl, and Friedrich Engels. 1955. *The Communist Manifesto*. New York: Appleton-Century-Crofts. Originally published in 1848.

Mashhour, Amira. 2005. "Islamic Law and Gender Equality—Could There Be a Common Ground?: A Study of Divorce and Polygamy in Sharia Law and Contemporary Legislation in Tunisia and Egypt." *Human Rights Quarterly* 27 (2) (May): 562–596.

Massell, Gregory. 1973. "Revolutionary Law in Soviet Central Asia," in Donald Black and Maureen Mileski (eds.), *The Social Organization of Law*, pp. 226–261. New York: Seminar Press.

Massing, Michael. 1998. *The Fix*. New York: Simon and Schuster.

Mathison, Sandra (ed.). 2005. *Encyclopedia of Education*. Thousand Oaks, CA: Sage.

Maticka-Tyndale, Eleanor, Jacqueline Lewis, and Megan Street. 2005. "Making a Place for Escort Work: A Case Study." *The Journal of Sex Research* 42 (1) (February): 46–53.

Matsumoto, David, and Linda Juang. 2004. *Culture and Psychology*. 3rd ed. Belmont, CA: Wadsworth/Thomson.

Mattei, Ugo. 1997. *Comparative Law and Economics*. Ann Arbor: University of Michigan Press.

Matthew, Roger, and Maggie O'Neill (eds.). 2003. *Prostitution*. Burlington, VT: Ashgate/Dartmouth.

Mawhinney, V. T. 1998. "Behavioral Maladaption Contagion in America: An Applied Theoretical Analysis." *Behavior and Social Issues* 8 (2): 159–185.

May, David A., and James E. Headley. 2004. *Identity Theft*. New York: Peter Lang.

Mayer, Ann Elizabeth. 1999. *Islam and Human Rights: Tradition and Politics*. Boulder, CO: Westview Press.

Mayhew, Leon H. 1971. "Stability and Change in Legal Systems," in Bernard Barber and Alex Inkeles (eds.), *Stability and Social Change*, pp. 187–210. Boston: Little, Brown.

Mays, Larry G., and Peter R. Gregware (eds.). 2001. *Courts and Justice, A Reader.* 2nd ed. Prospect Heights, IL: Waveland Press.

Mazur, B. 1989. "Access to Legal Education and the Profession in Canada," in R. Dhavan, N. Kibble, and W. Twining (eds.), *Access to Legal Education and the Legal Profession*, pp. 114–131. London: Butterworths.

McAdam, Doug, and David A. Snow (eds.). 1997. *Social Movements: Readings on Their Emergence, Mobilization, and Dynamics*. Los Angeles: Roxbury.

McAlinden, Anne-Marie. 2005. "The Use of 'Shame' With Sexual Offenders." *British Journal of Criminology* 45 (3) (May): 373–394.

McBarnet, Doreen. 2004. *Crime, Compliance and Control*. Burlington, VT: Ashgate/Dartmouth.

McCann, Charles R. 2004. *Individualism and the Social Order: The Social Element in Liberal Thought*. New York: Routledge.

McCarthy, John F. 2005. "Between Adat and State: Institutional Arrangements on Sumatra's Forest Frontier." *Human Ecology* 33 (1) (February): 57–82.

McCorkle, Suzanne, and Melanie Reese. 2005. *Mediation Theory and Practice*. Boston, MA: Allyn and Bacon.

McCormick, Peter. 1994. *Canada's Courts*. Toronto: James Lorimer. 2006. "Where Does the Supreme Court Caseload Come From? Appeals from the Atlantic Courts of Appeal, 2000–2005." Retrieved from www.cpsa-acsp.ca/papers-2006/McCormick.pdf.

McCormick, Peter, and Ian Greene. 1990. *Judges and Judging: Inside the Canadian Judicial System*. Toronto: James Lorimer.

McCullagh, Declan. 2002. "Report: Anti-Terror Efforts Pinch Privacy." CNET News.com (September 3). Retrieved from news.com.com/2102-1023-956286.html.

McGillivray, A., and B. Comaskey. 1999. *Black Eyes All of the Time: Intimate Violence, Aboriginal Women, and the Justice System*. Toronto: University of Toronto Press.

McGuire, Kevin T. 1994. "Amici Curiae and Strategies for Gaining Access to the Supreme Court." *Political Research Quarterly* 47 (4) (December): 821–838.

McIlroy, Anne. 2005. "One Law To Rule Them All." *Guardian Unlimited*. (September 14). Retrieved from www.guardian.co.uk/ elsewhere/journalist/story/0,7792,1569677, 00.html.

McIntyre, Lisa J. 1994. *Law in the Sociological Enterprise: A Reconstruction*. Boulder, CO: Westview Press. 2005. *Need to Know: Social Science Research Methods*. Boston: McGraw-Hill.

McIntyre, Sheila. 1995. "Gender Bias Within the Law School: 'The Memo' and Its Impact," in The Chilly Collective (eds.), *Breaking Anonymity: The Chilly Climate for Women Faculty*, pp. 211–264. Waterloo, ON: Wilfred Laurier University Press.

McLachlin, Beverley, The Honourable Madam Justice. 1992. "Rules and Discretion in the Governance of Canada." *Saskatchewan Law Review* 56: 168–179.

McLaren, Peter, and Ramin Farahmandpur. 2004. *Teaching Against the Tide: Essays in Critical Pedagogy*. Lanham, MD: Rowman and Littlefield.

McLellan, A. Anne. 2002. "Medical Marijuana." *National Post* (August 29): A19.

McMichael, Philip. 2004. *Development and Social Change*. 3rd ed. Thousand Oaks, CA: Pine Forge Press.

McMullan, John L. 1992. *Beyond the Limits of the Law: Corporate Crime and Law and Order*. Halifax: Fernwood.

Mead, Margaret (ed.). 1953. *Cultural Patterns and Technical Change*. Paris: UNESCO.

Mears, T. Lambert. 2004. *The Institutes of Gaius and Justinian: The Twelve Tables, and the CXVIIIth and CXVIIth Novels, with Introduction and Translation*. Clark, NJ: Lawbook Exchange.

Meenaghan, Thomas M., Keith M. Kilty, and John G. McNutt. 2004. *Social Policy Analysis and Practice*. Chicago: Lyceum Books.

Meier, Andrew. 1995. "The Chechen Mafia: The Real Reason Yeltsin Invaded." *New Republic* 212 (17) (April 24): 16–18.

Melling, Tom. 1994. "Dispute Resolution Within Legislative Institutions." *Stanford Law Review* 46 (6) (July): 1677–1715.

Menkel-Meadow, Carrie (ed.). 2003. *Dispute Processing and Conflict Resolution: Theory, Practice and Policy*. Burlington, VT: Ashgate.

Mermin, Samuel. 1992. *Law and the Legal System: An Introduction*. 2nd ed. Boston: Little, Brown.

Merton, Robert K. 1957. *Social Theory and Social Structure*. New York: Free Press.

Miceli, Thomas J. 1998. "Settlement Strategies." *Journal of Legal Studies* 27 (2) (June): 473–482.

Michaels, Priscilla. 1978. "Review of Black's The Behavior of Law." *Contemporary Sociology* 7 (1) (January): 10–11.

Miethe, Terance D. 1995. "Predicting Future Litigiousness." *Justice Quarterly* 12 (3): 562–581.

Milgram, Stanley. 1975. *Obedience to Authority.* New York: Harper Colophon Books.

Miller, Arthur Selwyn. 1979. *Social Change and Fundamental Law: America's Evolving Constitution.* Westport, CT: Greenwood Press.

Miller, J. M., and J. E. Shutt. 2001. "Considering the Need for Empirically Grounded Drug Court Screening Mechanisms." *Journal of Drug Issues* 1 (1): 91–106.

Miller, Mary Jane. 1995. "Mirrors in the Robing Room: Reflections of Lawyers and the Law in Canadian Television Drama." *Canadian Journal of Law and Society* 10 (2) (Fall): 55–71.

Miller, Susan L. (ed.). 1998. *Crime Control and Women: Feminist Implications of Criminal Justice Policy.* Thousand Oaks, CA: Sage.

Mills, C. Wright. 1957. *The Power Elite.* New York: Oxford University Press.

Milor, Vedat. (ed.). 1994. *Changing Political Economies: Privatization in Post-Communist and Reforming Communist States.* Boulder, CO: Lynne Rienner.

Milovanovic, Dragan. 2003. *A Primer in the Sociology of Law.* 3rd ed. New York: Criminal Justice Press.

Minda, Gary. 1997. "Law and Literature at Century's End." *Cardozo Studies in Law and Literature* 9 (2): 245–258.

Mink, Gwendolyn, and Rickie Solinger (eds.) 2004. *Welfare: A Documentary History of U.S. Policy and Politics.* New York: New York University Press.

Mitrovica, Andrew. 2002. *Covert Entry: Spies, Lies and Crimes Inside Canada's Secret Service.* Toronto: Random House.

Monahan, John, and Laurens Walker. 1991. "Judicial Use of Social Science Research." *Law and Human Behavior* 15 (6) (December): 571–584. 1998. *Social Science in Law: Cases and Materials.* 4th ed. Westbury, NY: Foundation Press.

Montesquieu, Baron de. 1748/1989. *The Spirit of the Law.* Translated and edited by Anne M. Cohler, Basia Carolyn Miller, and Harold Samuel Stone. Cambridge: Cambridge University Press.

Monture-Agnes, P. 1999. "Standing Against Canadian Law: Naming Omissions of Race, Culture, and Gender," in Elizabeth Comack (ed.), *Locating Law: Race/Class/Gender Connections*, pp. 76–97. Halifax, NS: Fernwood Books.

Moog, Robert. 1993. "Indian Litigiousness and the Litigation Explosion." *Asian Survey* 33 (12) (December): 1136–1151.

Mooney, Linda, David Knox, Caroline Schacht, and Adie Nelson. 2004. *Understanding Social Problems.* 2nd ed. Toronto: Nelson Thomson.

Moore, Christopher. 1997. *The Law Society of Upper Canada and Ontario Lawyers 1797–1997.* Toronto: University of Toronto Press.

Moore, Elizabeth, and Michael Mills. 1990. "The Neglected Victims and Unexamined Costs of White Collar Crime." *Crime and Delinquency* 36: 408–418.

Morales, Alfonso (ed.). 2003. *Renascent Pragmatism: Studies in Law and Social Sciences.* Burlington, VT: Ashgate.

Morawetz, T. 1993. "Ethics and Style: The Lessons of Literature for Law." *Stanford Law Review* 45: 497–521.

Morden, Reid. 2002. "Finding the Right Balance." *Policy Options* (September): 48

Morgan, Patricia A. 1978. "The Legislation of Drug Law: Economic Crisis and Social Control." *Journal of Drug Issues* 8: 53–62.

Morgenthau, Hans. 1993. *Politics Among Nations.* New York: McGraw-Hill. Revised by Kenneth W. Thompson.

Morgenthau, Robert M. 1995. "What Prosecutors Won't Tell You: Capital Punishment Is the

Enemy of Law Enforcement." *New York Times* (February 7): A25.

Morse, Janice M., and Peggy Anne Field. 1995. *Qualitative Research Methods*. 2nd ed. Thousand Oaks, CA: Sage Publicatons.

Morton, Desmond, and Morton Weinfeld (eds.). 1998. *Who Speaks for Canada? Words That Shape a Country*. Toronto: McClelland and Stewart.

Morton, F. L., and A. Allen. 2001. "Feminists and the Courts: Measuring Success in Interest Group Litigation in Canada." *Canadian Journal of Political Science* 34 (1): 55–84.

Moses, Jonathan, and Richard B. Schmitt. 1992. "Lawyer's Billing Practices Are Scrutinized." *Wall Street Journal* (April 6): B7.

Mossman, Mary Jane. 1994. "Gender Equality, Family Law, and Access to Justice." *International Journal of Law and the Family* 8 (3) (December): 357–373. 1998. "The Paradox of Feminist Engagement with Law," in Nancy Mandell (ed.), *Feminist Issues: Race, Class, and Sexuality*, pp. 180–207. 2nd ed. Scarborough, ON: Allyn and Bacon. 1999. "Legal Aid," in James H. Marsh (ed.), *The Canadian Encyclopedia*, pp. 1318–1319. Toronto: McClelland and Stewart.

Mousourakis, George. 2003. *The Historical and Institutional Context of Roman Law*. Burlington, VT: Ashgate/Dartmouth.

Moynihan, Daniel Patrick. 1969. *Maximum Feasible Misunderstanding*. New York: Free Press. 1979. "Social Science and the Courts." *Public Interest* 54 (Winter): 12–31. 1989. "Toward a Post-Industrial Social Policy." *Public Interest* 96 (Summer): 16–27. 1998. *Secrecy: The American Experience*. New Haven, CT: Yale University Press.

Mulcahy, Aogan. 1994. "The Justification of 'Justice': Legal Practitioners' Accounts of Negotiated Case Settlements in Magistrates' Courts (United Kingdom)." *British Journal of Criminology* 34 (4) (Autumn): 411–430.

Mullan, David. 2001. *Administrative Law*. Toronto: Irwin.

Mullard, Maurice, and Paul Spicker. 1998. *Social Policy in a Changing Society*. New York: Routledge.

Mullis, Jeffrey. 1995. "Medical Malpractice, Social Structure and Social Control." *Sociological Forum* 10 (1) (March): 135–163.

Mundy, Martha (ed.). 2002. *Law and Anthropology*. Aldershot, UK: Ashgate/Dartmouth.

Munger, Frank. 2001. "Inquiry and Activism in Law and Society." *Law and Society Review* 35 (1).

Murdocca, Carmela. 2004. "The Racial Profile: Governing Race Through Knowledge Production." *Canadian Journal of Law and Society* 19 (2): 153–167.

Myers, John E. B. 2002. "Liability Considerations in Child Welfare: Lessons from Canada." *Child Abuse and Neglect* 26 (10) (October): 1007–1009.

Myers, Ken. 1994. "Sometimes It's Not What You Know: Law Deans Debate Admitting Students for the Wealth and Influence They Bring." *National Law Journal* 17 (4) (September 26): A1.

Nadelmann, Ethan A. 2006. "An End to Marijuana Prohibition: The Drive to Legalize Pick Ups," in Thomas Hickey (ed.), *Taking Sides: Clashing Views in Crime and Criminology*. Dubuque, IA: McGraw-Hill.

Nader, Laura, and Harry F. Todd, Jr. 1978. "Introduction: The Disputing Process," in Laura Nader and Harry F. Todd, Jr. (eds.), *The Disputing Process—Law in Ten Societies*, pp. 1–40. New York: Columbia University Press.

Nader, Ralph. 1965. *Unsafe at Any Speed: The Designed-in Dangers of the American Automobile*. New York: Grossman. 1969. "Law Schools and Law Firms." *New Republic* (October 11): 21–23.

Naffine, Ngaire. 1990. *Law and the Sexes: Explorations in Feminist Jurisprudence*. Sydney, Australia: Allen and Unwin.

Nagel, Stuart S. (ed.). 1970. *Law and Social Change*. Beverly Hills, CA: Sage. 1993. *Legal Scholarship, Microcomputers, and Super-Optimizing Decision-Making*. Westport, CT: Quorum Books.

Nagel, Stuart S., and Marian Neef. 1977. *The Legal Process: Modeling the System*. Beverly Hills, CA: Sage.

Nagpaul, Hans. 1994. "The Legal Profession in Indian Society: A Case Study of Lawyers at a Local Level in North India." *International Journal of the Sociology of Law* 22: 59–76.

Nasheri, Hedie. 1998. *Betrayal of Due Process. A Comparative Assessment of Plea Bargaining in the United States and Canada*. Lanham, MD: University Press of America.

Nathan, Richard P. 2000. *Social Science in Government: The Role of Policy Researchers*, updated ed. Albany, NY: Rockefeller Institute Press.

National Post. 2005. "Robert Blake Ordered to Pay $30M in Damages for Shooting Death of Wife." (November 19): A3.

Naysnerski, Wendy, and Tom Tietenberg. 1992. "Private Enforcement of Federal Environmental Law." *Law Economics* 68 (1) (February): 28–48.

Neacsu, E. Dana. 2000. "CLS Stands for Critical Legal Studies, If Anyone Remembers." *Journal of Law and Policy* 8: 415.

Negley, Glenn. 1965. *Political Authority and Moral Judgment*. Durham, NC: Duke University Press.

Nelson, Adie. 1994. "'Employment Equity' and the Red Queen's Hypothesis: Recruitment and Hiring in Western Canadian Municipal Police Forces." *Canadian Police College Journal* 16 (3): 184–203. 1994. "Females Who Sexually Abuse Children: A Discussion of Gender Stereotypes and Symbolic Assailants." *Qualitative Sociology* 17 (1): 63–88.

Nelson, E. D., and Augie Fleras. 1995. *Social Problems in Canada: Issues and Challenges*. Scarborough, ON: Prentice Hall.

Nelson, Robert L. 2001. "Law, Democracy, and Domination: Law and Society Research as Critical." *Law and Society Review* 35 (1): 33–37.

Nemeth, Charles, and K. C. Poulin. 2005. *Private Security and Public Safety*. Upper Saddle River, NJ: Pearson.

Neusner, Jacob, and Tamara Sonn. 1999. *Comparing Religions Through Law: Judaism and Islam*. New York: Routledge.

Newsweek. 1989. "The Future of Abortion: The Court Drills a Crack in the Foundation of Roe." (July 17): 14–27. 1995a. "Slammer Suits" (August 7): 6. 2003. "Lawsuit Hell, How Fear of Litigation Is Paralyzing Our Professions." (December 15): 43–51.

New York Times. 1986. "Suing the Clergy." (September 2): 1F. 1995a. "Mere Fraction of Civil Cases End with Punitive Awards." (July 21): B12. 1995b. "Rising Concern About Stress in Lawyer's Lives." (March 10): B15. 1995c. "Can New York Live with It?" (February 26): F2. 1995d. "Handgun Use Rose in 1993, Report Shows." (July 10): A6.

Nimkoff, Meyer F. 1957. "Obstacles to Innovation," in Francis R. Allen, Hornell Hart, Delbert C. Miller, William F. Ogburn, and Meyer F. Nimkoff, *Technology and Social Change*, pp. 56–71. New York: Appleton-Century-Crofts.

Nisbet, Robert A. 1969. *Social Change and History*. New York: Oxford University Press. 2000. *Twilight of Authority*. Indianapolis, IN: Liberty Fund, with new introduction. Originally published in 1975, New York: Oxford University Press.

Nock, Steven L., and Paul W. Kingston. 1990. *The Sociology of Public Issues*. Belmont, CA: Wadsworth.

Nonet, Philippe. 1976. "For Jurisprudential Sociology." *Law and Society Review* 10 (4) (Summer): 525–545.

Nonet, Philippe, and Philip Selznick. 2001. *Law and Society in Transition: Toward Responsive Law*. New Brunswick, NJ: Transaction.

Nordlinger, Jay. 2002. "Impromptus." *National Review* Online (December 11). Retrieved from http://overlawyered.com/archives/02/jan1.html.

Noreau, Pierre. 2000. "Norm, Commandment and Law: Law as an Object of Interdisciplinary Analysis." *Politique et Societes* 19 (2–3): 153–177.

Nossel, Suzanne, and Elizabeth Westfall. 1998. *Presumed Equal: What America's Top Women Lawyers Really Think About Their Firms*. Franklin Lakes, NJ: Career Press.

Nussbaum, Martha C. 1999. *Sex and Social Justice.* New York: Oxford University Press.

O'Barr, William M. 1983. "The Study of Language in Institutional Contexts." *Journal of Language and Social Psychology* 2: 241–251. 1982. *Linguistic Evidence: Language, Power and Strategy in the Courtroom.* New York: Academic Press.

O'Barr, William M., and John M. Conley. 1985. "Litigant Satisfaction Versus Legal Adequacy in Small Claims Court Narratives." *Law and Society Review* 19: 661–701.

Oberschall, Anthony. 1973. *Social Conflict and Social Movements.* Englewood Cliffs, NJ: Prentice Hall.

O'Brien, Timothy L. 1998. "Gambling: Married to the Action, for Better or Worse." *New York Times* (November 8): WK3.

O'Connell, John P., Jr. 1995. "Throwing Away the Key (and State Money): Study Reveals Ineffectiveness of Mandatory Sentencing Policies." *Spectrum: The Journal of State Government* 68 (1) (Winter): 28–32.

O'Donovan-Polten, Sheelagh. 2001. *The Scales of Success: Constructions of Life-Career Success of Eminent Men and Women Lawyers.* Toronto: University of Toronto Press.

Office of the Registrar of Lobbyists. 2005. "Message from the Registrar of Lobbyists." Retrieved from strategis.ic.gc.ca/epic/internet/inlobbyist-lobbyiste.nsf/en/Home.

Official Guide to U.S. Law Schools 2000. 2000. New York: Times Books/Random House.

Ohlin, Lloyd E. 1975. "Report on the President's Commission on Law Enforcement and Administration of Justice," in Mirra Komarovsky (ed.), *Sociology and Public Policy: The Case of Presidential Commissions*, pp. 93–115. New York: Elsevier.

Okin, Susan. 1999. "Is Multiculturalism Bad for Women?" in Joshua Cohen, Matthew Howard, and Martha C. Nussbaum (eds.) *Is Multiculturalism Bad for Women?* pp. 9–24. Princeton, NJ: Princeton University Press. 1998. "Feminism and Multiculturalism: Some Tensions." *Ethics* 108 (4): 661–684.

Oleinik, Anton N. 2003. *Organized Crime, Prison and Post-Soviet Societies.* Burlington, VT: Ashgate.

Olivo, Laurence M. 2001. "Introduction to Legal Studies—Law as a Concept and System" in Laurence Olivo (ed.) *Introduction to Law in Canada*, pp. 1–19. Concord, ON: Captus Press. 2001a. "Types of Law," in Laurence Olivo (ed.), *Introduction to Law in Canada*, pp. 83–92. Concord, ON: Captus Press. 2004. "Sources of Law," in Laurence M. Olivo (ed.), *Introduction to Law in Canada*, pp. 63–82. Concord, ON: Captus Press.

Olson, Walter K. 1991a. *The Litigation Explosion.* New York: Dutton. 1991b. "The Selling of the Law." *American Enterprise* (January–February): 27–35. 2003. *The Rule of Lawyers: How the New Litigation Elite Threatens America's Rule of Law.* New York: St. Martin's Press. 2004. "Capped in Canada." (July 26). Retrieved from http://overlawyered.com/canada.

Ontario Law Reform Commission. 1991. *Report on Exemplary Damages.* Toronto: Queen's Printer Ontario.

Ontario Provincial Police Association. 1993. "A Symposium on Police: The Community and the Police, a Working Partnership." Symposium transcripts, January 26 and 27, Regal Constellation Hotel, Toronto.

Ontario Women's Justice Network. 2000. "*Jane Doe v. Board of Commissioners of Police of Toronto.*" Retrieved from www.owjn.org. 2001. "Important Jane Doe v. Toronto Police Service Developments." Retrieved from www.owjn.org.

O'Reilly, Robert C., and Edward T. Green. 1992. *School Law for the 1990s: A Handbook.* New York: Greenwood Press.

Orr, Larry L. 1998. *Social Experiments: Evaluating Public Programs with Experimental Methods.* Thousand Oaks, CA: Sage.

Osborn, Fairfield. 1948. *Our Plundered Planet.* Boston: Little, Brown.

Osborne, Philip H. 2003. *The Law of Torts:* 2nd Edition. Toronto: Irwin Law.

Ost, Francois. 2006. "The Law as Mirrored in Literature." *SubStance* 35 (1): 3–19.

Owen, Michelle. 2000. "'Not the Same Story': Conducting Interviews with Queer Community Activists." *Resources for Feminist Research* 28 (1-2) (Spring/Summer): 49–60.

Oxford English Dictionary. 2005. London, UK: Oxford University Press.

Pacienza, Angela. 2001. "Government Loses Bid To Appeal Paycheque for Hep C Lawyers." (January 24). Retrieved from http: //www. hepnet./com/hepc/news012401.html.

Packer, Herbert L., and Thomas Ehrlich. 1972. *New Directions in Legal Education*. New York: McGraw-Hill.

PACT (People Against Coercive Treatment). 2002. "The Tory Psychiatric State: A Few 'Mental Health' Facts." Retrieved from www.tao.ca/~pact/Mental_ Health_Fact_Sheet.html.

Palermo, George B., Maxine Aldridge White, Lew A. Wasserman, and William Hanrahan. 1998. "Plea Bargaining: Injustice for All?" *International Journal of Offender Therapy and Comparative Criminology* 42 (2) (June): 111–123.

Palmer, Michael, and Simon Roberts. 1998. *Dispute Processes: ADR and the Primary Forms of Decision Making*. London: Butterworths.

Palys, Ted, and John Lowman. 2002. "Anticipating Law: Research Methods, Ethics, and the Law of Privilege." *Sociological Methodology* 32: 1–17.

Panitch, Leo. 2002. "Violence as a Tool of Order and Change: The War on Terrorism and the Anti-Globalization Movement." *Policy Options* 23 (6) (September): 40–44.

Pap, Elliot. 2006. "Bertuzzi Now Facing Lawsuit in B.C. Too: Moore Files Another." *National Post* (March 8): S3.

Papke, David R. (ed.). 1991. *Narrative and the Legal Discourse*. Liverpool, UK: Deborah Charles. 1990. "Discharge as Document: Appreciating the Storytelling of Appellate Opinions." *Journal of Legal Education* 40: 145–159.

Paringaux, Roland-Pierre. 1998. "Prostitution Takes a Turn for the West." *Guardian Weekly* 158 (21) (May 24): 18.

Parsons, Talcott. 1962. "The Law and Social Control," in William M. Evan (ed.), *Law and Sociology: Exploratory Essays*, pp. 56–62. New York: Free Press. 1964. "Evolutionary Universals in Society." *American Sociological Review* 29 (3) (June): 339–357.

Passas, Nikos (ed.) 2003. *International Crimes*. Aldershot, UK: Ashgate.

Peach, Lucinda. 2002. *Legislating Morality: Pluralism and Religious Identity in Lawmaking*. New York: Oxford University Press.

Peak, Kenneth J., and Ronald W. Glensor. 2004. *Community Policing and Problem Solving: Strategies and Practices*. 4th ed. Upper Saddle River, NJ: Prentice Hall.

Pearce, Frank. 1976. *Crimes of the Powerful*. London: Pluto Press.

Pearce, Frank, and Steve Tombs. 1998. *Toxic Capitalism: Corporate Crime and the Chemical Industry*. Brookfield, VT: Ashgate.

Peay, Jill (ed.). 1998. *Criminal Justice and the Mentally Disordered*. Brookfield, VT: Ashgate.

Peeples, Ralph, Catherine T. Harris, and Thomas B. Metzloff. 2000. "Settlement Has Many Faces: Physicians, Attorneys and Medical Malpractice." *Journal of Health and Social Behavior* 41 (2): 333–346.

Pepinsky, Harold E. 1976. *Crime and Conflict: A Study of Law and Society*. New York: Academic Press.

Perelman, Michael. 2003. "The Political Economy of Intellectual Property." *Monthly Review* 54 (8) (January): 29–37.

Perlez, Jane. 1995. "Poles Dismayed at Unchecked Crime." *New York Times* (June 19): A5.

Peters, Julie Stone. 2005. "Law, Literature and the Vanishing Real: On the Future of an Interdisciplinary Illusion." *PMLA* 120 (2).

Petrunik, Michael. 2003. "The Hare and the Tortoise: Dangerousness and Sex Offender Policy in the United States and Canada."

Canadian Journal of Criminology and Criminal Justice 45 (1) (January): 43–72.

Pfennigstorf, Werner. 1993. *Personal Injury Compensation: A Comparative Analysis of Major European Jurisdictions*. London: Lloyd's of London Press.

Phillips, Scott. 2003. "The Social Structure of Vengeance: A Test of Black's Model." *Criminology* 41 (3) (August): 673–708.

Phillips, Scott, and Ryken Grattet. 2000. "Judicial Rhetoric, Meaning-Making and the Institutionalization of Hate Crime Law." *Law and Society Review* 34 (3): 567–606.

Phillips, Scott, and Mark Cooney. 2005. "Aiding Peace, Abetting Violence: Third Parties and the Management of Conflict." *American Sociological Review* 70 (2) (April): 334–354.

Piaget, Jean. 1965. *The Moral Judgment of the Child*. New York: Free Press. Originally published in 1932.

Picard, Cheryl A., and R. P. Saunders. 2002. "The Regulation of Mediation," in Michael Mac Neil, Neil Sargent, and Peter Swann (eds.), *Law, Regulation, and Governance*, pp. 223–238. Don Mills, ON: Oxford University Press.

Pierce, Jennifer L. 1995. *Gender Trials: Emotional Lives in Contemporary Law Firms*. Berkeley, CA: University of California Press.

Pierce, Richard J., Jr. 1995. "Seven Ways to Deossify Agency Rule Making." *Administrative Law Review* 47 (1) (Winter): 59–95.

Pitulla, Joanne. 1995. "Firm Commitments: Lawyers Cannot Ignore Duty to Report Ethics Violations by Colleagues." *ABA Journal* 81 (April): 108–109.

Piven, Frances Fox, and Richard A. Cloward. 1993. *Regulating the Poor: The Functions of Public Welfare*. Rev. ed. New York: Vintage Books.

Podgers, James. 1994. "Chasing the Ideal: As More Americans Find Themselves Priced out of the System, the Struggle Goes on to Fulfill the Promise of Equal Justice for All." *ABA Journal* 80 (August): 56–61. 1995. "Sorting

Out Image, Ads, Ethics." *ABA Journal* 81 (March): 94–95.

Podgor, Ellen S. 1994. "Corporate and White Collar Crime: Simplifying the Ambiguous." *American Criminal Law Review* 31 (3) (Spring): 391–401.

Podgorecki, Adam. 1974. *Law and Society*. London: Routledge and Kegan Paul. 1985. "Social Systems and Legal Systems—Criteria for Classification," in Adam Podgorecki, Christopher J. Whelan, and Dinesh Khosla (eds.), *Legal Systems and Social Systems*, pp. 1–24. London: Croom Helm.

Poel, Sari Van Der. 1995. "Solidarity as Boomerang: The Fiasco of the Prostitutes' Rights Movement in the Netherlands." *Crime, Law and Social Change* 23: 41–65.

Polinsky, Mitchell, and Daniel L. Rubinfeld. 1998. "Does the English Rule Discourage Low-Probability-of-Prevailing Plaintiffs?" *Journal of Legal Studies* 27 (January): 141–160.

Pollack, Ervin H. 1979. *Jurisprudence: Principles and Applications*. Columbus: Ohio State University Press.

Pollock, Ellen Joan, and Stephen J. Adler. 1992. "Justice for All? Legal System Struggles to Reflect Diversity, but Progress Is Slow." *Wall Street Journal* (May 8): 1, 4.

Pope, Maurice. 1989. "Upon the Country—Juries and the Principle of Random Selection." *Social Science Information* 28 (2): 265–289.

Popp, D., R. A. Donovan, M. Crawford, K. L. Marsh, and M. Peele. 2003. "Gender, Race and Speech Style Stereotypes." *Sex Roles* 48 (7/8) (April): 317–325.

Porter, John. 1965. *The Vertical Mosaic: An Analysis of Social Class and Power in Canada*. Toronto: University of Toronto Press.

Posner, Richard A. 1988. *Law and Literature: A Misunderstood Relation*. Cambridge, MA: Harvard University Press. 1990. *The Problems of Jurisprudence*. Chicago, IL: University of Chicago Press. 1995. "The Sociology of the Sociology of Law: A View from Economics." *European Journal of Law and Economics* 2 (4) (December): 263–284. 1996. *The Federal Courts: Challenge and*

Reform. Cambridge, MA: Harvard University Press. 1998. *Law and Literature*. 2nd ed. Cambridge, MA: Harvard University Press. 2001a. *Frontiers of Legal Theory*. Cambridge, MA: Harvard University Press. 2001b. "Security Versus Civil Liberties." *The Atlantic Monthly* (December). Retrieved from www.the-atlantic.com/issues/2001/12/posner.htm.

Pospisil, Leopold. 1971. *Anthropology of Law: A Comparative Theory*. New York: Harper and Row. 1978. *The Ethnology of Law*. 2nd ed. Menlo Park, CA: Cummings.

Pottage, Alain, and Martha Mundy (eds.). 2004. *Law, Anthropology and the Constitution of the Social: Making Persons and Things*. New York: Cambridge University Press.

Potvin, Maryse. 2005. "The Role of Statistics on Ethnic Origin and 'Race' in Canadian Anti-Discrimination Policy." *International Social Science Journal* 57 (1) (March): 27–42.

Pound, Roscoe. 1941. "Justice According to Law." *Columbia Law Review* 14 (1): 1–26. 1941. *In My Philosophy of Law*. St. Paul, MN: West. 1943. "A Survey of Social Interests." *Harvard Law Review* 57 (October): 1–39. 1959. *Jurisprudence*. Vols. 1 and 2. St. Paul, MN: West.

Poutanen, M. A. 2002. "Regulating Public Space in Early Nineteenth-Century Montreal: Vagrancy Laws and Gender in a Colonial Context." *Social History* 35 (69) (May): 35–58.

Prentice, Robert A., and Jonathan J. Koehler. 2003. "A Normality Bias in Legal Decision Making." *Cornell Law Review* 88 (3) (March): 583–651.

President's Commission on Law Enforcement and Administration of Justice. 1967. *The Challenge of Crime in a Free Society*. Washington, DC: U.S. Government Printing Office.

Priban, Jiri, Pauline Roberts, and James Young (eds.). 2003. *Systems of Justice in Transition: Central European Experiences Since 1989*. Burlington, VT: Ashgate.

Price, David E. 1972. *Who Makes the Law? Creativity and Power in Senate Committees*. Cambridge, MA: Schenkman.

Public Safety and Emergency Preparedness Canada. 2005. Corrections and Conditional Release Statistical Overview. December. Cat. No. PS1-3/2005E.

Pue, W. Wesley, and David Sugarman (eds.). 1999. *Lawyers' Culture and the Cultural Significance of Lawyers: Historical Perspectives*. Brookfield, VT: Ashgate. 2003. *Lawyers and Vampires: Cultural Histories of Legal Professions*. Portland, OR: Hart.

Quade, Vicki. 1995. "There Is No Sisterhood: Non-White Women Lawyers Say They're Still at the Bottom of the Heap." *Human Rights* 22 (1) (Winter): 8–13.

Quaile, Jennifer. 2002. "'At the Mercy' of Patriarchy: Women and the Struggle over Child Support," in T. Brettel Dawson (ed.), *Women, Law and Social Change: Core Readings and Current Issues*, pp. 238–257. 4th ed. Toronto: Captus Press.

Queen Street Outreach Society. 2002. "Mental Health Laws in Ontario." Retrieved from www.qsos.ca/mha.html.

Queen's New Centre. 2004. "Ontario Law Schools Attract a Great Diversity of Students." November 9. Retrieved from www.qnc.queensu.ca/story_loader.php?id=4191238807603.

Quinney, Richard. 1970. *The Social Reality of Crime*. Boston: Little, Brown. 1974a. *Criminal Justice in America*. Boston: Little, Brown. 1974b. *The Critique of Legal Order: Crime Control in Capitalist Society*. Boston: Little, Brown. 1975. *Criminology: Analysis and Critique of Crime in America*. Boston: Little, Brown. 2002. *Critique of Legal Order: Crime Control in Capitalist Society*. New Brunswick, NJ: Transaction Books.

R. v. P. (J.A.). 1991. 6 C.R. (4th) 126. R. v. P. (J.A.). NWTR [1991].

Rabe, Barry G. 1991. "Impediments to Environmental Dispute Resolution in the American Political Context," in Miriam K. Mills (ed.), *Alternative Dispute Resolution in the Public Sector*, pp. 143–163. Chicago: Nelson-Hall.

Rabinovitch, Jannit, and Susan Strega. 2004. "The PEERS Story: Effective Services Sidestep the

Controversies." *Violence Against Women* 10 (2) (February): 140–159.

Rabson, Mia. 2005. "Manitoba Lobbying Ottawa for Drug-Treatment Court." *Winnipeg Free Press* (April 11): A3.

Radelet, Michael L., Hugo Adam Bedau, and Constance E. Putnam. 1992. *In Spite of Innocence: Erroneous Convictions in Capital Cases.* Boston: Northeastern University Press.

Radelet, Michael L., and Ronald L. Akers. 1996. "Deterrence and the Death Penalty: The Views of the Experts." *Journal of Criminal Law and Criminology* 87 (1): 1–16. Retrieved from www.justiceblind.com/death/radelet.html.

Radin, Margaret Jane. 1991. "The Pragmatist and the Feminist," in Michael Brint and William Weaver (eds.), *Pragmatism in Law and Society*, pp. 127–153. Boulder, CO: Westview Press.

Raiffa, Howard. 1997. *Lectures on Negotiation Analysis.* Cambridge, MA: PON Books.

Randall, Kerry. 2002. *Effective Yellow Pages Advertising for Lawyers: The Complete Guide to Creating Winning Ads.* Chicago, IL: ABA Law Practice Management Section.

Rapping, Elayne. 2004. *Law and Justice as Seen on TV.* New York: New York University Press.

Ratnesar, Romesh. 1998. "Who Should Carry a Gun?" *Time* (July 6): 29.

Rawls, John. 2001. *Justice as Fairness: A Restatement* (ed. Erin Kelly). Cambridge, MA: Belknap Press/Harvard University Press.

Razack, Sherene. 1991. *Canadian Feminism and the Law: The Women's Legal Education and Action Fund and the Pursuit of Equality.* Toronto: Second Story Press. 1994. "What Is to Be Gained by Looking White People in the Eye? Culture, Race and Gender in Cases of Sexual Violence." *Signs* 19 (4) (Summer): 894–923. 1998. *Looking White People in the Eye: Gender, Race and Culture in the Courtrooms and Classroom.* Toronto: University of Toronto Press. 2002. "Gendered Racial Violence and Spatialized Justice: The Murder of Pamela George," in Sharene Razack (ed.), *Race, Space and the Law: Unmapping A White Settler Society*, pp. 121–156. Toronto: Between the Lines.

RCMP. 2006. "Integrated Proceeds of Crime." February 3. Retrieved from www.rcmp-grc.gc.ca/un/prog_serv/fed_serv/ipoc_e.htm.

Reason, Peter, and Hilary Bradbury (eds.). 2001. *Handbook of Action Research, Participative Inquiry and Practice.* Thousand Oaks, CA: Sage.

Reasons, Charles E. 1974. *The Criminologist: Crime and the Criminal.* Pacific Palisades, CA: Goodyear.

Reasons, Charles E., and Robert M. Rich (eds.). 1978. *The Sociology of Law: A Conflict Perspective.* Toronto: Butterworths.

Reed, B. J., and John W. Swain. 1997. *Public Finance Administration.* 2nd ed. Thousand Oaks, CA: Sage.

Reed, Douglas S. 1998. "Twenty-Five Years After Rodriguez: School Finance Litigation and the Impact of New Judicial Federalism." *Law and Society Review* 32 (1): 175–220.

Reed, O. Lee. 2005. *The Legal and Regulatory Environment of Business.* 13th ed. Boston, MA: McGraw-Hill/Irwin.

Rehbinder, Manfreid. 1975. *Sociology of Law: A Trend Report and Bibliography.* The Hague: Mouton.

Reichstein, Kenneth J. 1965. "Ambulance Chasing: A Case Study of Deviation and Control Within the Legal Profession." *Social Problems* 13 (1) (Summer): 3–17.

Reilly, J. Nolan. 1999. "Winnipeg General Strike," in James H. Marsh (ed.), *The Canadian Encyclopedia: Year 2000 Edition*, p. 2525. Toronto: McClelland and Stewart.

Reinerman, Craig. 1996. "The Social Construction of Drug Scares," in Earl Rubington and Martin S. Weinberg (eds.), *Deviance: The Interactionist Perspective*, pp. 77–89. 6th ed. Boston: Allyn and Bacon.

Reinow, R., and L. T. Reinow. 1967. *Moment in the Sun.* New York: Dial Press.

Reiss, Albert J., Jr. 1971. *The Police and the Public.* New Haven, CT: Yale University Press. 1992. "Police Organization in the Twentieth Century," in Michael Tonry and Norval Morris (eds.), *Modern Policing*, pp. 51–97. Chicago: University of Chicago Press.

Reiss, Albert J., Jr., and David J. Bordua. 1967. "Environment and Organization: A Perspective on the Police," in David J. Bordua (ed.), *The Police: Six Sociological Essays*, pp. 25–55. New York: John Wiley.

Reitox, Earl (European Information Network on Drugs and Drug Addiction). 2001. "International Comparisons." Drug Monitoring Center of Finland. Retrieved from www.stakes.fi/reitox/index.html.

Religious Tolerance.org. 2001. "Extraditing Accused Murderers to the U.S." Retrieved from www.religioustolerance.org/execut5.htm. 2005a. "Executing Innocent People: Studies of the Reliability of the Legal System in Capital Cases." Retrieved from www.religioustolerance.org/executg2.htm. 2005b. "World Map Showing Status of Death Penalty." Retrieved from www.religioustolerance.org/executh.htm.

Relis, Tamara. 2002. "Civil Litigation from Litigants' Perspectives: What We Know and What We Don't Know About the Litigation Experience of Individual Litigants." *Studies in Law, Politics and Society* 25 (1): 151–212.

Renner, Michael. 1996. *Fighting for Survival: Environmental Decline, Social Conflict, and the New Age of Insecurity*. New York: W. W. Norton.

Report of the Aboriginal Justice Inquiry of Manitoba. 1991. *The Justice System and Aboriginal People*. Vol.1. Winnipeg: Queen's Printer.

Reske, Henry J. 1994a. "Judges Irked by Tough-on-Crime Laws." *ABA Journal* 80 (October): 18. 1994b. "Ralph Nader's New Project: Law Centers to Help the Small Group Instead of the Little Guy." *ABA Journal* 80 (May): 32–33. 1995. "Victim-Offender Mediation Catching On: Advocates Say Programs, Typically for Nonviolent Offenders, Benefit Both Parties." *ABA Journal* 81 (February): 14–16.

Resnick, Judith. 1990. "Constructing the Canon." *Yale Journal of Law and the Humanities* 2 (1): 221–230.

Rhode, Deborah L., and Carol Sanger (eds.). 2005. *Gender Rights*. Burlington, VT: Ashgate.

Rich, Robert M. 1977. *The Sociology of Law: An Introduction to Its Theorists and Theories*. Washington, DC: University Press of America. 1978. *Crimes Without Victims: Deviance and the Criminal Law*. Washington, DC: University Press of America.

Richardson, Diane, and Steven Seidman (eds.). 2002. *Handbook of Lesbian and Gay Studies*. Thousand Oaks, CA: Sage.

Ringer, Fritz. 2004. *Max Weber—An Intellectual Biography*. Chicago: University of Chicago Press.

Ripley, Randall B. 1980. *Congress: Process and Policy*. 4th ed. New York: W. W. Norton.

Ritzer, George. 2001. *Explorations in the Sociology of Consumption: Fast Food, Credit Cards and Casinos*. Thousand Oaks, CA: Sage. 2005. *Enchanting a Disenchanted World: Revolutionizing the Means of Consumption*. 2nd ed. Thousand Oaks: CA: Pine Forge Press.

Roach, Steven C. 2005. "Arab States and the Role of Islam in the International Criminal Court." *Political Studies* 53 (1) (March): 143–161.

Roberts, Julian V. 2000. "Introduction to Criminal Justice in Canada," in Julian V. Roberts (ed.), *Criminal Justice in Canada: A Reader*, pp. 3–15. Toronto: Harcourt. 2001. "Sentencing, Parole, and Psychology," in Regina A. Schuller and James R. P. Ogloff (eds.), *Introduction to Psychology and Law*, pp. 188–213. Toronto: University of Toronto Press.

Roberts, Simon. 1979. *Order and Dispute: An Introduction to Legal Anthropology*. New York: St. Martin's Press.

Robinson, David, Frank J. Porporino, and William A. Millson. 1999. "A One-Day Snapshot of Inmates in Canada's Adult Correctional Facilities," in Canadian Centre for Justice Statistics, *The Juristat Reader: A Statistical Overview of the Canadian Justice System*, pp. 53–68. Toronto: Thompson.

Robson, Karen, and Jean E. Wallace. 2001. "Gendered Inequalities in Earnings: A Study of Canadian Lawyers." *Canadian Review of Sociology and Anthropology* 38 (1) (February): 75–95.

Robson, Ruthann. 1992. "Embodiment(s): The Possibilities of Lesbian Legal Theory in Bodies Problematized by Postmodernisms and Feminisms." *Law and Sexuality, A Review of Lesbian and Gay Legal Issues* 2 (Summer): 37–80. 1994. "Resisting the Family: Repositioning Lesbians in Legal Theory." *Signs* 19 (4) (Summer): 975–997. 1998. *Sappho Goes To Law School.* New York: Columbia University Press.

Rodgers, Harrell R., Jr., and Charles S. Bullock III. 1972. *Law and Social Change: Civil Rights Laws and Their Consequences.* New York: McGraw-Hill.

Rodriguez, Nancy. 2003. "The Impact of 'Strikes' in Sentencing Decisions: Punishment for Only Some Habitual Offenders." *Criminal Justice Policy Review* 14 (1): 106–127.

Rodrique, Isabelle. 2002. "Cauchon May Relax Canada's Marijuana Laws." *Toronto Star* (July 13): A6.

Roesch, Ronald, Steven D. Dart, and James R. P. Ogloff (eds.). 1999. *Psychology and the Law: The State of the Discipline.* New York: Plenum.

Roesch, Ronald, Stephen L. Golding, Valerie P. Hans, and N. Dickon Reppucci. 1991. "Social Science and the Courts: The Role of Amicus Curiae Briefs." *Law and Human Behavior* 15 (1) (February): 1–11.

Rogers, James M. 1988. *The Impact of Policy Analysis.* Pittsburgh, PA: University of Pittsburgh Press.

Roll, John M., et al. 2005. "Identifying Predictors of Treatment Outcome in a Drug Court Program." *American Journal of Drug and Alcohol Abuse* 31 (4): 641–656.

Rondos v. Wawrin, Manitoba Court of Appeal, 1968, 64, W.W.R. 690, 68, D.L.R. (2d) 658 (cited in G. H. L. Fridman [2002]. *The Law of Torts in Canada.* Toronto: Carswell and Thomson.)

Rooy, Alison Van. 2004. *The Global Legitimacy Game: Civil Society, Globalization, and Protest.* New York: Palgrave Macmillan.

Rosenbloom, David H., and Deborah G. Goldman. 1998. *Public Administration: Understanding Management, Politics, and Law in the Public Sector.* 4th ed. New York: McGraw-Hill.

Rosenthal, Elisabeth. 1998. "For One-Child Policy, China Rethinks Iron Hand." *New York Times* (November 1): Y1, Y16.

Rosett, Arthur, and Donald R. Cressey. 1976. *Justice by Consent: Plea Bargains in the American Courthouse.* Philadelphia: Lippincott.

Ross, E. Adamson. 1922. *Social Control.* New York: MacMillan. Originally published in 1901.

Ross, Laurence H. 1989. "Sociology and Legal Sanctions," in Martin Lawrence Friedland (ed.), *Sanctions and Rewards in the Legal System: A Multidisciplinary Approach*, pp. 36–49. Toronto: University of Toronto Press. 1980. *Settled Out of Court.* 2nd ed. Chicago: Aldine.

Ross, Rupert. 1992. *Dancing with a Ghost: Exploring Indian Reality.* Markham, ON: Octopus.

Ross, William H., and Donald E. Conlon. 2000. "Hybrid Forms of Third-Party Dispute Resolution: Theoretical Implications of Combining Mediation and Arbitration." *Academy of Management Review* 25 (2) (April): 416–427.

Rossi, Peter H., Mark W. Lipsey, and Howard E. Freeman. 2004. *Evaluation: A Systematic Approach.* 7th ed. Thousand Oaks, CA: Sage.

Rostow, Walt W. 1961. *The Stages of Economic Growth: A Non-Communist Manifesto.* New York: Cambridge University Press.

Rouland, Norbert. 1994. *Legal Anthropology.* Trans. Philippe G. Planel. Stanford, CA: Stanford University Press.

Rousseau, Cecile, et al. 2002. "The Complexity of Determining Refugeehood: A Multidisciplinary Analysis of the Decision-Making Process of the Canadian Immigration and Refugee Board." *Journal of Refugee Studies* 15 (1) (March): 43–70.

Royal Commission on Bilingualism and Biculturalism. 1965. Report. Ottawa: Queen's Printer.

Royal Commission on New Reproductive Technologies. 1993. Proceed with Care: Final Report of the Royal Commission on New Reproductive Technologies, Vol. 2. Ottawa: Minister of Government Services Canada.

Royal Commission on the Status of Women in Canada. 1970. Report of the Royal Commission on the Status of Women in Canada. Ottawa: Information Canada.

Rozell, Mark J., and Clyde Wilcox. 1999. *Interest Groups in American Campaigns: The New Face of Electioneering*. Washington, DC: CQ Press.

Rubin, Paul H. 1995. "Fundamental Reform of Tort Law." *Regulation: The Cato Review of Business and Government* 4: 26–33.

Rubinstein, Jonathan. 1973. *City Police*. New York: Farrar, Straus and Giroux.

Ruddell, Rick. 2005. "Social Disruption, State Priorities and Minority Threat: A Cross-National Study of Imprisonment." *Punishment and Society* 7 (1) (January): 7–28.

Rusche, Georg, and Otto Kurchheimer. 1968. *Punishment and Social Structure*. New York: Russell and Russell.

Ryan, Patrick J., and George E. Rush (eds.). 1997. *Understanding Organized Crime in a Global Perspective*. Thousand Oaks, CA: Sage.

Saeed, Abdullah. 2004. *Freedom of Religion, Apostasy and Islam*. Burlington, VT: Ashgate.

Sajo, Andras. 2003. "From Corruption to Extortion: Conceptualization of Post-Communist Corruption." *Crime, Law and Social Change* 40 (2/3) (October): 171–195.

Saks, Michael J., and Reid Hastie. 1978. *Social Psychology in Court*. New York: Van Nostrand Reinhold.

Salinger, Lawrence M. 2005. *The Encyclopedia of White Collar and Corporate Crime*. Thousand Oaks, CA: Sage.

Samper, Ernesto. 1995. "Colombia's War on Drugs." *Wall Street Journal* (June 30): A16.

Sampford, Charles. 1989. *The Disorder of Law: A Critique of Legal Theory*. Oxford: Basil Blackwell.

Sangster, Joan. 2002. *Girl Trouble: Female Delinquency in English Canada*. Toronto: Between the Lines.

Sarat, Austin. 1989. "Alternatives to Formal Adjudication," in Sheldon Goldman and Austin Sarat (eds.), *American Court Systems: Readings in Judicial Process and Behavior*, pp. 33–40. 2nd ed. New York: Longman. 2001. *When the State Kills: Capital Punishment and the American Condition*. Princeton, NJ: Princeton University Press. 2004. *Social Organization of Law*. Los Angeles: Roxbury.

Sarat, Austin, and William L. F. Felstiner. 1995. *Divorce Lawyers and Their Clients: Power and Meaning in the Legal Process*. New York: Oxford University Press.

Sarat, Austin, and Thomas R. Kearns (eds.). 1994. *The Rhetoric of Law*. Ann Arbor: University of Michigan Press. 2000. *Law in the Domains of Culture*. Ann Arbor: University of Michigan Press.

Sarat, Austin, and Stuart Scheingold (eds.). 1998. *Cause Lawyering: Political Commitments and Professional Responsibilities*. New York: Oxford University Press.

Sargent, Neil C. 2002. "Is There Any Justice in Alternative Justice?" in Michael Mac Neil, Neil Sargent, and Peter Swan (eds.), *Law, Regulation and Governance*, pp. 204–222. Don Mills, ON: Oxford University Press.

Saturday Review. 1979. "Getting Hot Under the Collar." (June 9): 7.

Sauvageau, Florian, David Scheiderman, and David Taras. 2006. *The Last Word: Media Coverage of the Supreme Court of Canada*. Vancouver: UBC Press.

Savell, Lawrence. 1994. "I'm Bill Low. File with Me and Win, Win, Win!" *National Law Journal* 17 (3) (September 19): A23.

Savelsberg, Joachim J. 1992. "Law That Does Not Fit Society: Sentencing Guidelines as a Neoclassical Reaction to the Dilemmas of Substantivized Law." *American Journal of Sociology* 97 (5) (March): 1346–1381.

Scallen, Eileen A. 1995. "American Legal Argumentation: The Law and Literature/ Rhetoric Movement." *Argumentation* 9: 705–717.

Schenk, Christopher. 2001. *From Poverty Wages to a Living Wage: Why We Must Move Beyond Today's Minimum Wage*. Toronto: CSJ Foundation for Research and Education and the Ontario Federation of Labour.

Scheppele, Kim Lane. 1994. "Legal Theory and Social Theory." *Annual Review of Sociology* (20): 383–407. 1996. "Narrative Resistance and the Struggle for Stories." *Legal Studies Forum* 20 (1–2). Retrieved from tarlton.law.utexas.edu/lpop/ etext/lsf/schepp20.htm.

Schmaus, Warren. 2004. *Rethinking Durkheim and His Tradition*. New York: Cambridge University Press.

Schmidt, Sara. 2001. "U of T Law School Looks at Raising Tuition to $25 000." *National Post* (December 12): A1, A17. 2003. "Half of Teens in Canada Gamble: Up to 15 Percent at Risk of Addiction." *The Vancouver Sun* (October 14): A1.

Schmidt, Steve. 2001. "Canadian Courts Restrict Drug Tests." *National Post* (December 19): A1, A8.

Schmidt, William E. 1992. "British Courts to Doff Wig? Verdict Asked." *New York Times* (August 23): 4Y.

Scholes, Laurie Lamoureux. 2002. "The Canadian Council of Muslim Women: A Profile of the First 18 Years." *Journal of Muslim Minority Affairs* 22 (2) (October): 413–425.

Schrag, Philip G., and Michael Meltsner. 1998. *Reflections on Clinical Legal Education*. Boston: Northeastern University Press.

Schram, Sanford E. 2002. *Praxis for the Poor: Piven and Cloward and the Future of Social Science in Social Welfare*. New York: New York University Press.

Schulenberg, Jennifer L. 2003. "The Social Context of Police Discretion with Young Offenders: An Ecological Analysis." *Canadian Journal of Criminology and Criminal Justice* 45 (2) (April): 127–158.

Schuller, Regina A., and Meagan Yarmey. 2001. "The Jury: Deciding Guilt and Innocence," in Regina A. Schuller and James R. P. Ogloff (eds.), *Introduction to Psychology and Law: Canadian Perspectives*, pp. 157–187. Toronto: University of Toronto Press.

Schur, Edward M. 1968. *Law and Society*. New York: Random House.

Schutt, Russell K. 2004. *Investigating the Social World, the Process and Practice of Research*. 4th ed. Thousand Oaks, CA: Pine Forge Press.

Schwartz, Bernard. 1974. *The Law in America: A History*. New York: McGraw-Hill. 1995. "'Shooting the Piano Player'? Justice Scalia and Administrative Law." *Administrative Law Review* 47 (1) (Winter): 1–57.

Schwartz, John. 2001. "U.S. Refuses to Disclose PC Tracking." *New York Times* (August 25): A1.

Schwartz, Louis B. 1984. "With Gun and Camera Through Darkest CRITS-Land." *Stanford Law Review* 36 (1 and 2) (January): 413–464.

Schwartz, Richard D., and James C. Miller. 1975. "Legal Evolution and Societal Complexity," in Ronald L. Akers and Richard Hawkins (eds.), *Law and Control in Society*, pp. 52–62. Englewood Cliffs, NJ: Prentice Hall.

Schwartz, Richard D., and Sonya Orleans. 1970. "On Legal Sanctions," in Richard D. Schwartz and Jerome A. Skolnick (eds.), *Society and the Legal Order*, pp. 533–547. New York: Basic Books.

Scott, Robert A., and Arnold R. Shore. 1979. *Why Sociology Does Not Apply: A Study of the Use of Sociology in Public Policy*. New York: Elsevier.

Scott, Steffanie. 2003. "Gender, Household Headship and Entitlements to Land: New Vulnerabilities in Vietnam's Decollectivization." *Gender, Technology and Development* 7 (2) (May-August): 233–263. *Seattle Times*. 2003. "Judge Orders Acid Attacker Be Blinded." (December 13): A8.

Sechzer, Jeri Altneu. 2004. "'Islam and Woman: Where Tradition Meets Modernity': History and Interpretations of Islamic Women's Status." *Sex Roles* 51 (5/6) (September): 263–272.

Seelye, Katharine Q. 2001. "Global Warming May Bring New Variety of Class Action." *New York Times* (September 6): A1, A6.

Seib, Gerald F. 1995. "You Can Get Away from Washington—But Not Government." *Wall Street Journal* (June 21): A1, A5.

Seidman, Robert B. 1978. *The State, Law and Development.* New York: St. Martin's Press.

Seligman, Daniel. 1995. "Advocates Unlimited." *Fortune* 131 (4) (March 6): 217.

Selznick, Philip. 1961. "Sociology and Natural Law." *Natural Law Forum* 6: 84–108. 1968. "Law: The Sociology of Law." *International Encyclopedia of the Social Sciences*, No. 9: 50–59. New York: Free Press. 1969. *Law, Society and Industrial Justice.* New York: Russell Sage Foundation.

Sentencing Project. 2005. "Sentencing Project Report Finds Record Numbers of Persons Serving Life Imprisonment." Retrieved from www.sentencingproject.org/lifers.cfm.

Shaffer, Martha. 2003. "The Battered Woman Syndrome Revisited: Some Complicating Thoughts Five Years After *R. v. Lavallee*," in T. Brettel Dawson (ed.), *Women, Law and Social Change: Core Readings and Current Issues*, pp. 207–213. Concord, ON: Captus Press.

Shaffer, Martha, and Nicholas Bala. 2004. "Protecting Children from Domestic Violence: The Canadian Experience," in Peter G. Jaffe, Linda L. Baker, and Alison J. Cunningham (eds.), in *Protecting Children from Domestic Violence: Strategies for Community Intervention*, pp. 171–187. New York: Guilford University Press.

Shapo, Marshall S. 1997. "A Social Contract Tort." *Texas Law Review* 75 (7): 1835–1848.

Shaver, Frances M. 1993. "Prostitution: A Female Crime?" in Ellen Adelberg and Claudia Currie (eds.), *In Conflict with the Law: Women and the Canadian Justice System*, pp. 153–173. Vancouver: Press Gang. 1999. "Prostitution," in James H. Marsh (ed.), *The Canadian Encyclopedia: Year 2000 Edition*,

pp. 1917–1919. Toronto: McClelland and Stewart.

Sheldon, Tony. 2000. "Cannabis Use Among Dutch Youth." *British Medical Journal* 321: 655.

Shelley, Louise I. 2002. "Can Russian Right Organized Crime and Corruption?" *The Tocqueville Review* 23 (2): 37–55.

Sheppard, R. Ronald, and Garry J. Smith. 1999. "Gambling," in James H. Marsh (ed.), *The Canadian Encyclopedia: Year 2000 Edition*, p. 946. Toronto: McClelland and Stewart.

Sher, Julian. 1983. *White Hoods: Canada's Ku Klux Klan.* Vancouver: New Star Books.

Sherman, Lawrence W. 1978. "Review of the Behavior of Law." *Contemporary Sociology* 7 (1) (January): 10–15. 1992. *Policing Domestic Violence: Experiments and Dilemmas.* New York: Free Press.

Sherwin, Richard K. 2000. *When Law Goes Pop: The Vanishing Line Between Law and Popular Culture.* Chicago: University of Chicago Press.

Shibutani, Tamotsu. 1961. *Society and Personality: An Interactionist Approach to Social Psychology.* Englewood Cliffs, NJ: Prentice Hall.

Shilling, Chris, and Philip A. Mellor. 1998. "Durkheim, Morality and Modernity: Collective Effervescence, Homo Duplex and the Sources of Moral Action." *British Journal of Sociology* 49 (2) (June): 193–209.

Shoemaker, Pamela J., James William Tankard, and Dominic L. Lasorsa. 2004. *How To Build Social Science Theories.* Thousand Oaks, CA: Sage.

Shover, Neal, and John Paul Wright (eds.). 2001. *Crimes of Privilege, Readings in White Collar Crime.* New York: Oxford University Press.

Shullins, Nancy. 1994. "Survey Says Let's Bash All the Lawyers." *St. Louis Post-Dispatch* (April 30): 1D, 3D.

Shuman, Daniel W., and Anthony Champagne. 1997. "Removing the People from the Legal Process: The Rhetoric and Research on Judicial Selection and Juries."

Psychology, Public Policy, and Law 3 (2–3) (June–September): 242–258.

Siegel, Larry J. 1998. *Criminology: Theories, Patterns, and Typologies*. 6th ed. Belmont, CA: Wadsworth.

Simmie, Scott, and Julie Nunes. 2001. *The Last Taboo: A Survival Guide to Mental Health Care in Canada*. Toronto: McClelland and Stewart Ltd.

Simon, Leonore, Bruce Sales, and Lee Sechrest. 1992. "Licensure of Functions," in Dorothy K. Kagehiro and William S. Laufer (eds.), *Handbook of Psychology and Law*, pp. 542–563. New York: Springer-Verlag.

Simonds, M. 1996. *The Convict Lover*. Toronto: Macfarlane, Walter and Ross.

Simpson, A. W. B. 1988. *Invitation to Law*. Oxford, UK: Basil Blackwell.

Singh, Basil R. 2002. "Problems and Possibilities of Ethnic Minority Traditional Rights Within Liberal Democracies." *The Social Science Journal* 39 (2): 221–234.

Single, Eric. 2003. "Estimating the Costs of Substance Abuse: Implications to the Estimation of the Costs and Benefits of Gambling." *Journal of Gambling Studies* 19 (2) (Summer): 215–233.

Situ, Yingyi, and David Emmons. 2001. *Environmental Crime: The Criminal Justice System's Role in Protecting the Environment*. Thousand Oaks, CA: Sage.

Skerry, Peter. 1998. "The Affirmative Action Paradox." *Society* 35 (6) (September–October): 8–16.

Skolnick, Jerome H. 1994. *Justice Without Trial: Law Enforcement in Democratic Society*. 3rd ed. New York: Macmillan.

Smigel, Erwin O. 1964. *The Wall Street Lawyer*. New York: Free Press.

Smith, Anne Kates. 1992. "Opinions with a Price: More-Complex Court Cases Mean Jobs for Expert Witnesses." *U.S. News and World Report* (July 20): 64–66.

Smith, Beverley. 1989. *Professional Conduct for Canadian Lawyers*. Toronto: Butterworths.

Smith, Dwayne M., and Margaret A. Zahn (eds.). 1998. *Homicide: A Sourcebook of Social Research*. Thousand Oaks, CA: Sage.

Smith, Jim. 1999. "Inmates: Prison chow's bad, videos are old." *Philadelphia Daily News* (October 8). Retrieved from http://over-lawyered.com/archives/99oct2.html.

Smolowe, Jill. 1996. "The Unmarrying Kind." *Time* (April 29): 68–69. *Snell v. Farrell*, Supreme Court of Canada, 1990, 2 S.C.R. 311, 72 D.L.R. (4th) 289.

Snider, Laureen. 1999. "White-Collar Crime," in James H. Marsh (ed.), *The Canadian Encyclopedia: Year 2000 Edition*, p. 2504. Toronto: McClelland and Stewart.

Snow, David A., Sarah A. Soule, and Hanspeter Kriesi (eds.). 2004. *The Blackwell Companion to Social Movements*. Malden, MA: Blackwell.

Sollors, Werner. 2000. *Interracialism: Black-White Intermarriage in American History, Literature and Law*. New York: Oxford University Press.

Solomon, Robert. 1999. "Alcohol and Drug Law," in *Canadian Profile 1999: Alcohol, Tobacco and Other Drugs*, pp. 295–315. Ottawa: Centre on Substance Abuse and Centre for Addiction and Mental Health.

Somer, Kristin L., Irwin A. Horowitz, and Martin J. Bourgeois. 2001. "When Juries Fail to Grasp the Law: Biased Evidence Processing in Individual and Group Decision Making." *Personality and Social Psychology Bulletin* 27 (3) (March): 309–320.

Sommers, E. K. 1995. *Voices from Within: Women Who Have Broken the Law*. Toronto: University of Toronto Press.

Souryal, Sam S., and Dennis W. Potts. 1994. "The Penalty of Hand Amputation for Theft in Islamic Justice." *Journal of Criminal Justice* 22 (3) (May-June): 249–265.

Spector, Malcolm. 1972. "The Rise and Fall of a Mobility Route." *Social Problems* 20 (2) (Fall): 173–185.

Spector, Malcolm, and John I. Kitsuse. 1973. "Social Problems: A Reformulation." *Social Problems* 21 (2) (Fall): 145–159.

Spence, Gerry. 1989. *With Justice for None*. New York: Times Books.

Spencer, Herbert. 1899. *The Principles of Sociology (II)*. New York: D. Appleton.

Spiteri, Melani. 2002. "Sentencing Circles for Aboriginal Offenders in Canada: Furthering the Idea of Aboriginal Justice Within a Western Framework." Paper presented at the Third International Conference on Conferencing, Circles and Other Restorative Practices, August 8–10, Minneapolis, Minnesota. Retrieved from www.iirp.org/library/mn02/mn02_spiteri.html.

Stamler, Rodney. 2000. "Organized Crime," in Rick Linden (ed.), *Criminology: A Canadian Perspective*, pp. 429–458. 4th ed. Toronto: Harcourt.

Statistics Canada. 1998. *Canada Yearbook 1999*. Ottawa: Minister of Industry. 1998b. "Average Earnings of Full-Year, Full-Time Workers in the 25 Highest-Paying and 25 Lowest-Paying Occupations, by Sex, Canada, 1995." *The Daily* (May 12). Retrieved from www.statcan.ca/Daily/English/990512/d980512.htm. 2002a. "Crime Statistics 2001." *The Daily* (July 17). Retrieved from www.statcan.cDaily/English/020717/d020717b.htm. 2002b. "Fact-Sheet on Gambling." *Perspectives on Labour and Income* 3 (7) (July): 1–5. Catalogue No. 75-001-XIE. Retrieved from www.statcan/english/indepth/indepth/freepub/82_221_XIE/00502/tables/htm/22142.htm. 2002c. "Gambling: An Update." *The Daily* (July 16). Retrieved from www.statcan.ca/Daily/English/020718/d020718c.htm. 2003a. "Earnings of Canadians: Making a Living in the New Economy." *The Daily* (March 11). Retrieved from www12.statcan.ca/english/census01/Products/Analytic/companion/earn/contents.cfm. 2003b. "Problem Gambling, 2002." *The Daily* (December 12). Retrieved from www.statcan.ca/Daily/English/031212/031212c.htm. 2004. "Trends in Drug Offences and the Role of Alcohol and Drugs in Crime." *The Daily* (February 23). Retrieved from www.statcan.ca/Daily/English/040223/d040223a.htm. 2004a. "Alcohol and Illicit Drug Dependence, 2002." *The Daily* (December 9). Retrieved from www.statcan.ca/Daily/English/041209/d041209b.htm. 2004b. "Health Reports: Use of Cannabis and Other Illicit Drugs, 2002." *The Daily* (July 21). Retrieved from www.statcan.ca/Daily/English/040721/d040721a.htm. 2004c. "Courts Personnel and Expenditures, 2002/03." *The Daily* (November 23). Retrieved from www.statcan.ca/Daily/English/041123/d041123e.htm. 2004d. "Private Security and Public Policy in Canada, 2001." *The Daily* (August 10). Retrieved from www.statcan.ca/Daily/English/040810/d040810b.htm. 2004e. "Study: The Union Movement in Transition." *The Daily* (August 31). Retrieved from www.statcan.ca/Daily/English/040831/d0408831b.htm. 2005. "Adult Correctional Services, 2003/04." *The Daily* (December 16). Retrieved from www.statcan.ca/Daily/English/051216/d051216b.htm. 2005a. "Crime Statistics, 2004." *The Daily* (July 21). Retrieved from www.statcan.ca/Daily/English/050721/d050721a.htm. 2005b. "Homicides, 2004." *The Daily*, (October 6). Retrieved from www.statcan.ca/Daily/English/051006/d051006b.htm. 2005c. "Adult Correctional Services." *The Daily* (December 16). Retrieved from www.statcan.ca/Daily/English/051216/d051216b.htm. 2005d. "Police Personnel and Expenditures, 2005." *The Daily* (December 15). Retrieved from www.statcan.ca/Daily/English/051215/d051215d.htm. 2005d. "Divorces, 2003." *The Daily* (March 9). Retrieved from www.statcan.ca/Daily/English/050309/d050309b.htm. 2005e. "Legal Aid 2003/2004: Resource and Caseload." *The Daily* (March 29). Retrieved from www.statcan.ca/Daily/English/050329/d050329d.htm. 2005f "General Social Survey: Criminal Victimization, 2004." *The Daily* (November 24). Retrieved from www.statcan.ca/Daily/English/051124/d051124b.htm. 2006. "Legal Aid: 2004/05." *The Daily* (February 7). Retrieved from www.statcan.ca/Daily/English/060207/d060207c.htm.

Stead, Deborah. 1994. "Crime and Punishment—And Now Trial by Jury." *Business Week* (January 17): 20–22.

Stefaniuk, Walter. 1996. *You Asked Us . . . About Canada*. Toronto: Doubleday.

Stein, Laura. 1999. *Sexual Harassment in America. A Documentary History*. Westport, CT: Greenwood.

Stephens v. Myers, Nisi Prius. (1830), 4 C.and P. 349, 172 E.R. 735 (cited in Allen M. Linden, Lewis N. Klar, and Bruce Feldthusen, [2004]. *Canadian Tort Law: Cases, Notes and Materials*. 12th ed. Toronto: LexisNexis and Butterworths).

Stephens, Sharon. 1998. "Reflections on Environmental Justice: Children as Victims and Actors," in Christopher Williams (ed.), *Environmental Victims*, pp. 48–71. London, UK: Earthscan.

Sterba, James P. (ed.). 2004. *Morality in Practice*. 7th ed. Belmont, CA: Thomson/Wadsworth.

Sterner, Thomas. 2003. *Policy Instruments for Environmental and Natural Resource Management*. Washington, DC: Resources for the Future.

Stevens, Robert. 1973. "Law Schools and Law Students." *Virginia Law Review* 59 (4) (April): 51–707. 1983. *Law School: Legal Education in America from the 1850s to the 1980s*. Chapel Hill, NC: The University of North Carolina Press.

St. Louis Post-Dispatch 1995. "Centers For Death-Row Appeals Run out of Time" (September 3): 4C. 1998a. "Group Still Wants Rushdie Murdered, Raises Reward" (October 13): A6. 1998b. "Britons Take off Jackets, Hang up Their Customs and Relax Dress Codes" (September 2): A2. 2001. "McVeigh Execution Is Planned to the Smallest Detail" (April 8): A5.

Stolzenberg, Lisa, and Stewart J. D'Alessio. 1997. "'Three Strikes and You're Out': The Impact of California's New Mandatory Law on Serious Crime Rates." *Crime and Delinquency* 43 (4) (October): 457–469. 2000. "Gun Availability and Violent Crime: New Evidence from the National Incident-Based Reporting System." *Social Forces* 78 (4) June: 1461–1482. (eds.). 2002. *Criminal Courts for the 21st Century*. Upper Saddle River, NJ: Prentice Hall.

Stone, Christopher D. 1978. "Social Control of Corporate Behavior," in M. David Ermann and Richard J. Lundman (eds.), *Corporate and Governmental Deviants: Problems of Organizational Behavior in Contemporary Society*, pp. 241–258. New York: Oxford University Press.

Stone, Julius. 1964. *Legal System and Lawyer's Reasonings*. Stanford: Stanford University Press. 1966. *Law and the Social Sciences in the Second Half Century*. Minneapolis, MN: University of Minnesota Press.

Stracher, Cameron. 2001. "How to Bill 25 Hours in One Day." *New York Times Magazine* (April 8): 74.

Strathern, Marilyn. 2005. "Experiments in Interdisciplinarity." *Social Anthropology* 13 (1) (February): 75–90.

Strauss, Marina, and Simon Tuck. 2005. "Tribunal Rules Sears Broke Law by Inflating Tire Savings." *Globe and Mail* (January 25): B1, B8.

Strick, Anne. 1977. *Injustice for All*. New York: Penguin.

Strickland, Ruth Ann. 2004. *Restorative Justice*. New York: Peter Lang Publisher.

Suchman, Edward A. 1967. *Evaluative Research: Principles and Practice in Public Service and Social Action Programs*. New York: Russell Sage.

Sudnow, David. 1975. "Normal Crimes: Sociological Features of the Penal Code in a Public Defender Office." *Social Problems* 12 (3) (Winter): 255–276.

Sugarman, S. D. 1985. "Alternative Compensation Schemes and Tort Theory: Doing Away with Tort." *California Law Review* 558: 603–611.

Sullum, Jacob. 2003. *Saying Yes: In Defense of Drug Use*. New York: J. P. Tarcher/Putnam.

Summers, Robert S., and George G. Howard. 1972. *Law: Its Nature, Functions and Limits*. 2nd ed. Englewood Cliffs, NJ: Prentice Hall.

Sumner, William Graham. 1906. *Folkways*. Boston: Ginn. 1886/1940. "The Challenge of Facts," in Maurice R. Davie (ed.), *Sumner Today*, pp. 67–93. New Haven, CT: Yale University Press. Originally published in 1886.

Sunstein, Cass R. 2003. *Why Societies Need Dissent*. Cambridge, MA: Harvard University

Press.

Sutherland, Edwin H. 1949. *White Collar Crime.* New York: Dryden Press.

Sutherland, Edwin H., and Donald C. Cressey. 1974. *Criminology.* 9th ed. Philadelphia: Lippincott.

Sutton, John R. 2001. *Law/Society: Origins, Interactions, and Change.* Thousand Oaks: CA: Pine Forge Press.

Suzuki, David, and Holly Dressel. 2002. *Good News for a Change: Hope for a Troubled Planet.* Toronto: Stoddart.

Swartz, Joel. 1978. "Silent Killers at Work," in M. David Ermann and Richard Landmann (eds.), *Corporate and Governmental Deviance,* pp. 114–128. New York: Oxford University Press.

Tanase, Takao. 1995. "The Management of Disputes: Automobile Accident Compensation in Japan," in Richard L. Abel (ed.), *The Law and Society Reader,* pp. 58–83. New York: New York University Press.

Tang, Alisa. 2003. "Drug Abuse: Just Say No Funeral. Threat of Ostracism Cleans Up Thailand Village." *Seattle Times* (October 27): A11.

Tangley, Lord. 1965. *New Law for a New World.* London, UK: Stephens and Sons.

Tao, Jingzhou. 2004. *Arbitration Law and Practice in China.* New York: Kluwer Law International.

Tappan, Paul W. 1960. *Crime, Justice, and Correction.* New York: McGraw-Hill.

Tashbrook, Linda. 2004. *Survey on Licensing.* Buffalo, NY: W. S. Hein.

Taylor, Judith. 2005. "Who Manages Feminist-Inspired Reform? An In-Depth Look at Title IX Coordinators in the United States." *Gender and Society* 19 (3) June: 358–375.

Tempest, Rone. 2005. "Death Row Often Means a Long Life." *Los Angeles Times* (March 6). Retrieved from www.deathpenalty.org/index.php?pid=cost.

Terrill, Richard J. 2003. *World Criminal Justice Systems: A Survey.* 5th ed. Cincinnati, OH: Anderson.

Thomas, Kenneth W. 1992. "Conflict and Conflict Management: Reflections and Update." *Journal of Organizational Behavior* 13 (3) (May): 265–274.

Thompson, Chris. 2005. "Man Wins $340,000 in Bottled Fly Lawsuit." *Windsor Star* (April 23): A1.

Thompson, Duncan C. 1979. *How to Become a Lawyer in Canada.* Edmonton, AB: Acorn Books.

Thorne, Barrie, and Nancy Henley (eds.). 1975. *Language and Sex: Difference and Dominance.* Rowley, MA: Newbury.

Thornton, Margaret. 1996. *Dissonance and Distrust: Women in the Legal Profession.* Melbourne, Australia: Oxford University Press.

Thornton, Patricia M. 2002. "Framing Dissent in Contemporary China: Irony, Ambiguity and Metonymy." *The China Quarterly* 171 (September): 661–681.

Thurman, Quint C., and Jihong Zhao. 2004. *Contemporary Policing: Controversies, Challenges, and Solutions: An Anthology.* Los Angeles: Roxbury.

Thurman, Quint, Jihong Zhao, and Andrew Giacomazzi. 2001. *Community Policing in a Community Area: An Introduction and Exploration.* Los Angeles: Roxbury.

Tibbetts, Janice. 2001. "Ottawa Quietly Pays Man $1M for Wrongful Conviction." *National Post* (December 19): A5.

Tigar, Michael E. 1977. *Law and the Rise of Capitalism.* New York: Monthly Review Press.

Tillinghast Towers Perrin. 2002. *US Tort Costs 2000: Trends and Findings on the Costs of the US Tort System.* Chicago, IL: TTP. 2004. *US Tort Costs: 2004 Update.* Chicago, IL: TTP.

Tismaneanu, Vladimir. 1992. *Reinventing Politics: Eastern Europe from Stalin to Havel.* New York: Free Press.

Tittle, Charles R. 1969. "Crime Rates and Legal Sanctions." *Social Problems* 16 (4) (Spring): 409–423.

Toffler, Alvin. 1970. *Future Shock*. New York: Random House.

Toffolon-Weiss, Melissa, and J. Timmons Roberts. 2004. "Toxic Torts, Public Interest Law, and Environmental Justice: Evidence From Louisiana." *Law and Policy* 26 (2) (April): 259–287.

Tomasic, Roman. 1985. *The Sociology of Law*. London, UK: Sage.

Tomkins, Adam. 2003. *Public Law*. New York: Oxford University Press.

Tomlins, Christopher. 2000. "Framing the Field of Law's Disciplinary Encounters: A Historical Narrative." *Law and Society Review* 34 (4): 911–972.

Tomossy, George F., and David N. Weisstub (eds.). 2003. *Human Experimentation and Research*. Burlington, VT: Ashgate.

Tone, Andrea. 2001. *Devices and Desires: A History of Contraceptives in America*. New York: Hill and Wang.

Tonry, Michael. 1996. *Sentencing Matters*. New York: Oxford University Press.

Tonry, Michael, and Kathleen Hatlestad (eds.). 1997. *Sentencing Reform in Overcrowded Times: A Comparative Perspective*. New York: Oxford University Press.

Towers Perrin. 2006a. "U.S. Tort Costs Reach a Record $260 Billion." (March). Retrieved from www.towersperrin.com/ tp/jsp/masterbrand_webcache_html. 2006b. U.S. Tort Costs and Cross-Border Perspectives: 2005 Update. Retrieved from www.towersperrin.com/tillinghast._

Treaster, Joseph B. 1995. "Drug Therapy: Powerful Tool Reaching Few Inside Prisons." *New York Times* (July 3): 1, 9.

Treasury Board of Canada Secretariat. 2004–2005. Royal Canadian Mounted Police: Performance Report 2004–2005. Retrieved from www.tbs-sct.gc.ca/rma/dprl/04-05/ RCMP-GRC/RCMPGRCd4504_3.asp#crime. 2006. "Accountability Restored with Landmark Legislation-Federal Accountability Act Introduced to Rebuild Confidence and Trust of Canadians." April 11. Retrieved from news.gc.ca/cfmx/view/en/ index.jsp?articleid=2-6459.

Trebilcock, Bob. 2006. "Child Molesters on the Internet: Are They in Your Home?" in Thomas Hickey (ed.), *Taking Sides: Clashing Views in Crime and Criminology*, pp. 192–198. Dubuque, IA: McGraw-Hill.

Tremblay, Luci. 2002. "Quebec City and the Summits of 2001: Priority on People, Concerns for Freedom." *Policy Options* 23 (6) (September): 51–53.

Trevaskes, S. 2004. "China Propaganda Work in Chinese Courts: Public Trials and Sentencing Rallies as Sites of Expressive Punishment and Public Education in the People's Republic of China." *Punishment and Society* 6 (1) (January 1): 5–22.

Trevino, A. Javier. 1996. *The Sociology of Law: Classical and Contemporary Perspectives*. New York: St. Martin's Press.

Trubek, David M. 1978. "Environmental Defense I: Introduction to Interest Group Advocacy in Complex Disputes," in Burton A. Weisbrod, Joel F. Handler, and Neil K. Komesar (eds.), *Public Interest Law: An Economic and Institutional Analysis*, pp. 151–194. Berkeley and Los Angeles: University of California Press. 1984. "Where the Action Is: CRITS and Empiricism." *Stanford Law Review* 36 (1 and 2) (January): 575–622.

Trubek, David M., and John Esser. 1989. "'Critical Empiricism' in American Legal Studies: Paradox, Program, or Pandora's Box?" *Law and Social Inquiry* 14 (1): 3–52.

Tufts, Jennifer. 2000. "Public Attitudes Toward the Criminal Justice System." *Juristat*, Catalogue No. 85-002-XPE, 20 (12), December.

Turk, Austin T. 1972. *Legal Sanctioning and Social Control*. Rockville, MD: National Institute of Mental Health. 1978. "Law as a Weapon in Social Conflict," in Charles E. Reasons and Robert M. Rich (eds.), *The Sociology of Law: A Conflict Perspective*, pp. 213–232. Toronto: Butterworths

Turner, Jonathan H. 1972. Patterns of Social Organization: A Survey of Social Institutions.

New York: McGraw-Hill. 1974. "A Cybernetic Model of Legal Development." *Western Sociological Review* 5: 3–16. 2003. *The Structure of Sociological Theory.* 7th ed. Belmont, CA: Wadsworth.

Turner, Jonathan H., and Alexandra R. Maryanski. 1979. *Functionalism.* Menlo Park, CA: Benjamin/Cummings. 1995. "Is 'Neofunctionalism' Really Functional?" in Donald McQuarie (ed.), *Readings in Contemporary Sociological Theory: From Modernity to Post-Modernity*, pp. 49–62. Upper Saddle River, NJ: Prentice Hall.

Turner, Ralph, and Lewis M. Killian. 1987. *Collective Behavior.* 3rd ed. Englewood Cliffs, NJ: Prentice Hall.

Turow, Scott. 1977. "The Trouble with Law School." *Harvard Magazine* 80 (1) (September–October): 60–64. 2004. *Ultimate Punishment: A Lawyer's Reflections on Dealing with the Death Penalty.* Waterville, ME: Thorndike Press.

Tushnet, Mark. 1992. "The Degradation of Constitutional Discourse." *Georgetown Law Journal* 81: 251–295.

Tyler, Patrick E. 1995. "Population Control in China Falls to Coercion and Evasion." *New York Times* (June 25): 1, 6.

Tyler, Tom R. 1990. *Why People Obey the Law.* New Haven, CT: Yale University Press.

Tyler, Tom R., Jonathan D. Casper, and Bonnie Fisher. 1988. "Maintaining Allegiance Toward Legal Authorities: The Role of Prior Attitudes and the Use of Fair Procedures." ABF Working Paper #8813. Chicago: American Bar Foundation.

Tyler, Tracey. 2002. "Pleading Case for Reform of Legal Aid System." *The Sunday Star* (October 6): A1, A14.

Unger, Roberto Mangabeira. 1976. *Law in Modern Society: Toward a Criticism of Social Theory.* New York: Free Press. 1986. *The Critical Legal Studies Movement.* Cambridge, MA: Harvard University Press. 1998. *Democracy Realized: The Progressive Alternative.* New York: Verso.

Unger, Roberto Mangabeira, and Cornel West. 1998. *The Future of American Progressivism: An Initiative for Political and Economic Reform.* Boston: Beacon Press.

United Nations Development Program. 1995. *Human Development Report 1995.* New York: Oxford University Press. 2005. *Human Development Report 2005.* Retrieved from www.hdr.undp.org/reports/global/2005/.

University of Waterloo. 2006. "Prof Leads Worldwide Tobacco Project." *Daily Bulletin* (February 7). Retrieved from www.adm. waterloo.ca/bulletin/2006/feb/07tu.html.

U.S. Department of Justice. 1986. *Attorney General's Commission on Pornography. Final Report. Vols. 1 and 2 (July).* Washington, DC: U.S. Government Printing Office.1992. "Prosecutors in State Courts, 1990." *Bureau of Justice Statistics Bulletin* (March). 1995a. "Prison Sentences and Time Served for Violence." *Bureau of Justice Statistics, Selected Findings 4* (April). 1995b. "Drugs and Crime Facts, 1994." *Bureau of Justice Statistics* (June).

U.S. News and World Report. 2004. "Exclusive Rankings, Schools of Law." (April 12): 69–71.

U.S. Office of Economic Opportunity. 1970. *Preliminary Results of the New Jersey Graduated Work Incentive Experiment* (February 18). Washington, DC: U.S. Government Printing Office.

Vago, Steven. 1979. "Consumer Rights in Academe." *Social Policy* 9 (5) (March–April): 39–43. 2004. *Social Change.* 5th ed. Upper Saddle River, NJ: Prentice Hall.

Van Loon, F., and E. Langerwerf. 1990. "Socioeconomic Development and the Evolution of Litigation Rates of Civil Courts in Belgium, 1835–1980." *Law and Society Review* 24 (2): 283–298.

Valdes, Francisco, Jerome McCristal Culp, and Angela P. Harris (eds.). 2002. *Crossroads, Directions, and a New Critical Race Theory.* Philadelphia: Temple University Press.

Vallis, Mary. 2003. "More Wealthy Sales, Ad Execs than Lawyers: Census Surprise." *National Post* (March 12): A1, A10.

Van Brunschot, Erin Gibbs. 2003. "Community Policing and 'John Schools.'" *Canadian*

Review of Sociology and Anthropology 40 (2) (May): 215–232.

Vancouver Sun. 1999. "Global Capitalism Update: A Eunuch Approach to Collecting Bad Debts." (May 29): E3.

Van Den Berghe, Pierre L. 1967. "Dialectic and Functionalism: Toward a Synthesis," in N. Demerath and R. A. Peterson (eds.), *System Change and Conflict: A Reader on Contemporary Sociological Theory and the Debate over Functionalism*, pp. 294–310. New York: Free Press.

Vandor, Les. 2001. *Legal Counsel*. Toronto: ECW Press.

Varese, Federico. 2001. "Is Sicily the Future of Russia? Private Protection and the Rise of the Russian Mafia." *Archives Européennes de Sociologie* 42 (1): 186–221.

Vatz, Richard. 1980. "Rhetoric and the Law," in Lee S. Weinberg and Judith W. Weinberg (eds.), *Law and Society: An Interdisciplinary Introduction*, pp. 160–163. Washington, DC: University Press of America.

Vaughan, Diane. 1998. "Rational Choice, Situated Action, and the Social Control of Organizations." *Law and Society Review* 32 (1): 23–57.

Verdun-Jones, Simon N., and Adamira A. Tijerino. 2002. "Victim Participating in the Plea Negotiation Process in Canada." Department of Justice Canada, Policy Centre for Victim Issues. Retrieved from www.justice.gc.ca/en/ps/rs/rep/2002/vppnpc/vppnpc.html. 2004. "Four Models of Victim Involvement During Plea Negotiations: Bridging the Gap Between Legal Reforms and Current Legal Practice." *Canadian Journal of Criminology and Criminal Justice* 46 (4) (July).

Vidmar, Neil (ed.). 2000. *World Jury Systems*. New York: Oxford University Press. 2002. "Case Studies of Pre- and Mid-trial Prejudice in Criminal and Civil Litigation." *Law and Human Behavior* 26 (1): 73–105.

Vidmar, Neil, and Regina A. Schuller. 2001. "The Jury: Selecting Twelve Impartial Peers," in Regina A. Schuller and James R. P. Ogloff (eds.), *Introduction to Psychology and Law: Canadian Perspectives*, pp.

126–156. Toronto: University of Toronto Press.

Vining, Joseph. 1986. *The Authoritative and the Authoritarian*. Chicago: University of Chicago Press.

Violanti, John M. 1995. "The Mystery Within: Understanding Police Suicide." *FBI Law Enforcement Bulletin* 64 (2) (February): 19–24.

Viviano, Frank. 1995. "The New Mafia Order, Organized Crime in Russia, Mexico, and Elsewhere." *Mother Jones* 20 (3) (May–June): 44–55.

Volti, Rudi. 2001. *Society and Technological Change*. 4th ed. New York: St. Martin's Press.

Wade, Larry L. 1972. *The Elements of Public Policy*. Columbus, OH: Merrill.

Wald, Matthew L. 1998. "F.A.A. Asks, Can Airliners Get Too Old To Fly Safely." *New York Times* (October 2): A20.

Waldick v. Malcolm, Supreme Court of Canada, 1991, 2, S.C.R. 456, 3 O.R.

Waldman, Peter. 1986. "Pre-Paid Legal Plans Offer Consultations, Follow-Up Calls and Referrals at Low Cost." *Wall Street Journal* (February 11): 33.

Walker, Nancy Perry, and Lawrence S. Wrightsman. 1991. *The Child Witness: Legal Issues and Dilemmas*. Newbury Park, CA: Sage.

Walker, Nigel, and Mike Hough (eds.). 1988. *Public Attitudes to Sentencing: Surveys from Five Countries*. Aldershot, UK: Gower.

Wallace, Jean B. 1997. "It's About Time: A Study of Hours Worked and Work Spillover Among Law Firm Lawyers." *Journal of Vocational Behavior* 50 (2) (April): 227–248. 2001. "The Benefits of Mentoring for Female Lawyers." *Journal of Vocational Behavior* 58 (3) (June): 366–391.

Wallerstein, Judith S. 1999. "Children of Divorce: A Society in Search of Policy," in Mary Ann Mason, Arlene Skolnick, and Stephen D. Sugarman (eds.), *All Our Families: New Policies for a New Century*, pp. 65–94. New York: Oxford University Press.

Walton-Roberts, Margaret. 2004. "Rescaling Citizenship: Gendering Canadian Immigration Policy." *Political Geography* 23 (2) (March): 265–281.

Ward, Lester F. 1906. *Applied Sociology.* Boston: Ginn.

Ward, Linda. 2002. "The Supreme Court of Canada." Retrieved from www.cbc.ca/news/features/supreme_court.html.

Warskett, Rosemary. 2002. "Law, Regulation, and Becoming 'Uncivil': Contestation and Reconstruction Within the Federal Administrative State," in Michael Mac Neil, Neil Sargent, and Peter Swan (eds.), *Law, Regulation, and Governance*, pp. 188–202. Don Mills, ON: Oxford University Press.

Wasby, Stephen L., and David C. Brody. 1997. "Studies of Repressed Memory and the Issue of Legal Validity." *Law and Human Behavior* 21 (6) (December): 687–692.

Watson, Goodwin. 1969. "Resistance to Change," in Warren G. Bennis, Kenneth D. Benne and Robert Chin (eds.), *The Planning of Change*, pp. 488–498. 2nd ed. New York: Holt, Rinehart and Winston.

Weber, Max. 1921/1968. *Economy and Society, 3 vols.* Trans. Guenther Roth and Claus Wittich. New York: Badminster Press. 1947. *The Theory of Social Economic Organizations.* Ed. Talcott Parsons. Glencoe, IL: Free Press. 1954. *Law in Economy and Society.* Ed. Max Rheinstein and trans. Edward Shils and Max Rheinstein. Cambridge, MA: Harvard University Press.

Weibe, R., and Y. Johnson. 1998. *Stolen Life: The Journey of a Cree Woman.* Toronto: Random House.

Weir, William. 2004. "Laws That Are Really out of This World." *The Seattle Times* (February 8): A14.

Weisberg, Richard. 1996. *Vichy Law and the Holocaust in France.* New York: New York University Press. 2005. "Two Recent Assessments of Law and Literature." (September 1). Retrieved from lawlit.blogspot.com/2005/90/two-recent-assessments-of-law-and.html.

Weisbrod, Carol, and Pamela Sheingorn. 1978. "*Reynolds v. U.S.:* Nineteenth-Century Forms of Marriage and the Status of Women." *Connecticut Law Review* 10 (4): 828–858.

Weisburd, David, Stanton Wheeler, Elin Waring, and Nancy Bode. 1991. *Crimes of the Middle Classes: White Collar Offenders in the Federal Courts.* New Haven, CT: Yale University Press.

Weiss, Carol. 1998. *Evaluation Research: Methods for Studying Programs and Policies.* 2nd ed. Upper Saddle River, NJ: Prentice Hall.

Welsh, Sandy, Myrna Dawson, and Annette Nierobisz. 2002. "Legal Factors, Extra-Legal Factors, or Changes in the Law? Using Criminal Justice Research to Understand the Resolution of Sexual Harassment Complaints." *Social Problems* 49 (4) (November): 605–623.

West, Mark D. 2003. "Losers: Recovering Lost Property in Japan and the United States." *Law and Society Review* 37 (2) (June): 369–423.

Westermann, Ted D., and James W. Burfeind. 1991. *Crime and Justice in Two Societies, Japan and the United States.* Pacific Grove, CA: Brooks/Cole.

Wheeler, Stanton, Bliss Cartwright, Robert A. Kagan, and Lawrence M. Friedman. 1987. "Do the 'Haves' Come Out Ahead? Winning and Losing in State Supreme Courts, 1870–1970." *Law and Society Review* 21 (3) (Fall): 403–445.

Wheeler, Stanton, Kenneth Mann, and Austin Sarat. 1988. *Sitting in Judgment: The Sentencing of White-Collar Criminals.* New Haven and London: Yale University Press.

White, G. Edward. 2000. *Oliver Wendell Holmes, Sage of the Supreme Court.* New York: Oxford University Press.

White, James Boyd. 1973. *Studies in the Nature of Legal Thought and Expression.* Boston: Little, Brown. 1984. *When Words Lose Their Meaning: Constitutions and Reconstitutions of Language, Character and Community.* Chicago: University of Chicago Press. 1985.

Heracles' Bow: Essays on the Rhetoric and Poetics of the Law. Madison: University of Wisconsin Press. 1990. *Justice as Translation: An Essay in Cultural and Legal Criticism*. Chicago: University of Chicago Press. 1994. *Acts of Hope: Creating Authority in Literature, Law and Politics*. Chicago: University of Chicago Press.

White, Lucy E. 1991. "Subordination, Rhetorical Survival Skills, and Sunday Shoes: Notes on the Hearing of Mrs. G." in Katherine T. Bartlett (ed.), *Feminist Legal Theory: Readings in Law and Gender*, pp. 404–428. Boulder, CO: Westview Press.

White, Michael. 1999. "GM Ordered to Pay Accident Victims $49 B." *National Post* (July 10): A1.

Whitelaw, Kevin. 2004. "Shocking and Awful: A Series of Horrific Images and a Big American Black Eye." *U.S. News and World Report* (May 17): 26–36.

Whitla, W. 1995. "A Chronology of Women in Canada," in Nancy Mandell (ed.), *Feminist Issues: Race, Class and Sexuality*, pp. 315–53. Scarborough, ON: Prentice Hall.

Whittemore, Karen E., and James R. P. Ogloff. 1995. "Factors That Influence Jury Decision Making: Disposition Instructions and Mental State at the Time of the Trial." *Law and Human Behavior* 19 (3) (June): 283–304.

Wiber, Melanie G. 2000. "Fishing Rights As an Example of the Economic Rhetoric of Privatization: Calling for an Implicated Economics." *Canadian Review of Sociology and Anthropology* 37 (3) (August): 267–288.

Wice, Paul B. 1978. *Criminal Lawyers: An Endangered Species*. Beverly Hills, CA: Sage.

Wigmore, John H. 1913. "Introduction, to John Marshall Gest," in *The Lawyer in Literature*, pp. ix-xii. Boston: Boston Book.

Wilensky, Harold L. 1964. "The Professionalization of Everyone?" *American Journal of Sociology* 70 (2) (September): 137–158.

Williams, Glanville. 1951. "The Aims of the Law of Tort," Current Legal Problems; Vol. 137 (cited in Allen M. Linden, Lewis N. Klar, and Bruce Feldthusen. 2004. *Canadian Tort Law: Cases, Notes and Materials*. 12th ed. Toronto: LexisNexis and Butterworths).

Williams, James W. 2005. "Reflections on the Private versus Public Policing of Economic Crime." *British Journal of Criminology* 45 (3) (May): 316–339.

Williams, Kipling D., Elizabeth F. Loftus, and Kenneth A. Deffenbacher. 1992. "Eyewitness Evidence and Testimony," in Dorothy K. Kagehiro and William A. Laufer (eds.), *Handbook of Psychology and Law*, pp. 141–166. New York: Springer-Verlag.

Williams, Patricia J. 2006. *The Rooster's Egg*. Cambridge, MA: Harvard University Press. 1991. *The Alchemy of Race and Rights: Diary of a Law Professor*. Cambridge, MA: Harvard University Press.

Williams, Susan H. 2004. *Truth, Autonomy and Speech: Feminist Theory and the First Amendment*. New York: New York University Press.

Williams, Wendy W. 1987. "American Equality Jurisprudence," in Sheilah L. Martin and Kathleen E. Mahoney (eds.), *Equality and Judicial Neutrality*, pp. 115–127. Toronto: Carswell. 1991. "The Equality Crisis: Some Reflections on Culture, Courts, and Feminism," in Katharine T. Bartlett and Rosanne Kennedy (eds.), *Feminist Legal Theory: Readings in Law and Gender*, pp. 15–34. Boulder, CO: Westview Press.

Williamson, John B., David A. Karp, and John R. Dalphin. 1982. The *Research Craft: An Introduction to Social Science Methods*. 2nd ed. Boston: Little, Brown.

Willock, I. D. 1974. "Getting on with Sociologists." *British Journal of Law and Society* 1 (1): 3–12.

Wilson, H. T. 2002. "Rationality and Capitalism in Max Weber's Analysis of Western Modernity." *Journal of Classical Sociology* 2 (1) (March): 93–106.

Wilson, James Q. 1968a. "The Police and the Delinquent in Two Cities," in Stanton Wheeler (ed.), *Controlling Delinquents*, pp. 9–30. New York: John Wiley. 1968b. *Varieties of Police Behavior*. Cambridge, MA: Harvard University Press.

Wines, Michael. 2001. "Russia's Latest Dictator Goes by the Name of Law." *New York Times* (January 21): WK3. 2004. "Crime Reports Defy Russian Claims of Greater Calm in Chechnya" *New York Times* (April 13): A2.

Wing, Adrien Katherine (ed.). 2003. *Critical Race Feminism: A Reader*. 2nd ed. New York: New York University Press.

Winterdyk, John. 2002. "Do the Rich Get Richer and the Poor Injustice?" *LawNow* 27 (2) (October/November): 19–20.

Wolfe, Ellen L., John Guydish and Jenna Termondt. 2002. "A Drug Court Outcome Evaluation Comparing Arrests in a Two-Year Follow-up Period." *Journal of Drug Issues* 32 (4) (Fall): 1155–1172.

Wolfenden Report. 1963. Report of the Committee on Homosexual Offenses and Prostitution. Briarcliff Manor, NY: Stein and Day.

Wolfgang, Marvin E. 1998. "We Do Not Deserve to Kill." *Crime and Delinquency* 44 (1) (January): 19–31.

Wollschlager, Christian. 1990. "Civil Litigation and Modernization: The Work of the Municipal Courts of Bremen, Germany, in Five Centuries, 1549–1984." *Law and Society Review* 24 (2): 261–282.

Wong, K. C. 1998. "Black's Theory on the Behavior of Law Revisited II: A Restatement of Black's Concept of Law." *International Journal of Sociology* 26 (1) (March): 75–120.

Woo, Junda. 1992a. "Mediation Seen as Being Biased Against Women." *Wall Street Journal* (August 4): B1, B9. 1992b. "Sexual Harassment Is Found in Study of Federal Courts in 9 Western States." *Wall Street Journal* (August 5): B3.

Woocher, Frederic D. 1977. "Did Your Eyes Deceive You?: Expert Psychological Testimony on the Unreliability of Eyewitness Identification." *Stanford Law Review* 29: 969–1030.

Wood, Peter B., and R. G. Dunaway. 2003. "Consequences of Truth-in-Sentencing: The Mississippi Case." *Punishment and Society* 5 (2): 139–154.

World Health Organization. 2000a. International Consortium on Psychiatric Epidemiology. "Cross-National Comparisons of the Prevalences and Correlates of Mental Disorders." *Bulletin of the World Health Organization* 78 (4): 413–426. Retrieved from www. who.int/bulletin/tableofcontents/2000/vol.78no.4.html. 2000b. *The World Health Report 2000*. Retrieved from www.who.int/whr2001/2001/archives/2000/en/index.htm. 2000c. *Female Genital Mutilation*. Retrieved from www.who.int/mediacentre/factsheets/fs241/en/print.html.

Worrall, John L. 1998. "Administrative Determinants of Civil Liability Lawsuits Against Municipal Police Departments: An Exploratory Analysis." *Crime and Delinquency* 44 (2) (April): 295–313.

Worrall, John L., and Craig Hemmens. 2005. *Criminal Evidence: An Introduction*. Los Angeles: Roxbury.

Wortley, Scot, and Julian Tanner. 2005. "Inflammatory Rhetoric? Baseless Accusations? A Response to Gabor's Critique of Racial Profiling Research in Canada." *Canadian Journal of Criminology and Criminal Justice* 47 (3) (July): 581–609.

Wright, Martin, and Burt Galaway (eds.). 1989. *Mediation and Criminal Justice*. London: Sage.

Wright, Cecil A. 1967. *Introduction to Cases on the Law of Torts* (cited in Allen M. Linden, Lewis N. Klar, and Bruce Feldthusen. 2004. *Canadian Tort Law: Cases, Notes and Materials*. 12th ed. Toronto: LexisNexis and Butterworths.)

Wrightsman, Lawrence S., Michael T. Nietzel, and Milliam H. Fortune. 1998. *Psychology and the Legal System*. 4th ed. Pacific Grove, CA: Brooks/Cole.

Wynn, Joan Ransohoff, and Clifford Goldman. 1974. "Gambling in New York City: The Case for Legalization," in Lee Rainwater (ed.), *Social Problems and Public Policy, Deviance and Liberty*, pp. 66–75. Chicago: Aldine.

Yant, Martin. 1991. *Presumed Guilty: When Innocent People Are Wrongly Convicted*. Buffalo, NY: Prometheus Books.

Yarnold, Barbara M. 1992. *Politics and the Courts: Toward a General Theory of Public Law*. New York: Praeger.

Yates, Jeff, Belinda Creel Davis, and Henry R. Glick. 2001. "The Politics of Torts: Explaining Litigation Rates in the American States." *State Politics and Policy Quarterly* 1 (2) (Summer): 127–143.

Yates, Richard A., Ruth Whidden Yates, and Penny Bain. 2000. *Introduction to Law in Canada*. 2nd ed. Scarborough, ON: Allyn and Bacon.

Yates, Simeon J. 2004. *Doing Social Science Research*. Thousand Oaks, CA: Sage.

Yellon, Rod. 2002. "Seeking to Prove the Word 'STOP' Isn't Sufficient Warning to Motorists." *Winnipeg Free Press* (January 5). Retrieved from http://overlawyered.com/archives/02feb1.html.

Yngvesson, Barbara B. 1978. "The Atlantic Fishermen," in Laura Nader and Harry F. Todd, Jr. (eds.), *The Disputing Process—Law in Ten Societies*, pp. 59–85. New York: Columbia University Press.

Yoshino, Kenji. 2005. "The City and the Poet." *Yale Law Journal* 114: 1835–1847.

Young, Karen. 2005. "Does the Australian Competition and Consumer Commission Engage in 'Trial by Media'?" *Law and Policy* 27 (4) (October): 549–577.

Young, Virginia, and Eric Stern. 2001. "Elderly Are Called Prone to Gambling Problems." *St. Louis Post-Dispatch* (August 6): 1, 7.

Zander, Michael. 1999. *The Law-Making Process*. 5th ed. London, UK: Butterworths.

Zatz, Marjorie S. 1994. *Producing Legality: Law and Socialism in Cuba*. New York: Routledge.

Zeisel, Hans. 1967. "The Law," in Paul F. Lazarsfeld, William H. Sewell, and Harold Wilensky (eds.), *The Uses of Sociology*, pp. 81–99. New York: Basic Books.

Zhang, Sheldon. 1998. "In Search of Hopeful Glimpses: A Critique of Research Strategies in Current Boot Camp Evaluation." *Crime and Delinquency* 44 (2) (April): 314–334.

Zhao, Jihong, and Quint C. Thurman. 1997. "Community Policing: Where Are We Now?" *Crime and Delinquency* 43 (3) (July): 345–357.

Zifcak, Spencer (ed.). 2005. *Globalisation and the Rule of Law*. New York: Routledge.

Zimring, Franklin E. 1989. "Methods for Measuring General Deterrence: A Plea for the Field Experiment," in Martin Lawrence Friedland (ed.), *Sanctions and Rewards in the Legal System: A Multidisciplinary Approach*, pp. 99–108. Toronto: University of Toronto Press.

Zimring, Franklin, and Gordon Hawkins. 1975. "The Legal Threat as an Instrument of Social Change," in Ronald L. Akers and Richard Hawkins (eds.), *Law and Control in Society*, pp. 329–339. Englewood Cliffs, NJ: Prentice Hall. 1997. *Crime Is Not the Problem: Lethal Violence in America*. New York: Oxford University Press.

Zitrin, Richard, and Carol M. Langford. 1999. *The Moral Compass of the American Lawyer: Truth, Justice, Power, and Greed*. New York: Random House.

Zobel, Hiller B. 1994. "In Love with Lawsuits." *American Heritage* 45 (7) (November):

Index